Microsoft® Office Professional 2010

Step by Step

Joyce Cox
Joan Lambert
Curtis Frye

PUBLISHED BY
Microsoft Press
A Division of Microsoft Corporation
One Microsoft Way
Redmond, Washington 98052-6399

Library of Congress Control Number: 2010932312

Printed and bound in Canada

2 3 4 5 6 7 8 9 10 11 TG 6 5 4 3 2 1

Microsoft Press books are available through booksellers and distributors worldwide. For further information about international editions, contact your local Microsoft Corporation office or contact Microsoft Press International directly at fax (425) 936-7329. Visit our Web site at www.microsoft.com/mspress. Send comments to mspinput@ microsoft.com.

Acquisitions Editor: Juliana Atkinson
Developmental Editor: Devon Musgrave
Project Editor: Joel Panchot
Editorial Production: Online Training Solutions, Inc.
Cover: Girvin

Body Part No. X17-08755

Contents

Part 1 Microsoft Office Professional 2010

What do you think of this book? We want to hear from you!

Microsoft is interested in hearing your feedback so we can continually improve our books and learning resources for you. To participate in a brief online survey, please visit:

microsoft.com/learning/booksurvey

Part 4   **Microsoft PowerPoint 2010**

Part 5 **Microsoft OneNote 2010**

19 Create and Configure Notebooks 539

20 Create and Organize Notes 563

23   Manage Scheduling   679

24   Track Tasks   715

Part 7   **Microsoft Access 2010**

Part 8   Microsoft Publisher 2010

What do you think of this book? We want to hear from you!

Microsoft is interested in hearing your feedback so we can continually improve our books and learning resources for you. To participate in a brief online survey, please visit:

microsoft.com/learning/booksurvey

Introducing Microsoft Office Professional 2010

Microsoft Office 2010 is a comprehensive system of programs, servers, services, and solutions, including a dozen desktop productivity programs that you can install on your computer, and four new online program versions. To meet the varying needs of individuals and organizations, Microsoft offers five different Office 2010 software suites, each consisting of a different subset of programs. The following table identifies the programs available in each of the software suites.

	Office Home and Student 2010	Office Home and Business 2010	Office Standard 2010	Office Professional 2010	Office Professional Plus 2010
Access				Yes	Yes
Communicator					Yes
Excel	Yes	Yes	Yes	Yes	Yes
InfoPath					Yes
OneNote	Yes	Yes	Yes	Yes	Yes
Outlook		Yes	Yes	Yes	Outlook with Business Contact Manager
PowerPoint	Yes	Yes	Yes	Yes	Yes
Publisher			Yes	Yes	Yes
SharePoint Workspace					Yes
Word	Yes	Yes	Yes	Yes	Yes
Office Web Apps			Yes		Yes

Office Standard and Office Professional Plus are available only to volume licensing subscribers. The Office Web Apps, which are available with Office Standard and Office Professional Plus, and available to the general public through Windows Live, are online versions of Word, Excel, PowerPoint, and OneNote. You can store documents online and work with them from within any Web browser window by using the Office Web Apps.

This book provides instructional material for the following programs, which together form the Office Professional 2010 software suite:

- **Microsoft Word 2010** A word-processing program with which you can quickly and efficiently author and format documents.

- **Microsoft Excel 2010** A spreadsheet program with which you can analyze, communicate, and manage information.

- **Microsoft PowerPoint 2010** A program with which you can develop and present dynamic, professional-looking slide presentations.

- **Microsoft OneNote 2010** A digital notebook program with which you can collect, organize, and quickly locate many types of electronic information.

- **Microsoft Outlook 2010** A personal information management program with which you can manage e-mail, contacts, meetings, tasks, and other communications.

- **Microsoft Access 2010** A database program with which you can collect information and output information for reuse in a variety of formats.

- **Microsoft Publisher 2010** A desktop publishing program with which you can lay out newsletters, cards, calendars, and other publications.

The information in this book applies to these programs in all the software suites. If you have a software suite other than Office Professional, or if you installed one or more of these programs independently of a software suite, this is the right book for you.

Certification

Desktop computing proficiency is increasingly important in today's business world. When screening, hiring, and training employees, more employers are relying on the objectivity and consistency of technology certification to ensure the competence of their workforce. As an employee or job seeker, you can use technology certification to prove that you already have the skills you need to succeed. A Microsoft Office Specialist (MOS) is an individual who has demonstrated worldwide skill standards through a certification exam in one or more of the Office 2010 programs, including Microsoft Access, Excel, Outlook, PowerPoint, or Word. To learn more about the MOS program, visit the Microsoft Office Specialist Certification page at go.microsoft.com/fwlink/?LinkId=193884.

For More Information

The chapters of this book that cover Microsoft Word 2010, Excel 2010, PowerPoint 2010, Outlook 2010, and Access 2010 are excerpted from the full-length *Step by Step* books written about those programs. This book provides an overview of each program and information to get you started. To learn more, refer to the following books.

Microsoft Word 2010 Step by Step

By Joyce Cox and Joan Lambert (Microsoft Press, 2010)
ISBN 978-0-7356-2693-5

Contents:

Microsoft Excel 2010 Step by Step

By Curtis Frye (Microsoft Press, 2010)
ISBN 978-0-7356-2694-2

Contents:

1 Setting Up a Workbook

2 Working with Data and Excel Tables

3 Performing Calculations on Data

4 Changing Workbook Appearance

5 Focusing on Specific Data by Using Filters

6 Reordering and Summarizing Data

7 Combining Data from Multiple Sources

8 Analyzing Alternative Data Sets

9 Creating Dynamic Worksheets by Using PivotTables

10 Creating Charts and Graphics

11 Printing

12 Automating Repetitive Tasks by Using Macros

13 Working with Other Microsoft Office Programs

14 Collaborating with Colleagues

Microsoft PowerPoint 2010 Step by Step

By Joyce Cox and Joan Lambert (Microsoft Press, 2010)
ISBN 978-0-7356-2691-1

Contents:

1 Explore PowerPoint 2010

2 Work with Slides

3 Work with Slide Text

4 Format Slides

5 Add Simple Visual Enhancements

Microsoft Outlook 2010 Step by Step

By Joan Lambert and Joyce Cox (Microsoft Press, 2010)
ISBN 978-0-7356-2690-4

Contents:

Microsoft Access 2010 Step by Step

By Joyce Cox and Joan Lambert (Microsoft Press, 2010)
ISBN 978-0-7356-2692-8

Contents:

Let's Get Started!

Office 2010 includes new features, new functionality, and an easy-to-use interface intended to streamline your computing experience and make it easier to learn new programs. We're excited to bring you this glimpse into the inner workings of selected features in the core Office programs. We'll start with the basics and work into the most interesting and necessary features of each program. If you are an experienced Office user, you can skim Chapter 1, "Explore Office 2010," skip Chapter 2, "Work with Files," and jump right into the program-specific chapters.

Modifying the Display of the Ribbon

The goal of the Microsoft Office 2010 working environment is to make working with Office files—including Microsoft Word documents, Excel workbooks, PowerPoint presentations, Outlook e-mail messages, and Access databases—as intuitive as possible. You work with an Office file and its contents by giving commands to the program in which the document is open. All Office 2010 programs organize commands on a horizontal bar called the *ribbon*, which appears across the top of each program window whether or not there is an active document.

Ribbon tabs   Ribbon groups

A typical program window ribbon.

Commands are organized on task-specific tabs of the ribbon, and in feature-specific groups on each tab. Commands generally take the form of buttons and lists. Some appear in galleries in which you can choose from among multiple options. Some groups have related dialog boxes or task panes that contain additional commands.

Throughout this book, we discuss the commands and ribbon elements associated with the program feature being discussed. In this section, we discuss the general appearance of the ribbon, things that affect its appearance, and ways of locating commands that aren't visible on compact views of the ribbon.

See Also For detailed information about the ribbon, see "Working in the Program Environment" in Chapter 1, "Explore Office 2010."

Tip Some older commands no longer appear on the ribbon but are still available in the program. You can make these commands available by adding them to the Quick Access Toolbar. For more information, see "Customizing the Quick Access Toolbar" in Chapter 1, "Explore Office 2010."

Dynamic Ribbon Elements

The ribbon is dynamic, meaning that the appearance of commands on the ribbon changes as the width of the ribbon changes. A command might be displayed on the ribbon in the form of a large button, a small button, a small labeled button, or a list entry. As the width of the ribbon decreases, the size, shape, and presence of buttons on the ribbon adapt to the available space.

For example, when sufficient horizontal space is available, the buttons on the Review tab of the Word program window are spread out and you're able to see more of the commands available in each group.

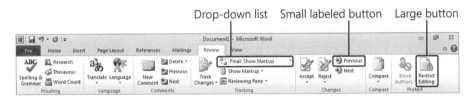

The Review tab of the Word program window at 1024 pixels wide.

If you decrease the width of the ribbon, small button labels disappear and entire groups of buttons are hidden under one button that represents the group. Click the group button to display a list of the commands available in that group.

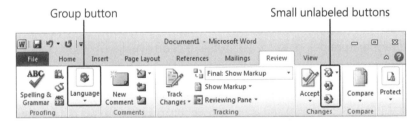

The Review tab of the Word program window at 675 pixels wide.

When the window becomes too narrow to display all the groups, a scroll arrow appears at its right end. Click the scroll arrow to display hidden groups.

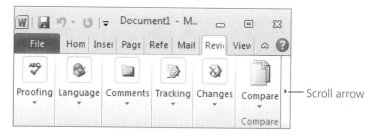

The Review tab of the Word program window at 340 pixels wide.

Changing the Width of the Ribbon

The width of the ribbon is dependent on the horizontal space available to it, which depends on these three factors:

- **The width of the program window** Maximizing the program window provides the most space for ribbon elements. You can resize the program window by clicking the button in its upper-right corner or by dragging the border of a non-maximized window.

  On a computer running Windows 7, you can maximize the program window by dragging its title bar to the top of the screen.

- **Your screen resolution** Screen resolution is the amount of information your screen displays, expressed as *pixels wide by pixels high*. The greater the screen resolution, the greater the amount of information that will fit on one screen. Your screen resolution options are dependent on your monitor. At the time of writing, possible screen resolutions range from 800 × 600 to 2048 × 1152. In the case of the ribbon, the greater the number of pixels wide (the first number), the greater the number of buttons that can be shown on the ribbon, and the larger those buttons can be.

On a computer running Windows 7, you can change your screen resolution from the Screen Resolution window of Control Panel.

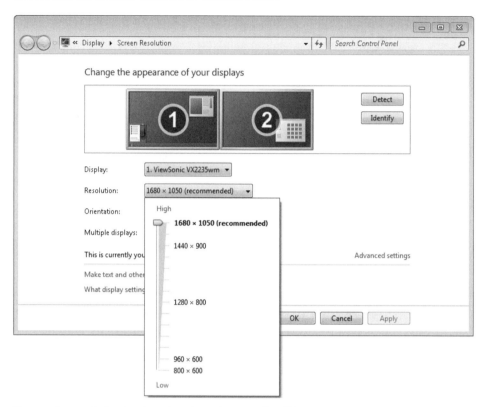

You set the resolution by dragging the pointer on the slider.

● **The density of your screen display** You might not be aware that you can change the magnification of everything that appears on your screen by changing the screen magnification setting in Windows. Setting your screen magnification to 125% makes text and user interface elements larger on screen. This increases the legibility of information, but it means that less information fits onto each screen.

On a computer running Windows 7, you can change the screen magnification from the Display window of Control Panel.

See Also For more information about display settings, refer to *Windows 7 Step by Step* (Microsoft Press, 2009), *Windows Vista Step by Step* (Microsoft Press, 2006), or *Windows XP Step by Step* (Microsoft Press, 2002) by Joan Lambert Preppernau and Joyce Cox.

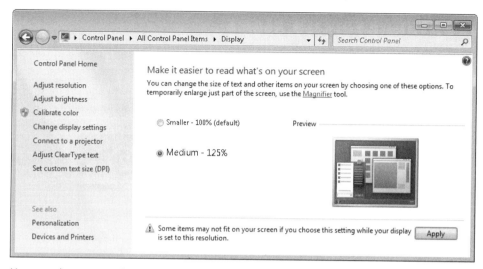

You can choose one of the standard display magnification options or create another by setting a custom text size.

The screen magnification is directly related to the density of the text elements on screen, which is expressed in dots per inch (dpi) or points per inch (ppi). (The terms are interchangeable, and in fact are both used in the Windows dialog box in which you change the setting.) The greater the dpi, the larger the text and user interface elements appear on screen. By default, Windows displays text and screen elements at 96 dpi. Choosing the Medium - 125% display setting changes the dpi of text and screen elements to 120 dpi. You can choose a custom setting of up to 500 percent magnification, or 480 dpi, in the Custom DPI Setting dialog box.

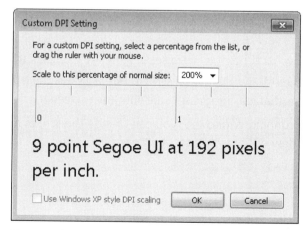

You can choose a magnification of up to 200 percent from the lists, or choose a greater magnification by dragging the ruler from left to right.

Adapting Exercise Steps

The screen images shown in the exercises in this book were captured at a screen resolution of 1024 × 768, at 100% magnification, and with the default text size (96 dpi). If any of your settings are different, the ribbon on your screen might not look the same as the one shown in the book. For example, you might see more or fewer buttons in each of the groups, the buttons you see might be represented by larger or smaller icons than those shown, or the group might be represented by a button that you click to display the group's commands.

When we instruct you to give a command from the ribbon in an exercise, we do it in this format:

● On the **Insert** tab, in the **Illustrations** group, click the **Chart** button.

If the command is in a list, we give the instruction in this format:

● On the **Page Layout** tab, in the **Page Setup** group, click the **Breaks** button and then, in the list, click **Page**.

The first time we instruct you to click a specific button in each exercise, we display an image of the button in the page margin to the left of the exercise step.

If differences between your display settings and ours cause a button on your screen to not appear as shown in the book, you can easily adapt the steps to locate the command. First, click the specified tab. Then locate the specified group. If a group has been collapsed into a group list or group button, click the list or button to display the group's commands. Finally, look for a button that features the same icon in a larger or smaller size than that shown in the book. If necessary, point to buttons in the group to display their names in ScreenTips.

If you prefer not to have to adapt the steps, set up your screen to match ours while you read and work through the exercises in the book.

Features and Conventions
of This Book

This book has been designed to lead you step by step through tasks you're likely to want to perform in Microsoft Word 2010, Excel 2010, PowerPoint 2010, OneNote 2010, Outlook 2010, Access 2010, and Publisher 2010. These programs are available as part of the Microsoft Office Professional 2010 software suite.

See Also This book, *Microsoft Office Professional 2010 Step by Step*, includes a selection of instructional content for each program in the Office Professional 2010 software suite. For more complete coverage of the features of each of these programs, refer to the corresponding program-specific *Step by Step* book.

Each chapter of this book includes self-contained topics that teach you about specific program features. Most topics conclude with a step-by-step exercise in which you practice using the program. The following features of this book will help you locate specific information:

- **Detailed table of contents** Scan the listing of the topics and sidebars within each chapter.

- **Chapter thumb tabs** Easily locate the beginning of each chapter by looking at the colored blocks on the odd-numbered pages.

- **Topic-specific running heads** Within a chapter, quickly locate a topic by looking at the running heads at the top of odd-numbered pages.

- **Glossary** Look up the meaning of a word or the definition of a concept. *The glossary for this book is available as online companion content. For more information, see go.microsoft.com/fwlink/?LinkID=192155.*

- **Detailed index** Look up specific tasks and features in the index, which has been carefully crafted with the reader in mind.

You can save time when reading this book by understanding how the *Step by Step* series shows exercise instructions, keys to press, buttons to click, and other information. These conventions are listed in the following table.

Convention	Meaning
SET UP	This paragraph preceding a step-by-step exercise indicates the practice files that you will use when working through the exercise. It also indicates any requirements you should attend to or actions you should take before beginning the exercise.
CLEAN UP	This paragraph following a step-by-step exercise provides instructions for saving and closing open files or programs before moving on to another topic. It also suggests ways to reverse any changes you made to your computer while working through the exercise.
1 2	Blue numbered steps guide you through hands-on exercises in each topic.
1 2	Black numbered steps guide you through procedures in sidebars and expository text.
See Also	This paragraph directs you to more information about a topic in this book or elsewhere.
Troubleshooting	This paragraph alerts you to a common problem and provides guidance for fixing it.
Tip	This paragraph provides a helpful hint or shortcut that makes working through a task easier.
Important	This paragraph points out information that you need to know to complete a procedure.
Keyboard Shortcut	This paragraph provides information about an available keyboard shortcut for the preceding task.
Ctrl+B	A plus sign (+) between two keys means that you must press those keys at the same time. For example, "Press Ctrl+B" means that you should hold down the Ctrl key while you press the B key.
	Pictures of buttons appear in the margin the first time the button is used in an exercise.
Black bold	In exercises that begin with SET UP information, the names of program elements, such as buttons, commands, windows, and dialog boxes, as well as files, folders, or text that you interact with in the steps, are shown in bold black type.
Blue bold	In exercises that begin with SET UP information, text that you should type is shown in bold blue type.

Using the Practice Files

Before you can complete the exercises in this book, you need to copy the book's practice files to your computer. These practice files, and other information, can be downloaded from the book's detail page, located at:

http://go.microsoft.com/fwlink/?Linkid=192155

Display the detail page in your Web browser and follow the instructions for downloading the files.

Important The Office Professional 2010 software suite is not available from this Web page. You should purchase and install that software suite before using this book.

The following table lists the practice files for this book.

Chapter	File
Chapter 1: Explore Office 2010	None
Chapter 2: Work with Files	Prices_start.docx
	Procedures_start.docx
	Rules_start.docx
Chapter 3: Edit and Proofread Text	Bamboo_start.docx
	Brochure_start.docx
	Letter_start.docx
	Orientation_start.docx
	RulesRegulations_start.docx
Chapter 4: Change the Look of Text	AgendaA_start.docx
	AgendaB_start.docx
	Information_start.docx
	OrientationDraft_start.docx
	RulesDraft_start.docx
Chapter 5: Organize Information in Columns and Tables	ConsultationA_start.docx
	ConsultationB_start.docx
	RepairCosts_start.docx
	RoomPlanner_start.docx

Chapter	File
Chapter 6: Add Simple Graphic Elements	Announcement_start.docx
	Authors_start.docx
	Flyer_start.docx
	Joan.jpg
	Joyce.jpg
	MarbleFloor.jpg
	OTSI-Logo.png
Chapter 7: Preview, Print, and Distribute Documents	InfoSheetA_start.docx
	InfoSheetB_start.docx
	InfoSheetC_start.docx
	OfficeInfo_start.docx
Chapter 8: Set Up a Workbook	ExceptionSummary_start.xlsx
	ExceptionTracking_start.xlsx
	MisroutedPackages_start.xlsx
	PackageCounts_start.xlsx
	RouteVolume_start.xlsx
Chapter 9: Work with Data and Excel Tables	2010Q1ShipmentsByCategory_start.xlsx
	AverageDeliveries_start.xlsx
	DriverSortTimes_start.xlsx
	Series_start.xlsx
	ServiceLevels_start.xlsx
Chapter 10: Perform Calculations on Data	ConveyerBid_start.xlsx
	ITExpenses_start.xlsx
	PackagingCosts_start.xlsx
	VehicleMiles_start.xlsx
Chapter 11: Change Workbook Appearance	CallCenter_start.xlsx
	Dashboard_start.xlsx
	ExecutiveSearch_start.xlsx
	HourlyExceptions_start.xlsx
	HourlyTracking_start.xlsx
	Phone.jpg
	Texture.jpg
	VehicleMileSummary_start.xlsx
Chapter 12: Focus on Specific Data by Using Filters	Credit_start.xlsx
	ForFollowUp_start.xlsx
	PackageExceptions_start.xlsx

Chapter	File
Chapter 13: Work with Slides	Projects.pptx
	ServiceA_start.pptx
	ServiceB_start.pptx
	ServiceC_start.pptx
	ServiceD_start.pptx
	ServiceOrientation.docx
Chapter 14: Work with Slide Text	BuyingTripsB_start.pptx
	BuyingTripsC_start.pptx
	CommunityServiceA_start.pptx
	CommunityServiceB_start.pptx
	CommunityServiceC_start.pptx
Chapter 15: Format Slides	BusinessTravelA_start.pptx
	BusinessTravelB_start.pptx
	ColorDesign_start.pptx
	CompanyMeetingA_start.pptx
	CompanyMeetingB_start.pptx
	LandscapingA_start.pptx
Chapter 16: Add Simple Visual Enhancements	Agastache.jpg
	JournalingA_start.pptx
	JournalingB_start.pptx
	Penstemon.jpg
	WaterConsumption.xlsx
	WaterSavingA_start.pptx
	WaterSavingB_start.pptx
	WaterSavingC_start.pptx
Chapter 17: Review and Deliver Presentations	Harmony_start.pptx
	Meeting_start.pptx
	SavingWater_start.pptx
	ServiceOrientationA_start.pptx
	ServiceOrientationB_start.pptx
	YinYang.png
Chapter 18: Explore OneNote 2010	None
Chapter 19: Create and Configure Notebooks	None

Chapter	File
Chapter 20: Create and Organize Notes	SBS Content Entry folder ADatumLogo.png Cabo.jpg California_Poppy.jpg Desert.jpg Landscaping.pptx
Chapter 21: Send and Receive E-Mail Messages	Brochure.docx StrategySession.pptx SBS First Draft message (created in this chapter)
Chapter 22: Store and Access Contact Information	Andrea Dunker, Andrew Davis, Idan Rubin, Nancy Anderson, and Sara Davis contact records (created in this chapter)
Chapter 23: Manage Scheduling	SBS Lunch with Jane and SBS Staff Meeting appointments, SBS Pay Day event (created in this chapter)
Chapter 24: Track Tasks	SBS First Draft and SBS Tradeshow Schedule messages (created in Chapter 21) SBS Dinner Reservations, SBS Order Brochures, and SBS Send Dinner Invitations tasks (created in this chapter)
Chapter 25: Explore an Access 2010 Database	GardenCompany01_start.accdb
Chapter 26: Create Databases and Simple Tables	None
Chapter 27: Create Simple Forms	GardenCompany03_start.accdb Logo.png
Chapter 28: Display Data	GardenCompany04_start.accdb
Chapter 29: Get Started with Publisher 2010	Importing.docx Logo.png Printing_start.pub
Chapter 30: Create Visual Interest	BirthdayGirl.jpg Blank_start.pub Text.docx
Chapter 31: Create Colorful Cards and Calendars	DataSource.xlsx Peaceful.jpg

Getting Help

Every effort has been made to ensure the accuracy of this book. If you do run into problems, please contact the sources listed in the following sections.

Getting Help with This Book

If your question or issue concerns the content of this book or its practice files, please first consult the book's errata page, which can be accessed at:

http://go.microsoft.com/fwlink/?Linkid=192155

This page provides information about known errors and corrections to the book. If you do not find your answer on the errata page, send your question or comment to Microsoft Press Technical Support at:

mspinput@microsoft.com

Getting Help with Office 2010

If your question is about one of the programs in the Microsoft Office Professional 2010 software suite, and not about the content of this book, your first recourse is the Help system for the individual program. This system is a combination of tools and files stored on your computer when you installed the software suite or program and, if your computer is connected to the Internet, information available from the Microsoft Office Online Web site. You can find Help information in the following ways:

- To find out about an item on the screen, you can display a ScreenTip. For example, to display a ScreenTip for a button, point to the button without clicking it. The ScreenTip gives the button's name, the associated keyboard shortcut if there is one, and some-times a description of what the button does when you click it.

- In the program window, you can click the Help button (a question mark in a blue circle) at the right end of the ribbon to display the program-specific Help window.

- At the right end of the title bars of some dialog boxes is a Help button (also a question mark) that you can click to display the program-specific Help window. Sometimes, topics related to the functions of that dialog box are already identified in the window.

To practice getting help, you can work through the following exercise.

 SET UP You don't need any practice files to complete this exercise. Start Word, and then follow the steps.

 1. At the right end of the ribbon, click the **Microsoft Word Help** button.

The Word Help window opens.

You can change the size of the font in the window by clicking the Change Font Size button on the toolbar.

If you are connected to the Internet, clicking any of the buttons below the Microsoft Office banner (Products, Support, Images, and Templates) takes you to a corresponding page of the Office Web site.

2. Below the bulleted list under **Browse Word 2010 support**, click **see all**.

   The window changes to display a list of Help topics.

3. In the list of topics, click **Activating Word**.

   Word Help displays a list of topics related to activating Microsoft Office programs. You can click any topic to display the corresponding information.

4. On the toolbar, click the **Show Table of Contents** button.

   The window expands to accommodate two panes. The Table Of Contents pane appears on the left. Like the table of contents in a book, it is organized in sections.

   If you're connected to the Internet, Word displays sections, topics, and training available from the Office Online Web site as well as those stored on your computer.

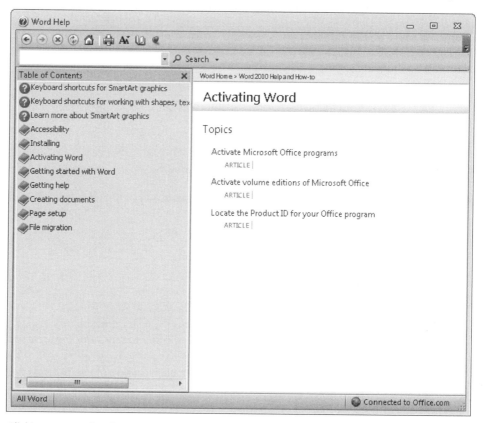

Clicking any section (represented by a book icon) displays that section's topics (represented by Help icons).

5. In the **Table of Contents** pane, click a few sections and topics. Then click the **Back** and **Forward** buttons to move among the topics you have already viewed.

6. At the right end of the **Table of Contents** title bar, click the **Close** button.

7. At the top of the **Word Help** window, click the **Type words to search for** box, type **saving**, and then press the Enter key.

The Word Help window displays topics related to the word you typed.

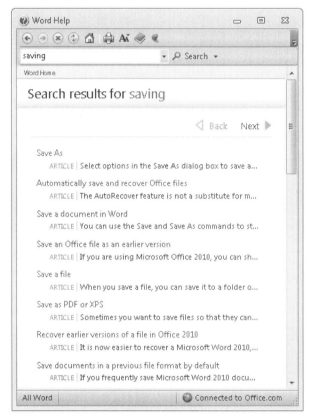

Next and Back buttons appear, making it easier to search for the topic you want.

8. In the results list, click the **Recover earlier versions of a file in Office 2010** topic.

   The selected topic appears in the Word Help window.

9. Below the title at the top of the topic, click **Show All**.

   Word displays any information that has been collapsed under a heading and changes the Show All button to Hide All. You can jump to related information by clicking hyperlinks identified by blue text.

   Tip You can click the Print button on the toolbar to print a topic. Only the displayed information is printed.

 **CLEAN UP** Click the Close button at the right end of the Word Help window.

More Information

If your question is about an Office 2010 program or another Microsoft software product and you cannot find the answer in the product's Help system, please search the appropriate product solution center or the Microsoft Knowledge Base at:

support.microsoft.com

In the United States, Microsoft software product support issues not covered by the Microsoft Knowledge Base are addressed by Microsoft Product Support Services. Location-specific software support options are available from:

support.microsoft.com/gp/selfoverview/

Microsoft Office Professional 2010

Chapter at a Glance

Work in the program environment, **page 4**

Change program settings, **page 17**

Customize the ribbon, **page 26**

Customize the Quick Access Toolbar, **page 31**

1 Explore Office 2010

In this chapter, you will learn how to

✔ Work in the program environment.

✔ Change program settings.

✔ Customize the ribbon.

✔ Customize the Quick Access Toolbar.

Microsoft Office 2010 programs have a common user interface—the way the program looks and the way you interact with it—which means that skills and techniques you learn in one program are also useful in the others.

Certain information that you provide in one Office 2010 program is made available to other Office 2010 programs so that you don't have to provide it individually in each program. Other settings are specific to the program you're working in. The basic Office 2010 user interface includes a standard method of giving commands by using tools gathered on a dynamic toolbar, called the ribbon. Commands are represented by buttons, by lists or galleries from which you choose settings, or by fields in task panes and dialog boxes in which you specify settings. You can customize some of the content that is available from the ribbon by hiding sets of commands (tabs) or by creating custom tabs. You can also collect frequently used buttons, lists, and galleries on a separate toolbar, the Quick Access Toolbar, so that they are available to you from anywhere in the program.

Each program has standard settings based on the way that most people work with the program. However, you can customize the settings to meet your specific needs and to fit the way that you work.

In this chapter, you'll first familiarize yourself with the standard Office 2010 program working environment. Then you'll customize the working environment, ribbon, and Quick Access Toolbar in Microsoft Word 2010, using techniques that are common to working in any Office 2010 program.

> **Practice Files** You don't need any practice files to complete the exercises in this chapter. For more information about practice file requirements, see "Using the Practice Files" at the beginning of this book.

Working in the Program Environment

The most common way to start any Office 2010 program is from the Start menu, displayed when you click the Start button at the left end of the Windows Taskbar. On the Start menu, click All Programs, click the Microsoft Office folder, and then click the program you want to start.

When you start Microsoft Word, Excel, or PowerPoint without opening a specific file, the program window appears, displaying a new blank document, workbook, or presentation. When you start Microsoft OneNote without opening a specific notebook, the program window displays the notebook you opened most recently.

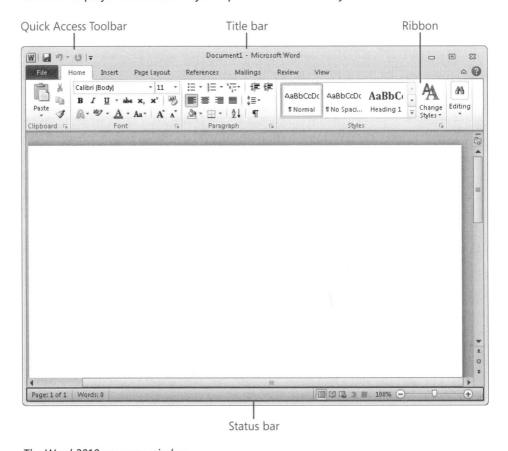

The Word 2010 program window.

See Also Windows 7 introduced many efficient new window-management techniques. For information about ways to work with a program window on a Windows 7 computer, refer to *Windows 7 Step by Step* by Joan Lambert Preppernau and Joyce Cox (Microsoft Press, 2009).

A typical Office 2010 program window contains the following elements:

● The title bar displays the name of the active document. At the left end of the title bar is the program icon, which you click to display commands to move, size, and close the program window. Three buttons at the right end of the title bar serve the same functions in all Windows programs: You can temporarily hide the program window by clicking the Minimize button, adjust the size of the window by clicking the Restore Down/Maximize button, and close the active document or exit the program by clicking the Close button.

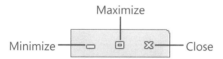

The default buttons on the Quick Access Toolbar in the Excel program window.

● By default, the Quick Access Toolbar appears to the right of the program icon at the left end of the title bar. Each program has a default set of Quick Access Toolbar buttons; most commonly, the default Quick Access Toolbar displays the Save, Undo, and Redo buttons. You can change the location of the Quick Access Toolbar and customize it to include any command to which you want to have easy access.

The default buttons on the Quick Access Toolbar in the Excel program window.

● Below the title bar is the ribbon. All the commands for working with file content are available from this central location so that you can work efficiently with the program.

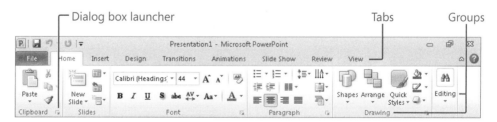

The ribbon in the PowerPoint program window.

See Also The appearance of buttons and groups on the ribbon changes depending on the width of the program window. For information about changing the appearance of the ribbon to match our images, see "Modifying the Display of the Ribbon" at the beginning of this book.

● Across the top of the ribbon is a set of tabs. Clicking a tab displays an associated set of commands.

Tip You might find it efficient to add all the commands you use frequently to the Quick Access Toolbar and display it below the ribbon, directly above the workspace. For information, see "Customizing the Quick Access Toolbar" later in this chapter.

● Commands related to managing the program and files (rather than file content) are gathered together in the Backstage view, which you display by clicking the colored File tab located at the left end of the ribbon. Commands available in the Backstage view are organized on named pages, which you display by clicking the page tabs located in the left pane.

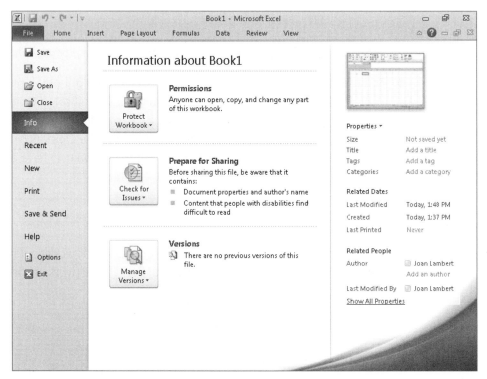

Clicking the File tab displays the Backstage view, where you can manage files and customize the program.

● Commands related to working with file content are represented as buttons on the remaining tabs. The Home tab is active by default.

Tip Don't be alarmed if your ribbon has tabs not shown in our screens. You might have installed programs that add their own tabs to the ribbon.

● On each tab, buttons are organized into named groups. Depending on your screen resolution and the size of the program window, the commands in a group might be displayed as labeled buttons, as unlabeled icons, or as one or more large buttons that you click to display the commands within the group. You might want to experiment with the screen resolution and width of the program window to understand their effect on the appearance of tab content.

● If a button label isn't visible, you can display the command, a description of its function, and its keyboard shortcut (if it has one) in a ScreenTip by pointing to the button.

ScreenTips can include the command name, description, and keyboard shortcut.

Tip You can control the display of ScreenTips and of feature descriptions in ScreenTips. Simply display the Backstage view, click Options to open the program's Options dialog box, and click the ScreenTip setting you want in the User Interface Options area of the General page. For more information, see "Changing Program Settings" later in this chapter.

● Related but less common commands might be available in a dialog box or task pane, which you display by clicking the dialog box launcher located in the lower-right corner of the group.

Tip You might find that less commonly used commands from earlier versions of a program are not available from the ribbon. However, these commands are still available. You can make missing commands accessible by adding them to the Quick Access Toolbar. For more information, see "Customizing the Quick Access Toolbar" later in this chapter.

● Some buttons include an integrated or separate arrow. To determine whether a button and arrow are integrated, point to the button or arrow to display its border. If a button and its arrow are integrated within one border, clicking the button will display options for refining the action of the button. If the button and arrow have separate borders, clicking the button will carry out the default action indicated by the button's current icon. You can change the default action of the button by clicking the arrow and then clicking the action you want.

The arrow of the Change Styles button is integrated, and the arrow of the Paste button is separate.

● Above the right end of the ribbon is the Minimize The Ribbon button. Clicking this button hides the commands but leaves the tab names visible. You can then click any tab name to temporarily display its commands. Clicking anywhere other than the ribbon hides the commands again. When the full ribbon is temporarily visible, you can click the button at its right end, shaped like a pushpin, to make the display permanent. When the full ribbon is hidden, you can click the Expand The Ribbon button to redisplay it.

Keyboard Shortcut Press Ctrl+F1 to minimize or expand the ribbon.

● Clicking the Help button at the right end of the ribbon displays the program-specific Help window in which you can use standard techniques to find information.

Keyboard Shortcut Press F1 to display the Help window for the active program.

See Also For information about the Help system, see "Getting Help" at the beginning of this book.

● Across the bottom of the program window, the status bar displays information about the current file and provides access to certain program functions. You can control the contents of the status bar by right-clicking it to display the Customize Status Bar menu, on which you can click any item to display or hide it.

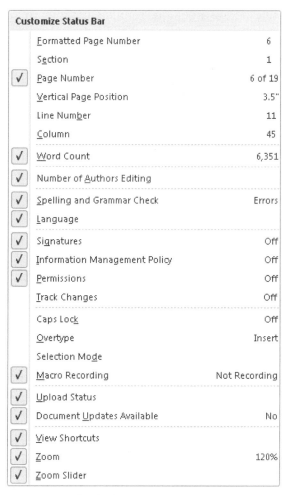

You can specify which items you want to display on the status bar.

● At the right end of the status bar in the Word, Excel, and PowerPoint program windows are the View Shortcuts toolbar, the Zoom button, and the Zoom slider. These tools provide you with convenient methods for adjusting the display of file content.

You can change the file content view by clicking buttons on the View Shortcuts toolbar and change the magnification by clicking the Zoom button or adjusting the Zoom slider.

See Also For information about changing the file content view, see "Viewing Files in Different Ways" in Chapter 2, "Work with Files."

The goal of all these features of the program environment is to make working in the program as intuitive as possible. Commands for tasks you perform often are readily available, and even those you might use infrequently are easy to find.

For example, when a formatting option has several choices available, they are often displayed in a gallery of thumbnails. These thumbnails display visual representations of each choice. If you point to a thumbnail in a gallery, the Live Preview feature shows you what that choice will look like if you apply it to the selected content.

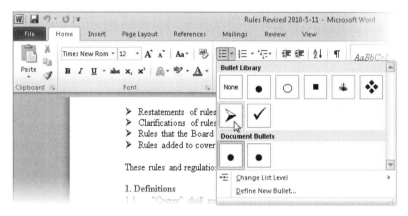

Live Preview shows the effect on the selected content of clicking the option you are pointing to.

In this exercise, you'll start Word and explore the tabs and groups on the ribbon. Along the way, you'll work with galleries and the Live Preview feature.

 SET UP You don't need any practice files to complete this exercise; just follow the steps.

1. On the **Start** menu, click **All Programs**, click **Microsoft Office**, and then click **Microsoft Word 2010**.

   Tip If this is the first time you've started an Office 2010 program, Office prompts you to enter your full name and initials. Office 2010 programs use this information when tracking changes, responding to messages, and so on. Next, Office prompts you to select the type of information you want to share over the Internet, and offers the option of signing up for automatic program updates from the Microsoft Update service. None of these options place you at risk, and all can be quite useful.

   The Word program window opens in Print Layout view, displaying a blank document. On the ribbon, the Home tab is active. Buttons related to working with document content are organized on this tab in five groups: Clipboard, Font, Paragraph, Styles, and Editing.

2. Point to each button on the **Home** tab.

   Word displays information about the button in a ScreenTip.

The ScreenTip for the Format Painter button displays the button's name, keyboard shortcut, and function.

Tip A button representing a command that cannot be performed on the selected file content is inactive (gray), but pointing to it still displays its ScreenTip.

3. Click the **Insert** tab, and then explore its buttons.

Buttons related to all the items you can insert into the document are organized on this tab in seven groups: Pages, Tables, Illustrations, Links, Header & Footer, Text, and Symbols.

The Insert tab of the ribbon.

4. Click the **Page Layout** tab, and then explore its buttons.

Buttons related to the appearance of the document are organized on this tab in five groups: Themes, Page Setup, Page Background, Paragraph, and Arrange.

The Page Layout tab of the ribbon.

5. In the **Page Setup** group, display the ScreenTip for the **Margins** button.

   The ScreenTip tells you how you can adjust the margins.

6. In the lower-right corner of the **Page Setup** group, click the **Page Setup** dialog box launcher.

   The Page Setup dialog box opens.

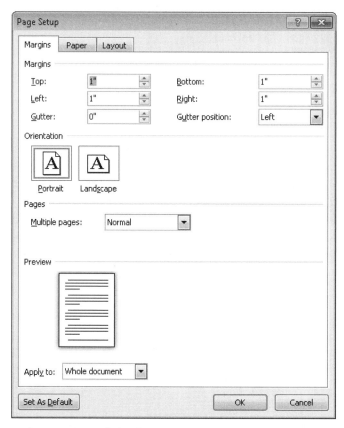

In the Page Setup dialog box, you can specify several page layout options in one location.

   Notice that you can preview the results of your changes before applying them.

7. Click **Cancel** to close the dialog box.

8. In the **Themes** group, click the **Themes** button.

The group expands to display a gallery of the available themes.

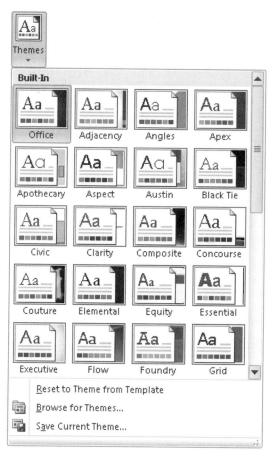

The theme controls the color scheme, fonts, and special effects applied to file content.

9. Press the Esc key to close the gallery without making a selection.

10. In the **Page Background** group, click the **Page Color** button, and then in the top row of the **Theme Colors** palette, point to each box in turn.

The blank document page shows a live preview of what it will look like if you click the color you are pointing to. You can see the effect of the selection without actually applying it.

11. Press Esc to close the palette without making a selection.

12. Click the **References** tab, and then explore its buttons.

    Buttons related to items you can add to documents are organized on this tab in six groups: Table Of Contents, Footnotes, Citations & Bibliography, Captions, Index, and Table Of Authorities. You will usually add these items to longer documents, such as reports.

The References tab of the ribbon.

13. Click the **Mailings** tab, and then explore its buttons.

    Buttons related to creating mass mailings are organized on this tab in five groups: Create, Start Mail Merge, Write & Insert Fields, Preview Results, and Finish.

The Mailings tab of the ribbon.

14. Click the **Review** tab, and then explore its buttons.

    Buttons related to proofreading documents, working in other languages, adding comments, tracking and resolving document changes, and protecting documents are organized on this tab in seven groups: Proofing, Language, Comments, Tracking, Changes, Compare, and Protect.

The Review tab of the ribbon.

15. Click the **View** tab, and then explore its buttons.

    Buttons related to changing the view and other aspects of the display are organized on this tab in five groups: Document Views, Show, Zoom, Window, and Macros.

The View tab of the ribbon.

16. On the ribbon, click the **File** tab, which is color-coded to match the logo color of the Word program.

    The Backstage view of Word 2010 is displayed. Commands related to managing documents (such as creating, saving, and printing) are available in this view.

17. If the **Info** page is not already displayed in the Backstage view, click **Info** in the left pane.

    On the Info page of the Backstage view, the middle pane provides options to control who can work on the document, to remove properties (associated information), and to access versions of the document automatically saved by Word. The right pane displays the associated properties, as well as dates of modification, creation, and printing, and the names of people who created and edited the document.

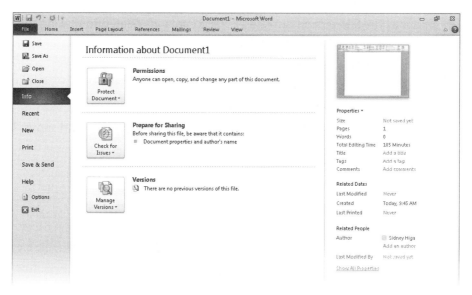

The Info page displays and provides commands for changing the information attached to a document.

See Also For information about working with properties, see "Preparing Documents for Electronic Distribution" in Chapter 7, "Preview, Print, and Distribute Documents."

18. In the left pane, click **Recent**.

    The Recent page displays the names of the documents you recently worked on. By default a maximum of 20 names is displayed. You can change this number on the Advanced page of the Word Options dialog box.

    See Also For information about the Options dialog box, see "Changing Program Settings" later in this chapter.

19. In the left pane, click **New**.

    The New page displays all the templates on which you can base a new document.

    See Also For information about creating documents, see "Creating and Saving Files" in Chapter 2, "Work with Files."

20. In the left pane, click **Print**.

    The Print page displays all print-related commands and provides a pane for pre-viewing the current document as it will appear when printed.

    See Also For information about printing, see Chapter 7, "Preview, Print, and Distribute Documents."

21. **In the left pane, click Share.**

    The Share page displays all the commands related to making the current document available to other people.

    See Also For information about working with shared documents, refer to *Microsoft Word 2010 Step by Step* by Joyce Cox and Joan Lambert (Microsoft Press, 2010).

22. In the left pane, click **Help**.

    The Help page displays all the ways you can get help and support for Word.

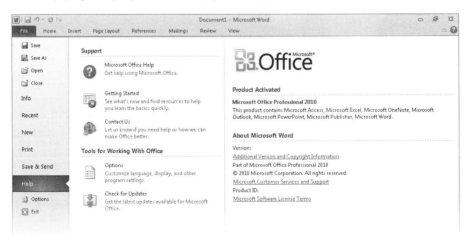

The right pane of the Help page displays your Office edition, its version number, and your product ID, which you will need if you contact Microsoft Product Support.

23. On the **Help** page, under **Tools for Working With Office**, click **Options**.

    The Word Options dialog box opens. In this dialog box are program settings that control the way the program looks and performs.

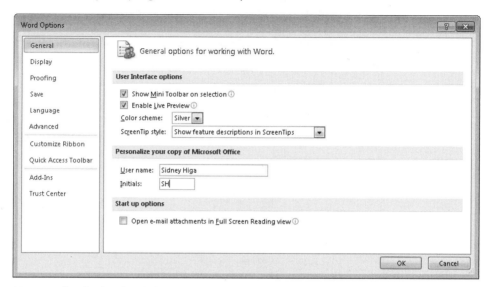

You can also display this dialog box by clicking Options in the left pane of the Backstage view.

See Also For information about the Options dialog box, see the next section, "Changing Program Settings."

24. At the bottom of the **Word Options** dialog box, click **Cancel**.

    You return to the blank document with the Home tab active on the ribbon.

 **CLEAN UP** Leave the blank document open if you're continuing directly to the next exercise.

Changing Program Settings

Earlier in this chapter, we mentioned that you can change settings in the Options dialog box for each program to customize the program environment in various ways. After you work with a program for a while, you might want to refine more settings to tailor the program to the way you work. Knowing your way around the Options dialog box makes the customizing process more efficient.

In this exercise, you'll open the Word Options dialog box and explore several of the available pages.

 SET UP You don't need any practice files to complete this exercise. Open a blank document if necessary, and then follow the steps.

1. On the **Home** tab, in the **Font** group, point to the **Bold** button.

   Word displays a ScreenTip that includes the button name, its keyboard shortcut, and a description of its purpose.

2. Display the Backstage view, and click **Options**.

   The Word Options dialog box opens, displaying the General page.

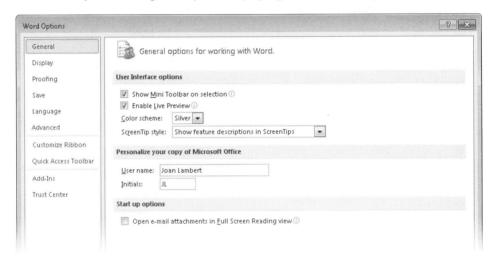

The General page of the Word Options dialog box.

If you prefer not to see the Mini Toolbar when you select text, you can disable that feature by clearing the Show Mini Toolbar On Selection check box. Similarly, you can disable the live preview of styles and formatting by clearing the Enable Live Preview check box.

3. Under **User Interface options**, display the **Color scheme** list, and click **Black**.

4. Display the **ScreenTip style** list, and click **Don't show feature descriptions in ScreenTips**.

5. Under **Personalize your copy of Microsoft Office**, verify that the **User Name** and **Initials** are correct, or change them to the way you want them to appear.

6. Click **OK** to close the **Word Options** dialog box.

   The program window elements are now black and shades of gray.

7. In the **Font** group, point to the **Bold** button.

   The ScreenTip now includes only the button name and its keyboard shortcut.

8. Open the **Word Options** dialog box, and in the left pane, click **Display**.

   On this page, you can adjust how documents look on the screen and when printed.

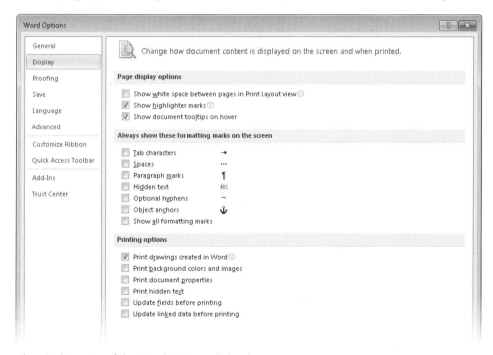

The Display page of the Word Options dialog box.

9. In the left pane, click **Proofing**.

This page provides options for adjusting the AutoCorrect settings and for refining the spelling-checking and grammar-checking processes.

See Also For information about AutoCorrect and checking spelling, see "Correcting Spelling and Grammatical Errors" in Chapter 3, "Edit and Proofread Text."

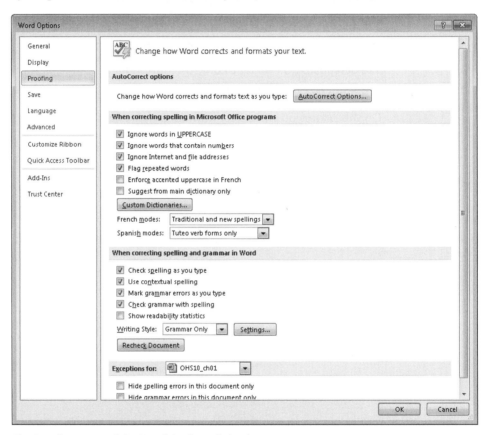

The Proofing page of the Word Options dialog box.

10. Display the **Save** page.

On this page, you can change the default document format; the location and save frequency of the AutoRecover file (a backup file created by Word while you're working in the file); the default location to which Word saves files you create; and the default location for files you check out from document management servers (such as Microsoft SharePoint) and drafts of those files saved while you are working offline.

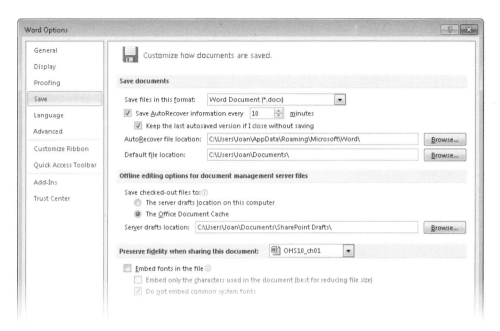

The Save page of the Word Options dialog box.

The Save page also has options for specifying whether you want the fonts used within the current document to be embedded in the document, in the event that someone who opens the document doesn't have those fonts on his or her computer.

11. Under **Save documents**, display the **Save files in this format** list.

Notice the many formats in which you can save files. One of these is the Word 97-2003 Document format that creates .doc files compatible with earlier versions of Word. If you upgraded to Word 2010 but your colleagues are still working in an earlier version of the program, you might want to select this option so that they will be able to view and work with any document you create.

Tip If you want to save just one document in a format that is compatible with earlier versions of the program, you can click Word 97-2003 in the Save As Type list of the Save As dialog box.

12. Click away from the list to close it, and then display the **Language** page.

If you create documents for international audiences, you can make additional editing languages available on this page. You can also specify the display, Help, and ScreenTip languages.

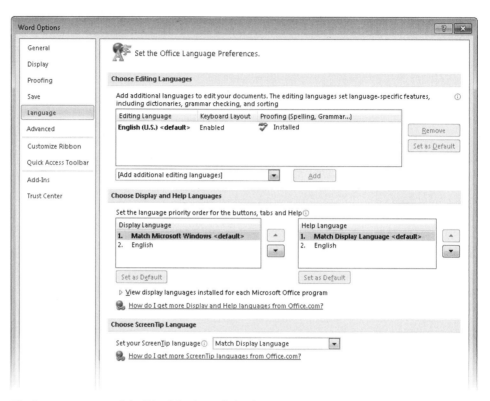

The Language page of the Word Options dialog box.

13. Display the **Advanced** page.

This page includes options related to editing document content; displaying documents on-screen; printing, saving, and sharing documents; and a variety of other options. Although these options are labeled *Advanced*, they are the ones you're most likely to want to adjust to suit the way you work.

See Also For information about advanced Word 2010 options that aren't discussed in this book, refer to *Microsoft Word 2010 Step by Step* by Joyce Cox and Joan Lambert (Microsoft Press, 2010).

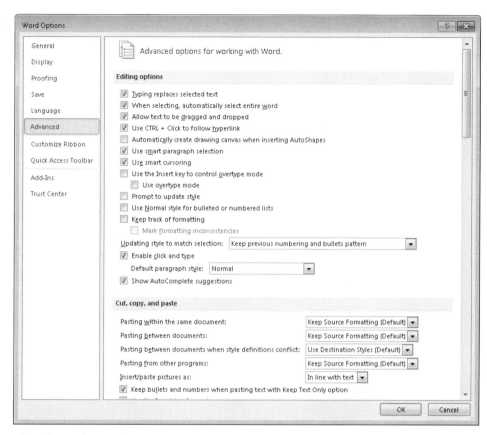

The Advanced page of the Word Options dialog box.

14. Take a few minutes to explore all the options on this page.

    In the General area at the bottom of the page are two buttons:

    ○ **File Locations** You click this button to change the default locations of various types of files associated with Word and its documents.

    ○ **Web Options** You click this button to adjust settings for converting a document to a Web page.

15. Skipping over the Customize Ribbon and Quick Access Toolbar pages, which we discuss in later topics in this chapter, click **Add-Ins**.

    This page displays all the active and inactive add-ins and enables you to add and remove them. (Add-ins are utility programs that provide additional functionality to an Office program.)

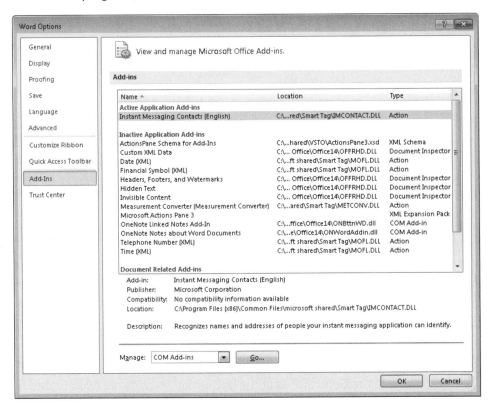

The Add-Ins page of the Word Options dialog box.

16. Display the **Trust Center** page.

    This page provides links to information about privacy and security. It also provides access to the Trust Center settings that control the actions Word takes in response to documents that are provided by certain people or companies, that are saved in certain locations, or that contain potentially harmful elements such as ActiveX controls or macros.

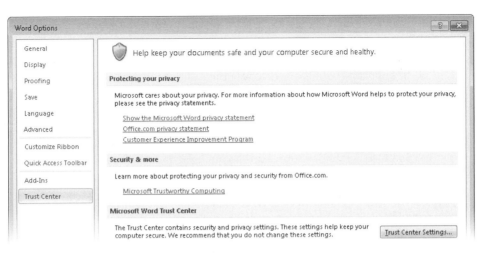

The Trust Center page of the Word Options dialog box.

17. Under **Microsoft Office Word Trust Center**, click **Trust Center Settings**, and then in the left pane of the **Trust Center** dialog box, click **Trusted Locations**.

On this page, you can specify the locations from which Word will not block content.

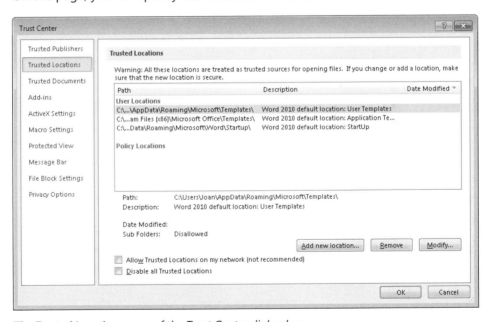

The Trusted Locations page of the Trust Center dialog box.

CLEAN UP Close the Trust Center dialog box. Reverse any changes you don't want to keep before moving on. Then close the Word Options dialog box. Leave the blank document open if you're continuing directly to the next exercise.

Customizing the Ribbon

The ribbon was designed to make all the commonly used commands visible so that people can more easily discover the full potential of an Office 2010 program. But many people use an Office program to perform the same set of tasks all the time, and for them, seeing buttons (or even entire groups of buttons) that they never use is just another form of clutter.

See Also For information about minimizing and expanding the ribbon, see "Customizing the Quick Access Toolbar" later in this chapter.

Would you prefer to see fewer commands than appear on the ribbon by default? Or would you prefer to see more specialized groups of commands? Well, you can. From the Customize Ribbon page of an Office 2010 program's Options dialog box, you can control the tabs that appear on the ribbon, and the groups that appear on the tabs.

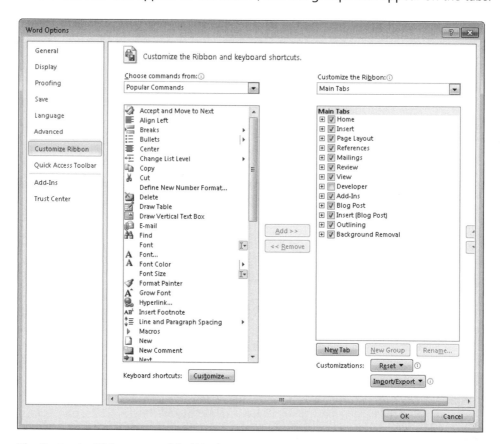

The Customize Ribbon page of the Word Options dialog box.

On this page, you can customize the ribbon in the following ways:

- If you rarely use a tab, you can turn it off.

- If you use the commands in only a few groups on each tab, you can remove the groups you don't use. (The group is not removed from the program, just from its tab.)

- You can move a predefined group by removing it from one tab and then adding it to another.

- You can duplicate a predefined group by adding it to another tab.

- You can create a custom group on any tab and then add commands to it. (You cannot add commands to a predefined group.)

- You can create a custom tab on the ribbon. For example, you might want to do this if you use only a few commands from each tab and you find it inefficient to flip between them.

Don't be afraid to experiment with the ribbon to come up with the configuration that best suits the way you work. If at any point you find that your new ribbon is harder to work with rather than easier, you can always reset everything back to the default configuration.

Tip If you upgraded from Office 2007 or an earlier version of Office, you might find that some commands present in the earlier version are not available on the ribbon. A few old features have been abandoned, but others that people used only rarely have simply not been exposed in the user interface. If you want to use one of these hidden features, you can make it a part of your program environment by adding it to the ribbon or to the Quick Access Toolbar. You can find a list of all the commands that do not appear on the ribbon but are still available in a program by displaying the Customize Ribbon page of the program's Options dialog box and then clicking Commands Not In The Ribbon in the Choose Commands From list.

In this exercise, you'll customize the ribbon in the Word program window by using techniques that are common to all Office 2010 programs. You'll turn off tabs, remove groups, create a custom group, and add a command to the group. Then you'll create a tab and move groups of buttons to it. Finally, you'll reset the ribbon to its default state.

SET UP You don't need any practice files to complete this exercise. Open a blank document if necessary, and then follow the steps.

1. Open the **Word Options** dialog box, and then click **Customize Ribbon**.

   The Customize Ribbon page is displayed.

2. In the list on the right, clear the check boxes of the **Insert**, **Page Layout**, **References**, **Mailings**, and **Review** tabs. Then click **OK**.

The ribbon now displays only the File, Home, and View tabs.

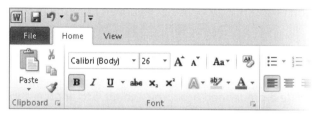

The only tab you can't customize is the File tab, which is your link to the Backstage view.

3. Redisplay the **Customize Ribbon** page of the **Word Options** dialog box, and in the right pane, select the **Page Layout** check box. Then click the plus sign to display the groups on this tab.

4. Above the left pane, click **Choose commands from** and then, in the list, click **Main Tabs**. In the **Main Tabs** list, click the plus sign adjacent to **Page Layout** to display the groups that are predefined for this tab.

5. In the right pane, click the **Paragraph** group, and then click **Remove**.

The group is removed from the Page Layout tab on the ribbon (the list on the right) but is still available in the list on the left. You can add it back to the Page Layout tab or add it to a different tab at any time.

6. In the right pane, click the plus sign adjacent to **Home** to display its groups, and then click the word **Home**.

7. Below the right pane, click **New Group**. When the **New Group (Custom)** group is added to the bottom of the Home group list, click **Rename**, type **Final** in the **Display name** box, and click **OK**. Then click the **Move Up** button until the **Final** group is at the top of the list.

Because of its location in the list, the new group will appear at the left end of the Home tab.

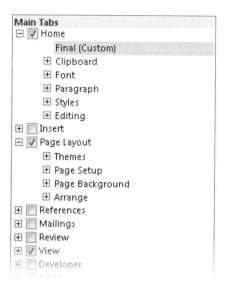

You have created a custom group on the Home tab.

8. In the **Choose commands from** list, click **File Tab**.

    The available commands list changes to include only the commands that are available in the Backstage view, which you display by clicking the File tab.

9. In the available commands list, click **Inspect Document**, and click **Add**. Then repeat this step to add **Mark as Final**.

    The two commands are added to the custom group.

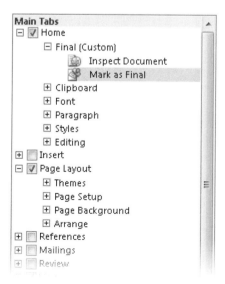

You can add commands to a custom group but not to a predefined group.

10. In the right pane, remove the **Font**, **Paragraph**, and **Styles** groups from the **Home** tab, and remove the **Page Background** group from the **Page Layout** tab.

11. Click the word **Home**, and then below the list, click **New Tab**.

    A new tab is added to the right pane and is selected for display on the ribbon. It has automatically been given one custom group.

12. Click **Remove** to remove the custom group.

13. Click **New Tab (Custom)**, and then click **Rename**. In the **Rename** dialog box, type **Formatting** in the **Display name** box, and click **OK**.

14. Display **Main Tabs** in the list on the left, and then expand the **Home** and **Page Layout** tabs.

15. With the **Formatting** tab selected in the right pane, add the **Font**, **Paragraph**, and **Styles** groups from **Home** in the left pane, and then add **Page Background** from **Page Layout**.

    The right pane shows the new configuration of the Home, Formatting, and Page Layout tabs.

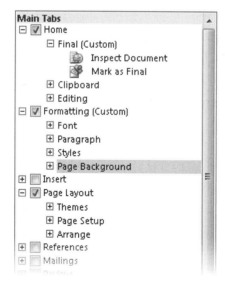

You have moved groups from the Home and Page Layout tabs to a new Formatting tab.

16. In the **Word Options** dialog box, click **OK**.

The Home tab displays the new Final group.

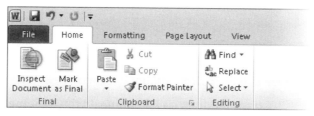

The custom Home tab.

17. Click the **Formatting** tab.

The formatting commands are now collected on the Formatting tab.

The custom Formatting tab.

18. Display the **Customize Ribbon** page of the **Word Options** dialog box. In the lower-right corner, click **Reset**, and then click **Reset all customizations**. Then in the message box asking you to confirm that you want to delete all ribbon and Quick Access Toolbar customizations, click **Yes**.

19. Click **OK** to close the **Word Options** dialog box.

The default ribbon configuration is restored.

✖ CLEAN UP Close the open document.

Customizing the Quick Access Toolbar

If you regularly use a few buttons that are scattered on various tabs of the ribbon and you don't want to switch between tabs to access the buttons or crowd your ribbon with a custom tab, you might want to add these frequently used buttons to the Quick Access Toolbar. They are then always visible in the upper-left corner of the program window.

Clicking Quick Access Toolbar in the left pane of a program's Options dialog box displays the page where you specify which commands you want to appear on the toolbar.

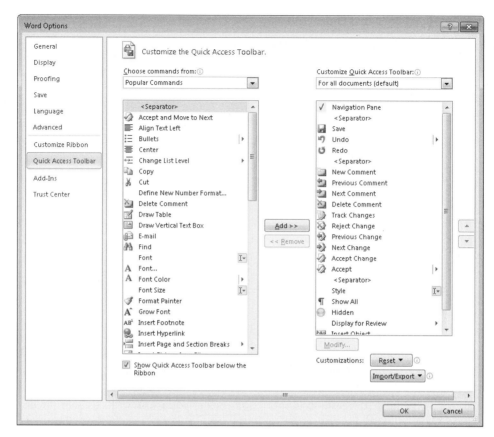

The Quick Access Toolbar page of the Word Options dialog box.

On this page, you can customize the ribbon in the following ways:

- You can define a custom Quick Access Toolbar for the program, or you can define a custom Quick Access Toolbar for a specific file.

- You can add any command from any group of any tab, including contextual tabs, to the toolbar.

- You can display a separator between different types of buttons.

- You can move buttons around on the toolbar until they are in the order you want.

- You can reset everything back to the default Quick Access Toolbar configuration.

If you never use more than a few buttons, you can add those buttons to the Quick Access Toolbar and then hide the ribbon by double-clicking the active tab or by clicking the Minimize The Ribbon button. Only the Quick Access Toolbar and tab names remain visible. You can temporarily redisplay the ribbon by clicking the tab you want to view.

You can permanently redisplay the ribbon by double-clicking any tab or by clicking the Expand The Ribbon button.

As you add buttons to the Quick Access Toolbar, it expands to accommodate them. If you add many buttons, it might become difficult to view the text in the title bar, or not all the buttons on the Quick Access Toolbar might be visible, defeating the purpose of adding them. To resolve this problem, you can move the Quick Access Toolbar below the ribbon by clicking the Customize Quick Access Toolbar button and then clicking Show Below The Ribbon.

In this exercise, you'll add a couple buttons to the Quick Access Toolbar for all documents, and then you'll test the buttons.

 SET UP You don't need any practice files to complete this exercise. Open a blank document, and then follow the steps.

1. Open the **Word Options** dialog box, and then click **Quick Access Toolbar**.

   The Customize The Quick Access Toolbar page displays a list of available commands on the left side, and a list of the currently displayed commands on the right side.

   Tip If you want to create a Quick Access Toolbar that is specific to the active file, click the arrow at the right end of the box below Customize Quick Access Toolbar, and then click For <file name>. Then any command you select will be added to a toolbar specific to that file instead of the toolbar for the program.

2. At the top of the available commands list on the left, double-click **Separator**.

3. Scroll down the available commands list, click the **Quick Print** command, and then click **Add**.

4. Repeat step 3 to add the **Text Highlight Color** command.

   The Text Highlight Color command is added to the list of commands that will appear on the Quick Access Toolbar.

The arrow to the right of the command indicates that clicking this button on the Quick Access Toolbar will display a menu of options.

5. Click **OK** to close the **Word Options** dialog box.

   The Quick Access Toolbar now includes the default Save, Undo, and Repeat buttons and the custom Quick Print and Text Highlight Color buttons, separated by a line.

   You have added two buttons to the Quick Access Toolbar.

   To print a document with the default settings, you no longer have to click the File tab to display the Backstage view. Click Print in the left pane, and then click the Print button.

6. If you want to test printing from the Quick Access Toolbar, ensure that your printer is turned on, and then on the Quick Access Toolbar, click the **Quick Print** button.

   Now let's see how easy it is to highlight or remove highlighting from text when you are working primarily with the commands on a tab other than the Home tab.

7. Click the **Review** tab. Then select the first highlighted paragraph, **Proof of notice of meeting**.

8. On the Quick Access Toolbar, click the **Text Highlight Color** arrow, and then click **No Color**.

   The yellow highlight is removed from the selection. The No Color option becomes the default for the Text Highlight Color button.

9. Select the next highlighted paragraph, and on the Quick Access Toolbar, click the **Text Highlight Color** button.

   The yellow highlight is removed from the selection.

10. Display the **Quick Access Toolbar** page of the **Word Options** dialog box, click **Reset**, and then click **Reset only Quick Access Toolbar**.

11. In the **Reset Customizations** message box, click **Yes** to return the Quick Access Toolbar to its default contents. Then click **OK** to close the **Word Options** dialog box.

 CLEAN UP Close the open document.

Key Points

- The Office 2010 program environment is flexible and can be customized to meet your needs.

- Most of the settings that control the working environment are gathered on the pages of the Options dialog box.

- You can customize the ribbon to make the development tools you need most often easily accessible.

- You can provide one-click access to any command by adding a button for it to the Quick Access Toolbar, either for the program or for one file.

Chapter at a Glance

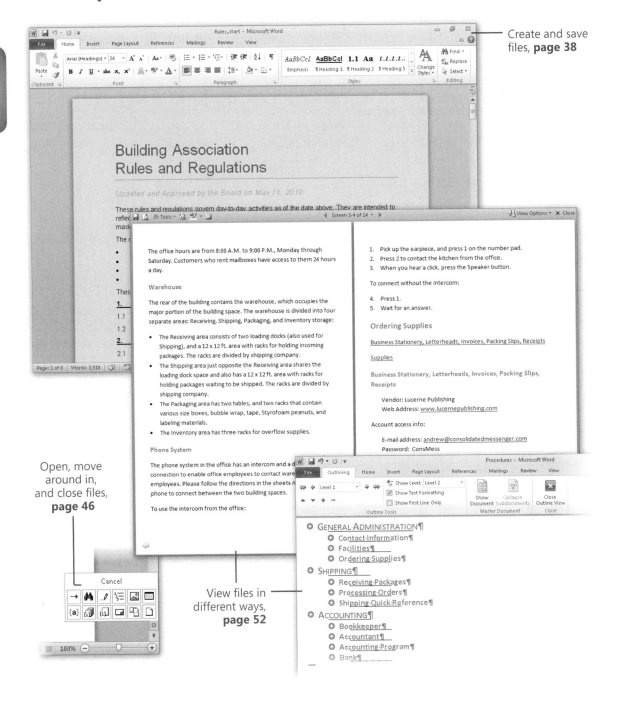

Create and save files, **page 38**

Open, move around in, and close files, **page 46**

View files in different ways, **page 52**

2 Work with Files

In this chapter, you will learn how to

✔ Create and save files.

✔ Open, move around in, and close files.

✔ View files in different ways.

When working in Microsoft Word, Excel, or PowerPoint, you save content in individual files. In each program, you can save files as different types depending on each file's purpose. The standard files are Word documents, Excel workbooks, and PowerPoint presentations. Regardless of the program or file type, you use similar techniques for creating, saving, moving around in, and viewing files in each program.

When working in OneNote, content is saved in individual files representing pages that are part of a notebook structure. OneNote creates the files for you and saves your changes as you work, so you don't need to. However, you use some of the same techniques for moving around in and viewing files as you do in other Microsoft Office 2010 programs.

In this chapter, you'll practice working with files in Word, using techniques that are common to working in files created in Word, Excel, or PowerPoint. First you'll create and save a document and then save an existing document in a different location. Then you'll open an existing document, move around in it, and close it. Finally, you'll explore various ways of viewing file content.

> **Practice Files** Before you can complete the exercises in this chapter, you need to copy the book's practice files to your computer. The practice files you'll use to complete the exercises in this chapter are in the Chapter02 practice file folder. A complete list of practice files is provided in "Using the Practice Files" at the beginning of this book.

Creating and Saving Files

When you start Word, Excel, or PowerPoint without opening a specific file, the program displays a blank document, workbook, or presentation in which you can start entering content. A blinking cursor (in the form of a vertical line) in the text pane or worksheet cell shows where the next character you type will appear.

When an Office 2010 program is running, you can create a new file from the New page of the Backstage view, which you display by clicking the File tab on the ribbon.

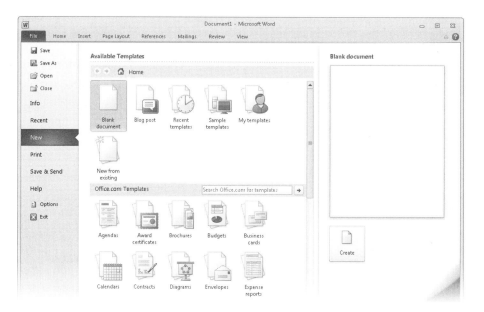

From the New page, you can create a document based on a preformatted template.

Tip More documents may be added to those available from Microsoft Office Online, so the templates available on your New page might be different from those shown here.

The documents listed on the New page are based on templates, which are sets of formats that have been saved in such a way that you can use them as a pattern for new documents. For example, in Word 2010 the icons in the top section of the Available Templates gallery are:

- **Blank document** Clicking this icon opens a document formatted with the standard settings. The document contains no content.

   Tip The standard Word document settings are based on a template named Normal, which is installed on your computer as part of the Office installation. You can make changes to the Normal template but it is not customary or advisable to do so.

- **Blog post** Clicking this icon opens a document containing the basic elements of a blog post in a document window. The document window includes additional functionality enabling you to easily post directly to an existing blog site from within Word.

- **Recent templates** Clicking this icon displays a page on which you can select from the most recent templates you have used.

  Tip Clicking the Back button or the Home button takes you back to the New page.

- **Sample templates** Clicking this icon displays a page on which you can select from sample documents that come with Word.

- **My templates** Clicking this icon displays a dialog box in which you can select a template you have created as the basis for a new document.

- **New from existing** Clicking this icon displays a dialog box in which you can select an existing document as the basis for a new document.

The icons in the Office.com Templates section represent categories of common types of files for the program you're working in. Depending on how many templates are available in a category, the icon might be a folder. Regardless, clicking one of these icons displays more templates that are available for download from the Microsoft Office Online Web site. You can also search for specific file types by entering the type you want in the Search Office.com For Templates box and clicking the Start Searching button.

See Also For information about document templates, refer to *Microsoft Word 2010 Step by Step* by Joyce Cox and Joan Lambert (Microsoft Press, 2010).

When you find a template you might want to use as the basis for your new file, clicking its icon displays a preview of that file in the right pane. You can then click the Create button in the right pane to create the file.

Tip Double-clicking an icon creates that type of file without first displaying it in the preview pane.

Each file you create from the New page of the Backstage view is temporary until you save it. To save a document, workbook, or presentation for the first time, you click the Save button on the Quick Access Toolbar or click Save in the Backstage view. Either action displays the Save As dialog box, where you can assign a name and storage location to the file.

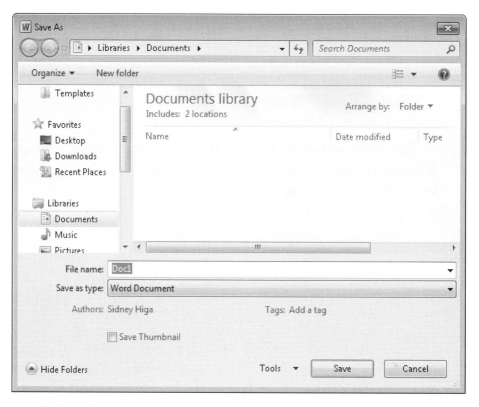

By default, the Save As dialog box displays the contents of your Documents library.

Troubleshooting This graphic shows the Save As dialog box as it appears when Word is running on Windows 7. If you are using a different version of the Windows operating system,
your dialog box will look different but the way you work in it will be similar.

If you want to save the file in a folder other than the one shown in the Address bar at
the top of the dialog box, you can click the arrow or chevrons in the Address bar or click
locations in the Navigation pane on the left to display the folder you want. If you want
to create a folder in which to store the file, you can click the New Folder button on the
toolbar.

If you want to save a file in a format other than the one shown in the Save As Type box,
click the Save As Type arrow and then, in the Save As Type list, click the file format you
want.

After you save a file the first time, you can save subsequent changes by clicking the Save button. The new version of the file then overwrites the previous version.

Keyboard Shortcut Press Ctrl+S to save the current document.

Tip Windows 7 automatically retains previous file versions. To view previous versions of a file on a computer running Windows 7, right-click the file in Windows Explorer, and then click Restore Previous Versions.

If you want to keep both the new version and the previous version, click Save As in the Backstage view, and then save the new version with a different name in the same location or with the same name in a different location. (You can't store two files of the same type with the same name in the same folder.)

Tip By default, each program periodically saves the file you're working on in case the program stops responding or you lose electrical power. To adjust the frequency at which the program saves the file, display the Backstage view, click Options, click the Save tab in the left pane of the Options dialog box, and specify the period of time in the box to the right of the Save AutoRecover Information Every check box. Then click OK.

In this exercise, you'll work with files in Word by using techniques that are common to all Office 2010 programs. You'll create a blank document, enter text, and save the document in a folder that you create.

 SET UP You don't need any practice files to complete this exercise. Start Word, and then follow the steps.

1. On the ribbon, click the **File** tab to display the Backstage view. Then in the left pane of the Backstage view, click **New**.

2. On the **New** page, double-click **Blank document**.

    Word creates a blank document temporarily called *Document2* and displays it in its own program window in Print Layout view. Document1 is still open, but its window is hidden by the Document2 window.

    Tip Word created Document1 when you started the program.

    See Also For information about switching between open windows, see "Viewing Files in Different Ways" later in this chapter.

3. With the cursor at the beginning of the new document, type **Parks Appreciation Day**, and then press the Enter key.

    The text appears in the new document.

4. Type the following sentence (including the period):

Help beautify our city by participating in the annual cleanup of Log Park, Swamp Creek Park, and Linkwood Park. This is a lot of fun! Volunteers receive a free T-shirt and barbeque lunch. Bring your own gardening tools and gloves.

Notice that you did not need to press Enter when the cursor reached the right margin because the text automatically continued on the next line.

Parks Appreciation Day

Help beautify our city by participating in the annual cleanup of Log Park, Swamp Creek Park, and Linkwood Park. This is a lot of fun! Volunteers receive a free T-shirt and barbecue lunch. Bring your own gardening tools and gloves.

You press Enter at the end of each paragraph; the Word Wrap feature takes care of wrapping each line.

Tip If a red or green wavy line appears under a word or phrase, Word is flagging a possible error in spelling or grammar. For now, ignore any errors.

5. Press Enter, and then type the following sentence (including the period):

The Service Committee is coordinating groups to participate in this event. If you are interested in spending time outdoors with your family and friends while improving the quality of our parks, contact Paul Shen at paul@treyresearch.net.

6. On the Quick Access Toolbar, click the **Save** button.

The Save As dialog box opens, displaying the contents of your Documents library. In the File Name box, Word suggests the first words in the document as a possible name.

7. Navigate to your **Chapter02** practice file folder.

New folder

8. On the dialog box's toolbar, click the **New folder** button, type **My New Documents** as the name of the new folder, and press Enter. Then double-click the **My New Documents** folder.

9. In the **File name** box, click anywhere in **Parks Appreciation Day** to select it, and then replace this name by typing **My Announcement**.

   Important Each type of file is identified by a specific file name extension. For example, the extension .docx identifies documents created in Word 2010 or Word 2007 that don't contain macros. Windows 7 does not display these extensions by default, and you don't need to type them in the Save As dialog box. When you save a file, Word automatically adds whatever extension is associated with the type of file selected in the Save As Type box.

10. Click **Save**.

    The Save As dialog box closes, Word saves the My Announcement document in the My New Documents folder, and the name of the document, My Announcement, appears on the program window's title bar.

11. Display the Backstage view, and then click **Save As**.

    The Save As dialog box opens, displaying the contents of the My New Documents folder, because that is the last folder you worked with.

12. In the **Address** bar of the **Save As** dialog box, to the left of **My New Documents**, click **Chapter02**.

    The dialog box now displays the contents of the Chapter02 practice file folder, which is the folder that contains the My New Documents folder.

    See Also For information about working with the file properties that appear at the bottom of the Save As dialog box, see "Preparing Documents for Electronic Distribution" in Chapter 7, "Preview, Print, and Distribute Documents."

13. Click **Save**.

    Word saves the My Announcement document in the Chapter02 practice file folder. You now have two versions of the document saved with the same name but in different folders.

✖ **CLEAN UP** At the right end of the title bar, click the Close button (the X) to close the My Announcement document. Leave Document1 open for use in the next exercise.

File Compatibility with Earlier Versions of Office Programs

The Office 2010 programs use file formats based on a programming language called extended markup language, or more commonly, XML. These file formats, called the *Microsoft Office Open XML Formats*, were introduced with Microsoft Office 2007.

The Office Open XML formats provide the following benefits:

- File size is smaller because files are compressed when saved, decreasing the amount of disk space needed to store the file, and the amount of bandwidth needed to send files in e-mail, over a network, or across the Internet.

- Recovering at least some of the content of damaged files is possible because XML files can be opened in a text program such as Notepad.

- Security is greater because the standard file formats cannot contain macros, and personal data can be detected and removed from the file. (Word 2010 and Word 2007 provide a different file format—.docm—for documents that contain macros.)

Each Office 2010 program offers a selection of file formats intended to provide specific benefits. The file formats and file name extensions for Word 2010 documents include the following:

- Word Document (.docx)
- Word Macro-Enabled Document (.docm)
- Word Template (.dotx)
- Word Macro-Enabled Template (.dotm)
- Word XML Document (.xml)

The file formats and file name extensions for Excel 2010 documents include the following:

- Excel Workbook (.xlsx)
- Excel Macro-Enabled Workbook (.xlsm)
- Excel Binary Workbook (.xlsb)
- Excel Template (.xltx)
- Excel Macro-Enabled Template (.xltm)
- Excel Add-In (.xlam)

The file formats and file name extensions for PowerPoint 2010 documents include the following:

- PowerPoint Presentation (.pptx)
- PowerPoint Macro-Enabled Presentation (.pptm)
- PowerPoint Template (.potx)
- PowerPoint Macro-Enabled Template (.potm)
- PowerPoint Show (.ppsx)
- PowerPoint Macro-Enabled Show (.ppsm)
- PowerPoint Add-In (.ppam)
- PowerPoint XML Presentation (.xml)
- PowerPoint Picture Presentation (.pptx)

Other non–program specific file types, such as text files, Web pages, PDF files, and XPS files, are available from the Save As dialog box of each program.

Tip OneNote notebooks are stored in folders. For information about the OneNote file formats, see "Navigating in the OneNote Program Window" in Chapter 18, "Explore OneNote 2010."

You can open a file created with Office 2003, Office XP, Office 2000, or Office 97 in an Office 2010 program, but new features will not be available. The file name appears in the title bar with *[Compatibility Mode]* to its right. You can work in Compatibility mode, or you can convert the document to the current file format by displaying the Info page of the Backstage view and clicking the Convert button in the Compatibility Mode section. You can also click Save As in the Backstage view to save a copy of the file in the current format.

If you work with people who are using Office 2003, Office XP, Office 2000, or Office 97, you can save your documents in a format that they will be able to open and use by choosing the corresponding *97-2003* file format in the Save As Type list, or they can download the Microsoft Office Compatibility Pack for Word, Excel, and PowerPoint File Formats from the Microsoft Download Center (located at download.microsoft.com) so that they can open current Office files in their version of Office.

Opening, Moving Around in, and Closing Files

If a program isn't already running, you can start the program and simultaneously open an existing file by double-clicking the file in Windows Explorer. While a program is running, you can open an existing document from the Backstage view. If you have recently worked on the document you want to open, you can display the Recent page and simply click the document you want in the list. If the document is not available on the Recent page, clicking Open in the left pane displays the Open dialog box.

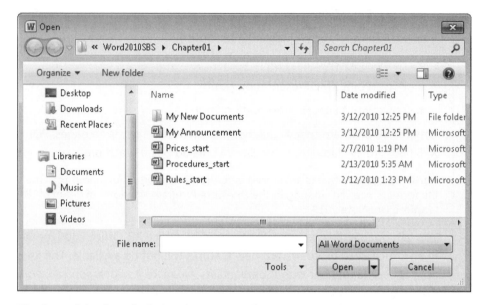

The Open dialog box, displaying the contents of a recently used folder.

By default, the Open dialog box displays your Documents library, with a combined view of your My Documents folder and the Public Documents folder. If you display the dialog box again in the same Word session, it displays the contents of the folder from which you last opened a file. To display the contents of a different folder, you can use the standard Windows techniques described in "Creating and Saving Files" earlier in this chapter. After you locate the document you want to work with, you can open it by clicking its file name and then clicking Open in the lower-right corner of the dialog box, or by simply double-clicking the file name.

Tip Clicking a file name and then clicking the Open arrow (not the button) displays a list of alternative ways in which you can open the file. To look through the file without making any inadvertent changes, you can open it as read-only, or you can open a separate copy of the file. After a computer crash or similar incident, you can open the file and attempt to repair any damage. You can also display the file in other versions and formats.

If you open a document that is too long to fit entirely on the screen, you can bring off-screen content into view without changing the location of the cursor by using the vertical scroll bar in the following ways:

- Click the scroll arrows to move up or down by one line.

- Click above or below the scroll box to move up or down by the height of one window.

- Drag the scroll box on the scroll bar to display the part of the document corresponding to the location of the scroll box. For example, dragging the scroll box to the middle of the scroll bar displays the middle of the document.

If the document is too wide to fit on the screen, Word displays a horizontal scroll bar that you can use in similar ways to move from side to side.

You can also move around in a document by moving the cursor. To place the cursor in a specific location, you simply click there. To move the cursor one page backward or forward, you click the Previous Page and Next Page buttons below the vertical scroll bar. You can also press a keyboard key to move the cursor. For example, pressing the Home key moves the cursor to the left end of a line.

Tip The location of the cursor is displayed on the status bar. You can also display its location by page, section, line, and column, and in inches from the top of the page. SImply select the option you want from the status bar shortcut menu.

The following table lists ways to use your keyboard to move the cursor.

Cursor movement	Key or keyboard shortcut
Left one character	Left Arrow
Right one character	Right Arrow
Down one line	Down Arrow
Up one line	Up Arrow
Left one word	Ctrl+Left Arrow
Right one word	Ctrl+Right Arrow
To the beginning of the current line	Home
To the end of the current line	End
To the beginning of the document	Ctrl+Home
To the end of the document	Ctrl+End
To the beginning of the previous page	Ctrl+Page Up
To the beginning of the next page	Ctrl+Page Down
Up one screen	Page Up
Down one screen	Page Down

In a long document, you might want to move quickly among elements of a certain type; for example, from graphic to graphic. Clicking the Select Browse Object button at the bottom of the vertical scroll bar displays a gallery of browsing options, such as Browse By Page and Browse By Graphic. (These options are also available on the Go To tab of the Find And Replace dialog box, which you display by clicking the Find arrow in the Editing group of the Home tab and then clicking Go To.) You can also display the Navigation task pane and move from heading to heading or page to page.

Keyboard Shortcut Press Ctrl+G to display the Go To tab of the Find And Replace dialog box.

See Also For information about using the Navigation task pane to search for specific content in a document, see "Finding and Replacing Text" in Chapter 3, "Edit and Proofread Text."

If more than one document is open, you can close the active document without exiting Word by clicking the Close button at the right end of the title bar. If only one document is open, clicking the Close button closes the document and also exits Word. If you want to close that document but leave Word running, you must click Close in the Backstage view.

In this exercise, you'll work with files in Word by using techniques that are common to all Office 2010 programs. You'll open an existing document, save a copy of the document, and explore various ways of moving around in it. Then you'll close the document.

SET UP You need the Rules_start document located in your Chapter02 practice file folder to complete this exercise. Continue from the previous exercise or exit and restart Word so that Document1 is the only open document. Then follow the steps.

1. Click the **File** tab to display the Backstage view, and then click **Open**.

   The Open dialog box opens, showing the contents of the folder you used for your previous open or save action.

2. Navigate to the location in which you saved the practice files for this book, and open the **Chapter02** folder.

3. Click the **Rules_start** document, and then click **Open**.

   The Rules_start document opens in the Word program window.

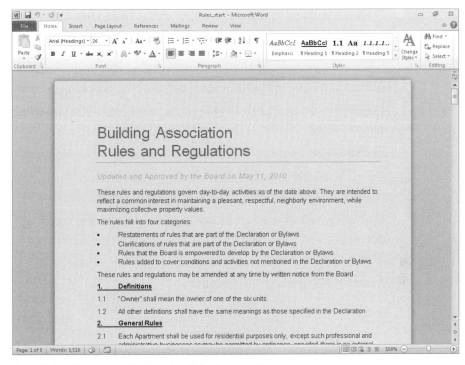

An existing document displayed in Print Layout view.

Troubleshooting The appearance of buttons and groups on the ribbon changes depending on the width of the program window. For information about changing the appearance of the ribbon to match our screen images, see "Modifying the Display of the Ribbon" at the beginning of this book.

4. Display the Backstage view, and in the left pane, click **Save As**. In the **Save As** dialog box, change the file name to **Rules**, and then click **Save**.

   Now you can experiment with the document without fear of overwriting the original.

5. In the second line of the document title, click at the end of the paragraph to position the cursor.

6. Press the Home key to move the cursor to the beginning of the line.

7. Press the Right Arrow key six times to move the cursor to the beginning of the word **and** in the heading.

8. Press the End key to move the cursor to the end of the line.

9. Press Ctrl+End to move the cursor to the end of the document.

10. Press Ctrl+Home to move the cursor to the beginning of the document.

11. At the bottom of the vertical scroll bar, click the **Next Page** button.

12. Click above the scroll box to change the view of the document by the height of one window.

13. Drag the scroll box to the top of the scroll bar.

    The beginning of the document comes into view. Note that the location of the cursor has not changed—just the view of the document.

14. Click to the left of the first row of the title to place the cursor at the top of the document, and then near the bottom of the vertical scroll bar, click the **Select Browse Object** button.

    A gallery of browsing choices opens.

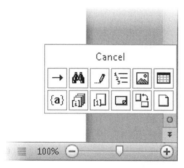

The Select Browse Object gallery.

15. Move the pointer over the buttons representing the objects among which you can browse.

    As you point to each button, the name of the browsing option appears at the top of the gallery.

16. Click the **Browse by Page** button.

    The cursor moves from the beginning of page 1 to the beginning of page 2.

17. Click the **View** tab, and then in the **Show** group, select the **Navigation Pane** check box.

    The Navigation task pane opens on the left side of the screen, displaying an outline of the headings in the document. The heading of the section containing the cursor is highlighted.

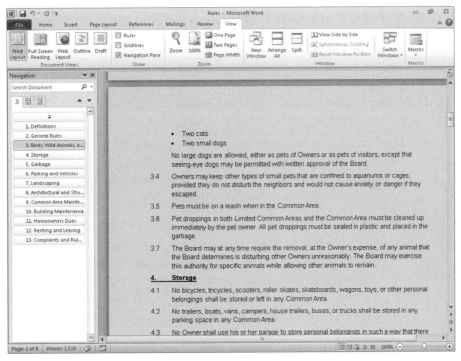

From the Navigation task pane, you can move from heading to heading or from page to page.

18. In the **Navigation** task pane, click the **Landscaping** heading.

   Word scrolls the document and moves the cursor to the selected heading.

19. In the **Navigation** task pane, click the **Browse the pages in your document** tab (the one with the icon of four small pages). Then scroll through the thumbnails in the task pane, and click page **5**.

20. At the right end of the **Navigation** task pane title bar, click the **Close** button.

21. At the right end of the program window title bar, click the **Close** button.

   The Rules document closes, and Document1 becomes the active document.

22. Display the Backstage view, and then click **Close**.

   Document1 closes, leaving Word running.

   Troubleshooting In step 22, if you click the Close button at the right end of the title bar instead of clicking Close in the Backstage view, you'll close the open Word document and exit the Word program. To continue working, start Word again.

✖ **CLEAN UP** If you're continuing directly to the next exercise, leave Word running.

Viewing Files in Different Ways

In each program, you can display the content of a file in a variety of views, each suited to a specific purpose. You switch the view by clicking the buttons in the Document Views group on the View tab, or those on the View Shortcuts toolbar in the lower-right corner of the program window. The views in each program are specific to that program's files.

Word 2010 includes the following views:

- **Print Layout view** This view displays a document on the screen the way it will look when printed. You can see page layout elements such as margins, page breaks, headers and footers, and watermarks.

- **Full Screen Reading view** This view displays as much of the content of the document as will fit on the screen at a size that is appropriate for reading. In this view, the ribbon is replaced by one toolbar at the top of the screen with buttons for saving and printing the document, accessing references and other tools, highlighting text, and making comments. You can move from page to page and adjust the view by selecting options from the View Options menu. You can edit the document only if you turn on the Allow Typing option on this menu, and you can switch views only by clicking the Close button to return to the previous view.

- **Web Layout view** This view displays the document the way it will look when viewed in a Web browser. You can see backgrounds and other effects. You can also see how text wraps to fit the window and how graphics are positioned.

- **Outline view** This view displays the structure of a document as nested levels of headings and body text, and provides tools for viewing and changing its hierarchy.

- **Draft view** This view displays the content of a document with a simplified layout so that you can type and edit quickly. You can't see page layout elements.

    See Also For information about Web Layout view and Outline view, refer to *Microsoft Word 2010 Step by Step* by Joyce Cox and Joan Lambert (Microsoft Press, 2010).

Excel 2010 includes the following views:

- **Normal view** This view displays the worksheet with column and row headers.

- **Page Layout view** This view displays the worksheet on the screen the way it will look when printed, including page layout elements.

- **Page Break Preview view** This view displays only the portion of the worksheet that contains content, and any page breaks. You can drag page breaks in this view to move them.

PowerPoint 2010 includes the following views:

- **Normal view** This view displays individual slides with active content objects such as text containers, and a separate pane into which you can enter notes.

- **Slide Sorter view** This view displays all the slides in a presentation. You can apply formatting to individual slides and to groups of slides, but you can't edit the slide content.

- **Notes Page view** This view displays each slide and its accompanying notes as they will look when printed in the Notes Page print layout.

- **Reading view** This view displays individual slides as they will appear on the screen, without active content objects. In this view, the ribbon is hidden. You can move from page to page and adjust the view by selecting options from a menu on the status bar. You can't edit slide content in this view.

See Also For information about OneNote 2010 notebook views, see Chapter 18, "Explore OneNote 2010."

When you want to focus on the layout of a document, worksheet, or slide, you can display rulers and gridlines to help you position and align elements. Simply select the corresponding check boxes in the Show group on the View tab. You can also adjust the magnification of the document by using the tools available in the Zoom group on the View tab, or the Zoom button or Zoom slider at the right end of the status bar. Clicking the Zoom button in either location displays a dialog box where you can select or type a percentage; or you can drag the Zoom slider to the left or right or click the Zoom Out or Zoom In button on either side of the slider to change the percentage incrementally.

You're not limited to working with one file at a time. You can easily switch between open files, and you can display more than one program window simultaneously. If you want to work with different parts of a document, you can open the document in a second window and display both, or you can split a window into two panes and scroll through each pane independently by using options in the Window group on the View tab.

Not represented on the View tab is a feature that can be invaluable when you are fine-tuning the layout of a document. Clicking the Show/Hide ¶ button in the Paragraph group on the Home tab turns the display of nonprinting and hidden characters on and off. Nonprinting characters, such as tabs and paragraph marks, control the layout of your document, and hidden characters provide the structure for behind-the-scenes processes, such as indexing. You can control the display of these characters for each window.

Tip You can hide any text by selecting it, clicking the Font dialog box launcher, selecting the Hidden check box, and clicking OK. When the Show/Hide ¶ button is turned on, hidden text is visible and is identified in the document by a dotted underline.

In this exercise, you'll work with files in Word by using techniques that are common to all Office 2010 programs. First you'll explore various ways that you can customize Print Layout view to make the work of developing documents more efficient. You'll turn white space on and off, zoom in and out, display the rulers and Navigation task pane, and view nonprinting characters and text. Then you'll switch to other views, noticing the differences so that you have an idea of which one is most appropriate for which task. Finally, you'll switch between open documents and view documents in more than one window at the same time.

SET UP You need the Procedures_start and Prices_start documents located in your Chapter02 practice file folder to complete this exercise. Open the Procedures_start document and save it as *Procedures*. Then follow the steps.

1. In **Print Layout** view, scroll through the document.

   As you can see, on all pages but the first, the printed document will have the title in the header at the top of the page, the page number in the right margin, and the date in the footer at the bottom of each page.

   See Also For information about headers and footers, refer to *Microsoft Word 2010 Step by Step* by Joyce Cox and Joan Lambert (Microsoft Press, 2010).

2. Point to the gap between any two pages, and when the pointer changes to two opposing arrows, double-click the mouse button. Then scroll through the document again.

   The white space at the top and bottom of each page and the gray space between pages are now hidden, as are the header and footer.

   Facilities

   Office

   Warehouse

   Phone System

   Office

   The Consolidated Messenger front office and lobby is located at the front of the building and serves as the main entrance for our office employees and our customers.

   Hiding white space between pages makes it quicker to scroll through a long document and easier to compare the content on two pages.

3. Restore the white space by pointing to the line that separates one page from the next and double-clicking the mouse button.

4. Press Ctrl+Home to move to the top of the document, and then near the right end of the status bar, click the **Zoom** button.

The Zoom dialog box opens.

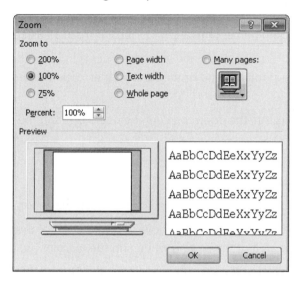

You can click a preset zoom percentage or specify your own.

5. Click **Many pages**. Then click the monitor button, click the second page thumbnail in the top row, and click **OK**.

The magnification changes so that you can see two pages side by side.

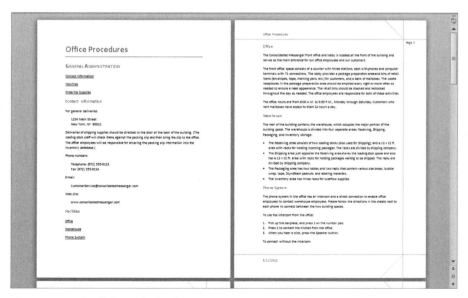

You can now scroll through the document two pages at a time.

100%

6. At the bottom of the vertical scroll bar, click the **Next Page** button to display the third and fourth pages of the document.

7. On the **View** tab, click the **Zoom** button. Then in the **Zoom** dialog box, click **75%**, and click **OK**.

   Notice that the Zoom percentage and slider position are adjusted to reflect the new setting.

8. On the status bar, at the left end of the **Zoom** slider, click the **Zoom Out** button two times.

   As you click the button, the Zoom percentage decreases and the slider moves to the left.

9. At the right end of the **Zoom** slider, click the **Zoom In** button until the magnification is 100 percent.

10. On the **View** tab, in the **Show** group, select the **Ruler** check box.

    Horizontal and vertical rulers appear above and to the left of the page. On the rulers, the content area of the page is white and the margins are blue.

11. On the **Home** tab, in the **Paragraph** group, click the **Show/Hide ¶** button.

    Nonprinting characters such as spaces, tabs, and paragraph marks are now visible.

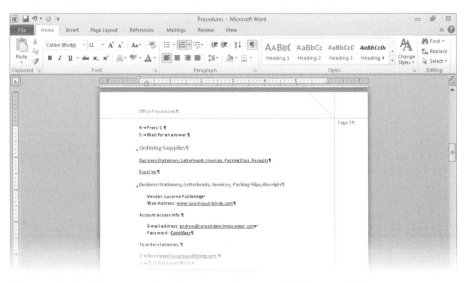

You can display the nonprinting characters that control the layout of the content.

12. On the **View Shortcuts** toolbar, click the **Full Screen Reading** button.

    Word displays the document in a format that's easy to read.

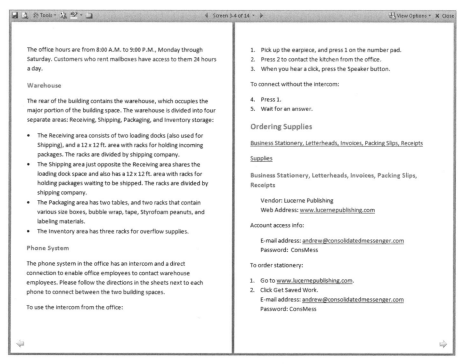

The office hours are from 8:00 A.M. to 9:00 P.M., Monday through Saturday. Customers who rent mailboxes have access to them 24 hours a day.

Warehouse

The rear of the building contains the warehouse, which occupies the major portion of the building space. The warehouse is divided into four separate areas: Receiving, Shipping, Packaging, and Inventory storage:

- The Receiving area consists of two loading docks (also used for Shipping), and a 12 x 12 ft. area with racks for holding incoming packages. The racks are divided by shipping company.
- The Shipping area just opposite the Receiving area shares the loading dock space and also has a 12 x 12 ft. area with racks for holding packages waiting to be shipped. The racks are divided by shipping company.
- The Packaging area has two tables, and two racks that contain various size boxes, bubble wrap, tape, Styrofoam peanuts, and labeling materials.
- The Inventory area has three racks for overflow supplies.

Phone System

The phone system in the office has an intercom and a direct connection to enable office employees to contact warehouse employees. Please follow the directions in the sheets next to each phone to connect between the two building spaces.

To use the intercom from the office:

1. Pick up the earpiece, and press 1 on the number pad.
2. Press 2 to contact the kitchen from the office.
3. When you hear a click, press the Speaker button.

To connect without the intercom:

4. Press 1.
5. Wait for an answer.

Ordering Supplies

Business Stationery, Letterheads, Invoices, Packing Slips, Receipts

Supplies

Business Stationery, Letterheads, Invoices, Packing Slips, Receipts

　Vendor: Lucerne Publishing
　Web Address: www.lucernepublishing.com

Account access info:

　E-mail address: andrew@consolidatedmessenger.com
　Password: ConsMess

To order stationery:

1. Go to www.lucernepublishing.com.
2. Click Get Saved Work.
　E-mail address: andrew@consolidatedmessenger.com
　Password: ConsMess

You can't edit content in Full Screen Reading view unless you set the view options to Allow Typing.

  13. In the lower-right corner of the window, click the **Forward** button.

You can now read the next two screens of information.

  14. To the right of the screen indicator at the top of the window, click the **Previous Screen** button.

15. Point to each button on the toolbar at the top of the window to display its ScreenTip. Then in the upper-right corner, click the **Close** button to return to **Print Layout** view.

  16. Press Ctrl+Home. Then on the **View Shortcuts** toolbar, click the **Web Layout** button, and scroll through the document.

In a Web browser, the text column will fill the window and there will be no page breaks.

  17. Press Ctrl+Home, and then on the **View Shortcuts** toolbar, click the **Outline** button.

Word displays the document's hierarchical structure, and the Outlining tab appears on the ribbon.

18. On the **Outlining** tab, in the **Outline Tools** group, click the **Show Level** arrow, and in the list, click **Level 2**.

The document collapses to display only the Level 1 and Level 2 headings.

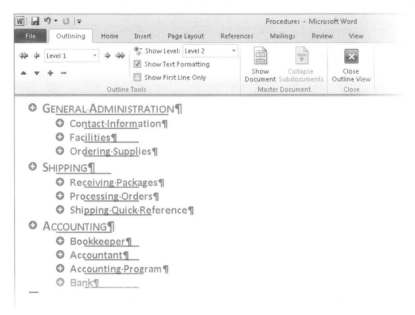

You can control the level of detail shown in the document's hierarchy.

19. On the **View Shortcuts** toolbar, click the **Draft** button, and then scroll through the document.

You can see the basic content of the document without any extraneous elements, such as margins and headers and footers. The active area on the ruler indicates the width of the text column, dotted lines indicate page breaks, and scrolling is quick and easy.

20. Display the Backstage view, click **Open**, and then in the **Open** dialog box displaying the contents of your **Chapter02** practice file folder, double-click **Prices_start**.

The Prices_start document opens in Print Layout view in its own window. Notice that the telephone number in the body of the memo has a dotted underline, which indicates that it is formatted as hidden.

21. Save the **Prices_start** document as **Prices** so that you can work with it without overwriting the original.

22. On the **Home** tab, in the **Paragraph** group, click the active **Show/Hide ¶** button to turn it off.

The telephone number is no longer visible.

23. On the **View** tab, in the **Window** group, click the **Switch Windows** button, and then in the list of open documents, click **Procedures**.

    The Procedures document is displayed in Draft view with nonprinting characters and hidden text turned on.

24. On the **View** tab, in the **Window** group, click the **Arrange All** button.

    The open windows are sized and stacked one above the other. Each window has a ribbon, so you can work with each document independently.

You can display more than one window at the same time.

Tip The ribbons in each window take up a lot of screen space. To see more of each document, you can click the Minimize The Ribbon button to hide all but the tab names.

25. At the right end of the **Document1** window title bar, click the **Close** button. Then in either open window, click the **Arrange All** button again.

    Word resizes the open windows to occupy the available space.

26. At the right end of the **Prices** window title bar, click the **Maximize** button.

    The window expands to fill the screen.

27. On the **View** tab, in the **Show** group, clear the **Ruler** check box.

 CLEAN UP Close the Procedures and Prices documents.

Key Points

- You create new documents, workbooks, presentations, and notebooks from the New page of the Backstage view. When creating documents, workbooks, and presentations, you can choose a blank template or a template that includes preset formatting and content placeholders.

- When you save a file, you specify its name, location, and file format in the Save As dialog box. Each program offers several file formats.

- The cursor indicates the location in which text will be inserted when you type. It's easy to move the cursor by clicking in the text or by pressing keys and keyboard shortcuts.

- You can view a file in a variety of ways, depending on your needs as you create the file and on the purpose for which you are creating it.

Microsoft Word 2010

Chapter at a Glance

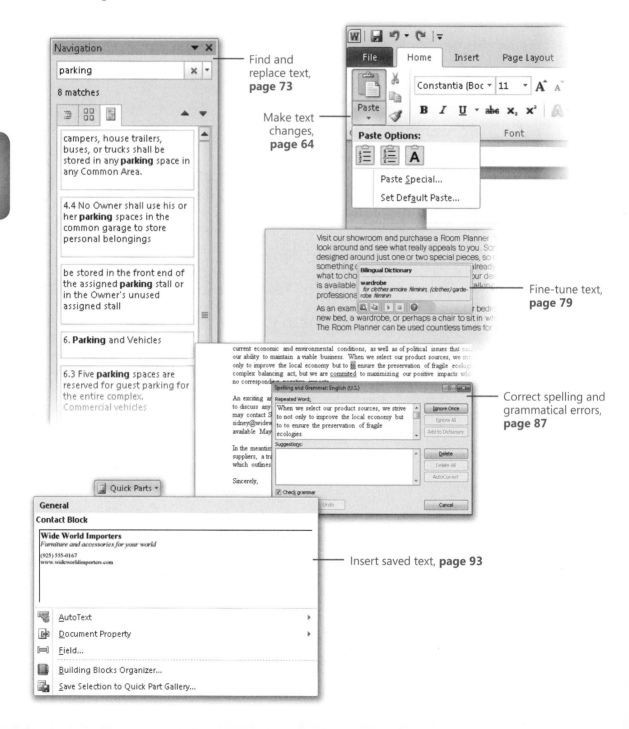

Find and replace text, **page 73**

Make text changes, **page 64**

Fine-tune text, **page 79**

Correct spelling and grammatical errors, **page 87**

Insert saved text, **page 93**

3 Edit and Proofread Text

In this chapter, you will learn how to

✔ Make text changes.

✔ Find and replace text.

✔ Fine-tune text.

✔ Correct spelling and grammatical errors.

✔ Insert saved text.

As you learned in Chapter 1, "Explore Office 2010," entering text is a simple matter of typing. However, even the most accurate typists occasionally make mistakes, also known as *typos* (for *typographical errors*). Unless the documents you create are intended for no one's eyes but your own, you need to ensure that they are not only correct but also persuasive. Whether you are a novice or experienced writer, Microsoft Word 2010 has several tools that make creating professional documents easy and efficient.

- **Editing tools** These tools provide quick-selection techniques and drag-and-drop editing to make it easy to move and copy text anywhere you want it.

- **Search tools** These tools can be used to locate and replace words, phrases, and special characters, either one at a time or throughout a document.

  See Also For information about using the search tools to find and replace formatting, see the sidebar "Finding and Replacing Formatting" in Chapter 4, "Change the Look of Text."

- **Research tools** These tools make it easy to find synonyms, look up information, and translate words and phrases.

- **AutoCorrect and Spelling And Grammar** These features make it easy to correct typographical and grammatical errors before you share a document with others.

- **Quick Parts** These building blocks can be used to save and recall specialized terms or standard paragraphs.

  Tip Word also includes formatted building blocks for document elements such as cover pages, headers, and footers. For information, see "Inserting Building Blocks" in Chapter 6, "Add Simple Graphic Elements."

In this chapter, you'll edit the text in a document by inserting and deleting text, copying and pasting a phrase, and moving a paragraph. Then you'll replace one phrase with another throughout the entire document. Next, you'll replace a word with a synonym and translate another word. You'll also add misspelled words to the AutoCorrect list and check the spelling and grammar of a document. Finally, you'll save a couple of building blocks for insertion later in a document.

> **Practice Files** Before you can complete the exercises in this chapter, you need to copy the book's practice files to your computer. The practice files you'll use to complete the exercises in this chapter are in the Chapter03 practice file folder. A complete list of practice files is provided in "Using the Practice Files" at the beginning of this book.

Making Text Changes

You'll rarely write a perfect document that doesn't require any editing. You'll almost always want to add or remove a word or two, change a phrase, or move text from one place to another. You can edit a document as you create it, or you can write it first and then revise it. Or you might want to edit a document that you created for one purpose so that you can use it for a different purpose. For example, a letter might make an ideal starting point for a flyer, or a report might contain all the information you need for a Web document.

Inserting text is easy; you click to position the cursor and simply begin typing. Any existing text to the right of the cursor moves to make room for the new text.

Deleting text is equally easy. If you want to delete only one or a few characters, you can simply position the cursor and then press the Backspace or Delete key until the characters are all gone. Pressing Backspace deletes the character to the left of the cursor; pressing Delete deletes the character to the right of the cursor.

To delete more than a few characters efficiently, you need to know how to select the text. Selected text appears highlighted on the screen. You can drag through a section of text to select it, or you can select specific items as follows:

- **Word** Double-click anywhere in the word. The word and the space immediately following it are selected, but not any punctuation following the word.

- **Sentence** Click anywhere in the sentence while holding down the Ctrl key. Word selects all the characters in the sentence, from the first character through the space following the ending punctuation mark.

- **Paragraph** Triple-click anywhere in the paragraph. Word selects the text of the paragraph and the paragraph mark.

- **Adjacent words, lines, or paragraphs** Position the cursor at the beginning of the text you want to select, hold down the Shift key, and then press the Arrow keys to select one character or line at a time; hold down the Shift and Ctrl keys and press the Arrow keys to select one word at a time; or click at the end of the text that you want to select.

- **Non-adjacent words, lines, or paragraphs** Make the first selection, and then hold down the Ctrl key while selecting the next text block.

Tip When you select text, Word displays a box called the *Mini Toolbar* so that you can quickly format the selection. You can ignore this toolbar for now. For more information, see "Manually Changing the Look of Characters" in Chapter 4, "Change the Look of Text."

As an alternative way of selecting, you can use an invisible area in the document's left margin, called the *selection area*, to select items.

- **Line** Click in the selection area to the left of the line.

- **Paragraph** Double-click in the selection area to the left of the paragraph.

- **Entire document** Triple-click in the selection area.

    Keyboard Shortcut Press Ctrl+A to select all the content in the body of the document.

Office Procedures

Page 2

throughout the day as needed. The office employees are responsible for both of these activities.

The office hours are from 8:00 A.M. to 9:00 P.M., Monday through Saturday. Customers who rent mailboxes have access to them 24 hours a day.

Warehouse

The rear of the building contains the warehouse, which occupies the major portion of the building space. The warehouse is divided into four separate areas: Receiving, Shipping, Packaging, and Inventory storage.

Selection area

In the selection area, the pointer becomes a right-pointing arrow.

After selecting the text you want to delete, press either Backspace or Delete.

Tip To release a selection, click anywhere in the window other than the selection area.

If you want to move or copy the selected text, you have three options:

- **Drag-and-drop editing** Use this feature, which is frequently referred to simply as *dragging*, when you need to move or copy text only a short distance—for example, within a paragraph. Start by using any of the methods described previously to select the text. Then point to the selection, hold down the mouse button, drag the text to its new location, and release the mouse button. To copy the selection, hold down the Ctrl key while you drag.

- **Cut, Copy, and Paste buttons** Use this method when you need to move or copy text between two locations that you cannot see at the same time—for example, between pages or between documents. Select the text, and click the Cut or Copy button in the Clipboard group on the Home tab. (The cut or copied item is stored in an area of your computer's memory called the *Microsoft Office Clipboard*, hence the name of the group.) Then reposition the cursor, and click the Paste button to insert the selection in its new location. If you click the Paste arrow instead of the button, Word displays a list of different ways to paste the selection.

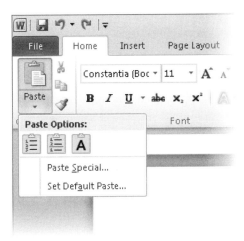

Under Paste Options, buttons represent the ways in which you can paste the item.

Pointing to a button under Paste Options displays a preview of how the cut or copied item will look when pasted into the text in that format, so you can experiment with different ways of pasting until you find the one you want.

See Also For more information about the Clipboard, see the sidebar "About the Clipboard" later in this chapter.

● **Keyboard shortcuts** It can be more efficient to press key combinations to cut, copy, and paste selections than to click buttons on the ribbon. The main keyboard shortcuts for editing tasks are shown in the following table.

Task	Keyboard shortcut
Cut	Ctrl+X
Copy	Ctrl+C
Paste	Ctrl+V
Undo	Ctrl+Z
Repeat/Redo	Ctrl+Y

Using a keyboard shortcut to cut or copy a selection stores the item on the Clipboard, just as if you had clicked the corresponding button.

Tip No matter which method you use, when you cut text, Word removes it from its original location. When you copy text, Word leaves the text in the original location and repeats it in the new location.

If you make a change to a document and then realize that you made a mistake, you can easily reverse the change. You can undo your last editing action by clicking the Undo button on the Quick Access Toolbar. To undo an earlier action, click the Undo arrow and then click that action in the list.

Tip Selecting an action from the Undo list undoes that action and all the editing actions you performed after that one. You cannot undo only one action other than the last one you performed.

If you make a change to a document and want to repeat that change elsewhere, you can click the Repeat button on the Quick Access Toolbar. If the last task you performed was to undo an action, the Repeat button is replaced by the Redo button. So if you change your mind about whatever you undid, you can click the Redo button to return the text to its previous state. You can't redo multiple actions by clicking them in a list as you can with the Undo button, but you can click the Redo button repeatedly until the text is restored to what you want.

In this exercise, you'll edit the text in a document. You'll insert and delete text, undo the deletion, copy and paste a phrase, and move a paragraph.

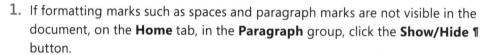 **SET UP** You need the Orientation_start document located in your Chapter03 practice file folder to complete this exercise. Open the Orientation_start document, and save it as *Orientation*. Then follow the steps.

1. If formatting marks such as spaces and paragraph marks are not visible in the document, on the **Home** tab, in the **Paragraph** group, click the **Show/Hide ¶** button.

   Keyboard Shortcut Press Ctrl+* to turn formatting marks on or off. (You need to hold down the Shift key to activate the * key. So in effect, you are pressing Ctrl+Shift+8.)

2. In the second bullet point under **Project Goals**, double-click the word **natural** to select it, and then press Backspace.

3. In the third bullet point, click to the left of the **a** in the word **and**, hold down the Shift key, and then click to the right of the **e** in the word **motivate**.

   Word selects the text between the two clicks.

   Troubleshooting If Word selects the word *Engage* as well, you clicked before the space instead of after it. Click anywhere in the document to release the selection, and then repeat step 3, being sure to click after the space but before the word *and*.

Community·Service·Committee¶
Employee·Orientation¶

Proposal↵
Last·updated:·January·25,·2010¶

Project·Goals¶
- → Familiarize·employees·with·the·concept·of·service.¶
- → Make·service·a·part·of·their·lives.¶
- → Engage·and·motivate·them.¶
- → Forge·a·sense·of·teamwork·among·all·employees·across·departments.¶
- → Provide·appropriate·skills·development·through·brainstorming,·planning,·and·leadership·
  opportunities.¶

You can use the Shift+click method to select as much text as you want.

4. Press Delete to delete the selection.

   Word also deletes the space after the selection.

5. In the fourth bullet point, double-click the word **Forge**, and then replace it by typing **Build**.

   Notice that you don't have to type a space after *Build*. Word inserts the space for you.

   Tip Word inserts and deletes spaces because the Use Smart Cut And Paste check box is selected on the Advanced page of the Word Options dialog box. If you want to be able to control the spacing yourself, click the Options button in the Backstage view, click Advanced, clear this check box (located in the Cut, Copy, And Paste area), and then click OK.

6. Scroll the page, and position the mouse pointer at the edge of the page to the left of the first bullet point under **Questions for Team Leaders**. Then with the pointer in the selection area, click to select the entire paragraph.

   Tip Clicking once selects this paragraph because it is only one line long. If the paragraph contained more than one line, you would need to double-click.

7. On the **Home** tab, in the **Clipboard** group, click the **Copy** button.

    The selection is copied to the Clipboard.

8. If you can't see the bulleted list under **Questions for Department Reps**, click the **Next Page** button below the vertical scroll bar to move to the beginning of the next page. Then click to the left of **What** in the first bullet point under **Questions for Department Reps**, and in the **Clipboard** group, click the **Paste** arrow.

    The Paste Options menu opens.

The Paste Options menu includes buttons representing pasting options.

9. Point to the **Merge List** button, notice how the text will look with this paste option implemented, and then click the button.

    The Paste Options button appears below and to the right of the inserted bullet point. You can click this button to display a list of paste options if you want to change the way the text has been pasted or the default way Word pastes. In this case, you can just ignore it.

10. In the **Set Up Team** section, triple-click anywhere in the paragraph that begins **The Committee will pursue** to select the entire paragraph.

11. In the **Clipboard** group, click the **Cut** button.

12. Press the Up Arrow key to move to the beginning of the preceding paragraph, and then in the **Clipboard** group, click the **Paste** button.

    The two paragraphs switch places.

13. On the Quick Access Toolbar, click the **Undo** arrow, and then in the **Undo** list, click the third action (**Paste Merge List**).

Word undoes the previous cut-and-paste operation and the pasting of the copied text.

14. Press Ctrl+Home to move to the top of the document. Then position the pointer in the selection area adjacent to the third bullet point under **Project Goals**, and click to select the paragraph.

15. Point to the selection, hold down the mouse button, and then drag the paragraph up to the left of the word **Make** at the beginning of the preceding bullet point.

   When you release the mouse, the bullet point moves to its new location.

16. With the text still selected, press the End key.

   Word releases the selection and moves the cursor to the end of the paragraph.

17. Press the Spacebar, and then press Delete.

   Word deletes the paragraph mark and merges the two bullet points.

Community·Service·Committee¶
Employee·Orientation¶

Proposal↵
Last·updated:··January·25,·2010¶

•Project·Goals¶
    •→ Familiarize·employees·with·the·concept·of·service.¶
    •→ Engage·them.·Make·service·a·part·of·their·lives.¶
    •→ Build·a·sense·of·teamwork·among·all·employees·across·departments.¶
    •→ Provide·appropriate·skills·development·through·brainstorming,·planning,·and·leadership·
      opportunities.¶
    •→ Meet·genuine·community·needs.¶

In the second bullet point, two bullets have now been combined into one.

✖ **CLEAN UP** If you prefer not to see formatting marks, turn them off. Then save and close the Orientation document.

About the Clipboard

You can view the items that have been cut or copied to the Clipboard in the Clipboard task pane, which you display by clicking the Clipboard dialog box launcher on the Home tab.

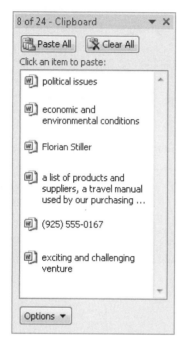

The Clipboard stores items that have been cut or copied from any Office program.

To paste an individual item at the cursor, you simply click the item in the Clipboard task pane. To paste all the items, click the Paste All button. You can point to an item, click the arrow that appears, and then click Delete to remove it from the Clipboard and the task pane, or you can remove all the items by clicking the Clear All button.

You can control the behavior of the Clipboard task pane by clicking Options at the bottom of the pane, and choosing the circumstances under which you want the task pane to appear.

To close the Clipboard task pane, click the Close button at the right end of its title bar.

Finding and Replacing Text

One way to ensure that the text in your documents is consistent and accurate is to use the Find feature to search for every occurrence of a particular word or phrase. For example, if you are responsible for advertising a trademarked product, you might want to search your marketing materials to check that every occurrence of the product's name is correctly identified as a trademark.

Clicking the Find button (not the arrow) in the Editing group on the Home tab displays the Navigation task pane with the Search tab active. As you type characters in the Search Document box at the top of the task pane, Word highlights all occurrences of those characters in the document and displays them in the search results list in the Navigation task pane.

Keyboard Shortcut Press Ctrl+F to display the Search tab of the Navigation task pane.

The Navigation task pane shows enough of the text surrounding the search term to identify its context.

When you point to a particular search result in the Navigation task pane, a ScreenTip displays the number of the page on which that result appears. You can click a search result to scroll the document to display the result's location.

Tip The beauty of the Navigation task pane is that you can continue editing your document as you normally would, without closing the pane.

If you want to be more specific about the text you are looking for—for example, if you want to look for occurrences that match the exact capitalization of your search term—click the arrow at the right end of the Search Document box in the Navigation task pane and then click Advanced Find to display the Find page of the Find And Replace dialog box. Clicking More in the lower-left corner expands the dialog box to make additional search options available.

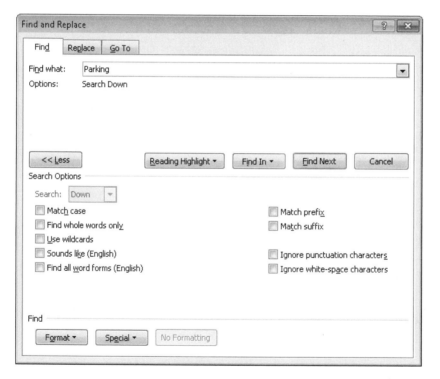

You can make a search more specific by using the criteria in the Search Options area of the Find And Replace dialog box.

In the expanded dialog box, you can do the following:

- Guide the direction of the search by selecting Down, Up, or All from the Search list.

- Locate only text that matches the capitalization of the Find What text by selecting the Match Case check box.

- Exclude occurrences of the Find What text that appear within other words by selecting the Find Whole Words Only check box.

- Find two similar words, such as *effect* and *affect* by selecting the Use Wildcards check box and then entering a wildcard character in the Find What box. The two most common wildcard characters are:

  - ?, which represents any single character in this location in the Find What text.

  - *, which represents any number of characters in this location in the Find What text.

  Tip To see a list of the available wildcards, use Help to search for the term *wildcards*.

- Find occurrences of the search text that sound the same but are spelled differently, such as *there* and *their*, by selecting the Sounds Like check box.

- Find occurrences of a particular word in any form, such as *try*, *tries*, and *tried*, by selecting the Find All Word Forms check box. You can match a prefix or a suffix, and you can ignore punctuation and white space.

- Locate formatting, such as bold, or special characters, such as tabs, by selecting them from the Format or Special list.

  See Also For information about finding and replacing formatting, see the sidebar "Finding and Replacing Formatting" in Chapter 4, "Change the Look of Text."

If you want to substitute a specific word or phrase for another, you can use the Replace feature. Clicking the Replace button in the Editing group of the Home tab displays the Replace page of the Find And Replace dialog box.

Correcting errors and inconsistencies is easy with the Replace feature.

Keyboard Shortcut Press Ctrl+H to display the Replace page of the Find And Replace dialog box.

Tip If the Navigation task pane is open, you can click the arrow at the right end of the Search Document box and then click Replace. The Find And Replace dialog box opens with the search term from the Navigation task pane already in the Find What box.

On the Replace page, you can click the following:

- **Find Next** Finds the first occurrence or leaves the selected occurrence as it is and locates the next one

- **Replace** Replaces the selected occurrence with the text in the Replace With box and moves to the next occurrence

- **Replace All** Replaces all occurrences with the text in the Replace With box

  Tip Before clicking Replace All, ensure that the replacement is clearly defined. For example, if you want to change *trip* to *journey*, be sure to tell Word to find only the whole word *trip*; otherwise, *triple* could become *journeyle*.

As on the Find page, clicking More displays the options you can use to carry out more complicated replacements.

In this exercise, you'll find a phrase and make a correction to the text. Then you'll replace one phrase with another throughout the entire document.

 SET UP You need the RulesRegulations_start document located in your Chapter03 practice file folder to complete this exercise. Open the RulesRegulations_start document, and save it as *RulesRegulations*. Then follow the steps.

1. With the cursor at the beginning of the document, on the **Home** tab, in the **Editing** group, click the **Find** button (not its arrow).

   The Navigation task pane opens, displaying the Search tab.

2. With the cursor in the **Search Document** box, type **Board**. (Don't type the period.)

The Navigation task pane displays 62 matches with the word *Board* and highlights every occurrence in the document.

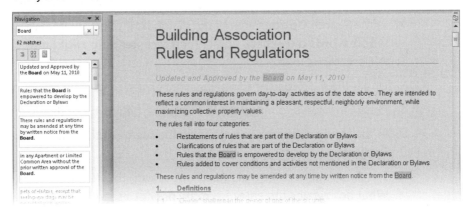

In the Navigation task pane, you can click each match to view its corresponding location in the document.

3. In the **Navigation** task pane, click the fifth match in the search results to jump to page **2**.

   Notice that under the heading *4. Storage*, Word has highlighted the *board* portion of *skateboards*. You need to restrict the search to the whole word *Board*.

4. In the **Navigation** task pane, click the arrow at the right end of the **Search Document** box.

   A menu of options for refining the search appears.

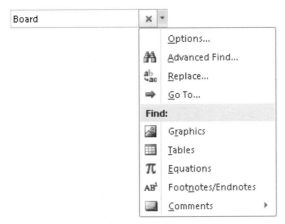

You can click options that allow you to find specific types of objects as well as text.

5. In the top part of the list, click **Advanced Find**.

   The Find And Replace dialog box opens with the Find page displayed. The Find What box already contains the search term from the Navigation task pane.

6. In the lower-left corner of the dialog box, click **More**.

   The dialog box expands to display options for refining the search.

7. In the **Search Options** area of the dialog box, select the **Match case** and **Find whole words only** check boxes. Then click **Reading Highlight**, click **Highlight All**, and click **Close**.

   Under the *4. Storage* heading, the word *skateboards* is no longer highlighted.

8. Press Ctrl+Home to move the cursor to the beginning of the document.

9. In the **Navigation** task pane, display the search options list again, and then click **Replace**.

   The Find And Replace dialog box opens with the Replace page active. The Find What box retains the entry from the previous search, and the Match Case and Find Whole Words Only check boxes are still selected.

10. Click **Less** to reduce the size of the box, and then drag the box by its title bar toward the top of the document.

11. Click the **Replace with** box, type **Association Board**, and then click **Find Next**.

    Word highlights the first occurrence of *Board*.

12. In the dialog box, click **Replace**.

    Word replaces the first occurrence of *Board* with *Association Board* and then finds the next occurrence.

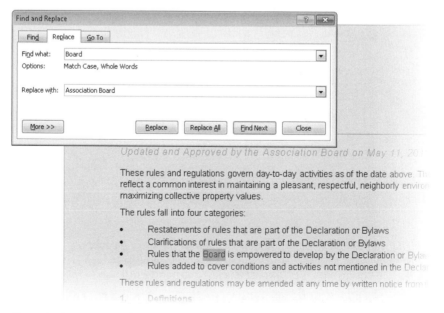

If you don't want to replace an occurrence, click Find Next to skip it.

13. Having tested the replacement, click **Replace All**.

14. When Word tells you how many replacements it made, click **OK** to close the message box. Then in the **Find and Replace** dialog box, click **Close**.

15. Press Ctrl+Home to move to the beginning of the document.

    In the *Updated and Approved* line of text, the word *Association* is now duplicated.

16. Use your new find and replace skills to replace any instances of **Association Association** in the document with **Association**.

✖ CLEAN UP Close the Navigation task pane. Then save and close the RulesRegulations document.

Fine-Tuning Text

Language is often contextual—you use different words and phrases in a marketing brochure than you would in a letter requesting immediate payment of an invoice or in an informal memo about a social gathering after work. To help you ensure that you're using the words that best convey your meaning in any given context, Word provides a thesaurus where you can look up alternative words, called *synonyms*, for a selected word. The Thesaurus is one of a set of research services provided by Word.

To look up alternatives for a word, you can right-click the word, and then click Synonyms to display a list from which you can choose the one you want. Alternatively, you can select the word and then click the Thesaurus button in the Proofing group on the Review tab. The Research task pane opens, displaying the selected word in the Search For box and synonyms for that word in the Thesaurus list.

Keyboard Shortcut Press Shift+F7 to open the Research task pane and display Thesaurus entries for the active word, which is also displayed in the Search For box.

You can click a synonym to display its synonyms and click again to repeat that process until you find exactly the word you want.

To replace the selected word with a synonym, point to your chosen synonym, click the arrow that appears, and then click Insert.

In addition to the Thesaurus, the Research task pane provides access to a variety of informational resources. You first open the Research task pane by clicking the Research button in the Proofing group and then enter a topic in the Search For box, specifying in the box below which resource Word should use to look for information about that topic.

Keyboard Shortcut Press the Alt key and click anywhere in the document to display the Research task pane.

You can choose a specific resource from the list or click All Reference Books or All Research Sites to widen the search.

Clicking Research Options at the bottom of the Research task pane displays the Research Options dialog box. In this dialog box, you can specify which of a predefined set of reference materials and other Internet resources will be available from the list.

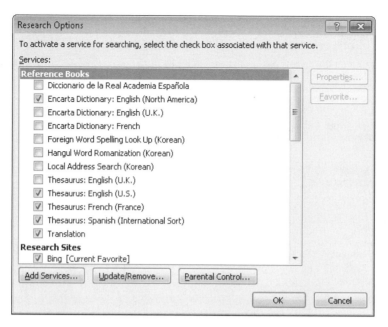

You can click Add Services to include your favorite reference resources in the list.

Word also comes with three translation tools with which you can quickly translate words and phrases, or even entire documents.

● **Mini Translator** You turn the Mini Translator on or off by clicking the Translate button in the Language group of the Review tab and then clicking Mini Translator. When the Mini Translator is turned on, you can point to a word or selected phrase to display a translation in the specified language. When the box containing the translation is displayed, you can click the Expand button to display the Research task pane, where you can change the translation language. You can also copy the translated word or phrase, or hear the word or phrase spoken for you.

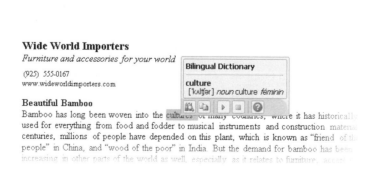

Using the Mini Translator is the quickest way to obtain the translation of a selection.

● **Online bilingual dictionary** To obtain the translation of a word that does not appear in the text of a document, you can click Translate Selected Text in the Translate menu to display the Research task pane, type the word in the Search For box, specify the language you want, and then click Start Searching. Word consults the online bilingual dictionary for the language you chose and displays the result. You can then click Insert to enter a translated word in the document at the cursor.

You can use the bilingual dictionary to translate a selected word or the word you type in the Search For box.

● **Online machine translator** To translate an entire document, you can click Translate Document on the Translate menu. When Word displays a message that the document will be sent for translation by the Microsoft Translator service (which is free), click Send. The document and its translation then appear side by side in your Web browser. You can set the translation from and translation to languages in the boxes at the top of the Web page and click buttons to change the view.

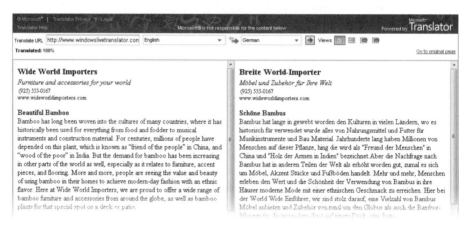

The Microsoft Translator service translates complete documents into the language you select.

To change the default language used by the Mini Translator or the machine translator, you click Choose Translation Language on the Translate menu. Then in the Translation Language Options dialog box, you can select different language pairs for each type of translator.

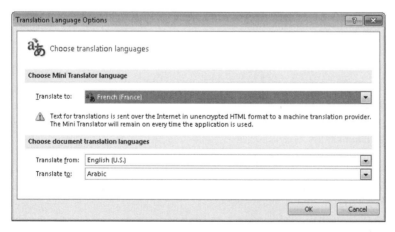

You can translate from and to many languages, including Arabic, Chinese, Greek, Hebrew, Italian, Japanese, Korean, Polish, Portuguese, Russian, Spanish, and Swedish.

In this exercise, you'll use the Thesaurus to replace one word with another. Then you'll experiment with the Mini Translator.

SET UP You need the Brochure_start document located in your Chapter03 practice file folder to complete this exercise. Open the Brochure_start document, and save it as *Brochure*. Then follow the steps.

1. Double-click the word **acclaimed** in the second line of the first paragraph.

2. On the **Review** tab, in the **Proofing** group, click the **Thesaurus** button.

   The Research task pane opens, listing synonyms for the word *acclaimed*.

3. In the task pane, under **much-admired**, click **commended**.

   The word *commended* replaces *acclaimed* in the Search For box at the top of the task pane.

Synonyms for commended *are now listed in the task pane.*

4. Point to the word **celebrated**, click the arrow that appears to its right, and then click **Insert**.

   The word *celebrated* replaces *acclaimed* in the document.

5. Close the **Research** task pane.

   Tip You can open the Research task pane at any time by clicking the Research button in the Proofing group on the Review tab.

6. In the **Language** group, click the **Translate** button, and then click **Choose Translation Language**.

   The Translation Language Options dialog box opens.

7. Under **Choose Mini Translator language**, click the **Translate to** arrow, click **French (France)** in the list, and then click **OK**.

8. In the **Language** group, click the **Translate** button, and then click **Mini Translator [French (France)]**.

   The Mini Translator is now turned on.

9. In the last paragraph of the document, point to the word **wardrobe**, and then move the pointer over the shadow box that appears above the word.

   The Mini Translator appears, showing two French translations for the word *wardrobe*: *armoire* and *garde-robe*.

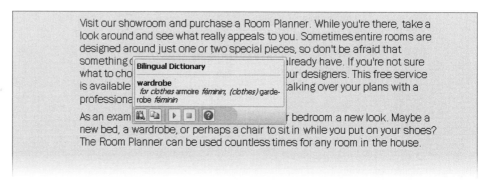

You can click the Play button to hear the translated word.

10. In the **Mini Translator** box, click the **Expand** button.

    The Research task pane opens, displaying the settings for translating from English into French.

11. Under **Bilingual Dictionary** in the **Research** task pane, double-click **armoire** to select it.

12. Right-click the selection, and click **Copy**.

13. In the document, double-click the word **wardrobe**.

14. Right-click the selection, and under **Paste Options** in the list, point to (don't click) the **Keep Text Only** button.

    Word displays a live preview of what the text will look like if you replace *wardrobe* with *armoire*.

15. Press the Esc key to close the shortcut menu and leave the word *wardrobe* in the text.

 CLEAN UP Close the Research task pane, and turn off the Mini Translator by clicking the Translate button in the Language group and clicking Mini Translator. Then save and close the Brochure document.

Correcting Spelling and Grammatical Errors

In the days of handwritten and typewritten documents, people might have tolerated a typographical or grammatical error or two because correcting such errors without creating a mess was difficult. Word-processing programs such as Word have built-in spelling and grammar checkers, so now documents that contain these types of errors are likely to reflect badly on their creators.

Tip Although Word can help you eliminate misspellings and grammatical errors, its tools are not infallible. You should always read through your document to catch any problems that the Word tools can't detect—for example, homonyms such as *their*, *there*, and *they're*.

Word provides these three tools to help you with the chore of eliminating spelling and grammar errors:

- **AutoCorrect** This feature corrects commonly misspelled words, such as *adn* to *and*, so that you don't have to correct them yourself. AutoCorrect comes with a long list of frequently misspelled words and their correct spellings. If you frequently misspell a word that AutoCorrect doesn't change, you can add it to the list in the AutoCorrect dialog box. If you deliberately mistype a word and don't want to accept the AutoCorrect change, you can reverse the correction by clicking the Undo button before you type anything else.

- **Error indicators** Word underlines potential spelling errors with red wavy underlines and grammatical errors with green wavy underlines. You can right-click an underlined word or phrase to display suggested corrections in a shortcut menu.

- **Spelling and Grammar dialog box** If you want to check the spelling or grammar of the entire document, you can click the Spelling & Grammar button in the Proofing group on the Review tab. Word then works its way through the document and displays the Spelling And Grammar dialog box if it encounters a potential error.

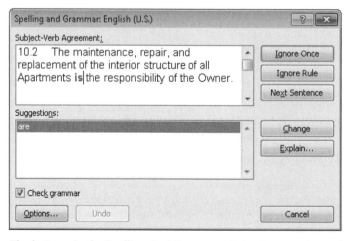

The buttons in the Spelling And Grammar dialog box are dynamic and reflect the type of error found.

Keyboard Shortcut Press F7 to start checking the spelling and grammar from your current location in the document.

If the error is a misspelling, the Spelling And Grammar dialog box suggests corrections; if the error is a breach of grammar rules, the Spelling And Grammar dialog box tells you which rule you have broken and suggests corrections. You can implement a suggestion by double-clicking it in the Suggestions box.

In this exercise, you'll change an AutoCorrect setting and add a word to the AutoCorrect list. You'll check the spelling in the document and add terms to the custom dictionary, and then you'll find, review, and correct a grammatical error.

SET UP You need the Letter_start document located in your Chapter03 practice file folder to complete this exercise. Open the Letter_start document, and save it as *Letter*. Then follow the steps.

1. Click immediately to the left of **negative** in the last line of the first paragraph, and then type **coresponding**, followed by a space.

   As soon as you press the Spacebar, AutoCorrect changes *coresponding* to *corresponding*.

2. Click the **File** tab to display the Backstage view, and then click **Options**.

3. In the left pane of the **Word Options** dialog box, click **Proofing**, and then on the **Proofing** page, click **AutoCorrect Options**.

   The AutoCorrect dialog box opens, displaying the AutoCorrect page.

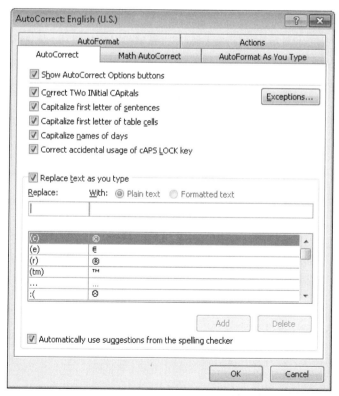

A selected check box indicates an error that AutoCorrect will automatically correct.

Tip You can clear the check box of any item you don't want corrected. For example, if you don't want AutoCorrect to capitalize the first letter that follows a period, clear the Capitalize First Letter Of Sentences check box.

4. In the **Replace** box, type **avalable**.

   Word scrolls the list below to show the entry that is closest to what you typed.

5. Press the Tab key to move the cursor to the **With** box, and then type **available**.

6. Click **Add** to add the entry to the correction list, and then click **OK**.

7. Click **OK** to close the **Word Options** dialog box.

8. Position the cursor at the end of the second paragraph, press the Spacebar, and then type **Sidney will not be avalable May 10-14** followed by a period.

   The word *avalable* changes to *available*.

9. In the first paragraph, right-click **sorces**, the first word with a red wavy underline.

   Word lists possible correct spellings for this word.

The shortcut menu also lists actions you might want to carry out, such as adding the word to the AutoCorrect list.

10. In the list, click **sources**.

    Word removes the red wavy underline and inserts the correction.

Tip Word's grammar checker helps identify phrases and clauses that don't follow traditional grammatical rules, but it's not always accurate. It's easy to get in the habit of ignoring green wavy underlines. However, it's wise to scrutinize them all to be sure that your documents don't contain any embarrassing mistakes.

11. Press Ctrl+Home to move to the beginning of the document, and then on the **Review** tab, in the **Proofing** group, click the **Spelling & Grammar** button.

    The Spelling And Grammar dialog box opens, with the duplicate word *to* in red in the Repeated Word box.

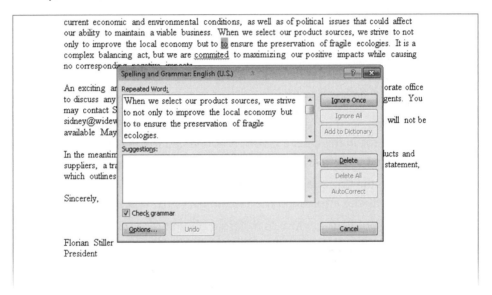

Behind the dialog box, Word has highlighted the duplicate to *in the document.*

Troubleshooting If the errors we mention don't appear to be in the practice file, click Options at the bottom of the Spelling And Grammar dialog box. Then in the Word Options dialog box, under When Correcting Spelling And Grammar In Word, click Recheck Document. Click Yes to reset the spelling and grammar checkers, and then click OK.

12. Click **Delete**.

    Word deletes the second *to* and then displays the first word it does not recognize, *commited*, in red in the Not In Dictionary box.

13. With **committed** selected in the **Suggestions** box, click **AutoCorrect**.

    Word adds the misspelling and the selected correction to the AutoCorrect list, so that the next time you type *commited* by mistake, the spelling will be corrected for you as you type. The program then identifies a possible grammatical error.

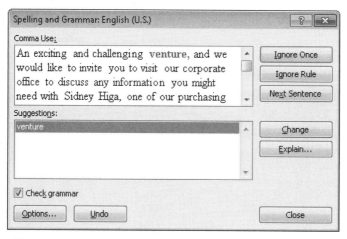

This grammatical error is identified as an incorrect use of a comma.

You need to read the sentence and then decide whether and how to correct the error. In this case, the error is not related to the comma after *venture* but to the fact that there is no verb in the first half of the sentence.

14. In the **Comma Use** box, double-click the word **An** at the beginning of the sentence with the error, and type **The import business is an**. Then click **Change**.

    Word flags *Contoso* as a word it doesn't recognize.

    Troubleshooting If Word does not proceed to the next potential error after you click Change, click Resume to tell Word to continue with the spelling and grammar check.

    Contoso is a proper noun and is spelled correctly. You could click Ignore All to cause Word to skip over any other instances of this word in this document. However, if this name appears frequently in your documents, you can prevent Word from continuing to flag it by adding the word to the custom dictionary.

15. Click **Add to Dictionary**.

    Word displays a message indicating that it has finished checking the spelling and grammar of the document.

16. Click **OK** to close the message box.

    Tip The grammar checker doesn't always catch awkward phrasing. For example, note the error in the second sentence of the first paragraph of the Letter document. It's a good example of why you should always proofread your documents, to catch the things that Word doesn't.

 CLEAN UP Save the Letter document, and then close it.

Viewing Document Statistics

As you type, Word keeps track of the number of pages and words in your document and displays this information at the left end of the status bar. To see the number of words in only part of the document, such as a few paragraphs, simply select that part. The status bar then displays the number of words in the selection, expressed as a fraction of the total, such as 250/800.

You can see more statistics in the Word Count dialog box, which you open by clicking the Word Count button in the Proofing group on the Review tab.

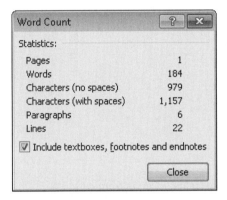

In addition to counting pages and words, Word counts characters, paragraphs, and lines.

Word also gives you the option of including or excluding words in text boxes, footnotes, and endnotes.

Inserting Saved Text

Another way to ensure consistency in your documents while also saving time is to use building blocks. These are saved items that are available for use in any document. Word 2010 comes with many built-in building blocks for formatted items such as cover pages, headers and footers, tables, and text boxes. You can also save your own building blocks by using the Quick Parts feature.

See Also For information about the building blocks that come with Word, see "Inserting Building Blocks" in Chapter 6, "Add Simple Graphic Elements."

A custom building block can be a simple phrase or sentence that you type often, or it can include multiple paragraphs, formatting, graphics, and so on. The trick is to first ensure that the text is exactly the way you want it. Then you can save the building block and use it confidently wherever you need it.

To create a building block, you select the item you want to save, click Quick Parts in the Text group on the Insert tab, and save the selection in the Quick Parts gallery with an assigned name. You can then insert the building block at the cursor by clicking Quick Parts to display the gallery and clicking the thumbnail of the building block you want. Or you can insert it elsewhere by right-clicking the thumbnail in the gallery and then clicking one of the specified locations.

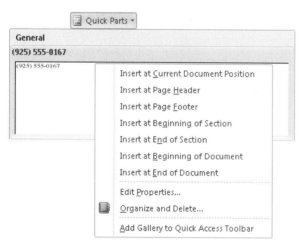

You can insert a custom building block by selecting a location from a list.

Tip In a document, you can type the name of any building block and then press the F3 key to insert it at the cursor.

When you create a custom building block, Word saves it in a special file called the *Building Blocks template*. When you exit Word, you'll be asked whether you want to save this template. If you want to discard the building blocks you have created in this Word session, click Don't Save. If you want them to be available for future documents, click Save.

In this exercise, you'll save a company contact-information block and the Latin name of a plant as building blocks so that you can insert them elsewhere in a document.

 SET UP You need the Bamboo_start document located in your Chapter03 practice file folder to complete this exercise. Open the Bamboo_start document, and save it as *Bamboo*. Then follow the steps.

1. At the top of the document, select the first four lines by using any of the selection techniques described earlier in this chapter.

 2. On the **Insert** tab, in the **Text** group, click the **Quick Parts** button, and then click **Save Selection to Quick Part Gallery**.

   The Create New Building Block dialog box opens.

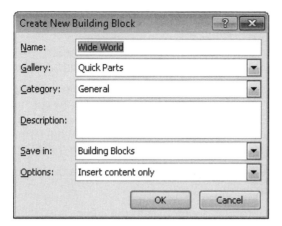

Word suggests the first few words of the selection as the name of the building block.

3. In the **Name** box, type **Contact Block**, and then click **OK**.

   Word saves the selection in the Quick Parts gallery.

4. In the third paragraph of the document, select **obatea acuminata aztectorum** (don't select the period). Then in the **Text** group, click the **Quick Parts** button.

   Notice that the company contact information now appears as a building block in the Quick Parts gallery.

The Quick Parts gallery displays only the building blocks you create. The built-in building blocks are available from other galleries, such as the Cover Page gallery.

5. Click **Save Selection to Quick Part Gallery**, type **oaa** in the **Name** box, and then click **OK**.

6. Press Ctrl+End to move the cursor to the end of the document, and then press the Spacebar.

7. Type **In particular, we recommend oaa** (don't type a period).

8. Press F3, and then type a period.

   Word replaces *oaa* with its building block, *obatea acuminata aztectorum*.

   Troubleshooting Pressing F3 substitutes the corresponding building block only if there is a space to the left of the building block name and the cursor is immediately to its right. If you want to enter a building block in existing text (rather than at the end of it), you need to ensure that there is a space after the cursor. Type two spaces, position the cursor between them, type the building block name, and then press F3.

9. Press Enter. Then in the **Text** group, click the **Quick Parts** button, and in the gallery, click the **Contact Block** entry.

   The company contact information appears at the cursor.

   very adaptable, with some species deciduous and others evergreen. Although there isn't yet a complete knowledge about this plant, there are believed to be between 1100 and 1500 different species of bamboo. The color range is from light green leaves and culms (stems) to dark, rich shades of green or some combination thereof.

   Because they are so easy to grow in such a variety of climates, there is a plant available for just about anyone who wishes to grow one in the backyard. Some dwarf species include chimonobambusa marmorea, indocalamus tessellatus, and pleioblastus chino vaginatus. Also suitable for the personal garden are those categorized as mid size. Examples of these types of plants are bambusa glaucophylla and otatea acuminata aztectorum. Plant starts and seeds are easier to find than ever, being available at nurseries and through mail order.

   Choosing bamboo as part of home or garden design makes sense on many levels. Not only does it have an appealing look, but it supports the environment as well as the countries that produce it. In particular, we recommend otatea acuminata aztectorum.

   Wide World Importers
   Furniture and accessories for your world

   (925) 555-0167
   www.wideworldimporters.com

   The two custom building blocks are inserted with just a few clicks.

✖ CLEAN UP Save the Bamboo document, and then close it. When you exit Word, remember to click Don't Save when you are asked whether you want to save changes to the Building Blocks template.

Inserting One Document into Another

Sometimes you'll want to insert one saved document into another document. For example, you might want to compile four quarterly reports so that you can edit them to create an annual report. In this situation, it would be tedious to have to select and copy the text of each report and then paste it into the annual document. Instead, you can have Word insert the existing documents for you. Here's how:

1. Position the cursor where you want to insert the existing document, and then on the Insert tab, in the Text group, click the Object arrow.

2. In the list, click Text From File.

   The Insert File dialog box opens.

3. Locate the file you want, and double-click it to insert it at the cursor.

Key Points

- You can cut or copy text and paste it elsewhere in the same document or in a different document. Cut and copied text is stored on the Clipboard.

- Undo one action or the last several actions you performed by clicking the Undo button (or its arrow) on the Quick Access Toolbar. Click the Redo button if you change your mind again.

- You can find each occurrence of a word or phrase and replace it with another.

- Rely on AutoCorrect to correct common misspellings. Correct other spelling and grammatical errors individually as you type or by checking the entire document in one pass.

- You don't have to type and proof the same text over and over again. Instead, save the text as a building block and insert it with a few mouse clicks.

Chapter at a Glance

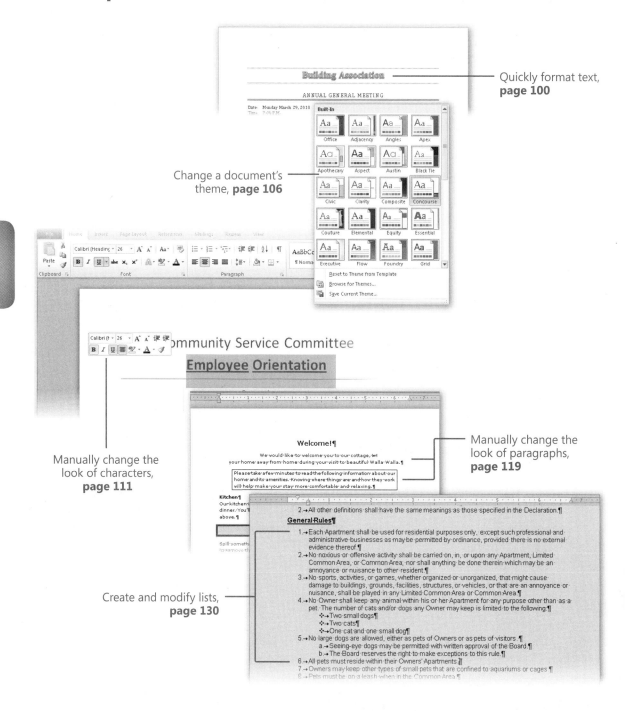

Quickly format text, **page 100**

Change a document's theme, **page 106**

Manually change the look of characters, **page 111**

Manually change the look of paragraphs, **page 119**

Create and modify lists, **page 130**

4 Change the Look of Text

In this chapter, you will learn how to

✔ Quickly format text.

✔ Change a document's theme.

✔ Manually change the look of characters.

✔ Manually change the look of paragraphs.

✔ Create and modify lists.

The appearance of your documents helps to convey their message. Microsoft Word 2010 can help you develop professional-looking documents whose appearance is appropriate to their contents. You can easily format the characters and paragraphs so that key points stand out and your arguments are easy to grasp. You can also change the look of major elements within a document by applying predefined sets of formatting called *Quick Styles*, and you can change the look of selected text by applying predefined combinations called *text effects*. In addition, you can change the fonts, colors, and effects throughout a document with one click by applying one of the built-in themes.

Tip A font consists of alphabetic characters, numbers, and symbols that share a common design.

In this chapter, you'll first experiment with built-in Quick Styles and text effects, and then you'll change the theme applied to a document. You'll change the look of individual words, and then you'll change the indentation, alignment, and spacing of individual paragraphs. You'll also add borders and shading to make paragraphs stand out. Finally, you'll create and format both bulleted and numbered lists.

> **Practice Files** Before you can complete the exercises in this chapter, you need to copy the book's practice files to your computer. The practice files you'll use to complete the exercises in this chapter are in the Chapter04 practice file folder. A complete list of practice files is provided in "Using the Practice Files" at the beginning of this book.

Quickly Formatting Text

You don't have to know much about character and paragraph formatting to be able to format your documents in ways that will make them easier to read and more professional looking. With a couple of mouse clicks, you can easily change the look of words, phrases, and paragraphs by using Quick Styles.

Word has several types of predefined Quick Styles, but the simplest are those you can apply to text.

- **Paragraph styles** You apply these to entire paragraphs, such as headings.

- **Character styles** You apply these to words.

- **Linked styles** You apply these to either paragraphs or words.

By default, Word makes just a few of the predefined Quick Styles available in the Quick Styles gallery in the Styles group on the Home tab. Quick Styles apply a combination of character formatting (such as font, size, and color) and paragraph formatting (such as line spacing).

The Quick Styles gallery.

The styles displayed as thumbnails in the Quick Styles gallery have been designed to go well together, so applying styles from the gallery produces a harmonious effect. After you apply styles from the current set of styles, you can easily change the look of the entire document by switching to a different style set. The Quick Style names are the same; only their defined formatting changes. So if you have applied the Heading 1 style to a paragraph, you can change its formatting simply by changing the style set.

You display the list of available style sets by clicking the Change Styles button and then clicking Style Set.

Clicking one of these style sets displays thumbnails of its styles in the Quick Styles gallery.

You can point to any style set in the list to see a live preview of how the applied styles in a set will look, and you can click a style set to apply its definitions to the document.

See Also For information about creating custom styles, refer to *Microsoft Word 2010 Step by Step*, by Joyce Cox and Joan Lambert (Microsoft Press, 2010).

In addition to applying Quick Styles to quickly change the look of paragraphs and characters, you can apply predefined text effects to a selection to add more zing. Clicking the Text Effects button in the Font group on the Home tab displays a gallery of effects to choose from.

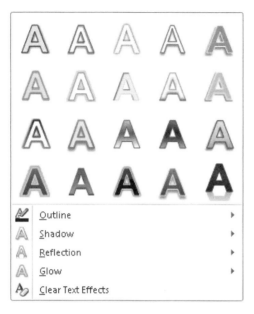

You can apply any predefined effect in the gallery to selected text, or you can click options at the bottom of the gallery and define a custom effect.

These effects are dramatic, so you'll probably want to restrict their use to document titles and similar elements to which you want to draw particular attention.

In this exercise, you'll experiment with Quick Styles and text effects.

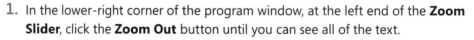 **SET UP** You need the AgendaA_start document located in your Chapter04 practice file folder to complete this exercise. Open the AgendaA_start document, and save it as *AgendaA*. Then follow the steps.

1. In the lower-right corner of the program window, at the left end of the **Zoom Slider**, click the **Zoom Out** button until you can see all of the text.

   For example, if your current view is 100% and your resolution is 1024x768, you can click the Zoom Out button three times to set the zoom percentage to 70%.

2. Ensure that the cursor is located at the top of the document, at the beginning of the **Building Association** paragraph. Then on the **Home** tab, in the **Styles** group, point to each thumbnail in the displayed row of the **Quick Styles** gallery.

   The formatting of the first line changes to show you a live preview of how its text will look if you click the style you are pointing to. You don't have to actually apply the formatting to see its effect.

3. Without making a selection, click the **Down** arrow to the right of the gallery.

   The next row of the Quick Styles gallery appears.

4. Point to each thumbnail in this row of the **Quick Styles** gallery.

Only the styles that are paragraph or linked styles affect the text. You cannot see a live preview of character styles unless the cursor is within a word or multiple words are selected.

5. To the right of the **Quick Styles** gallery, click the **More** button.

Word displays the entire Quick Styles gallery. The style applied to the paragraph containing the cursor is surrounded by a border.

6. In the gallery, click the **Title** thumbnail.

Word applies that style to the paragraph containing the cursor.

7. Click anywhere in the **ANNUAL GENERAL MEETING** line, and then in the gallery, click the **Heading 1** thumbnail.

8. Click anywhere in the **Agenda** line, and then in the gallery, click the **Heading 1** thumbnail.

Notice that although you applied the same Heading 1 style to *ANNUAL GENERAL MEETING* and *Agenda*, the first heading looks bigger because of the use of all capital letters.

Building Association

ANNUAL GENERAL MEETING
Date: Monday March 29, 2010
Time: 7:00 P.M.

Agenda
Preliminaries

Call to order

Proof of notice of meeting

The styles make it easy to distinguish information.

Tip We have hidden formatting marks for this exercise.

9. Point in the selection area to the left of the **Preliminaries** line, and click to select the line. Then hold down the Ctrl key while clicking adjacent to the following lines:

Approval of Minutes
Board Reports
Election of Board Members
New Business
Adjournment

10. Apply the **Heading 1** style to the selected lines. Then without moving the selection, click the **More** button and, in the gallery, click **Emphasis**.

    Applying the Emphasis character style on top of the Heading 1 paragraph style makes these headings italic, which looks lighter.

11. Select the **Date** and **Time** lines, and then in the **Quick Styles** gallery, click the **No Spacing** thumbnail.

12. Apply the **No Spacing** style to the three lines under **Preliminaries**, the two lines under **Board Reports**, and the two lines under **Election of Board Members**.

13. Press Ctrl+Home to release the selection and move the cursor to the top of the document.

    As you can see, the results look very professional.

Building Association

ANNUAL GENERAL MEETING
Date: Monday March 29, 2010
Time: 7:00 P.M.

Agenda

Preliminaries
Call to order
Proof of notice of meeting
Roll call to establish quorum

Approval of Minutes

Board Reports
Financial report
New rules and regulations

You have clearly defined the hierarchy of the agenda with just a few clicks.

14. In the **Styles** group, click the **Change Styles** button, point to **Style Set**, and then point to each style set in turn, watching the effect on the document.

15. When you finish exploring, click **Formal**.

    The formatting of the document changes and the headings and text take on the look assigned to this style set.

BUILDING ASSOCIATION

ANNUAL GENERAL MEETING

Date: Monday March 29, 2010
Time: 7:00 P.M.

AGENDA

Preliminaries

Call to order
Proof of notice of meeting
Roll call to establish quorum

Approval of Minutes

Board Reports

Financial report
New rules and regulations

*The Title, Heading 1, and Emphasis style definitions in the Formal style set produce
a different look from those in the default set.*

16. Select the document title. Then in the **Font** group, click the **Text Effects** button.

    Word displays the Text Effects gallery.

17. Point to each thumbnail in the gallery, observing the effect on the title behind the gallery.

18. Click the right-most thumbnail in the third row (**Fill - Red, Accent 2, Double Outline - Accent 2**). Then click away from the title to release the selection.

    The effect applied to the title makes it really stand out.

Building Association

ANNUAL GENERAL MEETING

Date: Monday March 29, 2010
Time: 7:00 P.M.

By using text effects, you can apply complex sets of formatting with a few clicks.

 CLEAN UP Save the AgendaA document, and then close it.

Changing a Document's Theme

To enhance the look of a Word document whose components have been styled, you can apply a predefined theme. A theme is a combination of colors, fonts, and effects that project a certain feeling or tone. For example, the Flow theme uses a palette of blues and greens, the Calibri and Constantia fonts, and understated effects. You apply a theme to the entire document by clicking the Themes button in the Themes group on the Page Layout tab, and then making a selection from the Themes gallery.

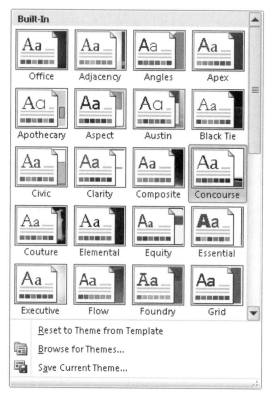

The Themes gallery.

If you like the colors of one theme and the fonts of another, you can mix and match theme elements. First apply the theme that most closely resembles the look you want, and then in the Themes group, change the colors by clicking the Theme Colors button or the fonts by clicking the Theme Fonts button.

If you create a combination of colors and fonts that you would like to be able to use with other documents, you can save the combination as a new theme. By saving the theme in the default Document Themes folder, you make the theme available in the Themes gallery. However, you don't have to store custom themes in the Document Themes folder; you can store them anywhere on your hard disk, on removable media, or in a network location. To use a theme that is stored in a different location, you click the Themes button, and then click Browse For Themes at the bottom of the gallery. Locate the theme you want in the Choose Theme Or Themed Document dialog box, and then click Open to apply that theme to the current document.

Tip The bottom section of the Themes gallery displays themes downloaded from the Microsoft Office Online Web site. You can visit this Web site at office.microsoft.com to find additional themes and templates created by Microsoft and by other people.

In this exercise, you'll apply a theme to an existing document and change the colors and fonts. Then you'll save the new combination as a custom theme.

SET UP You need the AgendaB_start document located in your Chapter04 practice file folder to complete this exercise. Open the AgendaB_start document, and save it as *AgendaB*. Then follow the steps.

1. On the **Page Layout** tab, in the **Themes** group, click the **Themes** button.

   The Themes gallery appears.

2. Point to each thumbnail in turn to display a live preview of the theme. (Scroll through the gallery so that you can explore all the themes.)

3. In the **Themes** gallery, click **Trek**.

   The colors and fonts change to those defined for the selected theme.

4. In the **Themes** group, click the **Theme Colors** button.

   The Theme Colors gallery appears. (The currently selected color set, which is not shown in the graphic on the next page, is indicated by a border.)

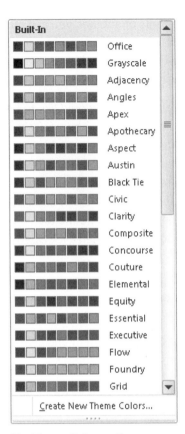

The Theme Colors gallery.

5. Preview any color set that interests you, and then in the gallery, click **Newsprint**.

   The Newsprint colors replace the Trek colors, but nothing else in the document changes.

6. In the **Themes** group, click the **Theme Fonts** button.

   The Theme Fonts gallery appears. The currently selected font set is highlighted. Each built-in option includes a set of two fonts—the first is used for headings and the second for body text.

The Theme Fonts gallery.

7. Preview any set of fonts that interests you, and then in the gallery, click **Apex**.

   The Apex fonts replace the Trek fonts, but the colors remain the same.

8. In the **Themes** group, click the **Themes** button, and then below the gallery, click **Save Current Theme**.

   The Save Current Theme dialog box opens and displays the contents of the Document Themes folder. (This dialog box resembles the Save As dialog box.) The Document Themes folder is the default location for saving any new themes you create.

9. In the **File name** box, replace the suggested name with **My Theme**, and then click **Save**.

10. In the **Themes** group, click the **Themes** button to display the gallery.

    Your new theme appears in the Custom section at the top of the gallery.

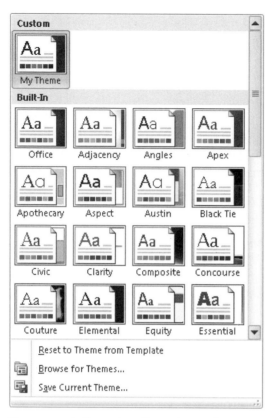

You can apply the custom theme to any document.

11. Click away from the gallery to close it without making a selection.

 **CLEAN UP** Save the AgendaB document, and then close it.

Tip If you want to delete the theme you created in this topic, open Windows Explorer and navigate to the C:\Users\<user name>\AppData\Roaming\Microsoft\Templates\Document Themes folder. (In Windows 7, you can click the Start button, type *Document Themes* in the Search box at the bottom of the Start menu, and then click the folder in the search results.) Then select My Theme, and press Delete.

Manually Changing the Look of Characters

As you have seen, Word 2010 makes changing the look of content in a styled document almost effortless. But styles can't do everything. To be able to precisely control the look of your text, you need to know how to manually change individual elements.

When you type text in a document, it is displayed in a particular font. By default the font used for text in a new Word document is Calibri, but you can change the font of any element at any time. The available fonts vary from one computer to another, depending on the programs installed. Common fonts include Arial, Verdana, and Times New Roman.

You can vary the look of a font by changing the following attributes:

- **Size** Almost every font comes in a range of sizes, which are measured in points from the top of letters that have parts that stick up (ascenders), such as *h*, to the bottom of letters that have parts that drop down (descenders), such as *p*. A point is approximately 1/72 of an inch (about 0.04 centimeters).

- **Style** Almost every font comes in a range of styles. The most common are regular (or plain), italic, bold, and bold italic.

- **Effect** Fonts can be enhanced by applying effects, such as underlining, small capital letters (small caps), or shadows.

- **Color** A palette of coordinated colors is available, and you can also specify custom colors.

- **Character spacing** You can alter the spacing between characters by pushing them apart or squeezing them together.

Although some attributes might cancel each other out, they are usually cumulative. For example, you might use a bold font in various sizes and various shades of green to make words stand out in a newsletter. Collectively, the font and its attributes are called *character formatting*.

You apply character formatting from one of three locations:

- **Mini Toolbar** Several common formatting buttons are available on the Mini Toolbar that appears when you point to selected text.

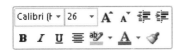

The Mini Toolbar is transparent until you point to it.

● **Font group on the Home tab** This group includes buttons for changing the font and most of the font attributes you are likely to use.

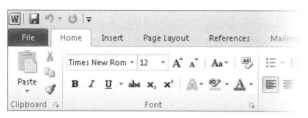

The Font group.

● **Font dialog box** If you are looking for an attribute, such as small caps, and don't see it in the Font group, click the Font dialog box launcher. All the attributes are gathered together on the Font page of the dialog box, except character spacing, which is on the Advanced page.

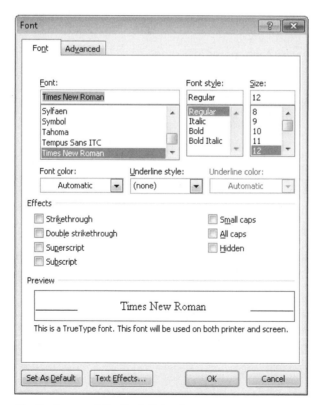

The Font page of the Font dialog box.

In this exercise, you'll format the text in a document by changing its font, style, size, color, and character spacing. You'll also highlight a few words. Then you'll return selected text to its original condition by clearing some formatting you no longer want.

 SET UP You need the OrientationDraft_start document located in your Chapter04 practice file folder to complete this exercise. Open the OrientationDraft_start document, and save it as *OrientationDraft*. Then follow the steps.

1. In the **Employee Orientation** heading, click anywhere in the word **Orientation**.

 2. On the **Home** tab, in the **Font** group, click the **Underline** button.

Keyboard Shortcut Press Ctrl+U to underline the active word or selection.

The word containing the cursor is now underlined. Notice that you did not have to select the entire word.

Tip If you click the Underline arrow, you can choose an underline style and color from the Underline gallery.

3. In the same heading, click anywhere in the word **Employee**, and then on the Quick Access Toolbar, click the **Repeat** button.

Keyboard Shortcut Press Ctrl+Y to repeat an action.

Word repeats the previous formatting command. Again, although you did not select the entire word, it is now underlined.

4. In the selection area, click adjacent to **Employee Orientation** to select the entire heading.

Word displays a transparent version of the Mini Toolbar. You can use the common commands on the Mini Toolbar to quickly change the look of the selection.

5. Point to the Mini Toolbar to make it fully visible. Then on the Mini Toolbar, click the **Bold** button.

Keyboard Shortcut Press Ctrl+B to make the active word or selection bold.

The heading is now bold. The active buttons on the Mini Toolbar and in the Font group on the Home tab indicate the attributes you applied to the selection.

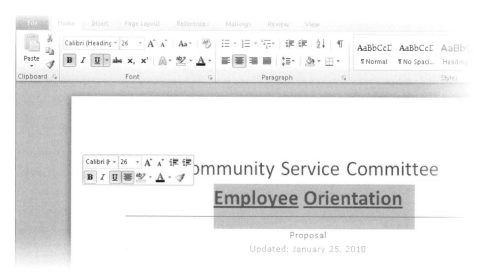

The ribbon reflects the settings in the Mini Toolbar.

Troubleshooting The appearance of buttons and groups on the ribbon changes depending on the width of the program window. For information about changing the appearance of the ribbon to match our screen images, see "Modifying the Display of the Ribbon" at the beginning of this book.

6. On the Mini Toolbar, click the **Format Painter** button. Then move the pointer into the selection area to the left of the **Proposal** heading, and click the mouse button.

    Tip The Format Painter button is also available in the Clipboard group on the Home tab.

    Word applies the formatting of *Employee Orientation* to *Proposal*.

7. Select **Employee Orientation**, and then on the **Home** tab, in the **Font** group, click the **Font** arrow.

    Calibri (Heading ▼)

    The Font gallery appears.

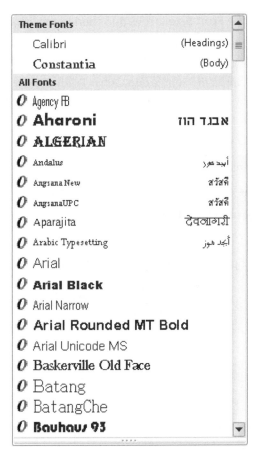

Word comes with many fonts.

8. Scroll through the gallery of available fonts, and then click **Impact**.

Troubleshooting If Impact is not available, select any heavy font that catches your attention.

The *Employee Orientation* heading now appears in the new font.

9. In the **Font** group, click the **Font Size** arrow, and then in the list, click **20**.

   The size of the heading text decreases to 20 points.

   Tip You can increase or decrease the font size in set increments by clicking the Grow Font and Shrink Font buttons in the Font group, or by clicking the same buttons on the Mini Toolbar that appears when you select text. You can also press Ctrl+> or Ctrl+<.

10. Click the **Font** dialog box launcher.

   Keyboard Shortcut Press Ctrl+Shift+F to display the Font dialog box.

   The Font dialog box opens.

11. Click the **Underline style** arrow, and then in the list, click **(none)**.

12. In the **Effects** area, select the **Small caps** check box.

13. Click the **Advanced** tab.

   Notice that the Spacing option is currently set to Expanded.

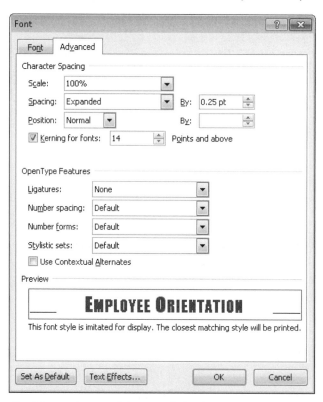

The Advanced page of the Font dialog box.

14. To the right of the **Spacing** option, in the **By** box, select **0.25 pt**, type **10 pt** (the *pt* stands for *points*), and click **OK**. Then press Home to release the selection.

The manually formatted text appears in small capital letters with the spacing between the characters expanded by 10 points.

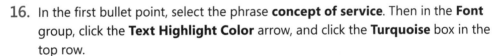

Community Service Committee
E M P L O Y E E   O R I E N T A T I O N

<u>**Proposal**</u>

You can expand and contract the spacing between letters to create different effects.

15. Select **Employee Orientation** again. In the **Font** group, click the **Font Color** arrow, and then under **Theme Colors** in the palette, click the box at the right end of the top row (**Lime, Accent 6**).

The selected words are now lime green.

> **Tip** To apply the Font Color button's current color, you can simply click the button (not its arrow). If you want to apply a color that is not shown under Theme Colors or Standard Colors, click More Colors at the bottom of the palette, and in the Colors dialog box, click the color you want in the color wheel.

16. In the first bullet point, select the phrase **concept of service**. Then in the **Font** group, click the **Text Highlight Color** arrow, and click the **Turquoise** box in the top row.

The selected phrase is now highlighted in turquoise, and the Text Highlight Color button shows turquoise as its active color.

> **Tip** If you click the Text Color Highlight button without first making a selection, the shape of the mouse pointer changes to a highlighter that you can drag across text. Click the button again, or press Esc, to turn off the highlighter.

17. In the fifth bullet point, double-click the word **brainstorming**. Then hold down the Ctrl key while double-clicking **planning** and **leadership**.

18. In the **Font** group, click the **Change Case** button, and click **UPPERCASE**. Then click away from the bullet point to release the selection.

The selected words now appear in all capital letters.

> # Community Service Committee
> ### E M P L O Y E E   O R I E N T A T I O N
>
> ## Proposal
> Updated: January 25, 2010
>
> **Project Goals**
> - Familiarize employees with the concept of service.
> - Make service a natural part of their lives.
> - Engage and motivate them.
> - Forge a sense of teamwork among all employees across departments.
> - Provide appropriate skills development through BRAINSTORMING, PLANNING, and LEADERSHIP opportunities.
> - Meet genuine community needs.

Instead of retyping, you can have Word change the case of words.

19. Select the **Proposal** line. Then on the **Home** tab, in the **Font** group, click the **Clear Formatting** button.

Keyboard Shortcut Press Ctrl+Spacebar to clear manually applied formatting.

The formatting of the selected text is removed.

Tip You cannot click the Clear Formatting button to remove highlighting. If the highlight is the same color as that shown on the Text Highlight Color button, you can select the text and click the button to remove the highlighting. If the button shows a different color, select the text, click the Text Highlight Color arrow, and then click No Color.

 CLEAN UP Save the OrientationDraft document, and then close it.

Character Formatting and Case Considerations

The way you use case and character formatting in a document can influence its visual impact on your readers. Used judiciously, case and character formatting can make a plain document look attractive and professional, but excessive use can make it look amateurish and detract from the message. For example, using too many fonts in the same document is the mark of inexperience, so don't use more than two or three.

Bear in mind that lowercase letters tend to recede, so using all uppercase (capital) letters can be useful for titles and headings or for certain kinds of emphasis. However, large blocks of uppercase letters are tiring to the eye.

Tip Where do the terms *uppercase* and *lowercase* come from? Until the advent of computers, individual characters made of lead were assembled to form the words that would appear on a printed page. The characters were stored alphabetically in cases, with the capital letters in the upper case and the small letters in the lower case.

Manually Changing the Look of Paragraphs

As you know, you create a paragraph by typing text and then pressing the Enter key. The paragraph can consist of one word, one sentence, or multiple sentences. You can change the look of a paragraph by changing its indentation, alignment, and line spacing, as well as the space before and after it. You can also put borders around it and shade its background. Collectively, the settings you use to vary the look of a paragraph are called *paragraph formatting*.

In Word, you don't define the width of paragraphs and the length of pages by defining the area occupied by the text; instead you define the size of the white space—the left, right, top, and bottom margins—around the text. You click the Margins button in the Page Setup group on the Page Layout tab to define these margins, either for the whole document or for sections of the document.

See Also For information about setting margins, see "Previewing and Adjusting Page Layout" in Chapter 7, "Preview, Print, and Distribute Documents." For information about sections, see "Controlling What Appears on Each Page" in the same chapter.

Although the left and right margins are set for a whole document or section, you can vary the position of the paragraphs between the margins. The quickest way to indent a paragraph from the left is to click the Increase Indent button; clicking the Decrease Indent button has the opposite effect. You cannot increase or decrease the indent beyond the margins.

Another way to control the indentation of lines is by dragging markers on the horizontal ruler to indicate where each line of text starts and ends.

- **First Line Indent** Begins a paragraph's first line of text at this marker

- **Hanging Indent** Begins a paragraph's second and subsequent lines of text at this marker at the left end of the ruler

- **Left Indent** Indents the text to this marker

- **Right Indent** Wraps the text when it reaches this marker at the right end of the ruler

You display the ruler by clicking the Ruler check box in the Show group on the View tab, or by clicking the View Ruler button located at the top of the vertical scroll bar.

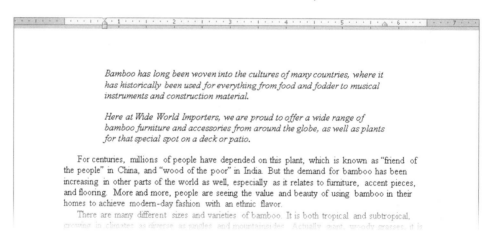

You can manually change a paragraph's indentation by moving markers on the horizontal ruler.

Setting a right indent indicates where the lines in a paragraph should end, but sometimes you might want to specify where only one line should end. For example, you might want to break a title after a particular word to make it look balanced on the page. You can end an individual line by inserting a text wrapping break (more commonly known as a *line break*). After positioning the cursor where you want the break to occur, you click the Breaks button in the Page Setup group on the Page Layout tab, and then click Text Wrapping. Word indicates the line break with a bent arrow. Inserting a line break does not start a new paragraph, so when you apply paragraph formatting to a line of text that ends with a line break, the formatting is applied to the entire paragraph, not just that line.

Keyboard Shortcut Press Shift+Enter to insert a line break.

You can also determine the positioning of a paragraph between the left and right margins by changing its alignment. You can click buttons in the Paragraph group on the Home tab to align paragraphs.

- **Align Left** Aligns each line of the paragraph at the left margin, with a ragged right edge

  Keyboard Shortcut Press Ctrl+L to left-align a paragraph.

- **Center** Aligns the center of each line in the paragraph between the left and right margins, with ragged left and right edges

  Keyboard Shortcut Press Ctrl+E to center-align a paragraph.

- **Align Right** Aligns each line of the paragraph at the right margin, with a ragged left edge

  Keyboard Shortcut Press Ctrl+R to right-align a paragraph.

- **Justify** Aligns each line between the margins, creating even left and right edges

  Keyboard Shortcut Press Ctrl+J to justify a paragraph.

Tip If you know that you want to create a centered paragraph, you don't have to type the text and then align the paragraph. You can use the Click And Type feature to create appropriately aligned text. Move the pointer to the center of a blank area of the page, and when the pointer's shape changes to an I-beam with centered text attached, double-click to insert the cursor in a centered paragraph. Similarly, you can double-click at the left edge of the page to enter left-aligned text and at the right edge to enter right-aligned text.

You can align lines of text in different locations across the page by using tab stops. The easiest way to set tab stops is to use the horizontal ruler. By default, Word sets left-aligned tab stops every half inch (1.27 centimeters), as indicated by gray marks below the ruler. To set a custom tab stop, you start by clicking the Tab button located at the left end of the ruler until the type of tab stop you want appears. You have the following options:

- **Left Tab** Aligns the left end of the text with the tab stop

- **Center Tab** Aligns the center of the text with the tab stop

- **Right Tab** Aligns the right end of the text with the tab stop

- **Decimal Tab** Aligns the decimal point in the text (usually a numeric value) with the tab stop

- **Bar Tab** Draws a vertical line at the position of the tab stop

After selecting the type of tab stop you want to set, you simply click the ruler where you want the tab stop to be. Word then removes any default tab stops to the left of the one you set.

This ruler has a custom left-aligned tab stop at the 1.5 inch mark and default tab stops every half inch to the right of the custom tab stop.

To change the position of an existing custom tab stop, you drag it to the left or right on the ruler. To delete a custom tab stop, you drag it away from the ruler.

To align the text to the right of the cursor with the next tab stop, you press the Tab key. The text is then aligned on the tab stop according to its type. For example, if you set a center tab stop, pressing Tab moves the text so that its center is aligned with the tab stop.

Tip To fine-tune the position of tab stops, click the Paragraph dialog box launcher on either the Home or Page Layout tab. In the Paragraph dialog box, click Tabs to display the Tabs dialog box. You might also open this dialog box if you want to use tab leaders—visible marks such as dots or dashes connecting the text before the tab with the text after it. For example, tab leaders are useful in a table of contents to carry the eye from the text to the page number.

To make it obvious where one paragraph ends and another begins, you can add space between them by adjusting the Spacing After and Spacing Before settings in the Paragraph group on the Page Layout tab. You can adjust the spacing between the lines in a paragraph by clicking the Line And Paragraph Spacing button in the Paragraph group on the Home tab.

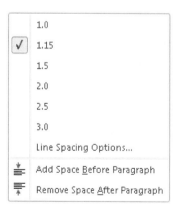

The Line Spacing options.

When you want to make several adjustments to the alignment, indentation, and spacing of selected paragraphs, it is sometimes quicker to use the Paragraph dialog box than to click buttons and drag markers. Clicking the Paragraph dialog box launcher on either the Home tab or the Page Layout tab opens the Paragraph dialog box.

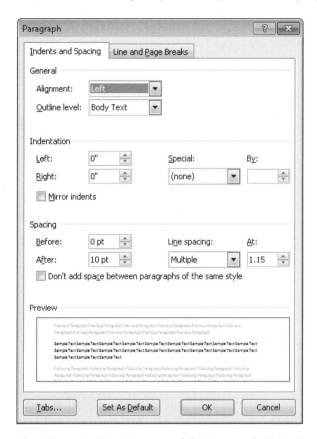

The Indents And Spacing page of the Paragraph dialog box.

You can do a lot with the options in the Paragraph dialog box, but to make a paragraph really stand out, you might want to put a border around it or shade its background. (For real drama, you can do both.) Clicking the Border arrow in the Paragraph group on the Home tab displays a gallery of border options.

The Borders gallery.

Clicking Borders And Shading at the bottom of the list displays the Borders And Shading dialog box, where you can select the style, color, width, and location of the border.

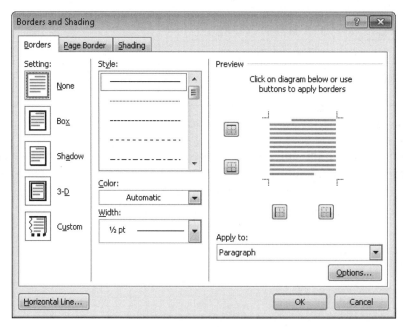

The Border page of the Borders And Shading dialog box.

In this exercise, you'll change text alignment and indentation, insert and modify tab stops, modify paragraph and line spacing, and add borders and shading to paragraphs.

 SET UP You need the Information_start document located in your Chapter04 practice file folder to complete this exercise. Open the Information_start document, and save it as *Information*. Then click the Show/Hide ¶ button to turn on the display of formatting marks, and follow the steps.

1. Set the zoom percentage so that you can see almost all of the paragraphs in the document. Then on the **View** tab, in the **Show** group, select the **Ruler** check box.

   Tip In the following steps, we give measurements in inches. You can substitute approximate measurements in your own measuring system. If you want to change the measuring system Word uses, display the Backstage view, click Options, and in the Word Options dialog box, display the Advanced page. Then under Display, click the system you want in the Show Measurements In Units Of list, and click OK.

 2. Select the first two paragraphs (**Welcome!** and the next paragraph). Then on the **Home** tab, in the **Paragraph** group, click the **Center** button.

   The lines are now centered between the margins.

   Tip When applying paragraph formatting, you don't have to select the entire paragraph.

 3. After the comma in the second paragraph, click to the left of **your**. Then on the **Page Layout** tab, in the **Page Setup** group, click the **Breaks** button, and click **Text Wrapping**.

   Word inserts a line break character and moves the part of the paragraph that follows that character to the next line.

The bent arrow after cottage indicates that you have inserted a line break.

   See Also For information about page and section breaks, see "Controlling What Appears on Each Page" in Chapter 7, "Preview, Print, and Distribute Documents."

 4. Click anywhere in the next paragraph, and then on the **Home** tab, in the **Paragraph** group, click the **Justify** button.

   Word inserts space between the words in the lines of the paragraph so that the edges of the paragraph are flush against both the left and right margins.

5. Without moving the cursor, on the horizontal ruler, drag the **Left Indent** marker to the **0.5** inch mark.

The First Line Indent and Hanging Indent markers move with the Left Indent marker.

6. At the right end of the ruler, drag the **Right Indent** marker to the **6** inch mark.

The paragraph is now indented a half inch in from each of the side margins.

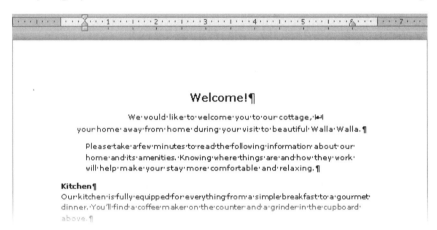

Left and right indents are often used to make paragraphs such as quotations stand out.

7. Click in the **Be careful** paragraph, and then in the **Paragraph** group, click the **Increase Indent** button.

8. Select the **Pillows**, **Blankets**, **Towels**, and **Dish towels** paragraphs, and with the **Left Tab** stop active at the left end of the ruler, click the ruler at the **2** mark.

Word removes the default tab stops (indicated by gray lines below the ruler) up to the 2-inch mark and inserts a custom left-aligned tab at that location on the ruler.

9. Click to the left of **There** in the **Pillows** paragraph, and press the Tab key. Then insert tabs to the left of **You**, **These**, and **There** in the next three paragraphs.

The part of each paragraph that follows the colon is now aligned at the 2-inch mark, producing more space than you need.

10. Select the four paragraphs containing tabs, and on the ruler, drag the **Left Tab** stop to the **1.25** mark.

11. Without changing the selection, on the ruler, drag the **Hanging Indent** marker to the **1.25** mark. Then press Home to release the selection.

The Left Indent marker has moved as well, causing the second line of the second selected paragraph to start in the same location as the tab stop.

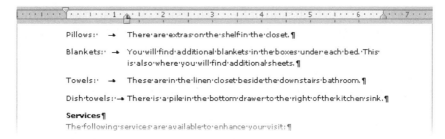

Hanging indents are often used to create table-like effects.

12. At the bottom of the document, select the three paragraphs containing dollar amounts. Where the horizontal and vertical rulers meet, click the **Tab** button until the **Decimal Tab** button is displayed and then click the ruler at the **3** mark.

13. Insert a tab to the left of each dollar amount.

    Word aligns the three paragraphs on the decimals.

14. Select the first paragraph containing tabs (**Pillows**), hold down the Ctrl key, and then select the paragraphs that begin with the following:

    Blankets
    Towels
    Limousine winery tour
    In-home massage

15. On the **Home** tab, in the **Paragraph** group, click the **Line Spacing** button, and click **Remove Space After Paragraph**. Then press the Home key.

    Now only the last paragraphs of the two lists have extra space after them.

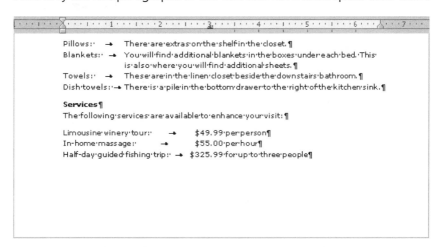

Removing internal space from lists makes them easier to read.

16. Scroll up until the top of the document is in view, and click anywhere in the **Please take a few minutes** paragraph. On the **Home** tab, in the **Paragraph** group, click the **Border** arrow, and then click **Outside Borders**.

17. Click anywhere in the **Be careful** paragraph, click the **Border** arrow, and then at the bottom of the list, click **Borders and Shading**.

    The Borders And Shading dialog box opens, with the Borders page displayed.

18. Under **Setting**, click the **3-D** icon to select that border style. Scroll through the **Style** list and click the fourth style from the bottom. Then click the **Color** arrow, and under **Theme Colors** in the palette, click the **Red, Accent 2** box.

    Tip If you want only one, two, or three sides of the selected paragraphs to have a border, click the buttons surrounding the image in the Preview area.

19. Click the **Shading** tab.

    You can use the options on this page to format the background of the selected paragraph.

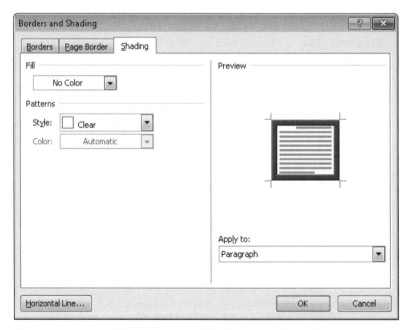

The Shading page of the Borders And Shading dialog box.

20. Click the **Fill** arrow, and under **Theme Colors**, click the lightest color in the red column (**Red, Accent 2, Lighter 80%**). Then click **OK** to close the **Borders and Shading** dialog box.

   A border surrounds the paragraph, and a light red color fills its background. The border stretches all the way to the right margin.

21. To achieve a more balanced look, in the **Paragraph** group, click the **Decrease Indent** button. Then click the **Center** button.

   The paragraph is now centered between the page margins and within its surrounding box.

A combination of a border and shading really makes text stand out. Don't overdo it!

 CLEAN UP Leave the rulers and formatting marks displayed for the next exercise, but change the zoom percentage back to 100%. Save the Information document, and then close it.

Finding and Replacing Formatting

In addition to searching for words and phrases in the Find And Replace dialog box, you can use the dialog box to search for a specific format and replace it with a different one.

See Also For information about finding and replacing text, see "Finding and Replacing Text" in Chapter 3, "Edit and Proofread Text."

To search for a specific format and replace it with a different format:

1. On the Home tab, in the Editing group, click the Replace button.

    Keyboard Shortcut Press Ctrl+H to display the Replace tab of the Find And Replace dialog box.

    The Find And Replace dialog box opens, displaying the Replace tab.

2. Click More to expand the dialog box. Then click Format, and on the Format menu, click either Font or Paragraph.

    Tip You can click Style to search for paragraph styles or character styles.

    The Find Font or Find Paragraph dialog box opens.

3. In the dialog box, click the format you want to find, and then click OK.

4. Click the Replace With text box, click Format, click Font or Paragraph, click the format you want to substitute for the Find What format, and then click OK.

5. Click Find Next to search for the first occurrence of the format, and then click Replace to replace that one occurrence or Replace All to replace every occurrence.

Creating and Modifying Lists

Lists are paragraphs that are usually formatted with a hanging indent so that the first line of each paragraph is longer than subsequent lines. Fortunately, Word takes care of the formatting of lists for you. You simply indicate the type of list you want to create. When the order of items is not important—for example, for a list of supplies needed to carry out a task—a bulleted list is the best choice. And when the order is important—for example, for the steps in a procedure—you will probably want to create a numbered list.

You can indicate the start of a list as follows:

● **Bulleted list** Type * (an asterisk) at the beginning of a paragraph, and then press the Spacebar or the Tab key before entering the list item text. Or click the Bullets button in the Paragraph group on the Home tab.

● **Numbered list** Type *1.* (the number 1 followed by a period) at the beginning of a paragraph, and then press the Spacebar or the Tab key before entering the list item text. Or click the Numbering button in the Paragraph group on the Home tab.

When you start a list in this fashion, Word automatically formats it as a bulleted or numbered list. When you press Enter to start a new item, Word continues the formatting to the new paragraph. Typing items and pressing Enter adds subsequent bulleted or numbered items. To end the list, press Enter twice; or click the Bullets arrow or Numbering arrow in the Paragraph group on the Home tab, and then in the library, click None.

Tip If you want to start a paragraph with an asterisk or number but don't want to format the paragraph as a bulleted or numbered list, click the AutoCorrect Options button that appears after Word changes the formatting, and then in the list, click the appropriate Undo option. You can also click the Undo button on the Quick Access Toolbar.

If you want to create a list that has multiple levels, you start off by creating the list in the usual way. Then when you want the next paragraph to be a level lower (indented more), you press the Tab key after pressing Enter and before you type the text of the item. If you want the next paragraph to be a level higher (indented less), you press Shift+Tab after pressing Enter. In the case of a bulleted list, Word changes the bullet character for each item level. In the case of a numbered list, Word changes the type of numbering used, based on a predefined numbering scheme.

Tip To create a multilevel numbered list with a scheme that is different from the default, you can click the Multilevel List button in the Paragraph group of the Home tab and then select a scheme from the List gallery. You can also define your own scheme.

If you type a set of paragraphs containing a series of items and then decide you want to turn the set into a list, you can select the paragraphs and then click the Bullets or Numbering button.

After you create a list, you can modify, format, and customize the list as follows:

● You can move items around in a list, insert new items, or delete unwanted items. If the list is numbered, Word automatically updates the numbers.

● You can sort items in a bulleted list into ascending or descending order by clicking the Sort button in the Paragraph group on the Home tab.

● For a bulleted list, you can change the bullet symbol by clicking the Bullets arrow in the Paragraph group and making a selection from the Bullets gallery. You can also define a custom bullet (even a picture bullet) by clicking Define New Bullet.

- For a numbered list, you can change the number style by clicking the Numbering arrow in the Paragraph group and making a selection from the Numbering gallery. You can also define a custom style by clicking Define New Number Format.

- You can modify the indentation of the list by dragging the indent markers on the horizontal ruler. You can change both the overall indentation of the list and the relationship of the first line to the other lines.

  See Also For information about paragraph indentation, see "Manually Changing the Look of Paragraphs" earlier in this chapter.

In this exercise, you'll create a bulleted list and a numbered list and then modify lists in various ways.

 SET UP You need the RulesDraft_start document located in your Chapter04 practice file folder to complete this exercise. Open the RulesDraft_start document, and save it as *RulesDraft*. Then follow the steps.

 1. With formatting marks and the rulers displayed, select the first four paragraphs under **The rules fall into four categories**, and then on the **Home** tab, in the **Paragraph** group, click the **Bullets** button.

   The selected paragraphs are reformatted as a bulleted list. Word indents the list and precedes each item with a bullet and a tab. The program also removes the space after all paragraphs except the last one.

 2. With the paragraphs still selected, in the **Paragraph** group, click the **Bullets** arrow.

   The Bullets gallery appears.

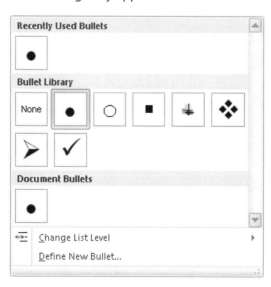

The Bullets gallery offers several predefined bullet choices.

3. Under **Bullet Library**, point to each bullet character to display a live preview of its effect on the selected list items, and then click the bullet composed of four diamonds.

The bullet character that begins each item in the selected list changes.

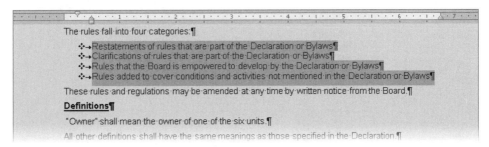

Different bullets are suited to different types of documents.

4. Select the two paragraphs below the **Definitions** heading, and then in the **Paragraph** group, click the **Numbering** button.

Word numbers the two selected paragraphs sequentially.

5. Select the first four paragraphs below the **General Rules** heading, and then click the **Numbering** button.

Word restarts the second numbered list from 1.

6. Select the next three paragraphs, and then in the **Paragraph** group, click the **Bullets** button.

Word formats the paragraphs as a bulleted list, using the symbol you specified earlier. These three bullets are a second-level list of the preceding numbered item and should be indented.

7. With the three bulleted items still selected, in the **Paragraph** group, click the **Increase Indent** button.

The bulleted paragraphs move to the right.

Tip You can also adjust the indent level of a bulleted list by selecting its paragraphs, and on the horizontal ruler, dragging the Left Indent marker to the left or right. You can move just the Hanging Indent marker to adjust the space between the bullets and their text.

8. Select the remaining three paragraphs, and click the **Numbering** button.

Word restarts this numbered list from 1, but you want it to continue the sequence of the previous numbered list.

9. Click anywhere in the **No large dogs** item, and then click the **Numbering** arrow.

The Numbering gallery appears.

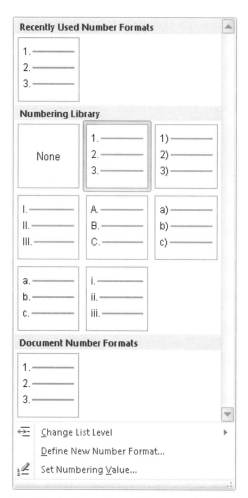

The Numbering gallery offers several predefined number formats.

10. At the bottom of the gallery, click **Set Numbering Value**.

    The Set Numbering Value dialog box opens.

In this dialog box, you specify how this numbered list relates to the previous one.

11. Change the **Set value to** setting to **5**, and then click **OK**.

    Word renumbers the list after the bullet items so that it continues from the previous list.

12. In the **No large dogs** numbered item, click to the left of **Seeing**, press Enter, and then press Tab.

    Word first creates a new number 6 item and renumbers all subsequent items. However, when you press Tab to make the item second level, Word changes the 6 to a, indents the item, and restores the original numbers to the subsequent items.

13. Press the End key, and then press Enter. Then type **The Board reserves the right to make exceptions to this rule.** (type the period), and press Enter.

14. Click the **Numbering** arrow, click **Change List Level** at the bottom of the gallery, and click the first **1.** option. Then in the new first-level item, type **All pets must reside within their Owners' Apartments.**

    The lists are now organized hierarchically.

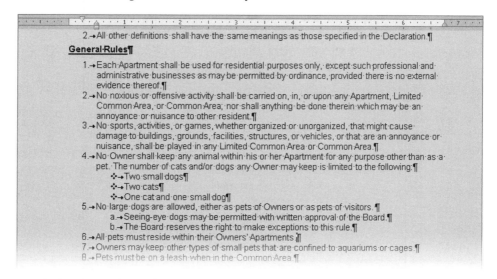

Word takes the work out of creating hierarchical lists.

15. Select the three bulleted paragraphs, and then in the **Paragraph** group, click the **Sort** button.

Formatting Text as You Type

The Word list capabilities are just one example of the program's ability to intuit how you want to format an element based on what you type. You can learn more about these and other AutoFormatting options by exploring the AutoCorrect dialog box. Display the Backstage view, click Options, click Proofing in the left pane of the Word Options dialog box, and then on the Proofing page, click AutoCorrect Options.

On the AutoFormat As You Type page, you can see the options Word implements by default, including bulleted and numbered lists. You can select and clear options to control AutoFormatting behavior.

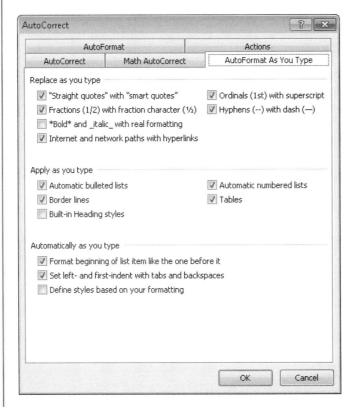

The AutoFormat As You Type page of the AutoCorrect dialog box.

One interesting option is Border Lines. When this check box is selected, typing three consecutive hyphens (-) or three consecutive underscores (_) and pressing Enter draws a single line across the page. Three consecutive equal signs (=) draw a double line, and three consecutive tildes (~) draw a zigzag line.

The Sort Text dialog box opens.

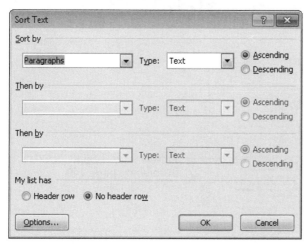

You can sort text in lists in ascending or descending order.

16. With the **Ascending** option selected, click **OK**.

The order of the bulleted items changes to ascending alphabetical order.

 **CLEAN UP** If you want, turn off the rulers and formatting marks. Then save and close the RulesDraft document.

Key Points

- Quick Styles and style sets make it simple to apply combinations of character and paragraph formatting to give your documents a professional look.

- The same document can look very different depending on the theme applied to it. Colors, fonts, and effects can be combined to create just the look you want.

- You can format characters with an almost limitless number of combinations of font, size, style, and effect. For best results, resist the temptation to use more than a handful of combinations.

- You can change the look of paragraphs by varying their indentation, spacing, and alignment and by setting tab stops and applying borders and shading. Use these formatting options judiciously to create a balanced, uncluttered look.

- Bulleted and numbered lists are a great way to present information in an easy-to-read, easy-to-understand format. If the built-in bulleted and numbered formats don't provide what you need, you can define your own formats.

Chapter at a Glance

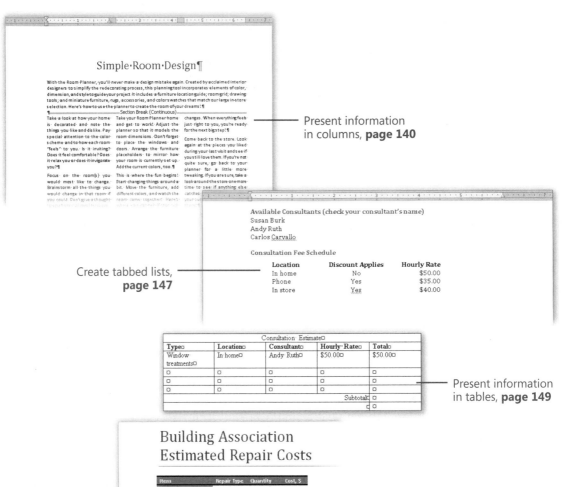

Present information in columns, **page 140**

Create tabbed lists, **page 147**

Present information in tables, **page 149**

Format tables, **page 160**

5 Organize Information in Columns and Tables

In this chapter, you will learn how to

- ✔ Present information in columns.
- ✔ Create tabbed lists.
- ✔ Present information in tables.
- ✔ Format tables.

Information in documents is most commonly presented as paragraphs of text. To make a text-heavy document more legible, you can flow the text in two or more columns, or you can display information in a table. For example, flowing text in multiple columns is a common practice in newsletters, flyers, and brochures; and presenting information in tables is common in reports.

When you need to present data in a document, using a table is often more efficient than describing the data in a paragraph, particularly when the data consists of numeric values. Tables make the data easier to read and understand. A small amount of data can be displayed in simple columns separated by tabs, which creates a tabbed list. A larger amount of data, or more complex data, is better presented in a table, which is a structure of rows and columns, frequently with row and column headings.

In this chapter, you'll first create and modify columns of text. Then you'll create a simple tabbed list. Finally, you'll create tables from scratch and from existing text, and format a table in various ways.

> **Practice Files** Before you can complete the exercises in this chapter, you need to copy the book's practice files to your computer. The practice files you'll use to complete the exercises in this chapter are in the Chapter05 practice file folder. A complete list of practice files is provided in "Using the Practice Files" at the beginning of this book.

Presenting Information in Columns

By default, Microsoft Word 2010 displays text in one column that spans the width of the page between the left and right margins. You can specify that text be displayed in two, three, or more columns to create layouts like those used in newspapers and magazines. When you format text to flow in columns, the text fills the first column on each page and then moves to the top of the next column. You can manually indicate where you want the text within each column to end.

The Columns gallery in the Page Setup group on the Page Layout tab displays several standard options for dividing text into columns. You can choose one, two, or three columns of equal width or two columns of unequal width. If the standard options don't suit your needs, you can specify the number and width of columns. The number of columns is limited by the width and margins of the page, and each column must be at least a half inch wide.

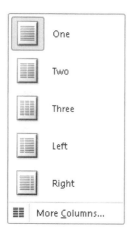

The Columns gallery displays the predefined column options.

No matter how you set up the columns initially, you can change the layout or column widths at any time.

You can format an entire document or a section of a document in columns. When you select a section of text and format it as columns, Word inserts section breaks at the beginning and end of the selected text to delineate the area in which the columnar formatting is applied. Within the columnar text, you can insert column breaks to specify where you want to end one column and start another. Section and column breaks are visible when you display formatting marks in the document.

Tip You can apply many types of formatting, including page orientation, to content within a specific section of a document without affecting the surrounding text. For information about sections, see "Controlling What Appears on Each Page" in Chapter 7, "Preview, Print, and Distribute Documents."

You can apply character and paragraph formatting to columnar text in the same way you would any text. Here are some formatting tips for columnar text:

● When presenting text in narrow columns, you can justify the paragraphs (align the text with the left and right edges) to achieve a neat and clean appearance. To justify the paragraphs, Word adjusts the spacing between words, essentially moving the empty space that would normally appear at the end of the line into the gaps between words.

● To more completely fill columns, you can have Word hyphenate the text to break words into syllables to fill up the gaps.

In this exercise, you'll flow the text in one section of a document into three columns. You'll justify the text in the columns, change the column spacing, and hyphenate the text. You'll then break a column at a specific location instead of allowing the text to flow naturally from one column to the next.

 SET UP You need the RoomPlanner_start document located in your Chapter05 practice file folder to complete this exercise. Open the RoomPlanner_start document, and save it as *RoomPlanner*. Then display formatting marks and the rulers, and follow the steps.

1. Click at the beginning of the paragraph that begins **Take a look** (do not click in the selection area). Then scroll down until you can see the end of the document, hold down the Shift key, and click to the right of the paragraph mark after **credit cards**.

   Word selects the text from the *Take a look* paragraph through the end of the last paragraph (but not the empty paragraph).

   Tip If you want to format an entire document with the same number of columns, you can simply click anywhere in the document—you don't have to select the text.

 2. On the **Page Layout** tab, in the **Page Setup** group, click the **Columns** button, and then in the **Columns** gallery, click **Three**.

   Word inserts a section break above the selected text and flows the text within the section into three columns.

3. Press Ctrl+Home to move to the top of the document.

    The section break is visible above the columns.

> # Simple·Room·Design¶
>
> With·the·Room·Planner,·you'll·never·make·a·design·mistake·again.··Created·by·acclaimed·interior·
> designers·to·simplify·the·redecorating·process,·this·planning·tool·incorporates·elements·of·color,·
> dimension,·and·style·to·guide·your·project.·It·includes·a·furniture·location·guide;·room·grid;·drawing·
> tools;·and·miniature·furniture,·rugs,·accessories,·and·color·swatches·that·match·our·large·in-store·
> selection.·Here's·how·to·use·the·planner·to·create·the·room·of·your·dreams!¶
>
> ¶ ═══════════════════════Section Break (Continuous)═══════════════════════
>
> Take·a·look·at·how·your·   love,·and·the·rest·will·fall·   design·for·a·day·or·two.·
> home·is·decorated·and·note·   into·place.¶   Then·review·it·again.·Does·it·
> the·things·you·like·and·   still·look·perfect,·or·is·
> dislike.··Pay·special·attention·   Take·your·Room·Planner·   something·not·quite·right?·
> to·the·color·scheme·and·to·   home·and·get·to·work!·   You·might·need·to·"live"·
> how·each·room·"feels"·to·   Adjust·the·planner·so·that·it·   with·the·new·plan·for·a·few·
> you.·Is·it·inviting?·Does·it·   models·the·room·   days,·especially·if·you've·
> feel·comfortable?·Does·it·   dimensions.·Don't·forget·to·   made·big·changes.·When·
> relax·you·or·does·it·   place·the·windows·and·   everything·feels·just·right·to·
> invigorate·you?¶   doors.·Arrange·the·furniture·   you,·you're·ready·for·the·
>   placeholders·to·mirror·how·   next·big·step!¶
> Focus·on·the·room(s)·you·   your·room·is·currently·set·

A continuous section break changes the formatting of the subsequent text but keeps it on the same page.

4. On the **Home** tab, in the **Editing** group, click the **Select** button, and then click **Select All**.

    Keyboard Shortcut Press Ctrl+A to select all the text in the document.

5. In the **Paragraph** group, click the **Justify** button.

    Keyboard Shortcut Press Ctrl+J to justify paragraphs.

    The spacing between the words changes to align all the paragraphs in the document with both the left and right margins. Because you applied the formatting to the entire document, the title is no longer centered. However, it is often quicker to apply format-ting globally and then deal with the exceptions.

6. Press Ctrl+Home to move to the paragraph containing the document title. Then in the **Paragraph** group, click the **Center** button.

   Keyboard Shortcut Press Ctrl+E to center text.

   Word centers the document title between the left and right margins.

7. Adjust the zoom percentage until you can see about two-thirds of the first page of the document.

   See Also For information about adjusting the zoom percentage, see "Viewing Files in Different Ways" in Chapter 2, "Work with Files."

8. Click anywhere in the first column.

   On the horizontal ruler, Word indicates the margins of the columns.

On the ruler, the indent markers show the indentation of the active column.

Tip If your rulers aren't turned on, select the Ruler check box in the Show group of the View tab.

9. On the **Page Layout** tab, display the **Columns** gallery, and click **More Columns**.

   The Columns dialog box opens. The spacing between columns is set by default to a half inch.

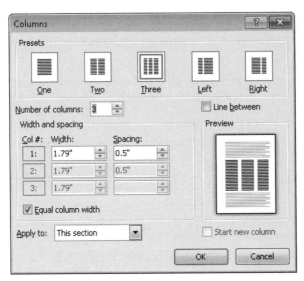

Because the Equal Column Width check box is selected, you can adjust the width and spacing of only the first column.

Tip To separate the columns with vertical lines, select the Line Between check box.

10. In the **Width and spacing** area, in the **Spacing** box for column 1, type or select **0.2"**.

    Word changes the measurement in the Spacing box for column 2, and widens all the columns in the Preview area to reflect the new setting.

11. Click **OK**.

    Word reflows the columns to fit their new margins.

Wider columns generally look neater on the page.

12. Click at the beginning of the **Take a look** paragraph. Then in the **Page Setup** group, click the **Hyphenation** button, and click **Automatic**.

Word hyphenates the text of the document, which fills in some of the large gaps between words.

13. Click anywhere in the **NOTE** paragraph in the third column.

14. On the horizontal ruler, at the left end of the third column, drag the **Hanging Indent** marker 0.25 inch (two marks) to the right.

All the lines in the *NOTE* paragraph except the first are now indented, offsetting the note from the paragraphs above and below it.

You can change the indentation of individual paragraphs within a column.

15. Display the bottom of page **1**. In the first column on page **1**, click at the beginning of the **Take your Room Planner home** paragraph. Then in the **Page Setup** group, click the **Breaks** button, and click **Column**.

Word inserts a column break. The text that follows the column break moves to the top of the second column.

16. At the bottom of the third column on page **1**, click at the beginning of the **If you're not sure** paragraph, and then on the Quick Access Toolbar, click the **Repeat Insertion** button to insert another column break.

Keyboard Shortcut Press Ctrl+Y to repeat the previous action.

Word inserts a column break. The text that follows the column break moves to the top of the first column on page 2.

✖ **CLEAN UP** Return the Zoom Level setting to 100%, and then save and close the RoomPlanner document.

Creating Tabbed Lists

If you have a relatively small amount of data to present, you might choose to display it in a tabbed list, which arranges text in simple columns separated by tabs. You can align the text within the columns by using left, right, centered, or decimal tab stops.

See Also For more information about setting tab stops, see "Manually Changing the Look of Paragraphs" in Chapter 4, "Change the Look of Text."

When entering text in a tabbed list, inexperienced Word users have a tendency to press the Tab key multiple times to align the columns of the list with the default tab stops. If you do this, you have no control over the column widths. To be able to fine-tune the columns, you need to set custom tab stops rather than relying on the default ones.

When setting up a tabbed list, you should press Tab only once between the items that you want to appear in separate columns. Next you apply any necessary formatting. And finally, you set the custom tab stops. Set left, right, centered, and decimal tabs to control the alignment of the column content, or set a bar tab to add a vertical line to visually separate list columns. By setting the tabs in order from left to right, you can check the alignment of the text within each column as you go.

In this exercise, you'll first enter text separated by tabs and format the text. Then you'll set custom tab stops to create a tabbed list.

 SET UP You need the ConsultationA_start document located in your Chapter05 practice file folder to complete this exercise. Open the ConsultationA_start document, and save it as *ConsultationA*. Then display formatting marks and the rulers, and follow the steps.

1. Set the zoom percentage to a level that is comfortable for you, and then press Ctrl+End to move the cursor to the blank line at the end of the document.

2. Type **Location**, press Tab, type **Discount Applies**, press Tab, type **Hourly Rate**, and then press Enter.

3. Add three more lines to the list by typing the following text, pressing the Tab and Enter keys where indicated.

In home *Tab* **No** *Tab* **$50.00** *Enter*
Phone *Tab* **Yes** *Tab* **$35.00** *Enter*
In store *Tab* **Yes** *Tab* **$40.00** *Enter*

The tab characters push the items to the next default tab stop, but because some items are longer than others, they do not line up.

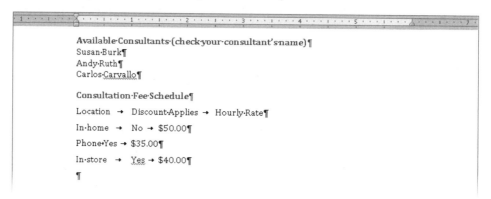

In a tabbed list, it's important to press the Tab key only once between items.

4. Select the first line of the tabbed list, and then on the Mini Toolbar that appears, click the **Bold** button.

Troubleshooting If the Mini Toolbar doesn't appear, click the Bold button in the Font group on the Home tab.

Keyboard Shortcut Press Ctrl+B to apply bold.

5. Select all four lines of the tabbed list, and then on the Mini Toolbar, click the **Increase Indent** button.

Tip It's more efficient to make all character and paragraph formatting changes to the text before setting tab stops. Otherwise, you might have to adjust the tab stops after applying the formatting.

6. With the tabbed list still selected, on the **Page Layout** tab, in the **Paragraph** group, under **Spacing**, change the **After** setting to **0 pt**.

7. Click the tab setting button at the junction of the horizontal and vertical rulers until the **Center Tab** button is active. (You will probably have to click only once.) Then click the **2.5** inch mark on the horizontal ruler.

On the ruler, Word sets a center-aligned tab stop that looks like the Center Tab icon. The items in the second column of the tabbed list center themselves at that position.

8. Click the tab setting button once.

   The Right Tab button is now active.

9. With the **Right Tab** button active, click the horizontal ruler at the **4.5** inch mark.

   On the ruler, Word sets a right-aligned tab stop that looks like the Right Tab icon. The items in the third column of the tabbed list right-align themselves at that position.

10. On the **Home** tab, in the **Paragraph** group, click the **Show/Hide ¶** button to hide the tabs, paragraph marks, and other formatting marks. Then click away from the tabbed list to see the results.

    The tabbed list resembles a simple table.

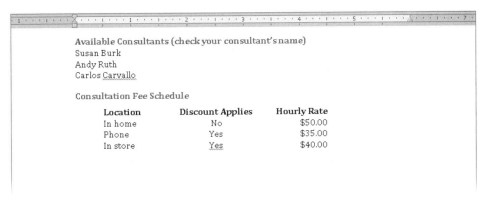

You have created a simple table-like layout with just a few clicks.

✖ CLEAN UP Save the ConsultationA document, and then close it.

Presenting Information in Tables

A table is a structure of vertical columns and horizontal rows. Each column and each row can be named with a heading, although some tables have only column headings or only row headings. At the junction of each column and row is a box called a *cell* in which data (text or numeric information) is stored.

You can create empty or predefined tables in a Word document in the following ways:

● The Insert Table gallery, which is available from the Tables group on the Insert tab, displays a simple grid.

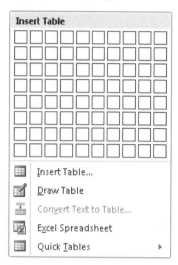

You can create a simple table from the grid in the Insert Table gallery.

Clicking a cell in the grid inserts an empty table the width of the text column. The table has the number of rows and columns you indicated in the grid, with all the rows one line high and all the columns of an equal width.

● To insert a more customized empty table, you can click Insert Table on the menu at the bottom of the Insert Table gallery to open the Insert Table dialog box, in which you can specify the number of rows and columns and customize the column width.

You can create a custom-width table from the Insert Table dialog box.

● To insert a less clearly defined empty table, you can click Draw Table below the grid in the Insert Table gallery. This command displays a pencil with which you can draw cells directly in the Word document to create a table. The cells you draw connect by snapping to a grid, but you have some control over the size and spacing of the rows and columns.

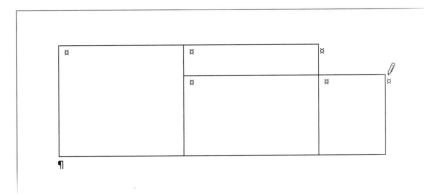

You can draw a table directly on the page.

See Also For information about drawing tables, refer to *Microsoft Word 2010 Step by Step*, by Joyce Cox and Joan Lambert (Microsoft Press, 2010).

● In addition to empty tables, you can insert any of the available Quick Tables, which are predefined tables of formatted data that you can replace with your own information. Built-in Quick Tables include a variety of calendars, simple tables, tables with subheadings, and tabbed lists. You can also save your own custom tables to the Quick Tables gallery so that you can easily insert a frequently used table structure and data into any document.

Enrollment in local colleges, 2010

College	New students	Graduating students	Change
Undergraduate			
Cedar University	110	103	+7
Elm College	223	214	+9
Maple Academy	197	120	+77
Pine College	134	121	+13
Oak Institute	202	210	-8
Graduate			
Cedar University	24	20	+4
Elm College	43	53	-10
Maple Academy	3	11	-8
Pine College	9	4	+5
Oak Institute	53	52	+1
Total	998	908	90

Source: Fictitious data, for illustration purposes only

The Quick Tables gallery includes a selection of predefined tables such as this one.

A new table appears in the document as a set of cells, usually bordered by gridlines. (In some Quick Tables, the gridlines are turned off.) Each cell contains an end-of-cell marker, and each row ends with an end-of-row marker. (The end-of-cell markers and end-of-row markers are identical in appearance, and are visible only when you display formatting marks in the document.) When you point to a table, a move handle appears in its upper-left corner and a size handle in its lower-right corner. When the cursor is in a table, two Table Tools contextual tabs—Design and Layout—appear on the ribbon.

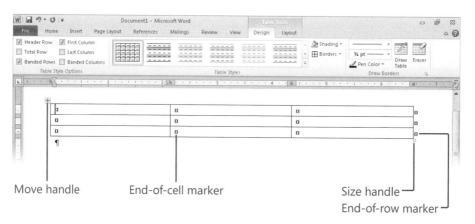

Move handle   End-of-cell marker   Size handle
                                                          End-of-row marker

A table has its own controls and its own contextual ribbon tabs.

Tip The move handle and size handle appear only in Print Layout view and Web Layout view.

After you create a table, you can enter data (such as text, numbers, or graphics) into the table cells and press the Tab key to move the cursor from cell to cell. Pressing Tab when the cursor is in the last cell of a row moves the cursor to the first cell of the next row. Pressing Tab when the cursor is in the last cell of the last row adds a new row to the table and moves the cursor to the first cell of that row.

Tip You can move and position the cursor by pressing the Tab key or the Arrow keys, or by clicking in a table cell.

If the data you want to present in a table already exists in the document, either as regular text or as a tabbed list, you can convert the text to a table by selecting it and then clicking Convert Text To Table in the Insert Table gallery. Conversely, you can convert an active table to regular text by clicking the Convert To Text button in the Data group on the Layout tab.

You can modify a table's structure by changing the size of the table, changing the size of one or more columns or rows, or adding or removing rows, columns, or individual cells.

Tip To change a table's structure, you often need to select the entire table or a specific column or row. The simplest way to do this is to position the cursor in the table, column, or row, click the Select button in the Table group on the Layout tab, and then click the table element you want. Alternatively, you can point to the top edge of a column or left edge of a row and, when the pointer changes to an arrow, click to select the column or row.

The basic methods for manipulating a table or its contents are as follows:

- **Insert a row or column** Click anywhere in a row or column adjacent to where you want to make the insertion. Then on the Layout tab, in the Rows & Columns group, click the Insert Above, Insert Below, Insert Left, or Insert Right button.

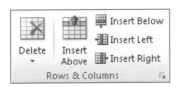

The Rows & Columns group of the Layout tab.

Selecting more than one row or column before you click an Insert button inserts that number of rows or columns in the table.

Tip You can insert cells by clicking the Rows & Columns dialog box launcher and specifying in the Insert Cells dialog box how adjacent cells should be moved to accommodate the new cells.

- **Delete a row or column** Click anywhere in the row or column, and in the Rows & Columns group, click the Delete button. Then click Delete Cells, Delete Columns, Delete Rows, or Delete Table.

- **Resize an entire table** Drag the size handle.

- **Resize a single column or row** Without selecting the column, drag its right border to the left or right. Without selecting the row, drag its bottom border up or down. (If you select a column or row and then drag its border, only the selected column or row changes.)

- **Move a table** Point to the table, and then drag the move handle that appears in its upper-left corner to a new location. Or use the Cut and Paste commands in the Clipboard group on the Home tab to move the table.

- **Merge cells** Create cells that span multiple columns or rows by selecting the cells you want to merge and clicking the Merge Cells button in the Merge group on the Layout tab. For example, to center a title in the first row of a table, you can merge all the cells in the row to create one merged cell that spans the table's width.

- **Split cells** Divide one cell into multiple cells by clicking the Split Cells button in the Merge group on the Layout tab and then specifying the number of columns and rows you want.

- **Sort information** Click the Sort button in the Data group on the Layout tab to sort the rows in ascending or descending order by the data in any column. For example, in a table that has the column headings Name, Address, ZIP Code, and Phone Number, you can sort on any one of those columns to arrange the information in alphabetical or numerical order.

In this exercise, you'll work with two tables. First you'll create an empty table, enter and align text in the table cells, add rows to the table, and merge cells. Then you'll create a second table by converting an existing tabbed list, change the width of a column, and change the width of the entire table.

SET UP You need the ConsultationB_start document located in your Chapter05 practice file folder to complete this exercise. Open the ConsultationB_start document, and save it as *ConsultationB*. Then display formatting marks and the rulers, and follow the steps.

1. Click to the left of the second blank paragraph below **Please complete this form**.

2. On the **Insert** tab, in the **Tables** group, click the **Table** button. Then in the **Insert Table** gallery, point to (don't click) the cell that is five columns to the right and five rows down from the upper-left corner of the grid.

   Word highlights the cells that will be in the table, indicates the table dimensions in the gallery header, and creates a temporary table in the document.

Table

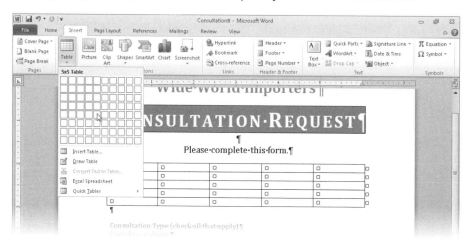

You can preview the table with the number of columns and rows you have specified.

3. Click the cell.

   Word creates a blank table consisting of five columns and five rows. The cursor is located in the first cell. Because the table is active, Word displays the Design and Layout contextual tabs.

4. In the selection area to the left of the table, point to the first row of the table, and then click once to select it.

5. On the **Layout** contextual tab, in the **Merge** group, click the **Merge Cells** button.

   Word combines the five cells in the first row into one cell.

6. With the merged cell selected, in the **Alignment** group, click the **Align Center** button.

   The end-of-cell marker moves to the exact center of the merged cell to indicate that anything you type there will be centered both horizontally and vertically.

7. Type **Consultation Estimate**.

   The table now has content that looks like a table title.

Consultation Estimate ⌷				
⌷	⌷	⌷	⌷	⌷
⌷	⌷	⌷	⌷	⌷
⌷	⌷	⌷	⌷	⌷
⌷	⌷	⌷	⌷	⌷

Merged cells are often used for table titles and column headings.

8. Click the first cell in the second row, type **Type**, and then press Tab.

9. Type **Location**, **Consultant**, **Hourly Rate**, and **Total**, pressing Tab after each entry.

   Pressing Tab after the *Total* heading moves the cursor to the first cell of the third row. The table now has a row of column headings.

10. Select the column heading row, and then on the Mini Toolbar, click the **Bold** button.

11. In the third row, type **Window treatments**, **In home**, **Andy Ruth**, **$50.00**, and **$50.00**, pressing Tab after each entry.

    You have entered a complete row of data.

12. Select the last two rows, and then on the **Layout** tab, in the **Rows & Columns**

    group, click the **Insert Below** button.

    Word adds two new rows and selects them.

13. In the last row, click the first cell, hold down the Shift key, and then press the Right Arrow key four times to select the first four cells in the row.

14. In the **Merge** group, click the **Merge Cells** button.

    Word combines the selected cells into one cell.

15. In the **Alignment** group, click the **Align Center Right** button.

16. Type **Subtotal**, and then press Tab twice.

    Word adds a new row with the same structure to the bottom of the table.

Consultation· Estimate¤				
Type¤	**Location**¤	**Consultant**¤	**Hourly·Rate**¤	**Total**¤
Window· treatments¤	In·home¤	Andy· Ruth¤	$50.00¤	$50.00¤
¤	¤	¤	¤	¤
¤	¤	¤	¤	¤
¤	¤	¤	¤	¤
			Subtotal¤	¤
			¤	¤

When you add a new row, it has the same format as the one it is based on.

17. Type **Add trip fee**, press Tab twice to add a new row, and then type **Total**.

    Now you'll create a different table by converting existing text.

18. Scroll down to the bottom of the document, and select the rows of the tabbed list beginning with **Distance** and ending with **$20.00**.

19. On the **Insert** tab, in the **Tables** group, click the **Table** button, and then click **Convert Text to Table**.

    The Convert Text To Table dialog box opens.

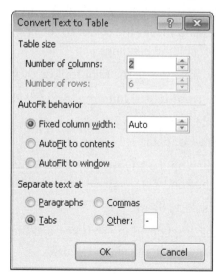

You can separate text into columns based on the symbol you specify.

20. Verify that the **Number of columns** box displays **2**, and then click **OK**.

    The selected text appears in a table with two columns and six rows.

21. Click anywhere in the table to release the selection, and then point to the right border of the table. When the pointer changes to two opposing arrows, double-click the border.

    Word adjusts the width of the right column to accommodate its longest cell entry.

    Tip You can also adjust the column width by changing the Table Column Width setting in the Cell Size group on the Layout tab.

22. Point to the **In-Home Trip Charge** table.

    Word displays the move handle in the upper-left corner and the size handle in the lower-right corner.

23. Drag the size handle to the right, releasing the mouse button when the right edge of the table aligns approximately with the **4** inch mark on the horizontal ruler.

    The width of the table expands.

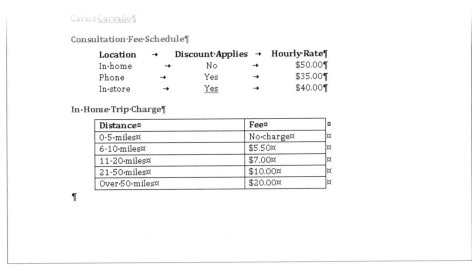

The table is now approximately as wide as the tabbed list above, creating a nice balance.

 CLEAN UP Save the ConsultationB document, and then close it.

Performing Calculations in Tables

When you want to perform calculations with the numbers in a Word table, you can create a formula that uses a built-in mathematical function. You construct a formula by using the tools in the Formula dialog box, which you display by clicking the Formula button in the Data group on the Layout contextual tab.

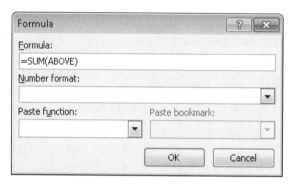

The Formula dialog box.

A formula consists of an equal sign (=), followed by a function name (such as SUM), followed by parentheses containing the location of the cells you want to use for the calculation. For example, the formula =SUM(Left) totals the cells to the left of the cell containing the formula.

To use a function other than SUM in the Formula dialog box, you click the function you want in the Paste Function list. You can use built-in functions to perform a number of calculations, including averaging (AVERAGE) a set of values, counting (COUNT) the number of values in a column or row, or finding the maximum (MAX) or minimum (MIN) value in a series of cells.

Although formulas commonly refer to the cells above or to the left of the active cell, you can also use the contents of specified cells or constant values in formulas. To use the contents of a cell, you type the cell address in the parentheses following the function name. The cell address is a combination of the column letter and the row number—for example, A1 is the cell at the intersection of the first column and the first row. A series of cells in a row can be addressed as a range consisting of the first cell and the last cell separated by a colon, such as A1:D1. For example, the formula =SUM(A1:D1) totals the values in row 1 of columns A through D. A series of cells in a column can be addressed in the same way. For example, the formula =SUM(A1:A4) totals the values in column A of rows 1 through 4.

Other Layout Options

You can control many aspects of a table in the Table Properties dialog box, which you display by clicking the Properties button in the Table group on the Layout tab. You can set the following options:

- On the Table page, you can specify the width of the entire table, as well as the way it interacts with the surrounding text.

- On the Row page, you can specify the height of each row, whether a row is allowed to break across pages, and whether a row of column headings should be repeated at the top of each page.

  Tip The Repeat As Header Row option is available only if the cursor is in the top row of the table.

- On the Column page, you can set the width of each column.

- On the Cell page, you can set the width of cells and the vertical alignment of text within them.

  Tip You can also control the widths of selected cells by changing the settings in the Cell Size group on the Layout tab.

- On either the Table page or Cell page, you can control the margins of cells (how close text comes to the cell border) by clicking Options and specifying top, bottom, left, and right settings.

  Tip You can also control the margins by clicking the Cell Margins button in the Alignment group on the Layout tab.

- On the Alt Text page, you can enter text that describes what the table is about.

Formatting Tables

Formatting a table to best convey its data can be a process of trial and error. With Word 2010, you can quickly get started by applying one of the table styles available in the Table Styles gallery on the Design contextual tab.

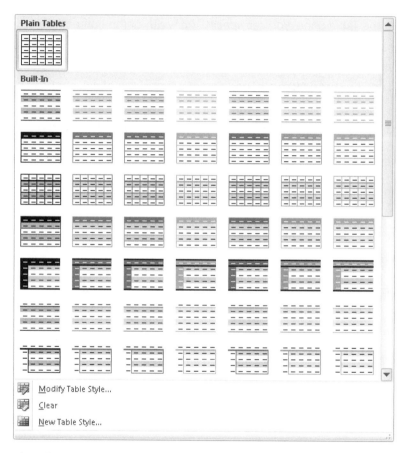

The table styles include a variety of borders, colors, and other attributes to give the table a professional look.

If you want to control the appearance of a table more precisely, you can use the commands on the Design and Layout tabs. You can also format the table content. As you saw in the previous exercise, you can apply character formatting to the text in tables just as you would to regular text, by clicking buttons on the Mini Toolbar. You can also click the buttons in the Font group on the Home tab. You can apply paragraph formatting, such as alignment and spacing, by clicking buttons in the Paragraph group on the Home tab. And you can apply both character and paragraph styles from the Quick Styles gallery.

In this exercise, you'll first apply a table style to a table. Then you'll format a table row and column. You'll also apply character and paragraph formatting to various cells so that the table's appearance helps the reader understand its data.

 SET UP You need the RepairCosts_start document located in your Chapter05 practice file folder to complete this exercise. Open the RepairCosts_start document, and save it as *RepairCosts*. If formatting marks are displayed, hide them, and then follow the steps.

1. Click anywhere in the table, and then on the **Design** tab, point to each thumbnail in the first row of the **Table Styles** gallery to see its live preview.

2. In the **Table Style Options** group, clear the **Banded Rows** check box, and select the **Total Row** check box.

   The table style thumbnails no longer have banded rows, reflecting your changes.

 3. In the **Table Styles** group, click the **More** button.

   The Table Styles gallery appears.

4. Preview all the styles in the gallery. When you finish exploring, click the second thumbnail in the fifth row (**Medium Shading 2 – Accent 1**).

   The style needs to be modified to suit the data, but it's a good starting point.

Building Association Estimated Repair Costs

Item	Repair Type	Quantity	Cost, $
Elastomeric Decks	Resurface	400 sq. ft.	1,600
Wood Decks	Replace	1,200 sq. ft.	6,500
Building Exterior	Repaint	9,000 sq. ft.	9,000
Roof	Reseal	5,000 sq. ft.	2,700
Entry Doors	Repaint	4	600
Carpet	Replace	150 sq. yds.	4,500
Intercom	Replace	1	2,500
Garage Door Opener	Replace	1	2,000
Steel Doors	Repaint	10	750
Exterior Trim	Repaint	800 ft.	4,500
Elevator Hydraulics	Replace	1	55,000
Fire Alarm System	Replace	1	3,000
TOTAL			110,550

This table style applies formatting to the header and total rows, the first column, and the text of the table.

5. Select all the cells in the last row by clicking in the selection area to its left. Then in the **Table Styles** group, click the **Borders** arrow, and click **Borders and Shading**.

   The Borders And Shading dialog box opens, displaying the borders applied to the selected cells.

6. On the **Borders** page of the dialog box, scroll to the top of the **Style** list, and click the thick black border.

7. In the **Preview** area, click the top border button once to remove the current border, and click again to apply the thick black border.

8. Click the **Shading** tab, and click the **Fill** arrow. Under **Theme Colors** in the palette, click the fifth box in the top row (**Blue, Accent 1**). Then click **OK**.

9. Without moving the selection, on the **Home** tab, in the **Font** group, click the **Font Color** arrow, and under **Theme Colors** in the palette, click the white box. Then press Home to release the selection.

   The table now has the same border at the top and bottom.

Building Association Estimated Repair Costs

Item	Repair Type	Quantity	Cost, $
Elastomeric Decks	Resurface	400 sq. ft.	1,600
Wood Decks	Replace	1,200 sq. ft.	6,500
Building Exterior	Repaint	9,000 sq. ft.	9,000
Roof	Reseal	5,000 sq. ft.	2,700
Entry Doors	Repaint	4	600
Carpet	Replace	150 sq. yds.	4,500
Intercom	Replace	1	2,500
Garage Door Opener	Replace	1	2,000
Steel Doors	Repaint	10	750
Exterior Trim	Repaint	800 ft.	4,500
Elevator Hydraulics	Replace	1	55,000
Fire Alarm System	Replace	1	3,000
TOTAL			110,550

You can customize a table style to meet your needs.

10. Point to the left side of the **Elastomeric Decks** cell, and when the pointer changes to a black right-pointing arrow, drag downward to select all the cells in the **Item** column *except* the **TOTAL** cell.

11. On the **Design** tab, in the **Table Styles** group, click the **Shading** arrow, and under **Theme Colors**, click the third box in the blue column (**Blue, Accent 1, Lighter 40%**).

12. Select all the cells containing amounts in the **Cost, $** column, including the cell with the total. Then on the **Layout** tab, in the **Alignment** group, click the **Align Center Right** button.

> **Tip** If the first row of your table has several long headings that make it difficult to fit the table on one page, you can turn the headings sideways. Simply select the heading row and click the Text Direction button in the Alignment group on the Layout tab.

Now you can judge how well the table displays its data.

Building Association Estimated Repair Costs

Item	Repair Type	Quantity	Cost, $
Elastomeric Decks	Resurface	400 sq. ft.	1,600
Wood Decks	Replace	1,200 sq. ft.	6,500
Building Exterior	Repaint	9,000 sq. ft.	9,000
Roof	Reseal	5,000 sq. ft.	2,700
Entry Doors	Repaint	4	600
Carpet	Replace	150 sq. yds.	4,500
Intercom	Replace	1	2,500
Garage Door Opener	Replace	1	2,000
Steel Doors	Repaint	10	750
Exterior Trim	Repaint	800 ft.	4,500
Elevator Hydraulics	Replace	1	55,000
Fire Alarm System	Replace	1	3,000
TOTAL			**110,550**

The total now stands out better, and the amounts are easier to read.

> **Tip** If you will need to use this formatted table with different data in the future, you can save it as a Quick Table. For information about saving customized tables for future use, see the sidebar "Quick Tables" on the next page.

 CLEAN UP Save the RepairCosts document, and then close it.

Quick Tables

With Word 2010, you can create Quick Tables—preformatted tables with sample data that you can customize. To create a Quick Table:

1. On the Insert tab, in the Tables group, click the Table button, and then point to Quick Tables.

   The Quick Tables gallery appears.

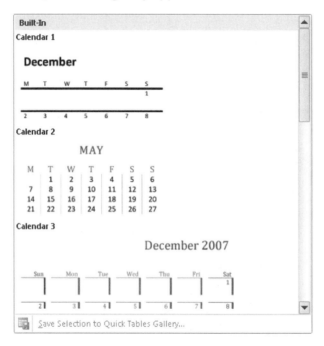

The predefined Quick Tables meet several common needs.

2. Scroll through the gallery, noticing the types of tables that are available, and then click the one you want.

   For example, this is the Matrix Quick Table.

City or Town¤	Point A¤	Point B¤	Point C¤	Point D¤	Point E¤	¤
Point A¤	—¤	¤	¤	¤	¤	¤
Point B¤	87¤	—¤	¤	¤	¤	¤
Point C¤	64¤	56¤	—¤	¤	¤	¤
Point D¤	37¤	32¤	91¤	—¤	¤	¤
Point E¤	93¤	35¤	54¤	43¤	—¤	¤
¶						

The Matrix Quick Table includes row and column headings, placeholder data, and no summary data, such as totals.

3. On the Design tab, apply formatting to tailor the Quick Table to your needs.

For example, here's the Matrix Quick Table after we formatted it.

City or Town	Point A	Point B	Point C	Point D	Point E
Point A	—				
Point B	87	—			
Point C	64	56	—		
Point D	37	32	91	—	
Point E	93	35	54	43	—

It is easy to customize a Quick Table for your own needs.

If you will use the table again, you can save it in the Quick Tables gallery. Select the table, display the Quick Tables gallery, and click Save Selection To Quick Tables Gallery. Then in the Create New Building Block dialog box, assign a name to the table, and click OK. Provided you save the Building Blocks template when Word prompts you to, the table will be available in the Quick Tables gallery for future use.

See Also For information about building blocks, see "Inserting Building Blocks" in Chapter 6, "Add Simple Graphic Elements."

Key Points

- To vary the layout of a document, you can divide text into columns. You can control the number of columns, the width of the columns, and the space between the columns.

- To clearly present a simple set of data, you can use tabs to create a tabbed list, with custom tab stops controlling the width and alignment of columns.

- You can create a table from scratch, or convert existing text to a table. You can control the size of the table and its individual structural elements.

- By using the built-in table styles, you can quickly apply professional-looking cell and character formatting to a table and its contents.

- You can enhance a table and its contents by applying text attributes, borders, and shading.

Chapter at a Glance

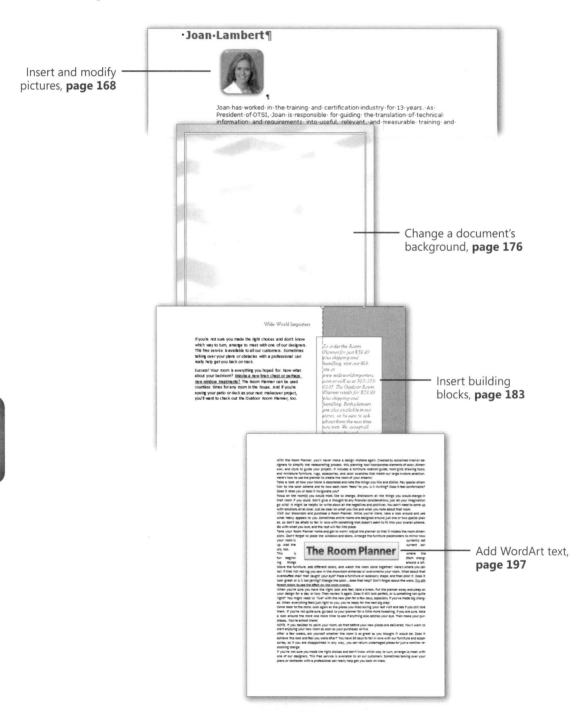

Insert and modify pictures, **page 168**

Change a document's background, **page 176**

Insert building blocks, **page 183**

Add WordArt text, **page 197**

6 Add Simple Graphic Elements

In this chapter, you will learn how to

✔ Insert and modify pictures.

✔ Change a document's background.

✔ Insert building blocks.

✔ Add WordArt text.

Some documents that you create in Microsoft Word 2010 are straightforward and require nothing more than words. Others might benefit from the addition of graphic elements to reinforce their concepts, to grab the reader's attention, or to make them more visually appealing. These graphic elements can include a wide variety of objects and effects, including:

- **Pictures** These objects are created outside of Word—photographs from digital cameras, clip art images, or files created on a computer with a graphics program. No matter what the origin of the picture, you can change its size and its position in relation to other content after you insert it in the Word document. For some types of pictures, you can make additional changes from within Word, such as cropping the picture or embellishing it by applying artistic effects.

- **Drawing objects** These objects are created within Word—text boxes, WordArt text, diagrams, charts, shapes, and other such objects. As with pictures, you can size, move, and format drawing objects from within Word.

    See Also For information about diagrams, charts, or shapes, refer to *Microsoft Word 2010 Step by Step*, by Joyce Cox and Joan Lambert (Microsoft Press, 2010).

- **Building blocks** You can draw attention to specific information and add graphic appeal by incorporating ready-made graphic building blocks (also called *Quick Parts*) into a document. These building blocks are combinations of drawing objects (and sometimes pictures) in a variety of formatting styles that you can select to insert elements such as cover pages, quotations pulled from the text (called *pull quotes*), and sidebars. You can also create your own building blocks, which then become available in the Quick Parts gallery.

- **Backgrounds** You can apply a variety of backgrounds to the pages of your document, including plain colors, gradients, textures, patterns, and pictures.

In this chapter, you'll first insert and modify pictures in a document. You'll experiment with page backgrounds, and then add three types of building blocks to a document. Finally, you'll have a bit of fun with WordArt.

> **Practice Files** Before you can complete the exercises in this chapter, you need to copy the book's practice files to your computer. The practice files you'll use to complete the exercises in this chapter are in the Chapter06 practice file folder. A complete list of practice files is provided in "Using the Practice Files" at the beginning of this book.

Inserting and Modifying Pictures

You can insert digital photographs or pictures created in almost any program into a Word document. You specify the source of the picture you want to insert by clicking one of these two buttons, which are located in the Illustrations group on the Insert tab:

- **Picture** Click this button to insert a picture that is saved as a file on your computer, or on a device (such as an external hard drive or a digital camera) that is connected to your computer.

- **Clip Art** Click this button to insert one of hundreds of clip art images, such as photos and drawings of people, places, and things.

  See Also For information about clip art, see the sidebar "About Clip Art" later in this chapter.

After you insert a picture in a document, you can modify the image by using commands on the Format contextual tab, which is displayed only when a picture or drawing object is selected. For example, you can click buttons in the Adjust group to change the picture's brightness and contrast, recolor it, apply artistic effects to it, and compress it to reduce the size of the document containing it. The Picture Styles group offers a wide range of picture styles that you can apply to a picture to change its shape and orientation, as well as add borders and picture effects. And finally, you can use the commands in the Size group for cropping and resizing pictures.

The Format contextual tab for pictures.

Troubleshooting The appearance of buttons and groups on the ribbon changes depending on the width of the program window. For information about changing the appearance of the ribbon to match our screen images, see "Modifying the Display of the Ribbon" at the beginning of this book.

See Also For information about using the commands in the Arrange group, refer to *Microsoft Word 2010 Step by Step*, by Joyce Cox and Joan Lambert (Microsoft Press, 2010).

In this exercise, you'll insert a couple of photographs and size and crop them. You'll modify one of them and then copy the modifications to the other one. Then you'll insert an illustration and apply an artistic effects to it.

SET UP You need the Authors_start document, the Joan and Joyce photographs, and the OTSI-Logo illustration located in your Chapter06 practice file folder to complete this exercise. Open the Authors_start document, and save it as *Authors*. Display the rulers and formatting marks, and then follow the steps.

1. Click to the left of the **Joyce has 30 years' experience** paragraph, press the Enter key, and press the Up Arrow key. Then on the **Insert** tab, in the **Illustrations** group, click the **Picture** button.

   The Insert Picture dialog box opens, displaying the contents of your Pictures library.

2. Navigate to the **Chapter06** practice file folder, and double-click the **Joyce** picture.

   Word inserts the picture at the cursor and displays the Format contextual tab on the ribbon.

   Troubleshooting If Word inserts a frame the size of the picture but displays only a sliver of the picture itself, Word cannot increase the line spacing to accommodate the picture because it is set to a specific amount. To correct this problem, click the Paragraph dialog box launcher, and in the Paragraph dialog box, change the Line Spacing setting to Single.

   Tip In this exercise, you insert pictures in blank paragraphs. By default, Word inserts the picture in-line with the text, meaning that Word increases the line spacing as necessary to accommodate the picture. If you were to type text adjacent to the picture, the bottom of the picture would align with the bottom of the text on the same line. After you insert a picture, you can change its position and the way text wraps around it.

   See Also For more information about positioning objects and wrapping text around them, see "Adding WordArt Text" later in this chapter. You can also refer to *Microsoft Word 2010 Step by Step*, by Joyce Cox and Joan Lambert (Microsoft Press, 2010).

3. In the lower-right corner of the picture, point to the handle (the circle). When the pointer changes to a double arrow, drag up and to the left until the right side of the picture's shadow frame is in line with the **1.75** inch mark on the horizontal ruler.

   When you release the mouse button, the picture assumes its new size.

Because the ratio of the picture's height to its width (called the aspect ratio*) is locked, the height and width change proportionally.*

Tip You can fine-tune the size of a graphic by adjusting the Shape Height and Shape Width settings in the Size group on the Format tab.

4. On the **Format** contextual tab, in the **Size** group, click the **Crop** button.

   Word surrounds the picture with crop handles.

5. Point to the bottom-middle handle, and when the pointer changes to a black T, drag upward until the picture is about 1 inch high.

   Word grays out the part of the picture you have cropped away.

Word will not actually crop the picture until you turn off the crop button.

6. Click the **Crop** button to turn it off.

   Word removes the crop handles and discards the gray part of the picture.

> **Tip** In addition to cropping a picture manually, you can click the Crop arrow and select from various options, including having Word crop a picture to fit a shape you select, cropping to a precise width:height ratio, filling an area with a picture, or fitting a picture to an area.

7. Click to the left of the **Joan has worked** paragraph, press Enter, and then press the Up Arrow key. Then repeat steps 1 through 6 to insert, size, and crop the **Joan** picture below the **Joan Lambert** heading.

8. With the **Joan** picture still selected, on the **Format** contextual tab, in the **Adjust** group, click the **Color** button.

The Color gallery appears.

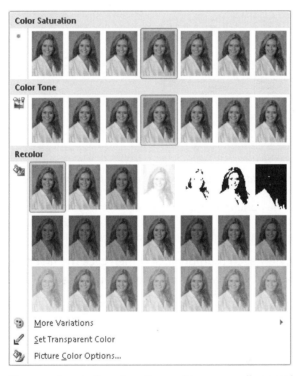

You can change the saturation and tone, as well as recolor the picture.

9. Under **Recolor** in the **Color** gallery, preview each option, and then click the second thumbnail in the first row (**Grayscale**).

The picture is grayscaled—that is, each color is converted into a shade of gray.

10. In the **Adjust** group, click the **Corrections** button. Then in the **Corrections** gallery, under **Brightness and Contrast**, preview each option, and then click the fourth thumbnail in the top row (**Brightness: +20% Contrast: -40%**).

11. In the **Picture Styles** group, click the **More** button.

The Picture Styles gallery appears.

You can apply frames, shadows, glows, and 3-D effects from the Picture Styles gallery.

Troubleshooting The number of thumbnails per row in your galleries might be different than ours, depending on the screen resolution and the width of the program window. In the steps, look for the thumbnail with the name specified.

12. In the gallery, preview each thumbnail, and then click the first thumbnail in the fifth row (**Bevel Rectangle**). Click away from the picture to see the effect.

The photograph now has a three-dimensional appearance.

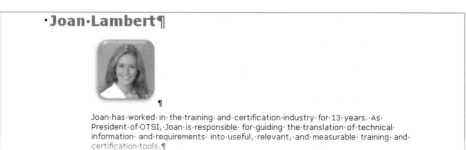

This picture style gives the effect of a padded square button.

13. Click the **Joan** picture to select it, and then on the **Home** tab, in the **Clipboard** group, click the **Format Painter** button.

14. If necessary, scroll up in the document, and click the **Joyce** picture.

    Word copies the grayscale format, color corrections, and picture style from one picture to the other.

15. Scroll down until the **Online Training Solutions, Inc. (OTSI)** heading is visible, click to the left of the **OTSI specializes** paragraph, press Enter, and then press Up Arrow.

16. On the **Insert** tab, in the **Illustration** group, click the **Picture** button. Then in the **Chapter06** folder displayed in the **Insert Picture** dialog box, double-click the **OTSI-Logo** graphic.

17. With the logo selected, on the **Format** contextual tab, in the **Adjust** group, click the **Artistic Effects** button.

18. In the **Artistic Effects** gallery, preview each thumbnail, and then click the last thumbnail in the fifth row (**Glow Edges**). Click away from the picture to see the effect.

    The logo now has a black-and-white stylized effect.

> ·**Online·Training·Solutions,·Inc.·(OTSI)**¶
>
> OTSI·specializes·in·the·design,·creation,·and·production·of·Office·and·Windows· training·products·for·office·and·home·computer·users.·For·more·information· about·OTSI,·visit·¶
>
> *www.otsi.com*¶

You can use artistic effects to make pictures look like paintings, pencil sketches, cutouts and more.

Tip To move a picture, simply drag it to the desired location. To copy a graphic, hold down the Ctrl key while you drag, releasing first the mouse button and then the Ctrl key. (If you release Ctrl first, Word will move the image instead of copying it.)

 CLEAN UP Save the Authors document, and then close it.

About Clip Art

If you want to dress up a document with a graphic but you don't have a suitable picture, you might want to search for a clip art image. Clip art comes in many different styles and formats, including illustrations, photographs, videos, and audio clips. The only thing the clips have in common is that they are free and available without any copyright restrictions.

Clicking the Clip Art button displays the Clip Art task pane, where you can enter a search term to look for an image on your computer or on the Office.com Web site. When clip art images matching your search term are displayed in the task pane, you can click an image to insert it in your document. If you don't want to insert an image at the cursor but want it to be available for use somewhere else, you can point to the image in the Clip Art task pane, click the arrow that appears, and then click Copy to store a copy of the image on the Microsoft Office Clipboard. If you find an image on Office.com and want to be able to insert it in documents when you are not online, you can point to the arrow, click Make Available Offline, and then store it in a clip art collection. You can also edit the keywords associated with an image and view its properties.

To find and insert a clip art image:

1. Position the cursor where you want the image to appear. Then on the Insert tab, in the Illustrations group, click the Clip Art button.

2. In the Clip Art task pane, select the current entry in the Search For box (or click in the box if there is no entry), and enter a keyword for the type of clip art you are looking for, such as *cats*. Then select the Include Office.com Content check box, and click Go.

   Tip You can restrict the search results to a particular type of clip art by selecting the type in the Results Should Be list.

   The task pane displays any clip art images that have your keyword associated with them.

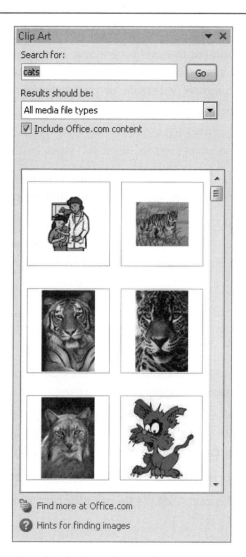

Cat-related clip art images from your computer and Office.com.

3. In the task pane, click the image you want to insert into the document.

You can then manipulate the clip art image the same way you would a picture.

Changing a Document's Background

Whether you're creating a document that will be printed, viewed on a computer, or published on the Internet and viewed in a Web browser, you can make your document stand out by adding a background color, texture, or picture to every page in a document. You can also add borders to every page.

See Also For information about creating documents for the Web, refer to *Microsoft Word 2010 Step by Step*, by Joyce Cox and Joan Lambert (Microsoft Press, 2010).

When it comes to backgrounds, the trick is to not overdo it. Your effects need to be subtle enough that they do not interfere with the text or other elements on the page.

In this exercise, you'll first apply a solid background color to every page. Then you'll create a two-color gradient across the pages. You'll fill the pages with one of the textures that come with Word and then fill them with a picture. Finally, you'll put a border around every page.

SET UP You need the MarbleFloor picture located in your Chapter06 practice file folder to complete this exercise. Open a blank document, turn off the rulers and formatting marks, and then follow the steps.

1. In the lower-right corner of the program window, click the **Zoom Level** button, and set the zoom percentage to display the whole page.

2. On the **Page Layout** tab, in the **Page Background** group, click the **Page Color** button, and then under **Theme Colors**, in the column of green boxes, click the second box from the top (**Olive Green, Accent 3, Lighter 60%**).

   The background of the document changes to the selected color.

3. In the **Page Background** group, click the **Page Color** button, and then click **Fill Effects**.

   The Fill Effects dialog box opens.

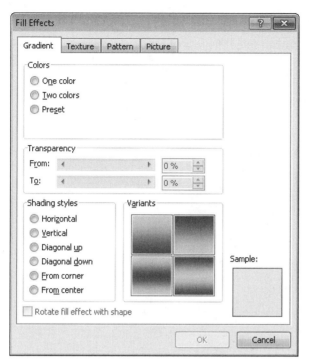

The Gradient page of the Fill Effects dialog box.

4. In the **Colors** area, click **Two colors**, and then leaving **Color 1** set to light green, click the **Color 2** arrow, and in the fifth column of boxes, select the top box (**Blue, Accent 1, Lighter 80%**).

   The Variants and Sample areas change to show graded combinations of the two colors.

5. In the **Shading styles** area, click each option in turn and observe the effects in the **Variants** and **Sample** areas. Then click **Diagonal Up**.

6. In the **Variants** area, click the option in the upper-left corner, and then click **OK**.

   The background of the document is now shaded from light green to light blue.

7. Display the **Fill Effects** dialog box again, and click the **Texture** tab.

On this page, you can select from a number of texture files that come with Word.

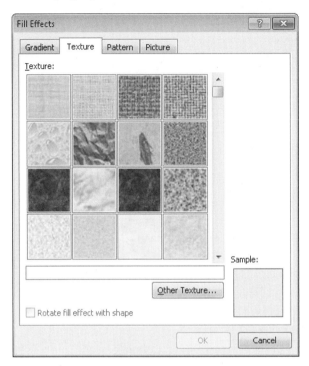

The Texture page of the Fill Effects dialog box.

8. Click the effect in the second column of the third row (**White Marble**), and then click **OK**.

The background changes to display the effect rather than the color.

The page with the White Marble texture applied to the background.

9. Display the **Fill Effects** dialog box again, and click the **Picture** tab. Then click **Select Picture**, and with the contents of your **Chapter06** practice file folder displayed in the **Select Picture** dialog box, double-click **MarbleFloor**. In the **Fill Effects** dialog box, click **OK**.

The background changes to display a blurred picture of a marble floor in the Doge's Palace in Venice.

The page with the MarbleFloor picture applied to the background.

Tip Word fills the page with as much of the picture as will fit. If one copy of the picture does not completely fill the page, Word inserts another copy, effectively "tiling" the image.

10. In the **Page Background** group, click the **Page Borders** button.

The Borders And Shading dialog box opens with the Page Border page active.

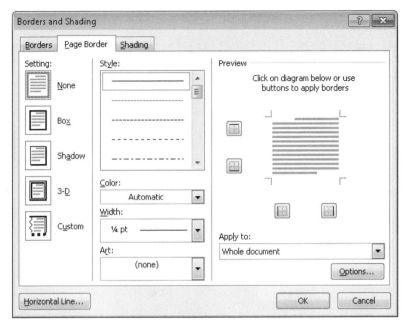

The Page Border page is almost the same as the Borders page, except that an Art option is available at the bottom of the center pane.

11. In the **Setting** area of the **Borders and Shading** dialog box, click **Box**. Then in the **Color** list, click the third box in the blue column (**Blue, Accent 1, Lighter 40%**).

12. In the **Art** list, scroll down, clicking any art option you like to see it applied to the page in the **Preview** pane. When you find a style you like, click **OK**.

We chose a classic double border near the bottom of the Art list.

The page with a double border applied on top of the picture background.

13. Press Ctrl+Enter to insert a page break, and then scroll to the second page.

    When you apply a background, it is reflected in all the pages of the document.

 **CLEAN UP** If you want, save the document as *PageBackground*, and then close it.

Inserting Building Blocks

To simplify the creation of professional-looking text elements, Word 2010 comes with ready-made visual representations of text, known as *building blocks*, which are available from various groups on the Insert tab. You can insert the following types of building blocks:

- **Cover page** You can quickly add a formatted cover page to a longer document such as a report by selecting a style from the Cover Page gallery. The cover page includes text placeholders for elements such as a title so that you can customize the page to reflect the content of the document.

  Tip You can also insert a blank page anywhere in a document—even in the middle of a paragraph—by positioning the cursor and then clicking the Blank Page button in the Pages group on the Insert tab.

- **Header and footer** You can display information on every page of a document in regions at the top and bottom of a page by selecting a style from the Header or Footer gallery. Word indicates the header and footer areas by displaying dotted borders and displays a Design contextual tab on the ribbon. You can enter information in the header and footer areas the same way you enter ordinary text. You can have a different header and footer on the first page of a document and different headers and footers on odd and even pages.

  Tip If your document contains section breaks, each successive section inherits the headers and footers of the preceding section unless you break the link between the two sections. You can then create a different header and footer for the current section. For information about sections, see "Controlling What Appears on Each Page" in Chapter 7, "Preview, Print, and Distribute Documents."

- **Page number** You can quickly add headers and footers that include only page numbers and require no customization by selecting the style you want from one of the Page Number galleries.

- **Text box** To reinforce key concepts and also alleviate the monotony of page after page of plain text, you can insert text boxes such as sidebars and quote boxes by selecting a style from the Text Box gallery. The formatted text box includes placeholder text that you replace with your own.

If you frequently use a specific element in your documents, such as a formatted title-subtitle-author arrangement at the beginning of reports, you can define it as a custom building block. It is then available from the Quick Parts gallery.

See Also For information about saving frequently used text as a custom building block, see "Inserting Saved Text" in Chapter 3, "Edit and Proofread Text."

You can see a list of all the available building blocks by clicking the Quick Parts button in the Text group on the Insert tab and then clicking Building Blocks Organizer.

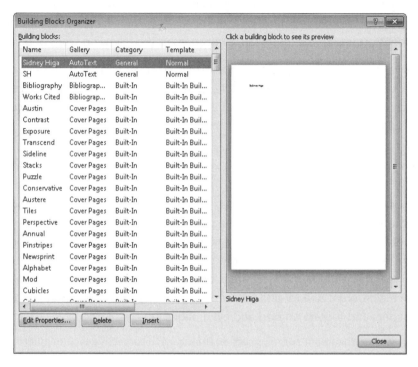

The Building Blocks Organizer dialog box.

Initially the building blocks are organized by type, as reflected in the Gallery column. If you want to insert building blocks of the same design in a document, you might want to sort the list alphabetically by design name, by clicking the Name column heading. For example, a cover page, footer, header, quote box, and sidebar are all available with the Pinstripes design. Some elements, such as bibliographies, equations, tables of contents, tables, and watermarks, are not part of a design family and have their own unique names.

Tip You can see more information about each building block by dragging the horizontal scroll box to display the right side of the Building Blocks list.

At the bottom of the Building Blocks Organizer dialog box, you can click Edit Properties to display a dialog box where you can see the information about a selected building block in a more readable format. If you are viewing the properties associated with a custom building block, you can change them in this dialog box, but we don't recommend changing the properties assigned to a building block that came with Word.

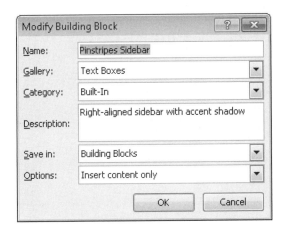

The Modify Building Block dialog box.

You can delete a selected custom building block from the list by clicking Delete at the bottom of the Building Blocks Organizer dialog box, and you can insert a selected building block into the document by clicking Insert.

In this exercise, you'll insert a cover page and add a header and footer to a document. You'll also insert two kinds of text boxes with the same design. Finally, you'll save a customized sidebar as a building block.

SET UP You need the Flyer_start document located in your Chapter06 practice file folder to complete this exercise. Open the Flyer_start document, and save it as *Flyer*. Then follow the steps.

1. Click the **Zoom Level** button in the lower-right corner of the program window. In the **Zoom** dialog box, click **Whole page**, and then click **OK**.

2. With the cursor at the top of the document, on the **Insert** tab, in the **Pages** group, click the **Cover Page** button.

The Cover Page gallery appears.

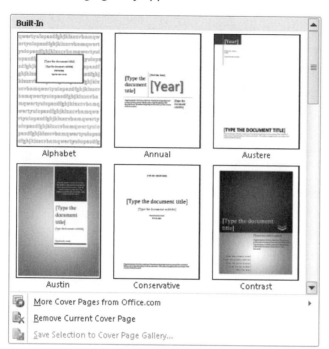

The thumbnails show the designs of the available cover pages.

3. Scroll through the **Cover Page** gallery to see the available options, and then click **Pinstripes**.

Word inserts the cover page at the beginning of the document and adds placeholders for the title, subtitle, date, company name, and author name.

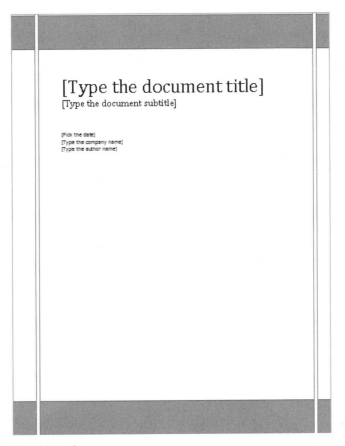

The selected cover page.

Tip If any of the required information is attached to the document as properties, Word inserts the information instead of the placeholder.

4. Click anywhere in the title placeholder, and type **Simple Room Design**. Then click the **Pick the date** placeholder, click the arrow that appears, and in the calendar, click today's date (indicated by a red box). Delete the remaining placeholder paragraphs.

5. On the **Insert** tab, in the **Header & Footer** group, click the **Header** button. Scroll through the **Header** gallery, and then click **Pinstripes**.

Word displays the Design contextual tab, dims the text of the document, and indicates the header and footer areas with dotted lines.

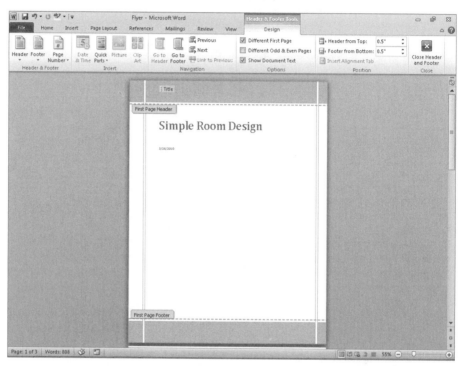

Because the Different First Page check box in the Options group on the Design tab is selected, the header area is labeled First Page Header.

6. In the **Navigation** group, click the **Next** button.

Word moves to the next section of the document, which is the page after the cover page.

7. Type **Wide World Importers**. Then on the **Home** tab, in the **Paragraph** group, click the **Center** button.

8. On the **Design** tab, in the **Navigation** group, click the **Go to Footer** button.

   The cursor moves to the footer area at the bottom of the page.

9. In the **Header & Footer** group, click the **Page Number** button, point to **Current Position** in the list, and then in the gallery, click **Large Color**.

   Except for the first page of the document, the pages now have a header and footer.

Headers and footers can include any information you want repeated on each page in a section, including graphics.

Tip To use a numbering scheme other than Arabic numerals, to number pages by chapter, or to control the starting number, click the Page Number button in the Header & Footer group, and then click Format Page Numbers. In the Page Number Format dialog box, click the Number Format arrow, and then in the list, click the format you want.

10. In the **Close** group, click the **Close Header and Footer** button.

11. At the top of the second page, delete **Simple Room Design**. Then on the **Insert** tab, in the **Text** group, click the **Quick Parts** button, and click **Building Blocks Organizer**.

   The Building Blocks Organizer shown at the beginning of this topic opens. The left pane displays a complete list of all the building blocks available on your computer. Clicking a building block in the left pane displays a preview in the right pane.

   Tip The Building Blocks list you see on your computer includes AutoText entries for your user name and initials. To change either of these entries, display the Backstage view, click Options, and then on the General page of the Word Options dialog box, update your information and click OK.

12. Scroll through the **Building blocks** list, previewing a few of the building blocks. Then click the **Name** column heading, and scroll through the list again.

   Notice that page elements of the same theme are coordinated.

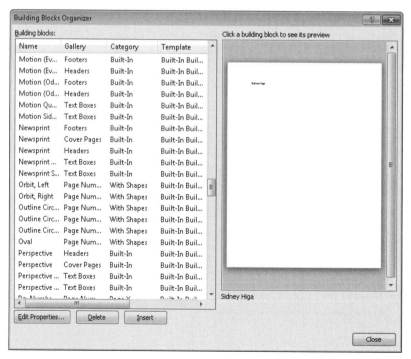

The Building Blocks Organizer dialog box, after the Name column has been sorted.

13. In the **Building blocks** list, click **Pinstripes Quote** (the first of the **Pinstripes** text boxes), and then below the list, click **Insert**.

Word inserts the quote box halfway down the right side of the page.

Placeholder text in the quote box tells you how to insert your own text and format the block.

14. Click the **Zoom Out** button on the **Zoom Slider** until you can read the text of the document. Then select and copy the last sentence of the fourth paragraph (**Go with what you love...**).

15. Click the quote box to select the placeholder text. Then on the **Home** tab, in the **Clipboard** group, click the **Paste** arrow, and under **Paste Options**, click the **Keep Text Only** button.

The copied text replaces the placeholder, and because it was pasted as unformatted text, it retains the formatting of the placeholder text. The quote box automatically resizes to fit its new contents.

See Also For information about text boxes, see the sidebar "Drawing Text Boxes" later in this chapter.

16. Display the whole page again. Then scroll to the last page of the document, and click anywhere on the page.

17. On the **Insert** tab, in the **Text** group, click the **Text Box** button, scroll through the gallery, and click **Pinstripes Sidebar**.

Word inserts the sidebar down the right side of the page.

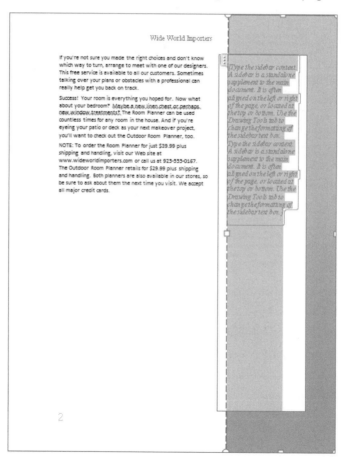

This sidebar consists of two overlapping, coordinated boxes.

18. If necessary, zoom out so that you can see the text well enough to edit it. Then at the beginning of the last paragraph of the document, delete **NOTE:** (including the colon and following space).

19. Select the last paragraph, and on the **Home** tab, in the **Clipboard** group, click the **Cut** button.

    Keyboard Shortcut Press Ctrl+X to cut the selected content to the Clipboard.

20. Click the sidebar to select the placeholder text. Then in the **Clipboard** group, click the **Paste** arrow, and under **Paste Options**, click the **Keep Text Only** button.

    The sidebar now contains the cut text.

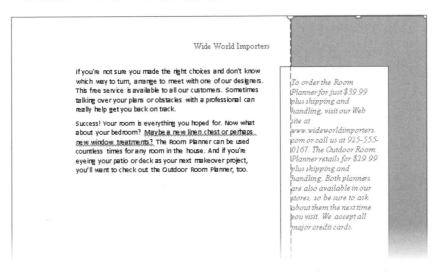

The pasted text takes on the formatting assigned to the text box.

21. To widen the sidebar so that the Web site address fits on one line, click the sidebar text, and drag the blue handle on the dotted line at the left side of the white box to the left, until it sits slightly to the left of the frame of the white box.

    If the Web site address still doesn't fit, adjust the width of the sidebar again.

22. Click at the top of the sidebar's blue box. Then on the **Insert** tab, in the **Text** group, click the **Quick Parts** button, and click **Save Selection to Quick Part Gallery**.

Troubleshooting If you click the text in the sidebar or elsewhere in the document after resizing the sidebar, the sidebar will no longer be selected and the Save Selection To Quick Part Gallery command will not be available.

The Create New Building Block dialog box opens.

23. Replace the text in the **Name** box with **Order Sidebar**, and then click **OK**.

You can now insert this custom sidebar from the Quick Parts gallery into other documents.

24. In the **Text** group, click the **Quick Parts** button.

The Quick Parts gallery appears.

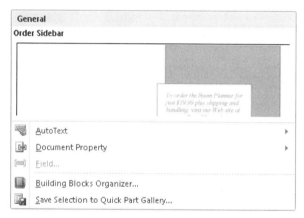

The Order Sidebar custom building block appears at the top of the gallery.

25. Click **Building Blocks Organizer**, and then in the **Building Blocks Organizer** dialog box, click the **Category** column heading to sort the **Building blocks** list by that column.

26. In the **Building blocks** list, scroll to the **General** category, and click **Order Sidebar** once.

The building block you just created appears in the preview pane.

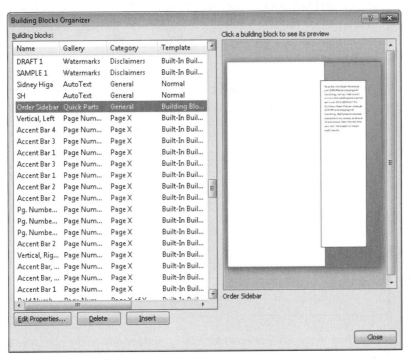

The General category includes your custom building block and the user name and initials AutoText entries.

 CLEAN UP If you want, delete the building block you just created before you close the Building Blocks Organizer dialog box. Then save the Flyer document, and close it.

Important When you exit Word after saving a custom building block, you'll be asked whether you want to save changes to the template in which you stored the building block. If you want the building block to be available for future documents, click Save; otherwise, click Don't Save.

Drawing Text Boxes

If none of the predefined text-box building blocks meets your needs, you can draw your own text box. At the bottom of the Text Box gallery, click Draw Text Box, and then drag a box the size you want anywhere on the page. You can immediately start typing at the blinking cursor, and you can format the text the way you would any other text.

When a text box is surrounded by a dashed border, it's selected for text editing. To manipulate the text box itself, you need to click its frame.

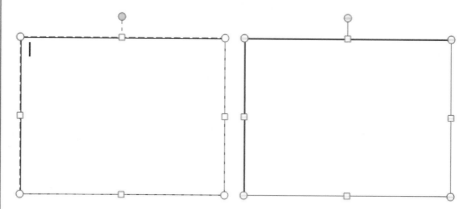

The text box on the left is selected for editing, and the one on the right is selected for manipulation.

When a text box has a solid border, you can reposition it by dragging it to another location, and you can change its size by dragging the size handles around its frame. You can change the outline and fill colors by using the commands in the Shape Styles group on the Format contextual tab.

You can link text boxes so that text flows from one to the next. To do so:

1. Click the first text box.

2. In the Text group on the Format contextual tab, click Create Link.

   The mouse pointer changes to a small pitcher.

3. Point to the second text box, and then when the mouse pointer changes to a pouring pitcher, click once.

   Note that the second text box must be empty.

Adding WordArt Text

If you're familiar with WordArt in earlier versions of Word, you're in for a surprise. WordArt has matured from the fun little tool you might have used in the past to create headings in molded shapes and gaudy colors. Its capabilities are now oriented toward creating more sophisticated display-text objects that you can position anywhere on the page. Although the WordArt object is attached to the paragraph that contained the cursor when you created it, you can move it independently from the text, even positioning it over the text if you want.

To insert a WordArt object, you click the WordArt button in the Text group on the Insert tab, and click a text style in the WordArt gallery. (The WordArt styles are the same as the text effects available in the Text Effects gallery in the Font group of the Home tab.) Then you enter your text in the text box that appears. You can edit the text, adjust the character formatting in the usual ways, and change the text style at any time.

Tip You can also select existing text before clicking the WordArt button to convert that text into a WordArt object.

See Also For information about character formatting, see "Manually Changing the Look of Characters" in Chapter 4, "Change the Look of Text." For information about text effects, see "Quickly Formatting Text" in the same chapter.

When a WordArt object is selected, the Format contextual tab appears on the ribbon. You can use the commands on this tab to format the WordArt object to meet your needs. For example, from the Format tab, you can add effects such as shadows and 3-D effects, change the fill and outline colors, and change the text direction and alignment. You can also position the WordArt object in any of several predefined locations on the page, as well as specify how the text should wrap around the object.

Tip Don't go too wild with WordArt formatting. Many WordArt Styles and Shape Styles take up space and can involve trial and error to produce a neat effect.

In this exercise, you'll insert a new WordArt object, modify it, and then position it on the page. Then you'll change the way it relates to the text on the page.

SET UP You need the Announcement_start document located in your Chapter06 practice file folder to complete this exercise. Open the Announcement_start document and save it as *Announcement*. Then with the rulers and formatting marks turned off, follow the steps.

1. On the **Insert** tab, in the **Text** group, click the **WordArt** button.

   The WordArt gallery appears, displaying the same formatted letters you see when you click the Text Effects button.

2. Click the third thumbnail in the fifth row (**Fill – Red, Accent 2, Warm Matte Bevel**).

   Word inserts a WordArt object with that text effect at the cursor. Because a graphic object is selected, the Format contextual tab appears on the ribbon.

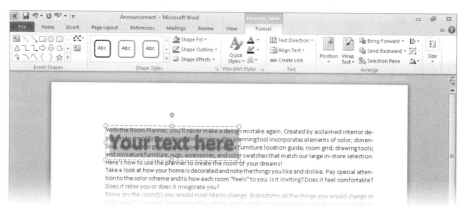

The WordArt object contains placeholder text in the style you chose.

   Tip If formatting marks are displayed, you see an anchor icon adjacent to the first paragraph. You can ignore it for now.

   See Also For information about anchoring objects, refer to *Microsoft Word 2010 Step by Step*, by Joyce Cox and Joan Lambert (Microsoft Press, 2010).

3. With **Your Text Here** selected, type **The Room Planner**. (Don't type the period.)

   Tip WordArt objects can accommodate multiple lines. Simply press Enter if you want to start a new line.

4. Without moving the cursor, on the **Home** tab, in the **Paragraph** group, click the **Center** button.

5. Click the border of the text box to select the box, and then change the zoom percentage so that you can see the whole page.

6. On the **Format** contextual tab, in the **Arrange** group, click the **Position** button.

   The Position gallery appears.

You can position the WordArt object in one of 10 predefined positions.

7. Point to each thumbnail in turn to preview where each option will place the object. Then under **With Text Wrapping**, click the second thumbnail in the second row (**Position in Middle Center with Square Text Wrapping**).

   The object moves to the middle of the page.

   Don't worry if the word *Planner* is now truncated. Because of the interaction of the object with its surrounding text, sometimes not all the WordArt text fits in its box after you position it. You'll fix that in a minute.

8. In the **Arrange** group, click the **Wrap Text** button.

   The Wrap Text gallery appears.

You can change the text wrapping without changing the position.

9. Point to each thumbnail in turn to preview their effects, and then click **Tight**.

10. In the **Arrange** group, click the **Wrap Text** button, and then click **More Layout Options**.

   The Layout dialog box opens with the Text Wrapping page active.

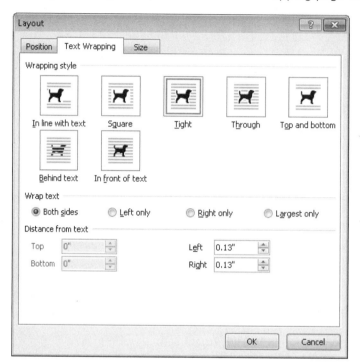

   If you know what kind of text wrapping you want, you can select it on this page of the dialog box, but you can't preview it.

11. In the **Distance from text** area, change the **Left** and **Right** settings to **0.3"**, and then click **OK**.

   The text outside the box is no longer encroaching on the box.

   If the word *Planner* was truncated in your box, the entire word should now be displayed. If it isn't, try increasing the Distance From Text settings to 0.4".

12. In the **WordArt Styles** group, display the **WordArt Quick Styles** gallery, and then click the fourth thumbnail in the third row (**Gradient Fill – Blue, Accent 1**).

   Troubleshooting Depending on your screen resolution and program window size, you might have to click the Quick Styles button to display the gallery.

13. In the **Shape Styles** group, display the **Shape Styles** gallery, and then click the fourth thumbnail in the fourth row (**Subtle Effect – Olive Green, Accent 3**).

14. Press Ctrl+Home.

Now you can see the effect of the WordArt text.

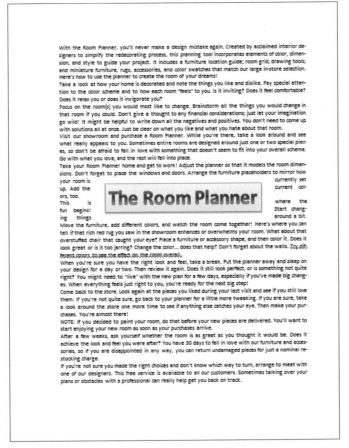

This simple text banner is a stylish alternative to a traditional title.

15. If you want, experiment with combinations of the styles and formatting available on the **Format** tab.

For example, you might want to try some of the Text Effects options, such as the molding effects available in the Transform gallery.

 CLEAN UP Save the Announcement document, and then close it.

Formatting the First Letter of a Paragraph

Many books, magazines, and reports begin the first paragraph of a section or chapter by using an enlarged, decorative capital letter. Called a *dropped capital*, or simply a *drop cap*, this effect can be an easy way to give a document a finished, professional look.

The Drop Cap gallery provides two basic drop-cap styles:

- **Dropped** Sits in the text column and displaces paragraph text
- **In margin** Hangs in the margin adjacent to the paragraph text

In either case, the drop cap is as tall as three lines of text and uses the same font as the rest of the paragraph.

To insert a drop cap:

1. Click anywhere in a paragraph of text, and then on the Insert tab, in the Text group, click the Drop Cap button.
2. Point to each thumbnail to display its live preview, and then click the one you want.

    Word inserts the first letter of the paragraph in a box. If you selected Dropped, Word rewraps the text to the right of the graphic.

For more options, click Drop Cap Options at the bottom of the Drop Cap gallery to open the Drop Cap dialog box. You can choose a font that is different from the paragraph and adjust the drop cap's height and distance from the text.

If you want to make the first word of the paragraph stand out, you can click to the right of the drop cap and type the rest of the word. If you do this, don't forget to delete the word from the beginning of the paragraph!

Key Points

- You can insert illustrations created with most graphics programs, as well as digital photos, into a Word document.

- A background color, texture, pattern, or picture can really give a document pizzazz, but be careful that it doesn't overwhelm the text.

- Word comes with predefined building blocks that quickly add graphic elements to a document.

- Using WordArt, you can easily add fancy text to a document and then format and position it for the best effect.

Chapter at a Glance

Preview and adjust page layout, **page 206**

Print documents, **page 217**

Control what appears on each page, **page 212**

Prepare documents for electronic distribution, **page 219**

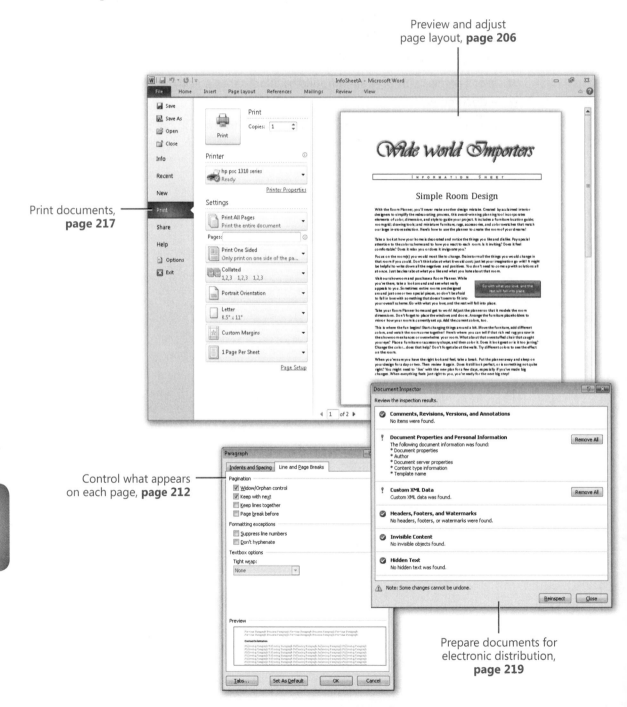

7 Preview, Print, and Distribute Documents

In this chapter, you will learn how to

✔ Preview and adjust page layout.

✔ Control what appears on each page.

✔ Print documents.

✔ Prepare documents for electronic distribution.

When you finish developing a document, you'll often want to distribute either a printed version or an electronic version. Before committing the document to paper, you should check that the pages are efficiently laid out and that there are no glaring problems, such as headings that print on separate pages from their text. Microsoft Word 2010 provides several tools you can use to manipulate how much text appears on each page and to control page layout. It also provides tools for finalizing an electronic document and ensuring that the end product of all your hard work contains no traces of personal or confidential information. When you are ready to print, you can control precisely how many copies and what parts of your document appear on paper.

In this chapter, you'll first preview a document and make some adjustments to improve its presentation. Then you'll look at the options available for controlling page breaks. You'll print a document, and finally, you'll inspect and finalize it for electronic distribution.

Practice Files Before you can complete the exercises in this chapter, you need to copy the book's practice files to your computer. The practice files you'll use to complete the exercises in this chapter are in the Chapter07 practice file folder. A complete list of practice files is provided in "Using the Practice Files" at the beginning of this book.

Previewing and Adjusting Page Layout

Usually while you're creating a document, you'll make decisions about the size of the margins and the direction of the page (called the *orientation*) to best suit your content. You can use the Margins and Orientation commands in the Page Setup group of the Page Layout tab to make any necessary adjustments to the document, and you can use the Size command to change the paper size.

You can also display the Page Setup dialog box, where you can make these basic layout changes all in one place.

You can adjust all the page layout settings in one place.

Working on your document in Print Layout view helps to ensure that the document looks tidy on the page. However, before you print the document, you'll almost always want to check how it will look on paper by previewing it. Previewing is essential for multipage documents but is helpful even for one-page documents. To preview a document, you display the Print page of the Backstage view and then page through the document displayed in the right pane. This view shows exactly how each page of the document will look when printed on the specified printer.

The Print page of the Backstage view.

If you don't like what you see in the preview pane of the Print page, you don't have to leave the Backstage view to make adjustments. The middle pane of the Print page provides tools for making the following changes:

- **Orientation** You can switch the direction in which a page is laid out on the paper. The default orientation is Portrait, in which the page is taller than it is wide. You can set the orientation to Landscape, in which the page is wider than it is tall.

- **Paper size** You can switch to one of the sizes available for the selected printer by making a selection from a list.

- **Margins** Changing the margins of a document changes where information can appear on each page. You can select one of Word's predefined sets of top, bottom, left, and right margins, or set custom margins.

  Tip All the pages of a document have the same orientation and margins unless you divide the document into sections. Then each section can have independent orientation and margin settings. For more information about sections, see "Controlling What Appears on Each Page" later in this chapter.

If your printer is capable of scaling the pages of your document, you'll also see an option to set the number of pages to print per sheet of paper, up to 16. You might use this option to print a booklet with two pages per sheet that will be folded in the middle. You might also be tempted to use this option to save paper, but bear in mind that the smaller the pages, the harder it is to read them.

You can also open the Page Setup dialog box from the Print page to make multiple adjustments in one place.

In this exercise, you'll preview a document, change the orientation, and adjust the margins.

SET UP You need the InfoSheetA_start document located in the Chapter07 practice file folder, and an active printer connection, to complete this exercise. Open the InfoSheetA_start document, and save it as *InfoSheetA*. Then follow the steps.

1. Display the Backstage view, and in the left pane, click **Print**.

   Keyboard Shortcut Press Ctrl+P to display the Print page of the Backstage view.

The Print page is displayed, with a preview of the document on the right. The shaded background of the document is not displayed because it will not be printed.

61%

2. In the lower-right corner of the preview pane, click the **Zoom** button, and then in the **Zoom** dialog box, click **Many pages**, click the monitor button, and click the second page icon in the top row of the grid (**1x2 Pages**). Then click **OK**.

Word displays the two pages of the document side by side.

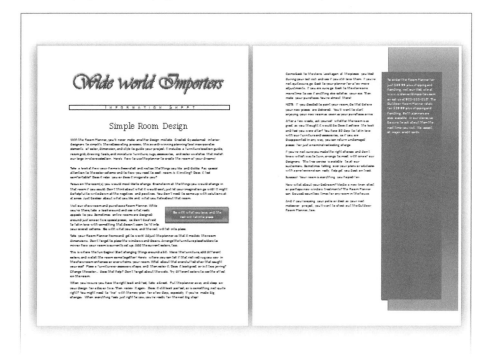

You can preview multiple pages.

Tip If you want to preview a multipage document as it will look when printed on both sides of the page and bound, add a blank page to the beginning of the document before previewing it.

3. Under **Settings** in the middle pane, click **Custom Margins**.

The gallery of margin options appears.

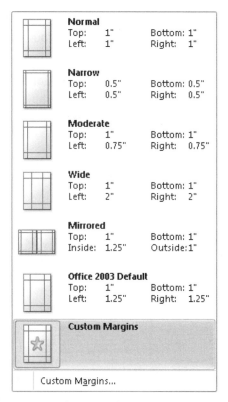

You can select predefined margins or set your own.

4. In the list, click **Wide**.

   The text rewraps within the new margins.

5. In the page range in the lower-left corner of the preview pane, click the **Next Page** button.

   The page range updates to show that the document now has three pages and that page 2 is the active page.

6. Click the **Next Page** button again to see the last page of the document.

7. At the bottom of the middle pane, click **Page Setup**.

   The Page Setup dialog box opens, displaying the Margins page. Notice that selecting Wide margins on the Print page set the left and right margins to 2 inches.

8. In the **Pages** area, display the **Multiple pages** list, and click **Mirror Margins**.

   The Preview area now displays two pages side by side, and in the Margins area, Left and Right have changed to Inside and Outside.

9. In the **Margins** area, change the value in the **Outside** box to **1"**.

   Tip You can either type a new value or click the down arrow at the right end of the box.

   In the pages in the Preview area, the width of the outside margins decreases.

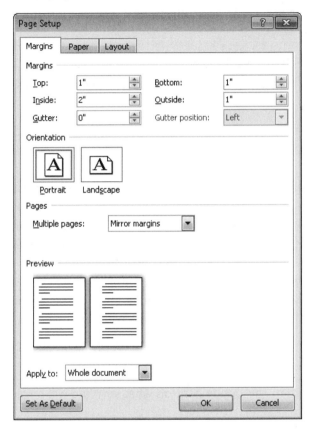

You might use the Mirror Margins setting if you were planning on printing on both sides of the paper and then stapling the pages.

10. Return the **Multiple pages** setting to **Normal**, and in the **Margins** area, change the value in the **Left** box to **1"**.

11. If you want, in the **Page Setup** dialog box, click the **Paper** tab and then the **Layout** tab, and notice the available options on those pages. Then click **OK**.

   On the Print page, the margins setting is now Normal Margins, and the page range indicator shows that the number of pages in the document has decreased to two.

 CLEAN UP Save the InfoSheetA document, and then close it.

Controlling What Appears on Each Page

When a document includes more content than will fit between its top and bottom margins, Word creates a new page by inserting a soft page break. If you want to break a page before Word would normally break it, you can insert a manual page break in one of three ways:

- Click Page Break in the Pages group on the Insert tab.
- Click Breaks in the Page Setup group on the Page Layout tab, and then click Page.
- Press Ctrl+Enter.

Tip As you edit the text in a document, Word changes the location of the soft page breaks, but the program cannot change the location of any manual page breaks you might have inserted.

If a paragraph breaks so that most of it appears on one page but its last line appears at the top of the next page, the line is called a *widow*. If a paragraph breaks so that its first line appears at the bottom of one page and the rest of the paragraph appears on the next page, the line is called an *orphan*. These single lines of text can make a document hard to read, so by default, Word specifies that a minimum of two lines should appear at the top and bottom of each page. However, on the Line And Page Breaks page of the Paragraph dialog box, you can change whether page breaks are allowed to create widows and orphans. You can also change the following options:

- **Keep with next** This option controls whether Word will break a page between the paragraph containing the cursor and the following paragraph.

- **Keep lines together** This option controls whether Word will break a page within a paragraph.

- **Page break before** This option controls whether Word will break a page before the paragraph containing the cursor.

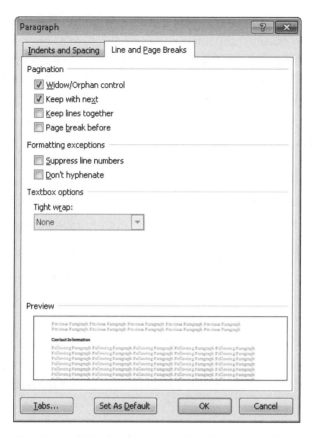

The Line And Page Breaks page of the Paragraph dialog box.

Tip You can apply these options to individual paragraphs, or you can incorporate them into the styles you define for document elements such as headings. For information about styles, refer to *Microsoft Word 2010 Step by Step*, by Joyce Cox and Joan Lambert (Microsoft Press, 2010).

In addition to page breaks, you can insert section breaks in your documents. A section break identifies a part of the document that has page settings, such as orientation or margins, that are different from those of the rest of the document. For example, you might want to put a large table in its own section so that you can turn it sideways by changing its orientation to Landscape.

You insert a section break by clicking Breaks in the Page Setup group on the Page Layout tab and then selecting from the following section types:

- **Next Page** Starts the following section on the next page
- **Continuous** Starts a new section without affecting page breaks
- **Even Page** Starts the following section on the next even-numbered page
- **Odd Page** Starts the following section on the next odd-numbered page

If formatting marks are displayed, a section break appears in Print Layout view as a double-dotted line from the preceding paragraph mark to the margin, with the words *Section Break* and the type of section break in the middle of the line.

Tip To remove a page or section break, click at the left end of the break and then press the Delete key.

In this exercise, you'll insert page and section breaks, and ensure that the pages break in logical places.

SET UP You need the OfficeInfo_start document located in the Chapter07 practice file folder to complete this exercise. Open the OfficeInfo_start document, and save it as *OfficeInfo*. Display formatting marks, and then follow the steps.

1. Scroll through the document, noticing any awkward page breaks, such as a topic or list that starts close to the bottom of a page.

2. On the **Home** tab, in the **Editing** group, click the **Select** button, and then click **Select All**.

3. Click the **Paragraph** dialog box launcher, and then in the **Paragraph** dialog box, click the **Line and Page Breaks** tab.

   Because different settings have been applied to different paragraphs in the document, all the check boxes have a solid filling.

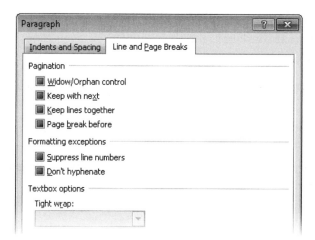

When multiple paragraphs are selected, solid check boxes indicate that the paragraphs have different settings.

4. Double-click all the check boxes to clear them.

5. Select the **Keep lines together** check box (click more than once if necessary), and then click **OK**.

   This setting ensures that none of the paragraphs will be broken across two pages. Word alerts you to the presence of this formatting by displaying a square symbol to the left of each paragraph.

6. Press Ctrl+Home to release the selection, and then scroll through the document, again looking for untidy page breaks.

7. Click to the left of the **Facilities** heading.

8. On the **Insert** tab, in the **Pages** group, click the **Page Break** button.

   Keyboard Shortcut Press Ctrl+Enter to insert a page break.

   Word breaks the page and moves the *Facilities* heading and the following text to the next page.

9. Scroll down to the bottom of page **3**, select the **Supplies** heading and the three lines that follow it (the third line is at the top of page **4**), and then display the **Line and Page Breaks** page of the **Paragraph** dialog box.

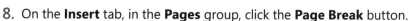

10. In the **Pagination** area, leave the **Keep lines together** check box selected, select the **Keep with next** check box, and then click **OK**.

   Word moves the selection to the next page.

11. Scroll down to page **9**, and click to the left of the **Shipping Quick Reference** heading.

   Tip If you drag the scroll box in the scroll bar, Word displays a ScreenTip with the number of the page that will be displayed if you release the mouse button.

12. On the **Page Layout** tab, in the **Page Setup** group, click the **Breaks** button, and then under **Section Breaks**, click **Next Page**.

   Word pushes the heading to the next page.

13. Scroll up until the text on page **9** is displayed.

   A double dotted line with the words *Section Break (Next Page)* appears at the right end of the paragraph preceding the section break.

   - 2.→ Send·the·invoice·to·the·customer.¶
   - 3.→ Enter·Tentative·in·the·customer's·Access·account·until·you·receive·the·check·and·the·check· has·cleared·the·bank.¶⎯⎯⎯⎯⎯⎯⎯⎯⎯ Section Break (Next Page) ⎯⎯⎯⎯⎯⎯⎯⎯⎯

   The section break indicator.

14. Scroll down to page **10**, and with the cursor in the **Shipping Quick Reference** heading, on the **Page Layout** tab, in the **Page Setup** group, click the **Margins** button. Then in the **Margins** gallery, click **Wide**.

   The table in the new section shrinks in width to fit between the wider margins.

15. On the **Insert** tab, in the **Header & Footer** group, click the **Header** button, and then click **Edit Header**.

   In the Navigation group of the Design contextual tab, the Link To Previous button is selected, meaning that the header of the new section has inherited the settings of the preceding section. Because the preceding section has no header on its first page, this one doesn't have one either.

16. On the **Design** contextual tab, in the **Options** group, clear the **Different First Page** check box. Then click the **Close Header and Footer** button.

Now the header from pages 2 through 9 of the preceding section is repeated on page 10 in this section.

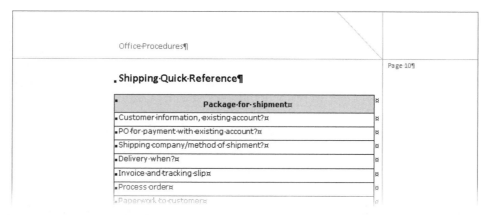

You might have to adjust the header settings after creating a new section.

 CLEAN UP Save the OfficeInfo document, and then close it.

Printing Documents

When you are ready to print a document, you display the Print page of the Backstage view, and then, to print one copy on the current printer with the settings shown, you simply click the Print button.

If you need to use settings other than the defaults, you can change the following:

- **Number of copies** Click the arrows or type the number you need.

- **Printer** Switch to a different printer, or click Printer Properties to change the printer options.

- **Print range** Print the entire document, the selected text, the current page, or a custom range of pages. (Point to the information icon to the right of the Pages box to see the format in which to enter a custom range.)

- **Sides of the paper** Print on one side or both sides, either manually or, if your printer has duplex capability, automatically.

- **Collation** For multiple copies of a multipage document, print all the pages in the document as a set or print all the copies of each page as a set.

If your printer has multiple paper trays or a manual paper feeder, you can select the paper source you want to use, on the Paper page of the Page Setup dialog box.

In this exercise, you'll see how to select a different printer before sending two copies of the current page of a document to be printed.

 SET UP You need the InfoSheetB_start document located in the Chapter07 practice file folder, and multiple active printer connections, to complete this exercise. Open the InfoSheetB_start document, and save it as *InfoSheetB*. Then follow the steps.

1. Display the Backstage view, and in the left pane, click **Print**.

   If you don't need to change any settings, you can simply click the Print button at the top of the middle pane of the Print page.

2. If you have more than one printer available and you want to switch printers, under **Printer** in the middle pane, click the option displaying the name of the default printer, and in the list, click the printer you want.

3. Point to the information icon to the right of the **Printer** area heading.

   Tip You can also point to the selected printer.

   Information about your printer's status is displayed.

Printer Status
Status: Ready
Type: hp psc 1310 series
Where: USB001
Comment:

   You can check your printer's status without leaving the Print page.

4. In the **Copies** box next to the **Print** button, change the number of copies to **2**.

5. Under **Settings**, click the arrow to the right of the first box to expand the list of print options, and then in the list, click **Print Current Page**.

6. Leaving the other settings as they are, click the **Print** button at the top of the middle pane.

   Word prints two copies of the document's first page on the designated printer, and returns you to the document.

 CLEAN UP Close the InfoSheetB document.

Preparing Documents for Electronic Distribution

When a document is complete, you can distribute it in two basic ways: on paper or electronically. If you distribute it electronically, you need to ensure that no private or inappropriate information is attached to the file and that it can be viewed by the people to whom you are sending it.

Many documents go through several revisions, and some are scrutinized by multiple reviewers. During this development process, documents can accumulate information that you might not want in the final version, such as the names of people who worked on the document, comments that reviewers have added to the file, or hidden text about status and assumptions. This extraneous information is not a concern if the final version is to be delivered as a printout. However, these days, more and more files are delivered electronically, making this information available to anyone who wants to read it.

To examine some of the attached information, you can display the document's properties on the Info page of the Backstage view. You can change or remove the information in either the Document Panel or the Properties dialog box. However, Word provides a tool called the *Document Inspector* to automate the process of finding and removing all extraneous and potentially confidential information. After you run the Document Inspector, you see a summary of its search results, and you have the option of removing all the items found in each category.

Word also includes two other finalizing tools:

- **Check Accessibility** Checks for document elements and formatting that might be difficult for people with certain kinds of disabilities to read.

- **Check Compatibility** Checks for the use of features not supported in earlier versions of Word.

After you have handled extraneous information and accessibility and compatibility issues, you can mark a document as final and make it a read-only file, so that other people know that they should not make changes to this released document.

In this exercise, you'll inspect a document for inappropriate information and mark it as final.

 SET UP You need the InfoSheetC_start document located in the Chapter07 practice file folder to complete this exercise. Open the InfoSheetC_start document, and save it as *InfoSheetC*. Then follow the steps.

1. Display the Backstage view, and in the left pane, click **Info**.

   In the right pane you see the properties that have been saved with the file. Some of the information, including the name of the author, was attached to the file by Word. Other information, such as the title, was added by a user.

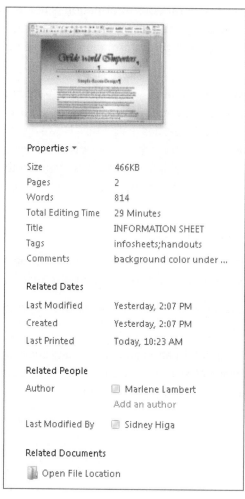

The properties attached to this document.

2. In the right pane, click the **Properties** button, and then in the list, click **Advanced Properties**.

    The Properties dialog box for this document opens. On the General page of the dialog box are properties maintained by Word.

3. Click the **Summary** tab.

    Notice that additional identifying information is displayed on this page.

These properties were entered by the people who worked on the document.

Tip To make a document easier to find in Windows Explorer, you can add tags in the Properties area of the Info page or keywords in the Properties dialog box.

4. Click **Cancel** to close the **Properties** dialog box.

5. In the **Prepare for Sharing** area of the **Info** page, click **Check for Issues**, and then click **Inspect Document**.

    Troubleshooting If Word asks whether you want to save changes to the file, click Yes.

    The Document Inspector dialog box opens, listing the items that will be checked.

6. Without changing the default selections in the **Document Inspector** dialog box, click **Inspect**.

The Document Inspector reports the presence of the properties you viewed earlier, as well as some custom XML data.

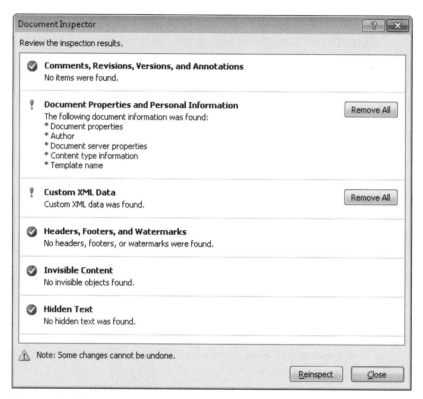

The results of the inspection.

7. To the right of **Document Properties and Personal Information**, click **Remove All**.

8. To the right of **Custom XML Data**, click **Remove All**.

9. Click **Reinspect**, and then click **Inspect**.

Word has removed the properties and XML data.

10. In the **Document Inspector** dialog box, click **Close**.

The right pane of the Info page now shows that there are no custom properties attached to the document.

11. In the **Permissions** area of the **Info** page, click **Protect Document**, and then click **Mark As Final**.

    A message tells you that the document will be marked as final and then saved.

12. Click **OK**.

    A message tells you that the document has been marked as final and that typing, editing commands, and proofing marks are turned off.

13. Click **OK**.

    The Permissions area now indicates that the file is final.

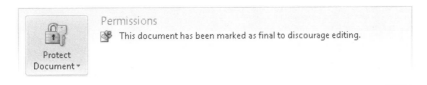

The Info page reminds people that the file is final.

14. Click the **Insert** tab.

    An orange bar appears, notifying you that the document has been marked as final.

15. Click the **Insert** tab again.

    The tab's groups and buttons are displayed, but all of the buttons are inactive.

    Tip If you really want to make changes to the document, you can click a tab to display the orange bar and then click the Edit Anyway button to unmark the file.

 CLEAN UP Save the InfoSheetC document, and then close it.

Tip If you need to distribute a document electronically but you don't want to share the actual file, you can "print" the document to a new file in XML Paper Specification (XPS) format. For information, refer to *Microsoft Word 2010 Step by Step*, by Joyce Cox and Joan Lambert (Microsoft Press, 2010).

Key Points

- You should always preview a document before printing it.

- You can use page and section breaks and page break options to ensure that pages break in logical places.

- All the printing options are now gathered together on the Print page of the Backstage view.

- Before distributing a document, you can use the Document Inspector to remove private or inappropriate information.

Part 3
Microsoft Excel 2010

Chapter at a Glance

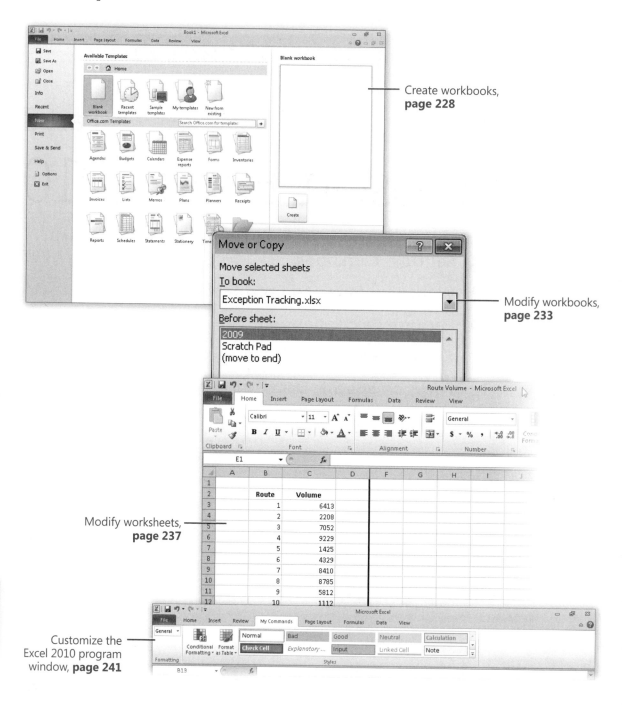

Create workbooks,
page 228

Modify workbooks,
page 233

Modify worksheets,
page 237

Customize the
Excel 2010 program
window, **page 241**

8 Set Up a Workbook

In this chapter, you will learn how to

✔ Create workbooks.

✔ Modify workbooks.

✔ Modify worksheets.

✔ Customize the Excel 2010 program window.

When you start Microsoft Excel 2010, the program presents a blank workbook that contains three worksheets. You can add or delete worksheets, hide worksheets within the workbook without deleting them, and change the order of your worksheets within the workbook. You can also copy a worksheet to another workbook or move the worksheet without leaving a copy of the worksheet in the first workbook. If you and your colleagues work with a large number of documents, you can define property values to make your workbooks easier to find when you and your colleagues attempt to locate them by using the Windows search facility.

Another way to make Excel easier to use is by customizing the Excel program window to fit your work style. If you have several workbooks open at the same time, you can move between the workbook windows quickly. However, if you switch between workbooks frequently, you might find it easier to resize the workbooks so they don't take up the entire Excel window. If you do this, you just need to click the title bar of the workbook you want to modify to switch to it.

The Microsoft Office User Experience team has enhanced your ability to customize the Excel user interface. If you find that you use a command frequently, you can add it to the Quick Access Toolbar so it's never more than one click away. If you use a set of commands frequently, you can create a custom ribbon tab so they appear in one place. You can also hide, display, or change the order of the tabs on the ribbon.

In this chapter, you'll learn how to create and modify workbooks, create and modify worksheets, make your workbooks easier to find, and customize the Excel 2010 program window.

> **Practice Files** Before you can complete the exercises in this chapter, you need to copy the book's practice files to your computer. The practice files you'll use to complete the exercises in this chapter are in the Chapter08 practice file folder. A complete list of practice files is provided in "Using the Practice Files" at the beginning of this book.

Creating Workbooks

Every time you want to gather and store data that isn't closely related to any of your other existing data, you should create a new workbook. The default new workbook in Excel has three worksheets, although you can add more worksheets or delete existing worksheets if you want. Creating a new workbook is a straightforward process—you just click the File tab, click New, identify the type of workbook you want, and click the Create button.

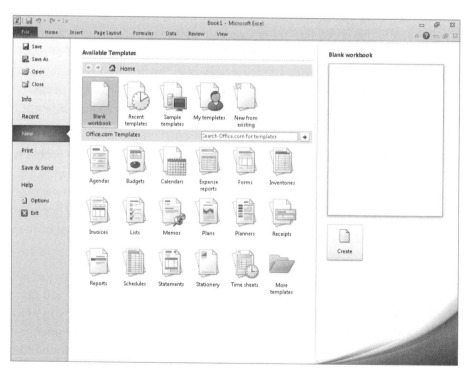

The New page of the Backstage view.

When you start Excel, the program displays a new, blank workbook; you can begin to type data into the worksheet's cells or open an existing workbook. In this book's exercises, you'll work with workbooks created for Consolidated Messenger, a fictional global shipping company. After you make changes to a workbook, you should save it to preserve your work.

Tip Readers frequently ask, "How often should I save my files?" It is good practice to save your changes every half hour or even every five minutes, but the best time to save a file is whenever you make a change that you would hate to have to make again.

When you save a file, you overwrite the previous copy of the file. If you have made changes that you want to save, but you also want to keep a copy of the file as it was when you saved it previously, you can use the Save As command to specify a name for the new file.

You also can use the controls in the Save As dialog box to specify a different format for the new file and a different location in which to save the new version of the file. For example, Lori Penor, the chief operating officer of Consolidated Messenger, might want to save an Excel file that tracks consulting expenses as an Excel 2003 file if she needs to share the file with a consulting firm that uses Excel 2003.

After you create a file, you can add information to make the file easier to find when you use the Windows search facility to search for it. Each category of information, or property, stores specific information about your file. In Windows, you can search for files based on the file's author or title, or by keywords associated with the file. A file tracking the postal code destinations of all packages sent from a vendor might have the keywords *postal*, *destination*, and *origin* associated with it.

To set values for your workbook's built-in properties, you can click the File tab, click Info, click Properties, and then click Show Document Panel to display the Document Properties panel just below the ribbon. The standard version of the Document Properties panel has fields for the file's author, title, subject, keywords, category, and status, and any comments about the file. You can also create custom properties by clicking the arrow located just to the right of the Document Properties label, and clicking Advanced Properties to display the Properties dialog box.

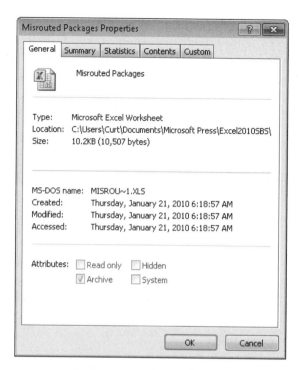

General workbook properties are based on the file and cannot be edited.

On the Custom page of the Properties dialog box, you can click one of the existing custom categories or create your own by typing a new property name in the Name field, clicking the Type arrow and selecting a data type (for example, Text, Date, Number, or Yes/No), selecting or typing a value in the Value field, and then clicking Add. If you want to delete an existing custom property, point to the Properties list, click the property you want to get rid of, and click Delete. After you finish making your changes, click the OK button. To hide the Document Properties panel, click the Close button in the upper-right corner of the panel.

In this exercise, you'll create a new workbook, save the workbook with a new name, assign values to the workbook's standard properties, and create a custom property.

SET UP You need the ExceptionSummary_start workbook located in your Chapter08 practice file folder to complete this exercise. Start Excel, and open the ExceptionSummary_start workbook. Then follow the steps.

1. Click the **File** tab, and then click **Close**.

    The ExceptionSummary_start workbook closes.

2. Click the **File** tab, and then click **New**.

    The New Workbook page of the Backstage view appears.

3. Click **Blank Workbook**, and then click **Create**.

   A new, blank workbook opens.

4. Click the **File** tab, and then click **Save As**.

   The Save As dialog box opens.

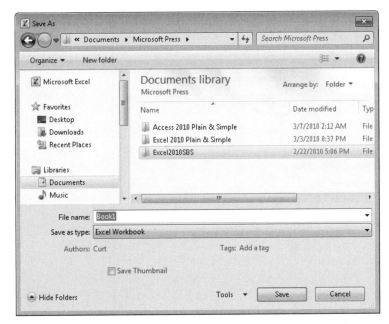

By default, the Save As dialog box displays the contents of your Documents library or the last folder you accessed from the dialog box.

5. Navigate to your **Chapter08** practice file folder. In the **File name** field, type **Exceptions 2010**.

6. Click the **Save** button.

   Excel 2010 saves your work, and the Save As dialog box closes.

7. Click the **File** tab, click **Info**, click **Properties**, and then click **Show Document Panel**.

   The Document Properties panel opens.

8. In the **Keywords** field, type **exceptions, regional, percentage**.

9. In the **Category** field, type **performance**.

10. Click the arrow at the right end of the Document Properties button, and then click **Advanced Properties**.

    The Exceptions 2010 Properties dialog box opens.

11. Click the **Custom** tab.

    The Custom page is displayed.

12. In the **Name** field, type **Performance**.

13. In the **Value** field, type **Exceptions**.

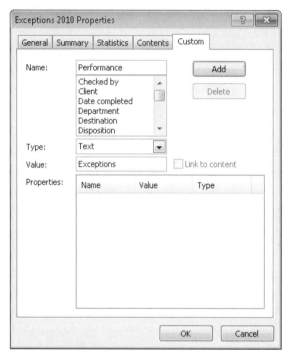

You can specify custom properties for a workbook.

14. Click the **Add** button, and then click **OK**.

    The Exceptions 2010 Properties dialog box closes.

15. On the Quick Access Toolbar, click the **Save** button to save your work.

    Keyboard Shortcut Press Ctrl+S to save a workbook.

 **CLEAN UP** Close the Exceptions 2010 workbook.

Modifying Workbooks

Most of the time, you create a workbook to record information about a particular activity, such as the number of packages that a regional distribution center handles or the average time a driver takes to complete all deliveries on a route. Each worksheet within that workbook should represent a subdivision of that activity. To display a particular worksheet, just click the worksheet's tab on the tab bar (just below the grid of cells).

In the case of Consolidated Messenger, the workbook used to track daily package volumes could have a separate worksheet for each regional distribution center. New Excel workbooks contain three worksheets; because Consolidated Messenger uses nine regional distribution centers, you would need to create six new ones. To create a new worksheet, click the Insert Worksheet button at the right edge of the tab bar.

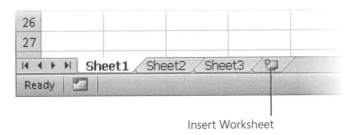

Insert Worksheet

When you create a worksheet, Excel assigns it a generic name such as Sheet4.

After you decide what type of data you want to store on a worksheet, you should change the default worksheet name to something more descriptive. For example, you could change the name of Sheet1 in the regional distribution center tracking workbook to *Northeast*. When you want to change a worksheet's name, double-click the worksheet's tab on the tab bar to highlight the worksheet name, type the new name, and press Enter.

Another way to work with more than one worksheet is to copy a worksheet from another workbook to the current workbook. One circumstance in which you might consider copying worksheets to the current workbook is if you have a list of your current employees in another workbook. You can copy worksheets from another workbook by right-clicking the tab of the sheet you want to copy and, on the shortcut menu, clicking Move Or Copy to display the Move Or Copy dialog box.

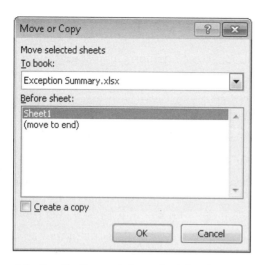

Selecting the Create A Copy check box leaves the copied worksheet in its original workbook, whereas clearing the check box causes Excel to delete the worksheet from its original workbook.

After the worksheet is in the target workbook, you can change the worksheets' order to make the data easier to locate within the workbook. To change a worksheet's location in the workbook, you drag its sheet tab to the desired location on the tab bar. If you want to remove a worksheet from the tab bar without deleting the worksheet, you can do so by right-clicking the worksheet's tab on the tab bar and clicking Hide on the context menu. When you want Excel to redisplay the worksheet, right-click any visible sheet tab and then click Unhide. In the Unhide dialog box, click the name of the sheet you want to display, and click OK.

To differentiate a worksheet from others, or to visually indicate groups or categories of worksheets in a multiple-worksheet workbook, you can easily change the color of a worksheet tab. To do so, right-click the tab, point to Tab Color, and then click the color you want.

Tip If you copy a worksheet to another workbook, and the destination workbook has the same Office Theme applied as the active workbook, the worksheet retains its tab color. If the destination workbook has another theme applied, the worksheet's tab color changes to reflect that theme. For more information on Office themes, see Chapter 11, "Change Workbook Appearance."

If you determine that you no longer need a particular worksheet, such as one you created to store some figures temporarily, you can delete the worksheet quickly. To do so, right-click its sheet tab, and then click Delete.

In this exercise, you'll insert and rename a worksheet, change a worksheet's position in a workbook, hide and unhide a worksheet, copy a worksheet to another workbook, change a worksheet's tab color, and delete a worksheet.

SET UP You need the ExceptionTracking_start workbook located in your Chapter08 practice file folder to complete this exercise. Open the ExceptionTracking_start file, and save it as *ExceptionTracking*. Then follow the steps.

1. On the tab bar, click the **Insert Worksheet** button.

   A new worksheet is displayed.

2. Right-click the new worksheet's sheet tab, and then click **Rename**.

   Excel highlights the new worksheet's name.

3. Type **2010**, and then press Enter.

4. On the tab bar, double-click the **Sheet1** sheet tab.

   Excel highlights the worksheet's name.

5. Type **2009**, and then press Enter.

6. Right-click the **2009** sheet tab, point to **Tab Color**, and then, in the **Standard Colors** area of the color palette, click the green square.

   Excel changes the 2009 sheet tab to green.

7. On the tab bar, drag the **2010** sheet tab to the left of the **Scratch Pad** sheet tab.

8. Right-click the **2010** sheet tab, and then click **Hide**.

   Excel hides the 2010 worksheet.

9. Right-click the **2009** sheet tab, and then click **Move or Copy**.

   The Move Or Copy dialog box opens.

You must specify the destination of the moved or copied worksheet.

10. Click the **To book** arrow, and then in the list, click **(new book)**.

11. Select the **Create a copy** check box.

12. Click **OK**.

    A new workbook opens, containing only the worksheet you copied into it.

13. On the Quick Access Toolbar, click **Save**.

    The Save As dialog box opens.

14. In the **File name** field, type **2009 Archive**, and then press Enter.

    Excel saves the workbook, and the Save As dialog box closes.

15. On the **View** tab, click the **Switch Windows** button, and then click **ExceptionTracking**.

    The ExceptionTracking workbook is displayed.

16. On the tab bar, right-click the **Scratch Pad** sheet tab, and then click **Delete**. In the dialog box that opens, click **Delete** to confirm the operation.

    The Scratch Pad worksheet is deleted.

17. Right-click the **2009** sheet tab, and then click **Unhide**.

    The Unhide dialog box opens.

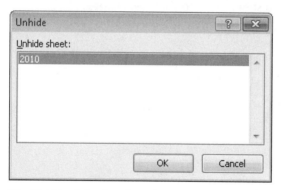

The Unhide dialog box lists all hidden worksheets.

18. Click **2010,** and then click **OK**.

    The Unhide dialog box closes, and the 2010 worksheet is displayed in the workbook.

 CLEAN UP Save and close the ExceptionTracking workbook and the 2009 Archive workbook.

Modifying Worksheets

After you put up the signposts that make your data easy to find, you can take other steps to make the data in your workbooks easier to work with. For example, you can change the width of a column or the height of a row in a worksheet by dragging the column's right border or the row's bottom border to the desired position. Increasing a column's width or a row's height increases the space between cell contents, making your data easier to read and work with.

Tip You can apply the same change to more than one row or column by selecting the rows or columns you want to change and then dragging the border of one of the selected rows or columns to the desired location. When you release the mouse button, all the selected rows or columns change to the new height or width.

Modifying column width and row height can make a workbook's contents easier to work with, but you can also insert a row or column between cells that contain data to make your data easier to read. Adding space between the edge of a worksheet and cells that contain data, or perhaps between a label and the data to which it refers, makes the workbook's contents less crowded. You insert rows by clicking a cell and clicking the Home tab on the ribbon. Then, in the Cells group, in the Insert list, click Insert Sheet Rows. Excel inserts a row above the row that contains the active cell. You insert a column in much the same way, by choosing Insert Sheet Columns from the Insert list. When you do this, Excel inserts a column to the left of the active cell.

When you insert a row, column, or cell in a worksheet that has had formatting applied, the Insert Options button appears. Clicking the Insert Options button displays a list of choices you can make about how the inserted row or column should be formatted. The following table summarizes your options.

Option	Action
Format Same As Above	Applies the formatting of the row above the inserted row to the new row
Format Same As Below	Applies the formatting of the row below the inserted row to the new row
Format Same As Left	Applies the formatting of the column to the left of the inserted column to the new column
Format Same As Right	Applies the formatting of the column to the right of the inserted column to the new column
Clear Formatting	Applies the default format to the new row or column

If you want to delete a row or column, right-click the row or column head and then, on the shortcut menu that appears, click Delete. You can temporarily hide rows or columns by selecting those rows or columns and then, on the Home tab, in the Cells group, clicking the Format button, pointing to Hide & Unhide, and then clicking either Hide Rows or Hide Columns. The rows or columns you selected disappear, but they aren't gone for good, as they would be if you'd used Delete. Instead, they have just been removed from the display until you call them back. To return the hidden rows to the display, select the row or column headers on either side of the hidden rows or columns. Then, on the Home tab, in the Cells group, click the Format button, point to Hide & Unhide, and then click either Unhide Rows or Unhide Columns.

Important If you hide the first row or column in a worksheet, you must click the Select All button in the upper-left corner of the worksheet (above the first row header and to the left of the first column header) or press Ctrl+A to select the entire worksheet. Then, on the Home tab, in the Cells group, click Format, point to Hide & Unhide, and then click either Unhide Rows or Unhide Columns to make the hidden data visible again.

Just as you can insert rows or columns, you can insert individual cells into a worksheet. To insert a cell, click the cell that is currently in the position where you want the new cell to appear. On the Home tab, in the Cells group, in the Insert list, click Insert Cells to display the Insert dialog box. In the Insert dialog box, you can choose whether to shift the cells surrounding the inserted cell down (if your data is arranged as a column) or to the right (if your data is arranged as a row). When you click OK, the new cell appears, and the contents of affected cells shift down or to the right, as appropriate. In a similar vein, if you want to delete a block of cells, select the cells, and on the Home tab, in the Cells group, in the Delete list, click Delete Cells to display the Delete dialog box—complete with options that enable you to choose how to shift the position of the cells around the deleted cells.

Tip The Insert dialog box also includes options you can click to insert a new row or column; the Delete dialog box has similar options for deleting an entire row or column.

If you want to move the data in a group of cells to another location in your worksheet, select the cells you want to move and use the mouse pointer to point to the selection's border. When the pointer changes to a four-pointed arrow, you can drag the selected cells to the desired location on the worksheet. If the destination cells contain data, Excel displays a dialog box asking whether you want to overwrite the destination cells' contents. If you want to replace the existing values, click OK. If you don't want to overwrite the existing values, click Cancel and insert the required number of cells to accommodate the data you want to move.

In this exercise, you'll insert a column and row into a worksheet, specify insert options, hide a column, insert a cell into a worksheet, delete a cell from a worksheet, and move a group of cells within the worksheet.

SET UP You need the RouteVolume_start workbook located in your Chapter08 practice file folder to complete this exercise. Open the RouteVolume_start workbook, and save it as *RouteVolume*. Then follow the steps.

1. On the **May 12** worksheet, select cell **A1**.

2. On the **Home** tab, in the **Cells** group, click the **Insert** arrow, and then in the list, click **Insert Sheet Columns**.

   A new column A appears.

3. In the **Insert** list, click **Insert Sheet Rows**.

   A new row 1 appears.

4. Click the **Insert Options** button that appears below the lower-right corner of the selected cell, and then click **Clear Formatting**.

   Excel removes the formatting from the new row 1.

5. Right-click the column header of column E, and then click **Hide**.

   Column E disappears.

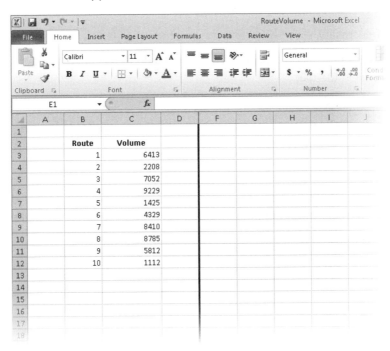

Hiding a row or column also hides the accompanying row or column header.

6. On the tab bar, click the **May 13** sheet tab.

   The worksheet named *May 13* appears.

7. Click cell **B6**.

8. On the **Home** tab, in the **Cells** group, click the **Delete** arrow, and then in the list, click **Delete Cells**.

   The Delete dialog box opens.

When deleting cells, you can specify whether to affect the column or row.

9. If necessary, click **Shift cells up**, and then click **OK**.

   The Delete dialog box closes and Excel deletes cell B6, moving the cells below it up to fill in the gap.

10. Click cell **C6**.

11. In the **Cells** group, in the **Insert** list, click **Insert Cells**.

    The Insert dialog box opens.

12. If necessary, click **Shift cells down**, and then click **OK**.

    The Insert dialog box closes, and Excel creates a new cell C6, moving cells C6:C11 down to accommodate the inserted cell.

13. In cell **C6**, type **4499**, and then press Enter.

14. Select cells **E13:F13**.

15. Point to the border of the selected cells. When your mouse pointer changes to a four-pointed arrow, drag the selected cells to cells **B13:C13**.

    The dragged cells replace cells B13:C13.

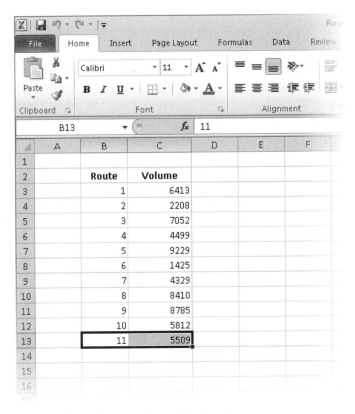

You can drag cell content to another location.

CLEAN UP Save the RouteVolume workbook, and then close it.

Customizing the Excel 2010 Program Window

How you use Excel 2010 depends on your personal working style and the type of data collections you manage. The Excel product team interviews customers, observes how differing organizations use the program, and sets up the user interface so that many users won't need to change it to work effectively. If you do want to change the Excel program window, including the user interface, you can. You can change how Excel displays your worksheets; zoom in on worksheet data; add frequently used commands to the Quick Access Toolbar; hide, display, and reorder ribbon tabs; and create custom tabs to make groups of commands readily accessible.

Zooming In on a Worksheet

One way to make Excel easier to work with is to change the program's zoom level. Just as you can "zoom in" with a camera to increase the size of an object in the camera's viewer, you can use the zoom setting to change the size of objects within the Excel 2010 program window. For example, if Peter Villadsen, the Consolidated Messenger European Distribution Center Manager, displayed a worksheet that summarized his distribution center's package volume by month, he could click the View tab and then, in the Zoom group, click the Zoom button to display the Zoom dialog box. The Zoom dialog box contains controls that he can use to select a preset magnification level or to type in a custom magnification level. He could also use the Zoom control in the lower-right corner of the Excel 2010 window.

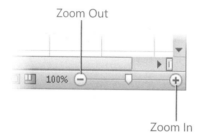

You can zoom in or out incrementally or set a specific magnification level.

Clicking the Zoom In control increases the size of items in the program window by 10 percent, whereas clicking the Zoom Out control decreases the size of items in the program window by 10 percent. If you want more fine-grained control of your zoom level, you can use the slider control to select a specific zoom level or click the magnification level indicator, which indicates the zoom percentage, and use the Zoom dialog box to set a custom magnification level.

The Zoom group on the View tab also contains the Zoom To Selection button, which fills the program window with the contents of any selected cells, up to the program's maximum zoom level of 400 percent.

Tip The minimum zoom level in Excel 2010 is 10 percent.

Arranging Multiple Workbook Windows

As you work with Excel, you will probably need to have more than one workbook open at a time. For example, you could open a workbook that contains customer contact information and copy it into another workbook to be used as the source data for a mass mailing you create in Microsoft Word 2010. When you have multiple workbooks open simultaneously, you can switch between them by clicking the View tab and then, in the Window group, clicking the Switch Windows button and clicking the name of the workbook you want to view.

You can arrange your workbooks within the Excel window so that most of the active workbook is shown but the others are easily accessible. To do so, click the View tab and then, in the Window group, click the Arrange All button. Then, in the Arrange Windows dialog box, click Cascade.

The best arrangement depends on the number and content of the open windows.

Many Excel 2010 workbooks contain formulas on one worksheet that derive their value from data on another worksheet, which means you need to change between two worksheets every time you want to see how modifying your data changes the formula's result. However, an easier way to approach this is to display two copies of the same workbook simultaneously, displaying the worksheet that contains the data in the original window and displaying the worksheet with the formula in the new window. When you change the data in either copy of the workbook, Excel updates the other copy. To display two copies of the same workbook, open the desired workbook and then, in the View tab's Window group, click New Window. Excel opens a second copy of the workbook. To display the workbooks side by side, on the View tab, in the Window group, click Arrange All. Then, in the Arrange Windows dialog box, click Vertical and then click OK.

If the original workbook's name is *Exception Summary*, Excel 2010 displays the name *Exception Summary:1* on the original workbook's title bar and *Exception Summary:2* on the second workbook's title bar.

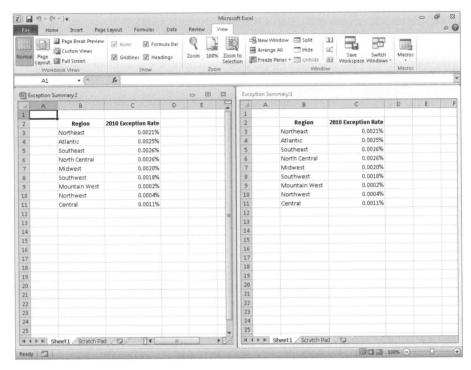

Arranging windows vertically.

Troubleshooting The appearance of buttons and groups on the ribbon changes depending on the width of the program window. For information about changing the appearance of the ribbon to match our images, see "Modifying the Display of the Ribbon" at the beginning of this book.

Adding Buttons to the Quick Access Toolbar

As you continue to work with Excel 2010, you might discover that you use certain commands much more frequently than others. If your workbooks draw data from external sources, for example, you might find yourself using the Refresh All button on the Data tab quite often than the program's designers might have expected. You can make any button accessible with one click by adding the button to the Quick Access Toolbar, located just above the ribbon.

To add a button to the Quick Access Toolbar, display the Customize The Quick Access Toolbar page of the Excel Options dialog box. This page contains two panes. The pane on the left lists all of the controls that are available within a given category, and the pane on the right lists the controls currently displayed on the Quick Access Toolbar. In the Choose Commands From list, click the category that contains the control you want to add. Excel 2010 displays the available commands in the box below the Choose Commands From field. Click the control you want, and then click the Add button.

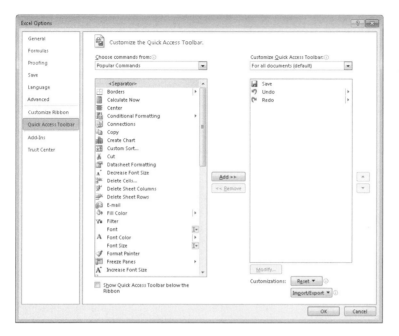

You can change a button's position on the Quick Access Toolbar by clicking its name in the right pane and then clicking either the Move Up or Move Down button at the right edge of the dialog box.

To remove a button from the Quick Access Toolbar, click the button's name in the right pane, and then click the Remove button. When you're done making your changes, click the OK button. If you prefer not to save your changes, click the Cancel button. If you saved your changes but want to return the Quick Access Toolbar to its original state, click the Reset button and then click either Reset Only Quick Access Toolbar, which removes any changes you made to the Quick Access Toolbar, or Reset All Customizations, which returns the entire ribbon interface to its original state.

You can also choose whether your Quick Access Toolbar changes affect all your work-books or just the active workbook. To control how Excel applies your change, in the Customize Quick Access Toolbar list, click either For All Documents to apply the change to all of your workbooks or For Workbook to apply the change to the active workbook only.

If you'd like to export your Quick Access Toolbar customizations to a file that can be used to apply those changes to another Excel 2010 installation, click the Import/Export button and then click Export All Customizations. Use the controls in the dialog box that opens to save your file. When you're ready to apply saved customizations to Excel, click the Import/Export button, click Import Customization File, select the file in the File Open dialog box, and click Open.

Customizing the Ribbon

Excel 2010 enhances your ability to customize the entire ribbon by enabling you to hide and display ribbon tabs, reorder tabs displayed on the ribbon, customize existing tabs (including tool tabs, which appear when specific items are selected), and to create custom tabs.

To begin customizing the ribbon, click the File tab and then click Options. In the Excel Options dialog box, click Customize Ribbon to display the Customize The Ribbon page.

The Customize The Ribbon page of the Excel Options dialog box.

To select which tabs appear in the tabs pane on the right side of the screen, click the Customize The Ribbon field's arrow and then click either Main Tabs, which displays the tabs that can appear on the standard ribbon; Tool Tabs, which displays the tabs that appear when you click an item such as a drawing object or PivotTable; or All Tabs.

Tip The procedures taught in this section apply to both the main tabs and the tool tabs.

Each ribbon tab's name has a check box next to it. If a tab's box is selected, then that tab appears on the ribbon. You can hide a tab by clearing the check box and bring it back by selecting the check box. You can also change the order in which the tabs are displayed on the ribbon. To do so, click the name of the tab you want to move and then click the Move Up or Move Down arrows to reposition the selected tab.

Just as you can change the order of the tabs on the ribbon, you can change the order of groups on a tab. For example, the Page Layout tab contains five groups: Themes, Page Setup, Scale To Fit, Sheet Options, and Arrange. If you use the Themes group infrequently, you could move the group to the right end of the tab by clicking the group's name and then clicking the Move Down button until the group appears in the desired position.

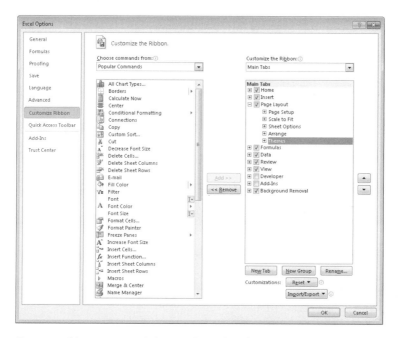

You can add, remove, and change the order of groups on a tab.

To remove a group from a built-in ribbon tab, click the name of the group in the right pane and click the Remove button. If you remove a group from a built-in tab and later decide you want to put it back on the tab, display the tab in the right pane. Then, click the Choose Commands From field's arrow and click Main Tabs. With the tab displayed, in the left pane, click the expand control (which looks like a plus sign) next to the name of the tab that contains the group you want to add back. You can now click the name of the group in the left pane and click the Add button to put the group back on the selected ribbon tab.

The built-in ribbon tabs are designed efficiently, so adding new command groups might crowd the other items on the tab and make those controls harder to find. Rather than adding controls to an existing ribbon tab, you can create a custom tab and then add groups and commands to it. To create a custom ribbon tab, click the New Tab button on the Customize The Ribbon page of the Excel Options dialog box. When you do, a new tab named New Tab (Custom), which contains a group named New Group (Custom), appears in the tab list.

You can add an existing group to your new ribbon tab by clicking the Choose Commands From field's arrow, selecting a collection of commands, clicking the group you want to add, and then clicking the Add button. You can also add individual commands to your ribbon tab by clicking a command in the command list and clicking the Add button. To add a command to your tab's custom group, click the new group in the right tab list, click the command in the left list, and then click the Add button. If you want to add another custom group to your new tab, click the new tab, or any of the groups within that tab, and then click New Group.

The New Tab (Custom) name doesn't tell you anything about the commands on your new ribbon tab, so you can rename it to reflect its contents. To rename any tab on the ribbon, display the Customize The Ribbon page of the Excel Options dialog box, click the tab you want to modify, and then click the Rename button. Type the tab's new name in the Rename dialog box, and click OK. To rename any group on the ribbon, click the name of the group, and then click Rename. When you do, a different version of the Rename dialog box appears. Click the symbol that you want to use to represent the group on the ribbon, type a new name for the group in the Display Name box, and click OK.

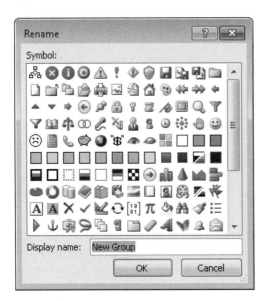

You can select a symbol to represent a group of commands on the ribbon.

If you'd like to export your ribbon customizations to a file that can be used to apply those changes to another Excel 2010 installation, click the Import/Export button and then click Export All Customizations. Use the controls in the dialog box that opens to save your file. When you're ready to apply saved customizations to Excel, click the Import/Export button, click Import Customization File, select the file in the File Open dialog box, and click Open.

When you're done customizing the ribbon, click the OK button to save your changes or click Cancel to keep the user interface as it was before you started this round of changes. You can also change a ribbon tab, or the entire ribbon, back to the state it was in when you installed Excel. To restore a single ribbon tab, click the tab you want to restore, click the Reset button, and then click Reset Only Selected Ribbon Tab. To restore the entire ribbon, including the Quick Access Toolbar, click the Reset button and then click Reset All Customizations.

Maximizing Usable Space in the Program Window

You can increase the amount of space available inside the program window by hiding the ribbon, the formula bar, or the row and column labels.

To hide the ribbon, double-click the active tab label. The tab labels remain visible at the top of the program window, but the tab content is hidden. To temporarily redisplay the ribbon, click the tab label you want. Then click any button on the tab, or click away from the tab, to rehide it. To permanently redisplay the ribbon, double-click any tab label.

Keyboard Shortcut Press Ctrl+F1 to hide and unhide the ribbon.

To hide the formula bar, clear the Formula Bar check box in the Show/Hide group on the View tab. To hide the row and column labels, clear the Headings check box in the Show/Hide group on the View tab.

In this exercise, you'll change your worksheet's zoom level, zoom in to emphasize a selected cell range, switch between multiple open workbooks, cascade multiple open workbooks within the Excel program window, add a button to the Quick Access Toolbar, and customize the ribbon.

SET UP You need the PackageCounts_start and MisroutedPackages_start workbooks located in your Chapter08 practice file folder to complete this exercise. Open the PackageCounts_start and MisroutedPackages_start workbooks, and save them as *PackageCounts* and *MisroutedPackages*, respectively. Then follow the steps.

1. In the **MisroutedPackages** workbook, in the lower-right corner of the Excel 2010 window, click the **Zoom In** control five times.

   The worksheet's zoom level changes to 150%.

2. Select cells **B2:C11**.

3. On the **View** tab, in the **Zoom** group, click the **Zoom to Selection** button.

   Excel displays the selected cells so they fill the program window.

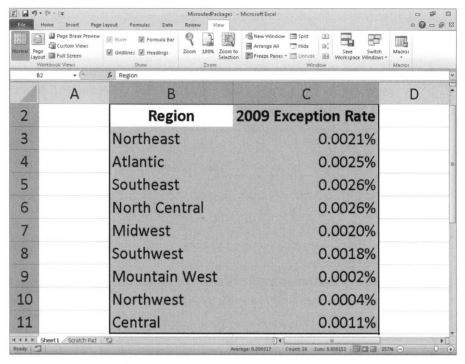

Magnifying selected cells.

4. On the **View** tab, in the **Zoom** group, click the **Zoom** button.

   The Zoom dialog box opens.

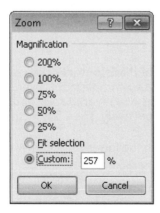

You can select a preset magnification level or enter a custom magnification level.

5. Click **100%**, and then click **OK**.

   The worksheet returns to its default zoom level.

6. On the **View** tab, in the **Window** group, click the **Switch Windows** button, and then click **PackageCounts**.

   The PackageCounts workbook opens.

7. On the **View** tab, in the **Window** group, click the **Arrange All** button.

   The Arrange Windows dialog box opens.

8. Click **Cascade**, and then click **OK**.

   Excel cascades the open workbook windows within the program window.

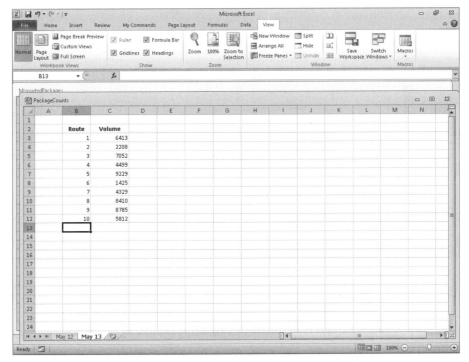

Switch among cascaded windows by clicking the visible part of a window frame.

9. Click the **File** tab, and then click **Options**.

   The Excel Options dialog box opens.

10. Click **Quick Access Toolbar**.

   The Customize The Quick Access Toolbar page opens.

11. Click the **Choose commands from** arrow, and then in the list, click **Review Tab**.

   The commands in the Review Tab category appear in the command list.

12. Click the **Spelling** command, and then click **Add**.

   Excel adds the Spelling command to the Quick Access Toolbar.

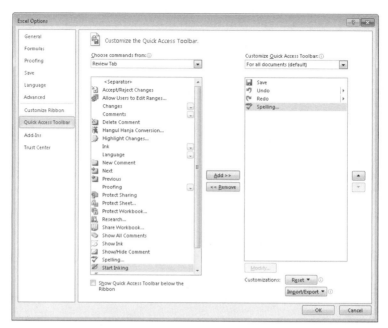

Adding commands to the Quick Access Toolbar.

13. Click **Customize Ribbon**.

    The Customize The Ribbon page of the Excel Options dialog box appears.

14. If necessary, click the **Customize the Ribbon** box's arrow and click **Main Tabs**. In the right tab list, click the **Review** tab and then click the **Move Up** button three times.

    Excel moves the Review tab between the Insert and Page Layout tabs.

15. Click the **New Tab** button.

    A tab named New Tab (Custom) appears below the most recently active tab in the Main Tabs list.

16. Click the **New Tab (Custom)** tab name, click the **Rename** button, type **My Commands** in the **Display Name** box, and click **OK**.

    The new tab's name changes to My Commands.

17. Click the **New Group (Custom)** group and then click **Rename**. In the **Rename** dialog box, click the icon that looks like a paint palette (second row, fourth from the right). Then type **Formatting** in the **Display name** box, and click **OK**.

    The new group's name changes to Formatting.

18. In the right tab list, click the **My Commands** tab name. Then, on the left side of the dialog box, click the **Choose Commands From** box's arrow and click **Main Tabs**.

    The Main Tabs group of ribbon tabs appears in the left tab list.

19. In the left tab list, click the **Home** tab's expand control, click the **Styles** group's name, and then click the **Add** button.

    The Styles group is added to the My Commands tab.

20. In the left tab list, under the **Home** tab, click the **Number** group's expand control.

    The commands in the Number group appear.

21. In the right tab list, click the **Formatting** group you created earlier. Then, in the left tab list, click the **Number Format** item and click the **Add** button.

    Excel 2010 adds the Number Format item to the Formatting custom group.

22. Click **OK** to save your ribbon customizations, and then click the **My Commands** tab on the ribbon.

Your custom tab.

> **Important** The remaining exercises in this book assume you are using Excel 2010 as it was installed on your computer.

 CLEAN UP Reset the ribbon to its original configuration, and then save and close all open workbooks. If you are not continuing directly to the next chapter, exit Excel.

Key Points

- Save your work whenever you do something you'd hate to have to do again.

- Assigning values to a workbook's properties makes it easier to find your workbook using the Windows search facility.

- Be sure to give your worksheets descriptive names.

- If you want to use a worksheet's data in another workbook, you can send a copy of the worksheet to that other workbook without deleting the original worksheet.

- You can delete a worksheet you no longer need, but you can also hide a worksheet in the workbook. When you need the data on the worksheet, you can unhide it.

- You can save yourself a lot of bothersome cutting and pasting by inserting and deleting worksheet cells, columns, and rows.

- Customize your Excel 2010 program window by changing how it displays your workbooks, zooming in on data, adding frequently used buttons to the Quick Access Toolbar, and rearranging or customizing the ribbon to meet your needs.

Chapter at a Glance

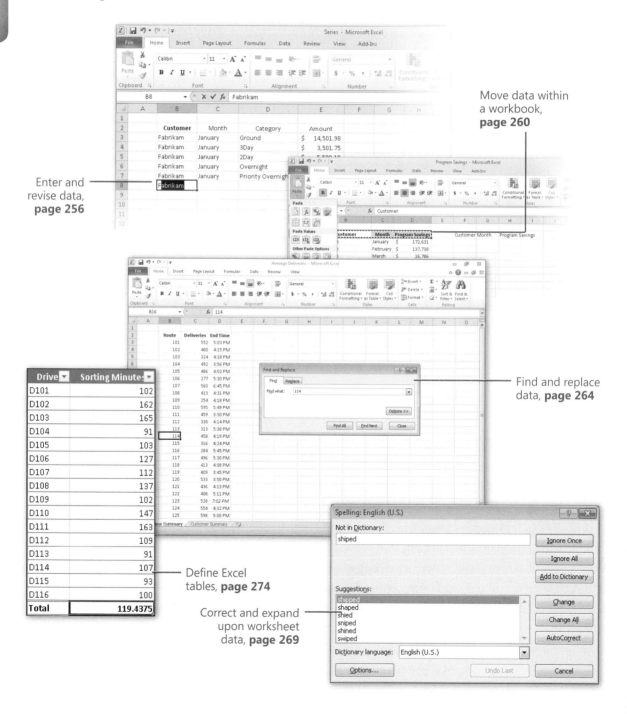

Move data within a workbook, **page 260**

Enter and revise data, **page 256**

Find and replace data, **page 264**

Define Excel tables, **page 274**

Correct and expand upon worksheet data, **page 269**

9 Work with Data and Excel Tables

In this chapter, you will learn how to

- ✔ Enter and revise data.
- ✔ Move data within a workbook.
- ✔ Find and replace data.
- ✔ Correct and expand upon worksheet data.
- ✔ Define Excel tables.

With Microsoft Excel 2010, you can visualize and present information effectively by using charts, graphics, and formatting, but the data is the most important part of any workbook. By learning to enter data efficiently, you will make fewer data entry errors and give yourself more time to analyze your data so you can make decisions about your organization's performance and direction.

Excel provides a wide variety of tools you can use to enter and manage worksheet data effectively. For example, you can organize your data into Excel tables, which enables you to store and analyze your data quickly and efficiently. Also, you can enter a data series quickly, repeat one or more values, and control how Excel formats cells, columns, and rows moved from one part of a worksheet to another with a minimum of effort. With Excel, you can check the spelling of worksheet text, look up alternative words by using the Thesaurus, and translate words to foreign languages.

In this chapter, you'll learn how to enter and revise Excel data, move data within a workbook, find and replace existing data, use proofing and reference tools to enhance your data, and organize your data by using Excel tables.

> **Practice Files** Before you can complete the exercises in this chapter, you need to copy the book's practice files to your computer. The practice files you'll use to complete the exercises in this chapter are in the Chapter09 practice file folder. A complete list of practice files is provided in "Using the Practice Files" at the beginning of this book.

Entering and Revising Data

After you create a workbook, you can begin entering data. The simplest way to enter data is to click a cell and type a value. This method works very well when you're entering a few pieces of data, but it is less than ideal when you're entering long sequences or series of values. For example, Craig Dewar, the Vice President of Marketing for Consolidated Messenger, might want to create a worksheet listing the monthly program savings that large customers can realize if they sign exclusive delivery contracts with Consolidated Messenger. To record those numbers, he would need to create a worksheet tracking each customer's monthly program savings.

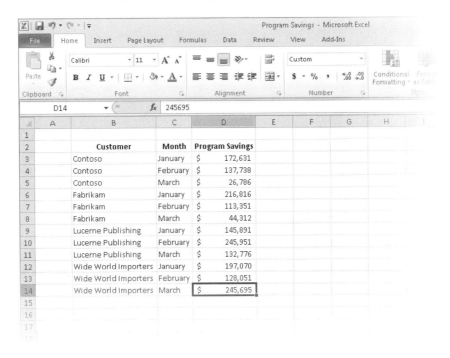

The process of entering repeated content can be simplified by using the AutoFill option.

Repeatedly entering the sequence January, February, March, and so on can be handled by copying and pasting the first occurrence of the sequence, but there's an easier way to do it: use AutoFill. With AutoFill, you enter the first element in a recognized series, click and hold the mouse button down on the fill handle at the lower-right corner of the cell, and drag the fill handle until the series extends far enough to accommodate your data. Using a similar tool, FillSeries, you can enter two values in a series and use the fill handle to extend the series in your worksheet. For example, if you want to create a series starting at 2 and increasing by 2, you can put 2 in the first cell and 4 in the second cell, select both cells, and then use the fill handle to extend the series to your desired end value.

You do have some control over how Excel extends the values in a series when you drag the fill handle. For example, if you drag the fill handle up (or to the left), Excel extends the series to include previous values. If you type *January* in a cell and then drag that cell's fill handle up (or to the left), Excel places *December* in the first cell, *November* in the second cell, and so on.

Another way to control how Excel extends a data series is by holding down the Ctrl key while you drag the fill handle. For example, if you select a cell that contains the value *January* and then drag the fill handle down, Excel extends the series by placing *February* in the next cell, *March* in the cell after that, and so on. If you hold down the Ctrl key while you drag the fill handle, however, Excel repeats the value *January* in each cell you add to the series.

Tip Be sure to experiment with how the fill handle extends your series and how pressing the Ctrl key changes that behavior. Using the fill handle can save you a lot of time entering data.

Other data entry techniques you'll use in this section are AutoComplete, which detects when a value you're entering is similar to previously entered values; Pick From Drop-Down List, from which you can choose a value from among the existing values in a column; and Ctrl+Enter, which you can use to enter a value in multiple cells simultaneously.

Troubleshooting If an AutoComplete suggestion doesn't appear as you begin typing a cell value, the option might be turned off. To turn on AutoComplete, click the File tab, and then click Options. In the Excel Options dialog box, display the Advanced page. In the Editing Options area of the page, select the Enable AutoComplete For Cell Values check box, and then click OK.

The following table summarizes these data entry techniques.

Method	Action
AutoFill	Enter the first value in a recognized series and use the fill handle to extend the series.
FillSeries	Enter the first two values in a series and use the fill handle to extend the series.
AutoComplete	Type the first few letters in a cell, and if a similar value exists in the same column, Excel suggests the existing value.
Pick From Drop-Down List	Right-click a cell, and then click Pick From Drop-Down List. A list of existing values in the cell's column is displayed. Click the value you want to enter into the cell.
Ctrl+Enter	Select a range of cells, each of which you want to contain the same data, type the data in the active cell, and press Ctrl+Enter.

Another handy feature in Excel is the AutoFill Options button that appears next to data you add to a worksheet by using the fill handle.

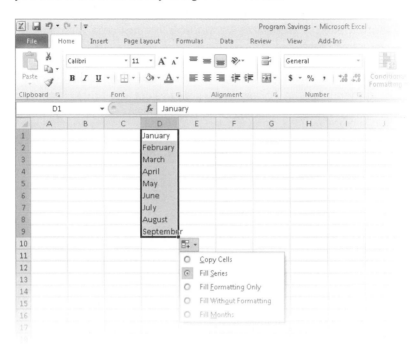

The AutoFill options allow you to specify the manner in which Excel fills a range of cells.

Clicking the AutoFill Options button displays a list of actions Excel can take regarding the cells affected by your fill operation. The options in the list are summarized in the following table.

Option	Action
Copy Cells	This copies the contents of the selected cells to the cells indicated by the fill operation.
Fill Series	This action fills the cells indicated by the fill operation with the next items in the series.
Fill Formatting Only	This copies the format of the selected cell to the cells indicated by the fill operation, but does not place any values in the target cells.
Fill Without Formatting	This action fills the cells indicated by the fill operation with the next items in the series, but ignores any formatting applied to the source cells.
Fill Days, Weekdays, and so on	The appearance of this option changes according to the series you extend. For example, if you extend the values *Wed*, *Thu*, and *Fri*, Excel presents two options, Fill Days and Fill Weekdays, and you can select the one you want. If you do not use a recognized sequence, this option does not appear.

In this exercise, you'll enter data by using multiple methods and control how Excel formats an extended data series.

SET UP You need the Series_start workbook located in your Chapter09 practice file folder to complete this exercise. Start Excel, open the Series_start workbook, and save it as *Series*. Then follow the steps.

1. On the **Monthly** worksheet, select cell **B3**, and then drag the fill handle down until it covers cells **B3:B7**.

   Excel repeats the value *Fabrikam* in cells B4:B7.

2. Select cell **C3**, hold down the Ctrl key, and drag the fill handle down until it covers cells **C3:C7**.

   Excel repeats the value *January* in cells C4:C7.

3. Select cell **B8**, and then type the letter **F**.

   Excel displays the characters *abrikam* in reverse colors.

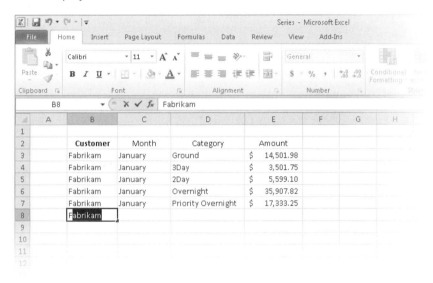

Excel suggests completed words based on those already present in the worksheet.

4. Press Tab to accept the value *Fabrikam* for the cell.

5. In cell **C8**, type **February**.

6. Right-click cell **D8**, and then click **Pick From Drop-down List**.

   A list of values in column D appears below cell D8.

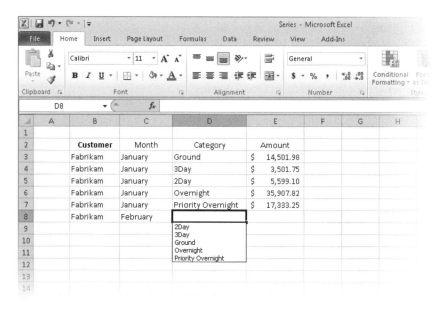

You can restrict cell entries by defining them in a drop-down list.

7. From the list, click **2Day**.

8. In cell **E8**, type **11802.14**, and then press Tab or Enter.

9. Select cell **B2**, and then drag the fill handle so that it covers cells **C2:E2**.

   Excel replaces the values in cells C2:E2 with the value *Customer*.

 10. Click the **AutoFill Options** button, and then click **Fill Formatting Only**.

   Excel restores the original values in cells C2:E2 but applies the formatting of cell B2 to those cells.

CLEAN UP Save the Series workbook, and then close it.

Moving Data Within a Workbook

You can move to a specific cell in lots of ways, but the most direct method is to click the desired cell. The cell you click will be outlined in black, and its contents, if any, will appear in the formula bar. When a cell is outlined, it is the active cell, meaning that you can modify its contents. You use a similar method to select multiple cells (referred to as a cell range)—just click the first cell in the range, hold down the left mouse button, and drag the mouse pointer over the remaining cells you want to select. After you select the cell or cells you want to work with, you can cut, copy, delete, or change the format of the contents of the cell or cells. For instance, Gregory Weber, the Northwest Distribution

Center Manager for Consolidated Messenger, might want to copy the cells that contain a set of column labels to a new page that summarizes similar data.

Important If you select a group of cells, the first cell you click is designated as the active cell.

You're not limited to selecting cells individually or as part of a range. For example, you might need to move a column of price data one column to the right to make room for a column of headings that indicate to which service category (ground, three-day express, two-day express, overnight, or priority overnight) a set of numbers belongs. To move an entire column (or entire columns) of data at a time, you click the column's header, located at the top of the worksheet. Clicking a column header highlights every cell in that column and enables you to copy or cut the column and paste it elsewhere in the workbook. Similarly, clicking a row's header highlights every cell in that row, enabling you to copy or cut the row and paste it elsewhere in the workbook.

When you copy a cell, cell range, row, or column, Excel copies the cells' contents and formatting. In previous versions of Excel, you would paste the cut or copied items and then click the Paste Options button to select which aspects of the cut or copied cells to paste into the target cells. The problem with using the Paste Options button was that there was no way to tell what your pasted data would look like until you completed the paste operation. If you didn't like the way the pasted data looked, you had to click the Paste Options button again and try another option.

With the new Paste Live Preview capability in Excel, you can see what your pasted data will look like without committing to the paste operation. To preview your data using Paste Live Preview, cut or copy worksheet data and then, on the Home tab of the ribbon, in the Clipboard group, click the Paste button's arrow to display the Paste gallery, and point to one of the icons. When you do,

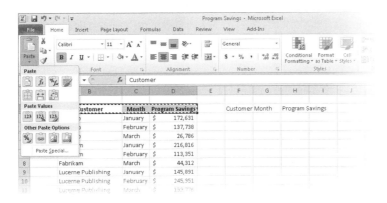

Excel displays a preview of how your data will appear if you click the paste option you're pointing to.

If you position your mouse pointer over one icon in the Paste gallery and then move it over another icon without clicking, Excel will update the preview to reflect the new option. Depending on the cells' contents, two or more of the paste options might lead to the same result.

Troubleshooting If pointing to an icon in the Paste gallery doesn't result in a live preview, that option might be turned off. To turn Paste Live Preview on, click the File tab and click Options to display the Excel Options dialog box. Click General, select the Enable Live Preview check box, and click OK.

After you click an icon to complete the paste operation, Excel displays the Paste Options button next to the pasted cells. Clicking the Paste Options button displays the Paste Options palette as well, but pointing to one of those icons doesn't generate a preview. If you want to display Paste Live Preview again, you will need to press Ctrl+Z to undo the paste operation and, if necessary, cut or copy the data again to use the icons in the Home tab's Clipboard group.

Troubleshooting If the Paste Options button doesn't appear, you can turn the feature on by clicking the File tab and then clicking Options to display the Excel Options dialog box. In the Excel Options dialog box, display the Advanced page and then, in the Cut, Copy, And Paste area, select the Show Paste Options Buttons When Content Is Pasted check box. Click OK to close the dialog box and save your setting.

After cutting or copying data to the Clipboard, you can access additional paste options from the Paste gallery and from the Paste Special dialog box, which you display by clicking Paste Special at the bottom of the Paste gallery.

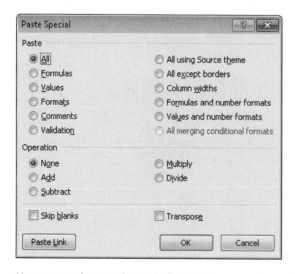

You can conduct mathematical operations on cut or copied content when you paste it into another location.

In the Paste Special dialog box, you can specify the aspect of the Clipboard contents you want to paste, restricting the pasted data to values, formats, comments, or one of several other options. You can perform mathematical operations involving the cut or copied data and the existing data in the cells you paste the content into. You can transpose data—change rows to columns and columns to rows—when you paste it, by clicking Transpose in the Paste gallery or by selecting the Transpose check box in the Paste Special dialog box.

In this exercise, you'll copy a set of data headers to another worksheet, move a column of data within a worksheet, and use Paste Live Preview to control the appearance of copied data.

 SET UP You need the 2010Q1ShipmentsByCategory_start workbook located in your Chapter09 practice file folder to complete this exercise. Open the 2010Q1ShipmentsByCategory_start workbook, and save it as *2010Q1ShipmentsByCategory*. Then follow the steps.

1. On the **Count** worksheet, select cells **B2:D2**.

2. On the **Home** tab, in the **Clipboard** group, click the **Copy** button.

    Excel copies the contents of cells B2:D2 to the Clipboard.

    Keyboard Shortcut Press Ctrl+C to copy worksheet contents to the Clipboard.

3. On the tab bar, click the **Sales** tab to display that worksheet.

4. Select cell **B2**.

5. On the **Home** tab, in the **Clipboard** group, click the **Paste** button's arrow, point to the first icon in the **Paste** group, and then click the **Keep Source Formatting** icon (the final icon in the first row of the **Paste** gallery.)

    Excel displays how the data would look if you pasted the copied values without formatting, and then pastes the header values into cells B2:D2, retaining the original cells' formatting.

6. Right-click the column header of column **I**, and then click **Cut**.

    Excel outlines column I with a marquee.

7. Right-click the header of column **E**, and then, under **Paste Options**, click **Paste**.

Excel pastes the contents of column I into column E.

Keyboard Shortcut Press Ctrl+V to paste worksheet contents exactly as they appear in the original cell.

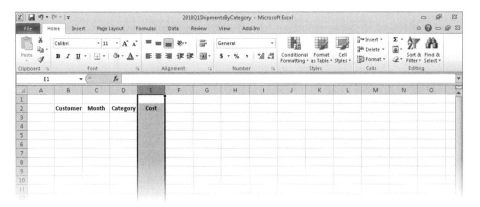

Cutting and pasting a column removes the column from its original location.

Troubleshooting The appearance of buttons and groups on the ribbon changes depending on the width of the program window. For information about changing the appearance of the ribbon to match our screen images, see "Modifying the Display of the Ribbon" at the beginning of this book.

 CLEAN UP Save the 2010Q1ShipmentsByCategory workbook, and then close it.

Finding and Replacing Data

Excel worksheets can hold more than one million rows of data, so in large data collections it's unlikely that you would have the time to move through a worksheet one row at a time to locate the data you want to find. You can locate specific data in an Excel worksheet by using the Find And Replace dialog box, which has two pages (one named *Find*, the other named *Replace*) that you can use to search for cells that contain particular values. Using the controls on the Find page identifies cells that contain the data you specify; using the controls on the Replace page, you can substitute one value for another. For example, if one of Consolidated Messenger's customers changes its company name, you can change every instance of the old name to the new name by using the Replace functionality.

When you need more control over the data that you find and replace, for instance, if you want to find cells in which the entire cell value matches the value you're searching for, you can click the Options button to expand the Find And Replace dialog box.

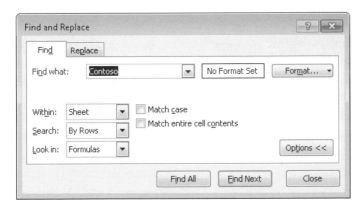

You can limit your search to the current worksheet or expand it to include all worksheets in the workbook.

One way you can use the extra options in the Find And Replace dialog box is to use a specific format to identify data that requires review. As an example, Consolidated Messenger's Vice President of Marketing, Craig Dewar, could make corporate sales plans based on a projected budget for the next year and mark his trial figures using a specific format. After the executive board finalizes the numbers, he could use the Find Format capability in the Find And Replace dialog box to locate the old values and change them by hand.

The following table summarizes the Find And Replace dialog box controls' functions.

Control	Function
Find What field	Contains the value you want to find or replace
Find All button	Selects every cell that contains the value in the Find What field
Find Next button	Selects the next cell that contains the value in the Find What field
Replace With field	Contains the value to overwrite the value in the Find What field
Replace All button	Replaces every instance of the value in the Find What field with the value in the Replace With field
Replace button	Replaces the highlighted occurrence of the value in the Find What field and highlights the next cell that contains that value
Options button	Expands the Find And Replace dialog box to display additional capabilities

(continued)

Control	Function
Format button	Displays the Find Format dialog box, which you can use to specify the format of values to be found or values to be replaced
Within box	Enables you to select whether to search the active worksheet or the entire workbook
Search box	Enables you to select whether to search by rows or by columns
Look In box	Enables you to select whether to search cell formulas or values
Match Case check box	When checked, requires that all matches have the same capitalization as the text in the Find What field (for example, *cat* doesn't match *Cat*)
Match Entire Cell Contents check box	Requires that the cell contain exactly the same value as in the Find What field (for example, *Cat* doesn't match *Catherine*)
Close button	Closes the Find And Replace dialog box

To change a value by hand, select the cell, and then either type a new value in the cell or, in the formula bar, select the value you want to replace and type the new value. You can also double-click a cell and edit its contents within the cell.

In this exercise, you'll find a specific value in a worksheet, replace every occurrence of a company name in a worksheet, and find a cell with a particular formatting.

 SET UP You need the AverageDeliveries_start workbook located in your Chapter09 practice file folder to complete this exercise. Open the AverageDeliveries_start workbook, and save it as *AverageDeliveries*. Then follow the steps.

1. If necessary, click the **Time Summary** sheet tab.

   The Time Summary worksheet is displayed.

2. On the **Home** tab, in the **Editing** group, click **Find & Select**, and then click **Find**.

   The Find And Replace dialog box opens with the Find tab displayed.

   Keyboard Shortcut   Press Ctrl+F to display the Find tab of the Find And Replace dialog box.

Find & Select ▾

3. In the **Find what** field, type **114**.

4. Click **Find Next**.

Excel highlights cell B16, which contains the value *114*.

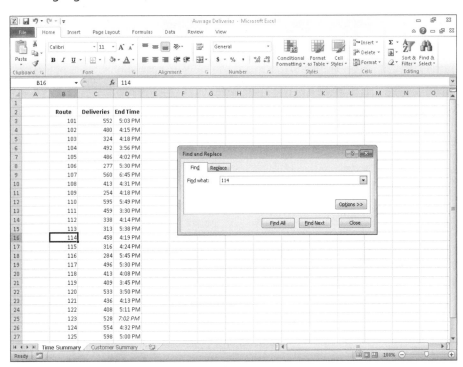

You can conduct a simple text search, or expand the dialog box and select other options.

5. Delete the value in the **Find what** field, and then click the **Options** button.

   The Find And Replace dialog box expands to display additional search options.

6. Click **Format**.

   The Find Format dialog box opens.

7. Click the **Font** tab.

   The Font page is displayed.

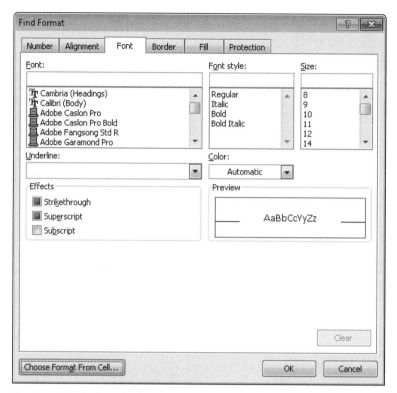

The Font list displays the fonts that are installed on your computer.

8. In the **Font style** list, click **Italic**.

9. Click **OK**.

   The Find Format dialog box closes.

10. Click **Find Next**.

    Excel highlights cell D25.

11. Click **Close**.

    The Find And Replace dialog box closes.

12. On the tab bar, click the **Customer Summary** sheet tab.

    The Customer Summary worksheet is displayed.

13. On the **Home** tab, in the **Editing** group, click **Find & Select**, and then click **Replace**.

    The Find And Replace dialog box opens with the Replace tab displayed.

    Keyboard Shortcut Press Ctrl+H to display the Replace tab of the Find And Replace dialog box.

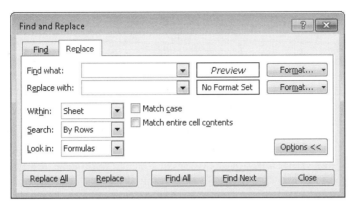

You can replace text, formatting, and formula elements.

14. Click the **Format** arrow to the right of the **Find what** field, and then in the list, click **Clear Find Format**.

    The format displayed next to the Find What field disappears.

15. In the **Find what** field, type **Contoso**.

16. In the **Replace with** field, type **Northwind Traders**.

17. Click **Replace All**.

    A message box appears, indicating that Excel made three replacements.

18. Click **OK** to close the message box.

19. Click **Close**.

    The Find And Replace dialog box closes.

 CLEAN UP Save the AverageDeliveries workbook, and then close it.

Correcting and Expanding Upon Worksheet Data

After you enter your data, you should take the time to check and correct it. You do need to verify visually that each piece of numeric data is correct, but you can make sure that your worksheet's text is spelled correctly by using the Excel spelling checker. When the spelling checker encounters a word it doesn't recognize, it highlights the word and offers suggestions representing its best guess of the correct word. You can then edit the word directly, pick the proper word from the list of suggestions, or have the spelling checker ignore the misspelling. You can also use the spelling checker to add new words to a custom dictionary so that Excel will recognize them later, saving you time by not requiring you to identify the words as correct every time they occur in your worksheets.

Tip After you make a change in a workbook, you can usually remove the change as long as you haven't closed the workbook. To undo a change, click the Undo button on the Quick Access Toolbar. If you decide you want to keep a change, you can use the Redo command to restore it.

If you're not sure of your word choice, or if you use a word that is almost but not quite right for your intended meaning, you can check for alternative words by using the Thesaurus. Several other research tools are also available, such as the Bing decision engine and the Microsoft Encarta dictionary, to which you can refer as you create your workbooks. To display those tools, on the Review tab, in the Proofing group, click Research to display the Research task pane.

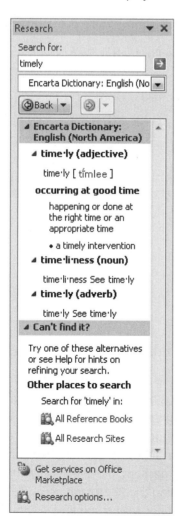

You can choose a research resource from the list in the top section of the Research task pane.

Finally, if you want to translate a word from one language to another, you can do so by selecting the cell that contains the value you want to translate, displaying the Review tab, and then, in the Language group, clicking Translate. The Research task pane opens (or changes if it's already open) and displays controls you can use to select the original and destination languages.

You can translate words and phrases into many different languages.

Important Excel translates a sentence by using word substitutions, which means that the translation routine doesn't always pick the best word for a given context. The translated sentence might not capture your exact meaning.

In this exercise, you'll check a worksheet's spelling, add terms to a dictionary, search the Thesaurus for an alternative word, and translate a word from English into French.

 SET UP You need the ServiceLevels_start workbook located in your Chapter09 practice file folder to complete this exercise. Open the ServiceLevels_start workbook, and save it as *ServiceLevels*. Then follow the steps.

1. On the **Review** tab, in the **Proofing** group, click **Spelling**.

   The Spelling dialog box opens.

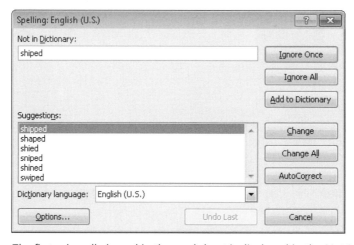

The first misspelled word in the worksheet is displayed in the Not In Dictionary field.

2. Verify that the word *shipped* is highlighted in the **Suggestions** pane, and then click **Change**.

   Excel corrects the word and displays the next questioned word: *withn*.

3. Click **Change**.

   Excel corrects the word and displays the next questioned word: *TwoDay*.

4. Click **Add to Dictionary**.

   Excel adds the word to the dictionary and displays the next questioned word: *ThreeDay*.

5. Click **Add to Dictionary**.

   Excel adds the word to the dictionary.

6. In the **Spelling** dialog box, click **Close**.

   A message box indicates that the spelling check is complete.

7. Click **OK** to close the message box.

8. Click cell **B6**.

9. On the **Review** tab, in the **Proofing** group, click **Thesaurus**.

The Research task pane opens.

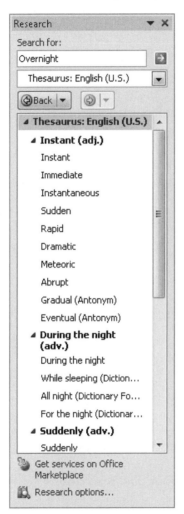

The Thesaurus displays synonyms for the word Overnight.

10. On the **Review** tab, in the **Language** group, click **Translate**.

The Research task pane displays the translation tools.

11. If necessary, in the **From** list, click **English (U.S.).**

12. In the **To** list, click **French (France).**

The Research task pane displays French words that mean *overnight.*

You can translate the same word into another language by choosing one from the To list.

 CLEAN UP Save the ServiceLevels workbook, and then close it.

Defining Excel Tables

With Excel, you've always been able to manage lists of data effectively, enabling you to sort your worksheet data based on the values in one or more columns, limit the data displayed by using criteria (for example, show only those routes with fewer than 100 stops), and create formulas that summarize the values in visible (that is, unfiltered) cells. In Excel 2007, the Excel product team extended your ability to manage your data by introducing Excel tables. Excel 2010 offers you the same capability.

Customer ▾	Month ▾	Program Savings ▾
Contoso	January	$ 172,631
Contoso	February	$ 137,738
Contoso	March	$ 26,786
Fabrikam	January	$ 216,816
Fabrikam	February	$ 113,351
Fabrikam	March	$ 44,312
Lucerne Publishing	January	$ 145,891
Lucerne Publishing	February	$ 245,951
Lucerne Publishing	March	$ 132,776
Wide World Importers	January	$ 197,070
Wide World Importers	February	$ 128,051
Wide World Importers	March	$ 245,695

Converting a data range to an Excel table provides many data-management capabilities.

To create an Excel table, type a series of column headers in adjacent cells, and then type a row of data below the headers. Click any header or data cell into which you just typed, and then, on the Home tab, in the Styles group, click Format As Table. In the gallery that opens, click the table style you want to apply. In the Format As Table dialog box, verify that the cells in the Where Is The Data For Your Table? field reflect your current selection and that the My Table Has Headers check box is selected, and then click OK.

Excel can also create an Excel table from an existing cell range as long as the range has no blank rows or columns within the data and there is no extraneous data in cells immediately below or next to the list. To create the Excel table, click any cell in the range and then, on the Home tab, in the Styles group, click the Format As Table button and select a table style. If your existing data has formatting applied to it, that formatting remains applied to those cells when you create the Excel table. If you want Excel to replace the existing formatting with the Excel table's formatting, right-click the table style you want to apply and then click Apply And Clear Formatting.

When you want to add data to an Excel table, click the rightmost cell in the bottom row of the Excel table and press the Tab key to create a new row. You can also select a cell in the row immediately below the last row in the table or a cell in the column immediately to the right of the table and type a value into the cell. After you enter the value and move out of the cell, the AutoCorrect Options action button appears. If you didn't mean to include the data in the Excel table, you can click Undo Table AutoExpansion to exclude the cells from the Excel table. If you never want Excel to include adjacent data in an Excel table again, click Stop Automatically Expanding Tables.

Tip To stop Table AutoExpansion before it starts, click the File tab, and then click Options. In the Excel Options dialog box, click Proofing, and then click the AutoCorrect Options button to display the AutoCorrect dialog box. Click the AutoFormat As You Type tab, clear the Include New Rows And Columns In Table check box, and then click OK twice.

You can add rows and columns to an Excel table, or remove them from an Excel table without deleting the cells' contents, by dragging the resize handle at the Excel table's lower-right corner. If your Excel table's headers contain a recognizable series of values (such as *Region1*, *Region2*, and *Region3*), and you drag the resize handle to create a fourth column, Excel creates the column with the label *Region4*—the next value in the series.

Excel tables often contain data you can summarize by calculating a sum or average, or by finding the maximum or minimum value in a column. To summarize one or more columns of data, you can add a Total row to your Excel table.

Customer	Month	Program Savings
Contoso	January	$ 172,631
Contoso	February	$ 137,738
Contoso	March	$ 26,786
Fabrikam	January	$ 216,816
Fabrikam	February	$ 113,351
Fabrikam	March	$ 44,312
Lucerne Publishing	January	$ 145,891
Lucerne Publishing	February	$ 245,951
Lucerne Publishing	March	$ 132,776
Wide World Importers	January	$ 197,070
Wide World Importers	February	$ 128,051
Wide World Importers	March	$ 245,695
Total		$ 1,807,068

The Total row automatically calculates the total of the preceding values.

When you add the Total row, Excel creates a formula that summarizes the values in the rightmost Excel table column. To change that summary operation, or to add a summary operation to any other cell in the Total row, click the cell, click the arrow that appears, and then click the summary operation you want to apply. Clicking the More Functions menu item displays the Insert Function dialog box, from which you can select any of the functions available in Excel.

Much as it does when you create a new worksheet, Excel gives your Excel tables generic names such as *Table1* and *Table2*. You can change an Excel table's name to something easier to recognize by clicking any cell in the table, clicking the Design contextual tab, and then, in the Properties group, editing the value in the Table Name box. Changing an Excel table name might not seem important, but it helps make formulas that summarize Excel table data much easier to understand. You should make a habit of renaming your Excel tables so you can recognize the data they contain.

See Also For more information about using the Insert Function dialog box and about referring to tables in formulas, see "Creating Formulas to Calculate Values" in Chapter 10, "Perform Calculations on Data."

If for any reason you want to convert your Excel table back to a normal range of cells, click any cell in the Excel table and then, on the Design contextual tab, in the Tools group, click Convert To Range. When Excel displays a message box asking if you're sure you want to convert the table to a range, click OK.

In this exercise, you'll create an Excel table from existing data, add data to an Excel table, add a Total row, change the Total row's summary operation, and rename the Excel table.

 SET UP You need the DriverSortTimes_start workbook located in your Chapter09 practice file folder to complete this exercise. Open the DriverSortTimes_start workbook, and save it as *DriverSortTimes*. Then follow the steps.

1. Select cell **B2**.

2. On the **Home** tab, in the **Styles** group, click **Format as Table**, and then select a table style.

   The Format As Table dialog box opens.

The dialog box automatically displays the data range that includes the selected cell.

3. Verify that the range =*$B$2:$C$17* is displayed in the **Where is the data for your table?** field and that the **My table has headers** check box is selected, and then click **OK**.

   Excel creates an Excel table from your data and displays the Design contextual tab.

4. In cell **B18**, type **D116**, press Tab, type **100** in cell **C18**, and then press Enter.

   Excel includes the data in your Excel table.

5. Select a cell in the table. Then on the **Design** contextual tab, in the **Table Style Options** group, select the **Total Row** check box.

   A Total row appears at the bottom of your Excel table.

6. Select cell **C19**, click the arrow that appears at the right edge of the cell, and then click **Average**.

   Excel changes the summary operation to Average.

Drive ▼	Sorting Minutes ▼
D101	102
D102	162
D103	165
D104	91
D105	103
D106	127
D107	112
D108	137
D109	102
D110	147
D111	163
D112	109
D113	91
D114	107
D115	93
D116	100
Total	119.4375

You can change the summary operation performed in a table.

7. On the **Design** contextual tab, in the **Properties** group, type the value **SortTimes** in the **Table Name** field, and then press Enter.

   Excel renames your Excel table.

8. On the Quick Access Toolbar, click the **Save** button to save your work.

 CLEAN UP Close the DriverSortTimes workbook. If you are not continuing directly to the next chapter, exit Excel.

Key Points

- You can enter a series of data quickly by typing one or more values in adjacent cells, selecting the cells, and then dragging the fill handle. To change how dragging the fill handle extends a data series, hold down the Ctrl key.

- Dragging a fill handle displays the Auto Fill Options button, which you can use to specify whether to copy the selected cells' values, extend a recognized series, or apply the selected cells' formatting to the new cells.

- With Excel, you can enter data by using a list, AutoComplete, or Ctrl+Enter. You should experiment with these techniques and use the one that best fits your circumstances.

- When you copy (or cut) and paste cells, columns, or rows, you can use the new Paste Live Preview capability to preview how your data will appear before you commit to the paste operation.

- After you paste cells, rows, or columns into your worksheet, Excel displays the Paste Options action button. You can use its controls to change which aspects of the cut or copied elements Excel applies to the pasted elements.

- By using the options in the Paste Special dialog box, you can paste only specific aspects of cut or copied data, perform mathematical operations, transpose data, or delete blank cells when pasting.

- You can find and replace data within a worksheet by searching for specific values or by searching for cells that have a particular format applied.

- Excel provides a variety of powerful proofing and research tools, enabling you to check your workbook's spelling, find alternative words by using the Thesaurus, and translate words between languages.

- With Excel tables, you can organize and summarize your data effectively.

Chapter at a Glance

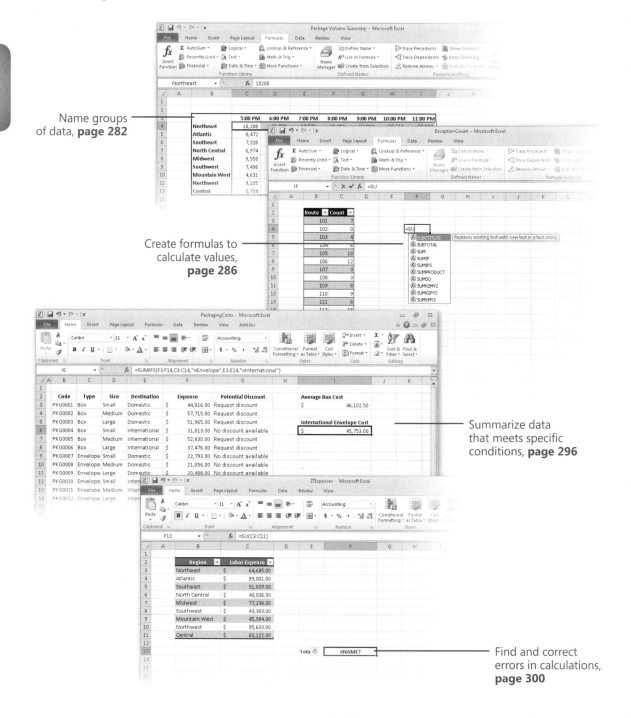

Name groups of data, **page 282**

Create formulas to calculate values, **page 286**

Summarize data that meets specific conditions, **page 296**

Find and correct errors in calculations, **page 300**

10 Perform Calculations on Data

In this chapter, you will learn how to

- ✔ Name groups of data.
- ✔ Create formulas to calculate values.
- ✔ Summarize data that meets specific conditions.
- ✔ Find and correct errors in calculations.

Microsoft Excel 2010 workbooks give you a handy place to store and organize your data, but you can also do a lot more with your data in Excel. One important task you can perform is to calculate totals for the values in a series of related cells. You can also use Excel to discover other information about the data you select, such as the maximum or minimum value in a group of cells. By finding the maximum or minimum value in a group, you can identify your best salesperson, product categories you might need to pay more attention to, or suppliers that consistently give you the best deal. Regardless of your bookkeeping needs, Excel gives you the ability to find the information you want. And if you make an error, you can find the cause and correct it quickly.

Many times, you can't access the information you want without referencing more than one cell, and it's also often true that you'll use the data in the same group of cells for more than one calculation. Excel makes it easy to reference a number of cells at once, enabling you to define your calculations quickly.

In this chapter, you'll learn how to streamline references to groups of data on your worksheets and how to create and correct formulas

> **Practice Files** Before you can complete the exercises in this chapter, you need to copy the book's practice files to your computer. The practice files you'll use to complete the exercises in this chapter are in the Chapter10 practice file folder. A complete list of practice files is provided in "Using the Practice Files" at the beginning of this book.

Naming Groups of Data

When you work with large amounts of data, it's often useful to identify groups of cells that contain related data. For example, you can create a worksheet in which cells C4:I4 hold the number of packages Consolidated Messenger's Northeast processing facility handled from 5:00 P.M. to 12:00 A.M. on the previous day.

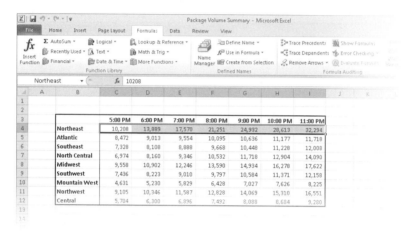

You can name a range of data and reference the entire range by using only the name.

Instead of specifying the cells individually every time you want to use the data they contain, you can define those cells as a range (also called a *named range*). For example, you can group the items from the cells described in the preceding paragraph into a range named *NortheastPreviousDay*. Whenever you want to use the contents of that range in a calculation, you can simply use the name of the range instead of specifying each cell individually.

Tip Yes, you could just name the range *Northeast*, but if you use the range's values in a formula in another worksheet, the more descriptive range name tells you and your colleagues exactly what data is used in the calculation.

To create a named range, select the cells you want to include in your range, click the Formulas tab, and then, in the Defined Names group, click Define Name to display the New Name dialog box. In the New Name dialog box, type a name in the Name field, verify that the cells you selected appear in the Refers To field, and then click OK. You can also add a comment about the range in the Comment field and select whether you want to make the name available for formulas in the entire workbook or just on an individual worksheet.

If the cells you want to define as a named range have labels in a row or column that's part of the cell group, you can use those labels as the names of the named ranges. For example, if your data appears in worksheet cells B4:I12 and the values in column B are the row labels, you can make each row its own named range. To create a series of named ranges from a group of cells, select all of the data cells, including the labels, display the Formulas tab and then, in the Defined Names group, click Create From Selection to display the Create Names From Selection dialog box. In the Create Names From Selection dialog box, select the check box that represents the labels' position in the selected range, and then click OK.

You can name ranges by their row or column labels.

A final way to create a named range is to select the cells you want in the range, click in the Name box next to the formula box, and then type the name for the range.

You can display the ranges available in a workbook by clicking the Name arrow.

To manage the named ranges in a workbook, display the Formulas tab, and then, in the Defined Names group, click Name Manager to display the Name Manager dialog box.

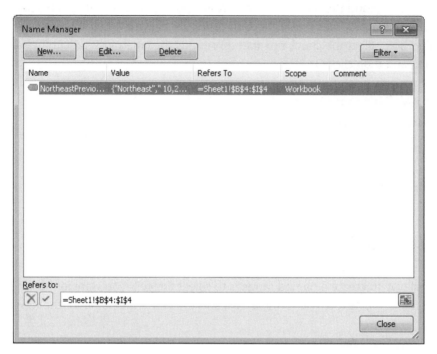

When you click a named range, Excel displays the cells it encompasses in the Refers To field.

Clicking the Edit button displays the Edit Name dialog box, which is a version of the New Name dialog box, enabling you to change a named range's definition; for example, by adding a column. You can also use the controls in the Name Manager dialog box to delete a named range (the range, not the data) by clicking it, clicking the Delete button, and then clicking OK in the confirmation dialog box that opens.

Tip If your workbook contains a lot of named ranges, you can click the Filter button in the Name Manager dialog box and select a criterion to limit the names displayed in the Name Manager dialog box.

In this exercise, you'll create named ranges to streamline references to groups of cells.

SET UP You need the VehicleMiles_start workbook located in your Chapter10 practice file folder to complete this exercise. Start Excel, open the VehicleMiles_start workbook, and save it as *VehicleMiles*. Then follow the steps.

1. Select cells **C4:G4**.

   You are intentionally leaving cell H4 out of this selection. You will edit the named range later in this exercise.

2. In the **Name** box at the left end of the formula bar, type **V101LastWeek**, and then press Enter.

   Excel creates a named range named *V101LastWeek*.

3. On the **Formulas** tab, in the **Defined Names** group, click **Name Manager**.

   The Name Manager dialog box opens.

4. Click the **V101LastWeek** name.

   The cell range to which the V101LastWeek name refers appears in the Refers To box at the bottom of the Name Manager dialog box.

5. Edit the cell range in the **Refers to** box to **=MilesLastWeek!$C$4:$H$4** (change the *G* to an *H*), and then click the check mark button to the left of the box.

   Excel changes the named range's definition.

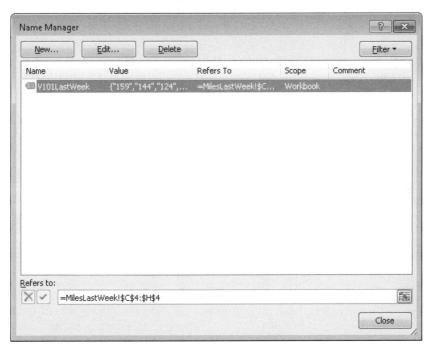

You can make changes to a named range in the Name Manager dialog box.

6. Click **Close**.

   The Name Manager dialog box closes.

7. Select the cell range **C5:H5**.

8. On the **Formulas** tab, in the **Defined Names** group, click **Define Name**.

   The New Name dialog box opens.

9. In the **Name** field, type **V102LastWeek**.

10. Verify that the definition in the **Refers to** field is **=MilesLastWeek!$C$5:$H$5**.

11. Click **OK**.

    Excel creates the name and closes the New Name dialog box.

 **CLEAN UP** Save the VehicleMiles workbook, and then close it.

Creating Formulas to Calculate Values

After you add your data to a worksheet and define ranges to simplify data references, you can create a formula, which is an expression that performs calculations on your data. For example, you can calculate the total cost of a customer's shipments, figure the average number of packages for all Wednesdays in the month of January, or find the highest and lowest daily package volumes for a week, month, or year.

To write an Excel formula, you begin the cell's contents with an equal (=) sign; when Excel sees it, it knows that the expression following it should be interpreted as a calculation, not text. After the equal sign, type the formula. For example, you can find the sum of the numbers in cells C2 and C3 by using the formula *=C2+C3*. After you have entered a formula into a cell, you can revise it by clicking the cell and then editing the formula in the formula box. For example, you can change the preceding formula to *=C3-C2*, which calculates the difference between the contents of cells C2 and C3.

Troubleshooting If Excel treats your formula as text, make sure that you haven't accidentally put a space before the equal sign. Remember, the equal sign must be the first character!

Typing the cell references for 15 or 20 cells in a calculation would be tedious, but Excel makes it easy to enter complex calculations. To create a new calculation, click the Formulas tab, and then in the Function Library group, click Insert Function. The Insert Function dialog box opens, with a list of functions, or predefined formulas, from which you can choose.

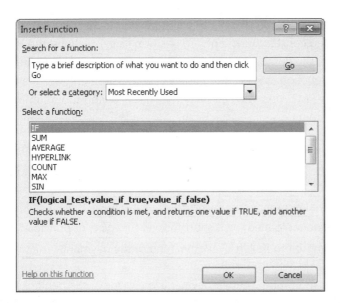

You can locate a function, if you don't know its name, by entering key descriptors in the Search For A Function box and then clicking Go.

The following table describes some of the most useful functions in the list.

Function	Description
SUM	Finds the sum of the numbers in the specified cells
AVERAGE	Finds the average of the numbers in the specified cells
COUNT	Finds the number of entries in the specified cells
MAX	Finds the largest value in the specified cells
MIN	Finds the smallest value in the specified cells

Two other functions you might use are the *NOW* and *PMT* functions. The *NOW* function displays the time Excel updated the workbook's formulas, so the value will change every time the workbook recalculates. The proper form for this function is *=NOW()*. To update the value to the current date and time, just press the F9 key or display the Formulas tab and then, in the Calculation group, click the Calculate Now button. You could, for example, use the *NOW* function to calculate the elapsed time from when you started a process to the present time.

The *PMT* function is a bit more complex. It calculates payments due on a loan, assuming a constant interest rate and constant payments. To perform its calculations, the *PMT* function requires an interest rate, the number of payments, and the starting balance. The elements to be entered into the function are called *arguments* and must be entered in a certain order. That order is written as *PMT(rate, nper, pv, fv, type)*. The following table summarizes the arguments in the *PMT* function.

Argument	Description
rate	The interest rate, to be divided by 12 for a loan with monthly payments, by 4 for quarterly payments, and so on
nper	The total number of payments for the loan
pv	The amount loaned (*pv* is short for *present value*, or principal)
fv	The amount to be left over at the end of the payment cycle (usually left blank, which indicates 0)
type	0 or 1, indicating whether payments are made at the beginning or at the end of the month (usually left blank, which indicates 0, or the end of the month)

If Consolidated Messenger wanted to borrow $2,000,000 at a 6 percent interest rate and pay the loan back over 24 months, you could use the *PMT* function to figure out the monthly payments. In this case, the function would be written =*PMT(6%/12, 24, 2000000)*, which calculates a monthly payment of $88,641.22.

You can also use the names of any ranges you defined to supply values for a formula. For example, if the named range NortheastPreviousDay refers to cells C4:I4, you can calculate the average of cells C4:I4 with the formula =*AVERAGE(NortheastPreviousDay)*. With Excel, you can add functions, named ranges, and table references to your formulas more efficiently by using the Formula AutoComplete capability. Just as AutoComplete offers to fill in a cell's text value when Excel recognizes that the value you're typing matches a previous entry, Formula AutoComplete offers to help you fill in a function, named range, or table reference while you create a formula.

As an example, consider a worksheet that contains a two-column Excel table named *Exceptions*. The first column is labeled *Route*; the second is labeled *Count*.

Route	Count
101	7
102	0
103	4
104	6
105	18
106	12
107	3
108	3
109	8
110	9
111	8
112	18
113	12
114	16
115	12
116	9
117	10
118	6
119	10
120	4

You can reference and entire column in a formula by using the column name.

You refer to a table by typing the table name, followed by the column or row name in square brackets. For example, the table reference *Exceptions[Count]* would refer to the Count column in the Exceptions table.

To create a formula that finds the total number of exceptions by using the *SUM* function, you begin by typing =*SU*. When you type the letter *S*, Formula AutoComplete lists functions that begin with the letter *S*; when you type the letter *U*, Excel narrows the list down to the functions that start with the letters *SU*.

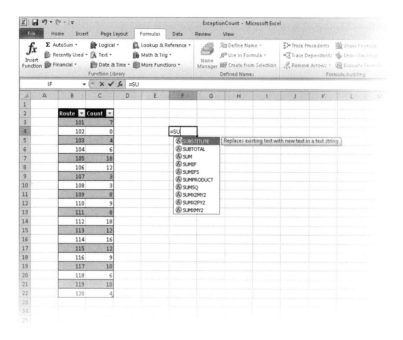

The AutoComplete list suggests functions that begin with the letters you type.

To add the *SUM* function (followed by an opening parenthesis) to the formula, click *SUM* and then press Tab. To begin adding the table reference, type the letter *E*. Excel displays a list of available functions, tables, and named ranges that start with the letter *E*. Click Exceptions, and press Tab to add the table reference to the formula. Then, because you want to summarize the values in the table's Count column, type a left square bracket and then, in the list of available table items, click Count. To finish creating the formula, type a right square bracket followed by a right parenthesis to create the formula *=SUM(Exceptions[Count])*.

If you want to include a series of contiguous cells in a formula, but you haven't defined the cells as a named range, you can click the first cell in the range and drag to the last cell. If the cells aren't contiguous, hold down the Ctrl key and select all of the cells to be included. In both cases, when you release the mouse button, the references of the cells you selected appear in the formula.

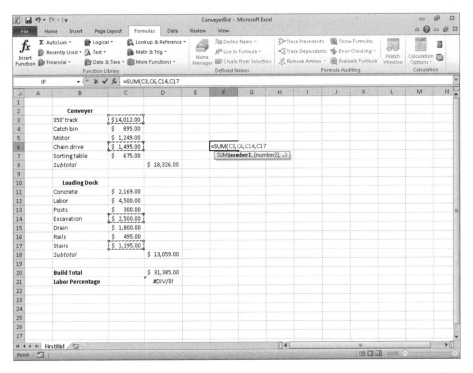

You can enter cells and cell ranges in a formula by selecting the cells while creating the formula.

Troubleshooting The appearance of buttons and groups on the ribbon changes depending on the width of the program window. For information about changing the appearance of the ribbon to match our screen images, see "Modifying the Display of the Ribbon" at the beginning of this book.

After you create a formula, you can copy it and paste it into another cell. When you do, Excel tries to change the formula so that it works in the new cells. For instance, suppose you have a worksheet where cell D8 contains the formula *=SUM(C2:C6)*. Clicking cell D8, copying the cell's contents, and then pasting the result into cell D16 writes *=SUM(C10:C14)* into cell D16. Excel has reinterpreted the formula so that it fits the surrounding cells! Excel knows it can reinterpret the cells used in the formula because the formula uses a relative reference, or a reference that can change if the formula is copied to another cell. Relative references are written with just the cell row and column (for example, *C14*).

Relative references are useful when you summarize rows of data and want to use the same formula for each row. As an example, suppose you have a worksheet with two columns of data, labeled *SalePrice* and *Rate*, and you want to calculate your sales representative's commission by multiplying the two values in a row. To calculate the commission for the first sale, you would type the formula *=B4*C4* in cell D4.

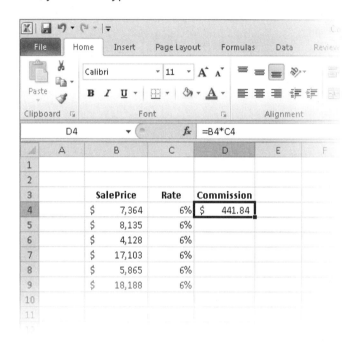

The formula is displayed in the formula bar, and its result is displayed in the cell.

Selecting cell D4 and dragging the fill handle until it covers cells D4:D9 copies the formula from cell D4 into each of the other cells. Because you created the formula using relative references, Excel updates each cell's formula to reflect its position relative to the starting cell (in this case, cell D4.) The formula in cell D9, for example, is *=B9*C9*.

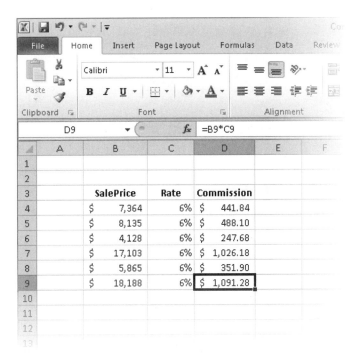

Copying a formula to other cells automatically updates cell references to reflect the new location.

You can use a similar technique when you add a formula to an Excel table column. If the sale price and rate data were in an Excel table and you created the formula *=B4*C4* in cell D4, Excel would apply the formula to every other cell in the column. Because you used relative references in the formula, the formulas would change to reflect each cell's distance from the original cell.

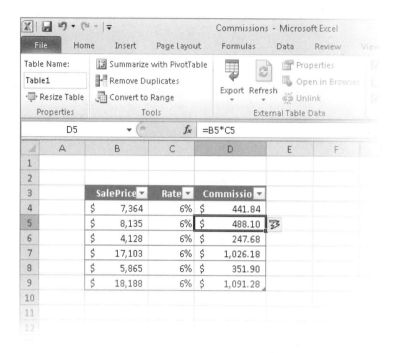

In an Excel table, changing a formula in one cell automatically changes it in related cells.

If you want a cell reference to remain constant when the formula using it is copied to another cell, you can use an absolute reference. To write a cell reference as an absolute reference, type $ before the row letter and the column number. For example, if you want the formula in cell D16 to show the sum of values in cells C10 through C14 regardless of the cell into which it is pasted, you can write the formula as *=SUM($C$10:$C$14).*

Tip Another way to ensure your cell references don't change when you copy the formula to another cell is to click the cell that contains the formula, copy the formula's text in the formula bar, press the Esc key to exit cut-and-copy mode, click the cell where you want to paste the formula, and press Ctrl+V. Excel doesn't change the cell references when you copy your formula to another cell in this manner.

One quick way to change a cell reference from relative to absolute is to select the cell reference in the formula box and then press F4. Pressing F4 cycles a cell reference through the four possible types of references:

● Relative columns and rows (for example, C4)

● Absolute columns and rows (for example, $C$4)

● Relative columns and absolute rows (for example, C$4)

● Absolute columns and relative rows (for example, $C4)

In this exercise, you'll create a formula manually, revise it to include additional cells, create a formula that contains an Excel table reference, create a formula with relative references, and change the formula so it contains absolute references.

 SET UP You need the ITExpenses_start workbook located in your Chapter10 practice file folder to complete this exercise. Open the ITExpenses_start workbook, and save it as *ITExpenses*. Then follow the steps.

1. If necessary, display the **Summary** worksheet. Then, in cell **F9**, type =**C4**, and press Enter.

   The value *$385,671.00* appears in cell F9.

2. Select cell **F9** and type =**SU**.

   Excel erases the existing formula, and Formula AutoComplete displays a list of possible functions to use in the formula.

3. In the **Formula AutoComplete** list, click **SUM**, and then press Tab.

   Excel changes the contents of the formula bar to *=SUM(*.

4. Select the cell range **C3:C8**, type a right parenthesis ( )) to make the formula bar's contents *=SUM(C3:C8)*, and then press Enter.

   The value *$2,562,966.00* appears in cell F9.

5. In cell **F10**, type =**SUM(C4:C5)**, and then press Enter.

6. Select cell **F10**, and then in the formula box, select the cell reference **C4**, and press F4.

   Excel changes the cell reference to *$C$4*.

7. In the formula box, select the cell reference **C5**, press F4, and then press Enter.

   Excel changes the cell reference to *$C$5*.

8. On the tab bar, click the **JuneLabor** sheet tab.

   The JuneLabor worksheet opens.

9. In cell **F13**, type =**SUM(J**.

   Excel displays JuneSummary, the name of the table in the JuneLabor worksheet.

10. Press Tab.

   Excel extends the formula to read *=SUM(JuneSummary*.

11. Type **[**, and then in the **Formula AutoComplete** list, click **Labor Expense**, and press Tab.

Excel extends the formula to read *=SUM(JuneSummary[Labor Expense*.

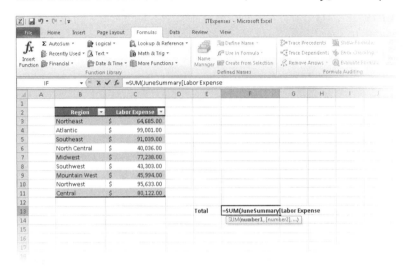

The Formula AutoComplete list suggests suitable formula elements.

12. Type **])** to complete the formula, and then press Enter.

The value *$637,051.00* appears in cell F13.

 **CLEAN UP** Save the ITExpenses workbook, and then close it.

Summarizing Data That Meets Specific Conditions

Another use for formulas is to display messages when certain conditions are met. For instance, Consolidated Messenger's Vice President of Marketing, Craig Dewar, might have agreed to examine the rates charged to corporate customers who were billed for more than $100,000 during a calendar year. This kind of formula is called a *conditional formula*; one way to create a conditional formula in Excel is to use the *IF* function. To create a conditional formula, you click the cell to hold the formula and open the Insert Function dialog box. From within the dialog box, click *IF* in the list of available functions, and then click OK. When you do, the Function Arguments dialog box opens.

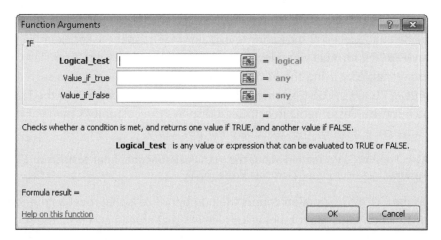

The IF function returns one value if a specified condition is true, and another if it is false.

When you work with an *IF* function, the Function Arguments dialog box has three boxes: Logical_test, Value_if_true, and Value_if_false. The Logical_test box holds the condition you want to check. If the customer's year-to-date shipping bill appears in cell G8, the expression would be *G8>100000*.

Now you need to have Excel display messages that indicate whether Craig Dewar should evaluate the account for a possible rate adjustment. To have Excel print a message from an *IF* function, you enclose the message in quotes in the Value_if_true or Value_if_false box. In this case, you would type *"High-volume shipper—evaluate for rate decrease."* in the Value_if_true box and *"Does not qualify at this time."* in the Value_if_false box.

Excel also includes several other conditional functions you can use to summarize your data, shown in the following table.

Function	Description
AVERAGEIF	Finds the average of values within a cell range that meet a given criterion
AVERAGEIFS	Finds the average of values within a cell range that meet multiple criteria
COUNT	Counts the number of cells in a range that contain a numerical value
COUNTA	Counts the number of cells in a range that are not empty
COUNTBLANK	Counts the number of cells in a range that are empty
COUNTIF	Counts the number of cells in a range that meet a given criterion
COUNTIFS	Counts the number of cells in a range that meet multiple criteria
IFERROR	Displays one value if a formula results in an error and another if it doesn't
SUMIF	Finds the sum of values in a range that meet a single criterion
SUMIFS	Finds the sum of values in a range that meet multiple criteria

You can use the *IFERROR* function to display a custom error message, instead of relying on the default Excel error messages to explain what happened. For example, you could use an *IFERROR* formula when looking up the CustomerID value from cell G8 in the Customers table by using the *VLOOKUP* function. One way to create such a formula is *=IFERROR(VLOOKUP(G8,Customers,2,false),"Customer not found")*. If the function finds a match for the CustomerID in cell G8, it displays the customer's name; if it doesn't find a match, it displays the text *Customer not found*.

See Also For more information about the VLOOKUP function, refer to *Microsoft Excel 2010 Step by Step*, by Curtis Frye (Microsoft Press, 2010).

Just as the *COUNTIF* function counts the number of cells that meet a criterion and the *SUMIF* function finds the total of values in cells that meet a criterion, the *AVERAGEIF* function finds the average of values in cells that meet a criterion. To create a formula using the *AVERAGEIF* function, you define the range to be examined for the criterion, the criterion, and, if required, the range from which to draw the values. As an example, consider a worksheet that lists each customer's ID number, name, state, and total monthly shipping bill.

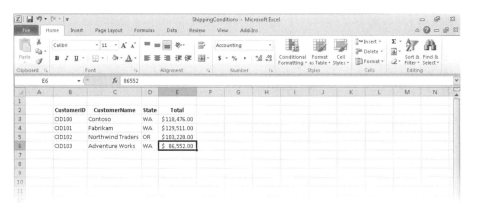

A sample worksheet containing values necessary to create a formula.

If you want to find the average order of customers from the state of Washington (abbreviated in the worksheet as WA), you can create the formula *=AVERAGEIF(D3:D6, "WA", E3:E6)*.

The *AVERAGEIFS, SUMIFS,* and *COUNTIFS* functions extend the capabilities of the *AVERAGEIF, SUMIF,* and *COUNTIF* functions to allow for multiple criteria. If you want to find the sum of all orders of at least $100,000 placed by companies in Washington, you can create the formula *=SUMIFS(E3:E6, D3:D6, "=WA", E3:E6, ">=100000").*

The *AVERAGEIFS* and *SUMIFS* functions start with a data range that contains values that the formula summarizes; you then list the data ranges and the criteria to apply to that range. In generic terms, the syntax runs *=AVERAGEIFS(data_range, criteria_range1, criteria1[,criteria_range2, criteria2...]).* The part of the syntax in square brackets (which aren't used when you create the formula) is optional, so an *AVERAGEIFS* or *SUMIFS* formula that contains a single criterion will work. The *COUNTIFS* function, which doesn't perform any calculations, doesn't need a data range—you just provide the criteria ranges and criteria. For example, you could find the number of customers from Washington who were billed at least $100,000 by using the formula *=COUNTIFS(D3:D6, "=WA", E3:E6, ">=100000").*

In this exercise, you'll create a conditional formula that displays a message if a condition is true, find the average of worksheet values that meet one criterion, and find the sum of worksheet values that meet two criteria.

SET UP You need the PackagingCosts_start workbook located in your Chapter10 practice file folder to complete this exercise. Open the PackagingCosts_start workbook, and save it as *PackagingCosts*. Then follow the steps.

1. In cell **G3**, type the formula **=IF(F3>=35000, "Request discount", "No discount available")**, and press Enter.

   Excel accepts the formula, which displays *Request discount* if the value in cell F3 is at least 35,000 and displays *No discount available* if not. The value *Request discount* appears in cell G3.

2. Click cell **G3**, and drag the fill handle down until it covers cell **G14**.

   Excel copies the formula in cell G3 to cells G4:G14, adjusting the formula to reflect the cells' addresses. The results of the copied formulas appear in cells G4:G14.

3. In cell **I3**, type the formula **=AVERAGEIF(C3:C14, "=Box", F3:F14)**, and press Enter.

   The value *$46,102.50*, which represents the average cost per category of boxes, appears in cell I3.

4. In cell **I6**, type **=SUMIFS(F3:F14, C3:C14, "=Envelope", E3:E14, "=International")**.

   The value *$45,753.00*, which represents the total cost of all envelopes used for international shipments, appears in cell I6.

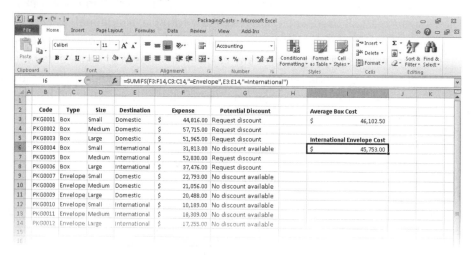

You can create a formula anywhere on a worksheet.

 CLEAN UP Save the PackagingCosts workbook, and then close it.

Finding and Correcting Errors in Calculations

Including calculations in a worksheet gives you valuable answers to questions about your data. As is always true, however, it is possible for errors to creep into your formulas. With Excel, you can find the source of errors in your formulas by identifying the cells used in a given calculation and describing any errors that have occurred. The process of examining a worksheet for errors is referred to as *auditing*.

Excel identifies errors in several ways. The first way is to display an error code in the cell holding the formula generating the error.

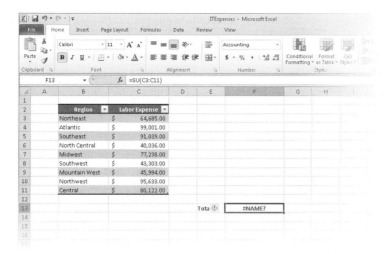

Error codes begin with a number sign (#).

When a cell with an erroneous formula is the active cell, an Error button is displayed next to it. Pointing to the Error button displays an arrow. Clicking the arrow displays a menu with options that provide information about the error and offer to help you fix it.

The following table lists the most common error codes and what they mean.

Error code	Description
#####	The column isn't wide enough to display the value.
#VALUE!	The formula has the wrong type of argument (such as text in a cell where a numerical value is required).
#NAME?	The formula contains text that Excel doesn't recognize (such as an unknown named range).
#REF!	The formula refers to a cell that doesn't exist (which can happen whenever cells are deleted).
#DIV/0!	The formula attempts to divide by zero.

Another technique you can use to find the source of formula errors is to ensure that the appropriate cells are providing values for the formula. For example, you might want to calculate the total number of deliveries for a service level, but you could accidentally create a formula referring to the service levels' names instead of their package quantities. You can identify the source of an error by having Excel trace a cell's *precedents*, which are the cells with values used in the active cell's formula. To do so, click the Formulas tab, and then in the Formula Auditing group, click Trace Precedents. When you do, Excel identifies those cells by drawing a blue tracer arrow from the precedents to the active cell.

You can also audit your worksheet by identifying cells with formulas that use a value from a given cell. For example, you might use one region's daily package total in a formula that calculates the average number of packages delivered for all regions on a given day. Cells that use another cell's value in their calculations are known as *dependents*, meaning that they depend on the value in the other cell to derive their own value. As with tracing precedents, you can click the Formulas tab, and then in the Formula Auditing group, click Trace Dependents.

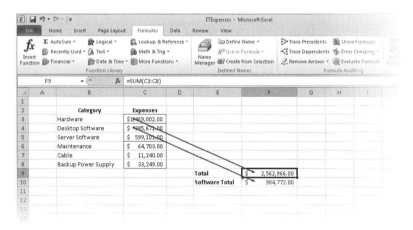

Excel draws blue arrows from the active cell to those cells that have calculations based on that value.

If the cells identified by the tracer arrows aren't the correct cells, you can hide the arrows and correct the formula. To hide the tracer arrows on a worksheet, display the Formulas tab, and then in the Formula Auditing group, click Remove Arrows.

If you prefer to have the elements of a formula error presented as text in a dialog box, you can use the Error Checking dialog box to view the error and the formula in the cell in which the error occurs. To display the Error Checking dialog box, display the Formulas tab, and then in the Formula Auditing group, click the Error Checking button. You can use the controls in the Error Checking dialog box to move through the formula one step at a time, to choose to ignore the error, or to move to the next or the previous error. If you click the Options button in the dialog box, you can also use the controls in the Excel Options dialog box to change how Excel determines what is an error and what isn't.

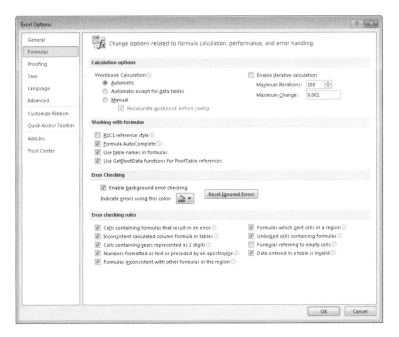

You can have the Error Checking tool ignore formulas that don't use every cell in a region
(such as a row or column).

Tip If you clear the Formulas That Omit Cells In A Region check box, you can create formulas
that don't add up every value in a row, column, or range without Excel displaying an error.

For times when you just want to display the results of each step of a formula and don't need
the full power of the Error Checking tool, you can use the Evaluate Formula dialog box to
move through each element of the formula. To display the Evaluate Formula dialog box,
you display the Formulas tab and then, in the Formula Auditing group, click the Evaluate
Formula button. The Evaluate Formula dialog box is much more useful for examining formulas that don't produce an error but aren't generating the result you expect.

Finally, you can monitor the value in a cell regardless of where in your workbook you are
by opening a Watch Window that displays the value in the cell. For example, if one of
your formulas uses values from cells in other worksheets or even other workbooks, you
can set a watch on the cell that contains the formula and then change the values in the
other cells. To set a watch, click the cell you want to monitor, and then on the Formulas
tab, in the Formula Auditing group, click Watch Window. Click Add Watch to have Excel
monitor the selected cell.

As soon as you type in the new value, the Watch Window displays the new result of the
formula. When you're done watching the formula, select the watch, click Delete Watch,
and close the Watch Window.

In this exercise, you'll use the formula-auditing capabilities in Excel to identify and correct errors in a formula.

SET UP You need the ConveyerBid_start workbook located in your Chapter10 practice file folder to complete this exercise. Open the ConveyerBid_start workbook, and save it as *ConveyerBid*. Then follow the steps.

1. Click cell **D20**.

2. On the **Formulas** tab, in the **Formula Auditing** group, click **Watch Window**.

   The Watch Window opens.

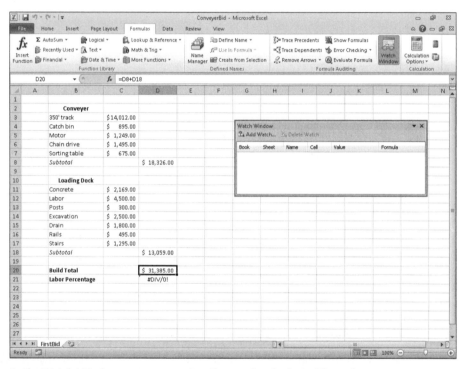

In the Watch Window, you can monitor the results of selected formulas.

3. Click **Add Watch**, and then in the **Add Watch** dialog box, click **Add**.

   Cell D20 appears in the Watch Window.

4. Click cell **D8**.

   =SUM(C3:C7) appears in the formula bar.

5. In the **Formula Auditing** group, click the **Trace Precedents** button.

   A blue arrow begins at the cell range C3:C7 and points to cell D8.

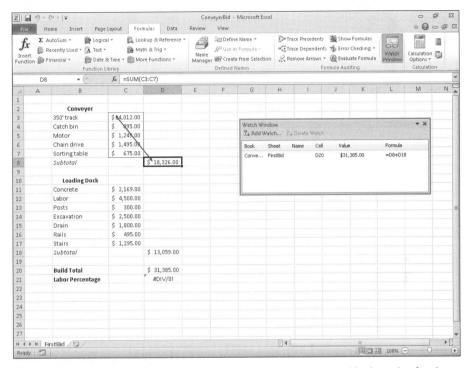

The auditing arrow indicates that the cells in the range C3:C7 provide the value for the formula in cell D8.

6. In the **Formula Auditing** group, click the **Remove Arrows** button.

 The arrow disappears.

7. Click cell **A1**.

8. In the **Formula Auditing** group, click the **Error Checking** button.

 The Error Checking dialog box opens.

The dialog box displays the error found in cell D1.

9. Click **Next**.

    Excel displays a message box indicating that there are no more errors in the worksheet.

10. Click **OK**.

    The message box and the Error Checking dialog box close.

11. In the **Formula Auditing** group, click the **Error Checking** arrow, and then in the list, click **Trace Error**.

    Blue arrows appear, pointing to cell D21 from cells C12 and D19. These arrows indicate that using the values (or lack of values, in this case) in the indicated cells generates the error in cell D21.

12. In the **Formula Auditing** group, click **Remove Arrows**.

    The arrows disappear.

13. In the formula box, delete the existing formula, type =**C12/D20**, and press Enter.

    The value *14%* appears in cell D21.

14. Click cell **D21**.

15. In the **Formula Auditing** group, click the **Evaluate Formula** button.

    The Evaluate Formula dialog box opens.

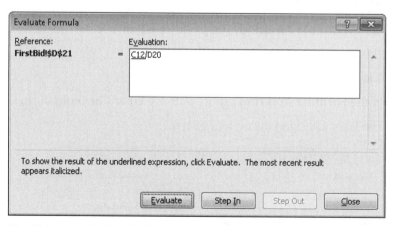

The dialog box displays the formula from cell D21.

16. Click **Evaluate** three times to step through the formula's elements, and then click **Close**.

    The Evaluate Formula dialog box closes.

17. In the **Watch Window**, click the watch in the list.

18. Click **Delete Watch**.

    The watch disappears.

19. On the **Formulas** tab, in the **Formula Auditing** group, click **Watch Window**.

    The Watch Window closes.

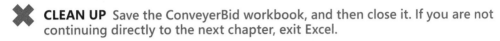 **CLEAN UP** Save the ConveyerBid workbook, and then close it. If you are not continuing directly to the next chapter, exit Excel.

Key Points

- You can add a group of cells to a formula by typing the formula, and then at the spot in the formula in which you want to name the cells, selecting the cells by using the mouse.

- By creating named ranges, you can refer to entire blocks of cells with a single term, saving you lots of time and effort. You can use a similar technique with table data, referring to an entire table or one or more table columns.

- When you write a formula, be sure you use absolute referencing ($A$1) if you want the formula to remain the same when it's copied from one cell to another, or use relative referencing (A1) if you want the formula to change to reflect its new position in the worksheet.

- Instead of typing a formula from scratch, you can use the Insert Function dialog box to help you on your way.

- You can monitor how the value in a cell changes by adding a watch to the Watch Window.

- To see which formulas refer to the values in the selected cell, use Trace Dependents; if you want to see which cells provide values for the formula in the active cell, use Trace Precedents.

- You can step through the calculations of a formula in the Evaluate Formula dialog box or go through a more rigorous error-checking procedure by using the Error Checking tool.

Chapter at a Glance

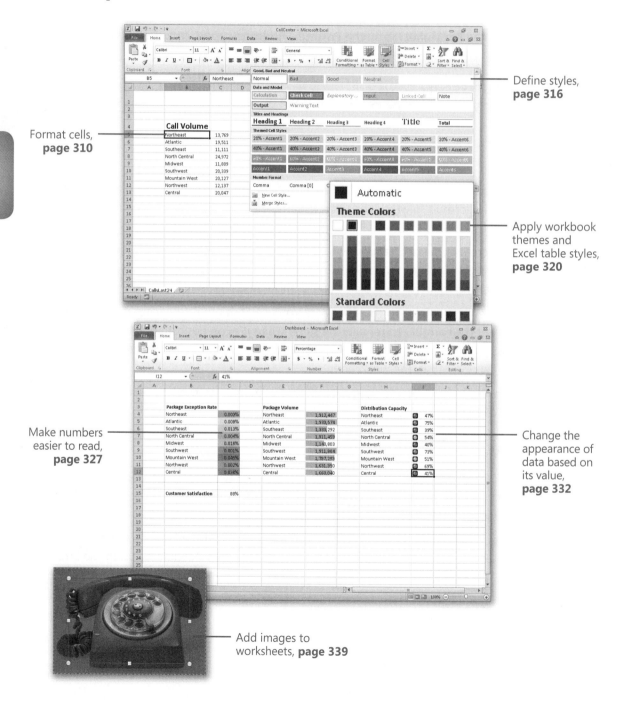

Format cells,
page 310

Define styles,
page 316

Apply workbook
themes and
Excel table styles,
page 320

Make numbers
easier to read,
page 327

Change the
appearance of
data based on
its value,
page 332

Add images to
worksheets, **page 339**

11 Change Workbook Appearance

In this chapter, you will learn how to

✔ Format cells.

✔ Define styles.

✔ Apply workbook themes and Excel table styles.

✔ Make numbers easier to read.

✔ Change the appearance of data based on its value.

✔ Add images to worksheets.

Entering data into a workbook efficiently saves you time, but you must also ensure that your data is easy to read. Microsoft Excel 2010 gives you a wide variety of ways to make your data easier to understand; for example, you can change the font, character size, or color used to present a cell's contents. Changing how data appears on a worksheet helps set the contents of a cell apart from the contents of surrounding cells. The simplest example of that concept is a data label. If a column on your worksheet contains a list of days, you can easily set apart a label (for example, *Day*) by presenting it in bold type that's noticeably larger than the type used to present the data to which it refers. To save time, you can define a number of custom formats and then apply them quickly to the desired cells.

You might also want to specially format a cell's contents to reflect the value in that cell. For example, Lori Penor, the chief operating officer of Consolidated Messenger, might want to create a worksheet that displays the percentage of improperly delivered packages from each regional distribution center. If that percentage exceeds a threshold, she could have Excel display a red traffic light icon, indicating that the center's performance is out of tolerance and requires attention.

In this chapter, you'll learn how to change the appearance of data, apply existing formats to data, make numbers easier to read, change data's appearance based on its value, and add images to worksheets.

> **Practice Files** Before you can complete the exercises in this chapter, you need to copy the book's practice files to your computer. The practice files you'll use to complete the exercises in this chapter are in the Chapter11 practice file folder. A complete list of practice files is provided in "Using the Practice Files" at the beginning of this book.

Formatting Cells

Excel spreadsheets can hold and process lots of data, but when you manage numerous spreadsheets it can be hard to remember from a worksheet's title exactly what data is kept in that worksheet. Data labels give you and your colleagues information about data in a worksheet, but it's important to format the labels so that they stand out visually. To make your data labels or any other data stand out, you can change the format of the cells that hold your data.

◢	A	B	C	D	E	F
1						
2						
3						
4		**Call Volume**				
5		Northeast	13,769			
6		Atlantic	19,511			
7		Southeast	11,111			
8		North Central	24,972			
9		Midwest	11,809			
10		Southwest	20,339			
11		Mountain West	20,127			
12		Northwest	12,137			
13		Central	20,047			
14						
15						
16						
17						

Include data labels to identify the data in a worksheet.

Most of the tools you need to change a cell's format can be found on the Home tab. You can apply the formatting represented on a button by selecting the cells you want to apply the style to and then clicking that button. If you want to set your data labels apart by making them appear bold, click the Bold button. If you have already made a cell's contents bold, selecting the cell and clicking the Bold button will remove the formatting.

Tip Deleting a cell's contents doesn't delete the cell's formatting. To delete a selected cell's formatting, on the Home tab, in the Editing group, click the Clear button (which looks like an eraser), and then click Clear Formats. Clicking Clear All from the same list will remove the cell's contents and formatting.

Buttons in the Home tab's Font group that give you choices, such as the Font Color button, have an arrow at the right edge of the button. Clicking the arrow displays a list of options accessible for that button, such as the fonts available on your system or the colors you can assign to a cell.

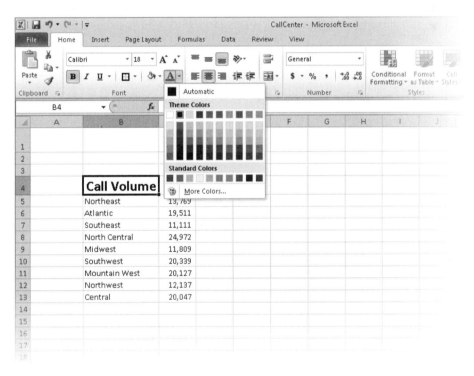

The Font Color gallery.

Another way you can make a cell stand apart from its neighbors is to add a border around the cell. To place a border around one or more cells, select the cells, and then choose the border type you want by selecting from the Border list in the Font group. Excel does provide more options: To display the full range of border types and styles, in the Border list, click More Borders. The Format Cells dialog box opens, displaying the Border page.

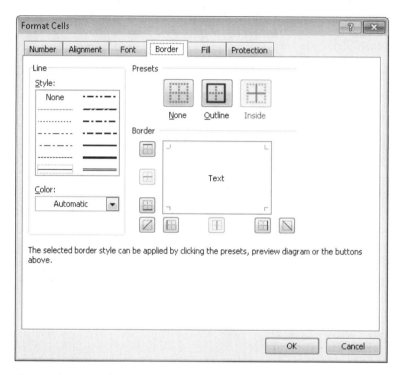

The Border page of the Format Cells dialog box contains the full range of tools you can use to define your cells' borders.

You can also make a group of cells stand apart from its neighbors by changing its shading, which is the color that fills the cells. On a worksheet that tracks total package volume for the past month, Lori Penor could change the fill color of the cells holding her data labels to make the labels stand out even more than by changing the labels' text formatting.

Tip You can display the most commonly used formatting controls by right-clicking a selected range. When you do, a Mini Toolbar containing a subset of the Home tab formatting tools appears above the shortcut menu.

If you want to change the attributes of every cell in a row or column, you can click the header of the row or column you want to modify and then select your desired format.

One task you can't perform by using the tools on the Home tab is to change the standard font for a workbook, which is used in the Name box and on the formula bar. The standard font when you install Excel is Calibri, a simple font that is easy to read on a computer screen and on the printed page. If you want to choose another font, click the File tab, and then click Options. On the General page of the Excel Options dialog box, set the values in the Use This Font and Font Size list boxes to pick your new display font.

Important The new standard font doesn't take effect until you exit Excel and restart the program.

In this exercise, you'll emphasize a worksheet's title by changing the format of cell data, adding a border to a cell range, and then changing a cell range's fill color. After those tasks are complete, you'll change the default font for the workbook.

SET UP You need the VehicleMileSummary_start workbook located in your Chapter11 practice file folder to complete this exercise. Start Excel, open the VehicleMileSummary_start workbook, and save it as *VehicleMileSummary*. Then follow the steps.

1. Click cell **D2**.

2. On the **Home** tab, in the **Font** group, click the **Bold** button.

   Excel displays the cell's contents in bold type.

3. In the **Font** group, click the **Font Size** arrow, and then in the list, click **18**.

   Excel increases the size of the text in cell D2.

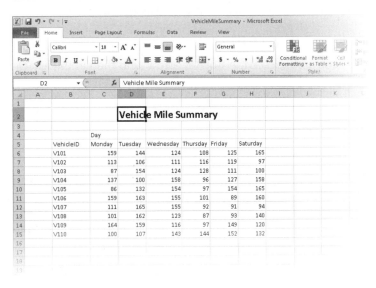

Larger text simulates a page header.

4. Click cell **B5**, hold down the Ctrl key, and click cell **C4** to select the non-contiguous cells.

5. On the **Home** tab, in the **Font** group, click the **Bold** button.

   Excel displays the cells' contents in bold type.

6. Select the cell ranges **B6:B15** and **C5:H5**.

7. In the **Font** group, click the **Italic** button.

   Excel displays the cells' contents in italic type.

⟋	A	B	C	D	E	F	G	H	I
1									
2				Vehicle Mile Summary					
3									
4			Day						
5		VehicleID	Monday	Tuesday	Wednesday	Thursday	Friday	Saturday	
6		V101	159	144	124	108	125	165	
7		V102	113	106	111	116	119	97	
8		V103	87	154	124	128	111	100	
9		V104	137	100	158	96	127	158	
10		V105	86	132	154	97	154	165	
11		V106	159	163	155	101	89	160	
12		V107	111	165	155	92	91	94	
13		V108	101	162	123	87	93	140	
14		V109	164	159	116	97	149	120	
15		V110	100	107	143	144	152	132	
16									
17									
18									

Local formatting such as bold and italic emphasizes cell content.

8. Select the cell range **C6:H15**.

9. In the **Font** group, click the **Border** arrow, and then in the list, click **Outside Borders**.

   Excel places a border around the outside edge of the selected cells.

10. Select the cell range **B4:H15**.

11. In the **Border** list, click **Thick Box Border**.

    Excel places a thick border around the outside edge of the selected cells.

12. Select the cell ranges **B4:B15** and **C4:H5**.

13. In the **Font** group, click the **Fill Color** arrow, and then in the **Standard Colors** area of the color palette, click the yellow button.

    Excel changes the selected cells' background color to yellow.

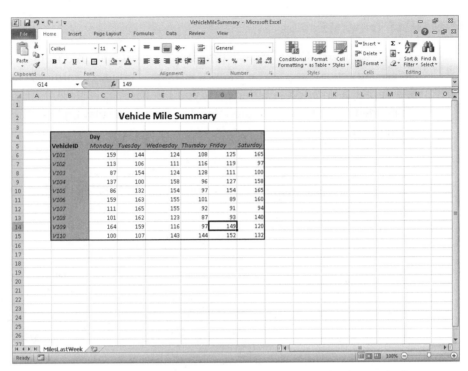

You can distinguish header cells from other cells by applying a background color.

Troubleshooting The appearance of buttons and groups on the ribbon changes depending on the width of the program window. For information about changing the appearance of the ribbon to match our screen images, see "Modifying the Display of the Ribbon" at the beginning of this book.

14. Click the **File** tab, and then click **Options**.

The Excel Options dialog box opens.

15. If necessary, click **General** to display the **General** page.

16. In the **When creating new workbooks** area, in the **Use this font** list, click **Verdana**.

Verdana appears in the Use This Font field.

17. Click **Cancel**.

The Excel Options dialog box closes without saving your change.

CLEAN UP Save the VehicleMileSummary workbook, and then close it.

Defining Styles

As you work with Excel, you will probably develop preferred formats for data labels, titles, and other worksheet elements. Instead of adding a format's characteristics one element at a time to the target cells, you can have Excel store the format and recall it as needed. You can find the predefined formats by displaying the Home tab, and then in the Styles group, clicking Cell Styles.

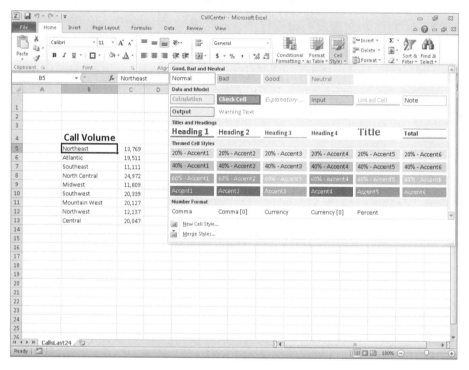

You can choose a style from the Cell Styles gallery, or create a custom style.

Clicking a style from the Cell Styles gallery applies the style to the selected cells, but Excel also displays a live preview of a format when you point to it. If none of the existing styles is what you want, you can create your own style by clicking New Cell Style at the bottom of the gallery to display the Style dialog box. In the Style dialog box, type the name of your new style in the Style Name field, and then click Format. The Format Cells dialog box opens.

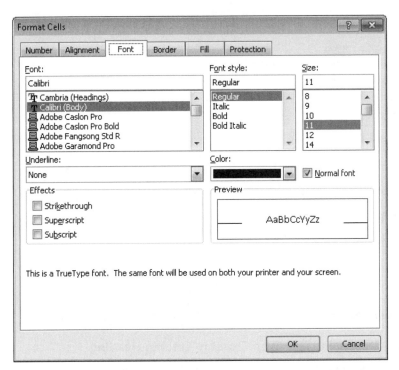

A custom style can include number, alignment, font, and border formatting.

After you set the characteristics of your new style, click OK to make your style available in the Cell Styles gallery. If you ever want to delete a custom style, display the Cell Styles gallery, right-click the style, and then click Delete.

If all you want to do is apply formatting from one cell to the contents of another cell, use the Format Painter tool in the Clipboard group on the Home tab. Just click the cell that has the format you want to copy, click the Format Painter button, and then click the cells to which you want to apply the copied format. To apply the same formatting to multiple cells, double-click the Format Painter button and then click the target cells. When you're done applying the formatting, press the Esc key.

In this exercise, you'll create a style and apply the new style to a data label.

SET UP You need the HourlyExceptions_start workbook located in your Chapter11 practice file folder to complete this exercise. Open the HourlyExceptions_start workbook, and save it as *HourlyExceptions*. Then follow the steps.

1. On the **Home** tab, in the **Styles** group, click **Cell Styles**, and then click **New Cell Style**.

   The Style dialog box opens.

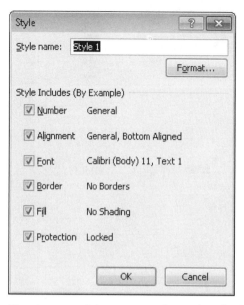

The elements of the current style are described in the Cell Style dialog box.

2. In the **Style name** field, type **Crosstab Column Heading**.

3. Click the **Format** button. In the **Format Cells** dialog box, click the **Alignment** tab.

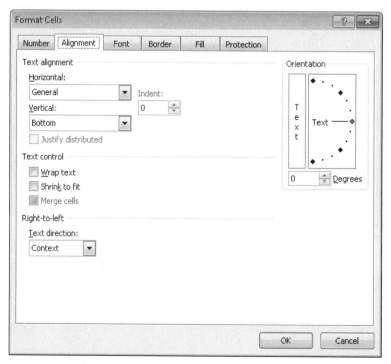

You can specify the alignment and direction of text.

4. In the **Horizontal** list, click **Center**.

5. Click the **Font** tab.

6. In the **Font style** list, click **Italic**.

   The text in the Preview pane appears in italicized text.

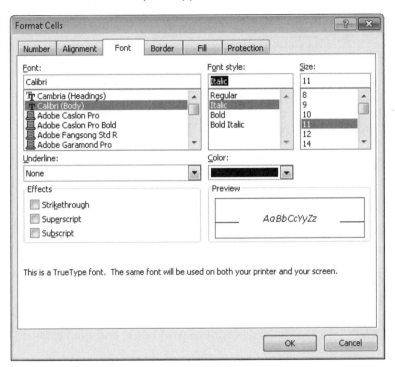

You can make changes on multiple pages of the Format Cells dialog box before closing it.

7. Click the **Number** tab.

   The Number page of the Format Cells dialog box is displayed.

8. In the **Category** list, click **Time**.

   The available time formats appear.

9. In the **Type** pane, click **1:30 PM**.

10. Click **OK** to save your changes.

    The Format Cells dialog box closes, and your new style's definition appears in the Style dialog box.

11. Click **OK**.

    The Style dialog box closes.

12. Select cells **C4:N4**.

13. On the **Home** tab, in the **Styles** group, click **Cell Styles**.

The Cell Styles gallery opens.

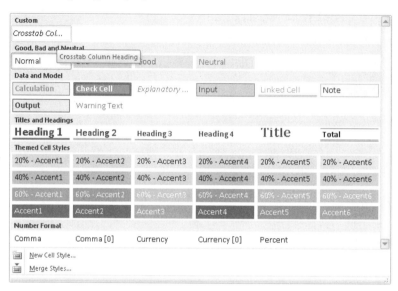

Your new style appears at the top of the gallery, in the Custom group.

14. Click the **Crosstab Column Heading** style.

Excel applies your new style to the selected cells.

✖ CLEAN UP Save the HourlyExceptions workbook, and then close it.

Applying Workbook Themes and Excel Table Styles

Microsoft Office 2010 includes powerful design tools that enable you to create attractive, professional documents quickly. The Excel product team implemented the new design capabilities by defining workbook themes and Excel table styles. A theme is a way to specify the fonts, colors, and graphic effects that appear in a workbook. Excel comes with many themes installed.

To apply an existing workbook theme, display the Page Layout tab. Then, in the Themes group, click Themes, and click the theme you want to apply to your workbook. By default, Excel applies the Office theme to your workbooks.

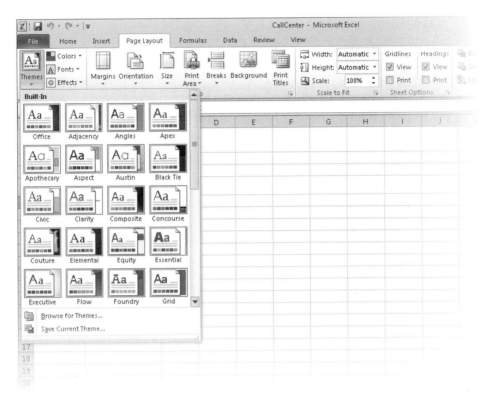

You can choose from among dozens of preformatted visual themes.

When you want to format a workbook element, Excel displays colors that are available within the active theme. For example, selecting a worksheet cell and then clicking the Font Color arrow displays a palette of colors. The theme colors appear at the top of the color palette—the standard colors and the More Colors link, which displays the Colors dialog box, appear at the bottom of the palette.

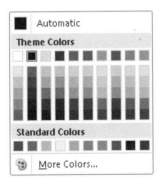

If you format workbook elements by using colors from the Theme Colors area, applying a different theme changes that object's colors.

You can change a theme's colors, fonts, and graphic effects by displaying the Page Layout tab and then, in the Themes group, selecting new values from the Colors, Fonts, and Effects lists. To save your changes as a new theme, display the Page Layout tab, and in the Themes group, click Themes, and then click Save Current Theme. Use the controls in the Save Current Theme dialog box that opens to record your theme for later use. Later, when you click the Themes button, your custom theme will appear at the top of the gallery.

Tip When you save a theme, you save it as an Office Theme file. You can apply the theme to other Office 2010 documents as well.

Just as you can define and apply themes to entire workbooks, you can apply and define Excel table styles. You select an Excel table's initial style when you create it; to create a new style, display the Home tab, and in the Styles group, click Format As Table. In the Format As Table gallery, click New Table Style to display the New Table Quick Style dialog box.

You can apply a standard Excel table style or create a custom table style.

Type a name for the new style, select the first table element you want to format, and then click Format to display the Format Cells dialog box. Define the element's formatting, and then click OK. When the New Table Quick Style dialog box reopens, its Preview pane displays the overall table style and the Element Formatting area describes the selected element's appearance. Also, in the Table Element list, Excel displays the element's name in bold to indicate it has been changed. To make the new style the default for new Excel tables created in the current workbook, select the Set As Default Table Quick Style For This Document check box. When you click OK, Excel saves the new table style.

Tip To remove formatting from a table element, click the name of the table element and then click the Clear button.

In this exercise, you'll create a new workbook theme, change a workbook's theme, create a new table style, and apply the new style to an Excel table.

SET UP You need the HourlyTracking_start workbook located in your Chapter11 practice file folder to complete this exercise. Open the HourlyTracking_start workbook, and save it as *HourlyTracking*. Then follow the steps.

1. If necessary, click any cell in the Excel table.

2. On the **Home** tab, in the **Styles** group, click **Format as Table**, and then click the style at the upper-left corner of the **Table Styles** gallery.

   Excel applies the style to the table.

3. On the **Home** tab, in the **Styles** group, click **Format as Table**, and then click **New Table Style**.

   The New Table Quick Style dialog box opens.

4. In the **Name** field, type **Exception Default**.

5. In the **Table Element** list, click **Header Row**.

6. Click **Format**.

   The Format Cells dialog box opens.

7. Click the **Fill** tab.

The Fill page is displayed.

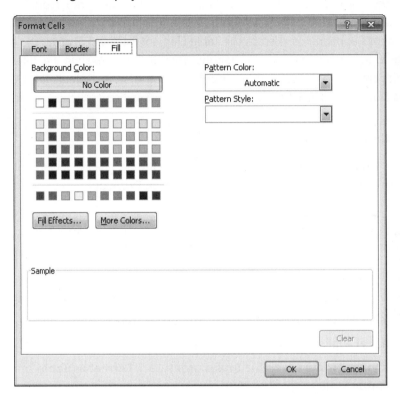

The fill colors shown in the palette are specific to the currently applied theme.

8. In the first row of color squares, just below the **No Color** button, click the third square from the left.

The new background color appears in the Sample pane of the dialog box.

9. Click **OK**.

The Format Cells dialog box closes. When the New Table Quick Style dialog box reopens, the Header Row table element appears in bold, and the Preview pane's header row is shaded.

10. In the **Table Element** list, click **Second Row Stripe**, and then click **Format**.

The Format Cells dialog box opens.

11. Just below the **No Color** button, click the third square from the left again.

The new background color appears in the Sample pane of the dialog box.

12. Click **OK**.

The Format Cells dialog box closes. When the New Table Quick Style dialog box reopens, the Second Row Stripe table element appears in bold, and every second row is shaded in the Preview pane.

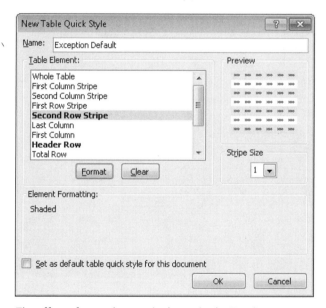

The effect of your changes is shown in the Preview area.

13. Click **OK**.

   The New Table Quick Style dialog box closes.

14. On the **Home** tab, in the **Styles** group, click **Format as Table**. In the gallery, in the **Custom** area, click the new format.

   Excel applies the new format.

15. On the **Page Layout** tab, in the **Themes** group, click the **Fonts** arrow, and then in the list, click **Verdana**.

   Excel changes the theme's font to Verdana (which is part of the Aspect font set).

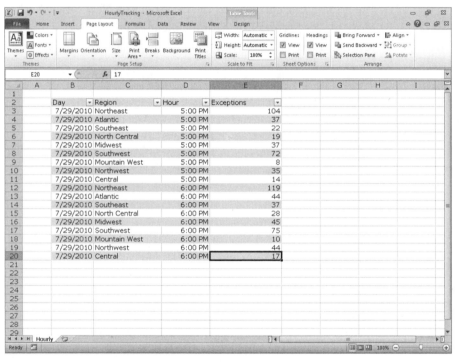

After changing a theme's colors, fonts, or effects, you can save the theme for reuse as a custom theme.

16. In the **Themes** group, click the **Themes** button, and then click **Save Current Theme**.

   The Save Current Theme dialog box opens.

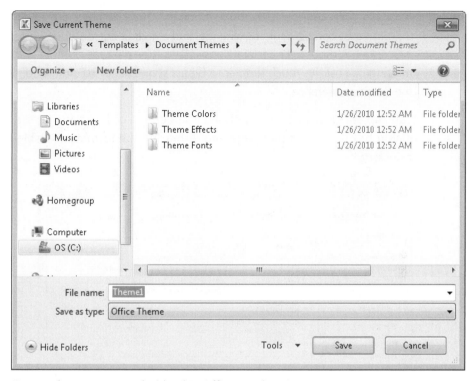

Custom themes are stored with other Office templates.

17. In the **File name** field, type **Verdana Office**, and then click **Save**.

Excel saves your theme.

18. In the **Themes** group, click the **Themes** button, and then click **Origin**.

Excel applies the new theme to your workbook.

✖ **CLEAN UP** Save the HourlyTracking workbook, and then close it.

Making Numbers Easier to Read

Changing the format of the cells in your worksheet can make your data much easier to read, both by setting data labels apart from the actual data and by adding borders to define the boundaries between labels and data even more clearly. Of course, using formatting options to change the font and appearance of a cell's contents doesn't help with idiosyncratic data types such as dates, phone numbers, or currency values.

As an example, consider U.S. phone numbers. These numbers are 10 digits long and have a 3-digit area code, a 3-digit exchange, and a 4-digit line number written in the form (###) ###-####. Although it's certainly possible to type a phone number with the expected formatting in a cell, it's much simpler to type a sequence of 10 digits and have Excel change the data's appearance.

You can tell Excel to expect a phone number in a cell by opening the Format Cells dialog box to the Number page and displaying the formats available for the Special category.

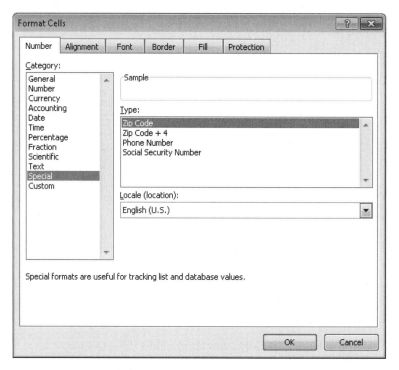

The Type list displays special formats that are specific to the location selected in the Locale list.

Clicking Phone Number in the Type list tells Excel to format 10-digit numbers in the standard phone number format. You can see this in operation if you compare the contents of the active cell and the contents of the formula box for a cell with the Phone Number formatting.

Troubleshooting If you type a 9-digit number in a field that expects a phone number, you won't see an error message; instead, you'll see a 2-digit area code. For example, the number 425550012 would be displayed as (42) 555-0012. An 11-digit number would be displayed with a 4-digit area code. If the phone number doesn't look right, you probably left out a digit or included an extra one, so you should make sure your entry is correct.

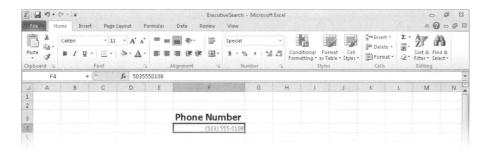

The Phone Number format applied to the number shown in the formula box.

Just as you can instruct Excel to expect a phone number in a cell, you can also have it expect a date or a currency amount. You can make those changes from the Format Cells dialog box by choosing either the Date category or the Currency category. The Date category enables you to pick the format for the date (and determine whether the date's appearance changes due to the Locale setting of the operating system on the computer viewing the workbook). In a similar vein, selecting the Currency category displays controls to set the number of places after the decimal point, the currency symbol to use, and the way in which Excel should display negative numbers.

Tip The Excel user interface enables you to make the most common format changes by displaying the Home tab of the ribbon and then, in the Number group, either clicking a button representing a built-in format or selecting a format from the Number Format list.

You can also create a custom numeric format to add a word or phrase to a number in a cell. For example, you can add the phrase *per month* to a cell with a formula that calculates average monthly sales for a year to ensure that you and your colleagues will recognize the figure as a monthly average. To create a custom number format, click the Home tab, and then click the Number dialog box launcher (found at the bottom right corner of the Number group on the ribbon) to display the Format Cells dialog box. Then, if necessary, click the Number tab.

In the Category list, click Custom to display the available custom number formats in the Type list. You can then click the base format you want and modify it in the Type box. For example, clicking the 0.00 format causes Excel to format any number in a cell with two digits to the right of the decimal point.

Tip The zeros in the format indicate that the position in the format can accept any number as a valid value.

To customize the format, click in the Type box and add any symbols or text you want to the format. For example, typing a dollar ($) sign to the left of the existing format and then typing *"per month"* (including quote marks) to the right of the existing format causes the number 1500 to be displayed as *$1500.00 per month*.

Important You need to enclose any text to be displayed as part of the format in quotes so that Excel recognizes the text as a string to be displayed in the cell.

In this exercise, you'll assign date, phone number, and currency formats to ranges of cells.

SET UP You need the ExecutiveSearch_start workbook located in your Chapter11 practice file folder to complete this exercise. Open the ExecutiveSearch_start workbook, and save it as *ExecutiveSearch*. Then follow the steps.

1. Click cell **A3**.

2. On the **Home** tab, click the **Font** dialog box launcher.

    The Format Cells dialog box opens.

3. If necessary, click the **Number** tab.

4. In the **Category** list, click **Date**.

    The Type list appears with a list of date formats.

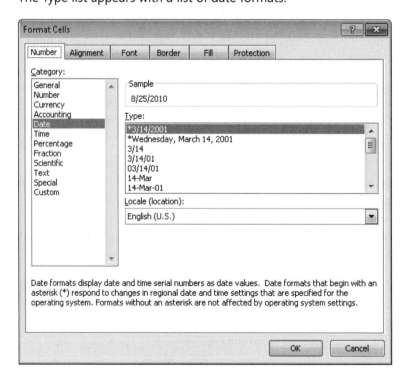

The Type list displays date formats that are specific to the location selected in the Locale list.

5. In the **Type** list, click **3/14/01**.

6. Click **OK** to assign the chosen format to the cell.

    Excel displays the contents of cell A3 to reflect the new format.

7. Click cell **G3**.

8. On the **Home** tab, in the **Number** group, click the **Number Format** button's down arrow and then click **More Number Formats**.

9. If necessary, click the **Number** tab in the **Format Cells** dialog box.

10. In the **Category** list, click **Special**.

    The Type list appears with a list of special formats.

11. In the **Type** list, click **Phone Number**, and then click **OK**.

    Excel displays the contents of the cell as (425) 555-0102, matching the format you selected, and the Format Cells dialog box closes.

12. Click cell **H3**.

13. Click the **Font** dialog box launcher.

14. In the **Format Cells** dialog box that opens, click the **Number** tab.

15. In the **Category** list, click **Custom**.

    The contents of the Type list are updated to reflect your choice.

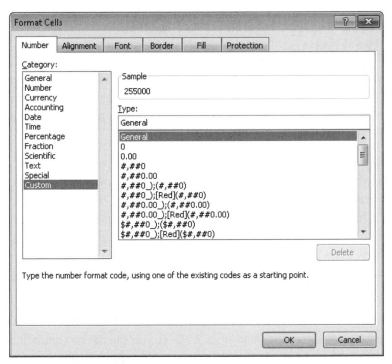

The Sample area displays a preview of the currently selected number format.

16. In the **Type** list, click the **#,##0** item.

17. In the **Type** box, click to the left of the existing format, and type $. Then click to the right of the format, and type " **before bonuses**" (note the space after the opening quote).

18. Click **OK**.

The Format Cells dialog box closes.

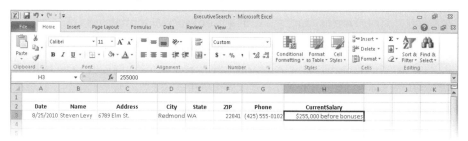

The custom number formatting is applied to the value in the active cell.

CLEAN UP Save the ExecutiveSearch workbook, and then close it.

Changing the Appearance of Data Based on Its Value

Recording package volumes, vehicle miles, and other business data in a worksheet enables you to make important decisions about your operations. And as you saw earlier in this chapter, you can change the appearance of data labels and the worksheet itself to make interpreting your data easier.

Another way you can make your data easier to interpret is to have Excel change the appearance of your data based on its value. These formats are called conditional formats because the data must meet certain conditions, defined in conditional formatting rules, to have a format applied to it. For example, if chief operating officer Lori Penor wanted to highlight any Thursdays with higher-than-average weekday package volumes, she could define a conditional format that tests the value in the cell recording total sales and changes the format of the cell's contents when the condition is met.

To create a conditional format, you select the cells to which you want to apply the format, display the Home tab, and then in the Styles group, click Conditional Formatting to display a menu of possible conditional formats. In Excel, you can define conditional formats that change how the program displays data in cells that contain values above or below the average values of the related cells, that contain values near the top or bottom of the value range, or that contain values duplicated elsewhere in the selected range.

When you select which kind of condition to create, Excel displays a dialog box that contains fields and controls you can use to define your rule. To display all of the rules for the selected cells, display the Home tab, and then in the Styles group, click Conditional Formatting. On the menu, click Manage Rules to display the Conditional Formatting Rules Manager.

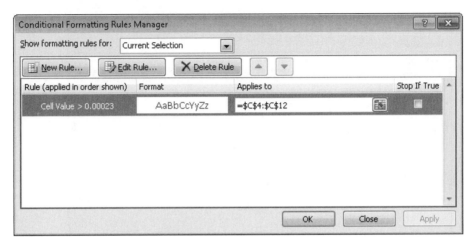

The Conditional Formatting Rules Manager.

The Conditional Formatting Rules Manager enables you to control your conditional formats in the following ways:

- Create a new rule by clicking the New Rule button.
- Change a rule by clicking the rule and then clicking the Edit Rule button.
- Remove a rule by clicking the rule and then clicking the Delete Rule button.
- Move a rule up or down in the order by clicking the rule and then clicking the Move Up button or Move Down button.
- Control whether Excel continues evaluating conditional formats after it finds a rule to apply by selecting or clearing a rule's Stop If True check box.
- Save any new rules and close the Conditional Formatting Rules Manager by clicking OK.
- Save any new rules without closing the Conditional Formatting Rules Manager by clicking Apply.
- Discard any unsaved changes by clicking Cancel.

Tip Clicking the New Rule button in the Conditional Formatting Rules Manager opens the New Formatting Rule dialog box. The commands in the New Formatting Rule dialog box duplicate the options displayed when you click the Conditional Formatting button in the Styles group on the Home tab.

After you create a rule, you can change the format applied if the rule is true by clicking the rule and then clicking the Edit Rule button to display the Edit Formatting Rule dialog box. In that dialog box, click the Format button to display the Format Cells dialog box. After you define your format, click OK to display the rule.

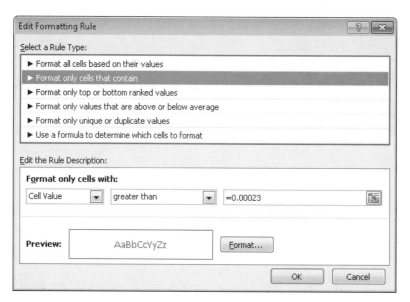

A basic conditional formatting rule. Rules can include multiple criteria.

Important Excel doesn't check to make sure that your conditions are logically consistent, so you need to be sure that you plan and enter your conditions correctly.

Excel also enables you to create three other types of conditional formats: data bars, color scales, and icon sets.

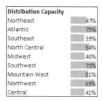

Data bars summarize the relative magnitude of values in a cell range by extending a band of color across the cell.

When data bars were introduced in Excel 2007, they filled cells with a color band that decreased in intensity as it moved across the cell. This gradient fill pattern made it a bit difficult to determine the relative length of two data bars because the end points weren't as distinct as they would have been if the bars were a solid color. Excel 2010 enables you to choose between a solid fill pattern, which makes the right edge of the bars easier to discern, and a gradient fill, which you can use if you share your workbook with colleagues who use Excel 2007.

Excel also draws data bars differently than was done in Excel 2007. Excel 2007 drew a very short data bar for the lowest value in a range and a very long data bar for the highest value. The problem was that similar values could be represented by data bars of very different lengths if there wasn't much variance among the values in the conditionally formatted range. In Excel 2010, data bars compare values based on their distance from zero, so similar values are summarized using data bars of similar lengths.

Tip Excel 2010 data bars summarize negative values by using bars that extend to the left of a baseline that the program draws in a cell. You can control how your data bars summarize negative values by clicking the Negative Value And Axis button, which can be accessed from either the New Formatting Rule dialog box or the Edit Formatting Rule dialog box.

Color scales compare the relative magnitude of values in a cell range by applying colors from a two-color or three-color set to your cells.

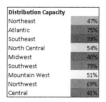

Distribution Capacity	
Northeast	47%
Atlantic	75%
Southeast	39%
North Central	54%
Midwest	40%
Southwest	73%
Mountain West	51%
Northwest	69%
Central	41%

The intensity of a cell's color reflects the value's tendency toward the top or bottom of the values in the range.

Icon sets are collections of images that Excel displays when certain rules are met.

Distribution Capacity		
Northeast		47%
Atlantic		75%
Southeast		39%
North Central		54%
Midwest		40%
Southwest		73%
Mountain West		51%
Northwest		69%
Central		41%

An icon set can consist of three, four, or five images.

When icon sets were introduced in Excel 2007, you could apply an icon set as a whole, but you couldn't create custom icon sets or choose to have Excel 2007 display no icon if the value in a cell met a criterion. In Excel 2010, you can display any icon from any set for any criterion or display no icon.

When you click a color scale or icon set in the Conditional Formatting Rules Manager and then click the Edit Rule button, you can control when Excel applies a color or icon to your data.

> **Important** Be sure to not include cells that contain summary formulas in your conditionally formatted ranges. The values, which could be much higher or lower than your regular cell data, could throw off your comparisons.

In this exercise, you'll create a series of conditional formats to change the appearance of data in worksheet cells displaying the package volume and delivery exception rates of a regional distribution center.

SET UP You need the Dashboard_start workbook located in your Chapter11 practice file folder to complete this exercise. Open the Dashboard_start workbook, and save it as *Dashboard*. Then follow the steps.

1. Select cells **C4:C12**.

Conditional Formatting ▾

2. On the **Home** tab, in the **Styles** group, click **Conditional Formatting**. On the menu, point to **Color Scales**, and then in the top row of the palette, click the second pattern from the left.

   Excel formats the selected range.

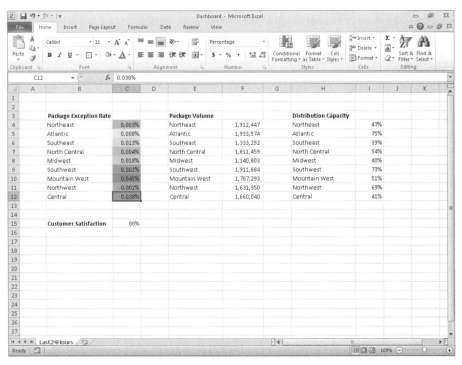

Color Scales conditional formatting applied to the first data range.

3. Select cells **F4:F12**.

4. On the **Home** tab, in the **Styles** group, click **Conditional Formatting**. On the menu, point to **Data Bars**, and then, in the **Solid Fill** group, click the orange data bar format.

    Excel formats the selected range.

5. Select cells **I4:I12**.

6. On the **Home** tab, in the **Styles** group, click **Conditional Formatting**. On the menu, point to **Icon Sets**, and then in the left column of the list of formats, click the three traffic lights with black borders.

    Excel formats the selected cells.

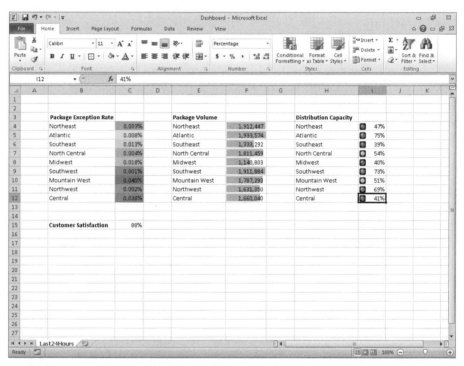

Three types of conditional formatting applied to the same data range.

7. With the range **I4:I12** still selected, on the **Home** tab, in the **Styles** group, click **Conditional Formatting**, and then click **Manage Rules**.

    The Conditional Formatting Rules Manager opens.

8. Click the **Icon Set** rule, and then click **Edit Rule**.

    The Edit Formatting Rule dialog box opens.

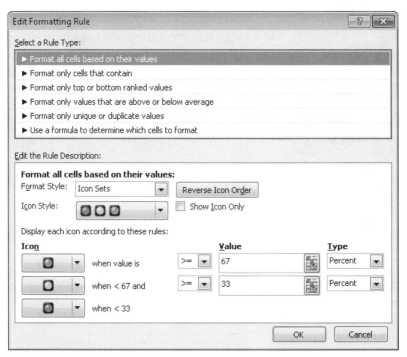

In the Edit Formatting Rule dialog box, you can customize conditional formatting.

9. Click the **Reverse Icon Order** button.

   Excel reconfigures the rules so the red light icon is at the top and the green light icon is at the bottom.

10. In the red light icon's row, in the **Type** list, click **Number**.

11. In the red light icon's **Value** field, type **0.7**.

12. In the yellow light icon's row, in the **Type** list, click **Number**.

13. In the yellow light icon **Value** field, type **0.5**.

14. Click **OK** twice to close the **Edit Formatting Rule** dialog box and the **Conditional Formatting Rules Manager**.

    Excel formats the selected cell range.

15. Click cell **C15**.

16. On the **Home** tab, in the **Styles** group, click **Conditional Formatting**. On the menu, point to **Highlight Cells Rules**, and then click **Less Than**.

    The Less Than dialog box opens.

17. In the left field, type **96%**.

18. In the **With** list, click **Red text**.

19. Click **OK**.

The Less Than dialog box closes, and Excel displays the text in cell C15 in red.

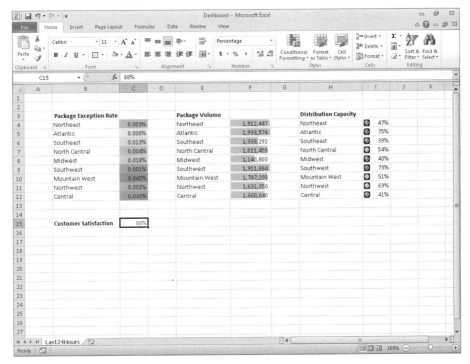

Custom conditional formatting includes cell and text colors.

✖ **CLEAN UP** Save the Dashboard workbook, and then close it.

Adding Images to Worksheets

Establishing a strong corporate identity helps customers remember your organization as well as the products and services you offer. Setting aside the obvious need for sound management, two important physical attributes of a strong retail business are a well-conceived shop space and an eye-catching, easy-to-remember logo. After you or your graphic artist has created a logo, you should add the logo to all your documents, especially any that might be seen by your customers. Not only does the logo mark the documents as coming from your company but it also serves as an advertisement, encouraging anyone who sees your worksheets to call or visit your company.

One way to add a picture to a worksheet is to display the Insert tab, and then in the Illustrations group, click Picture. Clicking Picture displays the Insert Picture dialog box, from which you can locate the picture you want to add from your hard disk. When you insert a picture, the Picture Tools Format contextual tab appears on the ribbon. You can use the tools on the Format contextual tab to change the picture's contrast, brightness, and other attributes. With the controls in the Picture Styles group, you can place a border around the picture, change the picture's shape, or change a picture's effects (such as shadow, reflection, or three-dimensional effects). Other tools, found in the Arrange and Size groups, enable you to rotate, reposition, and resize the picture.

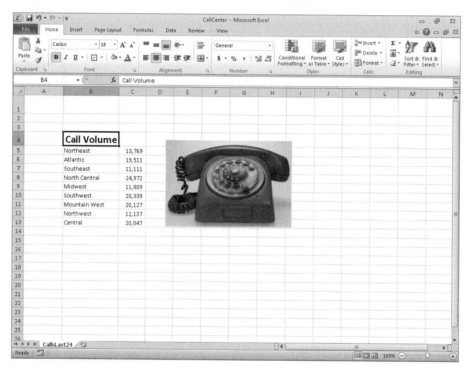

You can place an image anywhere on a worksheet.

You can also resize a picture by clicking it and then dragging one of the handles that appears on the graphic. If you accidentally resize a graphic by dragging a handle, just click the Undo button to remove your change.

Excel 2010 includes a new built-in capability that you can use to remove the background of an image you insert into a workbook. To do so, click the image and then, on the Format contextual tab of the ribbon, in the Adjust group, click Remove Background. When you do, Excel attempts to identify the foreground and background of the image.

You can display only the image subject by removing the image background.

You can drag the handles on the inner square of the background removal tool to change how the tool analyzes the image. When you have adjusted the outline to identify the elements of the image you want to keep, click the Keep Changes button on the Background Removal contextual tab of the ribbon to complete the operation.

If you want to generate a repeating image in the background of a worksheet to form a tiled pattern behind your worksheet's data, you can display the Page Layout tab, and then in the Page Setup group, click Background. In the Sheet Background dialog box, click the image that you want to serve as the background pattern for your worksheet, and click OK.

Tip To remove a background image from a worksheet, display the Page Layout tab, and then in the Page Setup group, click Delete Background.

To achieve a watermark-type effect with words displayed behind the worksheet data, save the watermark information as an image, and then use the image as the sheet background; you could also insert the image in the header or footer, and then resize or scale it to position the watermark information where you want it.

In this exercise, you'll add an image to an existing worksheet, change its location on the worksheet, reduce the size of the image, and then set another image as a repeating background for the worksheet.

SET UP You need the CallCenter_start workbook and the Phone and Texture images located in your Chapter11 practice file folder to complete this exercise. Open the CallCenter_start workbook, and save it as *CallCenter*. Then follow the steps.

Picture

1. On the **Insert** tab, in the **Illustrations** group, click **Picture**.

   The Insert Picture dialog box opens.

2. Navigate to the **Chapter11** practice file folder, and then double-click the **Phone** image file.

   The image appears on your worksheet.

Remove
Background

3. On the **Format** contextual tab, in the **Adjust** group, click **Remove Background**.

   Excel attempts to separate the image's foreground from its background.

4. Drag the handles at the upper-left and bottom-right corners of the outline until the entire phone, including the cord, is within the frame.

You resize an image on a worksheet by using the same techniques you do in a document.

5. On the **Background Removal** tab, click **Keep Changes**.

   Excel removes the highlighted image elements.

6. Move the image to the upper-left corner of the worksheet, click and hold the handle at the lower-right corner of the image, and drag it up and to the left until the image no longer obscures the **Call Volume** label.

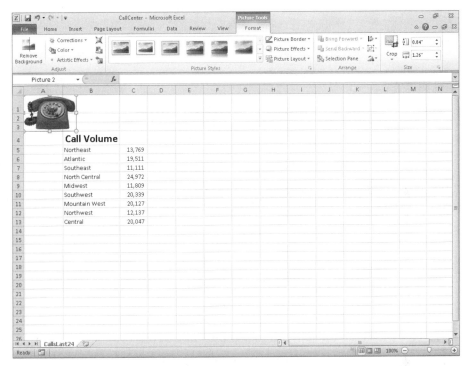

Images on worksheets are independent of worksheet cells.

7. On the **Page Layout** tab, in the **Page Setup** group, click **Background**.

The Sheet Background dialog box opens.

8. Navigate to the **Chapter11** practice file folder, and then double-click the **Texture** image file.

Excel repeats the image to form a background pattern.

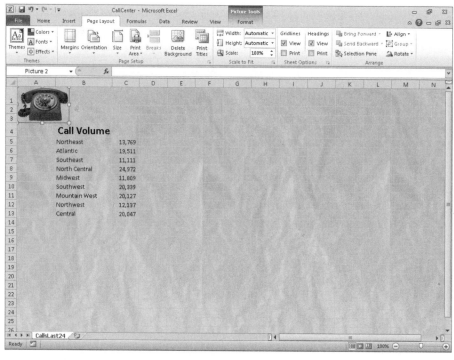

You can use an image file to create a worksheet background.

9. On the **Page Layout** tab, in the **Page Setup** group, click **Delete Background**.

Excel removes the background image.

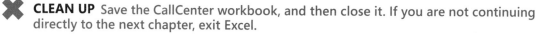

CLEAN UP Save the CallCenter workbook, and then close it. If you are not continuing directly to the next chapter, exit Excel.

Key Points

- If you don't like the default font in which Excel displays your data, you can change it.

- You can use cell formatting, including borders, alignment, and fill colors, to emphasize certain cells in your worksheets. This emphasis is particularly useful for making column and row labels stand out from the data.

- Excel comes with a number of existing styles that enable you to change the appearance of individual cells. You can also create new styles to make formatting your workbooks easier.

- If you want to apply the formatting from one cell to another cell, use the Format Painter to copy the format quickly.

- There are quite a few built-in document themes and Excel table formats you can apply to groups of cells. If you see one you like, use it and save yourself lots of formatting time.

- Conditional formats enable you to set rules so that Excel changes the appearance of a cell's contents based on its value.

- Adding images can make your worksheets more visually appealing and make your data easier to understand. Excel 2010 greatly enhances your ability to manage your images without leaving Excel.

Chapter at a Glance

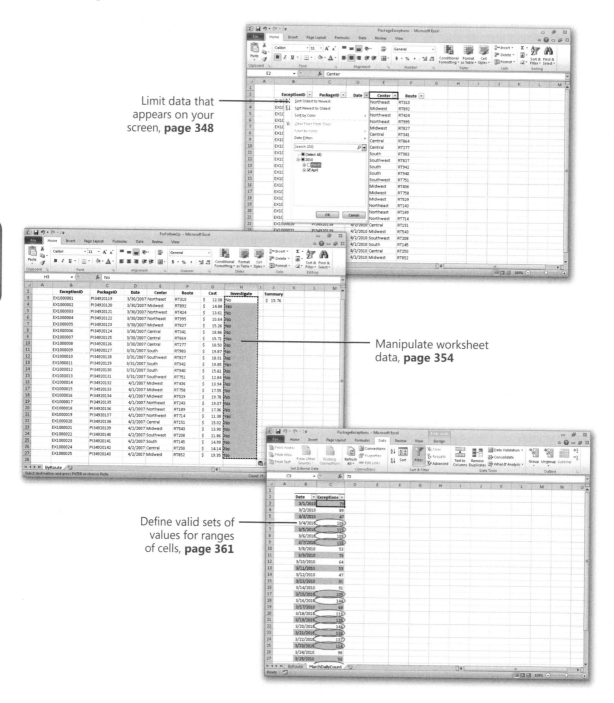

Limit data that appears on your screen, **page 348**

Manipulate worksheet data, **page 354**

Define valid sets of values for ranges of cells, **page 361**

12 Focus on Specific Data by Using Filters

In this chapter, you will learn how to

✔ Limit data that appears on your screen.

✔ Manipulate worksheet data.

✔ Define valid sets of values for ranges of cells.

With Microsoft Excel 2010, you can manage huge data collections, but storing more than 1 million rows of data doesn't help you make business decisions unless you have the ability to focus on the most important data in a worksheet. Focusing on the most relevant data in a worksheet facilitates decision making, whether that data represents the 10 busiest days in a month or revenue streams that you might need to reevaluate. Excel offers a number of powerful and flexible tools with which you can limit the data displayed in your worksheet. When your worksheet displays the subset of data you need to make a decision, you can perform calculations on that data. You can discover what percentage of monthly revenue was earned in the 10 best days in the month, find your total revenue for particular days of the week, or locate the slowest business day of the month.

Just as you can limit the data displayed by your worksheets, you can create validation rules that limit the data entered into them as well. Setting rules for data entered into cells enables you to catch many of the most common data entry errors, such as entering values that are too small or too large, or attempting to enter a word in a cell that requires a number. If you add a validation rule to worksheet cells after data has been entered into them, you can circle any invalid data so that you know what to correct.

In this chapter, you'll learn how to limit the data that appears on your screen, manipulate list data, and create validation rules that limit data entry to appropriate values.

Practice Files Before you can complete the exercises in this chapter, you need to copy the book's practice files to your computer. The practice files you'll use to complete the exercises in this chapter are in the Chapter12 practice file folder. A complete list of practice files is provided in "Using the Practice Files" at the beginning of this book.

Limiting Data That Appears on Your Screen

Excel spreadsheets can hold as much data as you need them to, but you might not want to work with all the data in a worksheet at the same time. For example, you might want to see the revenue figures for your company during the first third, second third, and final third of a month. You can limit the data shown on a worksheet by creating a filter, which is a rule that selects rows to be shown in a worksheet.

To create a filter, you click the cell in the data you want to filter and then, on the Home tab, in the Editing group, click Sort & Filter and then click Filter. When you do, Excel displays a filter arrow at the right edge of the top cell in each column of the data. The arrow indicates that the Excel AutoFilter capability is active.

Clicking the filter arrow displays a menu of filtering options and a list of the unique values in the column. The first few commands in the list are sorting commands, followed by the Clear Filter command and then the Filter By Color command. The next command that appears on the list depends on the type of data in the column. For example, if the column contains a set of dates, the command will be Date Filters. If the column contains several types of data, the command will be Number Filters. Clicking the command displays a list of commands specific to that data type.

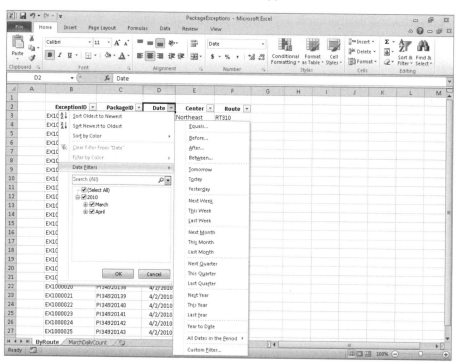

Excel displays only commands relevant to the type of data you're filtering.

Important When you turn on filtering, Excel treats the cells in the active cell's column as a range. To ensure that the filtering works properly, you should always have a label at the top of the column you want to filter. If you don't, Excel treats the first value in the list as the label and doesn't include it in the list of values by which you can filter the data.

After you click a filtering option, you define the filter's criteria. For example, you can create a filter that displays only dates after 3/31/2010.

You can filter an Excel table to display only very specific information.

Troubleshooting The appearance of buttons and groups on the ribbon changes depending on the width of the program window. For information about changing the appearance of the ribbon to match our screen images, see "Modifying the Display of the Ribbon" at the beginning of this book.

If you want to see the highest or lowest values in a data column, you can create a Top 10 filter. Choosing the Top 10 command from the menu doesn't just limit the display to the top 10 values. Instead, it opens the Top 10 AutoFilter dialog box. From within this dialog box, you can choose whether to show values from the top or bottom of the list, define the number of items you want to see, and choose whether the number in the middle box indicates the number of items or the percentage of items to be shown when the filter is applied. Using the Top 10 AutoFilter dialog box, you can find your top 10 salespeople or identify the top 5 percent of your customers.

Excel 2010 includes a new capability called the *search filter*, which you can use to type a search string that Excel uses to identify which items to display in an Excel table or a data list. To use a search filter, click a column's filter arrow and start typing a character string in the Search box. As you type the character string, Excel limits the items displayed at the bottom of the filter panel to those that contain the character or characters you've entered. When the filter list's items represent the values you want to display, click OK.

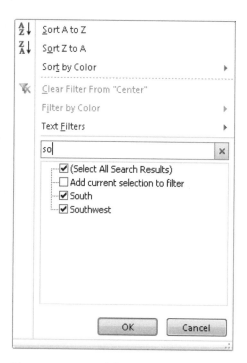

You can enter partial or entire words in the Text Filters box.

When you point to Text Filters and then click Custom Filter, you can define a rule that Excel uses to decide which rows to show after the filter is applied. For instance, you can create a rule that determines that only days with package volumes of less than 100,000 should be shown in your worksheet. With those results in front of you, you might be able to determine whether the weather or another factor resulted in slower business on those days.

Excel indicates that a column has a filter applied by changing the appearance of the column's filter arrow to include an icon that looks like a funnel. After you finish examining your data by using a filter, you can remove the filter by clicking the column's filter arrow and then clicking Clear Filter. To turn off filtering entirely and remove the filter arrows, display the Home tab and then, in the Editing group, click Sort & Filter and then click Filter.

In this exercise, you'll filter worksheet data by using a series of AutoFilter commands, create a filter showing the five days with the highest delivery exception counts in a month, create a search filter, and create a custom filter.

 SET UP You need the PackageExceptions_start workbook located in your Chapter12 practice file folder to complete this exercise. Start Excel, open the PackageExceptions_start workbook, and save it as *PackageExceptions*. Then follow the steps.

1. On the **ByRoute** worksheet, click any cell in the cell range **B2:F27**.

2. On the **Home** tab, in the **Editing** group, click **Sort & Filter**, and then click **Filter**.

   A filter arrow appears in each column's header cell.

3. Click the **Date** column filter arrow and then, from the menu that appears, clear the **March** check box.

   Excel changes the state of the Select All and 2010 check boxes to indicate that some items within those categories have been filtered.

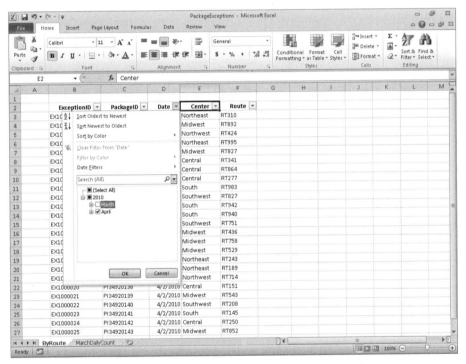

A gray check box indicates that the option is valid for some, but not all, items.

4. Click **OK**.

   Excel hides all rows that contain a date from the month of March.

5. Click the **Center** column filter arrow and then, from the menu that appears, clear the **Select All** check box.

   Excel clears all the check boxes in the list.

6. Select the **Midwest** check box, and then click **OK**.

   Excel filters the table.

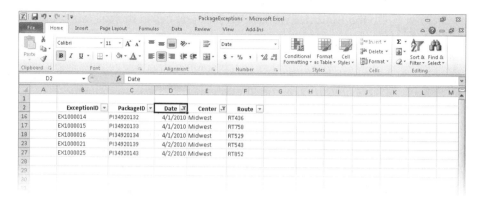

Excel displays only those exceptions that occurred in the Midwest distribution center during the month of April.

7. On the **Home** tab, in the **Editing** group, click **Sort & Filter**, and then click **Clear**.

   Excel clears all active filters but leaves the filter arrows in place.

8. Click the **Route** column header's filter arrow, and then type **RT9** in the **Search** box.

   The filter list displays only routes with identifiers that include the characters *RT9*.

9. Click **OK**.

   Excel applies the filter, displaying exceptions that occurred on routes with identifiers that contain the string *RT9*.

10. Click the **MarchDailyCount** sheet tab.

    The MarchDailyCount worksheet appears.

11. Click any cell in the Excel table.

12. Click the **Exceptions** filter arrow, click **Number Filters**, and then click **Top 10**.

    The Top 10 AutoFilter dialog box opens.

You can specify the rank, number, and type of items displayed by the Top 10 AutoFilter.

13. In the middle field, type **5**.

14. Click **OK**.

    Excel filters the table.

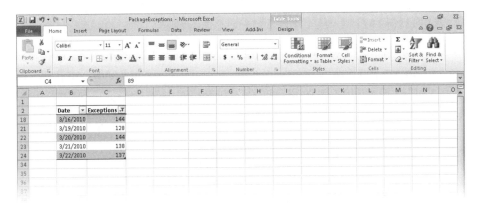

Excel displays the table rows that contain the five highest values in the column.

15. Click the **Exceptions** column filter arrow, and then click **Clear Filter from "Exceptions"**. Excel removes the filter.

16. Click the **Date** column filter arrow, click **Date Filters**, and then click **Custom Filter**. The Custom AutoFilter dialog box opens.

17. In the upper-left list, click **is after or equal to**. In the upper-right list, click **3/8/2010**. In the lower-left list, click **is before or equal to**. In the lower-right list, click **3/14/2010**.

18. Click **OK**.

    Excel filters the table.

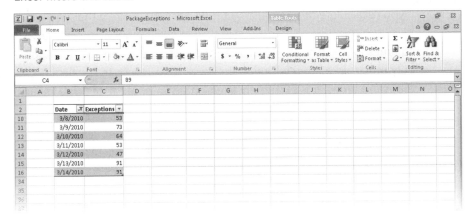

Because you left the AND option selected, Excel displays all table rows that contain a date from 3/8/2010 to 3/14/2010, inclusive.

19. On the Quick Access Toolbar, click the **Undo** button to remove your filter.

✖ **CLEAN UP** Save the PackageExceptions workbook, and then close it.

Manipulating Worksheet Data

Excel offers a wide range of tools you can use to summarize worksheet data. This section shows you how to select rows at random using the *RAND* and *RANDBETWEEN* functions, how to summarize worksheet data using the *SUBTOTAL* and *AGGREGATE* functions, and how to display a list of unique values within a data set.

Selecting List Rows at Random

In addition to filtering the data that is stored in your Excel worksheets, you can choose rows at random from a list. Selecting rows randomly is useful for choosing which customers will receive a special offer, deciding which days of the month to audit, or picking prize winners at an employee party.

To choose rows randomly, you can use the *RAND* function, which generates a random value between 0 and 1, and compare the value it returns with a test value included in the formula. As an example, suppose Consolidated Messenger wanted to offer approximately 30 percent of its customers a discount on their next shipment. A formula that returns a *TRUE* value 30 percent of the time would be *RAND<=0.3*; that is, whenever the random value was between 0 and 0.3, the result would be *TRUE*. You could use this formula to select each row in a list with a probability of 30 percent. A formula that displayed *TRUE* when the value was equal to or less than 30 percent, and *FALSE* otherwise, would be *=IF(RAND()<=0.3,"True","False")*.

If you recalculate this formula 10 times, it's very unlikely that you would see exactly three *TRUE* results and seven *FALSE* results. Just as flipping a coin can result in the same result 10 times in a row by chance, so can the *RAND* function's results appear to be off if you only recalculate it a few times. However, if you were to recalculate the function 10 thousand times, it is extremely likely that the number of *TRUE* results would be very close to 30 percent.

Tip Because the *RAND* function is a volatile function (it recalculates its results every time you update the worksheet), you should copy the cells that contain the *RAND* function in a formula and paste the formulas' values back into their original cells. To do so, select the cells that contain the *RAND* formulas and press Ctrl+C to copy the cell's contents. Then, on the Home tab, in the Clipboard group, in the Paste list, click Paste Values to replace the formula with its current result. If you don't replace the formulas with their results, you will never have a permanent record of which rows were selected.

The *RANDBETWEEN* function generates a random whole number within a defined range. For example, the formula *=RANDBETWEEN(1,100)* would generate a random integer value from 1 to 100, inclusive. The *RANDBETWEEN* function is very useful for creating sample data collections for presentations. Before the *RANDBETWEEN* function was introduced, you had to create formulas that added, subtracted, multiplied, and divided the results of the *RAND* function, which are always decimal values between 0 and 1, to create your data.

Summarizing Worksheets with Hidden and Filtered Rows

The ability to analyze the data that's most vital to your current needs is important, but there are some limitations to how you can summarize your filtered data by using functions such as *SUM* and *AVERAGE*. One limitation is that any formulas you create that include the *SUM* and *AVERAGE* functions don't change their calculations if some of the rows used in the formula are hidden by the filter.

Excel provides two ways to summarize just the visible cells in a filtered data list. The first method is to use AutoCalculate. To use AutoCalculate, you select the cells you want to summarize. When you do, Excel displays the average of values in the cells, the sum of the values in the cells, and the number of visible cells (the count) in the selection.

The AutoCalculate results are displayed on the status bar at the bottom of the Excel window.

To display the other functions you can use, right-click the status bar and select the function you want from the shortcut menu. If a check mark appears next to a function's name, that function's result appears on the status bar. Clicking a checked function name removes that function from the status bar.

AutoCalculate is great for finding a quick total or average for filtered cells, but it doesn't make the result available in the worksheet. Formulas such as *=SUM(C3:C26)* always consider every cell in the range, regardless of whether you hide a cell's row by right-clicking the row's header and then clicking Hide, so you need to create a formula by using either the *SUBTOTAL* function or the *AGGREGATE* function (which is new in Excel 2010) to summarize just those values that are visible in your worksheet. The *SUBTOTAL* function enables you to summarize every value in a range or summarize only those values in rows you haven't manually hidden. The *SUBTOTAL* function has this syntax: *SUBTOTAL(function_num, ref1, ref2, ...)*. The *function_num* argument holds the number of the operation you want to use to summarize your data. (The operation numbers are summarized in a table later in this section.) The *ref1, ref2*, and further arguments represent up to 29 ranges to include in the calculation.

As an example, assume you have a worksheet where you hid rows 20-26 manually. In this case, the formula *=SUBTOTAL(9, C3:C26, E3:E26, G3:G26)* would find the sum of all values in the ranges C3:C26, E3:E26, and G3:G26, regardless of whether that range contained any hidden rows. The formula =*SUBTOTAL(109, C3:C26, E3:E26, G3:G26)* would find the sum of all values in cells C3:C19, E3:E19, and G3:G19, ignoring the values in the manually hidden rows.

Important Be sure to place your *SUBTOTAL* formula in a row that is even with or above the headers in the range you're filtering. If you don't, your filter might hide the formula's result!

The following table lists the summary operations available for the *SUBTOTAL* formula. Excel displays the available summary operations as part of the Formula AutoComplete functionality, so you don't need to remember the operation numbers or look them up in the Help system.

Operation number (includes hidden values)	Operation number (ignores values in manually hidden rows)	Function	Description
1	101	AVERAGE	Returns the average of the values in the range
2	102	COUNT	Counts the cells in the range that contain a number
3	103	COUNTA	Counts the nonblank cells in the range
4	104	MAX	Returns the largest (maximum) value in the range
5	105	MIN	Returns the smallest (minimum) value in the range
6	106	PRODUCT	Returns the result of multiplying all numbers in the range
7	107	STDEV.S	Calculates the standard deviation of values in the range by examining a sample of the values
8	108	STDEV.P	Calculates the standard deviation of the values in the range by using all the values
9	109	SUM	Returns the result of adding all numbers in the range together
10	110	VAR.S	Calculates the variance of values in the range by examining a sample of the values
11	111	VAR.P	Calculates the variance of the values in the range by using all of the values

As the previous table shows, the *SUBTOTAL* function has two sets of operations. The first set (operations 1–11) represents operations that include hidden values in their summary, and the second set (operations 101–111) represents operations that summarize only values visible in the worksheet. Operations 1-11 summarize all cells in a range, regardless of whether the range contains any manually hidden rows. By contrast, the operations 101-111 ignore any values in manually hidden rows. What the *SUBTOTAL* function doesn't do, however, is change its result to reflect rows hidden by using a filter.

The new *AGGREGATE* function extends the capabilities of the *SUBTOTAL* function. With it, you can select from a broader range of functions and use another argument to determine which, if any, values to ignore in the calculation. *AGGREGATE* has two possible syntaxes, depending on the summary operation you select. The first syntax is *=AGGREGATE(function_ num, options, ref1...)*, which is similar to the syntax of the *SUBTOTAL* function. The other possible syntax, *=AGGREGATE(function_num, options, array, [k])*, is used to create *AGGREGATE* functions that use the *LARGE, SMALL, PERCENTILE.INC, QUARTILE.INC, PERCENTILE.EXC,* and *QUARTILE.EXC* operations.

The following table summarizes the summary operations available for use in the *AGGREGATE* function.

Number	Function	Description
1	AVERAGE	Returns the average of the values in the range.
2	COUNT	Counts the cells in the range that contain a number.
3	COUNTA	Counts the nonblank cells in the range.
4	MAX	Returns the largest (maximum) value in the range.
5	MIN	Returns the smallest (minimum) value in the range.
6	PRODUCT	Returns the result of multiplying all numbers in the range.
7	STDEV.S	Calculates the standard deviation of values in the range by examining a sample of the values.
8	STDEV.P	Calculates the standard deviation of the values in the range by using all the values.
9	SUM	Returns the result of adding all numbers in the range together.
10	VAR.S	Calculates the variance of values in the range by examining a sample of the values.
11	VAR.P	Calculates the variance of the values in the range by using all of the values.
12	MEDIAN	Returns the value in the middle of a group of values.
13	MODE.SNGL	Returns the most frequently occurring number from a group of numbers.
14	LARGE	Returns the k-th largest value in a data set; k is specified using the last function argument. If k is left blank, Excel returns the largest value.

(continued)

Number	Function	Description
15	*SMALL*	Returns the *k*-th smallest value in a data set; *k* is specified using the last function argument. If *k* is left blank, Excel returns the smallest value.
16	*PERCENTILE.INC*	Returns the *k*-th percentile of values in a range, where *k* is a value from 0 to 1, inclusive.
17	*QUARTILE.INC*	Returns the quartile value of a data set, based on a percentage from 0 to 1, inclusive.
18	*PERCENTILE.EXC*	Returns the *k*-th percentile of values in a range, where *k* is a value from 0 to 1, exclusive.
19	*QUARTILE.EXC*	Returns the quartile value of a data set, based on a percentage from 0 to 1, exclusive.

The second argument, *options*, enables you to select which items the *AGGREGATE* function should ignore. These items can include hidden rows, errors, and *SUBTOTAL* and *AGGREGATE* functions. The following table summarizes the values available for the options argument and the effect they have on the function's results.

Number	Description
0	Ignore nested *SUBTOTAL* and *AGGREGATE* functions
1	Ignore hidden rows and nested *SUBTOTAL* and *AGGREGATE* functions
2	Ignore error values and nested *SUBTOTAL* and *AGGREGATE* functions
3	Ignore hidden rows, error values, and nested *SUBTOTAL* and *AGGREGATE* functions
4	Ignore nothing
5	Ignore hidden rows
6	Ignore error values
7	Ignore hidden rows and error values

Finding Unique Values Within a Data Set

Summarizing numerical values can provide valuable information that helps you run your business. It can also be helpful to know how many different values appear within a column. For example, you might want to display all of the countries in which Consolidated Messenger has customers. If you want to display a list of the unique values in a column, click any cell in the data set, display the Data tab and then, in the Sort & Filter group, click Advanced to display the Advanced Filter dialog box.

You can filter the original list or create a filtered copy of the list.

In the List Range field, type the reference of the cell range you want to examine for unique values, select the Unique Records Only check box, and then click OK to have Excel display the row that contains the first occurrence of each value in the column.

Important Excel treats the first cell in the data range as a header cell, so it doesn't consider the cell as it builds the list of unique values. Be sure to include the header cell in your data range!

In this exercise, you'll select random rows from a list of exceptions to identify package delivery misadventures to investigate, create an *AGGREGATE* formula to summarize the visible cells in a filtered worksheet, and find the unique values in one column of data.

SET UP You need the ForFollowUp_start workbook located in your Chapter12 practice file folder to complete this exercise. Open the ForFollowUp_start workbook, and save it as *ForFollowUp*. Then follow the steps.

1. Select cells **G3:G27**.

   The average of the values in the selected cells, the number of cells selected, and the total of the values in the selected cells appear in the AutoCalculate area of the status bar.

2. In cell **J3**, enter the formula =**AGGREGATE(1,1,G3:G27)**.

   The value *$15.76* appears in cell J3.

 3. On the **Data** tab, in the **Sort & Filter** group, click **Advanced**.

   The Advanced Filter dialog box opens.

4. In the **List range** field, type **E2:E27**.

5. Select the **Unique records only** check box, and then click **OK**.

   Excel displays the rows that contain the first occurrence of each different value in the selected range.

Tip Remember that you must include cell E2, the header cell, in the List Range field so that the filter doesn't display two occurrences of Northeast in the unique values list. To see what happens when you don't include the header cell, try changing the range in the List Range field to E3:E27, selecting the Unique Records Only check box, and then clicking OK.

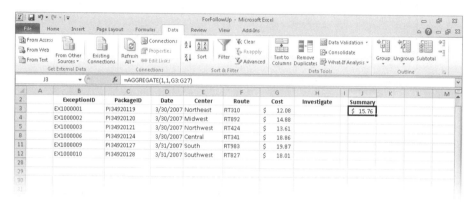

The Unique Records Only filter hides duplicate records.

6. On the **Data** tab, in the **Sort & Filter** group, click **Clear**.

   Excel removes the filter.

7. In cell **H3**, type the formula **=IF(RAND()<0.15,"Yes","No")**, and press Enter.

   A value of *Yes* or *No* appears in cell H3, depending on the *RAND* function result.

8. Select cell **H3**, and then drag the fill handle down until it covers cell **H27**.

   Excel copies the formula into every cell in the range H3:H27.

9. With the range **H3:H27** still selected, on the **Home** tab, in the **Clipboard** group, click the **Copy** button.

   Excel copies the cell range's contents to the Microsoft Office Clipboard.

10. Click the **Paste** arrow, and then in the **Paste** gallery that appears, click the first icon in the **Paste Values** group.

   Excel replaces the cells' formulas with the formulas' current results.

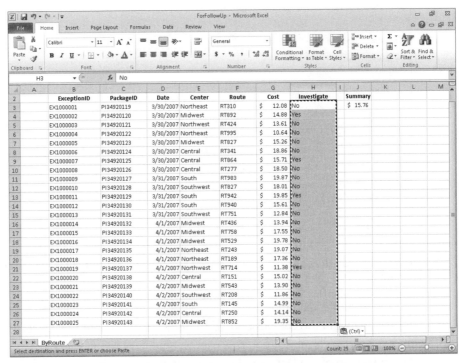

You can paste the results of formulas rather than the formulas themselves.

✖ CLEAN UP Save the ForFollowUp workbook, and then close it.

Defining Valid Sets of Values for Ranges of Cells

Part of creating efficient and easy-to-use worksheets is to do what you can to ensure the data entered into your worksheets is as accurate as possible. Although it isn't possible to catch every typographical or transcription error, you can set up a validation rule to make sure that the data entered into a cell meets certain standards.

To create a validation rule, display the Data tab on the ribbon and then, in the Data Tools group, click the Data Validation button to open the Data Validation dialog box. You can use the controls in the Data Validation dialog box to define the type of data that Excel should allow in the cell and then, depending on the data type you choose, to set the conditions data must meet to be accepted in the cell. For example, you can set the conditions so that Excel knows to look for a whole number value between 1000 and 2000.

Data validation rules are intended to ensure that worksheet users enter the correct information in a cell.

Setting accurate validation rules can help you and your colleagues avoid entering a customer's name in the cell designated to hold the phone number or setting a credit limit above a certain level. To require a user to enter a numeric value in a cell, display the Settings page of the Data Validation dialog box, and, depending on your needs, choose either Whole Number or Decimal from the Allow list.

If you want to set the same validation rule for a group of cells, you can do so by selecting the cells to which you want to apply the rule (such as a column in which you enter the credit limit of customers of Consolidated Messenger) and setting the rule by using the Data Validation dialog box. One important fact you should keep in mind is that, with Excel, you can create validation rules for cells in which you have already entered data. Excel doesn't tell you whether any of those cells contain data that violates your rule at the moment you create the rule, but you can find out by having Excel circle any worksheet cells containing data that violates the cell's validation rule. To do so, display the Data tab and then, in the Data Tools group, click the Data Validation arrow. On the menu, click the Circle Invalid Data button to circle cells with invalid data.

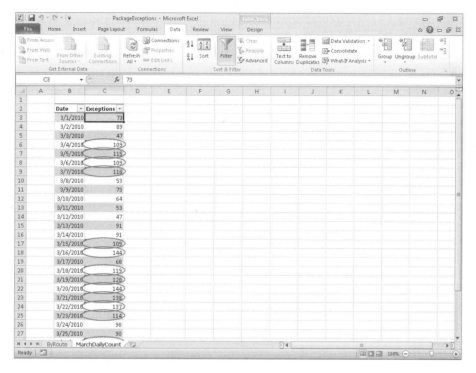

When you're ready to hide the data validation circles, click Clear Validation Circles in the Data Validation list.

Of course, it's frustrating if you want to enter data into a cell and, when a message box appears that tells you the data you tried to enter isn't acceptable, you aren't given the rules you need to follow. With Excel, you can create a message that tells the user which values are expected before the data is entered and then, if the conditions aren't met, reiterate the conditions in a custom error message.

You can turn off data validation in a cell by displaying the Settings page of the Data Validation dialog box and clicking the Clear All button in the lower-left corner of the dialog box.

In this exercise, you'll create a data validation rule limiting the credit line of Consolidated Messenger customers to $25,000, add an input message mentioning the limitation, and then create an error message if someone enters a value greater than $25,000. After you create your rule and messages, you'll test them.

 SET UP You need the Credit_start workbook located in your Chapter12 practice file folder to complete this exercise. Open the Credit_start workbook, and save it as *Credit*. Then follow the steps.

1. Select the cell range **J4:J7**.

   Cell J7 is currently blank, but you will add a value to it later in this exercise.

2. On the **Data** tab, in the **Data Tools** group, click **Data Validation**.

   ▣ Data Validation ▾   The Data Validation dialog box opens and displays the Settings page.

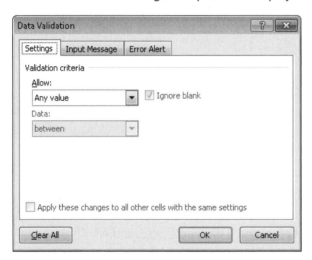

You can specify the type of data allowed in a cell.

3. In the **Allow** list, click **Whole Number**.

   Boxes labeled Minimum and Maximum appear below the Data box.

4. In the **Data** list, click **less than or equal to**.

   The Minimum box disappears.

5. In the **Maximum** box, type **25000**.

6. Clear the **Ignore blank** check box.

7. Click the **Input Message** tab.

   The Input Message page is displayed.

The input message is intended to provide guidance to the worksheet user.

8. In the **Title** box, type **Enter Limit**. In the **Input Message** box, type **Please enter the customer's credit limit, omitting the dollar sign and any commas**.

9. Click the **Error Alert** tab. On the **Error Alert** page, in the **Style** list, click **Stop**.

   The icon that appears on your message box changes to the Stop icon.

You can enter a custom error message or use the default message for this type of error.

10. In the **Title** box, type **Error**, and then click **OK**.

11. Click cell **J7**.

    A ScreenTip with the title *Enter Limit* and the text *Please enter the customer's credit limit, omitting the dollar sign and any commas* appears near cell J7.

12. Type **25001**, and press Enter.

   A stop box with the title Error opens. Leaving the Error Message box blank in the Data Validation dialog box causes Excel to use its default message.

   Clicking Retry enables you to edit the bad value; clicking Cancel deletes the entry.

13. In the **Error** box, click **Cancel**.

14. Click cell **J7**.

15. Type **25000**, and press Enter.

16. On the **Data** tab, in the **Data Tools** group, click the **Data Validation** arrow and then, in the list, click **Circle Invalid Data**.

   A red circle appears around the value in cell J4.

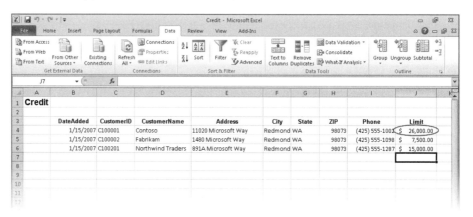

   A red data validation circle indicates invalid data.

17. In the **Data Validation** list, click **Clear Validation Circles**.

   The red circle around the value in cell K4 disappears.

CLEAN UP Save the Credit workbook, and then close it. If you are not continuing directly to the next chapter, exit Excel.

Key Points

- A number of filters are defined in Excel. (You might find the one you want is already available.)

- Filtering an Excel worksheet based on values in a single column is easy to do, but you can create a custom filter to limit your data based on the values in more than one column as well.

- With the new search filter capability in Excel 2010, you can limit the data in your worksheets based on characters the terms contain.

- Don't forget that you can get a running total (or an average, or any one of several other summary operations) for the values in a group of cells. Just select the cells and look on the status bar: the result will be there.

- Use data validation techniques to improve the accuracy of data entered into your worksheets and to identify data that doesn't meet the guidelines you set.

Part 4

Microsoft
PowerPoint 2010

Chapter at a Glance

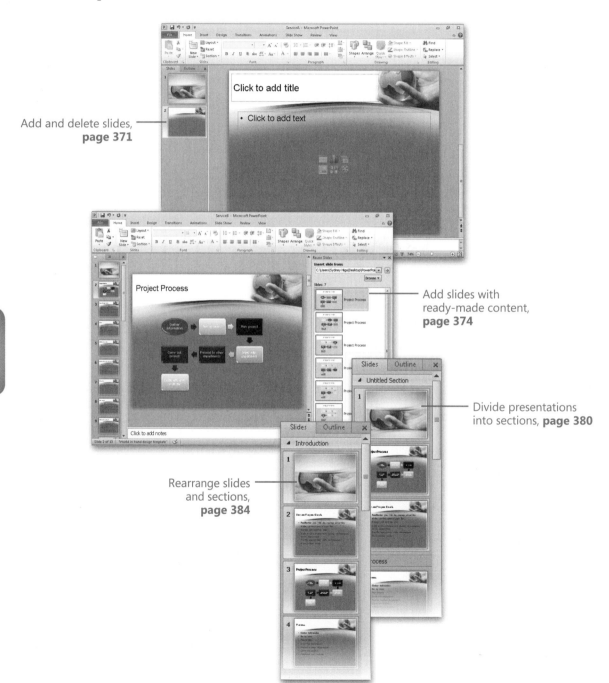

Add and delete slides, **page 371**

Add slides with
ready-made content,
page 374

Divide presentations
into sections, **page 380**

Rearrange slides
and sections,
page 384

13 Work with Slides

In this chapter, you will learn how to

- ✔ Add and delete slides.
- ✔ Add slides with ready-made content.
- ✔ Divide presentations into sections.
- ✔ Rearrange slides and sections.

For each slide to accomplish its purpose, it needs to present its content in the most effective way. The layout of individual slides and the order of slides in the presentation contribute significantly to the logical development of your message.

In this chapter, you'll add slides with different layouts, delete slides, and change the layout of a slide. You'll also divide a presentation into sections and collapse and expand sections. Finally, you'll rearrange slides and sections in a presentation.

> **Practice Files** Before you can complete the exercises in this chapter, you need to copy the book's practice files to your computer. The practice files you'll use to complete the exercises in this chapter are in the Chapter13 practice file folder. A complete list of practice files is provided in "Using the Practice Files" at the beginning of this book.

Adding and Deleting Slides

When you create a presentation, you add a slide by clicking the New Slide button in the Slides group on the Home tab. By default in a new presentation, a slide added after the title slide has the Title And Content layout. Thereafter, each added slide has the layout of the preceding slide. If you want to add a slide with a different layout, you can select the layout you want from the New Slide gallery.

If you change your mind about including a slide, you can easily delete it by selecting it either on the Slides tab of the Overview pane or in Slide Sorter view and then pressing the Delete key. You can also right-click the slide in either the pane or the view and then click Delete Slide. To select a series of slides, click the first slide in the series and hold down the Shift key while you click the last slide. To select noncontiguous slides, click the first one and hold down the Ctrl key as you click additional slides.

If you change your mind about the layout of a slide, you don't have to delete it and then add a new one with the layout you want. Instead, you can change the layout of an existing slide by selecting the new layout from the Layout gallery.

In this exercise, you'll add a slide with the default layout and add slides with other layouts. You'll delete first a single slide and then a series of slides. Then you'll change the layout of a slide.

 SET UP You need the ServiceA_start presentation located in your Chapter13 practice file folder to complete this exercise. Open the ServiceA_start presentation, and save it as *ServiceA*. Then follow the steps.

 1. With slide **1** displayed, on the **Home** tab, in the **Slides** group, click the **New Slide** button (not its arrow).

   Keyboard Shortcut Press Ctrl+M to add a slide to the presentation.

   PowerPoint adds slide 2 to the presentation with the default Title And Content layout.

This layout accommodates a title and either text or graphic content—a table, chart, diagram, picture, clip art image, or media clip.

Troubleshooting The appearance of buttons and groups on the ribbon changes depending on the width of the program window. For information about changing the appearance of the ribbon to match our screen images, see "Modifying the Display of the Ribbon" at the beginning of this book.

2. In the **Slides** group, click the **New Slide** arrow.

    The New Slide gallery appears.

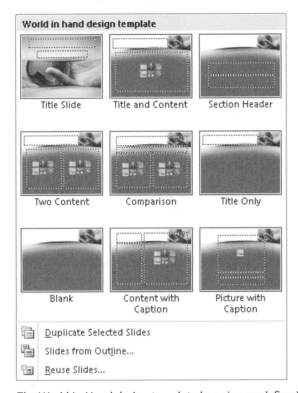

The World In Hand design template has nine predefined slide layouts.

3. In the gallery, click **Two Content**.

    PowerPoint adds slide 3, which has a placeholder for a title and two placeholders for text or graphic content.

4. In the **Slides** group, click the **New Slide** button.

    PowerPoint adds another slide with the Two Content layout.

    Tip You can also add new slides by pressing keyboard shortcuts while you're entering text on the Outline tab. For more information, see "Entering Text in Placeholders" in Chapter 14, "Work with Slide Text."

5. Continue adding slides from the IO gallery, selecting a different layout each time so that you can see what each one looks like.

   When you finish, the presentation contains 10 slides.

6. In the **Overview** pane, scroll to the top of the **Slides** tab. Then right-click slide **3**, and click **Delete Slide**.

   PowerPoint removes the slide from the presentation and renumbers all the subsequent slides.

7. On the **Slides** tab, click slide **5**. Then scroll to the bottom of the tab, hold down the Shift key, and click slide **9**.

8. With slides **5** through **9** selected, right-click the selection, and click **Delete Slide**.

   The presentation now has four slides.

 9. With slide **4** selected, on the **Home** tab, in the **Slides** group, click the **Layout** button.

   The Layout gallery appears. This gallery is the same as the New Slide gallery, but it applies the layout you choose to an existing slide instead of adding a new one.

10. In the gallery, click the **Title and Content** thumbnail.

 CLEAN UP Save the ServiceA presentation, and then close it without exiting PowerPoint.

Adding Slides with Ready-Made Content

If your presentation will contain information that already exists in a document created in Microsoft Word or another word processing program, you can edit that information into outline format and then import the outline into a PowerPoint presentation. The outline can be a Word document (.doc or .docx) or a Rich Text Format (RTF) file (.rtf).

For the importing process to work as smoothly as possible, the document must be formatted with heading styles. PowerPoint translates Heading 1 styles into slide titles, Heading 2 styles into bullet points, and Heading 3 styles into second-level bullet points, called *subpoints*.

If you often include a slide that provides the same basic information in your presentations, you don't have to re-create the slide for each presentation. For example, if you create a slide that shows your company's product development cycle for a new product presentation, you might want to use variations of that same slide in all new product presentations. You can easily tell PowerPoint to reuse a slide from one presentation in a different presentation. The slide assumes the formatting of its new presentation.

See Also For information about using a slide library to store slides for reuse, see the sidebar "Working with Slide Libraries" following this topic.

Within a presentation, you can duplicate an existing slide to reuse it as the basis for a new slide. You can then customize the duplicated slide instead of having to create it from scratch.

In this exercise, you'll add slides by importing a Word outline. Then you'll reuse a slide from an existing presentation. Finally, you'll duplicate an existing slide.

 SET UP You need the ServiceB_start and Projects presentations and the Service-Orientation document located in your Chapter13 practice file folder to complete this exercise. Open the ServiceB_start presentation, and save it as *ServiceB*. Then follow the steps.

1. On the **Home** tab, in the **Slides** group, click the **New Slide** arrow, and then below the gallery, click **Slides from Outline**.

   The Insert Outline dialog box opens. This dialog box resembles the Open dialog box.

2. Navigate to your **Chapter13** practice file folder, and then double-click the **ServiceOrientation** file.

   PowerPoint converts the outline into 12 slides.

3. In the **Overview** pane, click the **Outline** tab.

   On the Outline tab, each Heading 1 style from the ServiceOrientation document is now a slide title, each Heading 2 style is a bullet point, and each Heading 3 style is a subpoint.

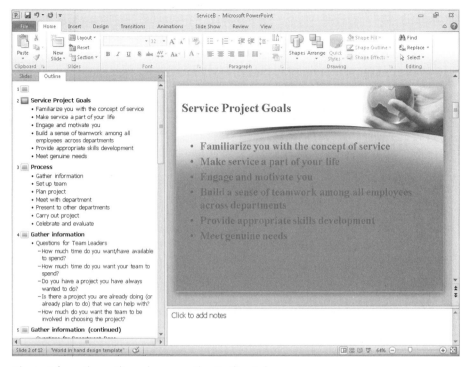

The text from the outline, shown on the Outline tab.

Tip You can start a new presentation from a Word outline. Click the File tab to display the Backstage view, and then click Open. In the Open dialog box, click All PowerPoint Presentations, and in the list of file types, click All Files. Then locate and double-click the outline document you want to use.

4. In the **Overview** pane, click the **Slides** tab, and then click the empty slide **1**.

5. On the **Home** tab, in the **Slides** group, click the **New Slide** arrow, and then below the gallery, click **Reuse Slides**.

   The Reuse Slides task pane opens on the right side of the window.

6. In the **Reuse Slides** task pane, click **Browse**, and then in the list, click **Browse File**.

   PowerPoint displays the Browse dialog box, which resembles the Open dialog box.

7. If the contents of your **Chapter13** practice file folder are not displayed, navigate to that folder now. Then double-click the **Projects** presentation.

   Thumbnails of all the slides in the presentation appear in the Reuse Slides task pane.

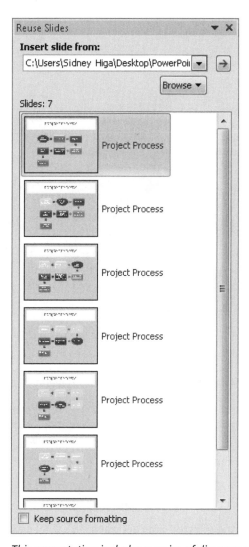

This presentation includes a series of diagrams related to a project workflow.

8. Scroll to the bottom of the task pane to see all the available slides, and then point to the last thumbnail.

    The thumbnail expands so that you can see the slide details, making it easier to select the slide you want.

9. Scroll back to the top of the task pane, and then click the first thumbnail.

    PowerPoint inserts the selected slide from the Projects presentation as slide 2 in the ServiceB presentation. The slide takes on the design of the presentation in which it is inserted.

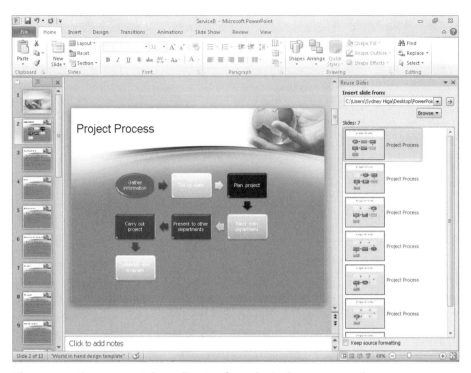

The presentation now contains a diagram from the Projects *presentation.*

Tip If you want the slide to retain the formatting from the Projects presentation instead of taking on the formatting of the ServiceB presentation, select the Keep Source Formatting check box at the bottom of the Reuse Slides task pane.

 10. Click the task pane's **Close** button.

11. With slide **2** selected on the **Slides** tab, in the **Slides** group of the **Home** tab, click the **New Slide** arrow. Then click **Duplicate Selected Slide**.

Tip You can also right-click the selected slide and then click Duplicate Slide.

PowerPoint inserts a new slide 3 identical to slide 2. You could now modify the existing slide content instead of creating it from scratch.

 CLEAN UP Save the ServiceB presentation, and then close it.

Working with Slide Libraries

If your organization is running Microsoft SharePoint Server and has enabled slide libraries, and if PowerPoint Professional Plus is installed on your computer, you and your colleagues can store slides or even entire presentations in a slide library so that they are available for use in any presentation.

For example, suppose a graphically gifted person has developed a slide with a sophisticated chart showing the percentage of income derived from the sale of different categories of merchandise. He or she can store the slide in a slide library so that other people can use it in their presentations without having to take the time to develop a similar chart. Larger organizations might even have people on staff with responsibility for creating this type of slide, so that they can ensure that all presentations convey the same information in the same professional way.

To store slides in a slide library:

1. Display the Backstage view, click Save & Send, and then click Publish Slides.

2. In the right pane, click the Publish Slides button.

   The Publish Slides dialog box opens.

3. In the Publish Slides dialog box, select the check box for the slide you want to store in the library.

4. If the URL of your SharePoint slide library does not appear in the Publish To box, click the box, and type the URL.

5. Click Publish to store the slide in the slide library.

To insert a slide from a slide library:

1. Click the slide after which you want the new slide to appear.

2. On the Home tab, in the Slides group, click the New Slide arrow, and then click Reuse Slides.

3. In the Reuse Slides task pane, in the Insert Slide From box, type the URL of your SharePoint slide library, and then click the Go arrow.

   You can also click Browse, click Browse Slide Library, and then navigate to the URL of the library in the Select A Slide Library dialog box.

4. Double-click the thumbnail of the slide you want to insert in the active presentation.

Exporting Presentations as Outlines

When you want to use the text from a presentation in another program, you can save the presentation outline as an .rtf file. Many programs, including the Windows and Macintosh versions of Word and older versions of PowerPoint, can import outlines saved in .rtf with their formatting intact.

To save a presentation as an .rtf file:

1. Display the Backstage view, and then click Save As.

   The Save As dialog box opens.

2. In the File Name box, specify the name of the file.

3. Display the Save As Type list, and click Outline/RTF.

4. Navigate to the folder in which you want to store the outline, and click Save.

   PowerPoint saves the presentation's outline in .rtf format with the designated name in the designated folder.

Dividing Presentations into Sections

New in PowerPoint 2010 is the ability to divide slides into sections. Sections appear as bars across the Slides tab of the Overview pane in Normal view and across the workspace in Slide Sorter view. They do not appear in other views, and they do not create slides or otherwise interrupt the flow of the presentation.

Dividing a presentation into sections can be a great tool during content development. Because you can hide whole sections of slides, the sections make it easier to focus on one part of a presentation at a time. If you are working on a presentation with other people, you can name one section for each person to delineate who is responsible for which slides.

In this exercise, you'll divide a presentation into two sections, adding one in Normal view and the other in Slide Sorter view. After naming the sections, you'll hide their slides and then display first one section and then both sections.

SET UP You need the ServiceC_start presentation located in your Chapter13 practice file folder to complete this exercise. Open the ServiceC_start presentation, and save it as *ServiceC*. Then follow the steps.

 1. With slide **1** displayed, on the **Home** tab, in the **Slides** group, click the **Section** button, and then click **Add Section**.

On the Slides tab of the Overview pane, PowerPoint adds a section bar before slide 1.

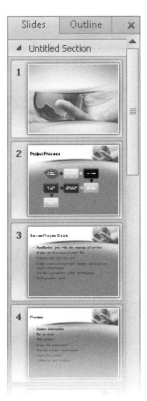

PowerPoint selects all the slides that are included in the new section.

 2. On the **View Shortcuts** toolbar, click the **Slide Sorter** button.

3. Click slide **4**, click the **Section** button, and then click **Add Section**.

PowerPoint adds a section bar before slide 4.

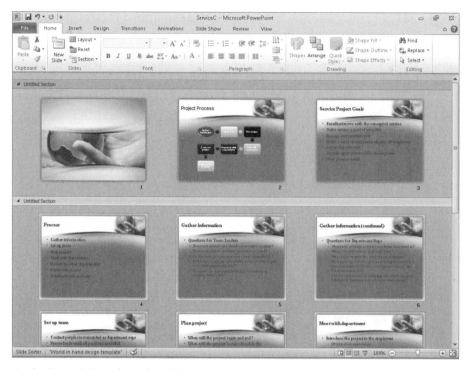

Again, PowerPoint selects the slides in the new section.

4. Right-click the second **Untitled Section** bar, and click **Rename Section**.

The Rename Section dialog box opens.

The current name is selected, ready to be replaced.

5. In the **Section name** box, type **Process**, and then click **Rename**.

6. On the **View Shortcuts** toolbar, click the **Normal** button.

7. On the **Slides** tab of the **Overview** pane, click the **Untitled Section** bar above slide **1**.

The section bar and all the slides in the section are selected.

You can select just one section of the presentation.

8. In the **Slides** group, click the **Section** button, and click **Rename Section**. Then in the **Rename Section** dialog box, type **Introduction** as the section name, and click **Rename**.

9. In the **Slides** group, click the **Section** button, and then click **Collapse All**.

   The slides are hidden under their section bars.

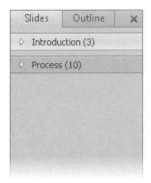

You can use sections to provide an "outline" of long presentations.

10. On the **Slides** tab, click the arrow to the left of **Introduction** to display only the slides in that section.

11. In the **Slides** group, click the **Section** button, and then click **Expand All**.

All the slides are now displayed.

 CLEAN UP Save the ServiceC presentation, and then close it.

Rearranging Slides and Sections

After you have created several slides, whether by adding them and entering text or by importing them from another presentation, you might want to rearrange the order of the slides so that they effectively communicate your message. You can rearrange a presentation in three ways.

● On the Slides tab, you can drag slides up and down to change their order.

● On the Slides tab, you can move entire sections up or down in a presentation.

● To see more of the presentation at the same time, you can switch to Slide Sorter view. You can then drag slide thumbnails or sections into the correct order.

In this exercise, you'll work on the Slides tab and in Slide Sorter view to logically arrange the slides in a presentation. You'll also delete a section you no longer need.

SET UP You need the ServiceD_start presentation located in your Chapter13 practice file folder to complete this exercise. Open the ServiceD_start presentation, and save it as *ServiceD*. Then follow the steps.

1. In the **Overview** pane, on the **Slides** tab, click the slide **2** thumbnail, and then drag it downward to the space above the thumbnail for slide **4**, but don't release the mouse button yet.

The thumbnail itself remains in place, but a bar indicates where the slide will move to when you release the mouse button.

2. Release the mouse button.

PowerPoint moves the slide to its new location in the Process section and switches the numbers of slides 2 and 3.

Tip You can move slides from one open presentation to another in Slide Sorter view. Display both presentations in Slide Sorter view, and then on the View tab, in the Window group, click the Arrange All button. Then drag slides from one presentation window to the other.

3. To the left of **Introduction** in the first section bar, click the black **Collapse Section** button. Then repeat this step for the **Process** section.

   Even with these two sections collapsed, you can't see all the slides.

4. On the **View Shortcuts** toolbar, click the **Slide Sorter** button.

5. Use the **Zoom Slider** at the right end of the status bar to adjust the zoom percentage so that you can see all the slides.

   We set the zoom percentage to 80%.

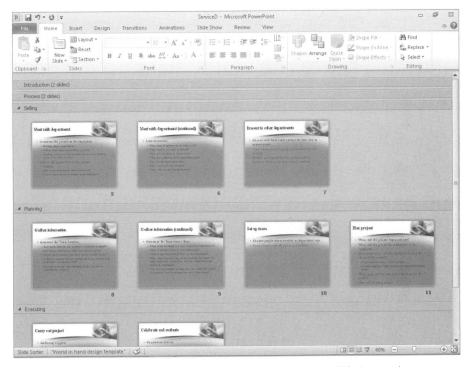

The sections you collapsed in Normal view are still collapsed in Slide Sorter view.

6. In the **Selling** section, click slide **7**, and then drag it to the left until its bar sits to the left of slide **5**.

   PowerPoint renumbers the slides in the section.

7. Point to the **Planning** section bar, right-click it, and then click **Move Section Up**.

   The Planning section bar and all its slides move above the Selling section. PowerPoint renumbers the slides in both sections.

8. Switch to Normal view.

9. Click the white **Expand Section** button to expand the **Introduction** and **Process** sections.

These two sections could easily be combined into one section.

10. Click the **Process** section bar. Then in the **Slides** group, click the **Section** button, and click **Remove Section**.

PowerPoint removes the Process section bar.

The Introduction section now contains four slides.

CLEAN UP Save the ServiceD presentation, and then close it.

Key Points

- You can add as many slides as you want. Most templates provide a variety of ready-made slide layouts to choose from.

- If you change your mind about a slide or its layout, you can delete it or switch to a different layout.

- You can create slides with content already in place by importing an outline or reusing existing slides. Both methods save time and effort.

- Grouping slides into sections makes it easy to focus on specific parts of the presentation.

- If you need to change the order of slides or sections, you can rearrange them on the Slides tab in Normal view or in Slide Sorter view.

Chapter at a Glance

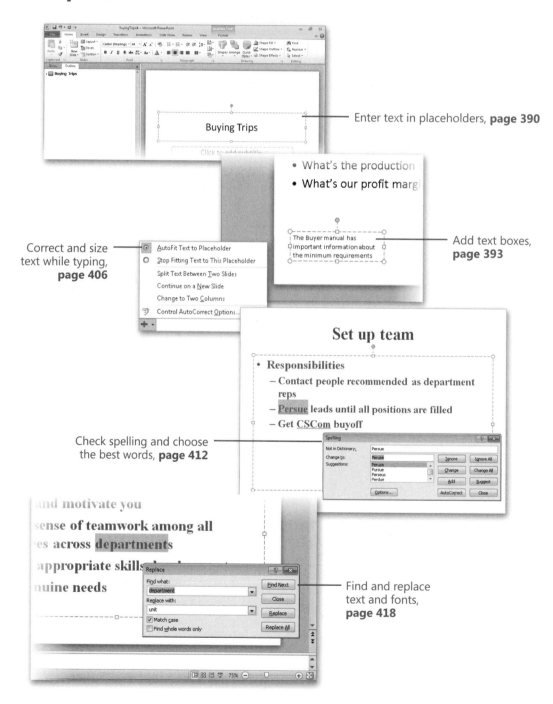

Enter text in placeholders, **page 390**

Add text boxes, **page 393**

Correct and size text while typing, **page 406**

Check spelling and choose the best words, **page 412**

Find and replace text and fonts, **page 418**

14 Work with Slide Text

In this chapter, you will learn how to

- ✔ Enter text in placeholders.
- ✔ Add text boxes.
- ✔ Edit text.
- ✔ Correct and size text while typing.
- ✔ Check spelling and choose the best words.
- ✔ Find and replace text and fonts.

In later chapters of this book, we show you ways to add fancy effects to electronic presentations so that you can really grab the attention of your audience. But no amount of animation, jazzy colors, and supporting pictures will convey your message if the words on the slides are inadequate to the task.

For most of your presentations, text is the foundation on which you build everything else. Even if you follow the current trend of building presentations that consist primarily of pictures, you still need to make sure that titles and any other words on your slides do their job, and do it well. So this chapter shows you various ways to work with text to ensure that the words are accurate, consistent, and appropriately formatted.

In this chapter, you'll learn how to enter and edit text on slides, on the Outline tab, and in text boxes. You'll see how the AutoCorrect feature helps you avoid typographical errors and the AutoFit feature makes the words you type fit in the available space. Then you'll see how the spell-checking feature can help you correct misspellings. Finally, you'll learn how to replace one word with another throughout a presentation by using the Find And Replace feature, which you also use to ensure the consistent use of fonts.

> **Practice Files** Before you can complete the exercises in this chapter, you need to copy the book's practice files to your computer. The practice files you'll use to complete the exercises in this chapter are in the Chapter14 practice file folder. A complete list of practice files is provided in "Using the Practice Files" at the beginning of this book.

Entering Text in Placeholders

When you add a new slide to a presentation, the layout you select indicates with placeholders the type and position of the objects on the slide. For example, a Title And Content slide has placeholders for a title and either a bulleted list with one or more levels of bullet points and subpoints or an illustration such as a table, chart, graphic, or movie clip. You can enter text directly into a placeholder on a slide in the Slide pane, or you can enter text on the Outline tab of the Overview pane, where the entire presentation is displayed in outline form.

When you point to a placeholder on a slide, the pointer changes to an I-beam. When you click the placeholder, a blinking cursor appears where you clicked to indicate where characters will appear when you type. As you type, the text appears both on the slide and on the Outline tab.

In this exercise, you'll enter slide titles, bullet points, and subpoints, both directly in placeholders on a slide and on the Outline tab.

 SET UP You don't need any practice files to complete this exercise. Open a new, blank presentation, and save it as *BuyingTripsA*. Then follow the steps.

1. In the **Slide** pane, click the slide's **Click to add title** placeholder.

   A selection box surrounds the title placeholder, and the cursor appears in the center of the box, indicating that the text you type will be centered in the placeholder.

2. Type **Buying Trips**. (Do not type the period.)

   By tradition, slide titles have no periods.

   Tip If you make a typing error while working through this exercise, press Backspace to delete the mistake, and then type the correct text. For information about more sophisticated ways of checking and correcting spelling, see "Correcting and Sizing Text While Typing" and "Checking Spelling and Choosing the Best Words," both later in this chapter.

3. In the **Overview** pane, click the **Outline** tab.

   Notice that the text you typed also appears there.

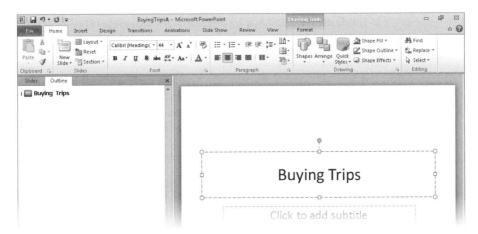

On the Outline tab, a slide icon appears adjacent to the slide title.

Troubleshooting The appearance of buttons and groups on the ribbon changes depending on the width of the program window. For information about changing the appearance of the ribbon to match our screen images, see "Modifying the Display of the Ribbon" at the beginning of this book.

4. In the **Slide** pane, click the **Click to add subtitle** placeholder.

5. Type **Ensuring Successful Outcomes**, and then press Enter to move the cursor to a new line in the same placeholder.

6. Type **Judy Lew, Purchasing Manager**.

   As you enter titles and bullet points throughout the exercises, don't type any ending punctuation marks.

7. On the Quick Access Toolbar, click the **Save** button.

   We won't tell you to save your work again in this exercise. Suffice it to say that you should save often.

8. Add a new slide with the **Title and Content** layout.

   See Also For information about adding slides, see "Adding and Deleting Slides" in Chapter 13, "Work with Slides."

   PowerPoint creates a slide with placeholders for a title and either a bulleted list or an illustration. The Outline tab now displays an icon for a second slide, and the status bar displays *Slide 2 of 2*.

9. Without clicking anywhere, type **Overview**.

   If you start typing on an empty slide without first selecting a placeholder, PowerPoint enters the text into the title placeholder.

10. On the **Outline** tab, click to the right of **Overview**, and then press Enter.

   PowerPoint adds a slide to the presentation, and an icon for slide 3 appears in the Outline pane.

11. Press the Tab key.

   The new slide changes to a bullet point on slide 2. The bullet is gray until you enter text for the bullet point.

12. Type **Preparing for a buying trip**, and then press Enter.

   PowerPoint adds a new bullet at the same level.

13. Type **Traveling internationally**, and then press Enter.

14. Type **Meeting the client**, and then press Enter.

15. Press Shift+Tab.

   On the Outline tab, the bullet changes into an icon for slide 3.

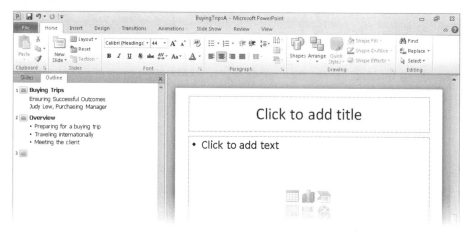

When you create a slide on the Outline tab, the new slide is displayed in the Slide pane.

16. Type **Preparing for a Buying Trip**, press Enter, and then press Tab.

17. Type **Know your needs**, and then press Enter.

 18. On the **Home** tab, in the **Paragraph** group, click the **Increase List Level** button.

   PowerPoint creates a subpoint.

   Tip You can use the Increase List Level button to change slide titles to bullet points and bullet points to subpoints, both in the Slide pane and on the Outline tab. You can also use the Decrease List Level button to change subpoints to bullet points and bullet points to slide titles in both places. However, when you're entering text on the Outline tab, it's quicker to use keys—Tab and Shift+Tab—to perform these functions than it is to take your hands off the keyboard to use your mouse.

19. Type **Know your customers**, press Enter, and then type **Know the current trends**.

20. Press Ctrl+Enter.

   Instead of creating another bullet, PowerPoint creates a new slide.

If you know what text you want to appear on your slides, it is often quicker to work on the Outline tab.

 CLEAN UP Save the BuyingTripsA presentation, and then close it.

Adding Text Boxes

The size and position of the placeholders on a slide are dictated by the slide's design. Every slide you create with a particular layout of a particular design has the same place-holders in the same locations, and the text you type in them has the same format.

If you want to add text that does not belong in a placeholder—for example, if you want to add an annotation to a graphic—you can create an independent text box and enter the text there. You can create a text box in two ways:

● You can click the Text Box button, click the slide where you want the text to appear, and then type. The text box grows to fit what you type on one line, even expanding beyond the border of the slide if necessary.

● You can click the Text Box button, drag a box where you want the text to appear on the slide, and then type. When the text reaches the right boundary of the box, the height of the box expands by one line so that the text can wrap. As you continue typing, the width of the box stays the same, but the height grows as necessary to accommodate all the text.

When you click inside a text box, the box is surrounded by a dashed border. You can then enter new text or edit existing text.

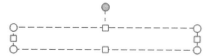

When the border is dashed, you can enter or edit text.

Clicking the dashed border changes it to a solid border. You can then manipulate the text box as a unit.

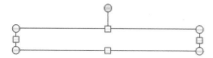

When the border is solid, you can manipulate the box.

You can move a text box by dragging its border, and you can copy it just as easily by holding down the Ctrl key while you drag. You can drag the blue squares and circles around the border of the box, which are called *sizing handles*, to change the size and shape of the text box. If you want the text in the text box to be oriented differently than the rest of the text on the slide, you can drag the green circle, which is called the *rotating handle*, to accomplish this purpose.

If you want to create a text box of a specific size or shape, you can right-click the box's border, click Format Shape, click Size in the Format Shape dialog box, and then change the settings. On the Text Box page of this dialog box, you can change the direction of text by displaying the Text Direction list and clicking one of the Rotate options. You can click Stacked in this list to keep the individual characters horizontal but make them run from top to bottom in the box instead of from left to right.

Tip If you want to change the size, shape, or behavior of a placeholder on an individual slide, you can use the same techniques as those you use with text boxes. If you want to make changes to the same placeholder on every slide, you should make the adjustments on the presentation's master slide. For more information about working with master slides, refer to *Microsoft PowerPoint 2010 Step by Step*, by Joyce Cox and Joan Lambert (Microsoft Press, 2010).

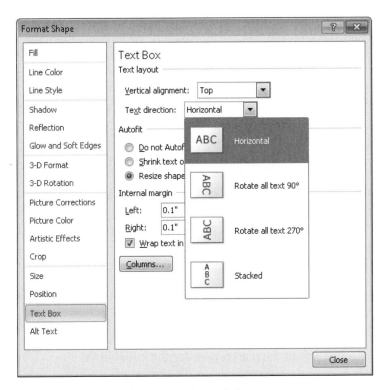

The Text Box page of the Format Shape dialog box.

On the Text Box page, you can also specify whether PowerPoint should shrink the text to fit the box if it won't all fit at the default size (18 points), and whether the text should wrap within the box.

To deselect the text box, you click a blank area of the slide. The border then disappears. If you want a text box to have a border when it's not selected, you can display the Format Shape dialog box, and on the Line Color page, select either Solid Line or Gradient Line. You can then fine-tune the border's color or gradient to achieve the effect you want.

In this exercise, you'll select and deselect a placeholder to see the effect on its border. You'll create one text box whose height stays constant while its width increases and another whose width stays constant while its height increases. You'll manipulate these text boxes by rotating and moving one of them and sizing the other.

SET UP You need the BuyingTripsB_start presentation located in your Chapter14 practice file folder to complete this exercise. Open the BuyingTripsB_start presentation, and save it as *BuyingTripsB*. Then follow the steps.

1. Move to slide **2**, and then on the slide, click the slide title.

   The cursor and dashed border indicate that the placeholder is selected for editing.

2. Point to the border of the placeholder, and when the pointer changes to a four-headed arrow, click the mouse button once.

   The placeholder is selected as a unit, as indicated by the solid border. Although you won't usually want to change the size or location of a text placeholder, while the placeholder has a solid border, you can size and move it just like any other text box. Your changes will affect only the placeholder on the current slide, not corresponding placeholders on other slides.

3. To deselect the placeholder, click outside it in a blank area of the slide.

4. Move to slide **5**, and then click anywhere in the bulleted list to display its placeholder.

5. On the **Insert** tab, in the **Text** group, click the **Text Box** button, and then point below and to the left of the placeholder for the bulleted list.

   The pointer shape changes to an upside-down *t*.

6. Click the slide to create a text box.

   A small, empty text box appears with a cursor blinking inside it.

Clicking the slide creates a single-line text box.

7. Type **Critical to get things off to a good start**.

   The width of the text box increases to accommodate the text as you type it.

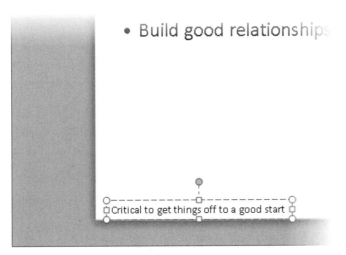

The text box grows horizontally.

8. To rotate the text so that it reads vertically instead of horizontally, point to the green rotating handle that is attached to the upper-middle handle of the text box, and drag it 90 degrees clockwise.

   Tip You can also rotate a text box by selecting the box for manipulation, and then on the Format contextual tab, in the Arrange group, clicking the Rotate button. In the list that appears, you can select an option to rotate the text box by 90 degrees to the left or right or to flip it horizontally or vertically.

9. Point to the border of the box (not to a handle), and then drag the box up and to the right, until it sits at the right edge of the slide.

10. Right-click the border of the box, and then click **Format Shape**.

11. In the **Format Shape** dialog box, click **Line Color**. Then click **Solid Line**.

    The page changes to allow you to pick the line color you want.

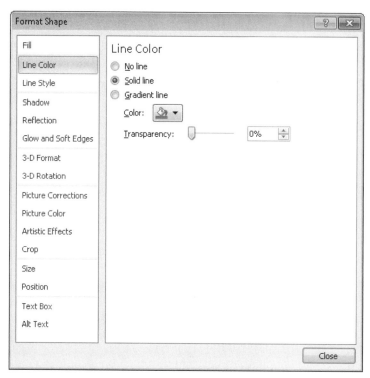

The Line Color page of the Format Shape dialog box.

12. Click the **Color** button, and in the top row of the **Theme Colors** palette, click the orange box (**Orange, Accent 6**). Then click **Close**.

13. Click a blank area of the slide to deselect the text box so that you can see the orange border.

14. Move to slide **6**, and then in the **Text** group, click the **Text Box** button. On the left side of the area below the bulleted list, drag approximately **2** inches to the right and **0.5** inch down.

No matter what height you make the box, it snaps to a standard height when you release the mouse button.

15. Type **The Buyer manual has important information about the minimum requirements**.

The width of the box does not change, but the height of the box increases to accommodate the complete entry.

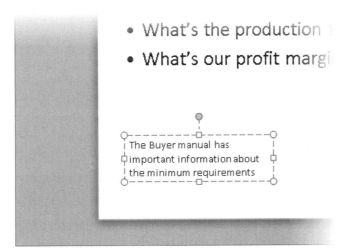

The text box grows vertically.

16. Click the border of the text box to select it as a unit. Then drag the solid border and the white sizing handles until the box is two lines high and the same width as the bullet points.

17. Click a blank area of the slide to deselect the text box.

    The border of the text box is no longer visible.

- What's the production time?
- **What's our profit margin?**

The Buyer manual has important information about
the minimum requirements

You can manually adjust the size and shape of a text box.

 CLEAN UP Save the BuyingTripsB presentation, and then close it.

Changing the Default Font for Text Boxes

When you create a text box, PowerPoint applies default settings such as the font, size, and style—regular, bold, and italic—as well as other effects, such as underline, small capitals, and embossing. To save yourself some formatting steps, you can change the default settings for the presentation you are working on.

To save the current settings as the new default:

1. In a new, blank presentation, create a text box and enter some text in it.

2. Select the text, and then on the Home tab, click the Font dialog box launcher.

3. Select the font, font style, size, color, underline style, and effects you want to apply to all the text boxes you create from now on in this presentation, and then click OK.

   You can also add other effects, such as a fill color, outline formatting, or a special effect.

   See Also For information about these other effects, refer to *Microsoft PowerPoint 2010 Step by Step*, by Joyce Cox and Joan Lambert (Microsoft Press, 2010).

4. Select the text box itself, right-click its border, and then click Set As Default Text Box.

5. Create another text box on the same slide, and then enter text in it.

   The text appears with the new default settings.

Editing Text

After you enter text in either a placeholder or a text box, you can change it at any time. You can insert new text by clicking where you want to make the insertion and simply typing. However, before you can change existing text, you have to select it by using the following techniques:

- **Word** Double-click the word to select the word and the space following it. Punctuation following the word is not selected.

- **Adjacent words, lines, or paragraphs** Drag through them. Alternatively, position the cursor at the beginning of the text you want to select, hold down the Shift key, and either press an arrow key to select characters one at a time or click at the end of the text you want to select.

- **Slide title** Click its slide icon on the Outline tab.

- **Bullet point or subpoint** Click its bullet on either the Outline tab or the slide.

- **All the text in a placeholder** Click inside the placeholder, click the Select button in the Editing group on the Home tab, and then click Select All.

  Keyboard Shortcut Press Ctrl+A after clicking inside the placeholder to select all the text.

- **All the objects on a slide** Select a placeholder (so that it has a solid border), click the Select button, and then click Select All. All the other objects on that slide are added to the selection. You can then work with all the objects as a unit.

  Tip Clicking Select and then Selection Pane displays the Selection And Visibility task pane, where you can specify whether particular objects should be displayed or hidden. You might want to hide an object if you're using the slide in similar presentations for two different audiences, one of which needs more detail than the other.

Selected text appears highlighted in the location where you made the selection—that is, on either the slide or the Outline tab.

To replace a selection, you type the new text. To delete the selection, you press either the Delete key or the Backspace key.

If you want to move or copy the selected text, you have three options:

- **Drag-and-drop editing** Use this feature, which is frequently referred to simply as *dragging*, when you need to move or copy text within the same slide or to a slide that is visible on the Outline tab without scrolling. Start by using any of the methods described previously to select the text. Then point to the selection, hold down the mouse button, drag the text to its new location, and release the mouse button. To copy the selection, hold down the Ctrl key while you drag.

- **Cut, Copy, and Paste buttons** Use this method when you need to move or copy text between two locations that you cannot see at the same time—for example, between slides that are not visible simultaneously on the Outline tab. Select the text, and click the Cut or Copy button in the Clipboard group on the Home tab. (The cut or copied item is stored in an area of your computer's memory called the *Microsoft Office Clipboard*, hence the name of the group.) Then reposition the cursor, and click the Paste button to insert the selection in its new location. If you click the Paste arrow instead of the button, PowerPoint displays a list of different ways to paste the selection.

Under Paste Options, buttons represent the ways in which you can paste the item.

Pointing to a button under Paste Options displays a preview of how the cut or copied item will look when pasted into the text in that format, so you can experiment with different ways of pasting until you find the one you want.

See Also For more information about the Clipboard, see the sidebar "About the Clipboard" later in this chapter.

● **Keyboard shortcuts** It can be more efficient to press key combinations to cut, copy, and paste selections than to click buttons on the ribbon. The main keyboard shortcuts for editing tasks are listed in the following table.

Task	Keyboard shortcuts
Cut	Ctrl+X
Copy	Ctrl+C
Paste	Ctrl+V
Undo	Ctrl+Z
Repeat/Redo	Ctrl+Y

Tip While moving and copying text on the Outline tab, you can collapse bullet points under slide titles so that you can see more of the presentation at one time. Double-click the icon of the slide whose bullet points you want to hide. Double-click again to redisplay the bullet points. To expand or collapse the entire outline at once, right-click the title of a slide, point to Expand or Collapse, and then click Expand All or Collapse All.

If you change your mind about a change you have made, you can reverse it by clicking the Undo button on the Quick Access Toolbar. If you undo an action in error, you can click the Redo button on the Quick Access Toolbar to reverse the change.

To undo multiple actions at the same time, you can click the Undo arrow and then click the earliest action you want to undo in the list. You can undo actions only in the order in which you performed them—that is, you cannot reverse your fourth previous action without first reversing the three actions that followed it.

Tip The number of actions you can undo is set to 20, but you can change that number by clicking the File tab to display the Backstage view, clicking Options to display the PowerPoint Options dialog box, clicking Advanced, and then in the Editing Options area of the Advanced page, changing the Maximum Number Of Undos setting.

In this exercise, you'll delete and replace words, as well as move bullet points and sub-points on the Outline tab and on slides.

SET UP You need the BuyingTripsC_start presentation located in your Chapter14 practice file folder to complete this exercise. Open the BuyingTripsC_start presentation, and save it as *BuyingTripsC*. Then follow the steps.

1. On the **Outline** tab, in the first bullet on slide **2**, double-click the word **buying**.

   When you select text on either the Outline tab or the slide, a small toolbar (called the *Mini Toolbar*) containing options for formatting the text appears. If you ignore the Mini Toolbar, it fades from view.

   See Also For information about using the Mini Toolbar, see "Changing the Alignment, Spacing, Size, and Look of Text" in Chapter 15, "Format Slides."

2. Press the Delete key.

3. In the slide **3** title, double-click **Buying**, and then press the Backspace key.

4. In the third bullet point on slide **5**, double-click **good**, and then type **lasting**, followed by a space.

   What you type replaces the selection. Notice that the text also changes in the Slide pane.

5. On slide **4**, click the bullet to the left of **Know the culture**.

   The entire bullet point is selected, including the invisible paragraph mark at the end.

   Tip When you want to work with a bullet point or subpoint as a whole, you need to ensure that the invisible paragraph mark at its end is included in the selection. If you drag across the text on the slide, you might miss the paragraph mark. As a precaution, hold down the Shift key and press End to be sure that the paragraph mark is part of the selection.

6. On the **Home** tab, in the **Clipboard** group, click the **Cut** button.

   Keyboard Shortcut Press Ctrl+X to cut the selection.

7. Click to the left of the word **Make** in the first bullet point on slide **5**, and then click the **Paste** button.

   Keyboard Shortcut Press Ctrl+V to paste the contents of the Clipboard.

   You have moved the bullet point from slide 4 to slide 5.

8. Display slide **3** in the **Slide** pane, and click the bullet point to the left of **Know your needs** to select the bullet point and its subpoints.

9. Drag the selection down and to the left of **Read the Buyer manual**.

   The bullet point and its subpoints move as a unit.

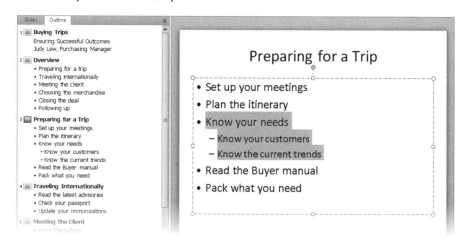

The change is reflected both on the slide and on the Outline tab.

10. On the Quick Access Toolbar, click the **Undo** button to reverse your last editing action.

    Keyboard Shortcut Press Ctrl+Z to undo the last editing action.

    The Redo button appears on the Quick Access Toolbar, to the right of Undo. When you point to the Undo or Redo button, the name in the ScreenTip reflects your last editing action—for example, Redo Drag And Drop.

11. On the Quick Access Toolbar, click the **Redo** button to restore the editing action.

    Keyboard Shortcut Press Ctrl+Y to restore the last editing action.

CLEAN UP Save the BuyingTripsC presentation, and then close it.

About the Clipboard

You can view the items that have been cut or copied to the Clipboard in the Clipboard task pane, which you display by clicking the Clipboard dialog box launcher on the Home tab.

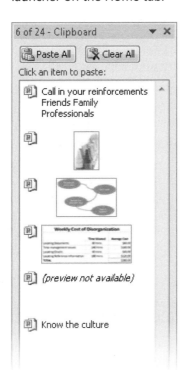

The Clipboard stores items that have been cut or copied from any presentation.

To paste an individual item at the cursor, you simply click the item in the Clipboard task pane. To paste all the items, click the Paste All button. You can point to an item, click the arrow that appears, and then click Delete to remove it from the Clipboard and the task pane, or you can remove all the items by clicking the Clear All button.

You can control the behavior of the Clipboard task pane by clicking Options at the bottom of the pane, and choosing the circumstances under which you want the task pane to appear.

To close the Clipboard task pane, click the Close button at the right end of its title bar.

Correcting and Sizing Text While Typing

We all make mistakes while typing text in a presentation. To help you ensure that these mistakes don't go uncorrected, PowerPoint uses the AutoCorrect feature to catch and automatically correct many common capitalization and spelling errors. For example, if you type *teh* instead of *the* or *WHen* instead of *When*, AutoCorrect immediately corrects the entry.

Tip If you don't want an entry you type to be corrected—for example, if you want to start a new paragraph with a lowercase letter—click the Undo button on the Quick Access Toolbar when AutoCorrect makes the change.

You can customize AutoCorrect to recognize misspellings you routinely type or to ignore text you do not want AutoCorrect to change. You can also create your own AutoCorrect entries to automate the typing of frequently used text. For example, you might customize AutoCorrect to enter the name of your organization when you type only an abbreviation.

In addition to providing the AutoCorrect feature to correct misspellings as you type, PowerPoint provides an AutoFit feature to size text to fit its placeholder. By default, if you type more text than will fit in a placeholder, PowerPoint reduces the size of the text so that all the text fits, and displays the AutoFit Options button to the left of the place-holder. Clicking this button displays a menu that gives you control over automatic sizing. For example, you can stop sizing text for the current placeholder while retaining the AutoFit settings for other placeholders.

Tip You can also change the AutoFit settings for a placeholder on the Text Box page of the Format Shape dialog box. In the Autofit area, you can change the default Shrink Text On Overflow setting to Do Not Autofit. You can also specify that instead of the text being sized to fit the placeholder, the placeholder should be sized to fit the text.

You can change the default AutoFit settings by clicking Control AutoCorrect Options on the AutoFit Options button's menu to display the AutoFormat As You Type page of the AutoCorrect dialog box.

Clear the AutoFit Title Text To Placeholder and AutoFit Body Text To Placeholder check boxes to stop making text fit in the placeholder.

In this exercise, you'll use AutoCorrect to fix a misspelled word and you'll add an AutoCorrect entry. Then you'll use AutoFit to size text so that it fits within its placeholder and to make a long bulleted list fit on one slide by converting its placeholder to a two-column layout.

 SET UP You need the CommunityServiceA_start presentation located in your Chapter14 practice file folder to complete this exercise. Open the Community-ServiceA_start presentation, and save it as *CommunityServiceA*. Then follow the steps.

1. Display slide **2**, and click the content placeholder.

2. Being careful for the purposes of this exercise to include the misspellings, type **Set up teh teem**, press the Enter key, and then type **Gather adn analyze data**.

   Almost immediately, AutoCorrect changes *teh* to *the* and *adn* to *and*. Notice that AutoCorrect does not change *teem* to *team*, or even flag it as a misspelling because *teem* is a legitimate word. PowerPoint cannot detect that you have used this homonym for *team* incorrectly. (A homonym is a word that sounds the same as another word but has a different meaning.)

3. Click the **File** tab to display the Backstage view, click **Options**, and then in the left pane of the **PowerPoint Options** dialog box, click **Proofing**.

4. In the **AutoCorrect options** area, click **AutoCorrect Options**.

The AutoCorrect dialog box opens.

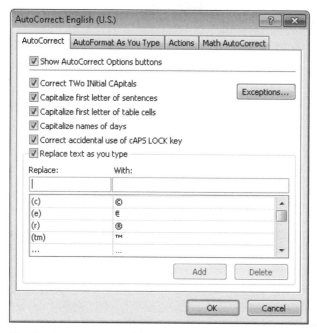

The AutoCorrect page of the AutoCorrect dialog box.

Troubleshooting If the AutoCorrect page is not active, click its tab to display its options.

The top part of the dialog box lists general rules for correcting errors such as capitalization mistakes. You can change any of these rules by clearing the associated check box.

5. In the lower part of the dialog box, scroll through the huge table of misspellings.

When you type one of the entries in the first column, PowerPoint automatically substitutes the correct spelling from the second column. For this exercise, suppose you often misspell the word *category* as *catigory*.

6. In the **Replace** box above the table, type **catigory**, and then press the Tab key.

The table below scrolls to show you similar words that are already in the AutoCorrect list.

7. In the **With** box, type **category**, and then click **Add**.

Now if you type *catigory* in any presentation, PowerPoint will replace it with *category*.

8. Click **OK** to close the **AutoCorrect** dialog box, and then click **OK** again to close the **PowerPoint Options** dialog box.

9. On slide **2**, with the cursor to the right of the word **data**, press Enter, type **Assign to a catigory**, and then press Enter.

   PowerPoint changes the word *catigory* to *category*.

10. Display slide **1**, click the subtitle placeholder, and type **Community Service Committee**.

11. Without moving the cursor, hold down the Shift key, and click to the left of **Community** to select the three words you just typed. Then press Ctrl+C to copy the words to the Clipboard.

12. Open the **PowerPoint Options** dialog box, and then open the **AutoCorrect** dialog box.

13. With the cursor in the **Replace** box, type **csc**. Then click the **With** box, press Ctrl+V to paste in the words you copied to the Clipboard, and click **Add**.

14. Close the **AutoCorrect** dialog box, and then close the **PowerPoint Options** dialog box.

15. Display slide **3**, and click to the left of **Responsibilities**. Then type **csc**, and press the Spacebar.

   PowerPoint changes the initials *csc* to *Community Service Committee*.

Set up team

- **Community Service Committee Responsibilities**
  - **Contact people recommended as department reps**

AutoCorrect makes the replacement if you follow csc *with a space or a punctuation mark.*

16. Display slide **1**, and click at the right end of the title.

   Notice that the setting in the Font Size box in the Font group on the Home tab is 44.

17. Type **:** (a colon), press Enter, and then type **Planning, Selling, and Executing a Project**.

When you type the word *Project*, AutoFit reduces the size of the title to 40 so that it fits in the title placeholder.

After AutoFit reduces the size of text, the AutoFit Options button appears to the left of the adjusted placeholder.

18. Click the **AutoFit Options** button.

A menu of options appears.

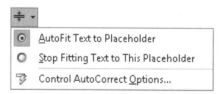

You can click Stop Fitting Text To This Placeholder to reverse the size adjustment and prevent future adjustments.

19. Press the Esc key to close the menu without making a selection.

20. Display slide **8**, click at the right end of the last subpoint, and notice that the font size is 28. Then press Enter, and type **How do we know if we are successful?**

The text size changes from 28 to 26.

21. Click the **AutoFit Options** button.

The menu of options appears.

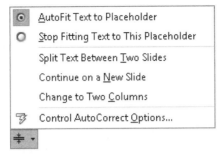

The menu for a bulleted list includes more options than the one for a title placeholder.

22. Click **Change to Two Columns**.

    The placeholder is instantly formatted to accommodate a two-column bulleted list.

23. Click a blank area of the slide.

    When the placeholder is not selected, it is easier to see the results.

Meet with department (continued)

* **Lead discussion with employees**
    – **What kind of project do we want to do?**
    – **What need do we want to address?**
    – **What are the goals of this project?**
    – **What do we need to do to meet those goals?**

    – **Who will perform these tasks?**
    – **What materials will we need?**
    – **When will the tasks be performed?**
    – **How do we stay on schedule?**
    – **How do we know if we are successful?**

A two-column bulleted list.

 CLEAN UP If you want, display the AutoCorrect dialog box, and remove the *catigory* and *csc* entries from the replacement table. Save the CommunityServiceA presentation, and then close it.

Checking Spelling and Choosing the Best Words

The AutoCorrect feature is very useful if you frequently type the same misspelling. However, most misspellings are the result of erratic finger-positioning errors or memory lapses. You can use two different methods to ensure that the words in your presentations are spelled correctly in spite of these random occurrences.

● By default, PowerPoint's spelling checker checks the spelling of the entire presentation—all slides, outlines, notes pages, and handout pages—against its built-in dictionary. To draw attention to words that are not in its dictionary and that might be misspelled, PowerPoint underlines them with a red wavy underline. You can right-click a word with a red wavy underline to display a menu with a list of possible spellings. You can choose the correct spelling from the menu or tell PowerPoint to ignore the word.

Tip To turn off this behind-the-scenes spell-checking, display the Backstage view, and click Options to open the PowerPoint Options dialog box. In the left pane, click Proofing, and then clear the Check Spelling As You Type check box.

● Instead of dealing with potential misspellings while you're creating a presentation, you can check the entire presentation in one session by clicking the Spelling button in the Proofing group on the Review tab. PowerPoint then works its way through the presentation, and if it encounters a word that is not in its dictionary, it displays the Spelling dialog box. After you indicate how PowerPoint should deal with the word, it moves on and displays the next word that is not in its dictionary, and so on.

The English-language version of Microsoft Office 2010 includes English, French, and Spanish dictionaries. If you use a word or phrase from a different language, you can mark it so that PowerPoint doesn't flag it as a misspelling.

You cannot make changes to the main dictionary in PowerPoint, but you can add correctly spelled words that are flagged as misspellings to the PowerPoint supplemental dictionary (called *CUSTOM.DIC*). You can also create and use custom dictionaries and use dictionaries from other Microsoft programs.

PowerPoint can check your spelling, but it can't alert you if you're not using the best word. Language is often contextual—the language you use in a presentation to members of a club is different from the language you use in a business presentation. To make sure you're using words that best convey your meaning in any given context, you can use the Thesaurus feature to look up alternative words, called *synonyms*, for a selected word.

Tip For many words, the quickest way to find a suitable synonym is to right-click the word, and point to Synonyms. You can then either click one of the suggested words or click Thesaurus to display the Research task pane.

In this exercise, you'll correct a misspelled word, mark a French phrase so that PowerPoint won't flag it as a misspelling, and check the spelling of an entire presentation. You'll then use the Thesaurus to replace a word on a slide with a more appropriate one.

 SET UP You need the CommunityServiceB_start presentation located in your Chapter14 practice file folder to complete this exercise. Open the Community-ServiceB_start presentation, and save it as CommunityServiceB. Then follow the steps.

1. Display slide **2**, and right-click **infermation**, which PowerPoint has flagged as a possible error with a red wavy underline.

   PowerPoint doesn't know whether you want to format the word or correct its spelling, so it displays both a Mini Toolbar and a menu.

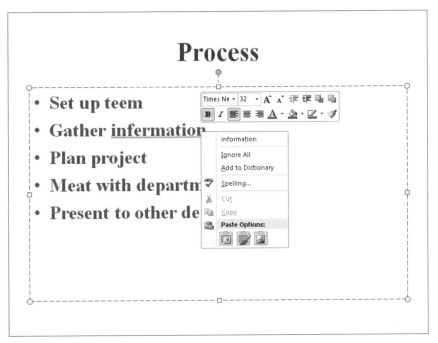

Right-clicking a flagged word displays options to format it or to correct it.

2. On the menu, click **information** to replace the misspelled word.

3. Move to slide **7**.

   The French words *Médecins* and *Frontières* have been flagged as possible errors.

 4. Select **Médecins Sans Frontières**, and then on the **Review** tab, in the **Language** group, click the **Language** button, and then click **Set Proofing Language**.

   The Language dialog box opens.

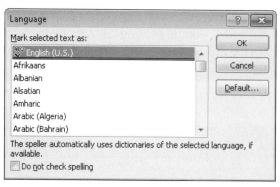

You can choose from a wide selection of languages in this dialog box.

5. Scroll down the list of languages, click **French (France)**, and then click **OK**.

   Behind the scenes, PowerPoint marks *Médecins Sans Frontières* as a French phrase, and the words no longer have red wavy underlines.

6. Click a corner of the slide so that no placeholders are selected, and then press Ctrl+Home.

7. On the **Review** tab, in the **Proofing** group, click the **Spelling** button.

   Keyboard Shortcut Press F7 to begin checking the spelling of a presentation.

   PowerPoint begins checking the spelling in the presentation. The spelling checker stops on the word *Persue* and displays the Spelling dialog box.

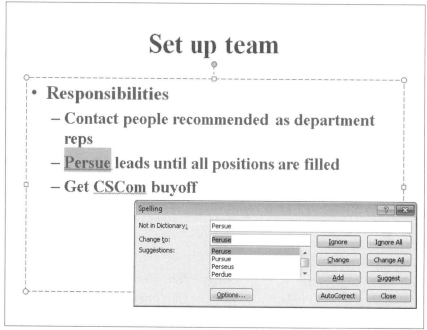

The words in the Suggestions list have the same capitalization as the possible misspelling.

8. In the **Suggestions** list, click **Pursue**, and then click **Change**.

The spelling checker replaces *Persue* with the suggested *Pursue* and then stops on the word *CSCom*, suggesting *Como* as the correct spelling. For purposes of this exercise, assume that this is a common abbreviation for *Community Service Committee*.

9. Click **Add**.

The term *CSCom* is added to the CUSTOM.DIC dictionary.

Tip If you do not want to change a word or add it to the supplemental dictionary, you can click Ignore or Ignore All. The spelling checker then ignores either just that word or all instances of the word in the presentation during subsequent spell checking sessions.

Next the spelling checker stops on *the* because it is the second of two occurrences of the word.

10. Click **Delete**.

The duplicated word is deleted. Now the spelling checker identifies *employes* as a misspelling.

11. In the suggestions list, click **employees**, and then click **AutoCorrect**.

PowerPoint adds the misspelling and the selected spelling to the AutoCorrect substitution table.

12. Click **Change** to change *succesful* to *successful*.

13. When a message box tells you that the spelling check is complete, click **OK**.

This presentation still has spelling problems—words that are spelled correctly but that aren't correct in context. We'll leave it to you to proof the slides and correct these errors manually. In the meantime, we'll finish the exercise by using the Thesaurus to find a synonym.

14. On slide **1**, select the word **Executing** (but not the space following the word).

15. On the **Review** tab, in the **Proofing** group, click the **Thesaurus** button.

Keyboard Shortcut Press Shift+F7 to activate the Thesaurus.

The Research task pane opens on the right side of the screen, displaying a list of synonyms for the selected word.

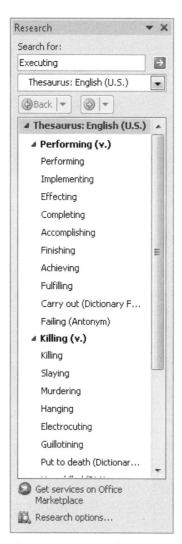

The synonyms have the same capitalization as the selected word.

16. Below **Performing**, point to **Completing**, click the arrow that appears, and then click **Insert**.

    Tip If you don't see an obvious substitute for the selected word, click a word that is close in the Thesaurus list to display synonyms for that word.

17. At the right end of the **Research** task pane, click the **Close** button.

CLEAN UP If you want, display the AutoCorrect dialog box, and remove the *employes* entry from the replacement table. To remove *CSCom* from the supplemental dictionary, display the Proofing page of the PowerPoint Options dialog box, and click Custom Dictionaries. Then in the Custom Dictionaries dialog box, click Edit Word List. Click CSCom, click Delete, and click OK three times. Then save and close the CommunityServiceB presentation.

Researching Information and Translating Text

In addition to the Thesaurus, the Research task pane provides access to a variety of informational resources. Display the Research task pane by clicking the Research button in the Proofing group and then enter a topic in the Search For box, specifying in the box below which resource PowerPoint should use to look for information about that topic. Clicking Research Options at the bottom of the Research task pane displays the Research Options dialog box, where you can specify which of a predefined set of reference materials and other Internet resources will be available from the list.

PowerPoint also comes with three translation tools with which you can quickly translate words and phrases, or even entire presentations.

- When the Mini Translator is turned on, you can point to a word or selected phrase to display a translation in the specified language. (You turn the Mini Translator on or off by clicking the Translate button in the Language group of the Review tab and then clicking Mini Translator.) When the box containing the translation is displayed, you can click the Expand button to display the Research task pane, where you can change the translation language. You can also copy the translated word or phrase, or hear it spoken for you.

  To change the default language used by the Mini Translator, click Choose Translation Language on the Translate menu. Then in the Translation Language Options dialog box, you can select from a list of languages, including Arabic, Chinese, Greek, Hebrew, Italian, Japanese, Korean, Polish, Portuguese, Russian, Spanish, and Swedish.

- To obtain the translation of a selected word, you can also click Translate Selected Text in the Translate menu to display the Research task pane. In the task pane, you can also type a word in the Search For box, specify the language you want, and then click Start Searching. PowerPoint consults the online bilingual dictionary for the language you chose and displays the result.

Finding and Replacing Text and Fonts

Sometimes a word you use might be correctly spelled but just not be the correct word. You can find and change specific text in a presentation by clicking the buttons in the Editing group on the Home tab to do the following:

- Click the Find button to locate each occurrence of a word, part of a word, or a phrase. In the Find dialog box, you enter the text, and then click Find Next. You can specify whether PowerPoint should locate only matches with the exact capitalization (also known as the *case*); in other words, if you specify *person*, you don't want PowerPoint to locate *Person*. You can also tell PowerPoint whether it should locate only matches for the entire text; in other words, if you specify *person*, you don't want PowerPoint to locate *personal*.

- Click the Replace button to locate each occurrence of a word, part of a word, or a phrase and replace it with something else. In the Replace dialog box, you enter the text you want to find and what you want to replace it with, click Find Next, and then click Replace to replace the found occurrence. You can also click Replace All to replace all occurrences. Again, you can specify whether to match capitalization and whole words.

You can also click the Replace arrow, and in the Replace list, click Replace Fonts to find and replace a font throughout a presentation. In the Replace Font dialog box, you can specify the font you want to change and the font you want PowerPoint to replace it with.

In this exercise, you'll first find and replace a word and then find and replace a font.

SET UP You need the CommunityServiceC_start presentation located in your Chapter14 practice file folder to complete this exercise. Open the Community-ServiceC_start presentation, and save it as *CommunityServiceC*. Then follow the steps.

1. On the **Home** tab, in the **Editing** group, click the **Replace** button.

   Keyboard Shortcut Press Ctrl+H to open the Replace dialog box.

   The Replace dialog box opens.

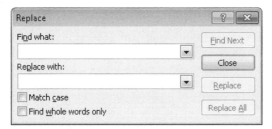

If you have already used the Find or Replace command, your previous Find What and Replace With entries carry over to this replace operation.

Tip To move a dialog box so that it doesn't hide the text, drag its title bar.

2. In the **Find what** box, type **department**, and then press Tab.

3. In the **Replace with** box, type **unit**.

4. Select the **Match case** check box to locate text that exactly matches the capitalization you specified and replace it with the capitalization you specified.

5. Click **Find Next**.

PowerPoint finds and selects part of the word *departments* on slide 2.

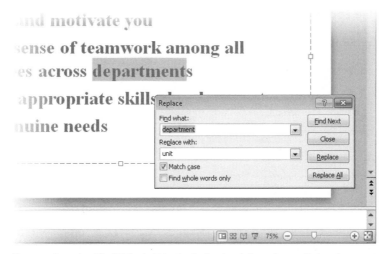

If you select the Find Whole Words Only check box, PowerPoint does not match this instance of department.

6. Click **Replace**.

   PowerPoint replaces *departments* with *units*, and then locates the next match.

7. Click **Replace All**.

   A message box tells you that PowerPoint has finished searching the presentation and that the replace operation changed nine occurrences of the text.

8. Click **OK**, and then in the **Replace** dialog box, click **Close**.

   Because you selected Match Case for this replace operation, one occurrence of *Department* has not been changed. We'll leave it to you to change it manually.

9. Click a blank area of the current slide so that no placeholder is selected, press Ctrl+Home to move to slide **1**, and then click the title.

   Notice that *Calibri (Headings)* is displayed in the Font box in the Font group.

10. Display slide **2**, and click first the title and then any bullet point.

    Notice that the font used for these elements is Times New Roman. Let's change this font to make it consistent with the title slide.

11. Click a corner of the slide so that no placeholder is selected.

12. In the **Editing** group, click the **Replace** arrow, and then click **Replace Fonts**.

    The Replace Font dialog box opens.

The default setting is to replace all instances of the Arial font with the Agency FB font.

13. Display the **Replace** list, and click **Times New Roman**.

    The Replace list includes only Arial and the fonts in the presentation.

14. Display the **With** list, and click **Calibri**.

    The With list includes all the fonts available on your computer.

15. Click **Replace**.

    All the Times New Roman text in the presentation changes to Calibri.

16. Click **Close** to close the **Replace Font** dialog box.

 CLEAN UP Save the CommunityServiceC presentation, and then close it.

Key Points

- You can enter and edit text both on the Outline tab or directly on a slide, depending on which is most efficient.

- You can place text wherever you want it on a slide by using text boxes.

- PowerPoint provides assistance by correcting common spelling errors and adjusting the size of text so that it fits optimally on a slide.

- The spelling checker flags possible misspellings so that you can take care of them as you type. Or you can check the spelling of an entire presentation.

- You can take advantage of the Find and Replace features to ensure consistent use of terms and fonts throughout a presentation.

Chapter at a Glance

Apply themes,
page 423

Use different color
and font schemes,
page 426

Change the slide
background,
page 429

Change the
look of
placeholders,
page 433

Change the
alignment,
spacing, size,
and look of
text, **page 437**

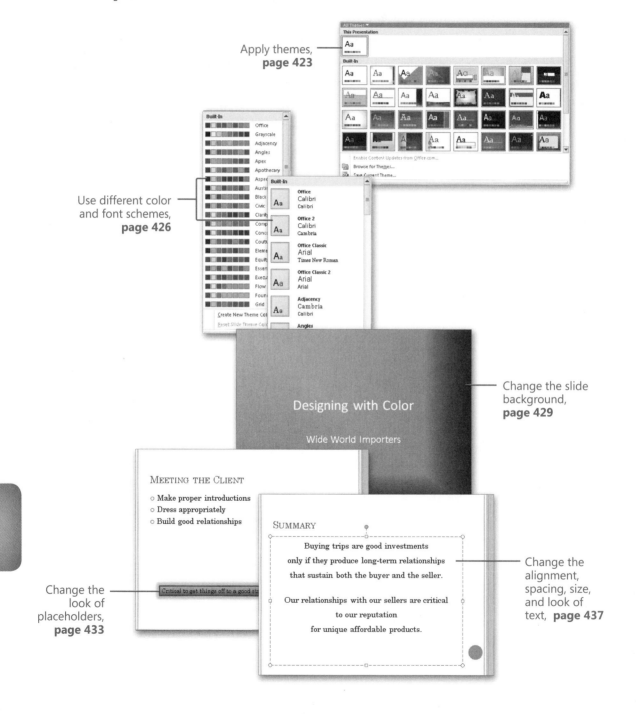

15 Format Slides

In this chapter, you will learn how to

- ✔ Apply themes.
- ✔ Use different color and font schemes.
- ✔ Change the slide background.
- ✔ Change the look of placeholders.
- ✔ Change the alignment, spacing, size, and look of text.

An overall consistent look, punctuated by variations that add weight exactly where it is needed, can enhance the likelihood that your message will be well received and absorbed by your intended audience. To make your Microsoft PowerPoint 2010 presentations visually appealing, you can add enhancements to the presentation as a whole or to individual slides.

In this chapter, you'll apply a theme to a presentation and then change the theme's color and font schemes. You'll add color and shading to the background of slides and to the background of placeholders. Finally, you'll change the look of specific text elements.

> **Practice Files** Before you can complete the exercises in this chapter, you need to copy the book's practice files to your computer. The practice files you'll use to complete the exercises in this chapter are in the Chapter15 practice file folder. A complete list of practice files is provided in "Using the Practice Files" at the beginning of this book.

Applying Themes

When you create a presentation based on a template or a ready-made design, the presentation includes a theme—a combination of colors, fonts, formatting, graphics, and other elements that gives the presentation a coherent look. Even a presentation developed from scratch has a theme; the Office theme is applied by default. This theme consists of a white background, a very basic set of colors, and the Calibri font.

If you want to change the theme applied to a presentation, you can choose one from the Themes gallery. By using the Live Preview feature, you can easily try different effects until you find the one you want.

See Also For information about creating your own themes, refer to *Microsoft PowerPoint 2010 Step by Step*, by Joyce Cox and Joan Lambert (Microsoft Press, 2010).

In this exercise, you'll change the theme applied to one presentation that was created from scratch and to another that was created from a template.

 SET UP You need the LandscapingA_start and CompanyMeetingA_start presentations located in your Chapter15 practice file folder to complete this exercise. Open the presentations, and save them as *LandscapingA* and *CompanyMeetingA*, respectively. Then follow the steps.

1. With the **LandscapingA** presentation active, on the **Design** tab, in the **Themes** group, click the **More** button.

   The Themes gallery appears, displaying all the available themes.

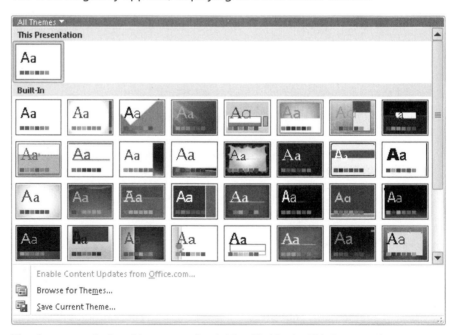

The theme attached to this presentation is identified in the This Presentation area.

2. Point to each theme thumbnail in turn to see a live preview of what the presentation will look like with that theme applied.

   Notice that the themes are organized alphabetically and that their names appear in ScreenTips when you point to them.

3. Click the **Austin** thumbnail to apply that theme to the entire presentation.

4. Click the **Home** tab, and then on slide **1**, click the presentation's title.

Instead of a white background with black text in the Calibri font, the presentation now has a green background design with title text in the Century Gothic font.

Most built-in themes have a distinctive title slide design that is modified for all the other slide layouts.

Troubleshooting The appearance of buttons and groups on the ribbon changes depending on the width of the program window. For information about changing the appearance of the ribbon to match our screen images, see "Modifying the Display of the Ribbon" at the beginning of this book.

5. On the **View** tab, in the **Window** group, click the **Switch Windows** button, and click **CompanyMeetingA** to switch to that presentation.

This presentation already has a theme applied to it.

6. Display the **Themes** gallery, and then click the **Urban** thumbnail.

The background of the presentation now has dark blue and teal accents, and the text is in blue Trebuchet and black Georgia.

 CLEAN UP Save and close the CompanyMeetingA and LandscapingA presentations.

Using Different Color and Font Schemes

Every presentation you create with PowerPoint 2010, even a blank one, has a set of colors, called a *color scheme*, associated with its theme. A color scheme consists of 12 complementary colors designed to be used for the following elements of a slide:

- **Text/Background** Use these four colors for dark text on a light background or light text on a dark background.

- **Accent 1 through Accent 6** Use these six colors for objects other than text.

- **Hyperlink** Use this color to draw attention to hyperlinks.

- **Followed Hyperlink** Use this color to indicate visited hyperlinks.

When you click color buttons such as the Font Color button in the Font group on the Home tab, the color palette displays 10 of the 12 colors with light to dark gradients. (The two background colors are not represented in these palettes.)

Understanding color schemes can help you create professional-looking presentations that use an appealing balance of color. You're not limited to using the colors in a presentation's color scheme, but because they have been selected by professional designers and are based on good design principles, using them ensures that your slides will be pleasing to the eye.

See Also For information about how scheme colors are allocated, refer to *Microsoft PowerPoint 2010 Step by Step*, by Joyce Cox and Joan Lambert (Microsoft Press, 2010). For information about using non-scheme colors, see the sidebar "Non–Color Scheme Colors" later in this chapter.

To view the color schemes you can apply to a presentation, you display the Colors gallery, which has Live Preview capabilities. When you find a color scheme you like, you simply click it to change the color scheme of all the slides in the presentation.

Tip To apply a color scheme only to a selected slide, right-click the scheme and then click Apply To Selected Slides

In addition to changing the color scheme, you can change the font scheme, which provides two complementary fonts for each theme. The Fonts gallery lists the combinations in alphabetical order by theme. In each combination, the top font (called the *heading font*) is used for slides titles, and the bottom font (called the *body font*) is used for other slide text.

If none of the color schemes is exactly what you're looking for, you can create your own by clicking Create New Theme Colors at the bottom of the Colors gallery and assembling colors in the Create New Theme Colors dialog box. You can also create a custom font scheme by clicking Create New Theme Fonts at the bottom of the Fonts gallery and then specifying the font combination you want in the Create New Theme Fonts dialog box.

After you save either type of custom scheme, you can apply it to one or all of the slides in a presentation.

When you apply a different color scheme or font scheme to a presentation, your changes are stored with the presentation and do not affect the underlying theme.

Tip Also associated with each theme is an effects scheme. This scheme ensures that the shapes in the presentation have a consistent look. Clicking the Effects button in the Themes group of the Design tab displays a gallery of effect combinations to choose from.

In this exercise, you'll apply a different color scheme to a presentation, create your own scheme, change the color scheme of one slide, and then apply a different font scheme.

 SET UP You need the CompanyMeetingB_start presentation located in your Chapter15 practice file folder to complete this exercise. Open the CompanyMeetingB_start presentation, and save it as *CompanyMeetingB*. Then follow the steps.

1. On the **Design** tab, in the **Themes** group, click the **Colors** button.

   The Colors gallery appears.

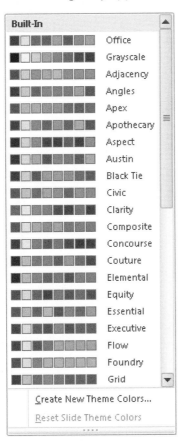

The color schemes show 8 of the 12 available colors.

2. In the gallery, point to a few color schemes, and watch the Live Preview effect on the active slide.

3. Click **Essential** to apply that color scheme to the presentation instead of the default color scheme of the Urban theme.

   Notice that the theme retains all of its other characteristics, such as the fonts and background graphic; only the colors change.

4. With slide **1** displayed, in the **Themes** group, click the **Colors** button.

5. Right-click the **Solstice** color scheme, and then click **Apply to Selected Slides**.

   PowerPoint applies the Solstice color scheme to only the title slide, changing its main background color from red to dark brown, but retaining the gold accent color.

6. On the **Design** tab, in the **Themes** group, click the **Fonts** button.

   The Fonts gallery appears.

Two fonts are assigned to each theme.

7. In the **Fonts** gallery, point to a few font schemes to display live previews of their effects on the active slide.

8. Click **Newsprint**.

   PowerPoint applies that font scheme to the presentation instead of the default font scheme of the Urban theme.

The title slide with the new font scheme.

 CLEAN UP Save the CompanyMeetingB presentation, and then close it.

Changing the Slide Background

In PowerPoint, you can customize the background of a slide by adding a solid color, a color gradient, a texture, or even a picture.

A color gradient is a visual effect in which a solid color gradually changes from light to dark or dark to light. PowerPoint offers several gradient patterns, each with variations. You can also choose a preset arrangement of colors from professionally designed backgrounds in which different colors gradually merge.

If you want something fancier than a solid color or a gradient, you can give the slide background a texture. PowerPoint comes with several built-in textures that you can easily apply to the background of slides. If none of these meets your needs, you might want to use a picture of a textured surface. For a dramatic effect, you can also incorporate an image or design of your own, although these are best reserved for small areas of the slide rather than the entire background.

In this exercise, you'll shade the background of one slide. Then you'll apply a textured background to all the slides in the presentation.

 SET UP You need the ColorDesign_start presentation located in your Chapter15 practice file folder to complete this exercise. Open the ColorDesign_start presentation, and save it as *ColorDesign*. Then follow the steps.

1. On the **Design** tab, in the **Background** group, click the **Background Styles** button.

   The Background Styles gallery appears.

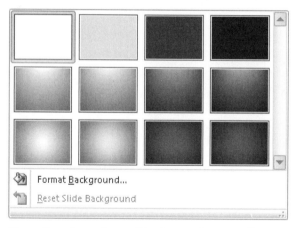

The gallery shows four solid colors and two gradients in each of four colors taken from the theme's color scheme.

2. In the gallery, point to each thumbnail in turn to see a live preview of its effects.

3. Click the third thumbnail in the second row (**Style 7**).

Instantly, the background of all the slides in the presentation change to a blue gradient.

4. Click the **Background Styles** button again, and then at the bottom of the gallery, click **Format Background**.

The Format Background dialog box opens.

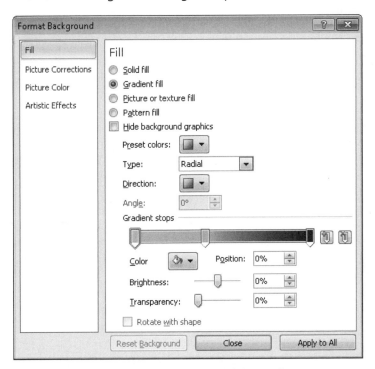

The Fill page shows the settings that control the gradient.

5. Click the **Type** arrow to display the list of options, and then click **Rectangular**.

Behind the dialog box, the active slide changes to reflect this setting.

6. Display the **Direction** list, and click the rightmost thumbnail (**From Top Left Corner**).

7. In the **Gradient stops** area, drag the middle handle on the slider (**Stop 2 of 3**) to the right until the **Position** setting is **80%**.

   Behind the dialog box, you can see that 80 percent of the slide is now a lighter shade, with the gradient to dark occupying only about 20 percent.

8. Display the **Color** list, and then under **Theme Colors**, click the third box in the purple column (**Purple, Accent 4, Lighter 40%**).

9. Click **Close**.

   PowerPoint applies the shaded background to the current slide only.

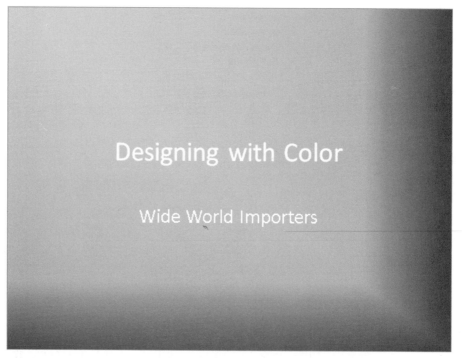

The title slide has a two-tone gradient that gives a raised effect.

10. Click the **Background Styles** button again, and then click **Format Background**.

11. In the **Format Background** dialog box, click **Picture or texture fill**.

    The active slide shows a live preview of the default texture.

12. Display the **Texture** gallery, and then click **Purple mesh**.

13. Click the **Apply to All** button, and then click **Close**.

    PowerPoint applies the textured background to all the slides in the presentation.

14. In the **Themes** group, click the **More** button.

    The Themes gallery appears.

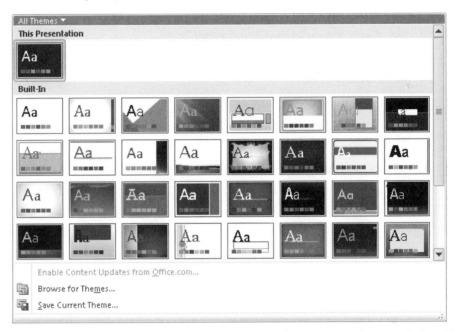

At the top of the gallery is a thumbnail reflecting the formatting you have applied to this presentation.

✖ **CLEAN UP** Save the ColorDesign presentation, and then close it.

Changing the Look of Placeholders

For a consistent look, you won't usually want to change the formatting of a presentation's placeholders. However, when you want to draw attention to an entire slide or an element of a slide, you can do so effectively by making specific placeholders stand out. You might also want to format text boxes that you have drawn manually on a slide.

See Also For information about drawing text boxes, see "Adding Text Boxes" in Chapter 14, "Work with Slide Text."

When you format a placeholder or a text box, you are essentially formatting a shape. You have the following options:

- Fill the background with a color, gradient, texture, pattern, or picture.
- Change the color and style of the shape's outline.
- Apply a style such as a shadow, reflection, or glow.
- Apply a three-dimensional effect.

In this exercise, you'll first apply a color to a text box. Then you'll change its border and give it a glow effect.

 SET UP You need the BusinessTravelA_start presentation located in your Chapter15 practice file folder to complete this exercise. Open the BusinessTravelA_start presentation, and save it as *BusinessTravelA*. Then follow the steps.

1. Display slide **5**, click anywhere in the free-standing text at the bottom of the slide, and then click the border of the text box to select the box for manipulation.

 2. On the **Format** contextual tab, in the **Shape Styles** group, click the **Shape Fill** arrow.

The Shape Fill palette appears.

Like other palettes, the Shape Fill palette reflects the theme's colors.

3. In the palette, point to a few colors in turn to see a live preview of its effects on the background of the text box.

4. Click the third shade in the orange column (**Orange, Accent 1, Lighter 40%**).

   The background of the text box is now a medium orange color.

5. Click the **Shape Fill** arrow again, and then below the palette, point to **Gradient**.

   The Gradient gallery appears.

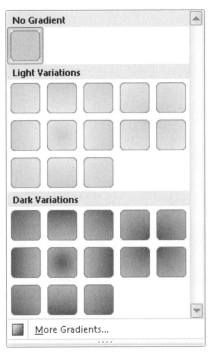

This gallery offers light and dark versions of gradients in different directions.

6. Under **Dark Variations**, click the second thumbnail in the third row (**Linear Up**).

7. In the **Shape Styles** group, click the **Shape Outline** arrow, and under **Standard Colors**, click the **Dark Red** box.

8. Click the **Shape Outline** arrow again. Then below the palette, point to **Weight**, and in the list, click **3 pt**.

   Tip The abbreviation *pt* stands for *point*. A point is a unit of measurement used in the design and publishing industries. There are 72 points to the inch.

9. In the **Shape Styles** group, click the **Shape Effects** button.

   A list of all the types of effects you can apply to the text box appears.

Many possible effects are available with a couple of mouse clicks.

10. In turn, display the options for each type, and point to a few to see their live previews.

11. When you have finished exploring, point to **Glow**, and then click the first thumbnail in the last row (**Orange, 18 pt glow, Accent color 1**).

12. Click away from the text box to release the selection.

    The text box is less likely to be overlooked now.

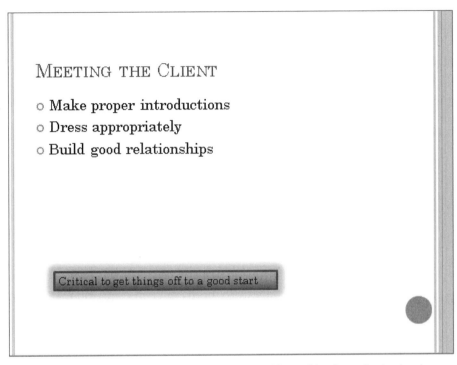

You can easily set off text boxes and placeholders with combinations of color, borders, and effects.

CLEAN UP Save the BusinessTravelA presentation, and then close it.

Changing the Alignment, Spacing, Size, and Look of Text

In most PowerPoint templates, text appears as either a slide title or a bulleted list. The alignment and spacing of the text are controlled by the design built into the template. You can override these settings, which are collectively called *paragraph formatting*. Click anywhere in the paragraph, and then do the following:

- **Lists** Click the Bullets arrow to display a gallery of alternative built-in bullet symbols. You can click None to remove bullet formatting and create an ordinary paragraph. To switch to a numbered list, click the Numbering arrow, and then click the numbering style you want.

- **Alignment** Click one of the following alignment buttons in the Paragraph group on the Home tab:

  ○ Click the Align Text Left button to align text against the placeholder's left edge. Left-alignment is the usual choice for paragraphs.

    Keyboard Shortcut Press Ctrl+L to left-align text.

  ○ Click the Center button to align text in the middle of the placeholder. Center-alignment is often used for titles and headings.

    Keyboard Shortcut Press Ctrl+E to center text.

  ○ Click the Align Text Right button to align text against the placeholder's right edge. Right-alignment isn't used much for titles and paragraphs, but you might want to use it in text boxes.

    Keyboard Shortcut Press Ctrl+R to right-align text.

  ○ Click the Justify button to align text against both the left and right edges, adding space between words to fill the line. You might justify a single, non-bulleted paragraph on a slide for a neat look.

- **Line spacing** Click the Line Spacing button in the Paragraph group, and make a selection.

- **Paragraph spacing** Open the Paragraph dialog box, either by clicking the Line Spacing button and then clicking Line Spacing Options at the bottom of the menu or by clicking the dialog box launcher in the lower-right corner of the Paragraph group. You can then adjust the Before and After settings for the entire paragraph.

In addition to changing the look of paragraphs, you can manipulate the look of individual words by manually applying settings that are collectively called *character formatting*. After selecting the characters you want to format, you can make changes by using the commands in the Font group on the Home tab, as follows:

- **Font** Override the font specified by the font scheme by making a selection in the Font box.

- **Size** Manually control the size of text either by clicking the Increase Font Size or Decrease Font Size button or by setting a precise size in the Font Size box.

  Keyboard Shortcut Press Ctrl+Shift+> or Ctrl+Shift+< to increase or decrease font size.

Tip If you turn off AutoFit so that you can manually size text, you have two ways to adjust the size of placeholders to fit their text: by manually dragging the handles around a selected placeholder, or by clicking Resize Shape To Fit Text on the Text Box page of the Format Shape dialog box. For information about AutoFit, see "Correcting and Sizing Text While Typing" in Chapter 14, "Work with Slide Text."

- **Style** Apply attributes such as bold, italic, underlining, and shadow and strikethrough effects to selected characters.

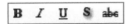

The character style buttons.

Keyboard Shortcut Press Ctrl+B to make text bold, Ctrl+I to make it italic, or Ctrl+U to underline it.

- **Color** Change the color of the selected characters by clicking the Font Color arrow and then clicking the color you want in the palette.

- **Case** Change the capitalization of the words—for example, you can change small letters to capital letters—by clicking the Change Case button and then clicking the case you want.

- **Character spacing** Increase or decrease the space between the letters in a selection by clicking the Character Spacing button and then clicking the option you want. You can also click More Spacing to display the Character Spacing page of the Font dialog box, where you can specify spacing more precisely.

Tip You can clear all manually applied character formatting from a selection by clicking the Clear All Formatting button.

To make it quick and easy to apply the most common paragraph and character formatting, PowerPoint displays the Mini Toolbar when you make a text selection. This toolbar contains the same buttons you'll find in the Font and Paragraph groups on the Home tab, but they're all in one place, adjacent to the selection. If you don't want to apply any of the Mini Toolbar formats, you can simply ignore it, and it will disappear.

The Mini Toolbar.

After you have formatted the text on a slide, you might find that you want to adjust the way lines break to achieve a more balanced look. This is often the case with slide titles, but bullet points and regular text can sometimes also benefit from a few manually inserted line breaks. You can simply press Shift+Enter to insert a line break at the cursor.

This fine-tuning should wait until you have taken care of all other formatting of the slide element, because changing the font, size, and attributes of text can affect how it breaks.

In this exercise, you'll experiment with changing various types of character formatting and paragraph formatting to achieve the look you want. You'll also insert a few line breaks to balance the text on a slide.

SET UP You need the BusinessTravelB_start presentation located in your Chapter15 practice file folder to complete this exercise. Open the BusinessTravelB_start presentation, and save it as *BusinessTravelB*. Then follow the steps.

1. Display slide **3**, and in the fourth bullet point, double-click **Buyer**.

   The Mini Toolbar appears.

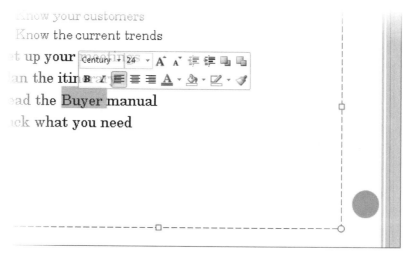

The Mini Toolbar is a shadow until you point to it.

2. Move the pointer over the Mini Toolbar to make it active, and then click the **Italic** button.

3. Display slide **4**, and in the **Slide** pane, drag diagonally across the four bullet points to select them.

4. On the **Home** tab, in the **Font** group, click the **Font Color** arrow. Then under **Standard Colors** in the palette, click the **Red** box.

5. Display slide **5**, and click anywhere in the bulleted list. Then in the **Editing** group, click the **Select** button, and click **Select All**.

All the text in the placeholder is selected. The text at the bottom is not selected because it is in a separate text box, not in the placeholder.

6. In the **Font** group, click the **Increase Font Size** button until the setting in the **Font Size** box is **44**.

Keyboard Shortcut Press Ctrl+Shift+> to increase the font size.

Using the Increase Font Size and Decrease Font Size buttons takes the guesswork out of sizing text.

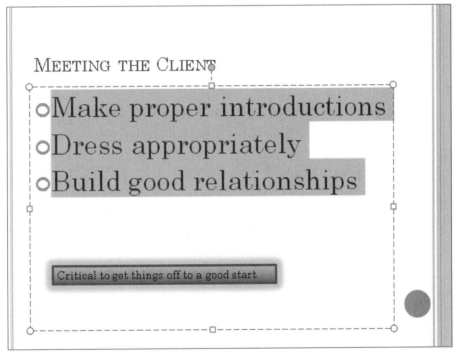

The first bullet point now spans the width of the placeholder.

7. In the **Font** group, click the **Clear All Formatting** button to return the font size to **24**.

8. Display slide **9**, and select both bullet points.

9. In the **Paragraph** group, click the **Bullets** arrow.

   The Bullets gallery appears.

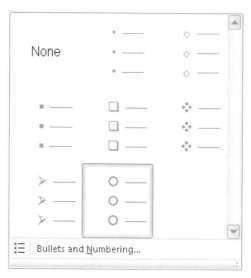

You can click Bullets And Numbering at the bottom of the gallery to create custom bullets.

10. In the gallery, click **None**.

    The bullet points are converted to regular text paragraphs.

11. With both paragraphs still selected, in the **Paragraph** group, click the **Line Spacing** button, and then click **Line Spacing Options**.

    The Paragraph dialog box opens.

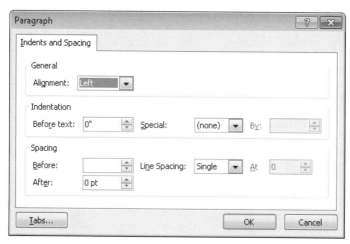

You can set alignment, indentation, line spacing, and paragraph spacing all in one place.

12. In the **General** area, change the **Alignment** setting to **Centered**.

13. In the **Spacing** area, change the **Before** setting to **0 pt** and the **After** settings to **24 pt**. Then change the **Line Spacing** setting to **1.5 lines**.

14. Click **OK**.

15. In the first paragraph, click to the left of the word **only**, and press Shift+Enter to insert a line break.

16. Repeat step 15 to insert another line break before the word **that**.

17. In the second paragraph, insert a line break before the word **to** and another before the word **for**.

The phrases of both paragraphs are now nicely balanced.

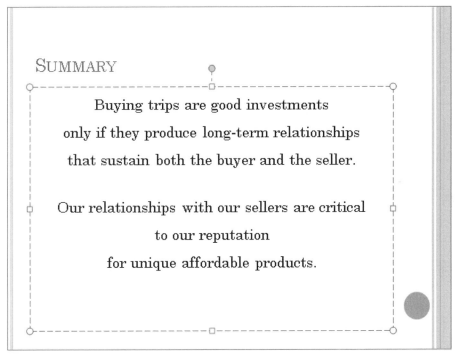

Line breaks can increase readability as well as the look of text on a slide.

 CLEAN UP Save the BusinessTravelB presentation, and then close it.

Non–Color Scheme Colors

Although working with the 12 colors of a harmonious color scheme enables you to create presentations with a pleasing design impact, you might want to use a broader range of colors. You can add colors that are not part of the color scheme by selecting the element whose color you want to change and then choosing a standard color from the Font Color palette or a custom color from the wide spectrum available in the Colors dialog box.

To apply a custom color:

1. Select text on a slide, and then on the Home tab, in the Font group, click the Font Color arrow.

2. At the bottom of the color palette, click More Colors.

   The Colors dialog box opens.

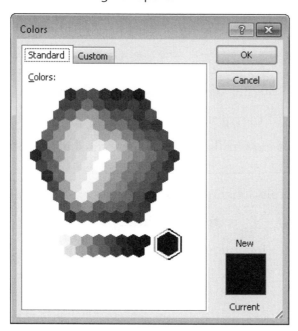

The Standard page of the Colors dialog box.

3. Click a color in the Colors spectrum, and then click OK.

   You can also click the Custom tab to display a color gradient where you can select a color based on precise Red/Green/Blue or Hue/Saturation/Luminescence settings.

After you use a color, it becomes available on all the palettes that appear when you click a button that applies color—for example, the Font Color button in the Font group on the Home tab. The color remains on the palettes even if you change the theme applied to the presentation.

Key Points

- Switching from one predefined theme to another is an easy way of changing the look of an entire presentation.

- You can apply a ready-made color scheme or font scheme to one or all the slides in a presentation, and you can create your own schemes.

- To dress up the background of one slide or of all the slides in a presentation, you can apply a solid color, a color gradient, a texture, or a picture.

- You can change the background, outline, and effect of specific placeholders or of text boxes.

- The formatting of paragraphs and text in a presentation can easily be changed by using the commands in the Focnt and Paragraph groups on the Home tab.

Chapter at a Glance

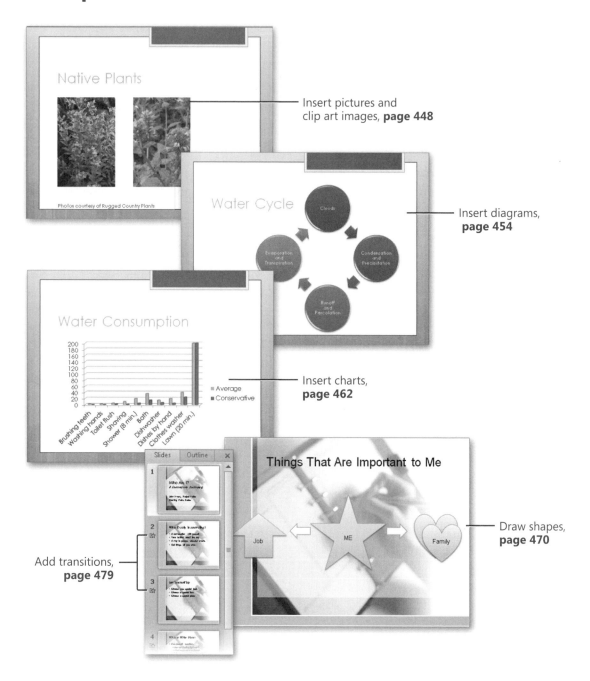

Insert pictures and clip art images, **page 448**

Insert diagrams, **page 454**

Insert charts, **page 462**

Draw shapes, **page 470**

Add transitions, **page 479**

16 Add Simple Visual Enhancements

In this chapter, you will learn how to

✔ Insert pictures and clip art images.

✔ Insert diagrams.

✔ Insert charts.

✔ Draw shapes.

✔ Add transitions.

With the ready availability of professionally designed templates, presentations have become more visually sophisticated and appealing. The words you use on your slides are no longer enough to guarantee the success of a presentation. These days, presentations are likely to have fewer words and more graphic elements. In fact, many successful presenters dispense with words altogether and use their slides only to graphically reinforce what they say when they deliver their presentations.

The general term *graphics* applies to several kinds of visual enhancements, including pictures, clip art images, diagrams, charts, and shapes. All of these types of graphics are inserted as objects on a slide and can then be sized, moved, and copied. For purposes of this chapter, we also consider transitions from one slide to another as a type of visual enhancement.

See Also For information about formatting and otherwise modifying graphics, refer to *Microsoft PowerPoint 2010 Step by Step*, by Joyce Cox and Joan Lambert (Microsoft Press, 2010).

In this chapter, you'll insert pictures and clip art images. You'll create a diagram and a chart, and you'll draw a simple illustration by using built-in shapes. Finally, you'll change the way slides move on and off the screen during a slide show.

> **Practice Files** Before you can complete the exercises in this chapter, you need to copy the book's practice files to your computer. The practice files you'll use to complete the exercises in this chapter are in the Chapter16 practice file folder. A complete list of practice files is provided in "Using the Practice Files" at the beginning of this book.

Inserting Pictures and Clip Art Images

You can add images created and saved in other programs as well as digital photographs to your Microsoft PowerPoint 2010 presentations. Collectively, these types of graphics are known as *pictures*. You might want to use pictures to make your slides more attractive and visually interesting, but you are more likely to use pictures to convey information in a way that words cannot. For example, you might display photographs of your company's new products in a presentation to salespeople.

If a slide has a content placeholder, you can insert a picture by clicking the Insert Picture From File button in the content placeholder. If the slide has no content placeholder, you can click the Picture button in the Images group on the Insert tab. Either way, the Insert Picture dialog box opens so that you can locate and insert the picture you want.

Tip Pictures you acquire from locations such as Web sites are often copyrighted, meaning that you cannot use them without the permission of the person who created them. Sometimes owners will grant permission if you give them credit. Professional photographers usually charge a fee to use their work. Always assume that pictures are copyrighted unless the source clearly indicates that they are license-free.

In addition to pictures you have acquired from various sources, you can insert clip art images into your slides. PowerPoint provides access to hundreds of professionally designed license-free clip art items that. These license-free graphics often take the form of cartoons, sketches, or symbolic images, but can also include photographs, animated drawings, and movies. In a PowerPoint presentation, you can use clip art to illustrate a point you are making, as interesting bullet characters, or to mark pauses in a presentation. For example, you might display a question mark image on a slide to signal a time in which you answer questions from the audience.

To add clip art to a slide, you can click the Clip Art button in a content placeholder, or you can click the Clip Art button in the Images group on the Insert tab. Either way, the Clip Art task pane opens. From this task pane, you can locate and insert the clip art image you want. You can search for clip art by keyword, search a specific Microsoft Clip Organizer collection, or search for specific files or media types, such as movies.

If your computer has an Internet connection, by default your search is expanded to include the thousands of free clip art images available on the Office.com Web site.

After you have inserted a picture, you can make it larger or smaller and position it anywhere you want on the slide.

Tip You can save PowerPoint slides as pictures that you can insert in other types of documents. Display the Save & Send page of the Backstage view, and click Change File Type in the center pane. Then click one of the formats listed under Image File Types in the right pane, and click Save As. In the Save As dialog box, specify a name and location, and then click Save. In the message box that appears, click Every Slide to save all the slides as images, or click Current Slide Only to save an image of the current slide.

In this exercise, you'll add pictures and clip art images to slides. After inserting them, you'll move and size them to fit their slides.

 SET UP You need the WaterSavingA_start presentation and the Penstemon and Agastache pictures located in your Chapter16 practice file folder to complete this exercise. Open the WaterSavingA_start presentation, and save it as *WaterSavingA*. Be sure you have an Internet connection so that you can connect to Office.com. Then follow the steps.

1. Press Ctrl+End to move to slide **11**, and delete **<show pictures>**.

   Because you have deleted the text from the content placeholder, PowerPoint redisplays the content buttons.

 2. In the content placeholder, click the **Insert Picture from File** button.

   The Insert Picture dialog box opens.

3. Navigate to your **Chapter16** practice file folder, click the **Penstemon** file, and then click **Insert**.

   Tip If a picture might change, you can ensure that the slide is always up to date by clicking the Insert arrow and then clicking Link To File to insert a link to the picture, or by clicking Insert And Link to both insert the picture and link it to its graphic file.

   PowerPoint inserts the picture in the middle of the content pane.

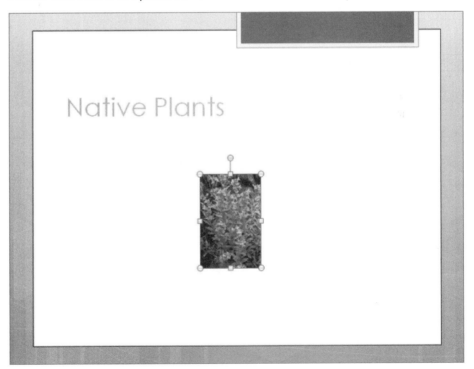

The picture is surrounded by a frame to indicate that it is selected. You use the handles around the frame to size and rotate the picture.

4. On the **View** tab, in the **Show** group, select the **Ruler** check box.

   Horizontal and vertical rulers are displayed across the top and down the left side of the Slide pane. The 0 mark on each ruler indicates the center of the slide. For clarity, we will refer to marks to the left of or above 0 as negative marks.

5. Point to the picture, and when you see a four-headed arrow attached to the pointer, drag to the left and down until its upper-left corner is almost level with the **−4** inch mark on the horizontal ruler and the **0.5** inch mark on the vertical ruler.

6. Point to the handle in the upper-right corner of the photo, and drag up and to the right until that corner sits about level with the **−1.5** inch mark on the horizontal ruler and the **1** inch mark on the vertical ruler.

   The photo increases in size. To make the picture smaller, you would drag in the opposite direction.

When you drag a corner handle, the photograph shrinks or grows proportionally.

7. On the **Insert** tab, in the **Images** group, click the **Picture** button, and then in the **Insert Picture** dialog box, double-click the **Agastache** file.

   You can add pictures or other images to a slide without an available content place-holder, and regardless of the slide layout.

8. Point to the handle in the lower-right corner of the photo, and drag down and to the right until the Agastache photo is about the same size as the Penstemon photo. Then click away from the photo to release the selection.

9. On the **Insert** tab, in the **Text** group, click the **Text Box** button, and then click below the lower-left corner of the Penstemon photo.

10. In the text box, type **Photos courtesy of Rugged Country Plants**. Then select the text, make it 14 points and purple, and click a blank area of the slide.

    These photographs came from ruggedcountryplants.com and are used with permission of the owners.

When you use photos you haven't taken yourself, you should always credit the source.

Clip
Art

11. Move to slide **4**, and on the **Insert** tab, in the **Images** group, click the **Clip Art** button.

The Clip Art task pane opens.

12. In the **Search for** box at the top of the task pane, type **protect**. Then with the **Include Office.com content** check box selected, click **Go**.

Thumbnails of any clip art, movies, and sounds stored on your computer or on the Office.com Web site that have the associated keyword *protect* or *protection* appear in the task pane.

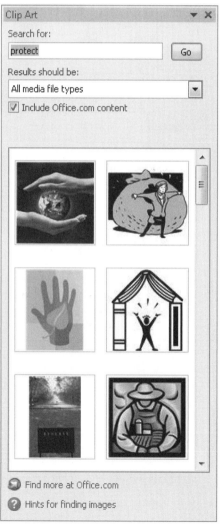

You can find free images of almost any concept by searching in the Clip Art task pane.

Tip If you don't see a suitable image, you can click Find More At Office.com at the bottom of the task pane, and search for additional images there.

13. Scroll down to see all the images that are available, and when you are ready, point to the green and blue drawing of hands protecting a plant.

A ScreenTip describes the image and gives its dimensions, file size, and format.

Hands framing plant
Provided By: Microsoft
537 (w) x 578 (h) pixels | 9 KB | WMF

This clip art file is in Windows Metafile (WMF) format.

14. Click the thumbnail once.

PowerPoint inserts the image in the center of the slide.

15. At the right end of the title bar of the **Clip Art** task pane, click the **Close** button.

16. Drag the image to the lower-right corner of the slide, and then drag the upper-left corner handle until the image occupies about half of the slide. Click a blank area to release the selection.

The image balances the text on the slide.

This image symbolizes people's efforts to protect plants.

 CLEAN UP Save the WaterSavingA presentation, and then close it.

Inserting Diagrams

Sometimes the concepts you want to convey to an audience are best presented in diagrams, which depict processes, hierarchies, cycles, or relationships. You can easily create a dynamic, visually appealing diagram for a slide by using SmartArt Graphics, a powerful tool that comes with the Microsoft Office 2010 programs. SmartArt provides predefined sets of formatting for effortlessly putting together any of the following types of diagrams:

- **Process** These visually describe the ordered set of steps required to complete a task—for example, the approval process for the launch of a new book series.

- **Hierarchy** These illustrate the structure of an organization or entity—for example, a company's top-level management structure.

- **Cycle** These represent a circular sequence of steps, tasks, or events; or the relationship of a set of steps, tasks, or events to a central, core element—for example, the looping process for continually improving a product based on customer feedback.

- **Relationship** These show convergent, divergent, overlapping, merging, or containing elements—for example, how organizing your e-mail, calendar, and contacts can converge to improve your productivity.

On a slide that includes a content placeholder, you can click the placeholder's Insert SmartArt Graphic button to start the process of creating a diagram. You can also click the SmartArt button in the Illustrations Group on the Insert tab to add a diagram to any slide. In either case, you then select the type of diagram you want to create and click a specific layout to see a picture and description. When you find the diagram that best conveys your information, you click OK to insert the diagram with placeholder text that you can replace in an adjacent Text pane.

Graphic Formats

You can use picture and clip art files in a variety of formats, including the following:

- **BMP (bitmap)** This format stores graphics as a series of dots, or pixels. There are different qualities of BMP, reflecting the number of bits available per pixel to store information about the graphic—the greater the number of bits, the greater the number of possible colors.

- **GIF (Graphics Interchange Format)** This format is common for images that appear on Web pages because they can be compressed with no loss of information and groups of them can be animated. GIFs store at most 8 bits per pixel, so they are limited to 256 colors.

- **JPEG (Joint Photographic Experts Group)** This compressed format works well for complex graphics such as scanned photographs. Some information is lost in the compression process, but often the loss is imperceptible to the human eye. Color JPEG images store 24 bits per pixel, so they are capable of displaying more than 16 million colors. Grayscale JPEG images store 8 bits per pixel.

- **TIFF (Tag Image File Format)** This format can store compressed images with a flexible number of bits per pixel. Using tags, a single multipage TIFF file can store several images, along with related information such as type of compression and orientation.

- **PNG (Portable Network Graphic)** This format has the advantages of the GIF format but can store colors with 8, 24, or 48 bits per pixel and grayscales with 1, 2, 4, 8, or 16 bits per pixel. A PNG file can also specify whether each pixel blends with its background color and can contain color correction information so that images look accurate on a broad range of display devices. Graphics saved in this format are smaller, so they display faster.

After you create a diagram, you can move and size it to fit the slide, and with a few clicks, you can change the colors and look of its shapes to achieve professional looking results.

In this exercise, you'll add a cycle diagram, enter text, and then move and size it. You'll also format its shapes in simple ways.

 SET UP You need the WaterSavingB_start presentation located in your Chapter16 practice file folder to complete this exercise. Open the WaterSavingB_start presentation, and save it as *WaterSavingB*. Display the rulers, and then follow the steps.

 1. Display slide **6**, and then click the **Insert SmartArt Graphic** button in the content placeholder.

The Choose A SmartArt Graphic dialog box opens.

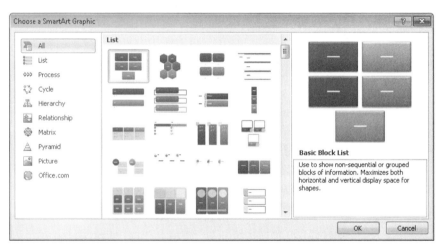

By default, all the available layouts are listed in the center pane, but you can filter them by category. A picture and description of the selected layout appear in the right pane.

2. In the left pane, click each layout type in turn to see all the available layouts of that type in the center pane, and then click **Cycle**.

3. In the center pane, click each layout in turn to view a picture and description in the right pane.

4. When you finish exploring, click the second layout (**Text Cycle**), and then click **OK**.

PowerPoint inserts a blank cycle diagram into the slide. The Design and Format contextual tabs appear on the ribbon.

5. On the **Design** tab, in the **Create Graphic** group, click the **Text Pane** button. The Text pane opens.

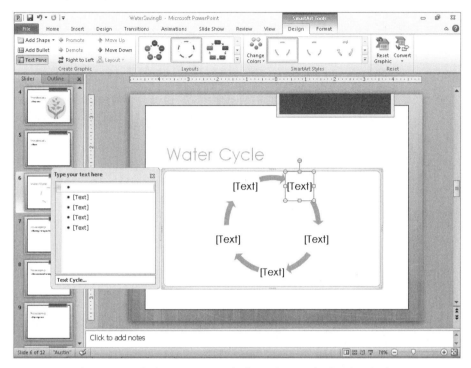

You can use the same techniques to create bullet points and subpoints in the Text pane as you would on the Outline tab of the Overview pane.

Troubleshooting The appearance of buttons and groups on the ribbon changes depending on the width of the program window. For information about changing the appearance of the ribbon to match our screen images, see "Modifying the Display of the Ribbon" at the beginning of this book.

6. With the first bullet in the **Text** pane selected, type **Clouds**, and then press the Down Arrow key to move to the next bullet.

Troubleshooting Be sure to press the Down Arrow key and not the Enter key. Pressing Enter will add a new bullet point (and a new shape).

7. Pressing Shift+Enter after each word, type **Condensation**, **and**, and **Precipitation**. Then press the Down Arrow key.

8. Repeat step 7 to add **Runoff**, **and**, and **Percolation**. Then repeat it again to add **Evaporation**, **and**, and **Transpiration**.

9. You don't need the last bullet point, so on the **Design** tab, in the **Create Graphic** group, click the **Text Pane** button to close the Text pane.

    Tip You can also click the Close button in the upper-right corner of the Text pane.

10. In the diagram, click the **Text** placeholder, and click the border of the empty shape to select it for manipulation. Then press the Delete key.

    The diagram now has four sets of text and arrows.

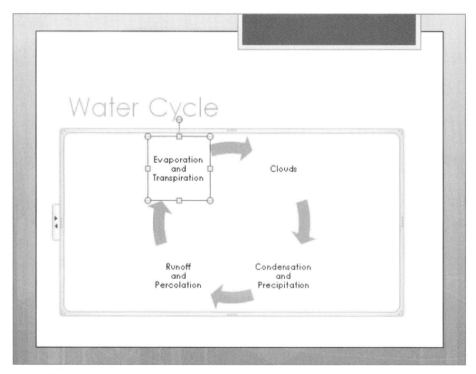

In this diagram, the arrows are more prominent than the text.

Tip You can click the tab with left and right arrows on the left side of the diagram's frame to open the Text pane.

11. In the **Layouts** group, click the **More** button to view the available Cycle diagram layouts, and then click the first thumbnail in the first row (**Basic Cycle**).

The diagram changes to the new layout.

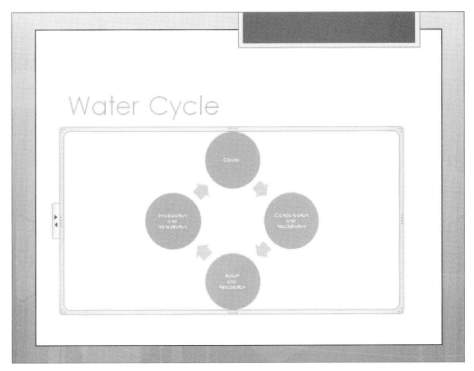

In this diagram, the text is contained in solid-color circles, and the arrows are less prominent.

12. Point to the handle (the four dots) in the middle of the right side of the diagram's frame, and when the pointer changes to a two-headed arrow, drag to the left until the frame is only as wide as the diagram. (Repeat the process as necessary.)

13. Point to a part of the frame where there is no handle, and when a four-headed arrow is attached to the pointer, drag the diagram until it sits in the lower-right corner of the white area of the slide.

14. Point to the handle in the upper-left corner of the frame and drag up and to the left until the frame sits at about the **−2.5** inch mark on both the horizontal and vertical rulers.

Troubleshooting Remember that the 0 mark on both rulers is centered on the slide. You want the 2.5-inch marks to the left of and above the 0 marks.

The diagram expands with its frame.

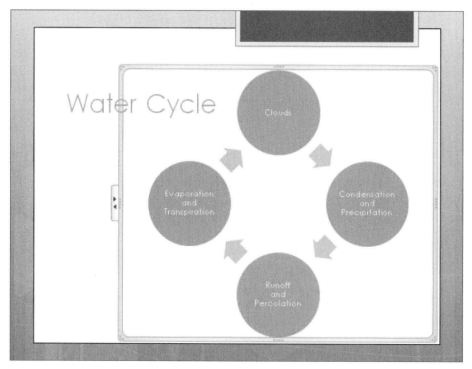

Because the diagram is an independent object, it can sit on top of the empty part of the title placeholder.

15. In the **SmartArt Styles** group, click the **Change Colors** button, and then in the gallery, under **Colorful**, click the second thumbnail (**Colorful Range - Accent Colors 2 and 3**).

The shapes in the diagram assume the colors of the selected scheme.

16. In the **SmartArt Styles** group, click the **More** button.

The SmartArt Styles gallery appears.

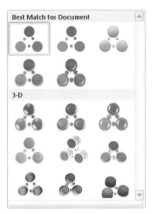

You can apply two-dimensional and three-dimensional styles from this gallery.

17. Under **3-D** in the gallery, click the first thumbnail in the first row (**Polished**).

18. Click outside the frame.

You can now see the final result.

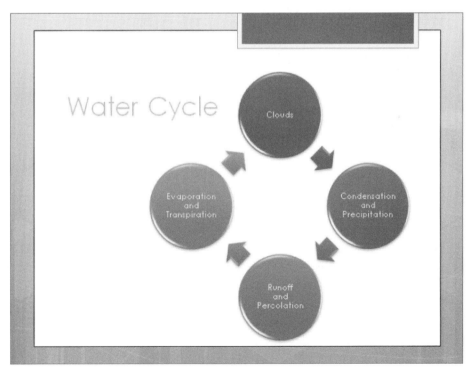

The colors and three-dimensional effect give the diagram pizzazz.

 CLEAN UP Save the WaterSavingB presentation, and then close it.

Converting Existing Bullet Points into Diagrams

You might decide after creating a bulleted list on a slide that a diagram would more clearly convey your point to your audience. You can easily convert a bulleted list to a SmartArt diagram with only a few clicks of the mouse button.

To create a diagram from an existing bulleted list:

1. Click anywhere in the placeholder containing the bulleted list you want to convert.

2. Right-click anywhere in the selected placeholder, and point to Convert To SmartArt.

3. Do one of the following:

   a. If the diagram layout you want appears in the gallery, click its thumbnail.

   b. If you don't see the layout you want, click More SmartArt Graphics. Then in the Choose A SmartArt Graphic dialog box, click the layout you want, and click OK.

4. Adjust the size, position, and look of the diagram in the usual way.

Inserting Charts

For those occasions when you want to display numeric data visually, you can add a chart to a slide. Charts make it easy to see trends that might not be obvious from looking at the numbers themselves.

On a slide that includes a content placeholder, you can click the placeholder's Insert Chart button to start the process of creating a chart. You can also click the Chart button in the Illustrations Group on the Insert tab to add a chart to any slide. In either case, you then select the type of chart you want. If your PowerPoint window is maximized, when you click OK, a sample chart of the type you selected is inserted in the current slide, and the PowerPoint window shrinks so that it occupies half the screen. An associated Microsoft Excel worksheet containing the data plotted in the sample chart is displayed in the other half. You use this worksheet to enter the information you want to plot, following the pattern illustrated by the sample data.

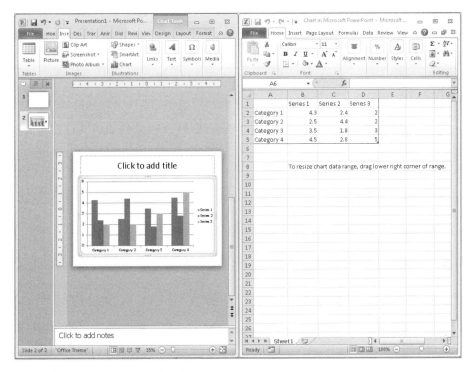

A sample chart and its associated worksheet.

The Excel worksheet is composed of rows and columns of cells that contain values, which in charting terminology are called *data points*. Collectively a set of data points is called a *data series*. Each worksheet cell is identified by an address consisting of its column letter and row number—for example, A2. A range of cells is identified by the address of the cell in the upper-left corner and the address of the cell in the lower-right corner, separated by a colon—for example, A2:D5.

When you replace the sample data in the worksheet, you immediately see the results in the chart in the adjacent PowerPoint window. Each data point in a data series is represented graphically in the chart by a data marker. The data is plotted against an x-axis—also called the *category axis*—and a y-axis—also called the *value axis*. (Three-dimensional charts also have a z-axis—also called the *series axis*.) Tick-mark labels along each axis identify the categories, values, or series in the chart. A legend provides a key for identifying the data series.

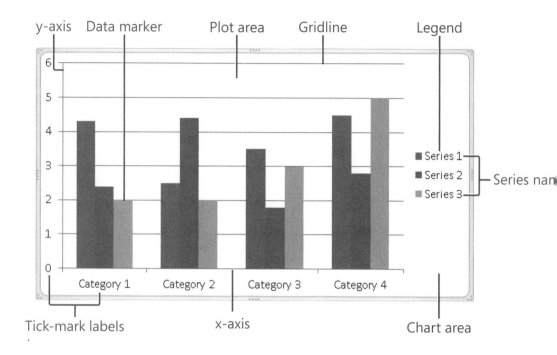

The major elements of a chart.

To enter data in a cell of the Excel worksheet, you first click the cell to select it. You can select an entire column by clicking the column header—the shaded box containing a letter at the top of each column—and an entire row by clicking the row header—the shaded box containing a number to the left of each row. You can select the entire work-sheet by clicking the Select All button—the box at the junction of the column and row headers.

Having selected a cell, you can enter your data by typing it directly. However, if your data already exists in an Excel worksheet or a Microsoft Access or Microsoft Word table, you don't have to retype it. You can copy the data from its source program and paste it into the Excel worksheet that is linked to the slide.

After you've plotted your data in the chart, you can move and size the chart to suit the space available on the slide. You can edit the data—both the values and the column and row headings—at any time, and PowerPoint will replot the chart to reflect your changes.

In this exercise, you'll create a chart by pasting existing data into the associated Excel worksheet. You'll then size the chart, and edit its data.

SET UP You need the WaterConsumption workbook and the WaterSavingC_start presentation located in your Chapter16 practice file folder to complete this exercise. From Windows Explorer, open the WaterConsumption workbook in Excel by double-clicking the workbook's file name. Then open the WaterSavingC_start presentation, and save it as *WaterSavingC*. Ensure that the PowerPoint program window is maximized, and then follow the steps.

1. Display slide **7**, and then in the content placeholder, click the **Insert Chart** button.

The Insert Chart dialog box opens.

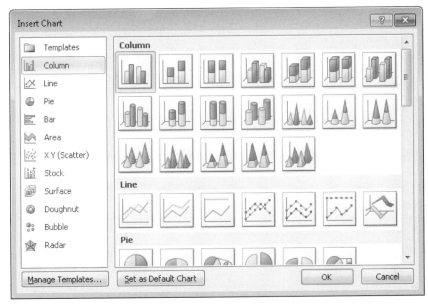

You can choose from many types of charts in this dialog box.

2. With **Column** selected in the left pane, click the first thumbnail in the second row (**Clustered Cylinder**), and then click **OK**.

PowerPoint inserts the chart into the slide and resizes its program window to occupy the left half of your screen. Excel starts and displays the data used to plot the chart in the right half of the screen.

3. From the Windows Taskbar, display the **WaterConsumption** worksheet. Then in the worksheet, point to cell **A3**, and drag down and to the right to cell **C13**.

Excel selects all the cells in the range A3:C13.

4. On the Excel **Home** tab, in the **Clipboard** group, click the **Copy** button.

5. From the Windows Taskbar, display the **Chart in Microsoft PowerPoint** worksheet. Then in the worksheet, click cell **A1**.

6. On the Excel **Home** tab, in the **Clipboard** group, click the **Paste** button. Then click **OK** to acknowledge the message that Excel has inserted rows in the worksheet to accommodate the copied data.

Excel pastes in the data, and PowerPoint immediately replots the chart.

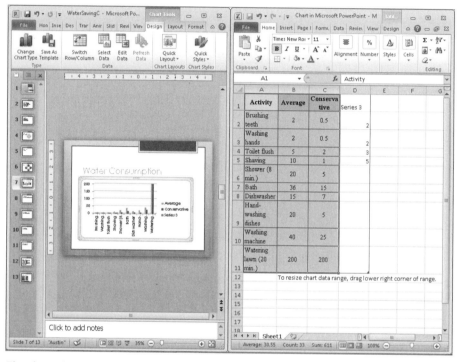

The chart plots all the data within the blue border in the worksheet.

7. To exclude the data in column D from the chart, in the worksheet, drag the handle in the lower-right corner of the blue border to the left, releasing it when cells **D1:D11** are shaded.

In the PowerPoint window, the chart now reflects the fact that only the Activity, Average, and Conservative columns are plotted.

8. In the upper-right corner of the Excel window, click the **Close** button to close the associated worksheet. Then close the **WaterConsumption** workbook.

The PowerPoint window expands, giving you a better view of the chart.

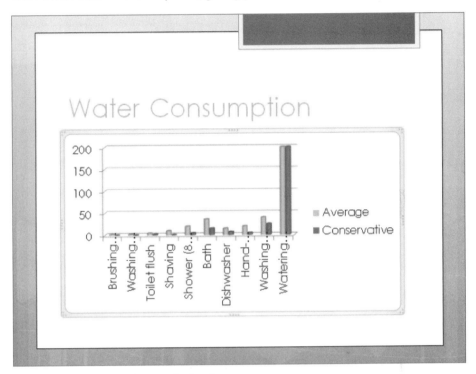

The copied data, plotted as a cylinder chart.

9. Point to the handle (the four dots) in the middle of the bottom of the frame, and drag downward until the frame sits at the bottom of the white area of the slide.

When you release the mouse button, the chart area expands, but not enough for the category labels to be displayed in their entirety.

10. On the **Design** contextual tab, in the **Data** group, click the **Edit Data** button.

The associated worksheet opens in Excel so that you can make changes to the plotted data.

11. Click cell **A9**, type **Dishes by hand**, and press Enter. Then in cell **A10**, type **Clothes washer**, and press Enter. Finally in cell **A11**, replace **Watering lawn (20 min.)** with **Lawn (20 min.)**, and press Enter. Then close the Excel worksheet.

Tip If the chart isn't selected (surrounded by a frame) in the PowerPoint window when you make changes to the data in the Excel window, the chart won't automatically update. If this happens, click the chart before proceeding.

PowerPoint replots the chart with the new category labels.

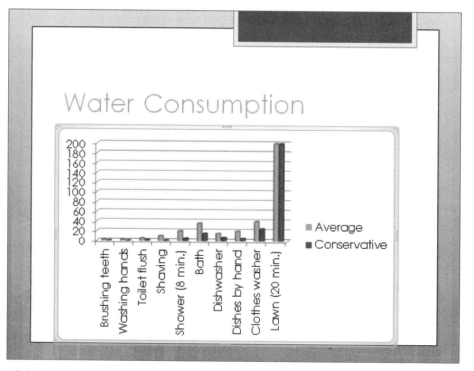

All the category labels now fit in the chart area.

12. Point to the handle in the middle of the right side of the frame, and drag to the right until the frame sits at the edge of the white area on that slide. Then click outside the chart frame.

PowerPoint has rotated the labels so that the chart area can expand even more.

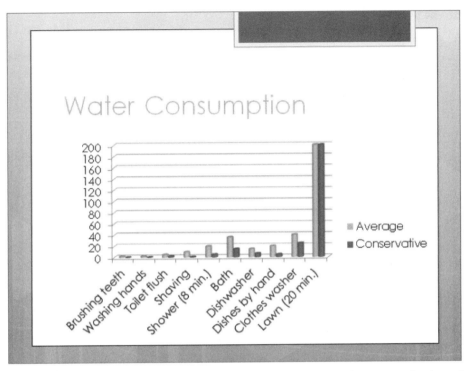

The chart shows that watering a lawn consumes much more water than most other household water usages.

Tip By default, the chart is plotted based on the series in the columns of the worksheet, which are identified in the legend. If you want to base the chart on the series in the rows instead, click the Switch Row/Column button in the Data group on the Design contextual tab. The worksheet must be open for the button to be active. (To open the worksheet, right-click the chart, and then click Edit Data.)

 CLEAN UP Save the WaterSavingC presentation, and then close it.

Drawing Shapes

To emphasize the key points in your presentation, you might want to include shapes in addition to text. PowerPoint provides tools for creating several types of shapes, including stars, banners, boxes, lines, circles, and squares. With a little imagination, you'll soon discover ways to create drawings by combining shapes.

To create a shape in PowerPoint, you click the Shapes button in the Illustrations group on the Insert tab, click the shape you want to insert, and then drag the crosshair pointer across the slide.

Tip To draw a circle or a square, click the Oval or a Rectangle shape, and hold down the Shift key while you drag.

After you draw the shape, it is surrounded by a set of handles, indicating that it is selected. (You can select a shape at any time by simply clicking it.) The handles serve the following purposes:

- You can drag the pale blue sizing handles to change the size of a shape.
- If a shape has a yellow diamond-shaped adjustment handle next to one of the sizing handles or elsewhere on the shape, the shape is adjustable. You can use this handle to alter the appearance of the shape without changing its size.
- You can drag the green rotating handle to adjust the angle of rotation of a shape.

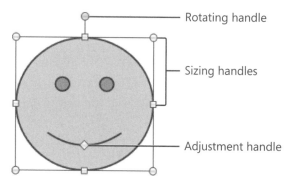

The three types of shape handles.

You can copy or cut a selected shape or multiple shapes and then paste the shapes elsewhere in the same presentation, in another presentation, or in any Office program.

To move a shape from one location to another on the same slide, you simply drag it. You can create a copy of a selected shape by dragging it while holding down the Ctrl key or by clicking the Copy arrow in the Clipboard group on the Home tab and then clicking Duplicate.

After drawing a shape, you can modify it by using the buttons on the Format contextual tab that appears when a shape is selected. For example, you can:

- Add text to a shape. PowerPoint centers the text as you type, and the text becomes part of the shape.
- Change the size and color of the shape and its outline.
- Apply special effects, such as making the shape look three-dimensional.

Having made changes to one shape, you can easily apply the same attributes to another shape by clicking the shape that has the desired attributes, clicking the Format Painter button in the Clipboard group on the Home tab, and then clicking the shape to which you want to copy the attributes. If you want to apply the attributes of a shape to all shapes in the active presentation, right-click the shape and then click Set As Default Shape. From then on, all the shapes you draw in the active presentation will have the new default attributes.

When you have multiple shapes on a slide, you can group them so that you can copy, move, and format them as a unit. You can change the attributes of an individual shape—for example, its color, size, or location—without ungrouping the shapes. If you do un-group the graphics, you can regroup the same shapes by selecting one of them and then clicking Regroup in the Group list.

In this exercise, you'll draw several shapes, add text to them, and change their colors. Then you'll duplicate and copy a shape and switch one shape for another.

SET UP You need the JournalingA_start presentation located in your Chapter16 practice file folder to complete this exercise. Open the JournalingA_start presentation, and save it as *JournalingA*. Display the rulers, and then follow the steps.

1. Display slide **5**, and on the **Insert** tab, in the **Illustrations** group, click the **Shapes** button.

   The Shapes gallery appears.

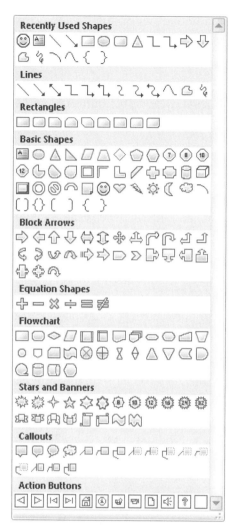

Many different types of shapes are grouped by category in the Shapes gallery.

2. Under **Stars and Banners** in the gallery, click the **5-Point Star** shape, and then drag the crosshair pointer in the middle of the slide to draw a star shape that spans the shadow of the hand in the background graphic.

   Tip If you click a shape button and then change your mind about drawing the shape, you can release the shape by pressing the Esc key.

   Pale blue handles surround the shape to indicate that it is selected.

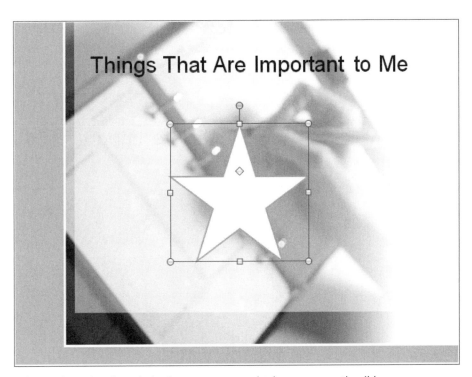

When a shape is selected, the Format contextual tab appears on the ribbon.

3. On the **Format** tab, in the **Insert Shapes** group, click the **More** button to display the **Shapes** gallery. Then under **Block Arrows**, click the **Right Arrow** shape, and draw a small arrow to the right of the star.

4. With the arrow still selected, hold down the Ctrl key, and drag a copy of the arrow to the left of the star.

   Troubleshooting Be sure to release the mouse button before you release the Ctrl key. Otherwise you'll move the shape instead of copying it.

5. With the shape still selected, in the **Arrange** group, click the **Rotate** button, and then click **Flip Horizontal**.

   You could have drawn a Left Arrow shape, but this technique ensures that the two arrows have the same proportions.

   Tip You can rotate or flip any type of image. Rotating turns a shape 90 degrees to the right or left; flipping turns a shape 180 degrees horizontally or vertically. You can also rotate a shape to any degree by dragging the green rotating handle.

6. Adjacent to the left arrow, add a scroll shape, and adjacent to the right arrow, add a heart shape.

All the shapes have the same outline and interior colors.

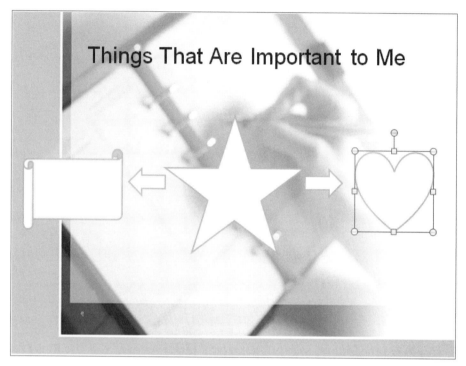

You can build a picture with the shapes available in the Shapes gallery.

7. With the heart selected, on the **Home** tab, in the **Clipboard** group, click the **Copy** arrow, and then in the list, click **Duplicate**.

PowerPoint pastes a copy of the shape on top of the original.

8. Point to the handle in the upper-left corner of the new shape, and drag down and to the right to make the second heart smaller than the first.

9. On the **Format** tab, in the **Insert Shapes** group, click the **Text Box** button, click the center of the star, and then type **ME**.

See Also For information about working with text boxes, see "Adding Text Boxes" in Chapter 14, "Work with Slide Text."

Don't worry that you can barely see the text; you'll fix that in a later step.

10. Repeat step 9 to add the word **Education** to the scroll shape and **Family** to the heart shape.

11. Click the scroll shape (don't click the text), hold down the Shift key, click the star shape, and then click the two hearts.

12. With all four shapes selected, in the **Shape Styles** group, click the **More** button to display the **Shape Styles** gallery.

13. Point to several thumbnails to see live previews of their effects, and then click the last thumbnail in the fourth row (**Subtle Effect – Light Blue, Accent 6**).

    The color of the interior and outline of the shapes changes, as does the color of the text.

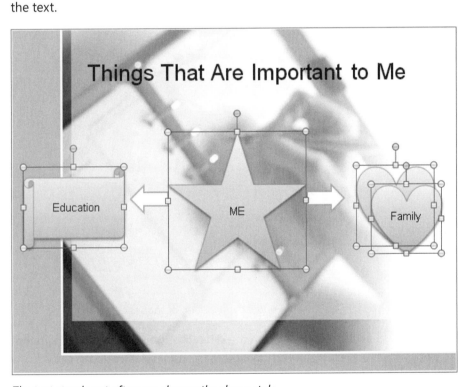

The text stands out after you change the shape style.

14. Click a blank area of the slide to release the selection, and then click the scroll shape (don't click its text).

15. In the **Insert Shapes** group, click the **Edit Shape** button, point to **Change Shape**, and under **Block Arrows**, click the third shape (**Up Arrow**).

    The scroll changes to the selected shape, with all formatting and text intact.

16. Double-click the word **Education**, and type **Job**. Then click outside the shape to release the selection.

    You can now see the results.

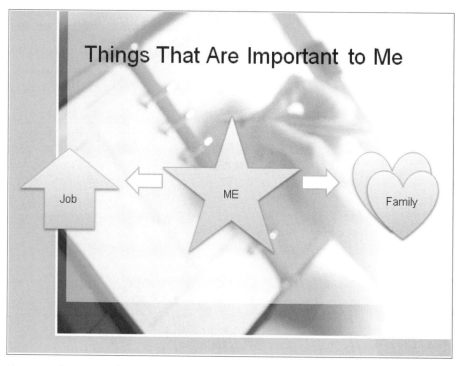

You can tell a story using a combination of shapes and text.

17. Select all the shapes on the slide. Then on the **Format** tab, in the **Arrange** group, click the **Group** button, and in the list, click **Group**.

    The shapes are grouped together as one object.

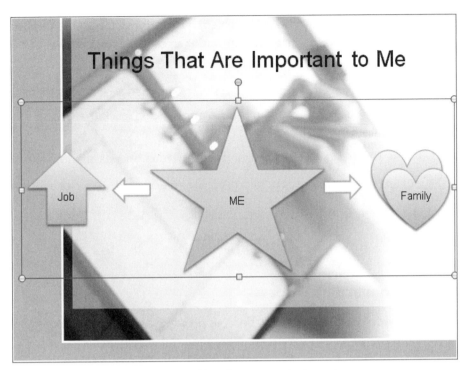

When shapes are grouped, one set of handles surrounds the entire group.

18. In the **Shape Styles** group, click the **Shape Outline** arrow, and then under **Standard Colors** in the palette, click the last color (**Purple**).

The outlines around the shapes change to purple.

19. Point to any shape in the group, and when the pointer has a four-headed arrow attached to it, drag downward about a half inch.

The entire group moves.

20. Click the left arrow. In the **Shape Styles** group, click the **Shape Fill** arrow and change the shape's color to purple.

Even though the shapes are grouped, you can still change the attributes of one of the shapes.

21. With the left arrow still selected, on the **Home** tab, in the **Clipboard** group, click the **Format Painter** button, and then click the right arrow.

   Both arrows are now purple.

22. Click away from the selected shape, and then click any shape to select the group.

23. On the **Format** tab, in the **Arrange** group, click the **Group** button, and then click **Ungroup**.

   The group is disbanded, and the individual shapes are now selected.

  CLEAN UP Save the JournalingA presentation, and then close it.

Connecting Shapes

If you want to show a relationship between two shapes, you can connect them with a line by joining special handles called *connection points*.

To connect shapes:

1. Click one of the shapes you want to connect. Then on the Format tab, in the Insert Shapes group, display the Shapes gallery, and under Lines, click one of the Connector shapes.

2. Point to the selected shape.

   Red connection points appear, and the pointer changes to a crosshair.

3. Point to a connection point, and then drag over to the other shape (don't release the mouse button).

4. When connection points appear on the other shape, point to a connection point, and release the mouse button.

   Red handles appear at each end of the line, indicating that the shapes are connected.

   Troubleshooting If a blue handle appears instead of a red one, the shapes are not connected. Click the Undo button on the Quick Access Toolbar to remove the connection line, and then redraw it.

Adding Transitions

When you deliver a presentation, you can move from slide to slide by clicking the mouse button or you can have PowerPoint replace one slide with the next at predetermined intervals. You can avoid abrupt breaks between slides by employing transitions that control the way slides move on and off the screen.

PowerPoint comes with the following categories of built-in transition effects:

- **Subtle** This category includes fades, wipes, and a shutter-like effect.

- **Exciting** This category includes more dramatic effects such as checkerboards, ripples, turning, and zooming.

The connector between two connection points.

After you have drawn the connector, you can format it by changing its color and weight. You can then set the formatted line as the default for all future connectors in this drawing. If you move a connected shape, the line moves with it, maintaining the relationship between the shapes.

- **Dynamic Content** This category holds the background of the slides still and applies a dynamic effect to the title and other content, such as rotating or flying onto the slide.

Each slide can have only one transition. You set transitions from the Transitions tab in Normal view or Slide Sorter view, for one slide at a time, for a group of slides, or for an entire presentation. This tab is new in PowerPoint 2010, reflecting the importance of transitions in ensuring a smooth flow for your presentations. (Previously, transitions were included on the Animations tab because they were considered just another form of animation.)

In addition to selecting the type of transition, you can specify the following:

- The sound
- The speed
- When the transition occurs

In this exercise, you'll apply a transition to a single slide, and apply the same transition to all the slides in the presentation. You'll also add sound to the transition and set the transition speed.

SET UP You need the JournalingB_start presentation located in your Chapter16 practice file folder to complete this exercise. Open the JournalingB_start presentation, and save it as *JournalingB*. Then follow the steps.

1. Display slide **2** in Normal view. Then on the **Transitions** tab, in the **Transition to This Slide** group, click each thumbnail in the gallery to see its effects.

 2. To the right of the gallery, click the **Down** button, and continue previewing the effects of each transition.

3. When you have finished exploring, click the **More** button to display the entire gallery, and then click the **Cover** thumbnail in the **Subtle** category.

PowerPoint demonstrates the Cover transition effect on slide 2 and indicates that the transition has been applied by placing an animation symbol below the slide number on the Slides tab of the Overview pane. (There is no indication on the slide itself.)

You have applied an animation to one slide.

Effect
Options ▾

4. In the **Transition to This Slide** group, click the **Effect Options** button, and then click **From Top-Left**.

5. In the **Timing** group, click the **Apply To All** button.

   An animation symbol appears below each slide number on the Slides tab.

6. On the **Slides** tab in the **Overview** pane, click the animation symbol below slide **3**.

   The Slide pane turns black, and then PowerPoint demonstrates the Cover transition from slide 2 to slide 3.

7. Display slide **1**. In the **Transition to This Slide** group, click the **More** button, and then in the **Transitions** gallery, click the **None** thumbnail.

   PowerPoint removes the animation symbol from below the slide 1 thumbnail.

Because you will usually start a presentation with the title slide displayed, there is no need for a transition on this slide.

8. On the **View Shortcuts** toolbar at the right end of the status bar, click the **Reading View** button.

   PowerPoint switches to Reading view and displays slide 1.

9. At the bottom of the screen, click the **Next** button repeatedly to see the transitions of the first few slides, and then press Esc to return to Normal view.

10. On the **View Shortcuts** toolbar, click the **Slide Sorter** button.

11. In **Slide Sorter** view, click slide **2**, hold down the Shift key, and then click slide **7** to select all the slides that have transitions.

12. In the **Timing** group, click the **Sound** arrow, and then click **Wind**.

   Tip If you want to associate a sound file of your own with a slide transition, click Other Sound at the bottom of the Sound list. Then in the Add Audio dialog box, find and select the sound file you want to use, and click Open.

13. In the **Timing** group, click the **Duration** up arrow until the duration shows as **02.00**.

14. In the **Preview** group, click the **Preview** button to preview the transition effect again. Then if you want, preview it again in Reading view.

PowerPoint demonstrates the transition of each selected slide with the sound specified in step 13.

✖ **CLEAN UP** Save the JournalingB presentation, and then close it.

Key Points

- When you add pictures or photographs to a slide, keep in mind that using pictures you don't own without permission, especially for business purposes, can breach the copyright of the owner. Limited use for non-commercial purposes is usually allowed as long as you acknowledge the source.

- Thousands of free clip art images are available to help you add visual interest to your slides.

- With SmartArt, you can create a variety of professional-looking diagrams with a few mouse clicks.

- Charts present numeric data in an easy-to-grasp visual format. You can choose from 11 types with many variations.

- Shapes can add interest to a slide and draw attention to key concepts. However, they can become tiresome and produce an amateurish effect if they are overused.

- Avoid abrupt transitions by having one slide smoothly replace another. You can control the transition type, its speed, and when it takes place.

Chapter at a Glance

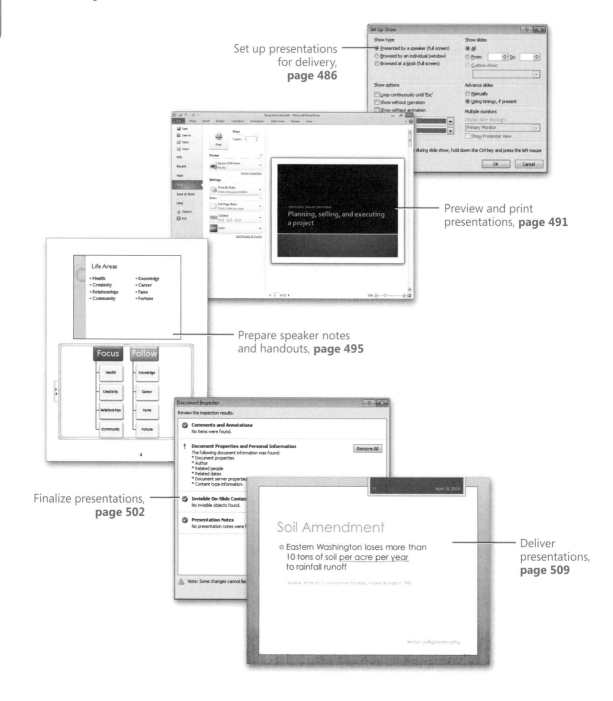

Set up presentations for delivery, **page 486**

Preview and print presentations, **page 491**

Prepare speaker notes and handouts, **page 495**

Finalize presentations, **page 502**

Deliver presentations, **page 509**

17 Review and Deliver Presentations

In this chapter, you will learn how to

✔ Set up presentations for delivery.

✔ Preview and print presentations.

✔ Prepare speaker notes and handouts.

✔ Finalize presentations.

✔ Deliver presentations.

When it is time to deliver the Microsoft PowerPoint 2010 presentation you have worked so hard to create, taking the time for a few final tasks helps to ensure a successful outcome.

Before exposing a new presentation to the eyes of the world, you should check a few settings and proof the text of the slides, preferably on paper, where typographic errors seem to stand out much better than they do on the screen. When you are satisfied that the presentation is complete, you can prepare for your moment in the spotlight by creating speaker notes. You might also want to create handouts to give to your audience, to remind them later of your presentation's message.

When all these tasks are complete, you should remove extraneous information before declaring the presentation final.

If you will deliver the presentation from your computer as an electronic slide show, it pays to become familiar with the tools available in Slide Show view, where instead of appearing in a window, the slide occupies the entire screen. You navigate through slides by clicking the mouse button or by pressing the Arrow keys, moving forward and backward one slide at a time or jumping to specific slides as the needs of your audience dictate. During the slide show, you can mark slides with an on-screen pen or highlighter to emphasize a point.

In this chapter, you'll set up a slide show for delivery, preview a presentation, and print selected slides. You'll remove the properties attached to a presentation and prevent other people from making further changes to it. Finally, you'll see how to deliver a presentation, including marking up slides while showing them.

> **Practice Files** Before you can complete the exercises in this chapter, you need to copy the book's practice files to your computer. The practice files you'll use to complete the exercises in this chapter are in the Chapter17 practice file folder. A complete list of practice files is provided in "Using the Practice Files" at the beginning of this book.

Setting Up Presentations for Delivery

In the old days, presentations were delivered by speakers with few supporting materials. Little by little, "visual aids" such as white board drawings or flip charts on easels were added, and eventually, savvy speakers began accompanying their presentations with 35mm slides or transparencies projected onto screens. To accommodate these speakers, early versions of PowerPoint included output formats optimized for slides of various sizes, including 35mm slides and the acetate sheets used with overhead projectors.

Although technology has evolved to the point where most presentations are now delivered electronically, PowerPoint 2010 still accommodates those output formats, as well as formats designed for printing on paper. Usually, you'll find the default on-screen format adequate for your needs. If you have a wide-screen monitor, or if you know you'll be using a delivery method other than your computer for your presentation, you should set the format of the presentation before you begin developing your content so that you place elements appropriately for the final size of your slides.

By default, slides are sized for an on-screen slide show with a width-to-height ratio of 4:3 (10 × 7.5 inches). The slides are oriented horizontally, with slide numbers starting at 1. You can change these settings in the Page Setup dialog box, where you can select from the following slide sizes:

- **On-screen Show** For an electronic slide show on screens of various aspects (4:3, 16:9, or 16:10)

- **Letter Paper** For a presentation printed on 8.5 × 11 inch U.S. letter-size paper

- **Ledger Paper** For a presentation printed on 11 × 17 inch legal-size paper

- **A3 Paper, A4 Paper, B4 (ISO) Paper, B5 (ISO) Paper** For a presentation printed on paper of various international sizes

- **35mm Slides** For 35mm slides to be used in a carousel with a projector

- **Overhead** For transparencies for an overhead projector

- **Banner** For a banner for a Web page

- **Custom** For slides that are a nonstandard size

If you want the same identifying information to appear at the bottom of every slide, you can insert it in a footer. You can specify the date and time, the slide number, and custom text in the Header And Footer dialog box, which shows a preview of where the specified items will appear on the slide.

If you are going to deliver a presentation before an audience and will control the progression of slides manually, the default settings will work well. However, provided the slides have been assigned advancement times on the Transitions tab, you can set up the presentation to run automatically, either once or continuously. For example, you might want to set up a product demonstration slide show in a store or at a tradeshow so that it runs automatically, looping until someone stops it. All it takes is a few settings in the Set Up Show dialog box.

In this exercise, you'll explore the Page Setup dialog box and experiment with slide orientation. You'll add footer information to every slide in a presentation, and then turn the presentation into a self-running slide show.

SET UP You need the ServiceOrientationA_start presentation located in your Chapter17 practice file folder to complete this exercise. Open the ServiceOrientationA_start presentation, and save it as *ServiceOrientationA*. Then follow the steps.

1. On the **Design** tab, in the **Page Setup** group, click the **Page Setup** button.

   The Page Setup dialog box opens.

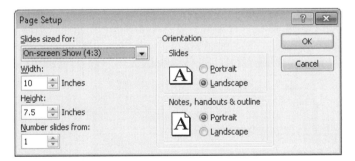

By default, the slides in a presentation are sized for an on-screen slide show with a width-to-height ratio of 4:3.

2. Display the **Slides sized for** list, and toward the bottom, click **35mm Slides**.

   The Width setting changes to 11.25 inches and the Height setting changes to 7.5 inches.

3. Display the **Slides sized for list** again, and click **Banner**.

The Width setting changes to 8 inches, and the Height setting changes to 1 inch. This format is useful if you want to design a presentation that will display in a frame across the top or bottom of a Web page.

Tip Obviously the current presentation with its long title and many bulleted lists is not suitable for the Banner format. If you want to create a banner, be sure to set the format before you begin developing the content of your presentation so that you choose words and graphics that fit within the space available.

4. Set the size of the slides to **On-screen Show (4:3)**. Then in the **Slides** area, click **Portrait**, and click **OK**.

The slide width changes to 7.5 and its height changes to 10 inches. This orientation is useful if you want to compare two presentations side by side in Reading view.

5. In the **Page Setup** group, click the **Slide Orientation** button, and then click **Landscape**.

6. On the **Insert** tab, in the **Text** group, click the **Header & Footer** button.

The Header And Footer dialog box opens with the Slide page displayed.

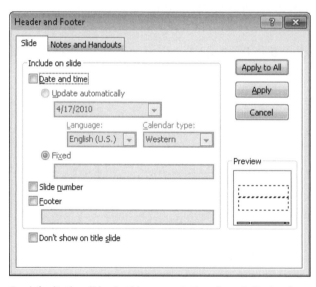

By default, the slides in this presentation do not display footer information.

7. In the **Include on slide** area, select the **Date and time** check box. Then with **Fixed** selected, type today's date in the text box.

   PowerPoint indicates on the thumbnail in the Preview area that the date will appear in the lower-left corner of the slide. The date will appear in the format in which you typed it.

8. Select the **Slide number** check box.

   The thumbnail in the Preview area shows that the slide number will appear in the lower-right corner.

9. Select the **Footer** check box, and then type your name in the text box.

   Your name will appear in the center of the slide.

10. Select the **Don't show on title slide** check box, and click **Apply to All**. Then display slide **2**.

    The specified footer information appears at the bottom of the slide.

Service project goals

- Familiarize you with the concept of service
- Make service a part of your life
- Engage and motivate you
- Build a sense of teamwork among all employees across units
- Provide appropriate skills development
- Meet genuine needs

April 17, 2010   Sidney Higa   2

You have entered footer information for all slides except the title slide.

Set Up
Slide Show

11. On the **Slide Show** tab, in the **Set Up** group, click the **Set Up Slide Show** button. The Set Up Show dialog box opens.

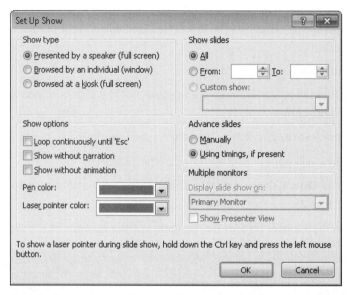

By default, the presentation is set for presenter delivery and to include all slides.

12. In the **Show type** area, click **Browsed at a kiosk (full screen)**.

When you click this option, the Loop Continuously Until 'Esc' check box in the Show Options area becomes unavailable so that you cannot clear it. Any narration or animation attached to the presentation will play with the presentation unless you select the Show Without Narration or Show Without Animation check box.

See Also For information about narration, and animation, refer to *Microsoft PowerPoint 2010 Step by Step*, by Joyce Cox and Joan Lambert (Microsoft Press, 2010).

13. Click **OK**.

14. To test the show, display slide **1**, and on the **View Shortcuts** toolbar, click the **Reading View** button.

The presentation runs continuously, using the transition effect and advancement time applied to all its slides.

See Also For information about transitions, see "Adding Transitions" in Chapter 16, "Add Simple Visual Enhancements."

Tip If the presentation has no advancement time applied to its slides, you should click Manually in the Advance Slides area of the Set Up Show dialog box.

15. When the presentation starts again at slide 1, press Esc to stop the slide show and return to Normal view.

    Now when you are ready to run the presentation, you can navigate to the folder where it is stored, and double-click it. When the presentation opens, switch to Slide Show view to start the presentation. You can press Esc to stop the slide show at any time.

 **CLEAN UP** Save the ServiceOrientationA presentation, and then close it.

Previewing and Printing Presentations

Even if you plan to deliver your presentation electronically, you might want to print the presentation to proof it for typographical errors and stylistic inconsistencies. Before you print, you can preview your presentation to see how the slides will look on paper. You preview a presentation on the Print page in the Backstage view, where the presentation appears in the right pane.

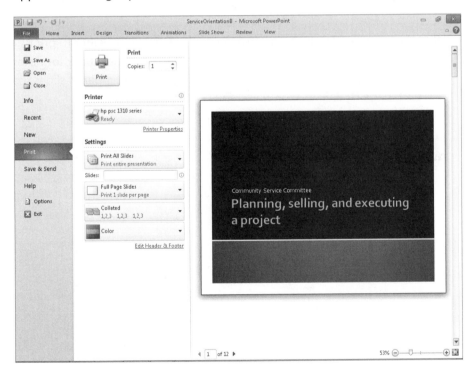

The Print page of the Backstage view.

You can click the Next Page or Previous Page button in the lower-left corner of the pane to move among the slides. To zoom in on part of a slide, click the Zoom In and Zoom Out buttons on the Zoom Slider in the lower-right corner. Click the Zoom To Page button to fit the slide to the pane.

If you will print a color presentation on a monochrome printer, you can preview in gray-scale or black and white to verify that the text is legible against the background.

Tip In Normal view, you can see how your slides will look when printed on a monochrome printer by clicking either the Grayscale or the Black And White button in the Color/Grayscale group on the View tab.

When you're ready to print, you don't have to leave the Backstage view. You can simply click the Print button to print one copy of each slide on the default printer. If the default settings aren't what you want, you can make the following changes on the Print page:

● **Number of copies** Click the arrows to adjust the Copies setting.

● **Which printer** If you have more than one printer available, specify the printer you want to use and set its properties (such as paper source and image compression).

● **Which slides to print** You can print all the slides, the selected slides, or the current slide. To print only specific slides, click the Slides box, and enter the slide numbers and ranges separated by commas (no spaces). For example, enter 1,5,10-12 to print slides 1, 5, 10, 11, and 12 .

● **What to print** From the Print Layout gallery, specify whether to print slides (one per page), notes pages (one half-size slide per page with space for notes), or an outline. You can also print handouts, specifying the number of slides that print on each page (1, 2, 3, 4, 6, or 9) and their order.

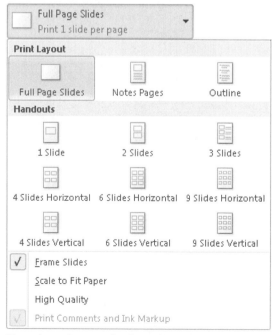

You select what to print from this gallery.

- **Whether to frame slides** Click this option below the Print Layout and Handouts galleries to put a frame around the slides on the printed page.

- **Whether to scale slides** If you haven't set the size of the slides to match the size of the paper in the printer, click this option to have PowerPoint automatically reduce or increase the size of the slides to fit the paper when you print them.

   See Also For information about setting the size of slides, see "Setting Up Presentations for Delivery" earlier in this chapter.

- **Print quality** Click this option if you want the highest quality printed output.

- **Print comments and ink markup** Click this option if electronic or handwritten notes are attached to the presentation and you want to review them along with the slides.

- **Collate multiple copies** If you're printing multiple copies of a presentation, specify whether complete copies should be printed one at a time.

- **Color range** Specify whether the presentation should be printed in color (color on a color printer and grayscale on a monochrome printer), grayscale (on either a color or a monochrome printer), or pure black and white (no gray on either a color or a monochrome printer).

- **Edit the header or footer** Click this option to display the Header And Footer dialog box.

   See Also For information about adding footers to slides, see "Setting Up Presentations for Delivery" earlier in this chapter.

In this exercise, you'll preview a presentation in grayscale, select a printer, and print a selection of slides.

SET UP You need the ServiceOrientationB_start presentation located in your Chapter17 practice file folder to complete this exercise. Open the ServiceOrientationB_start presentation, and save it as *ServiceOrientationB*. Then follow the steps.

1. Click the **File** tab to display the Backstage view, and then click **Print**.

   The right side of the Print page displays the first slide as it will print with the current settings.

2. Under **Settings**, click **Color**, and then click **Grayscale**.

   The preview shows the slide in black, white, and shades of gray.

3. Click the **Next Page** button to move through the slides, until slide **12** is displayed.

4. On the **Zoom Slider**, click the **Zoom In** button several times, and then use the horizontal scroll bar that appears to scroll all the way to the left.

It's easier to examine the date in the footer of the magnified slide.

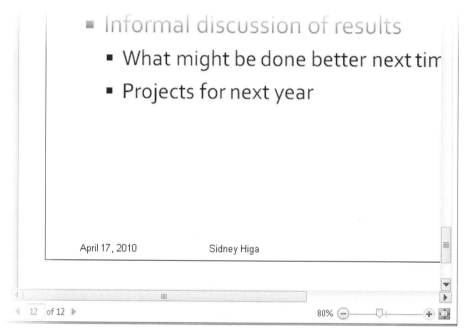

You can use the Zoom Slider to zoom in on parts of a slide.

5. Click the **Zoom to Page** button to return to the original zoom percentage.

6. In the middle pane, click the setting for your printer.

A list displays the names of all the printers installed on your computer.

7. In the list, click the printer you want to use.

Tip After choosing a printer, you can customize its settings for this particular print operation by clicking Printer Properties to display the Properties dialog box. For example, if the printer you have selected has duplex capabilities, you might want to specify that it should print slides on both sides of the page.

8. Under **Settings**, in the **Slides** box, type **1-3,5**, and then press Tab.

In the right pane, PowerPoint displays a preview of slide 1. Below the preview, the slide indicator changes to *1 of 4*, and you can now preview only the selected slides.

9. Click **Full Page Slides**, and below the gallery that appears, click **Frame Slides**.

10. At the top of the middle pane, click the **Print** button.

PowerPoint prints slides 1, 2, 3, and 5 with frames in shades of gray on the selected printer.

 CLEAN UP Save the ServiceOrientationB presentation, and then close it.

Preparing Speaker Notes and Handouts

If you will be delivering your presentation before a live audience, you might want some speaker notes to guide you. Each slide in a PowerPoint presentation has a corresponding notes page. As you create each slide, you can enter notes that relate to the slide's content by simply clicking the Notes pane and typing. If you want to include something other than text in your speaker notes, you must switch to Notes Page view by clicking the Notes Page button in the Presentation Views group on the View tab. When your notes are complete, you can print them so that they are readily available to guide the presentation.

Tip In Presenter view, you can see your notes on one monitor while you display the slides to your audience on another monitor. For information about Presenter view, see the sidebar "Setting Up Presenter View" later in this chapter.

As a courtesy for your audience, you might want to supply handouts showing the presentation's slides so that people can take notes. Printing handouts requires a few decisions, such as which of the nine available formats you want to use and whether you want to add headers and footers, but otherwise, you don't need to do anything special to create simple handouts.

Tip The layout of PowerPoint notes pages and handouts is controlled by a special kind of template called a *master*. Usually, you'll find that the default masters are more than adequate, but if you want to make changes, you can. For information about customizing masters, refer to *Microsoft PowerPoint 2010 Step by Step*, by Joyce Cox and Joan Lambert (Microsoft Press, 2010).

In this exercise, you'll enter speaker notes for some slides in the Notes pane. Then you'll switch to Notes Page view, and insert a graphic into one note and a diagram into another. Finally, you'll print both speaker notes and handouts.

 SET UP You need the Harmony_start presentation and the YinYang graphic located in your Chapter17 practice file folder to complete this exercise. Open the Harmony_start presentation, and save it as *Harmony*. Then follow the steps.

1. With slide **1** displayed, drag the splitter bar between the **Slide** pane and the **Notes** pane upward to enlarge the Notes pane.

2. Click anywhere in the **Notes** pane, type **Welcome and introductions**, and then press Enter.

3. Type **Logistics**, press Enter, and then type **Establish knowledge level**.

4. Display slide **2**, and in the **Notes** pane, type **Talk about the main concepts**.

5. Display slide **3**, and in the **Notes** pane, type **Complementary energies**, and then press Enter twice.

6. On the **View** tab, in the **Presentation Views** group, click the **Notes Page** button.

   Slide 3 is displayed in Notes Page view. The zoom percentage is set so that the entire notes page fits in the window.

7. On the **Insert** tab, in the **Images** group, click the **Picture** button.

8. In the **Insert Picture** dialog box, navigate to your **Chapter17** practice file folder, and then double-click the **YinYang** graphic.

9. Drag the image down below the note you typed in step 5.

   The picture is visible in Notes Page view.

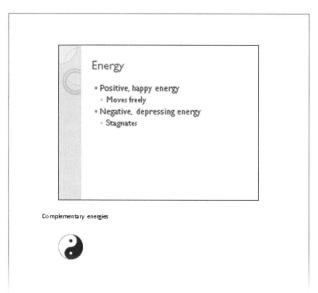

You might want to add images to your speaker notes to remind yourself of concepts you want to cover while the slide is displayed.

10. Below the scroll bar, click the **Next Slide** button to move to slide **4**. Then click the border around the text placeholder to select it, and press Delete.

11. On the **Insert** tab, in the **Illustrations** group, click the **SmartArt** button. In the left pane of the **Choose a SmartArt Graphic** dialog box, click **Hierarchy**, and then in the middle pane, double-click the second thumbnail in the last row (**Hierarchy List**).

    A diagram with six shapes and placeholder text is inserted into the page. Don't worry about its placement for now; you will fix that later.

    See Also For information about how to work with SmartArt diagrams, see "Inserting Diagrams" in Chapter 16, "Add Simple Visual Enhancements." For information about using SmartArt to customize diagrams, refer to *Microsoft PowerPoint 2010 Step by Step*, by Joyce Cox and Joan Lambert (Microsoft Press, 2010).

12. Open the **Text** pane, click the first placeholder in the hierarchy, and type the following, pressing the Down Arrow key or the Enter key as indicated:

    Focus (Down Arrow)

    > **Health** (Down Arrow)
    > **Creativity** (Enter)
    > **Relationships** (Enter)
    > **Community** (Down Arrow)

    Follow (Down Arrow)

    > **Knowledge** (Down Arrow)
    > **Career** (Enter)
    > **Fame** (Enter)
    > **Fortune**

    Tip If you have trouble seeing the notes at this zoom percentage, click the Zoom In button on the Zoom Slider in the lower-right corner of the window.

    The speaker notes now include a diagram expressing visually the concepts to be emphasized during the presentation.

13. Use the formatting options available in the **SmartArt Styles** group on the **Design** tab to format the diagram any way you want, and then move and size the diagram to fit in the space below the slide.

We used the Moderate Effect style and the Gradient Loop – Accent 1 colors.

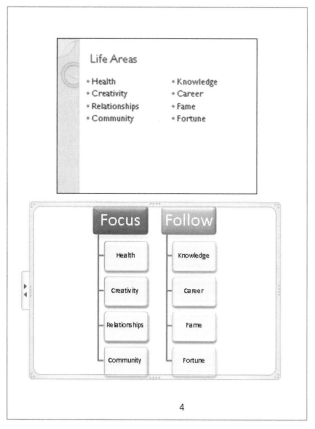

Diagrams can give you an at-a-glance reminder of important concepts.

14. On the **View** tab, in the **Presentation Views** group, click the **Normal** button.

The diagram is not visible in Normal view.

15. Display slide **3**.

The YinYang graphic is not visible in this view either.

16. Switch to Notes Page view, and then on the **Insert** tab, in the **Text** group, click the **Header & Footer** button.

The Header And Footer dialog box opens with the Notes And Handouts page displayed.

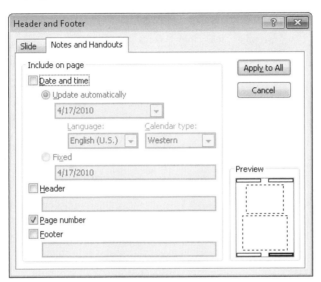

On the Notes And Handouts page, you can insert a header and a footer.

17. Select the **Date and Time** check box, and then click **Fixed**.

18. Select the **Header** check box, and then in the text box, type **Harmony in Your Home**.

19. Select the **Footer** check box, and then in the text box, type **Wide World Importers**.

20. Click **Apply to All**.

The notes page reflects your specifications.

21. Switch to Normal view, and then display the **Print** page of the Backstage view.

22. On the **Print** page, under **Settings**, click **Full Page Slides**, and then click **Notes Pages**.

23. Click the **Slides** box, type **1-4**, and then click the **Print** button.

    You now have a copy of the speaker notes to refer to during the presentation.

24. Display the **Print** page of the Backstage view again, and under **Settings**, click **Notes Pages**, and under **Handouts** in the gallery, click **3 slides**.

    The first page of the handouts is previewed in the right pane.

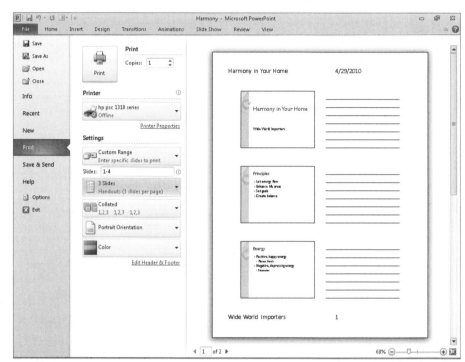

When you print three slides per page, PowerPoint adds lines for notes to the right of each slide image.

25. Change the **Slides** setting to **1-3**, and then click the **Print** button.

 CLEAN UP Save the Harmony presentation, and then close it.

Enhanced Handouts

If you want to provide audience handouts that include notes as well as pictures of the slides, you can send the presentation to a Microsoft Word document and then develop the handout content in Word.

To create handouts in Word:

1. Display the Save & Send page of the Backstage view, and under File Types in the middle pane, click Create Handouts.

2. In the right pane, click the Create Handouts button.

   The Send To Microsoft Word dialog box opens.

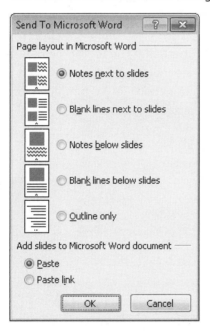

In two of the five available formats, you can enter notes along with the pictures of the slides.

3. Click the notes format you want.

4. If the slide content might change, under Add Slides To Microsoft Word Document, click Paste Link.

5. Click OK.

   Word starts and opens a document set up to contain the handout format you selected. If you selected Outline Only, the text of the presentation appears in the document as a bulleted list.

Finalizing Presentations

These days, many presentations are delivered electronically, either by e-mail or from a Web site. As you develop a presentation, it can accumulate information that you might not want in the final version, such as the names of people who worked on the presentation, comments that reviewers have added to the file, or hidden text about status and assumptions. If your presentation will never leave your computer, you don't have to worry that it might contain something that you would rather other people did not see. However, if the presentation file is going to be shared with other people, you will want to remove this identifying and tracking information before you distribute the presentation.

To examine some of the information attached to a presentation, you can display the properties on the Info page of the Backstage view. You can change or remove some of the properties in the Properties pane, or you can display the Document Panel or the Properties dialog box by clicking Properties at the top of the pane and clicking the option you want. However, to automate the process of finding and removing all extraneous and potentially confidential information, PowerPoint provides a tool called the *Document Inspector.*

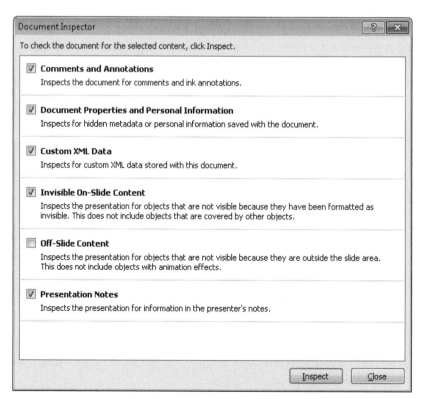

The Document Inspector removes many different types of information.

Tip When rearranging the objects on a slide, you might drag an object to one side while you decide whether to include it. The Off-Slide Content option in the Document Inspector dialog box detects any stray content that you might have overlooked. The Document Inspector also looks for invisible content on the slide. This is content you might have hidden by displaying the Selection And Visibility task pane and then clearing the object's check box. (To display the Selection And Visibility pane, click the Select button in the Editing group on the Home tab, and then click Selection Pane.)

After you run the Document Inspector, you see a summary of its search results, and you have the option of removing all the items found in each category.

PowerPoint also includes two other finalizing tools:

- **Check Accessibility** This tool checks for presentation elements and formatting that might be difficult for people with certain kinds of disabilities to read. It reports its findings in the Accessibility Checker task pane, and offers suggestions for fixing any potential issues.

- **Check Compatibility** This tool checks for the use of features not supported in earlier versions of PowerPoint. It presents a list of features that might be lost or degraded if you save the presentation in an earlier PowerPoint file format.

After you have handled extraneous information and accessibility and compatibility issues, you can mark a presentation as final and make it a read-only file, so that other people know that they should not make changes to this released presentation. This process does not lock the presentation, however; if you want to make additional changes to the presentation, you can easily turn off the final status.

In this exercise, you'll examine the properties attached to a presentation, remove personal information from the file, and then mark the presentation as final.

 SET UP You need the Meeting_start presentation located in your Chapter17 practice file folder to complete this exercise. Open the Meeting_start presentation, and save it as *Meeting*. Then follow the steps.

1. Display the **Info** page of the Backstage view.

   The Properties pane on the right side of the window displays the standard properties associated with this presentation.

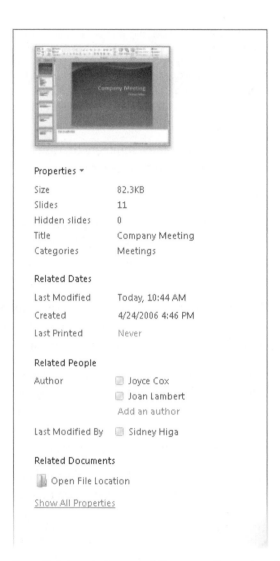

PowerPoint controls some of the properties, such as the size and dates; you can add and change others, such as the assigned categories and authors.

2. At the bottom on the **Properties** pane, click **Show All Properties**.

The pane expands to show all the properties.

3. Click the property adjacent to **Status**, and type **Done**.

4. At the top of the pane, click **Properties**, and click **Advanced Properties**. Then in the **Meeting Properties** dialog box, click the **Summary** tab.

   This page includes some of the properties you might want to change in a convenient format.

The Summary page of the Properties dialog box.

5. Click in the **Subject** box, type **Morale event**, and then click **OK**.

   The Subject property in the Properties pane reflects your change.

6. Save your changes to the presentation.

7. Display the **Info** page of the Backstage view again. Then in the center pane, click **Check for Issues**, and click **Inspect Document**.

   In the Document Inspector dialog box, you can inspect for six types of content.

8. Clear the **Custom XML Data** check box. Then with the **Comments and Annotations**, **Document Properties and Personal Information**, **Invisible On-Slide Content**, and **Presentation Notes** check boxes selected, click **Inspect**.

   The Document Inspector reports its findings.

This presentation includes properties that you might not want others to be able to view.

9. To the right of **Document Properties and Personal Information**, click **Remove All**.

   PowerPoint removes the presentation's properties.

10. Close the **Document Inspector** dialog box.

    In the Properties pane, all the properties have been cleared.

11. In the center pane of the **Info** page, click **Protect Presentation**, and then click **Mark as Final**.

    A message tells you that the presentation will be marked as final and then saved.

12. Click **OK** in the message box, and then click **OK** in the confirmation box that appears after the document is marked as final.

    The presentation's final status is now indicated on the Info page.

Marking as final discourages but does not prevent editing.

13. Click any tab on the ribbon to return to the presentation.

    The title bar indicates that this is a read-only file, and the ribbon tabs are hidden.

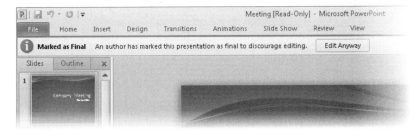

The information bar explains that this presentation has been marked as final.

14. Click the **Home** tab to display its commands, most of which are inactive.

15. On the title slide, double-click the word **Company**, and press the Delete key.

    Nothing happens. You cannot change any of the objects on the slides unless you click the Edit Anyway button in the information bar to remove the final status.

 **CLEAN UP** Close the Meeting presentation.

Setting Up Presenter View

If your computer can support two monitors, or if you will be presenting a slide show from your computer through a projector, you might want to check out Presenter view. In this view, you can control the presentation on one monitor while the audience sees the slides in Slide Show view on the delivery monitor or the projector screen.

To deliver a presentation on one monitor and use Presenter view on another:

1. Open the PowerPoint presentation you want to set up.

2. On the Slide Show tab, in the Set Up group, click Set Up Slide Show.

   The Set Up Show dialog box opens. When your computer is set up to use multiple monitors, the settings in the Multiple Monitors area are active.

3. In the Multiple Monitors area, click the Display Slide Show On arrow, and then in the list, click the name of the monitor you want to use to show the slides to your audience.

   The slides will display full-screen on the specified monitor.

4. Select the Show Presenter View check box, and then click OK.

5. With the title slide of the presentation active, switch to Slide Show view.

   The title slide is displayed full screen on the delivery monitor, and Presenter view is displayed on the control monitor. As the presenter, you can see details about what slide or bullet point is coming next, see your speaker notes, jump directly to any slide, black out the screen during a pause in the presentation, and keep track of the time.

6. On the control monitor, use the Presenter view tools to control the presentation.

Delivering Presentations

To deliver a presentation to an audience, you first click the Slide Show button to display the slides full screen. Then depending on how you have set up the presentation, you can either click the mouse button without moving the mouse to display the slides in sequence, or you can allow PowerPoint to display the slides according to the advancement timings you have set on the Transitions tab.

See Also For information about advancement timings, see "Adding Transitions" in Chapter 16, "Add Simple Visual Enhancements."

If you need to move to a slide other than the next one or the previous one, you can move the mouse pointer to display an inconspicuous navigation toolbar in the lower-left corner of the slide. You can use this toolbar in the following ways:

- To move to the next slide, click the Next button.
- To move to the previous slide, click the Previous button.
- To jump to a slide out of sequence, click the Navigation button, click Go To Slide, and then click the slide.

  Tip You can also display the Navigation button's menu by right-clicking the slide.

- To end the presentation, click the Navigation button, and then click End Show.

  Keyboard Shortcuts To display a list of keyboard shortcuts for carrying out presentation tasks, click the Navigation button, and then click Help. For example, you can press the Spacebar, the Down Arrow key, or the Right Arrow key to move to the next slide; press the Page Up key or the Left Arrow key to move to the previous slide; and press the Esc key to end the presentation.

During a presentation, you can reinforce your message by drawing on the slides with an electronic "pen" or changing the background behind text with a highlighter. You simply click the Pen button on the toolbar that appears when you move the mouse, click the tool you want, and then begin drawing or highlighting. The pen color is determined by the setting in the Set Up Show dialog box, but you can change the pen color during the presentation by clicking the Pen button, clicking Ink Color, and then selecting the color you want.

In this exercise, you'll move around in a presentation in various ways while delivering it. You'll also use a pen tool to mark up one slide, change the color of the markup, and then mark up another.

SET UP You need the SavingWater_start presentation located in your Chapter17 practice file folder to complete this exercise. Open the SavingWater_start presentation, and save it as *SavingWater*. Then follow the steps.

1. With slide **1** selected in Normal view, on the **View Shortcuts** toolbar, click the **Slide Show** button.

PowerPoint displays the title slide after implementing its applied transition effect.

2. Click the mouse button to advance to slide **2**.

The slide contents ripple onto the screen.

3. Press the Left Arrow key to move back to the previous slide, and then press the Right Arrow key to display the next slide.

4. Move the mouse.

The pointer appears on the screen, and barely visible in the lower-left corner, the shadow toolbar appears.

Troubleshooting If the pop-up navigation toolbar doesn't seem to appear, move the pointer to the lower-left corner of the screen and move it slowly to the right. The four toolbar buttons should become visible in turn. If they don't, press the Esc key to end the slide show. Then display the Backstage view, and click Options. In the PowerPoint Options dialog box, click Advanced, and in the Slide Show area, select the Show Popup Toolbar check box, and click OK.

5. Move the pointer to the bottom of the screen and to the left until the **Next** button appears. Then click the **Next** button to display slide **3**.

6. Right-click anywhere on the screen, and then click **Previous** to redisplay slide **2**.

7. Right-click anywhere on the screen, point to **Go to Slide**, and then in the list of slide names, click **11 Soil Amendment**.

8. Display the toolbar, click the **Navigation** button, and then click **Next** to display slide **12**.

9. Use various navigation methods to display various slides in the presentation until you are comfortable moving around.

10. Right-click anywhere on the screen, and then click **End Show**.

The active slide appears in Normal view.

Tip If you click all the way through to the end of the presentation, PowerPoint displays a black screen to indicate that the next click will return you to the previous view. If you do not want the black screen to appear at the end of a presentation, display the PowerPoint Options dialog box, and click Advanced. Then in the Slide Show area, clear the End With Black Slide check box, and click OK. Then clicking while the last slide is displayed will return you to the previous view.

11. Display slide **11**, and switch to Slide Show view.

12. Right-click anywhere on the screen, point to **Pointer Options**, and then click **Highlighter**.

   Tip When the pen or highlighter tool is active in Slide Show view, clicking the mouse button does not advance the slide show to the next slide. You need to switch back to the regular pointer to use the mouse to advance the slide.

13. On the slide, highlight the words **10 tons**.

14. Right-click anywhere on the screen, point to **Pointer Options**, and then click **Pen**.

15. On the slide, draw a line below the words **per acre per year**.

   PowerPoint draws the line in the color specified in the Set Up Show dialog box as the default for this presentation.

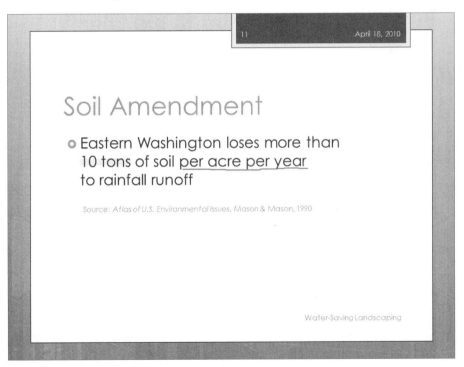

You can emphasize a point with the highlighter or pen.

16. Right-click the screen, point to **Pointer Options**, and then click **Erase All Ink on Slide**.

   The highlight and line are erased.

17. Press the Spacebar to move to the next slide.

18. Display the toolbar, click the **Pen** button, point to **Ink Color**, and then under **Standard Colors** in the palette, click the **Dark Red** box.

19. Draw a line below the words **Prevent erosion**.

20. Right-click anywhere on the screen, point to **Pointer Options**, and then click **Arrow**.

   The pen tool changes back to the regular pointer, and you can now click the mouse button to advance to the next slide.

21. Press Esc to stop the presentation.

   A message asks whether you want to keep your ink annotations.

22. Click **Discard**.

   The active slide is displayed in Normal view.

✖ CLEAN UP Save the SavingWater presentation, and then close it.

Key Points

- It's most efficient to set up your presentation in its intended output format before you begin adding content.

- To proof a presentation on paper, you can print it in color, grayscale, or black and white, depending on the capabilities of your printer.

- You can easily create speaker notes to facilitate a presentation delivery, or print handouts so that your audience can easily follow your presentation.

- Finalizing a presentation ensures that it doesn't contain personal or confidential information and that people are alerted before making further changes.

- Knowing how to use all the navigation toolbar buttons, commands, and keyboard shortcuts to navigate in Slide Show view is important for smooth presentation delivery.

- To emphasize a point, you can mark up slides during a presentation by using a pen in various colors or a highlighter.

Part 5

Microsoft
OneNote 2010

Chapter at a Glance

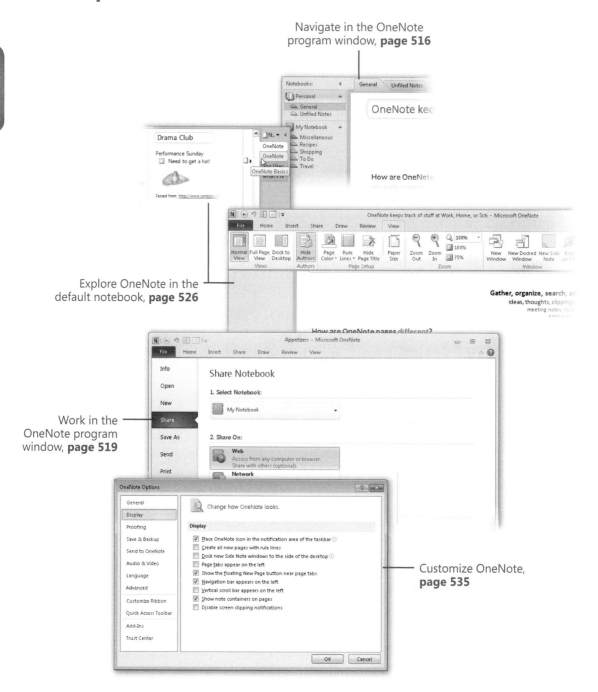

Navigate in the OneNote program window, **page 516**

Explore OneNote in the default notebook, **page 526**

Work in the OneNote program window, **page 519**

Customize OneNote, **page 535**

18 Explore OneNote 2010

In this chapter, you will learn how to

✔ Navigate in the OneNote program window.

✔ Work in the OneNote program window.

✔ Explore OneNote in the default notebook.

✔ Customize OneNote.

Microsoft OneNote 2010 is a handy program that makes it possible to electronically collect and store pieces of information. You can use OneNote to:

● Collect, save, and safeguard information in one place.

● Take notes in a class or meeting.

● Organize information in a way that is logical to you.

● Search for information when you need it.

After you spend a short time using OneNote, you will undoubtedly find many uses for it. OneNote 2010 is available in all editions of Microsoft Office 2010, and is equally useful for business and personal purposes.

As with all organizational systems, OneNote is most effective if you use it on a regular basis. By developing consistent data collection and storage practices, you will be able to most efficiently locate stored information whenever you need it. Eventually, you might even wonder how you ever survived without it.

In this chapter, you'll explore the OneNote working environment and storage structure, learn how to move around and work in OneNote, and look at the options for customizing OneNote to better fit the way you work.

> **Practice Files** You don't need any practice files to complete the exercises in this chapter. For more information about practice file requirements, see "Using the Practice Files" at the beginning of this book.

Navigating in the OneNote Program Window

In the same way that the Windows operating system information storage structure reflects that of a physical office, (with a desktop, folders, and files), the OneNote storage structure reflects that of a tabbed notebook. You might have a notebook for each project you work on, or one notebook in which you track business information and another in which you track personal information. Each notebook is divided into sections, and each section is divided into pages. If you want to extend the analogy, you can even format the background of a notebook page to resemble various types of ruled paper.

See Also For information about changing the background of a notebook page, see "Creating Sections and Pages," in Chapter 19, "Create and Configure Notebooks."

In Windows Explorer, each notebook is represented by a folder in your Documents\OneNote Notebooks folder. Each section of a notebook is stored as an .one file within the notebook folder. (Although you would usually move sections within OneNote itself, it is possible to move or copy a section to a different notebook in Windows Explorer by moving or copying the section file to a different notebook's folder.

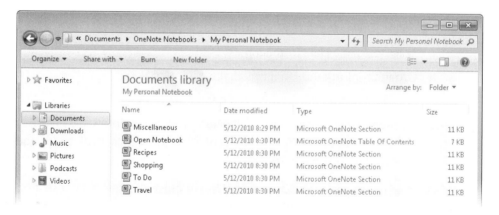

A typical OneNote notebook storage structure.

When you start OneNote 2010 for the first time, the program opens a sample notebook named Personal. Thereafter when you start OneNote, the notebook you worked with in the previous OneNote session opens.

Information about the content of open OneNote notebooks is shown in four areas of the OneNote program window.

Navigation Bar   Notebook header   Content pane   Page Tabs Bar

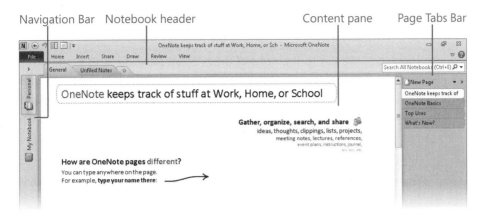

The default appearance of the OneNote program window.

● The Navigation Bar on the left side of the program window displays information about the notebooks that are stored in the default notebook location. When collapsed, as it is by default, the Navigation Bar displays a button for each notebook. When expanded, the Navigation Bar displays the hierarchical structure of each notebook. You expand and collapse the Navigation Bar by clicking the button in its upper-right corner.

Collapse Navigation Bar

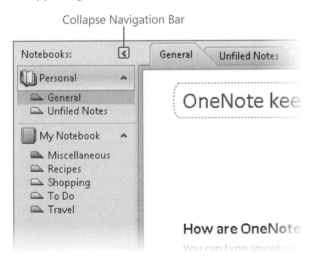

The expanded Navigation Bar.

● The content pane in the center of the program window displays the active notebook page. On pages that you create, the page title appears at the top of the page, along with the date and time the page was most recently modified.

- The notebook header above the content pane displays section tabs that you can click to move between sections of the active notebook.

- The Page Tabs Bar to the right of the content pane displays page tabs you can click to move between pages of the active section. By default, the Page Tabs Bar displays a tab for each page in the current section. You can filter the display of tabs to make it easier to locate specific content.

   You can collapse and expand the Page Tabs Bar by clicking the button in its upper-right corner.

   Keyboard Shortcuts Press Alt+Page Up to display the first page in the currently visible set of page tabs; press Alt+Page Down to display the last page in the currently visible set. Press Ctrl+Shift+[to increase the width of the Page Tabs Bar; press Ctrl+Shift+] to decrease the width of the Page Tabs Bar.

Working with Multiple Notebooks

You can have multiple notebooks open at one time, either in the same OneNote window or in separate OneNote windows.

Keyboard Shortcut Press Ctrl+M to open a second instance of the current OneNote window.

To open a notebook in the current OneNote window:

1. On the Open page of the Backstage view, click the Open Notebook button.

2. Browse to your Documents\OneNote Notebooks folder.

3. Click the folder representing the notebook you want to open, and click Open. In the notebook folder, click the Open Notebook file, and then click Open.

   Tip The Open Notebook file is a Table Of Contents file that contains pointers to the content within the notebook.

When you work with multiple notebooks in the same OneNote window, you can easily switch between them by clicking a notebook's button on the Navigation Bar.

Keyboard Shortcut Press Ctrl+G, the Down Arrow or Up Arrow key, and then Enter to switch to a different notebook on the Navigation Bar.

If you don't need to access an open notebook any more, you can close it. Closed notebooks do not appear on the Navigation Bar.

To close a notebook:

- On the Navigation Bar, right-click the notebook button, and then click Close This Notebook.

Working in the OneNote Program Window

As you do in other Office programs, you work with OneNote notebook content by using the commands on the ribbon and Quick Access Toolbar, and with the OneNote program, and OneNote notebook files in the Backstage view.

Working from the Ribbon and Quick Access Toolbar

Unlike in other Office 2010 programs, the ribbon in OneNote is collapsed by default to provide more space for the notebook page.

The OneNote ribbon includes the File tab and six other tabs:

- **Home** This tab includes buttons that represent commands for formatting note-book content, inserting and locating content tags, and coordinating notebook content with Microsoft Outlook 2010.

  See Also For information about content tags, see the sidebar "Tagging Content" in Chapter 20, "Create and Organize Notes."

The Home tab of the OneNote ribbon.

  Troubleshooting The appearance of buttons and groups on the ribbon changes depending on the width of the program window. For information about changing the appearance of the ribbon to match our screen images, see "Modifying the Display of the Ribbon" at the beginning of this book.

  See Also For information about interactions between OneNote and Outlook, see "Creating Sections and Pages" in Chapter 19, "Create and Configure Notebooks."

- **Insert** This tab includes commands for inserting, linking to, and attaching images, files, audio and video recordings, time stamps, and special symbols.

The Insert tab of the OneNote ribbon.

  See Also For information about inserting various types of content, see Chapter 20, "Create and Organize Notes."

● **Share** This tab includes commands for sharing a notebook with other OneNote users and for managing a multiuser notebook.

The Share tab of the OneNote ribbon.

See Also For information about multiuser notebooks, see "Creating a Notebook for Use by Multiple People" in Chapter 19, "Create and Configure Notebooks."

● **Draw** This tab includes commands for inserting and manipulating handwritten content.

The Draw tab of the OneNote ribbon.

See Also For information about writing in a notebook, see "Entering Content Directly onto a Page" in Chapter 20, "Create and Organize Notes."

● **Review** This tab includes commands for working with the of text stored on note-book pages, including checking spelling and grammar; researching word choices; and translating content either by using the Office translation tools or through an online service.

The Review tab of the OneNote ribbon.

See Also For information about reviewing content, see "Correcting Spelling and Grammatical Errors" in Chapter 3, "Edit and Proofread Text."

- **View** This tab includes commands for changing the appearance of the OneNote window and of notebook pages, for magnifying your view of notebook content, and for working with multiple program windows.

The View tab of the OneNote ribbon.

In OneNote, the default Quick Access Toolbar displays the Back, Undo, Dock To Desktop, and Full Page View buttons. As with other Office 2010 programs, you can change the location of the Quick Access Toolbar and customize it to include any commands to which you want to have one-click access.

Customize Quick Access Toolbar menu

The default OneNote Quick Access Toolbar.

From the Customize Quick Access Toolbar menu, you can add the Forward, Redo, Print, Print Preview, Favorite Pens, and Favorite Highlighter buttons. You can add other buttons from the Quick Access Toolbar page of the OneNote Options window or by right-clicking a command on the ribbon and then clicking Add To Quick Access Toolbar.

See Also For information about creating handwritten content with pens and highlighters, see "Entering Content Directly onto a Page" in Chapter 20, "Create and Organize Notes."

Tip If you prefer to work with the ribbon collapsed to maximize the available notebook page space, add all the commands you use frequently to the Quick Access Toolbar and display it below the ribbon, directly above the workspace. For information, see "Customizing the Quick Access Toolbar" in Chapter 1, "Explore Office 2010."

Working in the Backstage View

As with other Office 2010 programs, clicking the File tab at the left end of the OneNote ribbon displays the Backstage view. Commands related to managing OneNote and OneNote files (rather than notebook content) are organized on the following pages of the Backstage view:

- **Info** From this page, you can share, close, or view the properties of a notebook, view the synchronization status of your local copy of a shared notebook (the copy that is on your computer) with the original notebook (the copy that is in the central storage location), and open backup copies of notebooks.

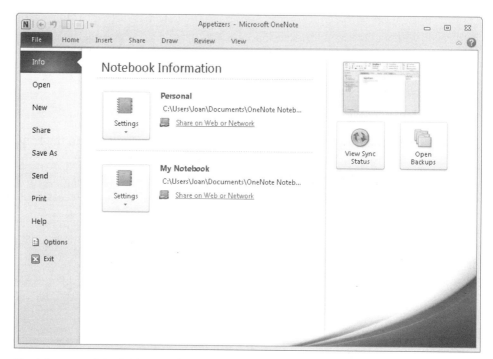

The Info page of the Backstage view.

- **Open** From this page, you can open an existing notebook either by browsing to and selecting the notebook's Table Of Contents file or by selecting a recently closed notebook from a list on the page.

- **New** From this page, you can create a new notebook on your local computer, on a computer that you access on your local network, on a SharePoint site, or on a Web site.

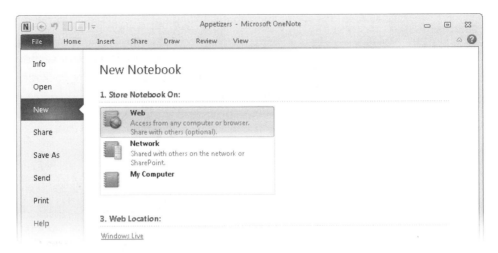

The New page of the Backstage view.

See Also For information about new notebooks, see "Creating a Notebook for Use by One Person" and "Creating a Notebook for Use by Multiple People" in Chapter 19, "Create and Configure Notebooks."

● **Share** From this page, you can share a notebook with other OneNote users by storing it on a computer that you access on your local network, on a SharePoint site, or on a Web site.

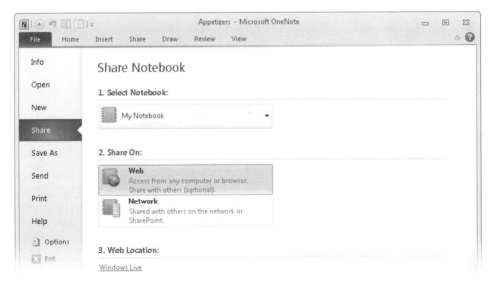

The Share page of the OneNote Backstage view.

See Also For information about sharing notebooks, see "Creating a Notebook for Use by Multiple People" in Chapter 19, "Create and Configure Notebooks."

- **Save As** From this page, you can save the current page or section in one of several file formats, or save the current notebook as a OneNote Package (a distributable OneNote file), a PDF file, or an XPS file.

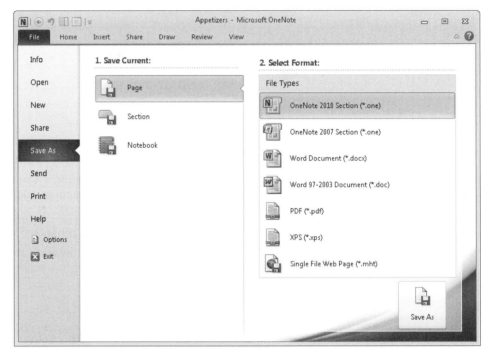

The Save As page of the Backstage view.

- **Send** From this page, you can send the current page content to Outlook or to Microsoft Word. If you want to send information from the current page to someone, you can embed the page content in the body of an e-mail message or attach the page to a message as a OneNote (.one) file, a Web (.mht) file, or a Portable Document Format (.pdf) file. You can copy the page content into a Word document, or if you use Word as your blog editor, you can copy the page content to a blog post form.

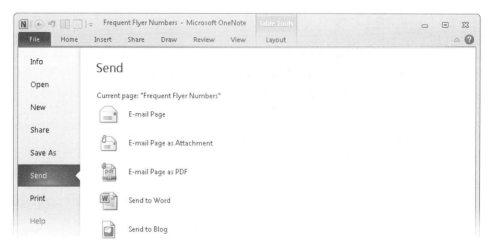

The Send page of the Backstage view.

● **Print** From this page, you can preview and print a notebook page, a group of pages, or an entire section of a notebook.

You can click Print and choose settings in the Print dialog box, or click Print Preview and choose settings in the Print Preview And Settings dialog box.

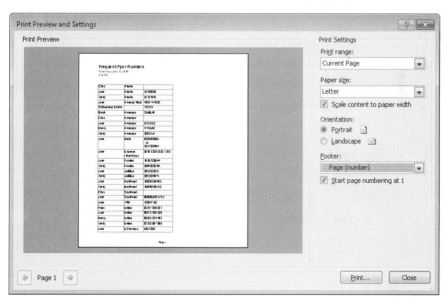

The Print Preview And Settings dialog box.

● **Help** From this page, you can access information about your Office installation, manage product activation and product keys, and access support resources, program options, and program updates.

Exploring OneNote in the Default Notebook

The default installation of OneNote 2010 includes one notebook, named *Personal*, which has one section, named *General*. This section has four pages of information about OneNote and examples of the types of information you can collect in OneNote and ways that you can work with it.

In this exercise, you'll take a quick tour of the Personal notebook while moving among sections and pages, and displaying different views of a page.

 SET UP You don't need any practice files to complete this exercise; just follow the steps.

1. On the **Start** menu, point to **All Programs**, click **Microsoft Office**, and then click **Microsoft OneNote 2010**.

   OneNote starts. If this is the first time you've used OneNote, the first page of the General section of the Personal notebook is displayed.

2. If the **Personal** notebook isn't open, do one of the following to open it:

   ○ If the **Personal** notebook is shown on the **Navigation Bar**, click its button.

   ○ If the **Personal** notebook is not shown on the **Navigation Bar**, display the **Open** page of the Backstage view, and click the **Open Notebook** button. In the **Open Notebook** dialog box, browse to your **Documents\OneNote Notebooks** folder, double-click the **Personal** folder, and then double-click **Open Notebook**.

   Troubleshooting If your school or organization has a specialized OneNote environment, the Personal notebook might not be available. You can follow along with this exercise by substituting any available notebook.

   With the default settings, the ribbon is collapsed at the top of the program window, the Navigation Bar is collapsed on the left side of the program window, and the Page Tabs Bar is open on the right side of the program window.

   Troubleshooting If the program window doesn't appear as described, don't worry; we'll show you how to adjust the settings in this exercise.

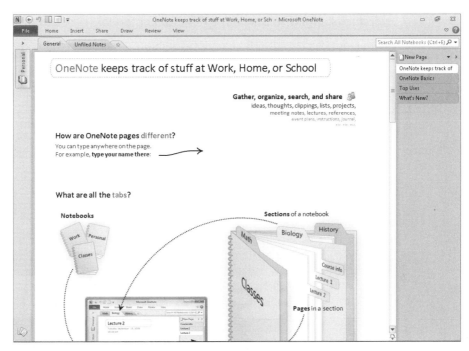

You can change the area available to the notebook page by opening and closing program window elements.

The current notebook is indicated by the active (boxed) notebook button on the Navigation Bar. The current section is indicated by the active (top) tab in the notebook header. The current page is indicated in the window title bar, in the dotted box at the top of the page, and on the active page tab.

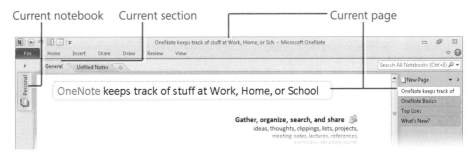

You can easily identify your location within the notebook organizational structure.

3. At the top of the **Navigation Bar**, click the **Expand Navigation Bar** button.

The expanded Navigation Bar displays the notebook and the two sections within it, which correspond to the tabs in the notebook header.

4. On the **Navigation Bar**, in the **Personal** notebook, click **Unfiled Notes**.

OneNote displays the Unfiled Notes section. This is a holding area for content that you send to OneNote from other programs. You can also create content directly in this section if you haven't decided on an organizational structure for the content.

Until you add content to the Unfiled Notes section, it is empty.

See Also For information about sending content to OneNote from other Office 2010 programs, see "Creating Sections and Pages" in Chapter 19, "Create and Configure Notebooks," and "Sending Content to OneNote" in Chapter 20, "Create and Organize Notes."

The Unfiled Notes section is part of the OneNote program rather than part of a specific notebook; you have only one Unfiled Notes section, and it is shared by all your notebooks.

Tip You can open the Unfiled Notes section when working in any notebook by clicking the Unfiled Notes button located at the bottom of the Navigation Bar.

 5. On the **Navigation Bar**, on the right side of the **Personal** notebook button, click the **Collapse** button.

The sections of the Personal notebook disappear from the Navigation Bar.

6. In the notebook header, point to the **General** tab.

A ScreenTip displays the complete path to the storage location of the section file (the .one file). Notice that the file name matches the section name.

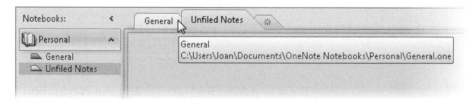

Point to a section tab to display its storage location.

7. Click the **General** tab to redisplay the **General** section of the **Personal** notebook. Then scroll down the page to view its content.

> **Tip** An image of a video thumbnail is embedded near the bottom of the page. Clicking the Click Here link to the right of the thumbnail displays a Web page from which you can play the video "How to organize stuff in OneNote 2010." This is a short video, without narrative, that provides a very basic overview of notebooks, sections, and pages.

8. At the top of the **Page Tabs Bar**, click the **Collapse Page Tabs** button.

The Page Tabs Bar shrinks to about half its former width. When truncated, the same name is displayed for the first and second pages.

9. In the **Page Tabs Bar**, point to the second page tab.

A ScreenTip displays the entire page title, *OneNote Basics*.

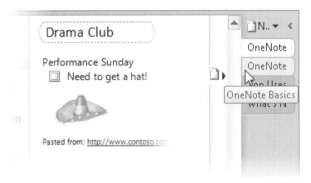

When the Page Tabs Bar is collapsed, pointing to any page tab displays the full page name.

> **See Also** For information about the New Page icon that appears to the left of the page tabs when you point to them, see "Creating Sections and Pages" in Chapter 19, "Create and Configure Notebooks."

10. Click the **OneNote Basics** page tab. Then scroll down the page to view its content.

At the top of the page are images of several types of content you can create in a notebook by using the tools that are built into OneNote.

You can create tables, charts, lists, equations, and more by using the tools in OneNote.

See Also For information about inserting and creating content on notebook pages, see Chapter 20, "Create and Organize Notes."

11. View the content of the **Top Uses** and **What's New** pages. Then display the **Info** page of the Backstage view, and click the **Settings** button for the **Personal** notebook.

A menu of actions you can take with the notebook expands.

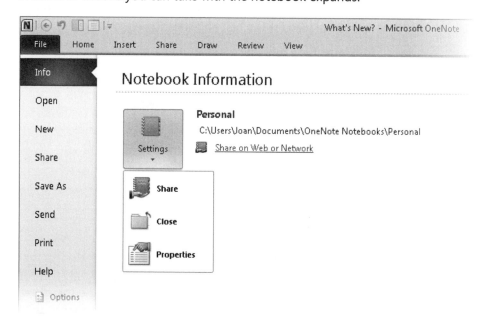

From the Info page, you can work with the currently active notebook.

12. On the **Settings** menu, click **Close**.

The Personal notebook closes. Only the Unfiled Notes section remains open in the OneNote program window.

13. Display the **Open** page of the Backstage view.

The Open page includes a list of notebooks you've recently closed.

Tip Clicking the pushpin button to the right of a notebook in the Recently Closed Notebooks list "pins" that notebook to the list so that it stays on the list regardless of how many other notebooks you close.

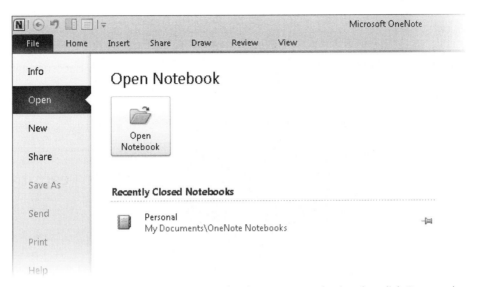

From the Open page, you can open a notebook you've recently closed or click Open and browse to a notebook.

14. In the **Recently Closed Notebooks** list, click **Personal**.

The Personal notebook reopens.

15. At the top of the program window, click the collapsed **View** tab of the ribbon.

The ribbon temporarily expands.

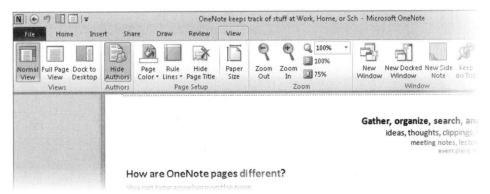

Options in the Views group change your view of the OneNote program window, not just of the selected notebook.

16. In the **Views** group, click the **Dock to Desktop** button.

Keyboard Shortcut Press Ctrl+Alt+D to dock the OneNote window.

The ribbon collapses. The OneNote program window becomes a vertical pane on the right side of the screen.

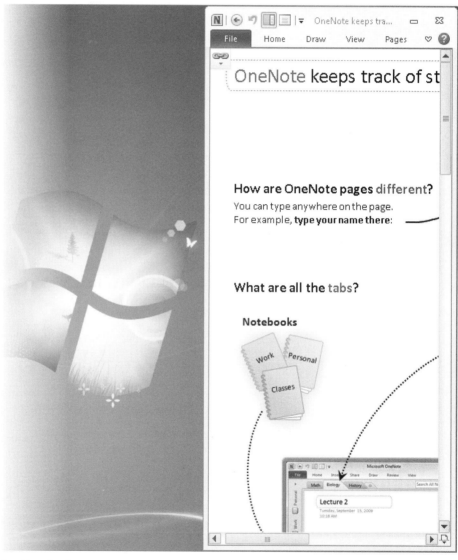

Docking the OneNote program window allows you to see more of your desktop.

17. Experiment with the docked OneNote window.

    You can't move the docked window by dragging its title bar. You can change the width of the window by dragging its left edge. When the window width is at its narrowest, the Quick Access Toolbar and ribbon tabs are not visible.

    Tip Other open windows on the screen might resize when you change the width of the docked OneNote window. Maximizing another window while OneNote is docked resizes that window to fill the entire screen other than the vertical space taken by the docked OneNote window. The docked window space is not available to other windows.

18. In the docked OneNote window, click the collapsed **View** tab.

    Only a subset of the commands previously available from this tab is available in the docked window.

19. In the **Views** group, click the **Normal View** button.

    The program window returns to its normal size.

    Tip You can also undock the window by clicking the active Dock To Desktop button on the Quick Access Toolbar.

20. On the Quick Access Toolbar, click the **Full Page View** button.

    Keyboard Shortcut Press F11 to enable or disable Full Page view.

    The Navigation Bar and Page Tabs Bar close entirely, and the content pane fills the width of the program window. The Pages tab appears on the ribbon.

21. Double-click the **Pages** tab to permanently expand it.

    The tab contains commands for moving among pages, locating content, and creating, deleting, or moving notebook pages.

22. In the **Navigate** group, click the **Next Page** button two times.

> **Keyboard Shortcut**   Press Ctrl+Page Down to display the next page in the current section. Press Ctrl+Page Up to display the previous page in the section. Press Alt+Home to display the first page in the section. Press Alt+End to display the last page in the section.

OneNote displays the Top Uses page in Full Page view.

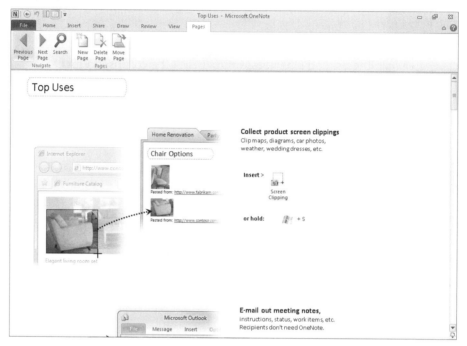

In Full Page view, the Navigation Bar and Page Tabs Bar are hidden.

23. On the Quick Access Toolbar, click the active **Full Page View** button.

OneNote returns to Normal view, and the Pages tab disappears from the ribbon.

 **CLEAN UP** Close the Personal notebook, but leave OneNote open.

Customizing OneNote

In this book, we discuss the default behavior of OneNote—the way the program works if you don't change any of its settings. As with all Office programs, there are a number of adjustments—major and minor—that you can make to modify the program to suit your needs. The majority of these are available from the OneNote Options dialog box, which you open by clicking Options in the Backstage view.

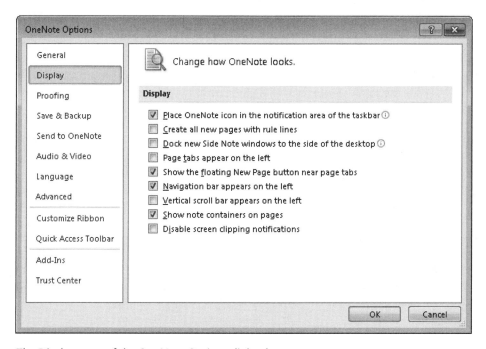

The Display page of the OneNote Options dialog box.

Like the Options dialog box in other Office 2010 programs, the OneNote Options dialog box presents a wide variety of settings divided into category-specific pages. Many of the settings you can control in OneNote are the same as those available in other Office programs. The OneNote Options dialog box includes the following pages:

- **General** On this page, you can set options that are common to the Office 2010 programs, including user interface options, the default font, and the user name and initials that identify changes you make to notebook content.

- **Display** On this page, you can change the location and appearance of OneNote features and tools.

- **Proofing** On this page, you can set the AutoCorrect options and spelling options for use in OneNote, as well as the spelling options that are common to the Office 2010 programs.

- **Save & Backup** On this page, you can specify the default locations in which OneNote saves files, configure automatic backup options or start a backup procedure, and configure file optimization options.

- **Send to OneNote** On this page, you can specify where OneNote stores content that you send from Outlook, send from a Web page, and print from a program to OneNote.

- **Audio & Video** On this page, you can specify audio and video recording settings and enable OneNote to search for spoken words within audio and video recordings.

- **Language** On this page, you can specify the languages used by the dictionary and spelling checker, the language priority order for buttons, tabs, and Help content, and the ScreenTip display language.

- **Advanced** On this page, you can set a variety of options including those for linking notes that you take from a docked OneNote window to other programs, optimizing OneNote operations when the computer is running on battery power, and working with tags and passwords.

Investigate this dialog box at your own convenience.

Key Points

- OneNote simplifies the process of collecting and storing electronic information.

- OneNote 2010 supports multiple notebooks, computers, and users, and has many useful new features.

- OneNote 2010 stores information in the Documents\OneNote Notebooks folder. Each "notebook" consists of a folder containing a .one file corresponding to each section within the notebook.

- The default OneNote 2010 installation includes a notebook containing examples and ideas for using OneNote in your home, school, or business environment.

- You can customize many aspects of the appearance and behavior of OneNote to fit your needs.

Chapter at a Glance

Create a notebook for use by one person, **page 540**

Create a notebook for use by multiple people, **page 543**

Create sections and pages, **page 550**

19 Create and Configure Notebooks

In this chapter, you will learn how to

✔ Create a notebook for use by one person.

✔ Create a notebook for use by multiple people.

✔ Create sections and pages.

In Chapter 18, "Explore OneNote 2010," we discussed the basic Microsoft OneNote 2010 data storage structure (notebooks, sections, and pages) and took a tour of the sample notebook that comes with OneNote. As you'll see in this chapter, there are many ways of structuring a notebook. The important thing is to create a structure that is easy for you to move around in so that you can easily find the information you want when you want it.

With OneNote 2010, you can create notebooks for your personal use on one computer, for use on multiple computers, and for use by multiple people. The ability to contribute and edit content in a shared notebook simultaneously with other people opens up many possibilities for collaboration.

In this chapter, you'll create a OneNote notebook on your computer and learn how to create a notebook that you can access from more than one computer or in which you can collaborate on content with other people. You'll create sections and section groups in your notebook, and add pages and subpages to the notebook so that you are ready to start storing information.

> **Practice Files** You don't need any practice files to complete the exercises in this chapter. For more information about practice file requirements, see "Using the Practice Files" at the beginning of this book.

Creating a Notebook for Use by One Person

OneNote 2007 included several notebook templates that created notebooks containing sections and pages customized for their intended use. OneNote 2010 doesn't include any notebook templates; you simply create a basic notebook and then create the sections and pages you want within it.

You can create a basic notebook, add content to it, and then organize the content into pages and sections, or you can create an organizational structure and then add content to the pages and sections. The best method will vary depending on the way you plan to use the notebook—whether you are collecting a wide variety of information or working on a highly structured.

If you work on only one computer, simply create the notebook in the default location (your Documents\OneNote Notebooks folder). If you work on more than one computer (such as a desktop computer and a portable computer) and have read/write access from both computers to a shared location, you can create a notebook that you can access from more than one computer. An appropriate shared location might be any of the following:

- A shared folder on your primary computer
- A folder on a shared network location
- A removable storage drive (such as a USB flash drive) that you move between computers
- A Microsoft SharePoint site document library
- A Web site

The first two locations are accessible only when you're working on the same network as the storage location; the last two are accessible only when you have an Internet connection; and the removable storage drive is accessible from any location.

See Also For information about sharing notebooks with other people over a network, on a SharePoint site, or on a Windows Live SkyDrive site, see "Creating a Notebook for Use by Multiple People" later in this chapter.

If you store the notebook in a shared folder on your primary computer, you can open it from any other computer for which you have the same logon credentials. Choose a storage location that will be available when you need it; for example, if you turn off your desktop computer while traveling with your portable computer, a notebook stored on the desktop computer might not be accessible.

In this exercise, you'll create a simple notebook in the default storage location on your computer.

 SET UP You don't need any practice files to complete this exercise. Start OneNote, and then follow the steps.

1. Display the Backstage view, and then in the left pane, click **New**.

   The New page displays options for creating local and shared notebooks.

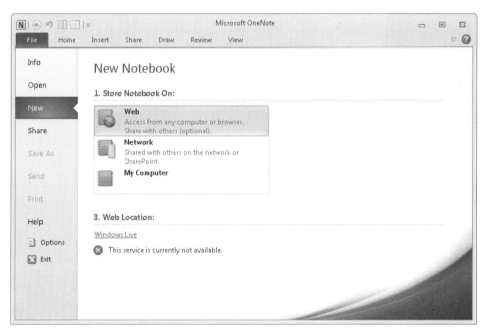

The New page is divided into numbered areas that lead you through the process of creating a notebook. Only steps 1 and 3 are visible until you select the storage location.

2. On the **New** page, under **1. Store Notebook On**, click **My Computer**.

   The page content changes to include options specific to creating a local notebook.

3. In the **2. Name** box, enter **My SBS Notes**

   Important The name of this notebook includes SBS, for *Step by Step*, so that you can easily differentiate it from your own notebooks.

4. In the **3. Location** box, confirm that the path specifies your **Documents\OneNote Notebooks** folder as the location of the new notebook.

This is all the information you need to provide to create the notebook.

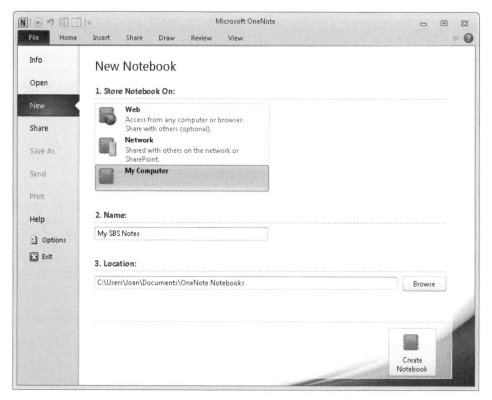

After you select the type of storage location, corresponding options appear on the page.

5. In the lower-right corner of the **New** page, click the **Create Notebook** button.

OneNote displays the new notebook.

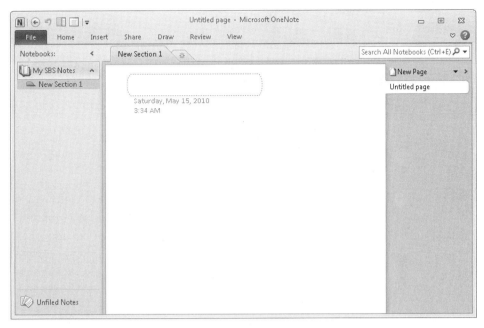

A new notebook includes one section and one untitled page.

✖ **CLEAN UP** Retain the My SBS Notes notebook for use in later exercises.

Creating a Notebook for Use by Multiple People

With Microsoft Office 2010, Microsoft has placed a strong emphasis on collaboration, specifically on the ability for multiple people (referred to as *authors*) to work together to create a document. OneNote is no exception—multiple people can access and contribute to an individual notebook that is stored in a central location.

OneNote creates an offline copy of the notebook on each computer from which the notebook is accessed. OneNote synchronizes each offline copy with the original notebook when the computer reconnects to the shared location and OneNote is running.

If you know in advance that you plan to share a notebook, you can do so at the time you create it; otherwise, you can share an existing notebook at any time.

Sharing a New or Existing Notebook

When creating a shared notebook, you select a storage location that is accessible either over your network or over the Internet, depending on the access requirements of the people with whom you want to share the notebook.

If you create a notebook for use on only one computer and later decide you want to share it with other authors, you can easily do so.

- If your primary computer can be accessed through a network or workgroup, you can share the notebook from its original location.

- If your primary computer cannot be accessed through a network or workgroup, or if you do not log on to your primary and secondary computers with the same credentials, you can move the notebook to a shared location.

To share the active notebook, follow these steps:

1. On the Share tab, in the Shared Notebook group, click Share This Notebook.

   The Share page of the Backstage view opens.

2. Select the location from which you want to share the notebook, as follows:

   ○ To share the notebook with any Internet user, click Web in the Share On section. Then in the Web Location section, click or browse to the site.

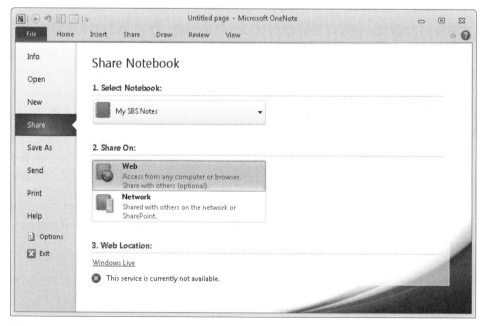

Sharing a notebook over the Web allows authors to access it from any location.

Troubleshooting When sharing a notebook over the Web, you should be able to do so by storing the notebook on a Windows Live SkyDrive site. At the time of writing this book, that option is unavailable, but hopefully it will be working by the time you read this.

○ To share the notebook with co-workers from a computer that is on your organization's internal network, click Network in the Share On section. In the Network Location section, enter the UNC address of the network location (in the format \\server\share\folder), click the location in the Recent Locations list, or click Browse and then, in the Select Folder dialog box, navigate to the network location and click Select.

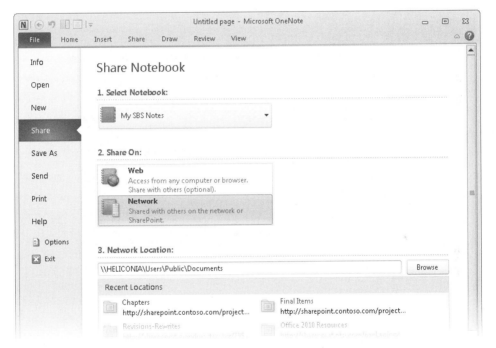

To share a notebook over a network, choose a network location to which all authors have access.

Tip If the Network Location box contains a SharePoint site address, clicking the Browse button opens that site; if you need to enter credentials to access the site, OneNote prompts you to do so.

○ To share the notebook with co-workers from a SharePoint document library, click Network in the Share On section. In the Network Location section, enter the URL of the document library or click the document library in the Recent Locations list.

3. On the Share page of the Backstage view, click the Share button.

OneNote saves the notebook in the selected location and displays a confirmation dialog box.

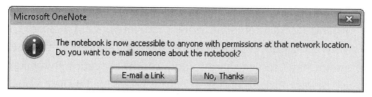

You can let other authors know the location of the shared notebook by sending an e-mail message initiated by OneNote.

4. If you want to inform other people about the location of the shared notebook at this time, click E-mail A Link. Otherwise, click No, Thanks.

If you click E-mail A Link, your default e-mail program starts, if it isn't already running, and creates an e-mail message with the subject *Invitation to OneNote notebook*. The message body includes a link to the shared notebook.

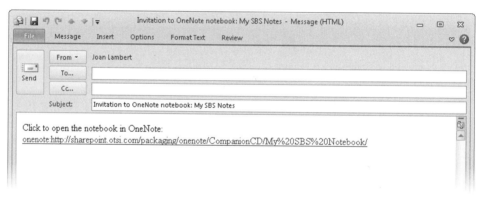

The standard e-mail message includes the location of the shared notebook.

After you share a notebook on a Web or network location, the Share page of the Backstage view changes to reflect that.

Other OneNote users can open a shared notebook either by clicking the link in the notification e-mail message or by browsing to the storage location of the shared notebook from the Open page of the Backstage view.

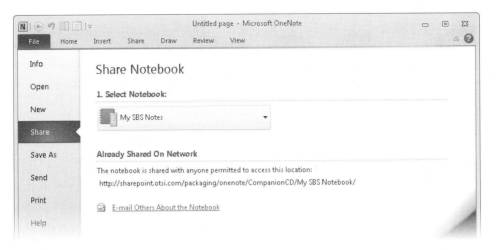

You can notify other people of the location of a shared notebook at any time by clicking the link on the Share page of the Backstage view.

To create a new notebook in a shared location, follow these steps:

1. Display the New page of the Backstage view.

2. Select the location in which you want to create the notebook, as follows:

   ○ To share the notebook with any Internet user from a Windows Live Sky Drive site, click Web in the Store Notebook On section. Then in the Web Location section, click or browse to the site.

   ○ To share the notebook with co-workers from a computer that is on your organization's internal network, click Network in the Store Notebook On section. In the Network Location section, enter the UNC address of the network location, click the location in the Recent Locations list, or click Browse and then, in the Select Folder dialog box, navigate to the network location and click Select.

   ○ To share the notebook with co-workers from a SharePoint document library, click Network in the Store Notebook On section. In the Network Location section, enter the URL of the document library or click the document library in the Recent Locations list.

3. On the New page of the Backstage view, click the Create Notebook button.

Managing a Shared Notebook

In OneNote, people who contribute to a notebook are referred to as *authors*. OneNote 2010 tracks the contributions of each notebook author. By default, other author's initials (as identified in the OneNote Options dialog box) are shown next to his or her edits; if you prefer, you can hide the authors' initials.

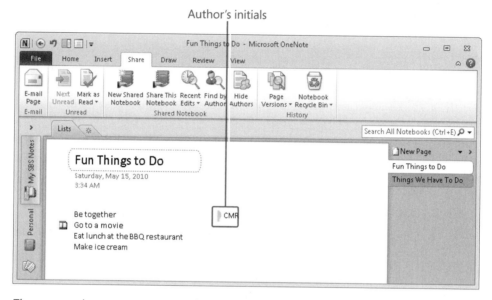

The commands you use to manage the shared notebook content are available from the Share tab on the ribbon.

Troubleshooting The appearance of buttons and groups on the ribbon changes depending on the width of the program window. For information about changing the appearance of the ribbon to match our screen images, see "Modifying the Display of the Ribbon" at the beginning of this book.

You can locate changes made to the notebook content within a specific time frame or by author. You can also view prior versions of a page, and roll back to a prior version if you want to discard the changes made since that version.

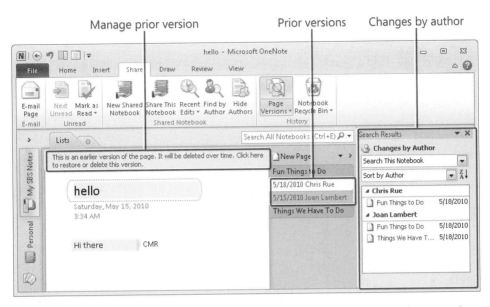

OneNote saves all prior versions of a page and indicates when and by whom they were changed.

By default, shared notebooks are synchronized when any author makes changes. You can check the synchronization status of your local copy of a shared notebook from the Shared Notebook Synchronization dialog box, which you open by clicking the View Sync Status button on the Info page of the Backstage view or by right-clicking the notebook on the Navigation Bar and then clicking Notebook Sync Status.

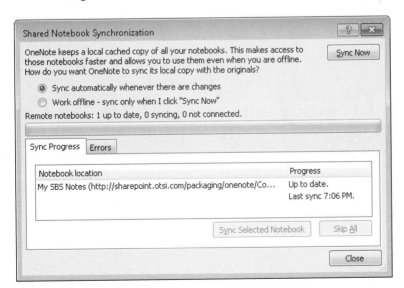

Your local copy of a shared notebook automatically reflects changes made by other authors unless you change the default setting in the Shared Notebook Synchronization dialog box.

The Sync Automatically Whenever There Are Changes option is selected by default. If you prefer, you can choose to work offline and sync only when you click the Sync Now button in this dialog box.

When the Navigation Bar is expanded, the ActiveSync icon to the right of the notebook name indicates the synchronization status of the shared notebook.

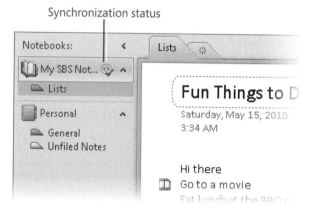

Synchronization status

A green check mark on the ActiveSync icon indicates that your local copy is synchronized with the shared notebook.

When OneNote is not actively synchronizing the primary notebook with the copies on other computers, one of the following indicators appears on the icon:

- A green check mark indicates a successful synchronization.
- A yellow caution triangle indicates a synchronization error.
- A red slashed circle indicates that the local copy of the notebook is offline.

Creating Sections and Pages

As we discussed briefly in the previous topic, you can create content and then move it into an organizational structure, or you can create an organizational structure and then create content within it. In this topic, we discuss creating storage structures within OneNote.

A new notebook contains one untitled section and one untitled page. You can easily create new pages on which to collect information and subdivide pages into subpages. You can also create new sections in which to organize the pages. You can further organize information by grouping sections together in section groups.

So how do you know whether to create a page, subpage, section, or section group? The answer is determined by the following:

- The nature of the information you are collecting. In a Customer Records notebook, you might want to include a section for each client, and in a Project Records notebook, you might want one section per project.

- The volume of information. There is no point in collecting information unless you can quickly and easily retrieve it when you need it. On an ideal page, all the information is visible at a glance, without too much scrolling. If you have to scroll, maybe some of the information should be organized on subpages. Similarly, in an ideal section, all the pages and subpages are visible at a glance on the Page Tabs Bar. If there are too many page tabs, maybe some of the pages should be organized in new sections. And if not all the sections are visible in the notebook header at a glance, maybe it's time to organize the sections in section groups.

The important thing to remember is that the organizational structure of a notebook should be dynamic—in other words, it should change as the information in the notebook changes.

Creating Pages and Subpages

When first created, each section contains one blank, untitled page. You can add plain blank pages, blank pages of a special size or with a special background, or specialized pages containing content templates for you to replace with your own content.

Blank page options include the following:

- Specific sizes, including Statement, Letter, Tabloid, Legal, A3–A6, B4–B6, Postcard, Index Card, and Billfold

- Simple backgrounds, including College Ruled, Small Grid, or 16 solid colors

- Nearly 70 decorative backgrounds displaying illustrated or photographic elements in the title bar, corner, margin, or background of an otherwise blank page

Specialized page options are based on content templates, which are divided into the following categories:

- Academic templates, including Simple and Detailed Lecture Notes, Lecture Notes And Study Questions, Math/Science Class Notes, and History Class Notes

- Business templates, including Project Overview and six types of Meeting Notes

- Planners templates, including three types of To Do Lists

You can quickly create a new page or subpage in the current section by selecting an option from the New Page menu at the top of the Page Tabs Bar.

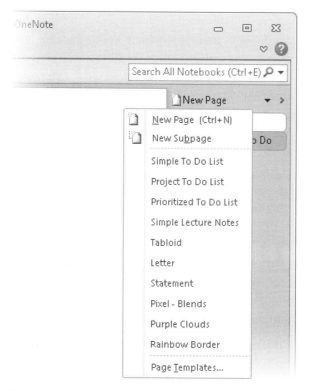

Common or recently selected page templates are available from the New Page menu.

Clicking Page Templates on the New Page menu displays the Templates task pane. You can preview any page template by clicking it in the list. The first time you click a template in the task pane, OneNote creates a page based on that template; subsequent clicks apply the selected template to the created page.

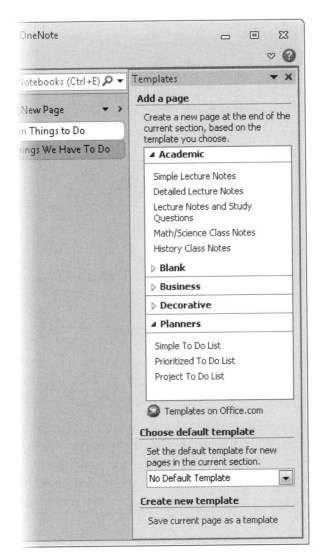

Additional page templates are available from Microsoft Office Online.

Tip You can't apply a template from the Templates task pane to an existing page, but you can apply a background color or create your own page template. For more information, see the "Formatting Notes, Pages, and Sections" section of "Entering Content Directly onto a Page" in Chapter 20, "Create and Organize Notes."

Naming Sections and Pages

A new section is named simply *New Section*, followed by a number to differentiate it from other new sections you create (New Section 1, New Section 2, and so on). To change the name of a section, right-click the section tab in the notebook header, click Rename, enter the section name you want, and then press Enter or click away from the section tab. A section name can have up to 50 characters.

A new page isn't named at all. OneNote identifies it as *Untitled page*. To assign a name to a page, you enter text in the title box located in the upper-left corner of the page.

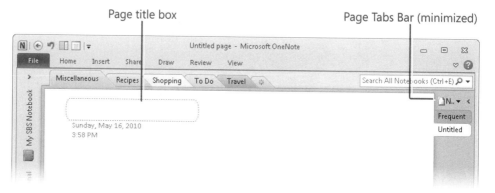

The date and time the page was created appear below the page title box.

You can enter as much text as you want in the title box; after the first eight characters, the box expands to fit the text. When the text exceeds the maximum for the page width, it wraps to the next line. You could enter thousands of characters in the title box, but we recommend that you keep page titles short. Because OneNote processes the title text each time it displays the page, long titles slow down the program response time, and you can't use the program while it is processing the text.

When the Page Tabs Bar is expanded at its default width, the first 21 characters of the page title appear on the page tab; when it's collapsed, only the first eight characters are visible. You can increase the width of the expanded Page Tabs Bar by pointing to the border between the active page and the tab area and then, when the cursor changes to a double-headed arrow, dragging the border to the left.

Keyboard Shortcuts Press Ctrl+Shift+[to increase the width of the Pages Tabs Bar. Press Ctrl+Shift+] to decrease the width of the Pages Tabs Bar.

The Page Tabs Bar is part of the program window, so when you switch between pages, sections, or notebooks, its width doesn't change. The configuration of common elements such as the Navigation Bar and Page Tabs Bar remains constant, and changing them for one page changes them for all pages.

Creating Sections and Section Groups

You have fewer options to consider when creating sections than when creating pages, because there is only one type of section. Unlike pages, sections don't have special templates. You can change a section color to differentiate it from other sections, perhaps as a visual reminder to yourself, and you can safeguard a section by assigning an access password to it.

See Also   For information about changing a section color, see the "Page and Section Backgrounds" section of "Entering Content Directly onto a Page" in Chapter 20, "Create and Organize Notes."

When a notebook contains a lot of information, you might want to create a section group. This useful organizational tool is an entirely separate set of sections and pages within a notebook. You can move sections to and among section groups.

In this exercise, you will rename existing sections and pages, add pages and subpages to a section, and then add a section and a section group to a notebook.

 SET UP   You need the My SBS Notes notebook you created earlier in this chapter to complete this exercise. Open the My SBS Notes notebook, expand the Navigation Bar and the Page Tabs Bar, and then follow the steps.

1. In the notebook header, right-click the **New Section 1** tab, and then click **Rename**.

    The tab name is selected for editing.

2. Type **Work**, and then press Enter.

    The section name changes on the section tab and on the Navigation Bar.

3. On the **Untitled** page, click in the page title box, and then type **Notes**

    As you type, the page name changes on the Page Tabs Bar.

 4. On the **Page Tabs Bar**, click the **New Page** arrow and then, in the list, click **Simple To Do List**.

    OneNote creates a new page, titled *To Do List*. On the Page Tabs Bar, the To Do List page tab follows the Notes page tab.

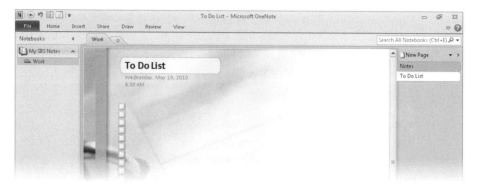

The To Do List page includes a background image and a checklist. You insert tasks in the space to the right of the check boxes.

Tip Scroll to the bottom of the To Do List page for information about reordering checklist items.

5. On the **Page Tabs Bar**, click the **New Page** arrow, and then click **Page Templates**.

   The Templates task pane opens on the right side of the program window.

6. In the **Templates** task pane, click the **Business** category and then, in the list, click **Simple Meeting Notes 1**.

   OneNote creates a page named *Meeting Title*. The page has a background image and a structure for basic meeting notes.

7. In the **Templates** task pane, in the **Business** category, click **Informal Meeting Notes 1**.

   The format of the existing Meeting Title page changes.

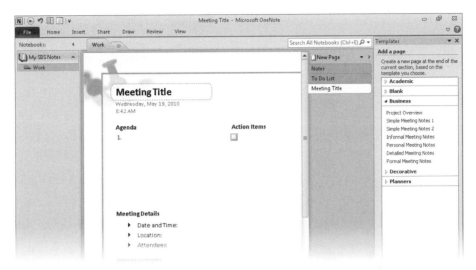

The Informal Meeting Notes 1 page includes a background image, a numbered agenda, an action item checklist, and areas for meeting details, announcements, discussion, summary, and notes about the next meeting.

8. In the upper-right corner of the **Templates** task pane, click the **Close** button.

The task pane closes.

9. On the **Page Tabs Bar**, point to the **Notes** page tab.

A New Page button appears on the right side of the content pane, to the left of the Page Tabs Bar. A black triangle points from the New Page button to the top of the page tab list.

10. Move the pointer down the page tab list to the **Meeting Title** page.

The New Page icon moves down the list with the pointer.

11. Point to the **New Page** button.

A thick black bar appears between the page tabs.

New Page   Insertion bar

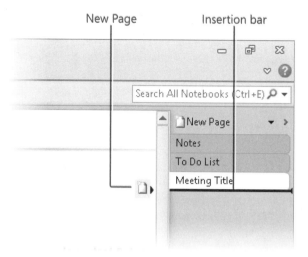

The bar indicates where a new page will be inserted when you click the button.

12. If necessary, move the pointer to position the insertion bar at the end of the page tab list. Then click the **New Page** button.

Keyboard Shortcut Press Ctrl+N to create a new page at the end of the current section. Press Ctrl+Alt+N to create a new page following the current page.

OneNote creates an untitled page at the location of the insertion bar.

13. On the **Page Tabs Bar**, right-click the **Untitled** page tab, and then click **Make Subpage**.

Keyboard Shortcut Press Ctrl+Alt+] to make the current page a subpage. Press Ctrl+Alt+[to bring a subpage up one level.

On the Page Tabs Bar, the name of the Untitled page tab is indented to indicate that it is now a subpage of the Meeting Title page.

Subpage

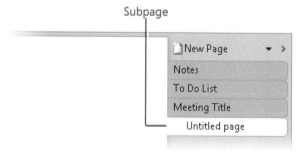

The page tabs of subpages are indented to differentiate them from page tabs.

14. Click the **Meeting Title** page tab. At the top of the **Page Tabs Bar**, click the **New Page** arrow, and then, in the list, click **New Subpage**.

Keyboard Shortcut   Press Ctrl+Shift+Alt+N to create a new subpage for the current page.

OneNote creates a second Untitled subpage.

15. Point to the **Meeting Title** page tab, and then click the **Collapse** button that appears at its right side.

The subpages collapse under the Meeting Title page tab.

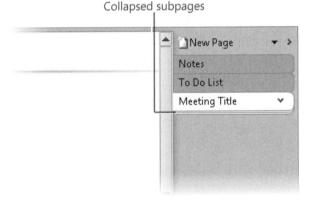

Collapsed subpages

You can collapse subpages to save space.

16. In the notebook header, to the right of the **Work** section tab, click the **Create New Section** button.

Keyboard Shortcut   Press Ctrl+T to create a new section.

OneNote creates a section containing one blank untitled page. The section name, *New Section 1*, is selected for editing.

17. Type **Ideas** and then press Enter.

18. In the **Navigation Bar**, right-click the **My SBS Notes** notebook, and then click **New Section Group**.

OneNote creates a section group and selects the section group's name for editing.

19. Type **Analysis** and then press Enter.

The section group appears on the Navigation Bar and in the notebook header, represented by a stack of section tabs.

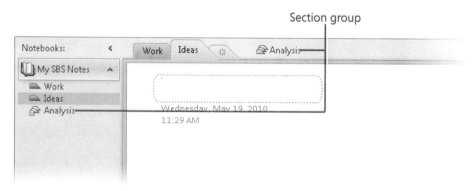

Section groups appear on the Navigation Bar at the same level as sections within the notebook.

20. On the **Navigation Bar** or the notebook header, click the **Analysis** section group.

The section group contains no sections or pages; it is only a container for sections.

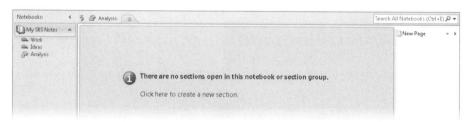

A new section group doesn't contain anything.

21. On the **Navigation Bar**, drag the **Ideas** section to the **Analysis** section group.

The selected section and its pages move to the section group.

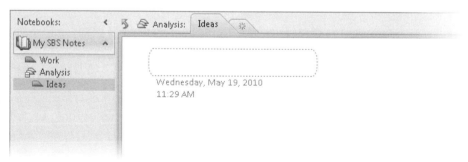

You can move sections to a section group or create new sections and pages directly in the section group.

 CLEAN UP Close the My SBS Notes notebook.

Key Points

- You can create a notebook for your own personal use on one computer or on multiple computers.

- When planning your information-storage system, you start with a blank notebook and add sections and pages.

- The organizational structure of a notebook is dynamic and can change to reflect the information you collect.

- You collect information on pages. When you have a lot of information on one page, individual items of information might be easier to find if you organize them on subpages.

- You can create pages based on decorative or functional page templates. Functional page templates include content templates that guide you in placing your own content.

- Pages are contained within sections. You can create additional sections to organize different types of information, and you can organize sections in section groups.

Chapter at a Glance

Work with note
containers, **page 564**

Enter content directly
onto a page, **page 565**

Send content to
OneNote, **page 579**

Capture audio and
video notes, **page 585**

20 Create and Organize Notes

In this chapter, you will learn how to

✔ Work with note containers.

✔ Enter content directly onto a page.

✔ Send content to OneNote.

✔ Capture audio and video notes.

✔ Take notes on the side.

In Chapter 19, "Create and Configure Notebooks," we discussed creating Microsoft OneNote notebooks, sections, and pages within which to store electronic information. In this chapter, we move on to the task of collecting and storing the information.

OneNote 2010 provides two primary ways to collect information: the OneNote program window and the OneNote Side Note utility. In addition, options in other programs—such as the Send To OneNote command on the Windows Internet Explorer Tools menu, and the Send To OneNote 2010 printer available when printing from any Windows program—make it easy to collect information without starting or switching to OneNote.

You can store almost any type of electronic information in a OneNote notebook, including text, graphics, photos, Web clippings and pages, hyperlinks, audio clips, and video clips. You can store as much or as little information as you want on each individual page.

In this chapter, you'll insert text, graphics, handwritten notes, screen clippings, Web notes, and media clips into note containers on pages of a OneNote notebook by using various methods.

> **Practice Files** Before you can complete the exercises in this chapter, you need to copy the book's practice files to your computer. The practice files you'll use to complete the exercises in this chapter are in the Chapter20 practice file folder. A complete list of practice files is provided in "Using the Practice Files" at the beginning of this book.

Working with Note Containers

Each piece of information you store on a notebook page exists within a note container. Similar to a text box that you might use to position text in a Microsoft Word document or on a Microsoft PowerPoint slide, a note container consists of a frame that has a move handle and a sizing handle. Each object (such as a text block, image, or URL) within the note container has an object selector.

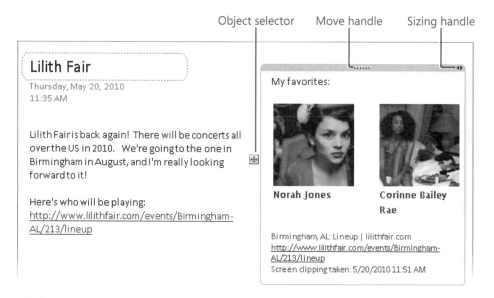

The frame, move handle, sizing handle, and object selector are visible only when you point to the content within the note container.

Unlike a text box in other programs, you don't have to insert a note container on the page before entering content into it—simply click anywhere on the page and type or paste content, or insert content from another source, to create the container. A note container can contain any sort of content, such as text, images, handwritten notes, screen clippings, or Web notes (Web page content you send to OneNote directly from Internet Explorer).

You can manipulate a note container on the page in the same way that you would manipulate a text box or other type of content frame in a word-processing or graphics program. You can change its size, relocate it on the page, and cut, copy, or delete it.

The contents of an entire page may be stored in one note container or in many note containers. While you work in OneNote, the frame of the active note container is visible, but the frames of the other note containers are not. Pointing to the content displays the note container's frame, and pointing to an object within the active container displays the object selector. You can manipulate individual objects within the container by dragging, clicking, or right-clicking the associated object selector.

Entering Content Directly onto a Page

The simplest type of information you will store in a OneNote notebook, and probably the most common, is text. You can enter text by typing directly on the notebook page or by pasting it from another source. But you aren't limited to simple text entry. You can insert attachments, formatted file contents, images, multimedia objects, and handwritten notes, all with a minimum amount of effort.

Tip When deciding how much information to include on a notebook page, consider whether you want to scroll down the page. If you want to see all the information at a glance, limit the content to about 30 lines of standard text.

Referencing External Files

When conducting research, you might identify an entire file of information—such as a document, image, or video clip—that you want to include in your notebook. You can store this information in the following three ways:

- Link to the external file on a local drive, network drive, or Web site by clicking the Link button in the Links group on the Insert tab, browsing to the file, and then clicking OK.

- Insert the file as an attachment by clicking the Attach File button in the Files group on the Insert tab, browsing to the file, and then clicking Insert.

  Keyboard Shortcut Press Alt+N+F to attach a document or file to the current page.

- Insert the file's contents on the page by clicking the File Printout button in the Files group on the Insert tab, browsing to the file, and then clicking OK.

  Keyboard Shortcut Press Alt+N+O to insert the contents of a document or file on the current page.

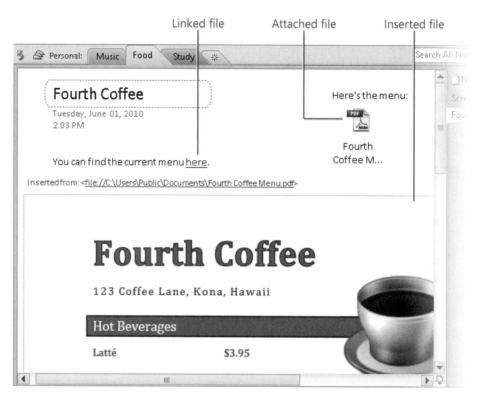

Opening a linked file requires access to the file location; attached and inserted files are part of the notebook.

Tip The name of the File Printout button is somewhat misleading. Clicking this button sends the contents of the external file that you select into the note container, in the same way that you send a file's contents to a printer. It does not print the OneNote page or notebook.

Tip OneNote automatically inserts the date and time when you send content from another source to OneNote. (For more information, see the sidebar "Inserting the Date & Time" later in this chapter.)

Creating Handwritten Notes

On any computer that has a mouse, you can enter "handwritten" notes by using a pen tool that you control with the mouse. On a Tablet PC, you can enter handwritten notes by using the tablet pen, just as you would in other handwriting-enabled programs.

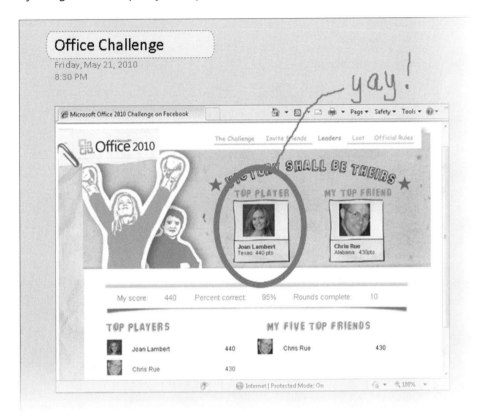

You can draw notes on a notebook page or on top of other content.

Tip OneNote automatically saves all your changes as you make them, so you don't need to. For this reason, you won't ever be prompted to choose whether to save a notebook when you close it.

Inserting Images

You can insert and attach image files just as you can document files. You can insert an image at a size that is scaled to fit the available space by using the Insert Picture command, or you can insert an image at its full size by using the File Printout command.

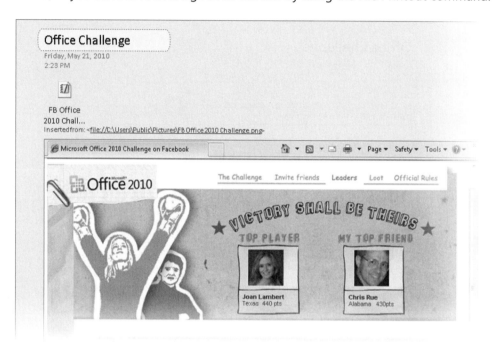

Inserting an image by using the File Printout command inserts an image icon, the image path, and the image.

To insert scaled versions of one or more photos or other image files onto a OneNote notebook page:

1. On the Insert tab, in the Images group, click the Picture button to insert the image at a size that is scaled to fit the available space.

2. In the Insert Picture dialog box, select the image file or image files that you want to insert on the page, and then click Insert.

You can easily change the size of an image on the page.

To change a scaled image to its full size:

● Right-click the image, and then click Restore To Original Size.

To manually resize an inserted image:

1. Click the image (not the note container).

    Sizing handles appear in the corners and at the center of each side of the image.

2. Drag a sizing handle to resize the image.

    ○ Drag a round corner sizing handle to maintain the image's aspect ratio.

    ○ Drag a square edge handle to resize the image in one direction only.

Using the new Screen Clipping tool, you can insert clip art (free graphics, photos, sounds, and movies) into your notes, but there is no built-in command for doing so. You must do one of the following:

- Insert the clip art into another Office document, such as a Word document, cut or copy the clip art from the document, and then paste it onto the notebook page.

- From the Start menu, open the Microsoft Office Clip Organizer, locate and copy the clip art you want, and then paste it onto the notebook page.

See Also For information about inserting screen clippings, see "Sending Content to OneNote" later in this chapter.

Formatting Notes, Pages, and Sections

You can change the appearance of text in notes in much the same way that you do in other Office 2010 programs. OneNote supports character-level formatting such as font, size, and color, and simple styles such as headings and titles.

Paragraph Formatting

OneNote 2010 provides several standard paragraph formatting options, including:

- Alignment (left, center, or right)

- Spacing (before, after, and within a paragraph)

- Lists (bulleted and numbered)

- Indent level

The paragraph formatting options settings aren't as complete as those in Word and the other Office 2010 programs, but they are a great improvement over what was available in OneNote 2007.

Outline Levels

You can assign outline levels (1 through 5) to paragraphs by indenting the paragraph. An icon appears to the left of each paragraph when you point to the paragraph. You can select all the content within the level headed by the paragraph by clicking the icon, and you can collapse or expand the content within the level by double-clicking the icon. You can also hide levels, which gives you the equivalent of an outline view.

To change the paragraph indentation for the purpose of assigning an outline level:

1. Click to place the cursor at the beginning of the paragraph, or drag to select multiple paragraphs.

2. Press the Tab key to increase the level, or press the Backspace key or Shift+Tab to decrease the level.

To select all text of a specific outline level within a note:

● Right-click the note container header, click Select, and then click the outline level you want to select.

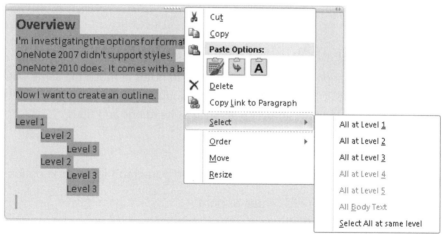

You can create an outline view by indenting paragraphs.

Keyboard Shortcuts Press Alt+Shift+*level number* (for example, Alt+Shift+1) to show all content through the specified outline level. Press Alt+Shift+0 to expand all outline levels. Press Alt+Shift+Plus Sign to expand a collapsed outline. Press Alt+Shift+Minus Sign to collapse an expanded outline.

Page and Section Backgrounds

By default, a OneNote notebook page has a blank white background. You can modify
the appearance of the page in several ways. For example, you can:

- Change the page size, orientation, and margins.
- Change the page background to any of 16 background colors. The available colors
  are muted so they don't obscure the page content.
- Display any of four horizontal rule line patterns (Narrow, College, Standard, and
  Wide) or four grid line patterns (Small, Medium, Large, and Very Large).

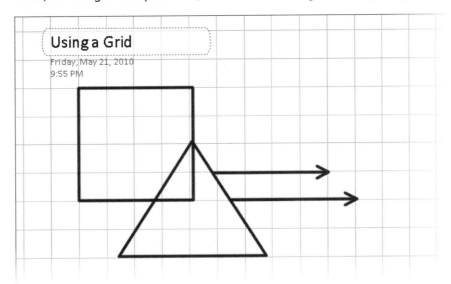

A notebook page displaying large grid rule lines that you can use to align content.

- Hide rule lines and grid lines (while leaving them in place for alignment purposes)
  or change the line color to any of 17 colors.

  Keyboard Shortcut Press Ctrl+Shift+R to show or hide rule lines.

These and other options are available on the View tab, in the Page Setup group.

Tip Changing the size, orientation, background, or other attribute of a page does not affect
other pages of the notebook.

You can change the color of a section tab and its Page Tabs area by right-clicking the
page tab, clicking Section Color, and clicking the color you want.

In this exercise, you'll enter text; insert, attach, and manipulate images; and create a handwritten note by using the OneNote writing tools.

 SET UP You need the SBS Content Entry notebook, the Landscaping presentation, and the Cabo, California_Poppy, Desert, and ADatumLogo images located in the Chapter20 practice file folder. Open the SBS Content Entry notebook, and then follow the steps.

1. On the **Text Notes** page, click to place the cursor on the page, and then type
   Collecting information in OneNote is easy!

   OneNote creates a visible note container when you type the first character and then expands the note container to fit the remaining text.

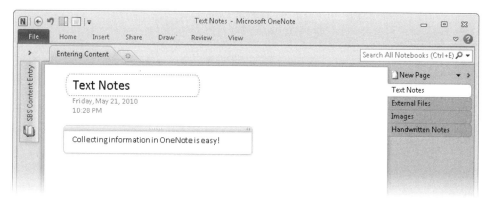

When working with simple text entries, you can increase the available page space by collapsing the ribbon.

2. In the **Page Tabs** area, click the **External Files** page tab.

3. On the **Insert** tab, in the **Files** group, click the **File Printout** button.

   The Choose Document To Insert dialog box opens.

   See Also For information about the File Printout button, see the "Referencing External Files" section of this topic.

4. Browse to the **Chapter20** practice file folder. Click the **Landscaping** presentation, and then click **Insert**.

   OneNote inserts the presentation file as an attachment, the *Inserted From* reference, and then each slide of the presentation, at its full size. Each slide is an individually sizable object.

   Tip When inserting an image on a blank page, you don't need to create a note container; OneNote does it for you.

5. In the **Page Tabs** area, click the **Images** page tab.

6. On the **Insert** tab, in the **Images** group, click the **Picture** button.

   The Insert Picture dialog box opens.

7. If necessary, browse to the **Chapter 20** practice file folder. Click the **ADatumLogo** image, and then click **Insert**.

   The inserted image appears on the page.

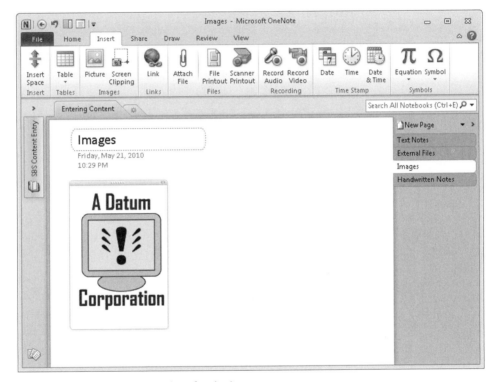

OneNote creates a note container for the image.

Troubleshooting The appearance of buttons and groups on the ribbon changes depending on the width of the program window. For information about changing the appearance of the ribbon to match our screen images, see "Modifying the Display of the Ribbon" at the beginning of this book.

8. Click the inserted image.

   Within the note container, a dotted outline appears around the image to indicate that it can be manually resized on the notebook page. Sizing handles appear on each side and in each corner of the inserted image.

9. Drag the bottom handles to change the height of the image, making it smaller and approximately square.

10. Right-click the image, and then click **Make Text in Image Searchable**.

Notice that by default, OneNote searches the text of the embedded image.

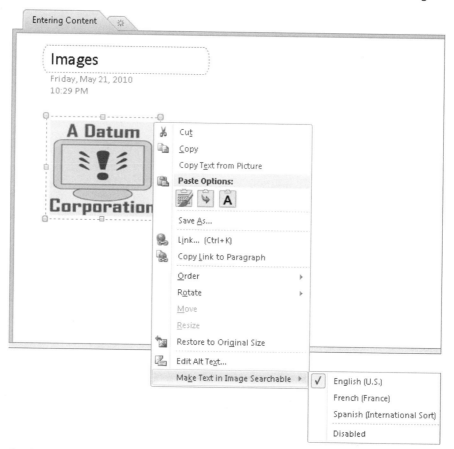

OneNote searches text in images, such as the words *A Datum Corporation shown in this image.*

11. Click to place the cursor to the right of the logo. Then on the **Insert** tab, in the **Files** group, click the **Attach File** button.

    The Choose A File Or A Set Of Files To Insert dialog box opens.

12. If necessary, browse to the **Chapter20** practice file folder. Click the **Cabo** image, hold down the Shift key, and then click the **Desert** image.

    The three images (the two you clicked and the one in-between) are selected in the dialog box.

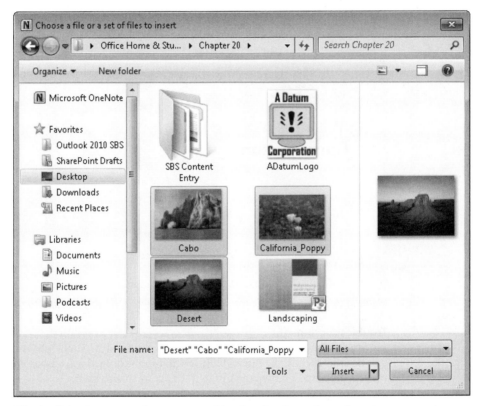

Files in dialog boxes may be represented by thumbnails as shown here, by program icons, or by words, depending on your Windows settings.

13. In the **Choose a file or a set of files to insert** dialog box, click **Insert**.

    The icons and file names representing the attached images appear on the page.

14. Point to the **California_Poppy** image.

    A ScreenTip containing file information is displayed.

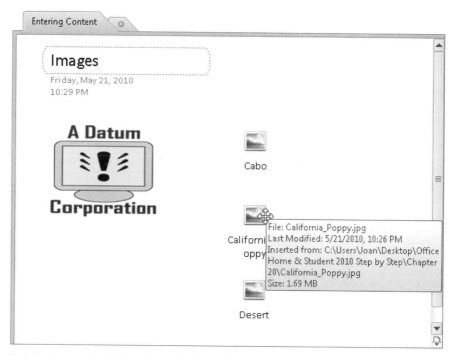

Pointing to an attached file icon displays a ScreenTip; double-clicking the icon opens the file.

Troubleshooting The displayed icons represent the program that is set up on your computer as the default program for this file type (the program in which the file opens when you double-click it). If your default programs are different from ours, the icons shown on your notebook page won't match the icons shown here.

15. Double-click the **California_Poppy** image. If a warning message appears, select the **Don't show this again** check box, and then click **OK**.

    The image opens in the default program for viewing .jpg files.

    Tip Unless you've changed the settings on your computer, the default program to view .jpg files is Windows Photo Viewer.

16. Close the image window to return to OneNote.

17. In the **Page Tabs** area, click the **Handwritten Notes** page tab.

18. On the **Draw** tab, in the **Tools** group, click the **Blue Pen (.05 mm)** button.

19. Point to the notebook page.

    The pointer shape changes from an arrow to a blue dot.

20. By dragging the pen on the notebook page, draw a picture depicting a possible business logo.

21. On the **Draw** tab, in the **Tools** group, click the **Select & Type** button.

22. Click to place the cursor on the page to the right of the note containing the logo (not in the same note container), and type **Logo idea**. Then drag the note container for the typed words to the left, to overlap the note container for the drawing.

    The content of both note containers is visible where they overlap.

You can move note containers on the page to arrange notes the way you want.

23. Experiment on your own with additional pens, colors, and commands from the Writing Tools toolbar.

 CLEAN UP Close the SBS Content Entry notebook.

Tagging Content

You can identify content that fits into specific categories by attaching a visual identifier, a *tag*, to the content. Tags are not only icons, however—they function as a property attached to the content. You can locate specific content based on the tags attached to it. OneNote 2010 includes nearly 30 built-in tags. You can modify any built-in tag, and also create your own tags.

The built-in content tags.

You apply a tag to a paragraph by right-clicking the paragraph, clicking Tag, and then clicking the tag you want to apply. You apply a tag to the active paragraph by clicking the tag in the Tags gallery on the Home tab.

Alternatively, you can use the keyboard shortcuts in the following table to work with tags.

To do this	Press this
Apply, mark, or clear the To Do tag	Ctrl+1
Apply or clear the Important tag	Ctrl+2
Apply or clear the Question tag	Ctrl+3
Apply or clear the Remember for later tag	Ctrl+4
Apply or clear the Definition tag	Ctrl+5
Apply or clear a custom tag	Ctrl+6
Apply or clear a custom tag	Ctrl+7
Apply or clear a custom tag	Ctrl+8
Apply or clear a custom tag	Ctrl+9
Remove all note tags from the selected notes	Ctrl+0
Move the selected page tab up	Alt+Shift+Up Arrow
Move the selected page tab down	Alt+Shift+Down Arrow
Move the insertion point to the page title	Ctrl+Shift+T

Sending Content to OneNote

The tools available in OneNote make collecting on-screen information in a OneNote notebook incredibly simple. You can send content from any screen to OneNote as a screen clipping, or send an entire Web page as a Web note. When viewing a Web page, you can send the entire page to your notebook without leaving Internet Explorer.

You can specify what you want OneNote to do with screen clippings, Web notes, and content that you print to OneNote from another program (by using the Print command and selecting the Send To OneNote 2010 printer) by setting the default action on the Send To OneNote page of the OneNote Options dialog box.

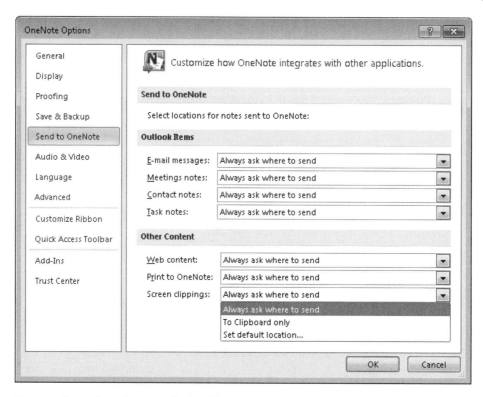

You can change how OneNote deals with content sent from other programs and from the Internet.

For Web notes and content printed to OneNote, the options are:

- **Always ask where to send** After capturing a Web note or printing to the OneNote Printer, you can select the section in which you want to save the content.

- **To current page** OneNote inserts the Web note into a new note container on the active notebook page.

- **To new page in current section** OneNote creates a new page in the active section and inserts the Web note into a note container at the top of the new page.

- **Set default location** You choose a specific location to which all Web notes and printed content are sent. This location is usually the Unfiled Notes section, from which you can move content into any notebook.

For screen clippings, the options are:

- **Always ask where to send** After capturing a screen clipping, you can select the section in which you want to save the clipping.

- **To Clipboard only** OneNote copies the screen clipping to the Microsoft Office Clipboard. You can paste it into OneNote or another program by using the Paste command in that program.

- **Set default location** You choose a specific location to which all Web notes are sent. This location is usually the Unfiled Notes section, from which you can move content into any notebook.

Collecting Screen Clippings

You can use the Screen Clipping tool to capture an image of anything that is visible on your computer screen. When the Screen Clipping tool is active, a transparent white overlay appears on the screen. Drag with your mouse (or pen, if you're using a Tablet PC) to define the area you want to "clip." As you drag, the white overlay becomes clear in the area you define. When you release the mouse button or lift the pen, the selected area is clipped.

Using the default settings, you can use one method to add a screen clipping to the active notebook page, and another method to send a screen clipping to a new page in any section of an active OneNote notebook.

To add a screen clipping to the active notebook page, follow these steps:

1. Display the content you want to clip.

2. Open the OneNote notebook and display the page to which you want to add the screen clipping.

3. On the Insert tab, in the Images group, click the Screen Clipping button.

   The OneNote window minimizes to the taskbar, and the Screen Clipping tool starts.

4. Capture the screen clipping you want.

   When you release the Screen Clipping tool, OneNote reappears, and the screen clipping is inserted into a note container on the page.

To send a screen clipping to a new page, follow these steps:

1. Display the content you want to clip.

2. In the notification area of the taskbar, right-click the OneNote icon, and then click Create Screen Clipping.

   Keyboard Shortcut Press the Windows logo key+S to start the Screen Clipping tool.

   The Screen Clipping tool starts.

3. Capture the screen clipping you want.

   When you release the Screen Clipping tool, the Select Location In OneNote dialog box opens.

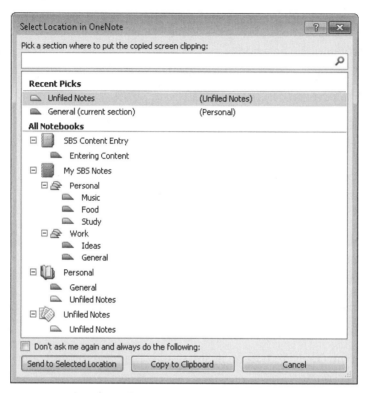

You can send a screen clipping to any section of an open notebook, or to the Unfiled Notes section.

Tip If you've selected a screen clipping option on the Send To OneNote page of the OneNote Options dialog box other than Always Ask Where To Send, the dialog box will not appear; instead, the option you selected will be invoked.

4. In the Select Location In OneNote dialog box, click the section to which you want to send the screen clipping, and then click Send To Selected Location. If the notebook to which you want to send the screen clipping is not open, click the Unfiled Notes section.

   See Also For more information about the Unfiled Notes section, see "Exploring OneNote in the Default Notebook" in Chapter 18, "Explore OneNote 2010."

5. Display OneNote.

   The selected section is active. The screen clipping appears on a new page in the section.

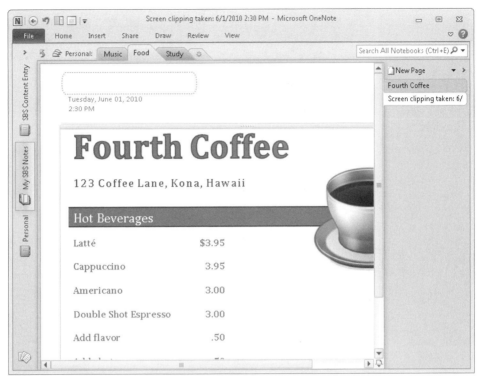

A screen clipping.

If you clipped content from a Web page, the notebook page tab name matches the Web page title. If you clipped content from the desktop or from another program, the notebook page tab name is *Screen clipping taken:*, followed by the date. In either case, the page title box at the top of the page is empty.

Collecting Web Notes

From Internet Explorer, you can send an entire Web page to OneNote.

To capture a Web note, follow these steps:

1. In Internet Explorer, display the Web page you want to send to OneNote.

2. On the Tools menu, click Send To OneNote.

3. In the Select Location In OneNote dialog box, click the section to which you want to send the screen clipping, and then click Send To Selected Location. If the notebook to which you want to send the screen clipping is not open, click the Unfiled Notes section.

   OneNote creates a new page in the selected section and inserts the Web page content in a note container on the page.

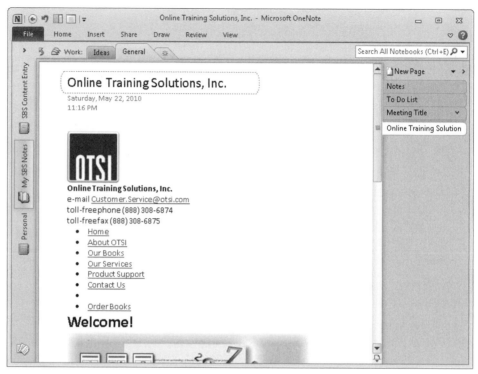

The Web page title is reflected in the notebook page title box and on the page tab.

Depending on the complexity of the content, the page layout in OneNote might not precisely reflect the on-screen layout.

Inserting the Date and Time

OneNote automatically inserts the date and time in certain locations, including the following:

- At the top of a notebook page, below the page title box, when you create a page
- In a note container, when you insert a screen clipping

You can insert date and time information in other locations.

To insert the date or time on a notebook page

1. Click to place the cursor where you want the date and time to appear on the page.
2. On the Insert tab, in the Time Stamp group, click the Date button, the Time button, or the Date & Time button.

   Keyboard Shortcuts Press Alt+N+D to insert the current date. Press Alt+Shift+T to insert the current time. Press Alt+Shift+F to insert the current date and time.

Capturing Audio and Video Notes

If your computer system includes a microphone, such as a built-in microphone or a free-standing or headset microphone, you can record audio directly into a file stored on a OneNote notebook page. (You'll get the best results by using a headset microphone.) Similarly, if your system includes a built-in or external webcam, you can record video directly into a file stored on a OneNote notebook page.

You can record audio that is playing on your computer, or audio that you speak, sing, or otherwise communicate through a microphone.

Tip If you haven't already configured your audio input device, you can do so by using the Microphone Setup Wizard available from the Speech Recognition window of Control Panel.

You can record video that you capture by using a webcam. The quality of the video you capture depends greatly on the webcam, lighting, and other factors not specific to OneNote. Many portable computers have built-in webcams that will automatically work with OneNote. If you don't have a built-in webcam, you can purchase one that connects to your desktop or portable computer through a USB cable.

Video is recorded and displayed in a window separate from the OneNote program window. You can move it around the screen by dragging its title bar, change its size by dragging the window frame, and minimize, maximize, or restore it by clicking the buttons on the window's title bar. If you're working on a Windows 7 computer, you can use the new window-management techniques such as Snap To Screen and Shake to manage the video window as you would any other.

The first time you record an audio or video clip, OneNote prompts you to indicate whether you want to configure the recordings so that OneNote can search the audio recording or the audio track of the video recording for spoken words. By enabling the Audio Search feature, spoken words matching the search criteria you enter in the Search box will be included in search results. For this feature to work effectively, the audio recording must be of a high quality, words must be spoken clearly, and the spoken language must match that of the OneNote user interface. Audio Search is currently supported for nine languages: English, Spanish, German, French, Italian, Traditional Chinese, Simplified Chinese, Japanese, and Korean.

In this exercise, you'll record and play back an audio clip and a video clip in OneNote.

 SET UP You don't need any practice files, but you do need to have a microphone and webcam installed to complete the exercise in its entirety. Display a blank notebook page, and then follow the steps.

1. In the page title box, type **My Recordings**. Then press Enter.

   OneNote creates a note container below the timestamp.

 2. On the **Insert** tab, in the **Recording** group, click the **Record Audio** button.

   If you haven't previously made an Audio Search selection, the Audio Search dialog box opens.

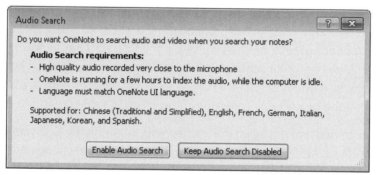

You can configure OneNote to search spoken words in audio and video recordings.

 3. If the **Audio Search** dialog box opens, and you want to make a selection at this time, click **Enable Audio Search** or **Keep Audio Search Disabled**. Otherwise, click the **Close** button on the window title bar, and OneNote will prompt you again later.

   Tip If you have a lot of audio and video content stored in a notebook, enabling the Audio Search feature can slow down the search process. You can change your Audio Search setting at any time by selecting or clearing the Enable Searching Audio And Video Recordings For Words check box on the Audio & Video page of the OneNote Options dialog box.

   OneNote inserts a Windows Media Audio (.wma) file icon, a file name that matches the page name, and the recording start time, and displays the Audio & Video Recording contextual tab of the ribbon. *(Recording...)* appears at the beginning of the page name in the program window title bar to indicate that you're currently recording an audio or video clip.

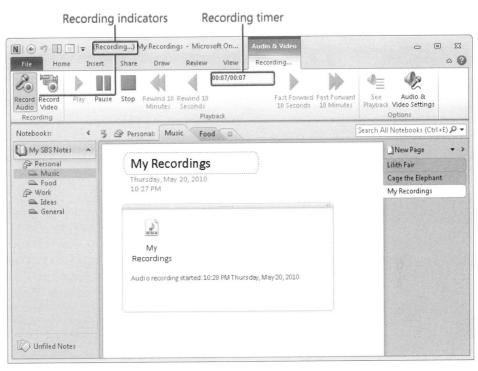

Recording indicators   Recording timer

You can pause a recording session.

4. Speak, sing, or otherwise deliver approximately 30 seconds of audio content. (Go ahead—take a chance on your favorite song!)

   As the recording progresses, the timer in the Playback group on the Recording tab indicates the length of the recording.

Stop

5. When you finish, click the **Stop** button in the **Playback** group on the **Recording** tab.

   Keyboard Shortcut Press Ctrl+Alt+S to stop the recording or playback of an audio or video clip.

   The Recording tab changes to the Playback tab.

6. Point to the **My Recordings** audio file icon.

   The note container becomes visible, and a Play button appears to the left of the note container. You can play a recording by clicking the Play button on the Playback tab or the Play button to the left of the note container.

7. Click the **Play** button.

Keyboard Shortcut Press Ctrl+Alt+P to play the most recently active audio or video recording on the page.

OneNote plays your audio recording. (If you can't hear it, check that your computer's speaker volume is turned up.) Additional commands for controlling the playback become active on the Playback tab.

You can skip backward and forward through a recording by clicking the Rewind and Fast Forward buttons.

8. On the **Playback** tab, in the **Playback** group, watch the progress of the timer. After the first 15 seconds of the recording, click the **Rewind 10 Seconds** button.

Keyboard Shortcuts Press Ctrl+Alt+Y to rewind the playback 10 seconds. Press Ctrl+Alt+U to fast forward the playback 10 seconds.

9. When the audio playback is finished, click the **Record Video** button in the **Recording** group on the **Playback** tab.

OneNote inserts a Windows Media Video (.wmv) file icon, a file name that matches the page name, and the recording start time. A video window opens on the page, displaying video captured by your webcam.

The recording controls for video recordings are the same as for audio recordings.

The Playback tab changes to the Recording tab, and *(Recording...)* appears at the beginning of the page name in the program window title bar.

10. Record a short video segment, and then click the **Pause** button.

    The picture in the video window freezes.

11. Click the **Pause** button again to restart the recording. Record another short video segment, and then click the **Stop** button.

12. On the **Playback** tab, in the **Playback** group, click the **Play** button to play your video recording.

    Note that there is no pause or transition between the two video segments you recorded.

CLEAN UP Retain the My Recordings page for future reference, if you want to, or delete it by right-clicking the page tab and then clicking Delete.

Missing the OneNote Icon?

If the OneNote icon does not appear in the notification area when the program is running, follow these steps to verify that the feature is turned on:

1. In the Backstage view, click Options.
2. In the left pane of the OneNote Options dialog box, click Display.
3. On the Display page, select the Place OneNote Icon In The Notification Area Of The Taskbar check box.
4. Click OK to close the dialog box and save your changes.

If the check box is selected and the icon still doesn't appear, follow these steps to verify that the icon is not hidden:

1. At the left end of the notification area of the status bar, click the Show Hidden Icons button, and then click Customize.
2. In the Notification Area Icons window of Control Panel, scroll down the Icons list to locate Microsoft OneNote Quick Launcher.
3. In the associated Behaviors list, click Show Icon And Notifications.

   The icon will now appear in the notification area at all times.

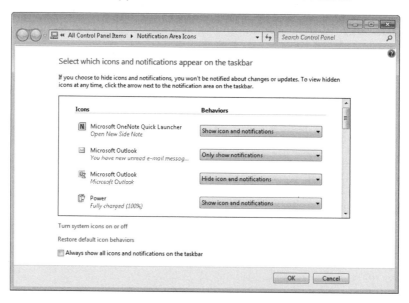

You can specify which icons appear in the notification area.

4. Click OK to close the dialog box and save your changes.

Taking Notes on the Side

It's not necessary to start OneNote each time you want to take notes or otherwise store information. You can also enter information into a Side Note—a simplified version of the OneNote program window. You can quickly open a Side Note by clicking the OneNote icon located in the notification area of the Windows Taskbar.

Keyboard Shortcut Press Ctrl+Shift+M to open a Side Note.

You can also open a Side Note from within the OneNote program window by clicking the New Side Note button, in the Window group, on the View tab.

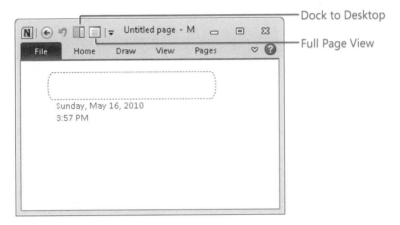

A standard Side Note is a minimized version of a OneNote page, with the Navigation Bar and Page Tabs area hidden, that displays a subset of the ribbon.

You can dock a Side Note to the desktop or display it in the full OneNote window by clicking the view buttons on the Quick Access Toolbar.

You work with content in a Side Note in the same way you work with it in the OneNote program window—because, in fact, that is precisely what you are doing. If you click the Full Page View button in the Side Note window (and then enlarge the window to provide perspective), you'll find yourself working on a page in the Unfiled Notes section.

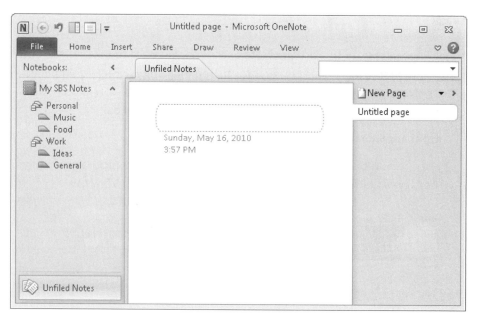

A new Side Note window is a page in the Unfiled Notes section; you can navigate to any notebook, section, or page from the Full Page view of the Side Note window.

The purpose of the Side Note window is to provide a small and easily accessible interface to OneNote. Because of the small size of the Side Note window, only a subset of the ribbon tabs may be visible at a time.

See Also For more information about the ribbon in OneNote, see "Working in the OneNote Program Window" and "Exploring OneNote in the Default Notebook" in Chapter 18, "Explore OneNote 2010."

When the Keep On Top button in the Window group on the View tab is active, you can position the Side Note in a convenient location on your screen, changing its size as necessary, and enter information as you want to. When the Side Note window is on top, it may get in the way of other windows, information, or commands that you might want to access, so you'll want to choose a location that doesn't interfere with your work. You can change the height or width of the window by dragging any side or corner of it.

Right-clicking the OneNote icon on the taskbar displays a list of options for collecting information.

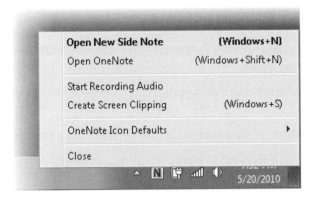

From the taskbar, you can start a variety of OneNote actions.

You can change the action that occurs when you click the OneNote icon to suit your needs. For example, if you frequently record audio, you might make that the default action. The available actions are Open New Side Note (the default), Open OneNote, Start Recording Audio, and Create Screen Clipping.

To change what happens when you click the OneNote icon:

● On the taskbar, right-click the OneNote icon, click OneNote Icon Defaults, and then click the action you want.

Collecting Information Outside of OneNote

You can collect information for use in OneNote when you're away from your primary computer by using either the OneNote Web App or OneNote Mobile 2010.

The OneNote Web App is part of the Office Web Apps, which are available through Windows Live. You can run the OneNote Web App in any Internet browser, on any computer; all you need is a Windows Live ID.

If you have a mobile device running Windows Mobile, such as a Windows phone, you can collect information by using OneNote Mobile 2010, which is available as part of Office Mobile 2010, and then synchronize data with a local or network notebook by using the built-in Microsoft ActiveSync software.

See Also For more information about the OneNote Web App, visit the Office Web Apps page at workspace.officelive.com/office-web-applications/. For more information about OneNote Mobile 2010, visit www.microsoft.com/office/2010/mobile/.

Key Points

- Notes are stored on a page in note containers. Each object within a note container can be manipulated separately.

- You can resize images inserted on a page and open file attachments directly from a page.

- You can use the OneNote writing tools to create handwritten notes and drawings.

- You can collect and store selected images of anything displayed on your screen by using the Screen Clipping tool.

- You can collect and store an entire Web page by using the Send To OneNote command on the Internet Explorer Tools menu.

- You can jot down quick notes without interfering with other program windows, by using Side Notes.

- You can display the OneNote icon in the notification area of the taskbar and choose the action that occurs when you click the icon.

Part 6

Microsoft Outlook 2010

Chapter at a Glance

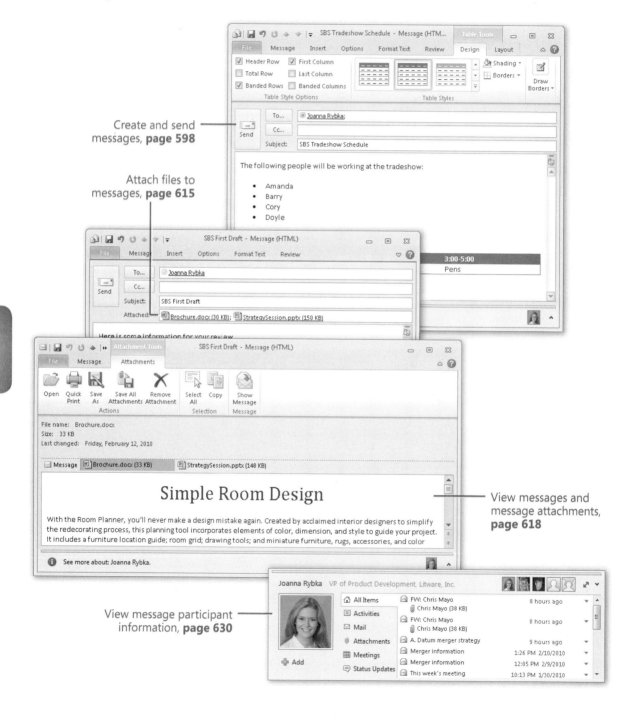

Create and send messages, **page 598**

Attach files to messages, **page 615**

View messages and message attachments, **page 618**

View message participant information, **page 630**

21 Send and Receive E-Mail Messages

In this chapter, you will learn how to

- ✔ Create and send messages.
- ✔ Attach files to messages.
- ✔ View messages and message attachments.
- ✔ Configure Reading Pane behavior.
- ✔ View message participant information.
- ✔ Respond to messages.

Although Microsoft Outlook 2010 helps you manage your calendar, contacts, tasks, and notes, the primary reason most people use Outlook is to send and receive e-mail messages. Over the past decade, e-mail (short for *electronic mail*) has become an accepted and even required form of business communication. And of course, many people use e-mail to keep in touch with friends and family, either from work or from home. Outlook makes it easy to connect to multiple e-mail accounts, either on a business network or over the Internet, and provides all the tools you need to send, respond to, organize, filter, sort, find, and otherwise manage e-mail messages.

Tip In this chapter and throughout this book, for expediency's sake, we sometimes refer to e-mail messages simply as *messages*. When referring to other types of messages we use full descriptions such as *instant messages* or *text messages*.

When sending messages from Outlook, you can format the text to suit your preferences, and include attachments such as documents, workbooks, and images. You can also personalize your message in these ways:

- ● Embed images, business graphics, and automatic signatures.
- ● Set message options such as voting buttons, importance, sensitivity, and reminders.
- ● Request electronic receipts when a message is delivered or opened.

See Also For information about Outlook 2010 features not covered in this book, refer to *Microsoft Outlook 2010 Step by Step* by Joan Lambert and Joyce Cox (Microsoft Press, 2010).

Outlook 2010 has several fancy new features that make it easy to display and track information about the people you correspond with. These features include presence icons that indicate whether a person is currently online, contact cards that appear when you point to a name in an e-mail message, and the People Pane at the bottom of the message window.

In this chapter, you'll create, send, and view messages, with and without attachments. You'll view information about message participants. Then you'll reply to and forward messages.

Practice Files Before you can complete the exercises in this chapter, you need to copy the book's practice files to your computer. The practice files you'll use to complete the exercises in this chapter are in the Chapter21 practice file folder. A complete list of practice files is provided in "Using the Practice Files" at the beginning of this book.

Important You'll use the messages you create in this chapter as practice files for exercises in later chapters of this book.

Creating and Sending Messages

Creating an e-mail message is a relatively simple process. The only information that is absolutely required is the recipient's e-mail address; however, you will usually provide information in the following fields:

● **To** Enter the e-mail address of the primary message recipient(s) in this field.

This is the only field that is absolutely required to send a message.

● **Subject** Enter a brief description of the message contents or purpose in this field.

The subject is not required, but it is important to provide information in this field, both so that you and the recipient can identify the message and so that the message isn't blocked as suspected junk mail by a recipient's e-mail program. Outlook will warn you if you try to send a message with no subject.

● **Message body** Enter your message to the recipient in this field, which is a large text box.

You can include many types of information including formatted text, hyperlinks, and graphics in the message body.

Addressing Messages

Addressing an e-mail message is as simple as inserting the intended recipient's e-mail address into an address box in the message header of a message composition window. You can enter e-mail recipients into any of three address boxes:

- **To** This address box is for primary message recipients. Usually, these are the people you want to respond to the message. Each message must have at least one address in the To box.

- **Cc** This address box is for "courtesy copy" recipients. These are usually people you want to keep informed about the subject of the e-mail message but from whom you don't require a response.

- **Bcc** This address box is for "blind courtesy copy" recipients. These are people you want to keep informed but whom you want to keep hidden from other message recipients. Bcc recipients are not visible to any other message recipients and therefore aren't included in message responses unless specifically added to one of the address boxes in the response message.

   Tip The Bcc address box is not displayed by default. You can display it in the message header by clicking the Bcc button, located in the Show Fields group on the Options tab of the message composition window.

You can insert an e-mail address into an address box in the following ways:

- Type the entire address.

- Type part of a previously used address and then select the address from a list.

- Click the address box label to display an address book from which you can select one or more addresses.

   See Also For information about address books, see "Saving and Updating Contact Information" in Chapter 22, "Store and Access Contact Information."

Tip Responding to a received message automatically fills in one or more of the address boxes in the new message window. For information, see "Responding to Messages" later in this chapter.

If your e-mail account is part of an Exchange network, you can send messages to another person on the same network by typing only his or her e-mail alias—for example, *joan*; the at symbol (@) and domain name aren't required. If you type only the name of a person whose e-mail address is in your address book, Outlook associates the name with the corresponding e-mail address, a process called *validating*, before sending the message.

Keyboard Shortcut Press Ctrl+K to force Outlook to validate addresses.

If you type only a name and Outlook cannot find that person's e-mail address in your address book, when you send the message, Outlook prompts you to select an address book entry or provide a full e-mail address.

Depending on how you enter a message recipient's name or e-mail address into an address box, Outlook either validates the name or address immediately (if you chose it from a list of known names) or validates it when you send the message. The validation process (also known as *resolving*) for each name or address has one of two results:

- If Outlook successfully resolves the name or address, an underline appears below it. If the name or address matches one stored in an address book, Outlook replaces your original entry with the content of the Display As field in the contact record, and then underlines it.

  See Also For information about contact record fields, see "Saving and Updating Contact Information" in Chapter 22, "Store and Access Contact Information."

- If Outlook is unable to resolve the name or address, the Check Names dialog box opens, asking you to provide additional information.

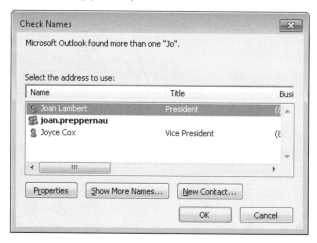

The Check Names dialog box might display No Suggestions, names that match the entry, or contact options saved in the contact record for the entered name.

In the Check Names dialog box, you can do one of the following:

- ○ Select from the suggested options.
- ○ Click Properties to learn more about the selected option.
- ○ Click Show More Names to display your address book.
- ○ Click New Contact to create a new contact record in your default address book, directly from the dialog box.

Troubleshooting Message Addressing

Outlook 2010 includes many features intended to simplify the process of addressing messages to recipients. As with any tool, these features can sometimes be more difficult to use than you'd like. In this section, we discuss troubleshooting tips for some common problems.

Troubleshooting the AutoComplete Address List

As you type a name or an e-mail address into the To, Cc, or Bcc box, Outlook displays matching addresses in a list below the box. You can insert a name or address from the list into the address box by clicking it or by pressing the arrow keys to select it and then pressing Tab or Enter.

From time to time, you might find that the address list contains incorrect e-mail addresses—for example, if you have previously sent a message to an incorrect e-mail address, or if a person changes his or her e-mail address. If you don't remove the incorrect address from the list, it can be easy to mistakenly accept Outlook's suggestion and send your message to the wrong address.

To clean up the AutoComplete Address list:

1. In the list, point to the name or address you want to remove.

2. Click the Delete button (the X) that appears to the right of the name or address.

Troubleshooting Multiple Recipients

By default, Outlook requires that you separate multiple e-mail addresses with semicolons. If you separate multiple addresses with another character such as a space or comma, or by pressing Enter, Outlook treats the addresses as one address and displays an error message when you attempt to send the message.

You can instruct Outlook to accept commas as address separators, in addition to semicolons. To do this, follow these steps:

1. In the Outlook program window or any item window, display the Backstage view, and then click Options.

2. In the left pane of the Outlook Options dialog box, click Mail.

3. On the Mail page, scroll to the Send Messages section.

4. Select the Commas Can Be Used To Separate Multiple Message Recipients check box, and then click OK.

Troubleshooting the Address Book

By default, Outlook first searches your Global Address List (the corporate directory provided with an Exchange account, if you're working with one), then searches the contact
records stored in the Contacts module of your default account and then searches the
Suggested Contacts list. If an e-mail address isn't located in one of those locations,
Outlook may search other address books such as those containing contact records
stored with secondary e-mail accounts or custom address books that you create.

If you have multiple address books, particularly multiple address books associated with
multiple accounts, Outlook does not, by default, search all of the address books and
therefore might not locate an e-mail address you have saved.

To change the order in which Outlook searches the address books, or to add address
books to the search list, follow these steps:

1. On the Home tab of the Outlook program window, in the Find group, click Address
   Book.

2. In the Address Book window, on the Tools menu, click Options.

   The Addressing dialog box opens.

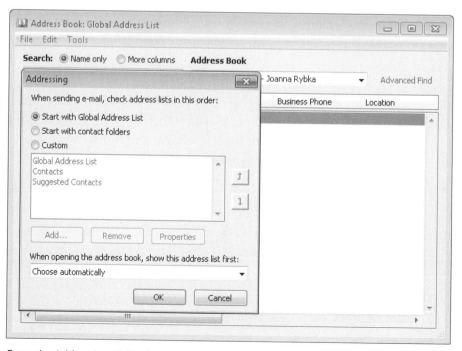

*From the Addressing dialog box, you can designate the order in which Outlook searches for
contacts in existing address books.*

3. In the Addressing dialog box, click Custom. Then do any of the following:

○ To search additional address books, click Add. Then in the Add Address List dialog box, click the address list you want to add, click Add, and click Close.

○ To change the order in which Outlook searches the address books in the list, click an address book and then click the Move Up or Move Down button.

○ If you're uncertain which address book is represented by a list entry, click the address book and then click Properties to display the account name and folder name of the address book.

4. In the Addressing dialog box, click OK, and then close the Address Book window.

Entering Content

As long as you have an Internet connection, you can send e-mail messages to people within your organization and around the world by using Outlook, regardless of the type of e-mail account you have. Outlook can send and receive e-mail messages in three message formats:

- **Hypertext Markup Language (HTML)** Supports paragraph styles (including numbered and bulleted lists), character styles (such as fonts, sizes, colors, weight), and backgrounds (such as colors and pictures). Most (but not all) e-mail programs support the HTML format—those that don't display HTML messages as Plain Text.

- **Rich Text Format (RTF)** Supports more paragraph formatting options than HTML, including borders and shading, but is compatible only with Outlook and Microsoft Exchange Server. Outlook converts RTF messages to HTML when sending them outside of an Exchange network.

- **Plain Text** Does not support the formatting features available in HTML and RTF messages but is supported by all e-mail programs.

E-mail message content isn't limited to simple text. You can create almost any type of content in an e-mail message that you can in a Word document. Because Outlook 2010 and Word 2010 share similar commands, you might already be familiar with processes for creating content such as lists and tables.

You can personalize your messages by using an individual font style or color and by inserting your contact information in the form of an e-mail signature or business card. (You can apply other formatting, such as themes and page backgrounds, but these won't always appear to e-mail recipients as you intend them to, and they can make your communications appear less professional.)

You can format the text of your message to make it more readable by including headings, lists, or tables, and you can represent information graphically by including charts, pictures, clip art, and other types of graphics. You can attach files to your message and link to other information, such as files or Web pages.

For the purposes of this book, we assume that you know how to enter, edit, and format content by using standard Microsoft Word techniques, so we don't discuss all of them in this book. We demonstrate many of these techniques within the step-by-step exercises, though, so keep an eye out for any new features that you aren't yet familiar with.

See Also For extensive information about entering and editing content and about formatting content by using character and paragraph styles, Quick Styles, and Themes, refer to *Microsoft Word 2010 Step by Step*, by Joyce Cox and Joan Lambert (Microsoft Press, 2010).

Tip You can also personalize a message by having Outlook add a predefined e-mail signature. You can specify different signatures for new messages and for replies and forwarded messages. For example, you might want to include your full name and contact information in the signature that appears in new messages, but only your first name in the signature that appears in replies and forwarded messages.

Saving and Sending Messages

At regular intervals while you're composing a message, Outlook saves a copy of the message in the Drafts folder. This is intended to protect you from losing messages that are in progress.

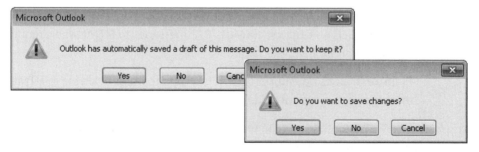

If you close a message composition window before sending the message, Outlook prompts you to save a draft or to save or discard the existing draft.

You can save a message draft at any time by clicking the Save button on the Quick Access Toolbar in the message window.

To resume working on a message that's been saved as a draft and closed, display the Mail module, click the Drafts folder in the Navigation Pane, and then double-click the message you want to work on.

After you finish composing a message, you can send it by clicking the Send button located in the message header or by pressing Ctrl+Enter. The first time you press this key combination, Outlook asks you to confirm that you want to designate this as the keyboard shortcut for sending messages.

When you send the message, Outlook deletes the message draft, if one exists, and stores a copy of the sent message in the Sent Items folder.

Tip Each account you access from Outlook has its own Drafts folder and its own Sent Items folder. Outlook automatically saves draft messages and sent messages in the folder affiliated with the e-mail account in which you compose or send the message.

You can change the location in which Outlook saves message drafts and sent messages from the Advanced E-mail Options dialog box.

In this exercise, you'll compose an e-mail message, save an interim message draft, and then send the message.

SET UP You don't need any practice files to complete this exercise. Display your Inbox, and then follow the steps.

1. On the **Home** tab, in the **New** group, click the **New E-mail** button.

    A new message window opens.

    Tip By clicking the New Items button, you can choose to create any type of Outlook item such as an appointment, contact, fax, message, note, or task, or an organizational item such as a contact group or data file, without leaving the module you're working in.

2. In the **To** box, type your own e-mail address.

3. In the **Subject** box, type **SBS Tradeshow Schedule**.

    Important The subject of this message begins with *SBS* (for *Step by Step*) so that you can easily differentiate it from other messages in your Inbox and Sent Items folders and can delete it later.

4. At the right end of the message window title bar, click the **Close** button.

    Outlook prompts you to save a message draft.

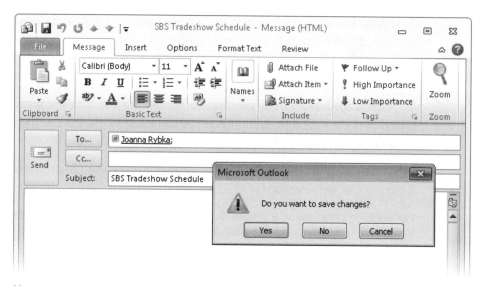

You can save a message that's in progress and return to it later.

Troubleshooting The appearance of buttons and groups on the ribbon changes depending on the width of the program window or item window. For information about changing the appearance of the ribbon to match our screen images, see "Modifying the Display of the Ribbon" at the beginning of this book.

5. In the **Microsoft Outlook** message box, click **Yes**.

    The message window closes. In the Navigation Pane, the number in the unread message counter to the right of the Drafts folder increases.

6. In the **Navigation Pane**, click the **Drafts** folder.

    Your message and its current content are in this folder.

A bold folder name indicates that the folder contains unread messages; the number of unread messages appears in parentheses to the right of the folder name.

7. In the **Mail** pane, double-click the message to open it for editing.

8. In the content pane, type **The following people will be working at the tradeshow:** and press the Enter key twice. Then type **Amanda**, **Barry**, **Cory**, and **Doyle**, pressing Enter once after each of the first three names, and twice after the fourth one.

The list of names is currently unformatted.

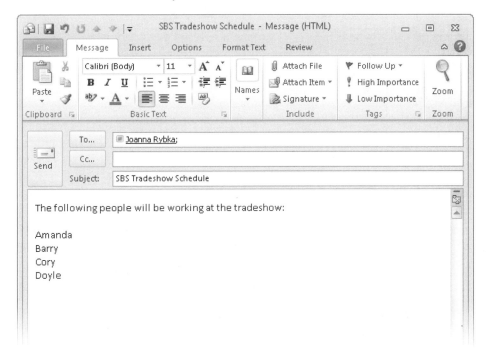

You enter text in a message the same way you do in a document.

9. Select the list of names. Then on the **Message** tab, in the **Basic Text** group, click the **Bullets** button (not its arrow).

Tip The Bullets button and other paragraph-formatting commands are also available in the Paragraph group on the Format Text tab.

Outlook converts the list of names to a simple bulleted list.

Tip In this book, when we give instructions to implement a command, we tell you on what tab and in which group the command button appears. When directing you to use multiple command buttons on the same tab, we might omit the tab name to avoid needless repetition.

10. With the bulleted list still selected, in the **Basic Text** group, click the **Bullets** arrow.

The Bullets gallery opens.

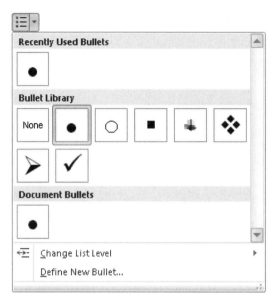

The Bullets gallery.

Notice the types of bullets available in the Bullet Library section of the gallery. You can change the list to use any of these bullets by clicking the bullet you want.

11. In the **Bullets** gallery, point to **Change List Level**.

    A menu illustrating bullets used by a multilevel list opens.

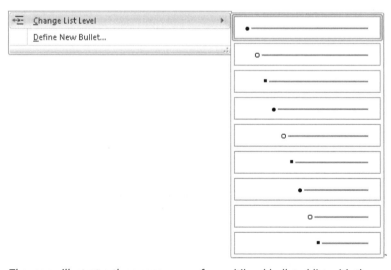

The menu illustrates the appearance of a multilevel bulleted list with the current settings.

You can demote (or promote) a list item to any of nine levels, differentiated by the bullet character and indent level.

12. Press Esc twice to close the **Bullets** gallery without making changes.

13. Press Ctrl+End to move the cursor to the end of the message. Type **Giveaways are:** and then press Enter twice.

14. On the **Insert** tab, in the **Tables** group, click the **Table** button.

    The Table gallery opens.

15. In the **Table** gallery, point to the third cell in the second row.

    A live preview of a three-column by two-row table appears at the cursor location in the message window.

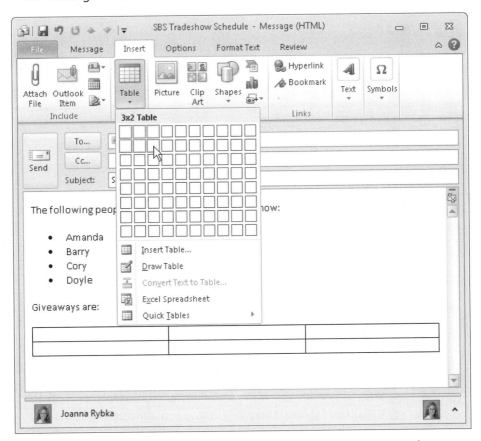

Outlook displays a preview of the effect of inserting a table with the current settings.

16. Click the selected cell to insert a three-column by two-row table in the message.

    The Table Tools contextual tabs, Design and Layout, appear on the Ribbon.

17. Enter the following information in the table, pressing Tab to move between table cells:

9:00-11:00	12:00-2:00	3:00-5:00
Mouse pads	**T-shirts**	**Pens**

The table and table content are currently unformatted.

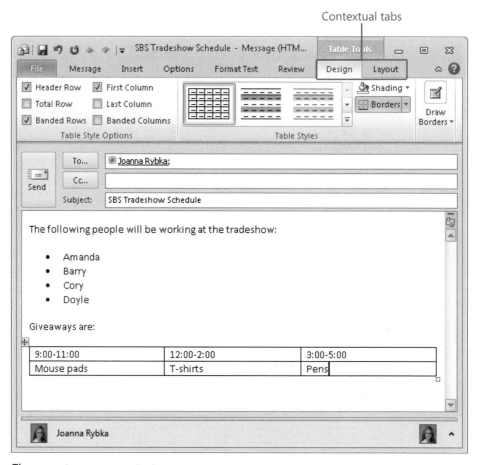

The current message content.

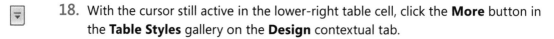

18. With the cursor still active in the lower-right table cell, click the **More** button in the **Table Styles** gallery on the **Design** contextual tab.

The Table Styles gallery opens. A box around the Plain Tables thumbnail indicates the formatting of the active table.

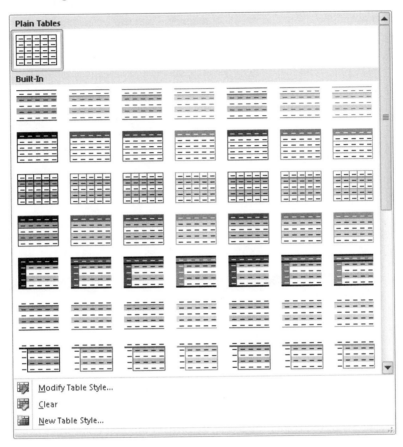

The Table Styles gallery.

19. In the **Built-In section** of the **Table Styles** gallery, point to the third thumbnail in the second row (the table with a red header row, identified by the ScreenTip *Light List – Accent 2*), and then click it.

Outlook displays a preview when you point to the thumbnail, and then applies the selected table style.

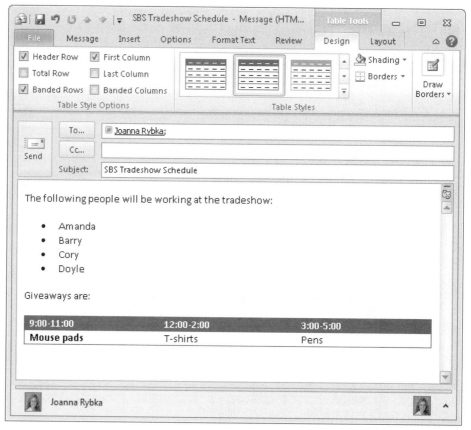

Applying a built-in table style.

Notice that the default table style formats the first column as bold.

20. On the **Design** tab, in the **Table Style Options** group, clear the **First Column** check box.

The content in the first row of the table is now bold, and the content of the second row is not.

21. In the message header, click the **Send** button.

Keyboard Shortcut Press Ctrl+Enter to send a message.

Outlook closes the message window and sends the message. The message draft disappears from the Drafts folder.

22. In the **Navigation Pane**, click the **Inbox** folder.

The received message is in this folder.

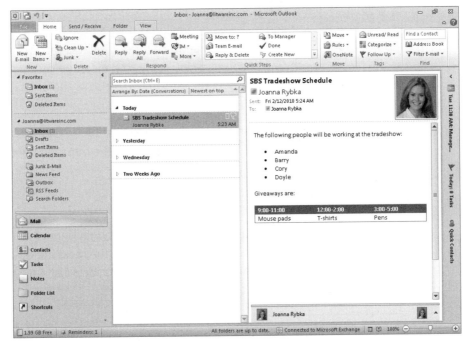

The formatted message content is shown in the Reading Pane.

Tip We're working with the To-Do Bar closed, so you can see more of the message content. To close the To-Do Bar in your Outlook program window, click the Minimize The To-Do Bar button in its upper-left corner.

23. In the **Navigation Pane**, click the **Sent Items** folder.

The sent message is in this folder.

CLEAN UP Display your Inbox. Retain the SBS Tradeshow Schedule message in your Inbox and Sent Items folders for use in later exercises.

Managing Multiple Accounts

If you have configured Outlook to connect to multiple e-mail accounts, you need to ensure that the message is being sent from the correct account.

By default, Outlook assumes that you intend to send a message from the account you're currently working in. If you begin composing a message while viewing the Inbox of your Work account, for example, Outlook selects the Work account as the message-sending account. If you reply to a message received by your Personal account, Outlook selects the Personal account as the message-sending account.

You can easily change the message-sending account. When Outlook is configured to use multiple accounts, a From button appears in the message header.

Tip If Outlook is configured to connect to only one account, you can display the From button by clicking From in the Show Fields group on the Options tab of a message composition window.

Clicking the From button displays a list of active accounts from which you can choose. If the account from which you want to send the message doesn't appear in the list, you can specify another account; however, you must have permission to send messages from that account.

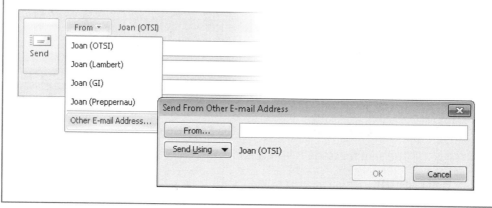

Attaching Files to Messages

A convenient way to distribute a file (such as a Microsoft Word document, Excel work-book, PowerPoint presentation, or picture) is by attaching the file to an e-mail message. Message recipients can preview or open the file from the Reading Pane, open it from the message window, forward it to other people, or save it to their computers.

Tip You can also e-mail Microsoft Office files from within the Office program you're working in, by using commands in the Backstage view.

For example, to send a Word document, open the document, display the Backstage view, click the Save & Send tab, and then click Send Using E-mail. Word offers the options of sending the document as an attached Word document, PDF file, or XPS file (Word converts the file for you before sending it), sending a link to the document (if it's saved in a shared location), or sending the document to a fax machine.

In this exercise, you'll send a Word document and a PowerPoint presentation as attachments to an e-mail message.

SET UP You need the Brochure document and the StrategySession presentation located in the Chapter21 practice file folder to complete this exercise. Display your Inbox, and then follow the steps.

1. On the **Home** tab, in the **New** group, click the **New E-mail** button.

2. In the **To** box of the new message window, type your own e-mail address.

   Tip If you completed the previous exercise, Outlook displays your e-mail address in a list as you begin typing. You can insert the address by clicking it or by pressing the Down Arrow key to select it (if necessary) and then pressing Enter.

3. In the **Subject** box, type **SBS First Draft**.

4. In the content pane, type **Here is some information for your review.** Then press Enter to move to the next line.

5. On the **Message** tab, in the **Include** group, click the **Attach File** button.

   Tip The Attach File button is also available in the Include group on the Insert tab.

   The Insert File dialog box opens, displaying the contents of your Documents library.

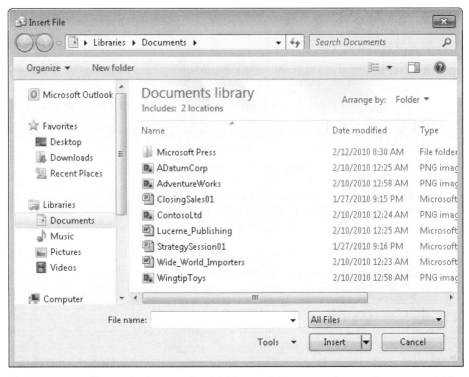

The Documents library displays top-level folders and files stored in your Documents folder and in the Public Documents folder.

Tip Your Insert File dialog box will reflect the contents of your own Documents library.

6. Navigate to your **Chapter21** practice file folder. In the **Chapter21** folder, click the **Brochure** document, hold down the Ctrl key, click the **StrategySession** presentation, and then click **Insert**.

The files appear in the Attached box in the message header.

Information about file attachments is visible to the sender and to the recipient.

7. In the message header, click the **Send** button.

Outlook closes the message window and sends the message.

 CLEAN UP When you receive the SBS First Draft message in your Inbox, retain it for use in later exercises.

Tip If you want to send personalized copies of the same e-mail message to several people, you can use the mail merge feature of Word 2010. For more information, refer to *Microsoft Word 2010 Step by Step* by Joyce Cox and Joan Lambert (Microsoft Press, 2010).

Troubleshooting File Types and Extensions

By default, Windows does not display file extensions in Explorer windows or dialog boxes such as the Insert File dialog box. You can usually differentiate file types by their icons—for example, the blue Word icon precedes the Brochure document name, and the red PowerPoint icon precedes the StrategySession presentation name.

You can display the file type as a field in specific views or as part of all file names.

- In a dialog box or Windows Explorer window, you can display the file type by clicking the Change Your View arrow on the toolbar and then clicking either Details or Tiles; each of these views includes the Type field.

- To display file extensions as part of all file names, click Organize on the toolbar of any Windows Explorer window, and then click Folder And Search Options. On the View tab of the Folder Options dialog box, clear the Hide Extensions For Known File Types check box, and then click Apply or OK.

Tip Many picture files are large, requiring a lot of bandwidth to send and a lot of storage space to receive. Instead of opening a message and then attaching a full-size picture file to it, you can send and simultaneously resize a picture by right-clicking the picture file in Windows Explorer, clicking Send To, and then clicking Mail Recipient. In the Attach Files dialog box that appears, choose from among five picture size options; the corresponding file size appears when you select a picture size. Then click Attach to open a message window in your default e-mail program.

Viewing Messages and Message Attachments

Each time you start Outlook and connect to your e-mail server, any new messages received since the last time you connected appear in your Inbox. Depending on your settings, Outlook downloads either the entire message to your computer or only the message header, which provides basic information about the message, such as:

- The item type (message, meeting request, task assignment, and so on)
- Who sent it
- When you received it
- The subject

Icons displayed in the message header indicate optional information such as:

- The most recent response action taken
- Whether files are attached
- If it has been digitally signed or encrypted
- If the sender marked it as being of high or low importance

The message header and icons provide information about the message.

There are three standard views of the message list:

- **Compact** The default view, which displays two lines of message properties, including the read status, subject, sender, time received, whether files are attached to the message, and any color categories or follow-up flags associated with the message.

- **Single** This one-line view displays the importance, reminder, item type or read status, whether files are attached to the message, sender, subject, received, size, category, and follow-up flags. The Reading Pane is open by default in this view.

- **Preview** This view displays from one to four lines of information about each message. For every message, Preview view displays the same information as Single view. For each unread message, Preview view also displays a part of the message content—specifically, the first 255 characters (including spaces). If a message contains fewer than 255 characters, <end> appears in the preview text. The Reading Pane is closed by default in this view.

These three standard views are available from the Change View gallery on the View tab.

Messages that you haven't yet read are indicated by closed envelope icons and bold headers. When you open a message, Outlook indicates that you have read it by changing the message icon from a closed envelope to an open envelope and changing the header font in the message list from bold to normal.

You can view the text of a message in several ways:

- You can open a message in its own window by double-clicking its header in the message list.

- You can read a message without opening it by clicking its header once in the message list to display the message in the Reading Pane.

- You can display the first three lines of each unread message under the message header by using the Preview feature. Scanning the first three lines of a message frequently gives you enough information to make basic decisions about how to manage it. The only drawback is that in Preview view, each unread message takes up five lines rather than the two lines in the default Messages view, so fewer messages are visible on your screen at one time.

You can view message attachments in several ways:

● You can preview certain types of attachments (including Excel spreadsheets, PowerPoint slideshows, Word documents, and Portable Document Format (PDF) files) directly in the Reading Pane by clicking the attachment in the message header.

   When you click the attachment, the message text is replaced by a preview of the attachment contents, and the Attachments contextual tab appears on the ribbon.

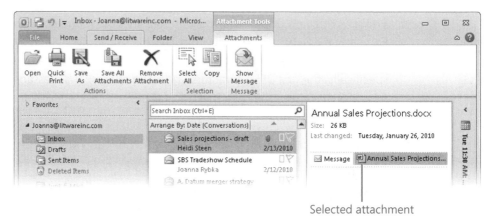

Selected attachment

From the Attachments tab, you can work with the attachment or toggle between the message content and attachment preview.

Tip You can turn off the Attachment Preview feature from the Attachment Handling page of the Trust Center window, which you open from the Outlook Options dialog box.

● You can open the attachment from the Reading Pane or from an open message window by double-clicking the attachment in the message header.

● You can save the attachment to your hard disk and open it from there. This strategy is recommended if you suspect an attachment might contain a virus because you can scan the file for viruses before opening it (provided that you have a virus scanning program installed).

See Also For information about protecting your computer from viruses, refer to *Windows 7 Step by Step* (Microsoft Press, 2009) or *Windows Vista Step by Step*, (Microsoft Press, 2007), both by Joan Lambert Preppernau and Joyce Cox.

If you receive a contact record or business card as a message attachment, you can add it to your primary address book by dragging the attachment from the e-mail message to the Contacts button in the Navigation Pane. To add the contact record to a secondary address book, expand the folder structure in the Navigation Pane and drag the attachment to that folder.

If you want to concentrate on reading messages without the distraction of other information typically presented in the Outlook program window, you can quickly reconfigure the program window to optimize message reading by clicking the Reading View button on the status bar, to the left of the zoom controls.

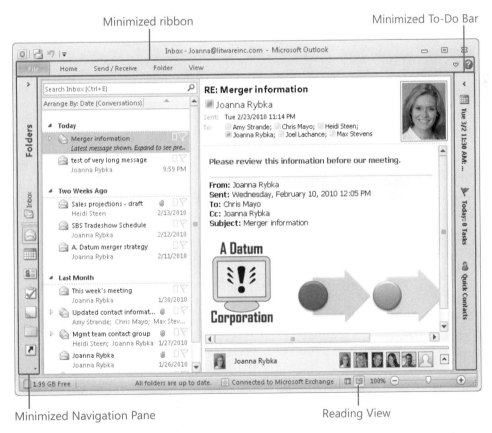

In Reading view, the Navigation Pane, To-Do Bar, and ribbon are hidden to maximize the size of the Reading Pane.

In this exercise, you'll preview and open a message and two types of attachments.

SET UP You need the SBS First Draft message you created earlier in this chapter to complete this exercise. If you did not create that message, you can do so now, or you can substitute any received message with an attachment in your Inbox. Display your Inbox, and then follow the steps.

1. On the **View** tab, in the **Current View** group, click the **Change View** button, and then click **Preview**.

   Troubleshooting If the Preview icon on the Change View menu is shaded, this feature is already turned on.

   The Reading Pane closes, and the first 255 characters of each message appear in the Inbox below the message header.

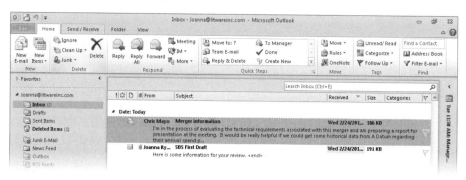

Preview view displays the first 255 characters of each unread message.

2. On the **View** tab, in the **Change View** list, click **Single**.

   The preview text disappears, and the Reading Pane reopens.

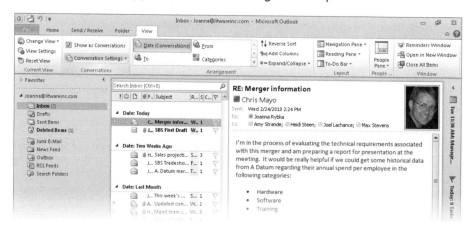

3. Locate the **SBS First Draft** message in your Inbox, and then click the message.

   Outlook displays the message in the Reading Pane. Below the message header area, the Reading Pane displays a Message button (which looks rather more like just the word Message than it does like a button) and the names of the attached files (Brochure.docx and StrategySession.pptx).

4. In the **Reading Pane**, point to (don't click) the **Message** button below the message header.

   Troubleshooting If you are working through this exercise with a message that does not have an attachment, the header does not include a Message button.

   A ScreenTip displays the total number of attachments.

   Message button

   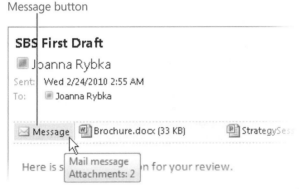

   Pointing to the Message button displays information about attached files.

   Tip If more files are attached than can be seen in the message header, you can use the scroll bar at the right end of the Attachments box to see them all.

5. Point to the **Brochure.docx** attachment.

   A ScreenTip displays the name, type, and size of the attached file.

   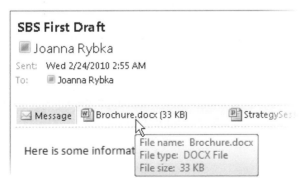

   Pointing to an attached file displays information about the file.

6. Click the **Brochure.docx** attachment once.

The Attachments contextual tab appears on the ribbon, and the fully formatted Word 2010 document appears in the Reading Pane.

The message header changes to display properties of the attached file.

You can scroll through the entire document within this pane, without starting Word.

Tip Clicking certain types of attachments displays an interim warning message in the Reading Pane, rather than immediately displaying the attached file's content. After reading the message, you can click Preview File to display the usual file preview.

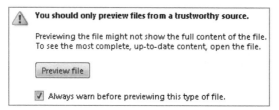

You can give Outlook permission to display previews of a specific type of file by clearing the Always Warn Before Previewing This Type Of File check box before clicking Preview File.

7. Click the **StrategySession.pptx** attachment.

Word starts the PowerPoint previewer and displays the title slide of the presentation in the Reading Pane. You can move among the presentation's slides by clicking the Previous Slide and Next Slide buttons in the lower-right corner of the pane.

8. In the lower-right corner of the Reading Pane, click the **Next Slide** button.

   The presentation transitions to the second slide, exactly as it would if you were displaying the slide show in PowerPoint. The slide currently displays only a title.

9. At the bottom of the vertical scroll bar, click the **Next** button once.

   An animated graphic appears on the slide. The animation works in the Reading Pane the same way it would within the PowerPoint program window.

When previewing a PowerPoint presentation, you can navigate through the presentation by using the scroll bar and the controls in the lower-right corner of the Reading Pane or by using the scroll wheel on the mouse.

10. In the **Reading Pane**, click the **Message** button (or, in the **Message** group on the **Attachments** tab, click **Show Message**).

    The message text reappears in the Reading Pane.

11. In the **Reading Pane**, double-click the **StrategySession.pptx** attachment (or, in the **Actions** group on the **Attachments** tab, click **Open**).

PowerPoint 2010 starts and opens the presentation, which is titled *The Master Plan*.

See Also For an introduction to the features of PowerPoint 2010, refer to *Microsoft PowerPoint 2010 Step by Step* by Joyce Cox and Joan Lambert (Microsoft Press, 2010).

12. Close the presentation to return to your Inbox.

13. In the message list, double-click the **SBS First Draft** message.

The message opens in its own window. The Message button and attachments are shown below the message header in the message window, as they are in the Reading Pane.

14. In the **Attachments** area below the message header, click the **Brochure.docx** attachment once.

The Attachments contextual tab appears on the ribbon, and a preview of the document appears in the message content pane exactly as it did in the Reading Pane.

You use the same techniques to preview and open attachments from the message window that you do from the Reading Pane.

 CLEAN UP Close the SBS First Draft message window, and retain it in your Inbox for use in later exercises. Then reset the program window to its default view by clicking Compact in the Change View gallery.

Viewing Conversations

Conversation view was first introduced in Outlook 2007 as a way of viewing in one place a series of received messages that stem from the same original message. This feature made it easy to locate various responses to a message and to identify separate branches of a conversation (referred to as *message threads*).

In Outlook 2010, the original Conversation view has been expanded to present an even clearer method of tracking message threads and to include not only received messages but also sent messages. Conversation view is considered such a useful organizational tool that it is designated as the default view of the Inbox and other message folders.

Except when discussing alternative views of messages, the graphics in this book depict messages arranged in Conversation view. A conversation of multiple messages is indicated by an arrow to the left of the conversation message header.

Configuring Reading Pane Behavior

You will frequently read and work with messages and other Outlook items in the Reading Pane. You can display the Reading Pane to the right of or below the module content pane.

Viewing Reading Pane Content

You might find it difficult to read the text in the Reading Pane at its default size, particularly if your display is set to a high screen resolution, as is becoming more and more common. You can change the size of the content displayed in the Reading Pane by using the Zoom controls located at the right end of the program window status bar to change the pane's magnification level.

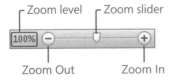

In the program window, the Zoom controls change the size of the content in the Reading Pane.

You can change the magnification of the Reading Pane contents in the following ways:

● To set a specific magnification level, click the Zoom Level button to open the Zoom dialog box.

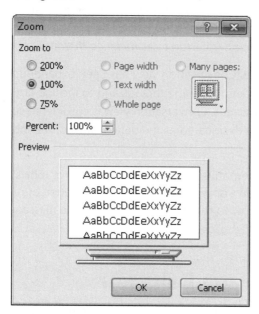

Select one of the three predefined magnification levels, or select or type a specific magnification level in the Percent box.

● To change the zoom level in 10 percent increments, click the Zoom Out and Zoom In buttons.

● To quickly change the zoom level to any setting between 10 percent and 500 percent, move the Zoom slider to the left or right.

Marking Messages as Read

By default, Outlook does not change the read status of a message when you preview it in the Reading Pane. If you commonly read your messages in the Reading Pane rather than opening them in message windows, you can keep better track of read and unread messages by changing the default setting.

To instruct Outlook to mark a message as read after you have previewed it in the Reading Pane:

1. Display the Backstage view, and then click Options.

2. On the Mail page of the Outlook Options dialog box, in the Outlook Panes area, click Reading Pane.

The Reading Pane dialog box opens.

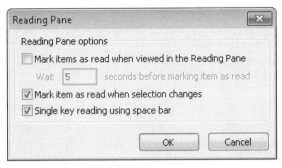

You can configure the way Outlook handles messages displayed in the Reading Pane.

3. In the Reading Pane dialog box, select the check box corresponding to the way you want Outlook to handle messages you view in the Reading Pane.

○ **Mark items as read when viewed in the Reading Pane** Outlook will mark the item as read after it has been displayed in the Reading Pane for five seconds or an alternative amount of time (up to 999 seconds) that you specify.

○ **Mark item as read when selection changes** Outlook will mark the item as read when you select another item.

4. Click OK in the Reading Pane dialog box and in the Outlook Options dialog box.

Single Key Reading

You can scroll through a long message in the Reading Pane in the following ways:

● Scroll at your own pace by dragging the vertical scroll bar that appears at the right side of the Reading Pane.

● Move up or down one line at a time by clicking the scroll arrows.

● Move up or down one page at time by clicking above or below the scroll box.

● Move up or down one page at a time by pressing the Spacebar. When you reach the end of a message by using this feature, called Single Key Reading, pressing the Spacebar again displays the first page of the next message. This option is very convenient if you want to read through several consecutive messages in the Reading Pane, or if you find it easier to press the Spacebar than to use the mouse.

Tip Single Key Reading is turned on by default. If you find it distracting, you can turn it off by clearing the Single Key Reading Using Space Bar check box in the Reading Pane dialog box.

Viewing Message Participant Information

After you receive a message (or after Outlook validates a recipient's name in a message that you're sending), you can easily display contact information and a history of your communications with that person.

Presence Icons

If presence information is available, a square presence icon appears to the left of each message participant's name. The presence icon (more casually referred to as a *jelly bean*) is color-coded to indicate the availability or online status of the message participant, as follows:

- Green indicates that the message recipient is available.
- Red indicates that the message recipient is busy.
- Orange indicates that the message recipient is away.
- White indicates that the message recipient is offline.

Tip This set of presence icons is used in Outlook, Windows Live Messenger, and Microsoft Office Communicator to provide a consistent user experience.

Depending on the environment, Outlook uses presence information from Office Communications Server or from Windows Live Messenger.

Contact Cards

Pointing to a presence icon displays an interactive contact card of information that includes options for contacting the person by e-mail, instant message, or telephone; for scheduling a meeting; and for working with the person's contact record.

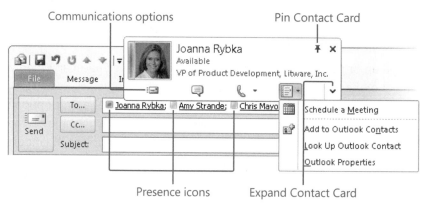

Pinning the contact card keeps it open even if you send or close the e-mail message.

Clicking the Expand Contact Card button displays a more extensive range of information and interaction options.

Place a telephone call

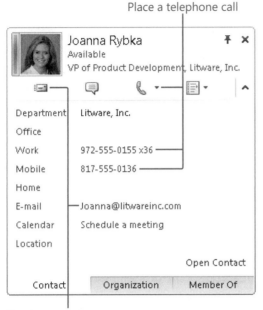

Send an e-mail message

From the expanded contact card, you can view the contact's position within the organization and which distribution lists he or she is a member of.

Tip A distribution list is a membership group created through Exchange and available from an organization's Global Address List. You can't create distribution lists, but you can create contact groups, which are membership groups saved in the Outlook Contacts module.

Clicking any of the blue links initiates contact with the person through the stored telephone number or e-mail address, initiates a meeting request, or, if the person is in your address book, opens his or her contact record.

When available, the Organization tab displays information about the contact's manager and direct reports. The Member Of tab displays information about distribution lists the contact is a member of. This information is available only for Exchange accounts.

The People Pane

The People Pane at the bottom of the message window displays extensive information about your previous communications with each message participant.

In its collapsed state, the People Pane displays small thumbnails representing each message participant. If a person's contact record includes a photograph, the photo appears in the People Pane. If no photograph is available, a silhouette of one person represents an individual message participant, and a silhouette of three people represents a distribution list.

Resizing bar

Distribution group

Contact without associated picture

The collapsed People Pane.

You can expand the People Pane either by clicking the Expand button at the right end of the pane or by dragging the horizontal bar that appears at the top of the pane. The People Pane can occupy only a certain percentage of the message window, so the amount you can manually adjust the height of the People Pane is dependent on the height of the message window.

In its expanded state, the People Pane displays either large thumbnails or a tabbed breakdown of communications for each message participant.

Toggle button

Click on a photo to see social network updates and email messages from this person.

| Chris Mayo | Amy Strande | Heidi Steen | Joan Lambert |
| Chief Technical Officer | Director of Marketing | Account Manager | VP of Product Develop... |

Scroll to view additional message participants

The simple view of the expanded People Pane.

You can switch between the simple view and the detailed view by clicking the Toggle button located near the right end of the expanded People Pane header.

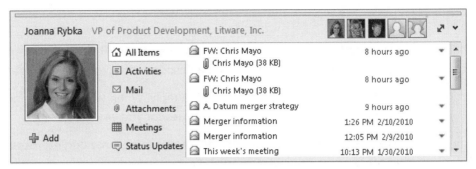

The detailed view of the expanded People Pane for messages in an Exchange account. Click Add to set up a connection from Outlook to an online social network.

The All Items tab of the detailed view displays all your recent communications with the selected person. If you're looking for a specific item, such as a meeting request or a document attached to a message, you can filter the item list by clicking any of the tabs to the left of the list.

Tip The detailed People Pane is available for all types of e-mail accounts. The images in this book depict the People Pane for an Exchange account. The People Pane for a POP3 account is identical except that the tabs are labeled with icons only rather than icons and words.

Troubleshooting the People Pane

When working with an Exchange account, you can display the People Pane in detailed view only if the Cached Exchange Mode feature is enabled. If the Toggle button isn't visible in the expanded People Pane when you're viewing an Exchange account message, the likely problem is that Cached Exchange Mode is not enabled.

To enable Cached Exchange Mode, follow these steps:

1. In the Backstage view of the Outlook program window, click Account Settings, and then in the list that appears, click Account Settings.

2. On the E-mail page of the Account Settings dialog box, click your Exchange account, and then click Change.

3. On the Server Settings page of the Change Account wizard, select the Use Cached Exchange Mode check box, click Next, and then on the wizard's final page, click Finish.

The Toggle button should now be visible in the header of the expanded People Pane.

Responding to Messages

You can respond to most e-mail messages that you receive by clicking a response button either within the message window or in the Respond group on the Message tab.

The most standard response to a message is a reply. When you reply to a message, Outlook fills in one or more of the address boxes for you, as follows:

- **Reply** Creates an e-mail message, addressed to only the original message sender, that contains the original message text.

- **Reply All** Creates an e-mail message, addressed to the message sender and all recipients listed in the To and Cc boxes, that contains the original message text. The message is not addressed to recipients of blind courtesy copies (Bcc recipients).

- **Reply with Meeting** Creates a meeting invitation addressed to all message recipients. The message text is included in the meeting window content pane. Outlook suggests the current date and an upcoming half-hour time slot for the meeting.

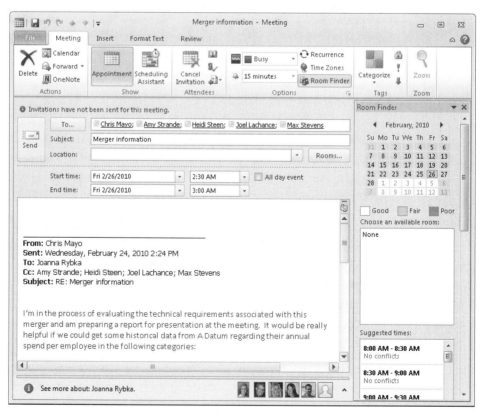

A meeting invitation created from a message.

Message replies include the original message header and text, preceded by a space in which you can respond. Replies do not include any attachments from the original message.

You can add, change, and delete recipients from any reply before sending it.

You can forward a received message to any e-mail address (regardless of whether the recipient uses Outlook) provided the message was not sent with restricted permissions. Outlook 2010 has the following message-forwarding options:

● **Forward** Creates a new message that contains the text of the original message and retains any attachments from the original message.

● **Forward As Attachment** Creates a blank message that contains no text but includes the original message as an attachment. The original message text and any attachments are available to the new recipient when he or she opens the attached message.

● **Forward As Text Message** Creates a text message to be sent by an SMS text messaging account to a mobile device, such as a mobile phone or a Windows Phone.

> **Troubleshooting** The Forward As Text Message response option works only if you have access to an SMS account.

Forwarded messages include the original message header and text, preceded by a space in which you can add information. Forwarded messages include attachments from the original message.

When you forward a message, Outlook does not fill in the recipient boxes for you (the assumption being that you want to forward the message to someone who wasn't included on the original message).

If you reply to or forward a received message from within the message window, the original message remains open after you send your response. You can instruct Outlook to close original messages after you respond to them—you'll probably be finished working with the message at that point. To do so, display the Mail page of the Outlook Options dialog box, select the Close Original Message Window When Replying Or Forwarding check box in the Replies And Forwards area, and then click OK.

> **Tip** When responding to an e-mail message, take care to use good e-mail etiquette. For example, if your response is not pertinent to all the original recipients of a message, don't reply to the entire recipient list, especially if the message was addressed to a distribution list that might include hundreds of members.

You can prevent other people from replying to all recipients of a message you send by addressing the message to yourself and entering other recipients in the Bcc box. Then the recipient list will not be visible to anyone.

If your organization runs Office Communications Server, you may also have these additional response options:

● **Call** Uses the telephone calling functionality of Office Communicator to place Voice Over IP (VOIP) calls from your computer, over the Internet, to the telephone number of the original message sender.

● **Call All** Uses the telephone calling functionality of Office Communicator to initiate a VOIP conference call to the telephone numbers of the original message sender and other message recipients.

● **Reply With IM or Reply All With IM** Opens an Office Communicator chat window with the original message subject as its title and the message sender or sender and recipients as the chat participants.

An Office Communicator IM session created from a message.

Troubleshooting The response options available in your Outlook installation might vary from those described here. The available response options always feature prominently on the main ribbon tab in the item window.

Nonstandard messages have alternative response options, such as the following:

- A meeting request includes options for responding to the request.

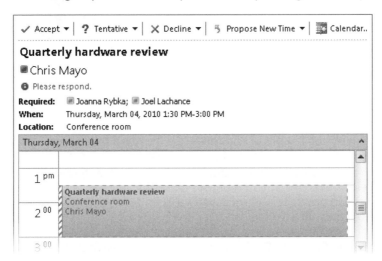

Responding to a meeting request from the Reading Pane.

See Also For information about meeting requests, see "Scheduling Meetings" in Chapter 23, "Manage Scheduling."

- A task assignment includes options for accepting or declining the assignment.

Responding to a task assignment from the Reading Pane.

See Also For information about task assignments, see "Managing Task Assignments" in Chapter 24, "Track Tasks."

- If a message contains voting buttons, you can respond by opening the message, clicking the Vote button in the Respond group on the Message tab, and then clicking the response you want to send. Or you can click the Info bar (labeled *Click here to vote*) in the Reading Pane and then click the response you want.

What color should the new logo be?

Heidi Steen

🛈 Click here to vote.

		Vote: Red
Sent:	Fri 2/26/2010 1	
To:	Amy Strande	Vote: Purple	Steen; Joanna Rybka;
	Joel Lachanc	Vote: Gold

We have narrowed the choice down to three colors. Please indicate your preference by voting.

Voting from the Reading Pane.

In this exercise, you'll reply to and forward a message that has an attachment.

SET UP You need the SBS First Draft message you created earlier in this chapter to complete this exercise. If you did not create that message, you can do so now, or you can substitute any received message with an attachment in your Inbox. Display your Inbox, and then follow the steps.

1. Open the **SBS First Draft** message in a message window.

   The message includes two attachments. The message window ribbon displays only the Message tab containing all the commands you use with a received message.

Reply

2. On the **Message** tab, in the **Respond** group, click the **Reply** button.

   Outlook creates a response, already addressed to you (the original sender). If the message had been sent to any other people, the reply would not include them.

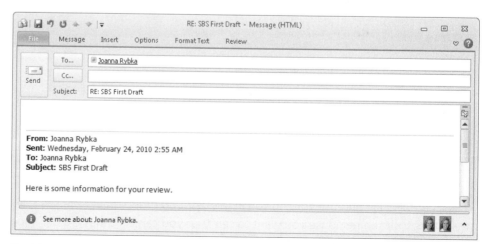

Replying to a message generates a new message addressed to the original sender.

The *RE:* prefix appears at the beginning of the message subject to indicate that this is a response to an earlier message. Note that the response does not include the original attachments (and in fact there is no indication that the original message had any). The original message, including its header information, appears in the content pane separated from the new content by a horizontal line.

3. With the cursor at the top of the content pane, type the following sentence:

   We'll need to get approval from the Marketing team before proceeding.

4. In the response header, click the **Send** button.

   Outlook sends your reply, which appears in your Inbox as the active message in the SBS First Draft conversation. The original message remains open on your screen.

5. In the original message, in the **Respond** group, click the **Forward** button.

   Troubleshooting If the original message closes, select the message in your Inbox and then click the Forward button in the Respond group on the Home tab.

   Outlook creates a new version of the message that is not addressed to any recipient. The *FW:* prefix at the beginning of the message subject indicates that this is a forwarded message. The files that were attached to the original message appear in the Attached box. The message is otherwise identical to the earlier response.

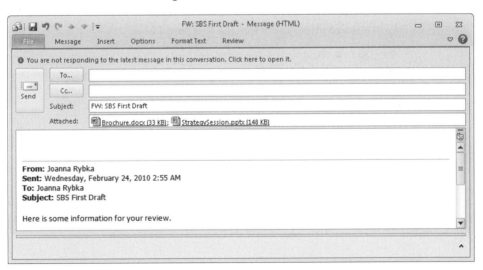

The MailTip at the top of the message header indicates that another message (your response) has been added to the conversation, so the message you're forwarding isn't technically the most current.

You address and send a forwarded message as you would any other.

6. In the **To** box, enter your e-mail address.

7. Click to position the cursor at the top of the content pane, and then type the following sentence:

   Don't forget to review these!

8. Send the message, and then close the original message window.

9. When the second message appears in your Inbox, compare the two messages and note the similarities and differences.

   For example, the Subject prefixes are different, and the forwarded message includes the original message attachments.

 **CLEAN UP** Close any open message windows. Retain the SBS First Draft conversation for use in later exercises.

Key Points

- You can easily create e-mail messages that include attachments.
- By default, messages you receive appear in your Inbox.
- You can see the first few lines of each message in Preview view, open a message in its own window, or preview messages in the Reading Pane. You can preview message attachments in the Reading Pane.
- You can reply to the message sender only or to the sender and all other recipients. You can also forward a message and its attachments to other people.

Resending and Recalling Messages

If you want to send a new version of a message you've already sent—for example, a status report in which you update details each week—you can *resend* the message. Resending a message creates a new version of the message with none of the extra information that might be attached to a forwarded message. To resend a message, follow these steps:

1. From your Sent Items folder, open the message you want to resend. (Or, if you copied yourself on the message, you can open it from your Inbox.)

2. On the Message tab, in the Actions group, click the Other Actions button, and then in the list, click Resend This Message.

Outlook creates a new message form identical to the original. If you want, you can change the message recipients, subject, attachments, or content before sending the new message.

If, after sending a message, you realize that you shouldn't have sent it—for example, if the message contained an error or was sent to the wrong people—you can *recall* it by instructing Outlook to delete or replace any unread copies of the message. To recall a message, follow these steps:

1. From your Sent Items folder, open the message you want to recall.

2. On the Message tab, in the Actions group, click the Other Actions button, and then click Recall This Message.

3. In the Recall This Message dialog box, click the option to delete unread copies of the message or the option to replace unread copies with a new message, and then click OK.

Message recall is available only for Exchange Server accounts.

Troubleshooting You may want to test the message recall functionality within your organization before you have occasion to need it for an important recall. Quite frequently, the message recall feature can result in a received message being flagged as Recalled, but remaining in the recipient's Inbox.

Chapter at a Glance

Save and update contact information, **page 644**

Display different views of contact records, **page 659**

Print contact records, **page 667**

22 Store and Access Contact Information

In this chapter, you will learn how to

- ✔ Save and update contact information.
- ✔ Communicate with contacts.
- ✔ Display different views of contact records.
- ✔ Print contact records.

Having immediate access to current, accurate contact information for the people you need to interact with—by e-mail, telephone, mail, or otherwise—is important for timely and effective communication. You can easily build and maintain a detailed contact list, or address book, in the Microsoft Outlook 2010 Contacts module. From your address book, you can look up information, create messages, and share contact information with other people. You can also keep track of your interactions with a person whose contact information is stored in Outlook.

If you need to take contact information with you in a non-electronic format, you can print an address book or selected contact records, in many different formats.

In this chapter, you'll create and edit contact records and view them in different ways. Then you'll print a contact record and a list of contact information.

> **Practice Files** You don't need any practice files to complete the exercises in this chapter. For more information about practice file requirements, see "Using the Practice Files" at the beginning of this book.

Saving and Updating Contact Information

You save contact information for people and companies by creating a contact record in an address book.

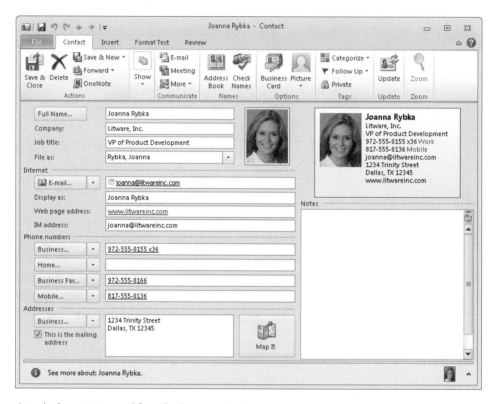

A typical contact record for a business contact.

Tip You can create a personalized electronic business card for yourself or for any of your contacts. For information about Outlook 2010 features not covered in this book, refer to *Microsoft Outlook 2010 Step by Step* by Joan Lambert and Joyce Cox (Microsoft Press, 2010).

You can store the following types of contact information in a contact record:

- Name, company name, and job title
- Business, home, and alternate addresses
- Business, home, mobile, pager, and other telephone numbers
- Business, home, and alternate fax numbers
- Web page address (URL), instant messaging (IM) address, and up to three e-mail addresses

- Photo or other identifying image
- General notes, which can include text and illustrations such as photos, clip art images, SmartArt diagrams, charts, and shapes

You can also store personal and organization-specific details for each contact, such as the following:

- Professional information, including department, office location, profession, manager's name, and assistant's name
- Personal information, including nickname, spouse or partner's name, birthday, anniversary, and the title (such as Miss, Mrs., or Ms.) and suffix (such as Jr. or Sr.) for use in correspondence

Creating Contact Records

You typically create a contact record by displaying the Contacts module and then clicking the New Contact button in the New group on the Home tab. In the contact record window that opens, you insert the information you want to save. After you save the contact record, it is displayed in the Contacts pane.

You can create a contact record containing only one piece of information (for example, a name or company name), or as much information as you want to include. You can quickly create contact records for several people who work for the same company by cloning the company information from an existing record to a new one. And of course, you can add to or change the information stored in a contact record at any time.

The order in which Outlook displays contact records in the Contacts pane is controlled by the *File As* setting. By default, Outlook files contacts by last name (Last, First order). If you prefer, you can change the order for new contacts to any of the following:

- First, Last
- Company
- Last, First (Company)
- Company (Last, First)

To set the filing order for all your contacts, display the Backstage view, click Options, and then on the Contacts page of the Outlook Options dialog box, click the Default "File As" Order arrow and select an order from the list. You can change the filing order for an individual contact by selecting the order you want in the File As list in the contact record.

Tip In addition to individual contact records, you can create groups of contacts so that you can manage messaging to multiple people through one e-mail address.

Address Books

Outlook stores contact information from different sources in separate address books. Some are created by Outlook, some by your e-mail server administrator, and others by you.

Contacts and Suggested Contacts Address Books

Outlook automatically creates a Contacts address book and a Suggested Contacts address book for each account you connect to. These address books are available from the My Contacts list in the Navigation Pane of the Contacts module.

The default Navigation Pane of the Contacts module.

The Contacts address book of your default e-mail account is your main address book, and it is the address book that appears by default in the Contacts module. The Contacts address book is empty until you add contact records to it.

If you correspond with someone who isn't already in your Contacts address book, Outlook automatically adds that person to the Suggested Contacts address book. You can work with the contact information saved in this address book, or you can move the information from the Suggested Contacts address book to create an official contact record for that person in a different address book.

Tip If you have an Outlook Mobile Service account, Outlook automatically creates a Mobile Address Book containing all the contacts in your Contacts address book for whom mobile phone numbers are listed. For more information, refer to *Microsoft Outlook 2010 and Office Communications Server Inside Out* by Jim Boyce (Microsoft Press, 2010).

Custom Address Books

You can create additional address books; for example, you might want to keep contact information for family and friends in an address book separate from client contact information, or you might maintain an address book for team members working on a specific project.

You create an address book by creating a folder and specifying that the folder will contain contact items.

An address book is a folder designed specifically to contain contact records and contact groups.

When you display the Folder List in the Navigation Pane, your custom address books appear along with other folders you create, and you can organize them in the same manner—for example, at the same level as your Inbox, as a subfolder of the Contacts address book, or inside a project folder. All address books are available from the My Contacts list in the Navigation Pane of the Contacts module.

Tip If your organization stores contact information in a SharePoint Contacts List, you can import the list contents from SharePoint into Outlook as an address book.

Global Address Lists

If you have an Exchange account, you also have access to an official address book called the *Global Address List* (or *GAL*). The GAL is maintained by your organization's Exchange administrator and may include information about individuals within your organization, distribution lists, and resources (such as conference rooms and media equipment) that you can reserve when you schedule meetings. It can also include organizational information (each person's manager and direct subordinates) and group membership information (the distribution lists each person belongs to).

The GAL doesn't appear in the My Contacts list shown in the Navigation Pane of the Contacts module. To display the GAL, click the Address Book button located in the Find group on the Home tab of the Contacts module or the Address Book button located in the Names group on the Message tab of a message composition window. Outlook users can view the GAL but not change its contents.

Dialing Rules

The first time you enter a phone number for a contact, the Location Information dialog box opens, prompting you to enter your own country, area code, and any necessary dialing information, such as a carrier code.

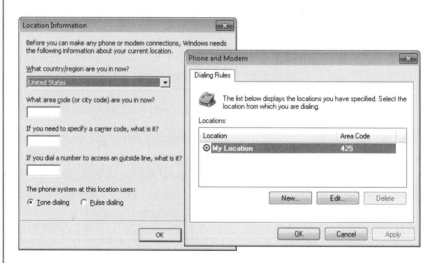

The Location Information and Phone And Modem dialog boxes collect information required by phone and fax programs.

Outlook sets up dialing rules based on the information you enter. You *must* enter at least your country and area code in the dialog box and then click OK; you can't close the dialog box without entering the requested information.

In this exercise, you'll create and edit a contact record in your main address book.

SET UP You don't need any practice files to complete this exercise. Display the Contacts module, and then follow the steps.

New Contact

1. On the **Home** tab, in the **New** group, click the **New Contact** button.

   A new contact record window opens.

2. In the **Full Name** box, type **Sara Davis**, and then press the Tab key to move to the **Company** box.

   Outlook transfers the name to the File As box and displays it in the default order (Last, First). The name also appears on the contact record window title bar and in the business card representation.

Entering a contact's name in the Full Name box distributes it to multiple areas of the contact record.

Troubleshooting The appearance of buttons and groups on the ribbon changes depending on the width of the program window or item window. For information about changing the appearance of the ribbon to match our screen images, see "Modifying the Display of the Ribbon" at the beginning of this book.

3. In the **Company** box, type **Wingtip Toys**.

4. In the **Job title** box, type **Assembly Plant Manager**.

5. In the **Internet** area, type **sara@wingtiptoys.com** in the **E-mail** box, and press Tab.

   Outlook automatically formats the e-mail address as a hyperlink and then enters the contact's name, followed by the e-mail address in parentheses, in the Display As box. This box indicates the way the contact will appear in the headers of e-mail messages you exchange with this contact.

6. In the **Display as** box, select the e-mail address inside the parentheses and then type **Work**.

7. Click the **E-mail** arrow (not the button).

A list displays the e-mail address fields available in the contact record.

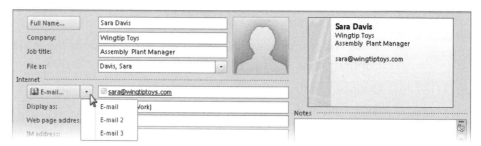

Groups of related contact information fields are indicated by an arrow button to the right of the field name.

8. In the **E-mail** list, click **E-mail 2**.

The E-mail 2 field replaces the E-mail field. The e-mail address you entered in the E-mail field, and its associated Display As text, disappears.

9. In the **E-mail 2** field, enter **sara@thephone-company.com**, and then press Tab.

Outlook enters the original name and the second e-mail address in the Display As field. Although the field name doesn't change to indicate it, this information is specific to the E-mail 2 field.

10. In the **Display as** box, select the e-mail address inside the parentheses and then type **Personal**.

The business card representation displays both e-mail addresses.

11. In the **Web page address** box, type **www.wingtiptoys.com**.

Outlook automatically formats the text as a hyperlink.

12. In the **Phone numbers** area, type **9725550101** in the **Business** box, and then press Tab. If the **Location Information** dialog box opens, enter your country and area code, and click **OK**. Then in the **Phone and Modem** dialog box, with the location associated with your area code selected, click **OK**.

See Also For information about the Location Information dialog box, see the sidebar "Dialing Rules" earlier in this topic.

Outlook formats the series of numbers you entered as a telephone number, using the regional settings governed by Windows.

13. In the **Addresses** area, click in the text box to the right of **Business**, type 4567 **Main Street**, press the Enter key, and then type **Dallas, TX 98052**.

    Tip In a new contact record, a selected check box to the left of the Business address field indicates that it is the default mailing address for the contact.

14. Click the **Business** arrow to display the **Addresses** list and then, in the list, click **Home**.

    The button label changes to indicate that you are displaying Sara's home address information.

15. In the text box, type 111 **Magnolia Lane**, press Enter, and then type **Flower Mound, TX 98053**.

    The contact record now contains both business and personal contact information.

    Tip If you record multiple addresses for a contact and want to specify one as the default mailing address, display that address and then select the This Is The Mailing Address check box.

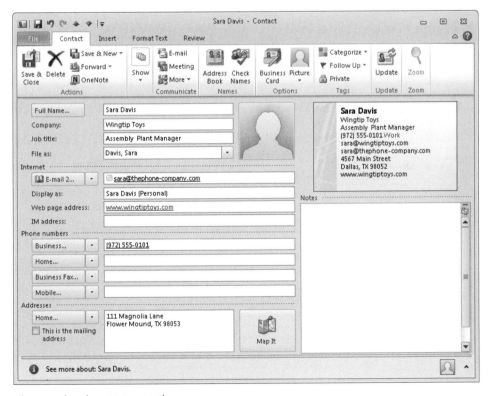

The completed contact record.

16. On the **Contact** tab, in the **Actions** group, click the **Save & Close** button.

    The contact record window closes. The Contacts pane now includes the new contact record for Sara Davis.

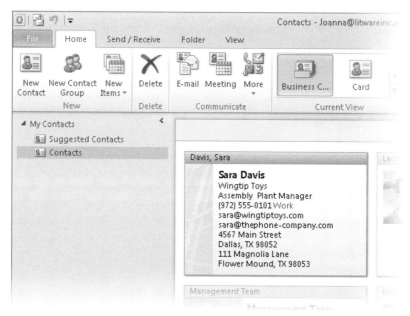

A business card view of the new contact record is visible in the Contacts pane.

17. In the **Contacts** pane, double-click the contact record for **Sara Davis**.

18. On the **Contact** tab, in the **Show** group (or in the **Show** list, if the **Show** group is compacted), click the **Details** button.

    Outlook displays the Details page of the contact record.

    Tip You can assign follow-up flags to contact entries, and link contact entries to e-mail messages, appointments, tasks, and other Outlook items. For more information, see "Creating Tasks from Outlook Items" in Chapter 24, "Track Tasks." You can view all items linked to a contact on the Activities page of the contact record.

19. In the **Spouse/Partner** box, type **Andrew**.

20. Click the **Birthday** arrow, scroll the calendar to **July**, and then click **31**.

The Birthday box displays the day and date information for July 31 of the current year.

The Details page of the contact record provides space for recording business and personal information.

Tip The birthday or anniversary date you select in the calendar defaults to the current calendar year. You can change the year by selecting it in the text box and then typing the year you want.

21. In the **Actions** group, click the **Save & New** arrow (not the button), and then in the list, click **Contact from the Same Company**.

Troubleshooting Clicking the Save & New button rather than the Save & New arrow opens a new, blank contact record. If this occurs, close the new contact record window to return to Sara Davis's contact record, and repeat step 21.

Outlook creates a new contact record that already contains the company name, Web page address, business phone number, and business address from Sara Davis's contact record.

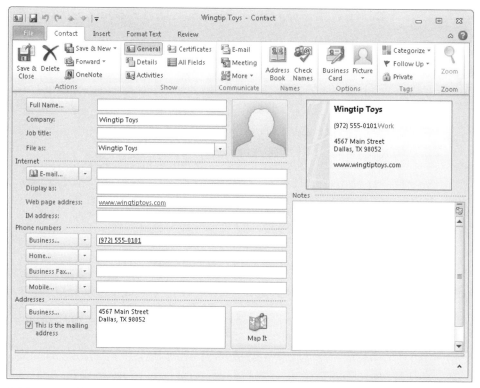

Without any changes, the new contact record could be saved as a contact record for the company rather than for a specific person.

Because no person's name has been provided, the File As name is currently set to the company name.

22. In the **Full Name** box, type **Andrea Dunker**, and in the **Job title** box, type **Sales Associate**.

23. In the **E-mail** box, type **andrea@wingtiptoys.com**. Leave the default **Display As** text.

24. Save and close the open contact records.

25. Use the techniques described in this exercise to create contact records for the following people:

Full name	Company	Job title	E-mail address
Andrew Davis	Trey Research	Account Manager	andrew@treyresearch.net
Idan Rubin	Trey Research	Research Associate	idan@treyresearch.net
Nancy Anderson	Trey Research	Research Associate	nancy@treyresearch.net

The Contacts pane now includes the five records you've created.

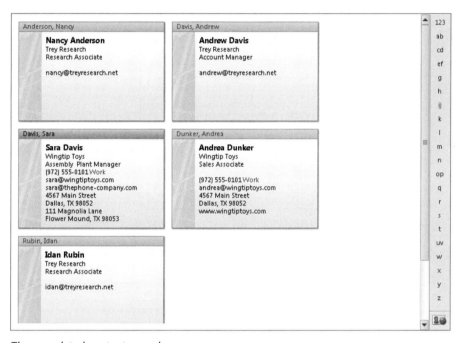

The completed contact records.

 CLEAN UP Save and close any open contact records to return to the Contacts pane. Retain the Nancy Anderson, Andrew Davis, Sara Davis, Andrea Dunker, and Idan Rubin contact records for use in later exercises.

Tip You can create a contact record for the sender of a message you have received by right-clicking the sender's name in the message header—either in the Reading pane or the open message item—and then clicking Add To Outlook Contacts. Outlook creates a contact record with the name and e-mail address already filled in. Add any other information you want to record, and then save the contact record.

Conforming to Address Standards

When you finish entering information in the Addresses area, Outlook verifies that the address conforms to a standard pattern. If Outlook detects irregularities in the address you enter, the Check Address dialog box opens, prompting you to enter the street address, city, state or province, postal code, and country in separate fields from which it reassembles the address.

The Check Address dialog box validates the address against standard patterns.

The intention of this feature is to verify that you have the information necessary to send mail to the contact. If you determine that the information in the Check Address dialog box is correct, you can click Cancel to close the dialog box without making changes.

Communicating with Contacts

Saving contact information for people in a physical or electronic address book is useful because it centralizes the information in one place so that you no longer have to remember the information or where to find it. The added benefit of saving contact information in an Outlook address book is that it makes the process of initiating communication with a contact much more efficient.

Initiating Communication from Contact Records

Contact records aren't useful only for storing information; you can also initiate a number of actions that are specific to a selected contact. Commands for initiating communication are available in the Communicate group on the Contact tab of an open contact record.

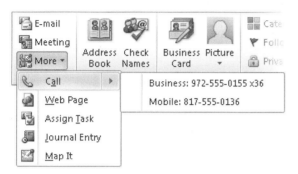

The commands available in the Communicate group may vary based on your specific Outlook configuration.

You can perform many actions from within a contact record by using the commands in the Communicate group on the Contact tab, including the following:

- Create an e-mail message addressed to the contact by clicking the E-mail button.

- Create a meeting request that includes the contact by clicking the Meeting button.

- Initiate a chat session with the contact by clicking the Reply With IM button. (Requires Office Communicator.)

- Place a call to the contact by clicking the Call arrow and then, in the list, clicking the telephone number you would like Outlook to dial. (Requires Internet telephone capabilities.)

- Display the contact's Web site by clicking the Web Page button.

- Create a task assigned to the contact by clicking the Assign Task button.

- Create a journal entry assigned to the contact by clicking the Journal Entry button.

- Display a map of the contact's address by clicking the Map It button in the Addresses area.

If Microsoft OneNote 2010 is installed on your computer, you can create a OneNote notebook entry linked to the contact record by clicking the OneNote button in the Actions group on the Contact tab.

Selecting Message Recipients from Address Books

When you send an e-mail message to a person whose contact information is stored in one of your address books, you can quickly address the message to that person by entering his or her name exactly as it appears in the address book and letting Outlook validate the address. If you don't know the exact spelling of the name, follow these steps:

1. In the message composition window, click the Address Book button in the Names group on the Message tab.

   The Select Names dialog box opens.

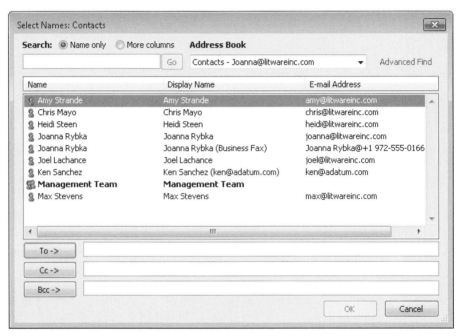

To insert names from an address book, you must open the address book from the message composition window.

2. In the Address Book list, click the arrow, and then click the address book you want to search.

3. Scroll through the Name list, and locate the person's name.

   Tip You can enter the first few letters of the person's name to scroll to entries beginning with those letters.

4. To add the person in the To box as a primary message recipient, double-click the name, or click it and then press Enter. To add the person as a secondary or private recipient, click in the Cc or Bcc box at the bottom of the dialog box and then double-click the name, or click it and press Enter.

Tip If you click the To, Cc, or Bcc box in the message header before clicking the Address Book button, double-clicking the name adds the person to that box. You can also click the Cc or Bcc box and then click the adjacent button to open the Select Names dialog box with that box active.

5. After selecting all message recipients from the address book, click OK to close the Select Names dialog box and return to the message composition window.

See Also For information about creating e-mail messages, see "Creating and Sending Messages" in Chapter 21, "Send and Receive E-Mail Messages."

Displaying Different Views of Contact Records

You can view all your address books in the Contacts module. You can also display a list of the contacts in an address book in one of these ways:

- Click the Address Book button in the Find group on the Home tab of the program window in any module to open the Address Book window.

- Click the Address Book button in the Names group on the Contact tab of a contact record window to open the Select Name dialog box.

In either case, you can expand the Address Book list and then click the name of the address book you want to display.

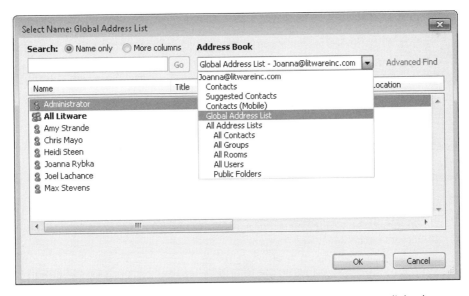

You can display any of the available address books from the Select Name dialog box.

You can view an address book in many different formats. You can choose any standard view from the Current View gallery on the Home tab of the Contacts module.

The Current View gallery of the Contacts module.

Each view presents information from your contact records either as cards or in a list:

- **Business Card** This view displays the business card associated with each contact record—either the default card created by Outlook or a custom card if you have one. Business cards are displayed in alphabetical order by first or last name, depending on the File As selection.

- **Card** This view displays contact information as truncated business cards that include limited information, such as job title and company name.

- **Phone** This view displays a columnar list including each contact's name, company, and contact numbers.

- **List** This view displays a columnar list with contact records arranged in groups. You can choose the grouping you want from the Arrangements gallery on the View tab.

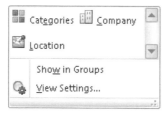

Buttons in the Arrangements gallery of the Contacts module are available only while contact records are displayed in a list view.

In any list view, you can expand and collapse the groups or select and take action on an entire group of contacts. You can also enter information directly into any contact record field displayed in the list.

You can search and filter your contact records in any view by using the Instant Search feature. You can sort contact records by any displayed column in a list view by clicking the column header.

You can change the fields displayed in each view; the way records are grouped, sorted, and filtered; the display font; the size of business cards; and other settings to suit your preferences. You can personalize a view from the Advanced View Settings dialog box, which you open by clicking View Settings in the Current View group on the View tab.

The options available in the Advanced View Settings dialog box vary depending on the currently displayed view.

In this exercise, you'll look at different views of contact records within the Contacts pane, add and remove columns in a list view, and reset a customized view.

 SET UP This exercise uses the Nancy Anderson, Andrew Davis, Sara Davis, Andrea Dunker, and Idan Rubin contact records you created in the exercise "Saving and Updating Contact Information," earlier in this chapter. If you didn't complete that exercise, you can do so at this time or use contact records of your own. Display the Contacts module, and then follow the steps.

1. On the **Home** tab, in the **Current View** gallery, click the **Business Card** button if that view isn't already selected.

   In Outlook 2010, this default Contacts module view displays standard business cards for each contact, as well as any personalized business cards you have saved. The cards are organized by File As name, which by default is alphabetically by last name.

2. On the alphabet bar located on the right side of the Contacts pane, click the letter **r**.

The Contacts pane scrolls as necessary to display the business card for Idan Rubin (or the first contact record in your Contacts module that is filed under R).

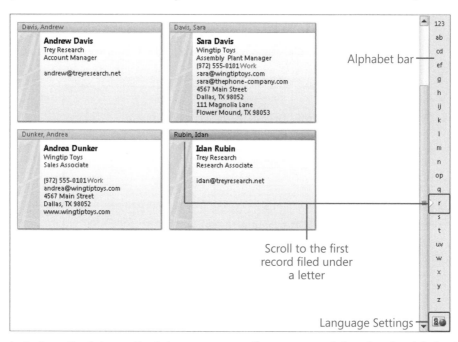

In Business Card view or Card view, you can scroll contact records by using the alphabet bar.

Tip You can display an additional alphabet in the alphabet bar. Options include Arabic, Cyrillic, Greek, Thai, and Vietnamese—other alphabets might be available depending on the version of Outlook and any language packs you have installed. To get started, click the Language Settings button at the bottom of the alphabet bar.

3. In the **Current View** gallery, click the **Card** button.

4. If the card columns are not wide enough to display the information saved with the contact records, click the **Zoom In** button at the right end of the status bar until the information is visible.

Outlook displays your contact records in a card-like format that includes only text and no additional graphic elements.

Anderson, Nancy

Full Name:	Nancy Anderson
Job Title:	Research Associate
Company:	Trey Research
E-mail:	nancy@treyresearch.net

Davis, Andrew

Full Name:	Andrew Davis
Job Title:	Account Manager
Company:	Trey Research
E-mail:	andrew@treyresearch.net

Davis, Sara

Full Name:	Sara Davis
Job Title:	Assembly Plant Manager
Company:	Wingtip Toys
Business:	4567 Main Street Dallas, TX 98052
Home:	111 Magnolia Lane Flower Mound, TX 98053
Business:	(972) 555-0101
E-mail:	sara@wingtiptoys.com
E-mail 2:	sara@thephone-company.com
Business Home Page:	www.wingtiptoys.com

Dunker, Andrea

Full Name:	Andrea Dunker
Job Title:	Sales Associate
Company:	Wingtip Toys
Business:	4567 Main Street Dallas, TX 98052
Business:	(972) 555-0101
E-mail:	andrea@wingtiptoys.com
Business Home Page:	www.wingtiptoys.com

Rubin, Idan

Full Name:	Idan Rubin
Job Title:	Research Associate
Company:	Trey Research
E-mail:	idan@treyresearch.net

Card view displays the available primary contact information, including name, telephone and fax numbers, postal and e-mail addresses, and notes.

Phone

5. In the **Current View** gallery, click the **Phone** button.

   Outlook displays your contact records in a grid of columns and rows organized in ascending order based on the File As column.

6. Click the **Full Name** column heading.

   Outlook sorts the contact records in ascending order based on the Full Name field, as indicated by the upward-pointing sort arrow to the right of the column heading. You can reverse the sort order by clicking the active heading again.

Sort order

Click any column header to sort by that column or to reverse the sort order.

7. Click the **Company** column heading.

   Outlook sorts the contact records in ascending order based on the Company field.

   Tip You can add a contact to your address book in any list view by clicking the box under the Full Name header (labeled Click Here To Add A New Contact) and entering the contact's information.

8. Right-click the **Company** column header, and then click **Field Chooser**.

   The Field Chooser window opens.

9. Scroll down the **Field Chooser** list until the **Job Title** field is visible. Drag the **Job Title** field from the **Field Chooser** dialog box to the column heading area, and when the red arrows indicate that it will be inserted between the **Company** and **File As** fields, release the mouse button.

   The list view now includes a column displaying the Job Title for each contact.

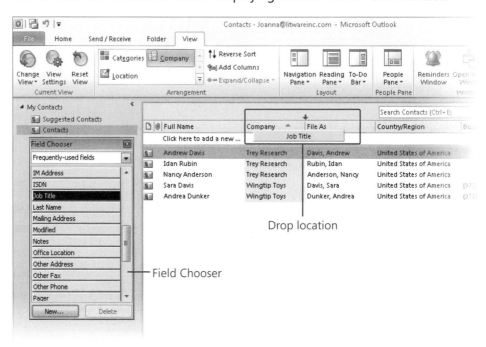

You can add any field to a list view from the Field Chooser.

10. Point to the column separator between **Job Title** and **File As**. When the cursor changes to a double-headed arrow, double-click.

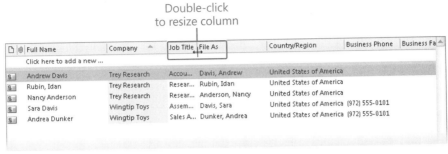

Double-clicking a column separator resizes the column to the left of the separator.

The column width changes to accommodate its contents.

11. Drag the **Country/Region** column header down from the column heading row until a black X appears. Then release the mouse button.

You can remove a column from a list view by dragging its column header away from the column header row.

The Country/Region column is removed from the list view.

12. On the **View** tab, in the **Current View** group, click the **Reset View** button. Then in the **Microsoft Outlook** dialog box that asks whether you want to reset the view to its original settings, click **Yes**.

The view returns to its original settings.

CLEAN UP Return the Contacts module to the default Business Card view. Retain the Nancy Anderson, Andrew Davis, Sara Davis, Andrea Dunker, and Idan Rubin contact records for use in later exercises.

User-Defined Fields

If you'd like to save information that doesn't fit into the default contact record fields, you can create a custom field. A custom field can contain information such as text, numbers, percentages, currency, Yes/No answers, dates, times, durations, keywords, and formulas.

You can create a custom information field from any view of the All Fields page by clicking the New button in the lower-left corner of the page and then specifying the name, type, and format of the field in the New Column dialog box that opens.

Custom fields can be formatted to contain many specific types of information.

Custom fields appear when you filter the All Fields page on User-Defined Fields In This Folder. When you enter information in the custom field for a specific contact, it also appears in the User-Defined Fields In This Item list within that contact record.

Printing Contact Records

You can print an address book or individual contact records, either on paper or to an electronic file (such as a PDF file or an XPS file), from any address book view. Depending on the view, Outlook offers a variety of print styles, such as those described in the following table.

Style	Description	Available in these views
Card	Contact information displayed alphabetically in two columns. Letter graphics appear at the top of each page and the beginning of each letter group	Business Card, Card
Small Booklet	Contact information displayed alphabetically in one column. Formatted to print eight numbered pages per sheet. Letter graphics appear at the top of each page and the beginning of each letter group, and a contact index at the side of each page indicates the position of that page's entries in the alphabet. Print double-sided if possible.	Business Card, Card
Medium Booklet	Contact information displayed alphabetically in one column. Formatted to print four numbered pages per sheet. Letter graphics appear at the top of each page and the beginning of each letter group, and a contact index at the side of each page indicates the position of that page's entries in the alphabet. Print double-sided if possible.	Business Card, Card
Memo	Contact information displayed under a memo-like header containing your name. One record per sheet.	Business Card, Card
Phone Directory	Contact names and telephone numbers displayed in two columns. Letter graphics appear at the top of each page and the beginning of each letter group.	Business Card, Card
Table	Contact information displayed in a table that matches the on-screen layout.	Phone, List

You can customize the layout of most of the default print styles, as well as save custom print styles.

In this exercise, you'll set up Outlook to print a phone list and then to print individual address cards.

 SET UP This exercise uses the Nancy Anderson, Andrew Davis, Sara Davis, Andrea Dunker, and Idan Rubin contact records you created in the exercise "Saving and Updating Contact Information," earlier in this chapter. If you didn't complete that exercise, you can do so at this time or use contact records of your own. Display the Contacts module in Card view, and then follow the steps.

1. Display the Backstage view, and then click **Print**.

   The Backstage view displays the current Print settings.

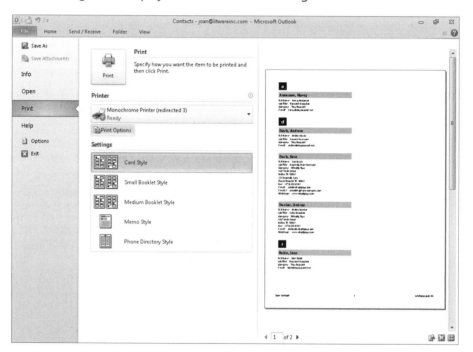

In Card view, many print styles are available in the Settings list.

Tip The Backstage view on your computer reflects your individual printer settings and might display more print options than shown here.

The preview pane displays the way the cards will appear if printed in the default Card Style, with the current settings. The page indicators at the bottom of the preview pane indicate that the cards will be printed on two pages.

> **Important** To fully complete this exercise, you must have a printer installed. If you don't have a printer installed, you can perform all the steps of the exercise other than printing.
>
> To install a printer, click the Start button, click Devices And Printers, and then on the toolbar, click Add A Printer. Follow the wizard's instructions to install a local or network printer. If you are working on a corporate network, your administrator can provide the information you need to install a printer.

2. In the lower-right corner of the preview pane, click the **Multiple Pages** button.

   The preview pane displays both pages. The second page contains a series of lines and illegible text.

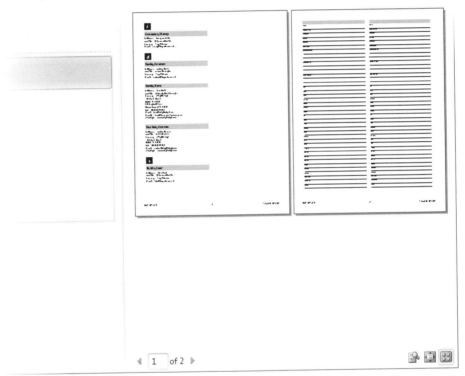

   You can display all pages of a document as they will be printed, to peruse the overall document layout.

3. In the lower-right corner of the preview pane, click the **Actual Size** button.

   The preview pane displays a full-size version of the document. The magnified text is large enough to read.

4. At the bottom of the preview pane, to the right of the number of pages, click the right arrow.

The preview pane displays the second page, which provides an area for you to record information about an additional contact. Outlook refers to this page of the print style as a *blank page*.

Certain print layouts include blank pages on which you can record information about new contacts.

5. In the middle pane, click **Print Options**.

The Print dialog box opens, displaying the options for the Card Style print style.

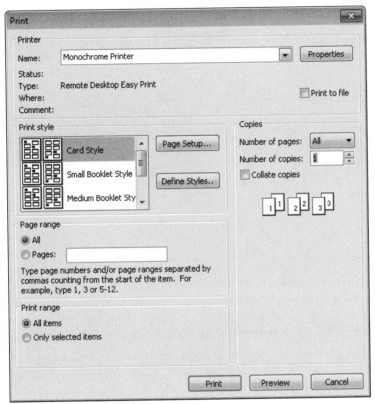

When printing contact records in the Card Style print style, you can select specific contact records (items) to be printed.

6. In the **Print** dialog box, click **Page Setup**.

The Page Setup: Card Style dialog box opens, displaying the Format page.

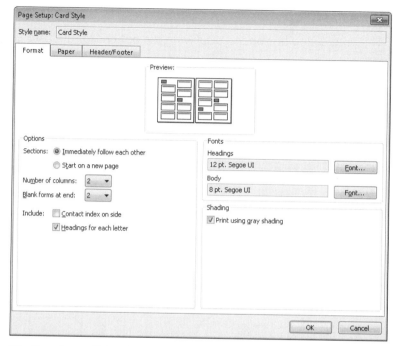

The Page Setup dialog box contents vary depending on the selected print style.

7. Look at the settings available on each of the dialog box pages.

   For all print styles, you can change the fonts, paper size, page orientation and margins, header and footer, and other basic settings. For this print style you can also change the layout of cards on the page, the number of blank forms to be printed, and how the alphabetical division of the cards is indicated.

8. In the **Page Setup** dialog box, in the **Options** area of the **Format** page, click **None** in the **Blank forms at end** list. Select the **Contact index on side** check box, and then clear the **Headings for each letter** check box.

9. Click **OK** in the **Page Setup** dialog box, and then click **Preview** in the **Print** dialog box.

   The preview pane displays the previously selected Actual Size view of the card list, which is now only one page.

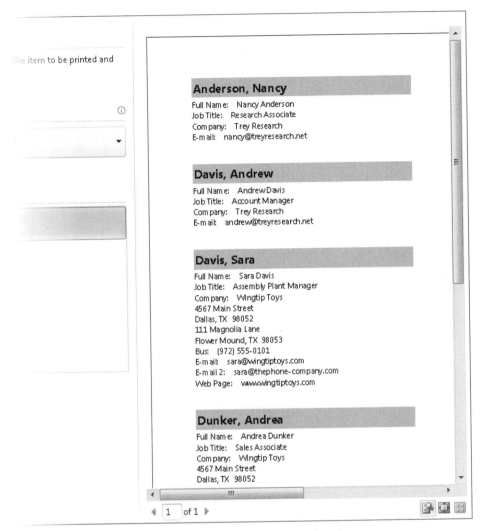

the item to be printed and

Alphabetical headings no longer precede the contact record cards.

10. In the lower-right corner of the preview pane, click the **One Page** button.

    The preview pane displays the entire card list as it will appear when printed.

11. If you want to print the card list, click the **Print** button.

    After printing the card list, Outlook returns to the Contacts module.

12. On the **Home** tab, in the **Current View** gallery, click the **List** button.

13. In the **Contacts** pane, click the **Sara Davis** contact record to select it, press and hold the Ctrl key, and then click the **Andrea Dunker** contact record to add it to the selection.

14. Display the **Print** page of the Backstage view.

    The Settings list displays only two options—Table Style and Memo Style. Memo Style is selected by default.

If the preview pane can't automatically display the multiple selected records, a Preview button appears in the preview pane instead.

15. If the **Preview** button appears in the preview pane, click it to display the previews of the two selected contact records.

16. In the **Settings** list, click **Table Style**.

    The preview of Table Style indicates that all contact records will be printed rather than only the two you selected.

17. In the middle pane, click **Print Options**.

    The Print dialog box opens, displaying the options for the Table Style.

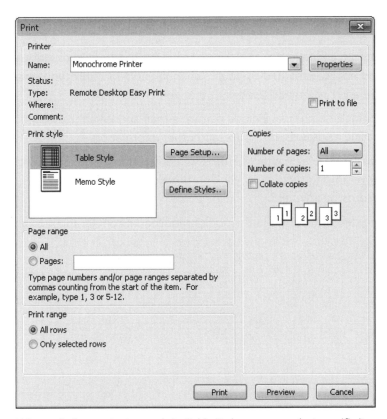

When printing contact records in Table Style, you can select specific items to be printed.

18. In the **Print range** area, click **Only selected rows**. Then click **Preview**.

The preview pane changes to display only the two contact records you selected.

19. If you want to print the two records, click the **Print** button.

Outlook prints a page displaying only the selected contacts.

20. Experiment with the other ways in which you can print your contact records and your address book.

CLEAN UP Return to the default Business Card view or your preferred view of the Contacts module before continuing to the next chapter. Retain the Nancy Anderson, Andrew Davis, Sara Davis, Andrea Dunker, and Idan Rubin contact records for use in later exercises.

Key Points

- You can create and access different types of address books including the Global Address List provided by your Exchange Server account, your main address book, and any custom address books that you create.

- Contact records can include names, e-mail and IM addresses, phone numbers, mailing addresses, birthdays, and other information.

- You can display contact records in many different views. In card views, you can move among records by clicking the alphabet bar. In list views, you can sort records by any field.

- You can print your address book or individual contact records in several formats.

Chapter at a Glance

Schedule and change appointments, **page 680**

Schedule and change events, **page 689**

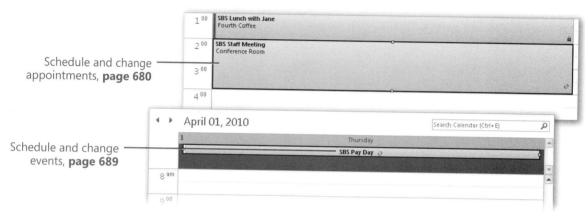

Display different views of a calendar, **page 701**

23 Manage Scheduling

You can use the Microsoft Outlook 2010 calendar to organize your daily activities and to remind you of important tasks and events. If you're a busy person and use the Outlook calendar to its fullest potential, it might at times seem as though the calendar runs your life—but that isn't necessarily a bad thing! Using the calendar effectively can help you stay organized, on task, and on time. You can schedule and track appointments, meetings, and events, and block time as a reminder to yourself to take care of tasks.

If you have a Microsoft Exchange Server account, an Outlook calendar has already been created for you. If you have configured Outlook to connect to a different type of account, you can manually create a calendar within that account. You can easily create appointments, events, and meetings on your Outlook calendar.

In this chapter, you'll schedule an appointment and an event on your own calendar and work with appointment options including recurrence, reminders, and availability. You'll schedule a meeting with another person, and learn about responding to, updating, and canceling meeting requests. Then you'll experiment with different ways of looking at your calendar to find the view that is most effective for your daily working style.

> **Practice Files** You don't need any practice files to complete the exercises in this chapter. For more information about practice file requirements, see "Using the Practice Files" at the beginning of this book.

Important The exercises in this chapter assume that you're working with an Exchange account. Some functionality may be unavailable if you're working with a calendar that's part of another type of account.

Scheduling and Changing Appointments

Appointments are blocks of time you schedule for only yourself (as opposed to meetings, to which you invite other Outlook users). An appointment has a specific start time and a specific end time (as opposed to an event, which occurs for one or more full 24-hour periods).

To schedule an appointment, you enter, at the minimum, a subject and time in an appointment window. The basic appointment window also includes a field for the appointment location and a free form notes area in which you can store general information, including formatted text, Web site links, and even file attachments so that they are easily available to you at the time of the appointment.

When creating an appointment, you indicate your availability (referred to as Free/Busy time) by marking it as Free, Tentative, Busy, or Out Of Office. The appointment time is color-coded on your calendar to match the availability you indicate. Your availability is visible to other Outlook users on your network, and is also displayed when you share your calendar or send calendar information to other people.

Tip When viewing your calendar in Day, Work Week, or Week view, each item on your Outlook task list appears in the Tasks section below its due date. You can schedule specific time to complete a task by dragging it from the Tasks area to your calendar.

See Also For information about adding the contents of a received message to your calendar, see the sidebar "Creating an Appointment from a Message" later in this chapter. For information about Outlook 2010 features not covered in this book, refer to *Microsoft Outlook 2010 Step by Step* by Joan Lambert and Joyce Cox (Microsoft Press, 2010).

By default, Outlook displays a reminder message 15 minutes before the start time of an appointment—you can change the reminder to occur as far as two weeks in advance, or you can turn it off completely if you want to. If you synchronize your Outlook installation with a mobile device, reminders also appear on your mobile device. This is very convenient when you are away from your computer.

If you have the same appointment on a regular basis—for example, a bimonthly haircut or a weekly exercise class—you can set it up in your Outlook calendar as a *recurring appointment*. A recurring appointment can happen at almost any regular interval, such as every Tuesday and Thursday, every other week, or the last day of every month. Configuring an appointment recurrence creates multiple instances of the appointment in your calendar at the time interval you specify. The individual appointments are linked. When making changes to a recurring appointment, you can choose to update all occurrences or only an individual occurrence of the appointment.

You can specify the time zone in which an appointment starts and ends. You might want to have different time zones if, for example, your "appointment" is an airplane flight that starts and ends in different time zones, and you want the flight to show up correctly wherever you're currently located.

In this exercise, you'll schedule an appointment and a recurring appointment, and you'll update appointments by using commands in the appointment window.

SET UP You don't need any practice files to complete this exercise. Display the Calendar module in the default Day view, minimize the To-Do Bar, and then follow the steps.

1. In the **Date Navigator** at the top of the **Navigation Pane**, click tomorrow's date.

   See Also For information about the default Calendar module view and the Date Navigator, see "Displaying Different Views of a Calendar" later in this chapter.

   Outlook displays tomorrow's schedule.

2. In the **Calendar** pane, point to the **12:00 P.M.** time slot (or, if you already have an appointment scheduled at 12:00 P.M., to another time when you have 30 minutes available).

   Click to add appointment appears in the time slot.

3. Click once to activate the time slot.

   In this default mode, you can enter basic appointment details directly in the Calendar pane.

4. Type **SBS Lunch with Jane**, and then press Enter.

   Important The subject of each appointment, meeting, or event you create while working through the exercises in this book begins with *SBS* so that you can easily differentiate the practice items you create from other items on your calendar.

   Outlook creates a half-hour appointment beginning at 12:00 P.M.

5. Drag the appointment from the 12:00 P.M. time slot to the **1:00 P.M.** time slot (or, if you already have an appointment scheduled at 1:00 P.M., to another time when you have an hour available).

   Outlook changes the appointment start time.

6. Point to the bottom border of the appointment, and when the pointer changes to a double-headed arrow, drag down one time slot so that the appointment ends at **2:00 P.M.**

   While the appointment is selected in the calendar, the Appointment contextual tab is available.

Date Navigator

Active appointment

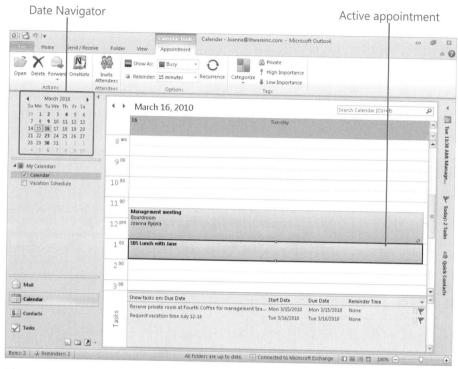

The most common appointment settings are available on the Appointment contextual tab.

Troubleshooting The appearance of buttons and groups on the ribbon changes depending on the width of the program window or item window. For information about changing the appearance of the ribbon to match our screen images, see "Modifying the Display of the Ribbon" at the beginning of this book.

You can add more details to the appointment and change the default settings from within the appointment window.

7. Double-click the **SBS Lunch with Jane** appointment.

   The appointment window opens. The subject, start time, and end time are set according to the information you entered in the Calendar pane.

8. In the **Location** box, type **Fourth Coffee**.

9. On the **Appointment** tab of the appointment window (not the Appointment contextual tab in the Calendar module), in the **Options** group, click the **Show As** arrow, and then in the list, click **Out of Office**.

10. In the **Options** group, click the **Reminder** arrow, and then in the list, click **1 hour**.

11. In the **Tags** group, click the **Private** button.

    Marking an appointment, event, or meeting as Private hides the details from anyone you share your calendar with.

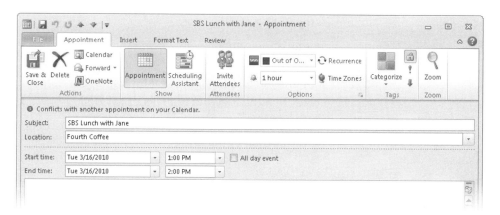

All of these settings other than the location are available from the Appointment contextual tab in the Calendar module.

12. In the **Actions** group, click the **Save & Close** button.

When the appointment window closes, Outlook applies your changes to the appointment shown on the calendar. Your availability is indicated by the colored bar on the left side of the appointment.

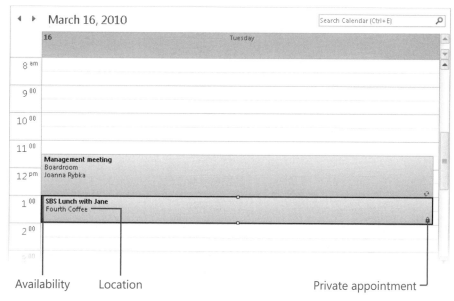

Availability   Location   Private appointment

Outlook might display messages about the appointment based on other calendar information.

The settings on the Appointment contextual tab also reflect the changes you made to the appointment.

13. Double-click the **2:00 P.M.** time slot.

    Outlook opens an appointment window with the appointment start time set to 2:00 P.M. and the end time set 30 minutes later. Because this immediately follows the lunch appointment you just created, the information bar at the top of the meeting window indicates that the meeting is adjacent to another on your calendar.

14. In the **Subject** box, type **SBS Staff Meeting**. In the **Location** box, type **Conference Room**. Then in the notes area, type the following sentence:

    Bring status reports.

Recurrence

15. On the **Appointment** tab, in the **Options** group, click the **Recurrence** button.

    The Appointment Recurrence dialog box opens.

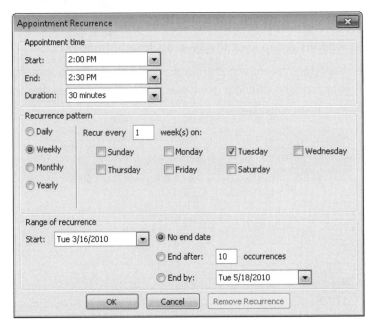

When configuring a weekly recurrence, you can change the time, day, frequency, and duration from the Appointment Recurrence dialog box.

The default appointment recurrence is weekly on the currently selected day of the week. You can set the appointment to recur until further notice, to end after a certain number of occurrences, or to end by a certain date.

16. In the **End** list, click **4:00 PM (2 hours)**. In the **Range of recurrence** area, click **End after**, and then in the box, replace **10** with **2**.

17. To indicate that you want to create a 2-hour appointment beginning at 2:00 P.M. on the selected day of the week, this week and next week only, click **OK** in the **Appointment Recurrence** dialog box.

In the appointment window, the Start Time and End Time fields disappear and are replaced by the recurrence details.

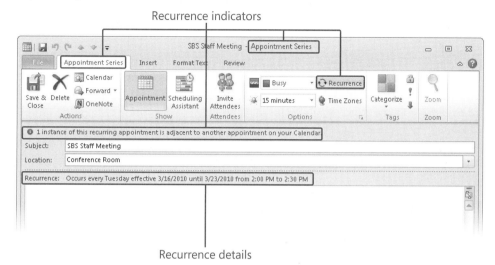

Several aspects of the appointment window change to reflect that this is now a series of recurring appointments.

18. On the **Appointment Series** tab, in the **Actions** group, click the **Save & Close** button.

    The new appointment appears on your calendar.

19. If necessary, scroll the **Calendar** pane to display the entire appointment.

    The circling arrow icon at the right end of the time slot indicates the recurrence.

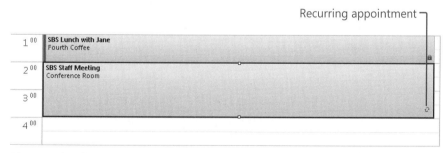

The completed appointments.

20. In the **Date Navigator**, click the weekday of the appointment in each of the next two weeks, to verify that the appointment appears on your calendar next week, but not the following week.

 **CLEAN UP** Retain the SBS Lunch with Jane and SBS Staff Meeting appointments in your calendar for use as practice files later in this chapter.

Adding National Holidays to Your Calendar

You can easily add the local holidays of any of over 80 countries to your Outlook calendar.

To add national holidays to your Outlook calendar, follow these steps:

1. Open the Outlook Options dialog box.

2. On the Calendar page of the Outlook Options dialog box, under Calendar Options, click Add Holidays.

   The Add Holidays to Calendar dialog box opens.

More than 80 countries are available in the Add Holidays To Calendar dialog box.

3. Select the check boxes of the countries whose holidays you want to add to your calendar, and then click OK.

   Tip If you've already added the holidays for a selected country to your calendar, Outlook prompts you to verify that you want to install a second instance of each holiday. Assuming that you do not want to do this, click No.

4. After Outlook adds the selected country's holidays to your calendar, click OK in the confirmation message box and in the Outlook Options dialog box.

Outlook 2010 assigns a color category named *Holiday* to all the local holidays it adds to your calendar. To view all the holidays on your calendar, enter *category:holiday* in the Search box. Note that Outlook adds each holiday for the next 20 years to the calendar, so the entire list of results might not be displayed immediately (only the first 200 results). If the search returns more than 200 results, add search criteria to narrow down the field (for example, *start:2012* to view all holidays in 2012) or click the information bar at the top of the search results list to display the entire list. You can narrow your search by using any of the displayed column headers followed by a colon and a search specification.

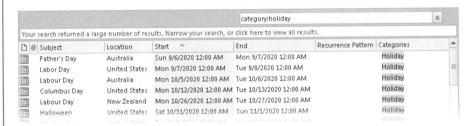

A basic search returns only the first 200 results; click the information bar to display all the results.

To remove national holidays from your calendar, follow these steps:

1. Use the Search function to locate the holidays you want to remove.

2. Select individual holidays you want to remove; or click any holiday in the list to activate the list, and then press Ctrl+A to select all the holidays in the search results.

3. Press the Delete key.

Tip If you inadvertently add two sets of holidays from one country to the calendar, the easiest way to rectify the situation is to remove all of that country's holidays and then add them again.

Creating an Appointment from a Message

Many e-mail messages that you receive result in your wanting or needing to schedule an appointment on your calendar based on the information in the message—for example, a friend or co-worker might send you a message containing the details of the grand opening for a local art gallery that you want to add to your calendar. Outlook provides a convenient method of creating a Calendar item (an appointment, event, or meeting request) based on an e-mail message; you simply drag the message to the Calendar button in the Navigation Pane. When you release the mouse button, an appointment window opens, already filled in with the message subject as the appointment subject, the message text in the content pane, and any message attachments attached to the appointment. The start and end times are set to the next half-hour increment following the current time. You can convert the appointment to an event or meeting in the same way that you would create an event or meeting from within the Calendar module. You can retain any or all of the message information as part of the Calendar item so that you (or other meeting participants) have the information on hand when you need it. After creating the Calendar item, you can delete the actual message from your Inbox.

To create an appointment from an e-mail message:

1. Drag the message from the Mail pane to the Calendar button in the Navigation Pane, but don't release the mouse button.

   As you hold the dragged message over the Calendar button, the Navigation Pane changes to display the Calendar module information instead of the Mail module information.

2. After the Navigation Pane content changes, release the mouse button to create an appointment based on the message.

   You can convert the appointment to an event by selecting the All Day Event check box, or convert it to a meeting by inviting other people to attend. You can edit the information in the content pane without affecting the content of the original message, and you can move or delete the original message without affecting the appointment.

3. In the appointment window, click the Save & Close button to save the appointment to your calendar.

See Also For information about adding message content to your To-Do List, see "Creating Tasks" in Chapter 24, "Track Tasks."

Scheduling and Changing Events

Events are day-long blocks of time that you schedule on your Outlook calendar—for example, a birthday, a payroll day, or anything else occurring on a particular day but not at a specific time. In all other respects, creating an event is identical to creating an appointment, in that you can specify a location, indicate recurrence, indicate your availability, and attach additional information to the event item.

You can create an event directly on the calendar when viewing your calendar in Day, Work Week, Week, or Month view.

In this exercise, you'll schedule an event and convert it to a recurring event by using the commands in the Calendar module.

 SET UP You don't need any practice files to complete this exercise. Display the Calendar module in Day view, and then follow the steps.

1. In the **Date Navigator** at the top of the **Navigation Pane**, click the first day of next month.

   The Date Navigator changes to display the next month.

2. In the **Calendar** pane, point to the blank space below the day header and above the time slots.

   Click to add event appears in the space.

3. Click once to activate the event slot. The event space changes to display a darker background color, and an event placeholder becomes active.

   In this mode, you can enter basic event details directly in the Calendar pane.

4. Type **SBS Pay Day**, and then press Enter.

5. On the **Appointment** contextual tab, in the **Options** group, click the **Recurrence** button.

   The Appointment Recurrence dialog box opens. The default recurrence for events is the same as for appointments—weekly on the currently selected day of the week. Note that the Start and End times are set to 12:00 AM and the Duration to 1 day, indicating that this is an all-day event.

6. In the **Recurrence pattern** area, click **Monthly**.

   Tip If you have an Exchange account and a mobile device that supports connections to Exchange accounts (such as a Windows 7 Phone, BlackBerry, or iPhone), it's easy to keep your calendar and reminders at your fingertips wherever you are by configuring your mobile device to connect to your Exchange account.

You can schedule a monthly event to recur on a specific date of the month or on a selected (first, second, third, fourth, or last) day of the month. Monthly events can recur every month or less often (for example, every third month).

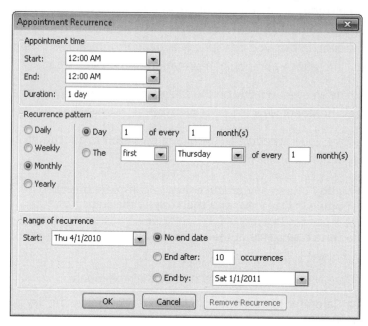

When configuring a monthly recurrence, you can change the day or date of the month, frequency, and duration from the Appointment Recurrence dialog box.

7. To create a recurring appointment on the first day of each month, with no specific end date, click **OK**.

The contextual tab changes to reflect that this is now a recurring event, and the recurrence icon appears to the right of the event subject.

In Day view, events appear above the schedule for the day.

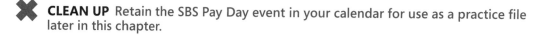 **CLEAN UP** Retain the SBS Pay Day event in your calendar for use as a practice file later in this chapter.

Scheduling Meetings

A primary difficulty when scheduling a meeting is finding a time that works for all the people who need to attend it. Scheduling meetings through Outlook is significantly simpler than scheduling meetings by discussing times and locations with the participants, particularly when you need to accommodate the schedules of several people. Outlook displays the individual and collective schedules of people within your own organization, and of people outside of your organization who have published their calendars to the Internet. You can review attendees' schedules to locate a time when everyone is available, or have Outlook find a convenient time for you.

You can send an Outlook meeting invitation (referred to as a meeting request) to any person who has an e-mail account—even to a person who doesn't use Outlook. You can send a meeting request from any type of e-mail account (such as an Exchange account or an Internet e-mail account).

The meeting window has two pages: the Appointment page and the Scheduling Assistant (or Scheduling) page. The Appointment page is visible by default. You can enter all the required information directly on the Appointment page, or use the additional features available on the Scheduling Assistant page to find the best time for the meeting.

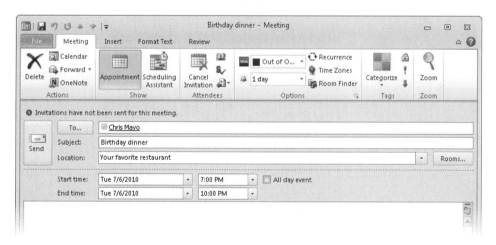

The Appointment page of a meeting window.

People you invite to meetings are referred to as *attendees*. By default, the attendance of each attendee is indicated as Required. You can inform non-critical attendees of the meeting by marking their attendance as Optional. You can invite entire groups of people by using a contact group or distribution list. You can also invite managed resources, such as conference rooms and audio/visual equipment, that have been set up by your organization's Exchange administrator.

A meeting request must have at least one attendee other than you, a start time, and an end time. It should also include a subject and a location, but Outlook will send the meeting request without this information if you specifically allow it. The body of a meeting request can include text and Web links, as well as file attachments. This is a convenient way to distribute meeting information to attendees ahead of time.

The secondary page of the meeting window is the Scheduling Assistant page, if your e-mail account is part of an Exchange Server 2010 or Exchange Server 2007 network. Otherwise, the secondary page is the Scheduling page, which doesn't include the Room Finder feature we discuss below. If you're organizing a meeting for a large number of people and want to view collective information about their schedules, you do so on the Scheduling or Scheduling Assistant page.

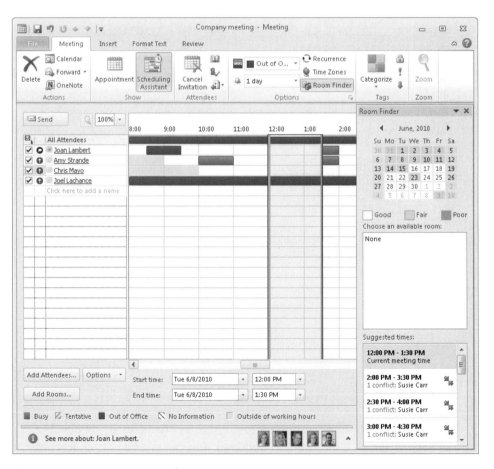

The Scheduling Assistant page of a meeting window.

The Scheduling and Scheduling Assistant pages include a group schedule that shows the status of each attendee's time throughout your working day. Outlook indicates your suggested meeting time on the group schedule with green (start time) and red (end time) vertical bars. If free/busy information is available for meeting attendees, their time is shown as white (Available), blue (Busy), or purple (Out of Office). Their Tentative bookings are indicated by light-blue diagonal stripes. If no information is available (either because Outlook can't connect to an attendee's calendar or because the proposed meeting is further out than the scheduling information stored on the server), Outlook shows the time with gray diagonal stripes. The row at the top of the schedule, to the right of the All Attendees heading, indicates the collective schedule of all the attendees.

Tip You can enter additional attendees in the To box on the Appointment page or in the All Attendees list on the Scheduling or Scheduling Assistant page.

You can change the time and duration of the meeting to work with the displayed schedules by selecting a different time in the Start Time and End Time lists, by dragging the green and red vertical bars (the start time and end time bars) in the group schedule, or by clicking the time you want in the Suggested Times list.

On the right side of the Scheduling Assistant page, the Room Finder task pane is open by default. The monthly calendar at the top of the Room Finder task pane indicates the collective availability of the group on each day, as follows:

- Dates that occur in the past and non-working days are gray.
- Days when all attendees are available are white (Good).
- Days when most attendees are available are light blue (Fair).
- Days when most attendees are not available are medium blue (Poor).

Tip The Room Finder task pane is available only for Exchange accounts. You can display or hide the Room Finder task pane on the Appointment page or on the Scheduling Assistant page by clicking the Room Finder button in the Options group on the Meeting tab.

Managed conference rooms that are available at the indicated meeting time are shown in the center of the Room Finder task pane. At the bottom of the Room Finder task pane, the Suggested Times list displays attendee availability for appointments of the length of time you have specified for the meeting.

Selecting a date in the calendar displays the suggested meeting times for just that day. (Scheduling suggestions are not provided for past or nonworking days.) Clicking a meeting time in the Suggested Times list updates the calendar and the meeting request.

See Also For information about creating a meeting request from an e-mail message, see the sidebar "Creating an Appointment from a Message" earlier in this chapter.

Outlook tracks responses from attendees and those responsible for scheduling the resources you requested, so you always have an up-to-date report of how many people will attend your meeting. The number of attendees who have accepted, tentatively accepted, and declined the meeting request appears in the meeting header section when you open a meeting in its own window. In this exercise, you'll create and send a meeting request.

 SET UP You don't need any practice files to complete this exercise. Display your default calendar and inform two co-workers or friends that you are going to practice inviting them as attendees to a meeting. Ask the attendees not to respond to the meeting request that they receive. Then follow the steps.

1. In the **Date Navigator**, click tomorrow's date. Then in the **Calendar** pane, click the **3:00 P.M.** time slot (or if you have a conflicting appointment, click a time when you have 30 minutes available).

2. On the **Home** tab, in the **New** group, click the **New Meeting** button.

   An untitled meeting window opens. The selected date and times are shown in the Start Time and End Time boxes above the notes pane.

3. In the **To** box, type the e-mail address of the first co-worker or friend with whom you arranged to practice.

4. In the **Subject** box, type **SBS Get-Together**.

5. In the **Location** box, type **Test meeting** to indicate that the meeting request is for testing purposes only.

   You have provided all the standard information for a meeting request.

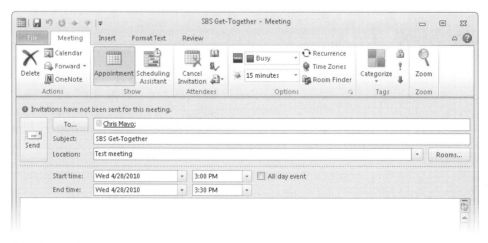

A basic meeting request.

6. On the **Meeting** tab, in the **Show** group, click the **Scheduling Assistant** button.

   The All Attendees list on the Scheduling Assistant page includes you and the attendee you entered in the To box (showing the attendee's e-mail address or, if the attendee has an entry in your Address Book, the associated name). The icon next to your name, a magnifying glass in a black circle, indicates that you are the meeting organizer. The icon next to the attendee's name, an upward-pointing arrow in a red circle, indicates that he or she is a required attendee.

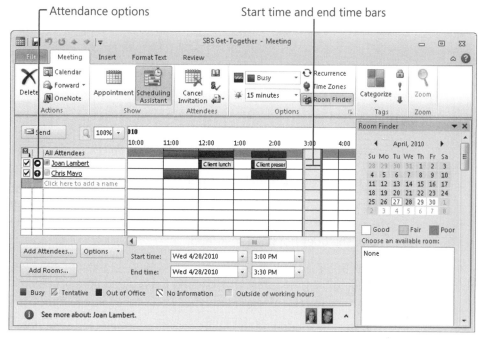

When you are the meeting organizer, the Scheduling Assistant displays the subject of each appointment on your schedule that is not marked as Private.

7. If necessary, scroll to the bottom of the **Room Finder** task pane to display the **Suggested times** list.

   The times shown are based on your schedule and the schedule information that is available for the first attendee.

8. In the **All Attendees** list, click **Click here to add a name**, enter the e-mail address of the second person with whom you arranged to practice, and then press Tab.

   The Suggested Times list in the Room Finder task pane is updated to reflect any schedule conflicts for the second attendee.

9. Click the **Required Attendee** icon to the left of the second attendee's name.

   A list of attendance options expands.

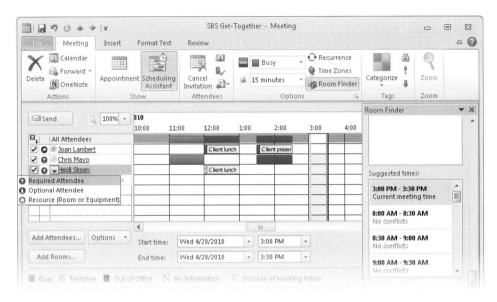

You can extend a courtesy invitation to optional attendees.

10. In the list, click **Optional Attendee**.

    The second attendee's icon changes to the letter i (for *information*) in a blue circle to indicate that you're sending the meeting request for his or her information, but he or she does not need to attend.

11. In the group schedule, experiment with changing the meeting time and duration by dragging the green start time bar and the red end time bar. Then in the **Suggested times** list, select a meeting time that works for all three attendees.

    The start time and end time bars move to the selected time slot.

    You can change the Show As and Reminder settings, create recurrences, assign color categories, and make any other changes you want. The availability specified in the Show As list will apply to all attendees who accept your meeting request.

12. After you select the meeting time you want, click the **Appointment** button in the **Show** group.

    On the Appointment page, the second attendee has been added to the To box, and the Start Time and End Time boxes display the meeting time you selected.

13. Verify the meeting details, and then click the **Send** button.

    The meeting appears in your calendar, and your co-workers or friends receive the meeting request.

 CLEAN UP Remind your attendees not to respond to the meeting request. Retain the SBS Get-Together meeting in your calendar for use in later exercises.

Updating and Canceling Meetings

You might find it necessary to change the date, time, or location of a meeting after you send the meeting request. As the meeting organizer, you can change any information in a meeting request at any time, including adding or deleting invited attendees, or canceling the meeting.

To edit a meeting request, double-click the meeting on your calendar. If the meeting is one of a series (a recurring meeting), Outlook prompts you to indicate whether you want to edit the meeting series or only the selected instance of the meeting. Make the changes you want, and then save and close the meeting window.

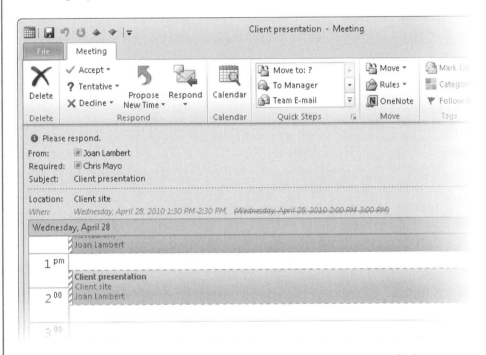

Changes to meeting details are tracked so that attendees can quickly identify them.

To cancel a meeting, click the meeting on your calendar and then click the Delete button in the Actions group on the Meeting or Meeting Series tab, or open the meeting window and then click the Delete button in the Delete group on the Meeting tab.

After you edit or cancel a meeting, Outlook sends an updated meeting request to the invited attendees to keep them informed. If the only change you make is to the attendee list, Outlook gives you the option of sending an update only to the affected attendees.

Responding to Meeting Requests

When you receive a meeting request from another Outlook user, the meeting appears on your calendar with your time scheduled as Tentative. Until you respond to the meeting request, the organizer doesn't know whether you plan to attend.

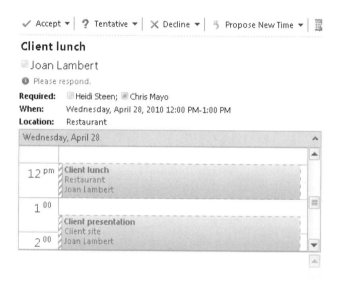

Unaccepted meeting requests in the Reading Pane.

You can respond to a meeting request in one of these four ways:

- You can accept the request. Outlook deletes the meeting request and adds the meeting to your calendar.

- You can tentatively accept the request, which indicates that you might be able to attend the meeting but are undecided. Outlook deletes the meeting request and shows the meeting on your calendar as tentatively scheduled.

- You can propose a new meeting time. Outlook sends your request to the meeting organizer for confirmation and shows the meeting with the original time on your calendar as tentatively scheduled.

- You can decline the request. Outlook deletes the meeting request and removes the meeting from your calendar.

If you don't respond to a meeting request, the meeting remains on your calendar with your time shown as tentatively scheduled.

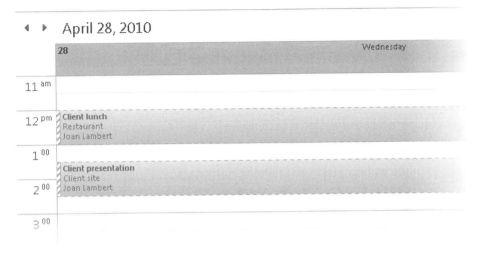

Tentatively scheduled time is indicated by diagonal striping.

If you're unsure whether a meeting time works for you, you can click the Calendar button within the meeting window. Your Outlook calendar for the suggested meeting day opens in a separate window so that you can view any conflicting appointments.

When accepting or declining a meeting, you can choose whether to send a response to the meeting organizer. If you don't send a response, your acceptance will not be tallied, and the organizer will not know whether you are planning to attend the meeting. If you do send a response, you can add a message to the meeting organizer before sending it.

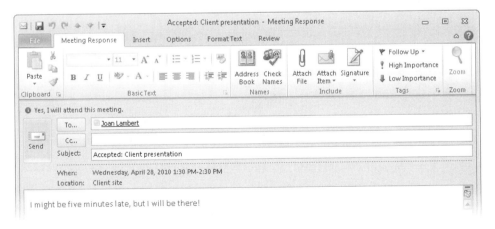

You can add a note to the meeting organizer or attach a document that pertains to the meeting subject.

To respond to a meeting request:

1. In the meeting window, in the Reading Pane, or on the shortcut menu that appears when you right-click the meeting request, click Accept, Tentative, or Decline.

2. Choose whether to send a standard response, a personalized response, or no response at all.

To propose a new time for a meeting:

1. In the meeting window, in the Reading Pane, or on the shortcut menu that appears when you right-click the meeting request, click Propose New Time, and then click Tentative And Propose New Time or Decline And Propose New Time.

   The Propose New Time dialog box opens.

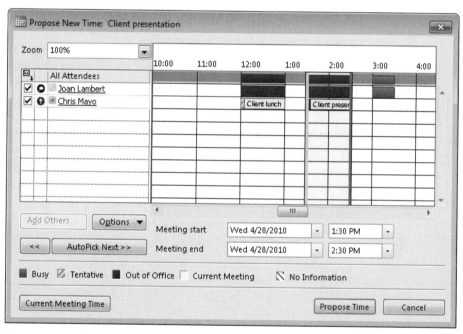

You can respond to a meeting request by proposing a different meeting time.

2. In the schedule area of the Propose New Time dialog box, change the meeting start and end times to the times you want to propose, and then click the Propose Time button.

3. In the meeting response window that opens, enter a message to the meeting organizer if you want to, and then click Send.

   Outlook sends your response and adds the meeting to your calendar as tentatively scheduled for the original meeting time. If the meeting organizer approves the meeting time change, you and other attendees will receive updated meeting requests showing the new meeting time.

Displaying Different Views of a Calendar

You can select a view and an arrangement for the display of your calendar. The default view is Calendar, and the default arrangement is Day. Most exercises in this chapter have shown the calendar in this default view and arrangement, which we refer to simply as *Day view*.

Tip Because Outlook 2010 coordinates your scheduled tasks to your calendar, you can look at your calendar in Day view or Week view to see the tasks that need to be completed that day or that week, and you can track your progress by marking tasks as complete when you finish them.

Views

The Calendar module offers four distinct views of content, which are available from the Change View list in the Current View group on the View tab. These views are:

- **Calendar** This is the standard view in which you display your Outlook calendar. In the Day, Work Week, or Week arrangement, Calendar view displays the subject, location, and organizer (if space allows) of each appointment, meeting, or event, as well as the availability bar and any special icons, such as Private or Recurrence.

- **Preview** In the Day, Work Week, or Week arrangement, Preview view displays additional information, including information from the notes area of the appointment window, as space allows.

- **List** This list view displays all appointments, meetings, and events on your calendar.

- **Active** This list view displays only future appointments, meetings, and events.

When working in a list view, you can group calendar items by selecting a field from the Arrangement gallery on the View tab.

Important In this book, we assume you are working in Calendar view, and refer to the standard Calendar view arrangements as *Day view*, *Work Week view*, *Week view*, and *Schedule view*. For information about changing and resetting views, see "Displaying Different Views of Contact Records" in Chapter 22, "Store and Access Contact Information."

Arrangements

By default, your calendar is shown in the Day arrangement of Calendar view. However, this arrangement displays your schedule only for the current day and doesn't keep you apprised of upcoming appointments later in the week or month. To help you stay on top of your schedule, you can display several different arrangements of your calendar:

- **Day** Displays one day at a time separated into half-hour increments.

- **Work Week** Displays only the days of your work week. The default work week is Monday through Friday from 8:00 A.M. to 5:00 P.M. Time slots that fall within the work week are white on the calendar; time slots outside of the work week are colored.

- **Week** Displays one calendar week (Sunday through Saturday) at a time.

- **Month** Displays one calendar month at a time, as well as the preceding and following weeks (for a total of six weeks, the same as the Date Navigator). When displaying Month view, you can choose one of three detail levels:

  - **Low Detail** Displays a calendar that is blank except for events.

  - **Medium Detail** Displays events and shaded, unlabeled bars to indicate appointments and meetings.

  - **High Detail** Displays events and labeled bars to indicate appointments and meetings.

- **Schedule view** Displays a horizontal view of the calendar for the selected time period. Schedule view, which is new in Outlook 2010, is very useful for comparing multiple calendars such as those of the members of a calendar group.

You switch among arrangements by clicking the buttons in the Arrangement group on the View tab of the Calendar module ribbon.

Tip If you've made changes to any view (such as the order in which information appears) and want to return to the default settings, click the Reset View button in the Current View group on the View tab. If the Reset View button is unavailable, the view already displays the default settings.

You can display a specific day, week, or month in the Calendar pane by using these techniques:

- In Month view, you can click the week tab at the left edge of a week to display only that week.

- In Month, Week, or Work Week view, you can display a specific day in Day view by double-clicking the header for that day.

- You can display the previous or next time periods by clicking the Back button or the Forward button next to the date or date range.

- You can display the current day by clicking the Today button in the Go To group on the Home tab.

Using the Date Navigator

You can use the Date Navigator to change the day or range of days shown on the calendar.

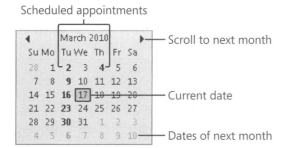

The default Date Navigator.

By default, the Date Navigator displays six weeks at a time. The current date is indicated by a red border. The days of the selected month are black. Days of the previous month and the next month are gray, but you can still select them in the Date Navigator. Bold dates indicate days with scheduled appointments, meetings, or events.

You can display a specific day, week, or month in the Calendar pane by selecting it in the Date Navigator. Use these techniques to work with the Date Navigator:

- To display a day, click that day.

   If you're displaying the calendar in Day, Work Week, or Week view, the day appears and is highlighted in the current view. If you're displaying the calendar in Month view, the display changes to Day view.

- To display a week, click the margin to the left of that week. Or, if you display week numbers in the Date Navigator and Calendar, click the week number to display that week.

   In any calendar view, selecting a week in the Date Navigator changes the display to Week view.

   Tip Specific weeks are referred to in some countries by number to simplify the communication of dates. (For example, you can say you'll be out of the office "Week 24" rather than "June 7-11.") Week 1 is the calendar week in which January 1 falls, Week 2 is the following week, and so on through to the end of the year. Because of the way the weeks are numbered, a year can end in Week 52 or (more commonly) in Week 53.

   To display week numbers in the Date Navigator and in the Month view of the calendar, select the Show Week Numbers... check box on the Calendar page of the Outlook Options dialog box.

● To display a month, click the Previous or Next button to scroll one month back or forward, or click the current month name and hold down the mouse button to display a range of months, point to the month you want to display, and then release the mouse button. To scroll beyond the seven-month range displayed by default, point to the top or bottom of the month list.

In Month view, scrolling the month displays the entire month; in Day view it displays the same date of the selected month, and in Week or Work Week view it displays the same week of the selected month.

In every Outlook module, the Date Navigator is located at the top of the To-Do Bar. In the Calendar module, if you close the To-Do Bar, the Date Navigator moves to the top of the Navigation Pane. In either location, you can display additional months by increasing the width or height of the area allocated to the Date Navigator. You can allocate up to 50 percent of the program window to the Navigation Pane or To-Do Bar.

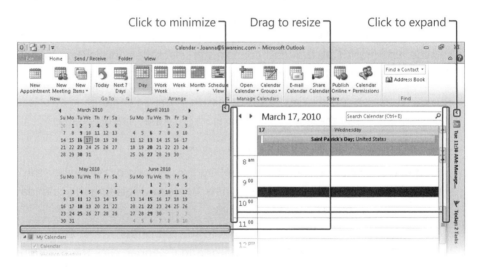

Expanding the Date Navigator in the Navigation Pane.

When the Date Navigator displays more than one month, each month shows either five or six weeks at a time—whichever is necessary to show all the days of the currently selected month in a Sunday through Saturday calendar format and to match the height of any other month displayed next to it. Only the first and last months include the days of the preceding or following month (in gray).

In this exercise, you'll first display different periods of time in your calendar and reset a customized view to its default settings. Then you'll change the display of the Daily Task List and of the To-Do Bar. Finally, you'll navigate through your calendar by using the Date Navigator, and display different levels of information about scheduled appointments and events.

 SET UP You need the SBS Lunch with Jane and SBS Staff Meeting appointments and the SBS Pay Day event you created in the previous exercises in this chapter. If you did not complete those exercises, you can do so now, or use any appointments, meetings, or events on your own calendar. Display the Calendar module in any Calendar view, and then follow the steps.

1. On the **Home** tab, in the **Arrange** group, click the **Work Week** button.

   Keyboard Shortcut Press Ctrl+Alt+2 to display your calendar in the Work Week arrangement.

   The Calendar pane displays your currently configured work week and highlights the corresponding days in the Date Navigator. The Daily Task List is open at the bottom of the pane. The first time slot of your work day appears at the top of the pane.

2. Scroll the **Calendar** pane to display one hour prior to the start of your work day.

   Time slots within your work day are white; time slots outside of your work day are shaded.

3. In the **Go To** group, click the **Today** button.

   If the Calendar pane wasn't previously displaying the current week, it does so now. The times displayed remain the same. The current day and the current time slot are highlighted.

Work week time slots ⎯⎯⎯ Current day ⎯⎯⎯ Non–work week time slots

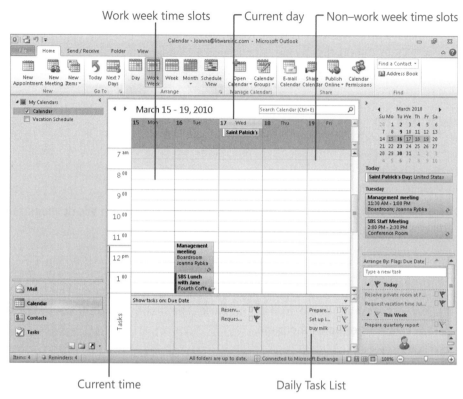

Current time ⎯⎯⎯ Daily Task List

When the To-Do Bar is open, the Date Navigator appears at the top of the To-Do Bar and not in the Navigation Pane.

4. On the **View** tab, in the **Current View** group, click the **Reset View** button.

A message box prompts you to confirm that you want to reset the view.

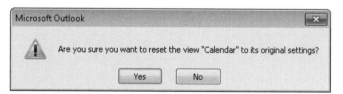

The Reset View command resets only the current view.

5. In the **Microsoft Outlook** message box, click **Yes**.

   The Calendar pane changes to display today's schedule in the default Day arrangement, with the Daily Task List open at the bottom of the pane.

6. On the **View** tab, in the **Layout** group, click the **Daily Task List** button, and then in the list, click **Minimized**.

   The Daily Task List changes to a single row at the bottom of the Calendar pane. The minimized Daily Task List displays a count of your total, active, and completed tasks for the day.

7. In the **Layout** group, click the **To-Do Bar** button, and then in the list, click **Minimized**.

   The To-Do Bar changes to a single column at the right side of the program window. The minimized To-Do Bar displays your next appointment and the number of tasks due today (from the To-Do Bar Task List).

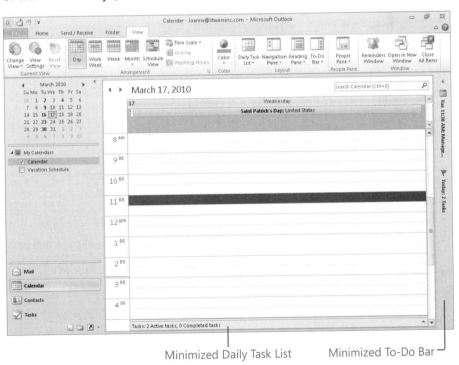

When the To-Do Bar is minimized, the Date Navigator moves to the Navigation Pane.

8. In the **Date Navigator**, which now appears at the top of the **Navigation Pane**, click a bold date to display your calendar for a day on which you have scheduled appointments or meetings.

9. In the **Date Navigator**, point to the left edge of a calendar row that contains one or more bold dates. When the cursor changes to point toward the calendar, click once.

The Calendar pane displays the selected seven-day week.

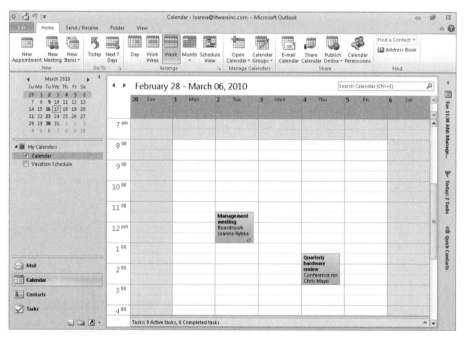

The days shown in the Calendar pane are shaded in the Date Navigator.

10. On the **Home** tab, in the **Arrange** group, click the **Month** button (not its arrow).

Keyboard Shortcut Press Ctrl+Alt+4 to display your calendar in the Month arrangement.

Outlook displays your calendar for the month. Alternating months are shaded to provide an obvious visual indicator of the change. The Daily Task List is not available in Month view.

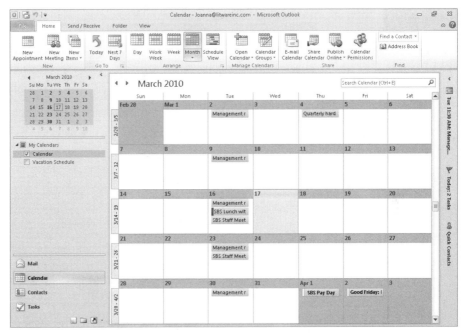

You can display a different month by scrolling the Calendar pane, or by clicking the month you want to view, in the Date Navigator.

11. In the **Arrange** group, click the **Month** arrow, and then click **Show Medium Detail**.

The calendar changes to display only events as readable items; appointments and meetings appear as horizontal lines, with the width of the line indicating the amount of time scheduled for that item.

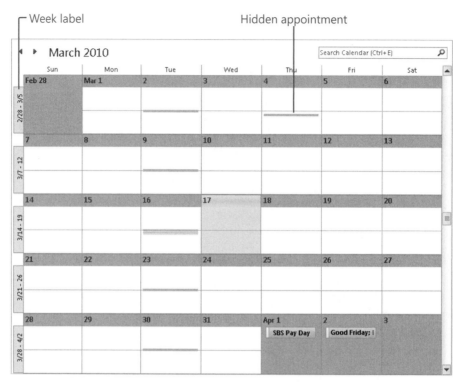

Week label   Hidden appointment

In Medium Detail view, items assigned to color categories are represented by lines in the category color.

12. In the **Month** list, click **Show Low Detail** to hide appointments and meetings entirely.

    The calendar changes to display only events; appointments and meetings are hidden entirely.

13. Click one of the week labels that appear along the left edge of the **Calendar** pane.

    Outlook displays the selected week in Week view. (If you had more recently displayed a Work Week view, the week would be shown in that view.) The calendar item details are no longer hidden.

14. To the left of the date range in the calendar header, click the **Forward** button.

    The calendar moves forward one week.

15. Use any of the available navigation methods to display the week containing one of the **SBS Staff Meeting** appointments.

Change
View ▾

16. On the **View** tab, in the **Current View** group, click the **Change View** button and then in the gallery, click **Preview**.

    The notes saved with the recurring appointment appear on the calendar.

17. Click the day label at the top of the day on which the **SBS Staff Meeting** appointment occurs.

    Outlook returns to Day arrangement, but still displays the Preview view.

11 00	
	Management meeting
	Boardroom
12 pm	Joanna Rybka
	Please have all reports from the previous week ready for this meeting.
	Lunch will be provided.
1 00	
2 00	**SBS Staff Meeting**
	Conference Room
	Bring status reports.
3 00	

In Preview view, the calendar displays any notes saved with the appointment.

18. In the **Change View** gallery, click **Calendar**.

    The Calendar pane returns to its default settings.

✖ **CLEAN UP** Retain the SBS Lunch With Jane and SBS Staff Meeting appointments and the SBS Pay Day event on your calendar for use in later exercises.

Key Points

- You can create and manage appointments and all-day events in your calendar.

- Other people in your organization can see whether you are free, busy, or out-of-office as a result of the appointments, events, and meetings scheduled in your calendar.

- You can personalize the display of your available working hours, and mark appointments as private to hide the details from other people.

- You can use Outlook to set up meetings, invite participants, and track their responses.

- Outlook can identify a meeting time based on participants' schedules.

- If your organization is running Exchange Server 2010 or Exchange Server 2007, you can use the Scheduling Assistant features to quickly identify meeting times of a specific duration during which your planned attendees are available.

- You can display many different views of your calendar. You can change the dates and date ranges displayed in the Calendar pane by using the Date Navigator, by using navigational buttons within the Calendar pane, or by using commands on the ribbon.

Chapter at a Glance

Create tasks, **page 716**

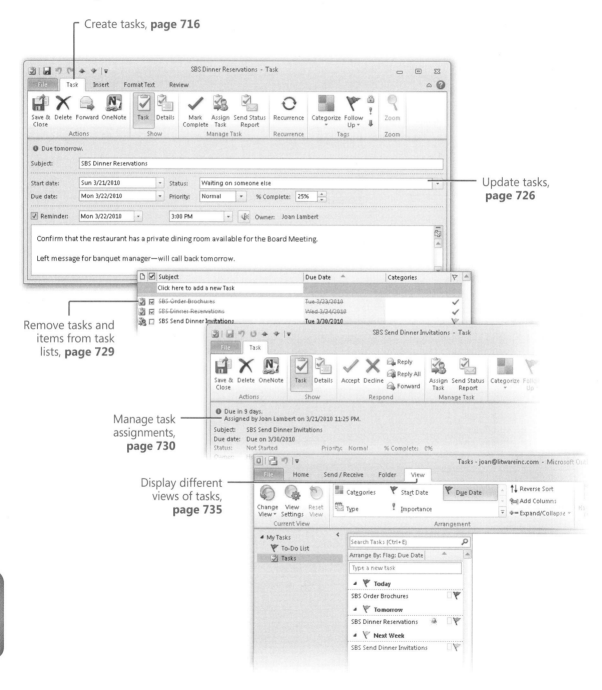

Update tasks, **page 726**

Remove tasks and items from task lists, **page 729**

Manage task assignments, **page 730**

Display different views of tasks, **page 735**

24 Track Tasks

In this chapter, you will learn how to

- ✔ Create tasks.
- ✔ Update tasks.
- ✔ Remove tasks and items from task lists.
- ✔ Manage task assignments.
- ✔ Display different views of tasks.

Many people keep one or more task lists going at all times, listing things to do, things to buy, people to call, and so on. You might cross off tasks as you complete them, transfer unfinished tasks to other lists, create multiple lists for multiple purposes, or follow a specialized system designed by an efficiency expert. You probably write these task lists on pieces of paper, even though you've undoubtedly experienced the pitfalls of that age-old system. Paper crumples, tears, and frequently ends up in the lint tray of the clothes dryer (even when you are sure you checked all the pockets before you put your pants in the laundry).

If you use Microsoft Outlook 2010 on a daily basis, you might find it far easier to use its built-in task list, called the *To-Do List*. You can add tasks, assign due dates, receive reminders, and mark tasks as complete when you finish them. You can even assign tasks to other people, and if those people use Outlook, you can view their progress on assigned tasks as they track progress milestones.

You can view the task list associated with your default e-mail account in several locations within Outlook, including the Tasks module, the To-Do Bar Task List, the Daily Task List that appears in selected calendar views, and the Outlook Today page. You can view other Outlook task lists in the Tasks module.

In this chapter, you'll create tasks from scratch and learn how to delegate tasks to other people and manage task assignments. You'll also review different ways of arranging, organizing, and locating tasks, and you'll remove tasks from your list by marking them as complete or deleting them.

> **Practice Files** The exercises in this chapter use Outlook items you created in exercises in previous chapters. If an exercise requires an item that you don't have, you can complete the exercise in which you create the item before beginning the exercise, or you can substitute a similar item of your own. A complete list of practice files is provided in "Using the Practice Files" at the beginning of this book.

See Also For information about the Daily Task List, see "Displaying Different Views of a Calendar" in Chapter 23, "Manage Scheduling." For information about the To-Do Bar and the To-Do Bar Task List, see "Displaying Different Views of Tasks" later in this chapter.

Creating Tasks

If you use your Outlook task list to its fullest potential, you'll frequently add tasks to it. You can create one-time or recurring tasks from scratch in different ways, or you can add an existing Outlook item (such as a message) to your task list. Regardless of how or where you create a task, all tasks are available in the Tasks module and in the To-Do Bar Task List. Only individual tasks are available in the Tasks List.

Tip Another way to add a task to your list is by accepting an assigned task. For more information, see "Managing Task Assignments" later in this chapter.

You can attach files to task items, and you can include text, tables, charts, illustrations, hyperlinks, and other content in the task window content pane by using the same commands you use in other Outlook item windows and in other Microsoft Office 2010 programs, such as Microsoft Word. You can also set standard Outlook item options such as recurrence, color categories, reminders, and privacy.

Tip You can maintain multiple task lists by creating folders to contain task items. For information about creating task folders, see the sidebar "Finding and Organizing Tasks" later in this chapter.

Creating Tasks from Scratch

You can create a task item from scratch by using one of several methods.

In the Tasks module:

- Click the New Task button on the Home tab, enter the task details in the task window that opens, and then save and close the task.

- When you display your To-Do List, enter the task description in the Type A New Task box at the top of the list, and then press Enter to create a task with the default settings.

- When you display your Tasks List, enter the task description in the Click Here To Add A New Task box, press Tab to move to subsequent fields, fill in other information, and then press Enter.

   Tip The fields available in the Tasks List vary based on the list view you're displaying. For information about the available views, see "Displaying Different Views of Tasks" later in this chapter.

In any module:

- Click the New Items button on the Home tab and then, in the list, click Task.

- In the To-Do Bar, enter the task description in the Type A New Task box at the top of the To-Do Bar Task List.

From any view of the task list, you can assign the task to a category, change the due date, add a reminder, mark the task as complete, or delete the task entirely. To access these commands, right-click the task name, category, or flag, and then click the option you want.

Tip By default, Outlook doesn't automatically set a reminder for tasks as it does for calendar items. You can turn on reminders from the Outlook Options dialog box. For more information about Outlook 2010 features not covered in this book, refer to *Microsoft Outlook 2010 Step by Step* by Joan Lambert and Joyce Cox (Microsoft Press, 2010).

Task Options

When you create a task item, the only information you must include is the subject. As with many other types of Outlook items, you can set several options for tasks to make it easier to organize and identify tasks.

- **Start date and due date** You can display tasks on the various Outlook task lists on either the start date or the due date. The color of the task flag indicates the due date.

- **Status** You can track the status of a task to remind yourself of your progress. Specific status options include Not Started, In Progress, Completed, Waiting On Someone, or Deferred. You also have the option of indicating what percentage of the task is complete. Setting the percentage complete to 25%, 50%, or 75% sets the task status to In Progress. Setting it to 100% sets the task status to Complete.

- **Priority** Unless you indicate otherwise, a task is created with a Normal priority level. You can set the priority to add a visual indicator of a task's importance. Low priority displays a blue downward pointing arrow and High priority displays a red exclamation point. You can sort and filter tasks based on their priority.

- **Recurrence** You can set a task to recur on a regular basis; for example, you might create a Payroll task that recurs every month. Only the current instance of a recurring task appears in your task list. When you mark the current task as complete, Outlook creates the next instance of the task.

- **Category** Tasks use the same category list as other Outlook items. You can assign a task to a category to associate it with related items such as messages and appointments.

- **Reminder** You can set a reminder for a task in the same way you do for an appointment. The reminder appears until you dismiss it or mark the task as complete.

- **Privacy** Marking a task as private ensures that other Outlook users to whom you delegate account access can't see the task details.

None of the options are required, but they can be helpful to you when sorting, filtering, and prioritizing your tasks.

Creating Tasks from Outlook Items

You frequently need to take action based on information you receive in Outlook—for example, information in a message or in a meeting request. You might want to add information from another Outlook item to your task list, to ensure that you complete any necessary follow-up work.

Depending on the method you use, you can either create a new task from an existing item or simply transfer the existing item to your task list by flagging it.

To create a new task from a message, contact, or note:

- Drag the message to the Tasks button at the bottom of the Navigation Pane, pause until the Navigation Pane changes to display the Tasks module content, and then release the mouse button.

This method opens a task window that already has information filled in from the original item. You can change settings, add information and attachments, assign the task to other people, and so on.

To transfer an existing e-mail message to your task list without creating an individual task:

- Click the flag icon to the right of a message in the Mail pane. This method, referred to as *flagging a message for follow-up*, adds the message to your task lists with the default due date specified in the Quick Click settings, and adds an information bar to the message. However, it does not create a separate task item, so to retain the task, you must retain the message—you can move the message between mail folders, but deleting the message deletes the task as well.

- Right-click the flag icon to the right of a message in the Mail pane, and then specify a due date: Today, Tomorrow, This Week, Next Week, No Date, or Custom (which allows you to set specific start and end dates).

   Tip Flagged messages appear on your task list under the default due date header. You can change the default due date either by setting the Quick Click flag in the Outlook Options dialog box or by right-clicking the flag and then clicking Set Quick Click. In the Set Quick Click dialog box, click the due date you want to appear by default, and then click OK.

- Drag the message to the To-Do Bar Task List and drop it under the heading for the due date you want to assign it to. (If the desired due date doesn't already have a heading in the To-Do Bar Task List, you need to drop the message under another heading and then assign the due date you want.) This method also adds the message to your task list but doesn't create a separate task item.

You can flag a contact record for follow-up by clicking the contact record in the Contacts pane and then clicking the Follow-Up button in the Tags group on the Home tab.

If you frequently want to create message-based tasks with special settings, such as a task with the original message attached to it, with specific follow-up settings or categories, and with specific assignments, you can create a Quick Step to accomplish all of these steps with one click.

In this exercise, you'll flag a message for follow-up and create tasks from the To-Do Bar Task List and from the Tasks pane.

 **SET UP** This exercise uses the SBS Tradeshow Schedule and SBS First Draft messages you created in Chapter 21, "Send and Receive E-Mail Messages." If you didn't create those messages, you can do so now, or you can substitute any messages in your Inbox. Display your Inbox, and expand the To-Do Bar if it is minimized. Locate the SBS Tradeshow Schedule message, and then follow the steps.

 1. In the message list, to the right of the **SBS Tradeshow Schedule** message, click the transparent **Quick Click** flag.

   The Quick Click flag changes from transparent to red, and a task named *SBS Tradeshow Schedule* appears in the Today category on your To-Do Bar Task List.

   Tip For the purposes of this exercise, we assume that you haven't yet created other tasks and Today is the only due date heading in the To-Do Bar Task List at this time.

2. In the **To-Do Bar Task List**, point to the **SBS Tradeshow Schedule** task.

A ScreenTip appears displaying the start date, reminder time, due date, the folder in which the message appears, and any categories assigned to the message.

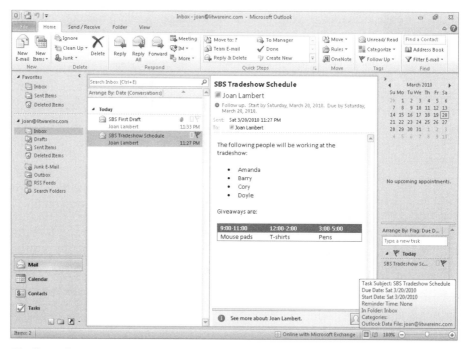

The flagged message appears in the To-Do Bar Task List. Pointing to the message displays additional information.

Troubleshooting The appearance of buttons and groups on the ribbon changes depending on the width of the program window or item window. For information about changing the appearance of the ribbon to match our screen images, see "Modifying the Display of the Ribbon" at the beginning of this book.

3. In the **To-Do Bar Task List**, double-click the **SBS Tradeshow Schedule** task.

The flagged message opens in a message window. The message header indicates that you need to follow up on this message. The start and due dates given are today's date.

Follow-up information

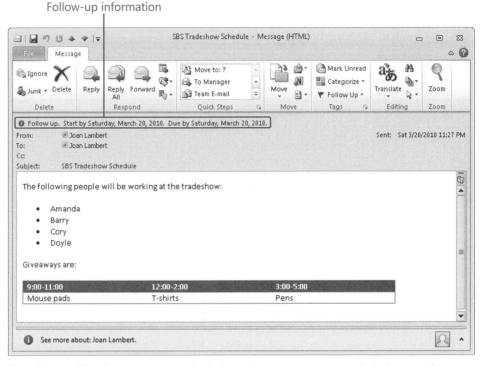

The ribbon of the flagged message includes only message commands; it does not have additional task-related tabs or commands.

4. Close the message window.

5. In the message list, locate the **SBS First Draft** message. Drag the message from the message list to the **To-Do Bar Task List**, and drop it under the **Today** heading.

    In the message list, the Quick Click flag in the right margin of the SBS First Draft message changes from transparent to red.

    Tip If you can't see all of your tasks, you can increase the height of the To-Do Bar Task List by dragging the horizontal divider between the calendar information and the task information upward.

6. In the **To-Do Bar Task List**, right-click (don't click) the red flag to the right of the **SBS First Draft** message.

    Troubleshooting Clicking an active flag marks the item as complete in the Inbox, and removes it from the To-Do Bar Task List. For more information, see "Removing Tasks and Items from Task Lists" later in this chapter.

    A list of due date options appears and, because a task has been activated, the Task List contextual tab appears on the ribbon.

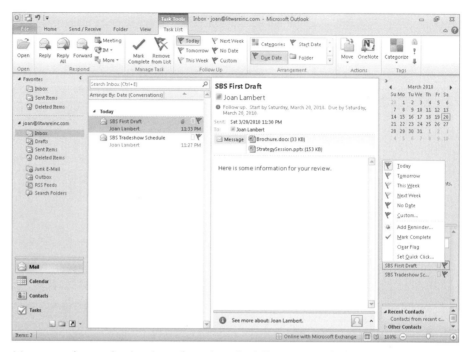

It's easy to change the due date of a task or the follow-up date for a flagged message in the To-Do Bar Task List.

7. In the list, click **This Week**.

   Tip Flagging a task for completion This Week or Next Week sets the start date to the first working day of the specified week and the due date to the last working day of the week. The default work week is Monday through Friday but the start and due dates reflect your own work week configuration.

   A new This Week due date heading appears in the To-Do Bar Task List with the message under the heading. In the message list and in the To-Do Bar Task List, the Quick Click flag to the right of the SBS First Draft message changes from red to light pink.

   Troubleshooting If the This Week heading doesn't automatically appear, click the Today heading to refresh the list.

8. At the top of the **To-Do Bar Task List**, click **Type a new task**, enter **SBS Order Brochures**, and then press Enter.

   Tip The tasks you create while working through the exercises in this book begin with *SBS* so that you can differentiate them from any real tasks you create.

   The new task appears in the Today section of the To-Do Bar Task List.

9. In the **Navigation Pane**, click the **Tasks** button.

The Tasks module opens, displaying your active tasks in the To-Do List. The icon preceding each item in the list indicates whether it is a standard task, a flagged e-mail message, and so on. Message icons match those shown in the Inbox, indicating whether the message is read or unread and whether you've replied to or forwarded the message.

10. In the **To-Do List**, click the **SBS Tradeshow Schedule** message.

    The Reading Pane displays the flagged message contents.

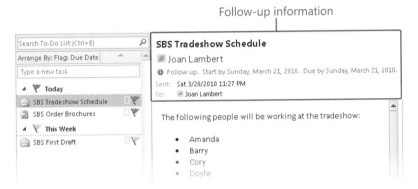

The To-Do List and Reading Pane of the Tasks module, displaying a flagged message.

11. In the **To-Do List**, click **SBS Order Brochures**.

    The Reading Pane displays the task item contents. You can't edit the task settings directly in the Reading Pane.

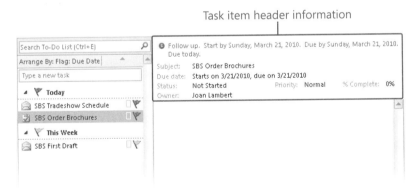

The To-Do List and Reading Pane, displaying a task item.

12. At the top of the **To-Do List**, click **Type a new task**, enter **SBS Dinner Reservations**, and then press Enter.

    The task appears in the Today section of both the To-Do List and the To-Do Bar Task List.

Next Week

13. In the **To-Do List**, click the **SBS Dinner Reservations** task. Then on the **Home** tab, in the **Follow Up** group, click **Next Week**.

In both task lists, the task appears under the Next Week heading. In the Reading Pane, the due date changes to Friday of the next week.

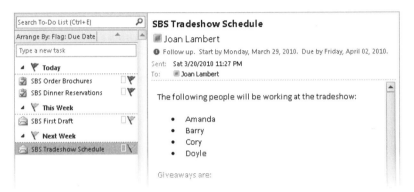

Setting the due date to Next Week puts the task under the Next Week heading but assigns an actual due date of the last working day of the next week.

14. Double-click the **SBS Dinner Reservations** task to open it in a task window.

15. In the notes pane, enter the following sentence:

Confirm that the restaurant has a private dining room available for the Board Meeting.

As with other Outlook items, you can add many types of content to the notes pane and format the text in the notes pane.

You can add notes, links, and attachments in the notes pane.

16. On the **Task** tab, in the **Actions** group, click the **Save & Close** button.

    The task window closes.

17. On the **Home** tab, in the **New** group, click the **New Task** button.

    An untitled task window opens.

18. In the **Subject** box, enter the following sentence:

    SBS Send Dinner Invitations.

19. Click the **Due date** arrow.

    A calendar appears.

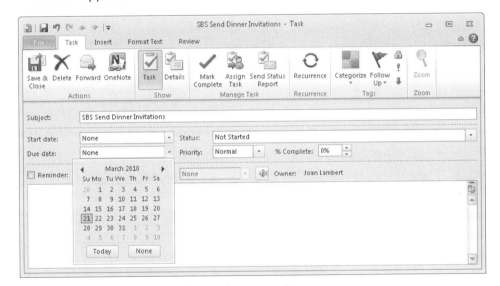

On the calendar, a red outline indicates the current date.

20. On the calendar, click the **Tuesday** of the next week (not of the current week).

    Tip You can't assign to a task a due date that has already passed.

21. Select the **Reminder** check box, click the **Reminder** arrow, and then in the calendar, click the **Monday** of the next week.

22. In the notes pane, enter the following sentence:

    Invite all Board members and their spouses.

23. In the **Actions** group, click the **Save & Close** button.

    Outlook adds the task to your task list, and it appears in the Next Week group in both the To-Do Bar Task List and the To-Do List.

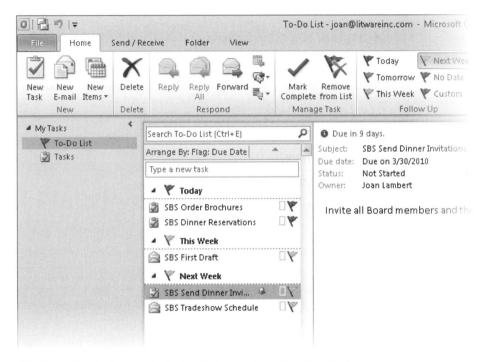

A bell next to a task name indicates that a reminder is set for the task.

 CLEAN UP Retain the SBS Order Brochures, SBS Dinner Reservations, and SBS Send Dinner Invitations tasks, and the flagged SBS Tradeshow Schedule and SBS First Draft messages, for use in later exercises.

Updating Tasks

Tasks generally appear on the Outlook task lists by start date or due date. You can change the details or dates of a task, or track the progress you've made on it.

To update the status of a task:

1. Open the task window.

2. In the % Complete list, type or select (by clicking the arrows) the percentage of the project you estimate as complete.

   Outlook changes the status to reflect your selection. Tasks that are 0% complete are Not Started, tasks that are 1% to 99% complete are In Progress, and tasks that are 100% complete are Completed.

3. If you want to manually change the task status—for example, to Waiting on someone else or Deferred—click that option in the Status list.

4. Save and close the task.

     Outlook updates the task both in your own task list and in the task originator's task list.

You can't track the status of a flagged message.

In this exercise, you'll update the status and due date of a task on your task list.

SET UP You need the SBS Dinner Reservations task you created earlier in this chapter to complete this exercise. If you didn't create that task, you can do so now, or you can substitute any task in your default task list. Display your To-Do List in the Tasks module, and then follow the steps.

1. In the **Tasks** pane, double-click the **SBS Dinner Reservations** task.

     For the purposes of this exercise, assume that you are waiting for the banquet manager to confirm whether a private dining room is available. You want to update the task to reflect your progress, change the task due date, and also remind yourself to call again if you don't hear from her by the end of the day.

2. Click the **Start date** arrow, and then on the calendar, click **Today**.

3. Click the **Status** arrow, and then in the list, click **Waiting on someone else**.

4. In the **% Complete** box, type or select (by clicking the arrows) **25%**.

5. In the notes pane, on a new line, type the following sentence:

     Left message for banquet manager—will call back tomorrow.

6. Click the **Due date** arrow, and then on the calendar, click the next day.

     The information bar at the top of the task header changes to reflect the new due date.

7. Select the **Reminder** check box. Click the first **Reminder** arrow, and then on the calendar, click the due date.

8. Click the second **Reminder** arrow, and then in the list, click **3:00 PM**.

     Outlook is set to display a reminder on the afternoon of the new due date.

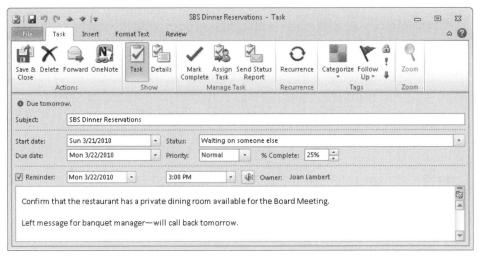

You can easily update a task to reflect its current completion status.

9. On the **Task** tab, in the **Actions** group, click the **Save & Close** button.

   In the To-Do List, the SBS Dinner Reservations task moves under the Tomorrow heading.

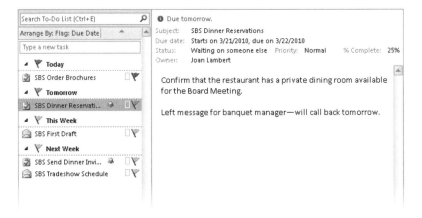

The changes you made in the task window are reflected in the Reading Pane.

✖ **CLEAN UP** Retain the SBS Dinner Reservations task for use in later exercises.

Removing Tasks and Items from Task Lists

When you complete a task or follow up on a flagged item, you have three options for managing its presence on your task list: marking the task or flagged item as complete, removing the flag from a flagged item, or deleting the task or flagged item entirely.

Marking a task or flagged item as complete retains a record of the item on your task list. Completed tasks are visible only in certain task list views.

To mark a task as complete:

- In the Tasks module, click the task to make it active, and then on the Home tab, in the Manage Task group, click the Mark Complete button.

- In views that include a check box preceding the task subject (most list views), select the check box to delete the task.

- In views that include a colored flag, click the flag once.

- In any view, right-click the task, and then click Mark Complete.

- In the task window, change the Status to Completed or the % Complete setting to 100%.

Whichever method you use, in your task list, the completed task is crossed through, the Complete check box is selected, and the flag changes to a check mark. In the task window for the completed task, Status is set to Completed and % Complete is set to 100%. (In other words, doing any one thing accomplishes all the others.)

Completed tasks appear in certain views of your Tasks List but not in your To-Do List.

After you mark an instance of a recurring task as complete, Outlook generates a new instance of the task at whatever interval you specified when creating the task.

Removing the flag from a flagged item such as a message or contact record retains the item in its original location but removes it from your task list entirely.

To remove the flag from an item:

- Display the Tasks module, click the flagged item to select it, and then click the Remove From List button in the Manage Tasks group on the Home tab.

- Click the flagged item in the To-Do Bar Task List and then click the Remove From List button in the Manage Tasks group on the Task List contextual tab.

- Right-click the flagged item, click Follow-up, and then click Clear Flag.

Deleting a task or flagged item moves the task or the original item to the Deleted Items folder; it is permanently deleted when you empty that folder. No record of it remains on your task list or in its original location (such as your Inbox).

To delete a task or flagged item:

- In the Tasks module, click the task to make it active and then on the Home tab, in the Delete group, click the Delete button.

- In any view, right-click the task, and then click Delete.

Managing Task Assignments

You can assign tasks from your Outlook task list to other people within your organization and outside of your organization (and other people can assign tasks to you). Outlook indicates assigned tasks in your task list by adding blue arrow pointing to a person on the task icon, similar to that of a shared folder in Windows Explorer.

Tasks You Assign to Others

You can assign tasks to people on your Microsoft Exchange Server network, to people on other Exchange Server networks, and to people running e-mail programs other than Outlook.

- When you assign a task to a person on your Exchange Server network, Outlook sends a task request, similar to a meeting request, to the person you designated. The assignee can accept or decline the task assignment by clicking the corresponding button in the Reading Pane or in the task window header. Outlook indicates the status of the task in your task list as Assigned.

- When you assign a task to a person who is on another Exchange Server network or is using an e-mail program other than Outlook, Outlook sends a message that the assignee can respond to manually. Until you change the task status, it is Waiting For Response From Recipient, rather than Assigned.

When you assign a task, you can choose whether to keep a copy of the task on your own task list or transfer it entirely to the assignee's task list. Either way, the task remains on your own task list until accepted, so you won't lose track of it. (If the recipient declines the task, you can return it to your task list or reassign it.)

Tip You can assign only actual task items; you can't assign flagged messages that appear in your task list.

After you assign a task to someone else, ownership of the task transfers to that person, and you can no longer update the information in the task window. (The assignee becomes the task owner and you become the task originator.) If you keep a copy of the task on your task list, you can follow the progress as the assignee updates the task status and details, and you can communicate information about the task to the owner by sending status reports. Unless you choose otherwise, Outlook automatically sends you a status report on an assigned task when the assignee marks the task as complete.

To delegate a task to another Outlook user:

1. In the task window, on the Task tab, in the Manage Task group, click the Assign Task button.

2. In the To box that appears in the task header, enter the e-mail address of the person you want to assign the task to.

3. In the task header, click the Send button. If a message box notifies you that the task reminder has been turned off, click OK.

   Outlook sends the task request, and notifies you when the assignee accepts or declines the task.

You can view the status of tasks you have assigned to other people by displaying your task list in Assignment view.

See Also For information about task list views, see "Displaying Different Views of Tasks" later in this chapter.

If you assign a task and the assignee declines the assignment, the task doesn't automatically return to your task list; you need to either reclaim it (return it to your own task list) or reassign it.

To reclaim or reassign a declined task:

1. Open the declined task assignment (indicated in your Inbox by a task icon with a red X).

   The Manage Task group on the Task tab of the ribbon includes commands specific to managing the declined task.

Declined task   Task management options

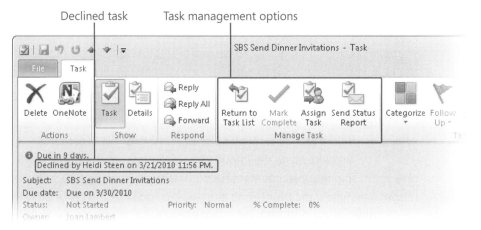

When an assignee declines a task, you can reclaim or reassign it.

2. In the Manage Task group, click the Return To Task List button to reclaim the task, or the Assign Task button to reassign it.

Tasks Other People Assign to You

When another person assigns a task to you, you receive a task assignment request.

To accept, decline, respond to, or reassign a task assignment request:

1. Open the task assignment request (indicated in your Inbox by a task icon with an outstretched hand).

   The Task tab of the ribbon includes commands specific to managing the task assignment request.

Assigned task   Task response options

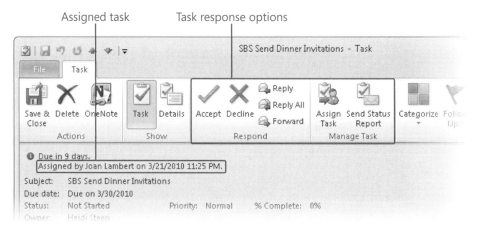

You can respond in several ways to a task assignment.

2. Take one of the following actions:

   ○ In the Respond group, click the Accept button to accept the task or the Decline button to decline the task, and send the associated response to the task owner.

   ○ In the Respond group, click Reply to send a message to the task owner without accepting or declining the task, or the Forward button to forward the task content to another person without reassigning the task.

   ○ In the Manage Task group, click the Assign Task button, and follow the process described earlier in this topic to assign the task to another person.

You can update the details of a task assigned to you by someone else in the same way that you do tasks that you create.

To send a status report about a task assigned to you by someone else:

1. Open the task window.

2. On the Task tab, in the Manage Task group, click the Send Status Report button.

   Outlook generates an e-mail message with the task information in the Subject field and message body.

3. Address the message to the people you want to send the report to, and then send the message.

In this exercise, you'll assign a task to another person.

SET UP You need the SBS Send Dinner Invitations task you created earlier in this chapter to complete this exercise. If you didn't create that task, you can do so now, or you can substitute any task in your default task list. Choose a co-worker or other e-mail contact to practice assigning tasks to, and let him or her know to expect a task assignment. Then display your To-Do List in the Tasks module, and follow the steps.

1. In the **Tasks** pane, double-click the **SBS Send Dinner Invitations** task.

   The task opens in a task window.

2. In the **Manage Task** group, click the **Assign Task** button.

   A To box and Send button appear in the task header, and the Manage Task group changes to display only the Cancel Assignment button.

3. In the **To** box, enter the e-mail address of the person to whom you want to assign the task.

Note that the Keep An Updated Copy Of This Task On My Task List and Send Me A Status Report When This Task Is Complete check boxes are selected by default.

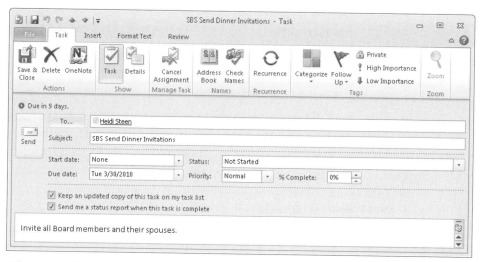

When you assign a task, you have the option of keeping it on your task list or removing it.

4. In the task header, click the **Send** button.

   A message box notifies you that the task reminder previously set for this task will be turned off when you assign it to another person.

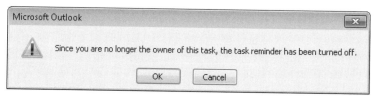

You don't receive reminders when tasks you assigned to others are overdue.

5. In the **Microsoft Outlook** message box, click **OK**.

   Outlook sends the task request. Your co-worker or contact receives a task assignment request.

6. Ask your co-worker or contact to accept the task.

   Outlook notifies you when the assignee accepts or declines the task.

 **CLEAN UP** Retain the SBS Send Dinner Invitations task for use in later exercises.

Displaying Different Views of Tasks

Outlook 2010 makes it simple to keep your task list at your fingertips. You can view tasks in several different locations, including the following:

- In the Tasks module, you can display either the To-Do List, which includes both tasks and flagged messages, or the Tasks List, which includes only tasks. There are many options for viewing and arranging each list.

- In any module, the expanded To-Do Bar displays the To-Do Bar Task List, where tasks are grouped and sorted under due date headings. (You can also sort this list by category, start date, folder, type, or importance, or you can create a custom arrangement.) You can scroll through the list to display all your tasks or collapse the groups you don't want to view. To increase the space available for your task list, you can close the Date Navigator or show fewer or no appointments.

  The minimized To-Do Bar displays only your next appointment (if you choose to display appointments) and the number of incomplete tasks due today (if you choose to display tasks). You switch between views of the To-Do Bar by clicking the Minimize or Expand button on its header.

- In the Calendar module, the Daily Task List appears at the bottom of the Calendar pane in Day, Work Week, or Week view. When expanded, the Daily Task List at displays the tasks due, including the category and task type, during the displayed time period. In Day view, the start date, due date, and reminder time also appear.

  Tip If you don't see the Daily Task List in Day, Work Week, or Week view, click the Daily Task List button in the Layout group on the View tab, and then click Normal.

  Like the Navigation Pane and the To-Do Bar, you can minimize the Daily Task List so that it displays only the number of active and completed tasks and provides more space for you to work. You can switch between views of the Daily Task List by clicking the Minimize or Expand button on its header.

  You can schedule a specific block of time to complete a task by dragging it from the Daily Task List to your calendar. When you mark the task complete, Outlook removes it from your calendar.

- On the Outlook Today page, the tasks due today are listed in the Tasks area. (This page was previously the "home page" of Outlook. You display the Outlook Today page by clicking your top-level account in the Navigation Pane.)

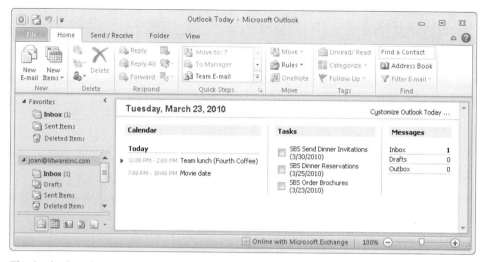

The Outlook Today page summarizes your activities for the current day.

So far in this chapter, we've been working in your To-Do List, which is the default Tasks module view and displays both tasks and flagged messages. You can display more comprehensive information about the tasks on a task list by clicking the Tasks entry for that account in the Tasks module Navigation Pane. As you can with your calendar, you can display different views of your Tasks List and within each view, different arrangements of the tasks.

You can change the view from the Change View gallery in the Current View group on the Home tab, or from the Change View gallery in the Current View group on the View tab. Tasks List views include:

- Active
- Assigned
- Completed
- Detailed
- Next 7 Days
- Overdue
- Prioritized
- Server Tasks
- Simple List
- Today
- To-Do List

The default view for the Tasks List is Simple List view, with tasks arranged by due date. Not surprisingly, the default view for the To-Do List is To-Do List.

From the Arrangements gallery in the Arrangement group on the View tab, you can select from the following standard arrangements of items within the To-Do List or a Tasks List view:

- Assignment
- Categories
- Due Date
- Folder (Available in the To-Do List only, this view separates tasks and flagged messages that are stored in different folders.)

  See Also For information about organizing tasks in custom folders, see the sidebar "Finding and Organizing Tasks" later in this chapter.

- Importance
- Modified Date
- Start Date
- Type

You can reorder the tasks in any list view by clicking the heading of the field you want to sort on. You can add and remove fields from the list view by using the Field Chooser, in the same way that you would from the list view of contact records.

See Also For information about adding and removing fields in a list view, see "Displaying Different Views of Contact Records" in Chapter 22, "Store and Access Contact Information."

Completed tasks remain in the Tasks List until you actually delete them, so they are available there if you want to view them.

Tip The Tasks List views don't by default display the Reading Pane. If you want, you can display it at the bottom of the Tasks pane so that you don't lose horizontal screen space and obscure task details. Click the Reading Pane button in the Layout group on the View tab, and then click Bottom.

In this exercise, you'll look at different views of tasks and flagged messages within the Tasks module.

 SET UP This exercise uses the SBS Order Brochures, SBS Dinner Reservations, and SBS Send Dinner Invitations tasks, and the SBS First Draft and SBS Tradeshow Schedule flagged messages you created and assigned earlier in this chapter. If you didn't create those tasks and messages, you can do so now, or you can substitute any tasks and flagged messages in your task list. Display the To-Do List in the Tasks module, in the default To-Do List view, and then follow the steps.

1. With the **To-Do List** displayed in the **Tasks** pane, click the **Change View** button in the **Current View** group on the **Home** tab.

   The Change View gallery expands. The To-Do List button is selected to indicate the current view.

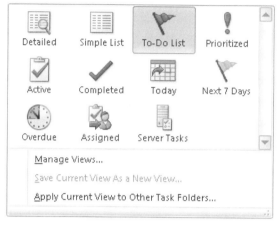

The Change View gallery.

2. In the **Change View** gallery, click **Detailed**.

   The To-Do List changes to a list view displaying many different task fields. The Reading Pane, which by default is open to the right of the Tasks pane in To-Do List view, closes.

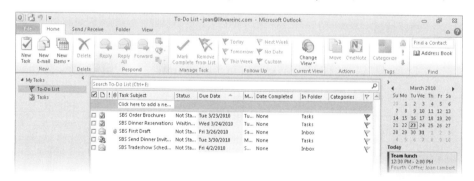

The To-Do List displayed in the Detailed view.

In this view, the To-Do List resembles the Tasks List.

3. In the **Navigation Pane**, click **Tasks**.

   The Tasks List appears in the Tasks pane. Only the tasks appear in the list; the flagged messages are absent.

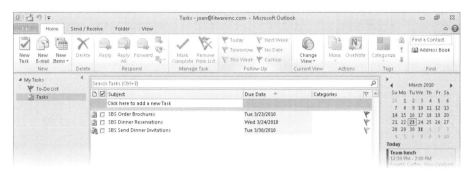

The Tasks List, displayed in Simple List view and arranged by due date.

The Tasks List displays its default Simple List view rather than the Detailed view you chose for the To-Do List. The arrow in the Due Date header indicates the current arrangement.

4. On the **View** tab, in the **Arrangement** gallery, click the **More** button.

The gallery expands to display additional arrangements.

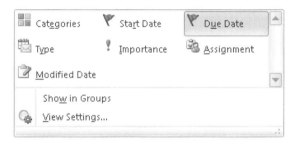

The Arrangement gallery.

5. In the **Arrangement** gallery, click **Assignment**.

The order of the tasks changes slightly, although it's not entirely obvious how or why.

6. In the **Arrangement** gallery, click **Show in Groups**.

The list changes to clearly distinguish tasks that you've assigned to other people from tasks that you own. If you have assigned tasks to multiple people, each assignee has a group.

You can group tasks by the current arrangement.

7. In the **Current View** group, in the **Change View** gallery, click **Assigned**.

The list changes to display only the task that you assigned in a previous exercise. Although only one task is visible in the Tasks List, the To-Do Bar Task List still displays all the tasks and flagged messages, so you can feel confident that you're looking at a filtered view and haven't accidentally deleted the other tasks.

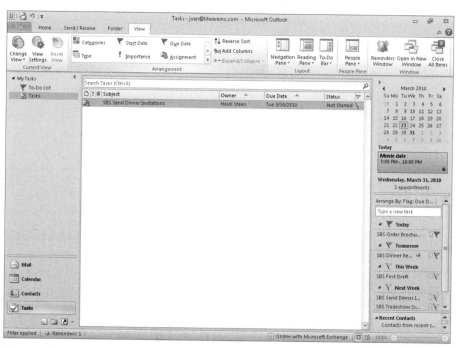

You can filter a task list to display tasks that meet very specific criteria.

8. In the **Change View** gallery, click **To-Do List**.

The Tasks pane displays all the active tasks in the same format as the default To-Do List. The arrangement changes to Due Date.

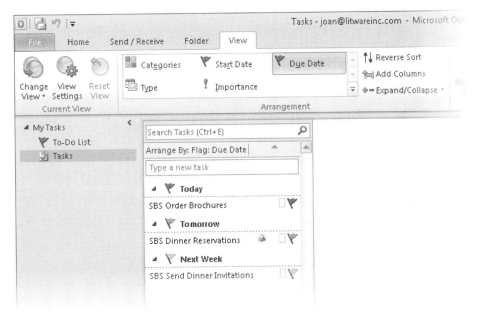

The Reading Pane is open by default in the To-Do List view of the Tasks pane.

Note, however, that this is not the real To-Do List—it doesn't include the flagged messages.

9. In the **Navigation Pane**, click **To-Do List**.

The flagged messages reappear in the Tasks pane.

✖ CLEAN UP Return to the Tasks List, and change the view back to the default Simple List view. Retain the SBS Order Brochures, SBS Dinner Reservations, and SBS Send Dinner Invitations tasks, and the flagged SBS Tradeshow Schedule and SBS First Draft messages, for use in later exercises.

Finding and Organizing Tasks

You can use the Outlook 2010 Search feature to quickly locate tasks by searching on any text in the task or in a file attached to the task. Type the word or other information you want to find in the Search box at the top of the Tasks pane header, in any view. Outlook filters the tasks as you type, displaying only those containing the search criteria you enter, and highlighting the matching criteria in the tasks.

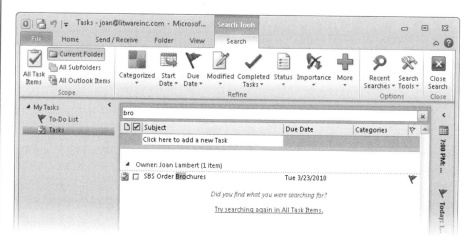

You can modify your search by using the tools on the contextual Search tab.

To help you organize your tasks, you can assign them to color categories in the same way that you do any other Outlook item.

If your task list gets too big, or if you want to maintain separate task lists for different purposes, you can organize tasks into separate folders. To create a task folder:

1. On the Folder tab, in the New group, click the New Folder button.

2. In the Create New Folder dialog box, enter the name and select the location of the folder.

3. In the Folder Contains list, click Task Items, and then click OK.

You can then drag existing tasks into the folder.

Tip If you drag a task into a Mail, Calendar, Contact, or Note Items folder, a message, meeting, contact, or note window opens with the task's subject entered in the Subject field and details of the task in the message body or notes pane.

Key Points

- You can create tasks for yourself and assign tasks to other people.
- Outlook displays tasks in the Tasks pane, in the Daily Task List in the Calendar pane, and on the To-Do Bar, which is available from any Outlook pane.
- You can organize tasks by grouping them in additional task folders or by categorizing them.
- When you assign tasks, Outlook sends a task request to the designated person, who can accept or decline the task. If you keep a copy of the assigned task, it is automatically updated when the person you assigned the task to updates the original.
- You can update tasks assigned to you and send status reports to the person who assigned the task.
- A task can have a status of Not Started, Deferred, Waiting, Complete, or the percentage completed.
- You can create one-time or recurring tasks. Outlook creates a new occurrence of a recurring task every time you complete the current occurrence.
- You can set a reminder to display a message at a designated time before a task is due.
- When you complete a task you can mark it as complete, remove it from your task list, or delete it.

Microsoft Access 2010

Chapter at a Glance

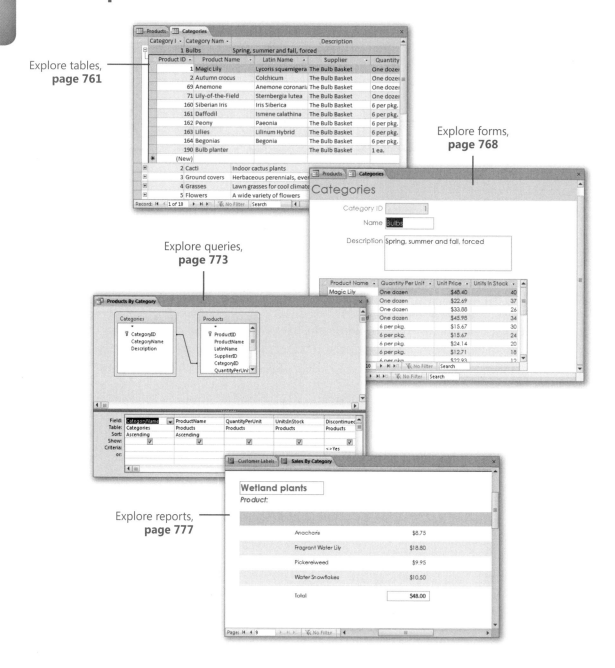

Explore tables,
page 761

Explore forms,
page 768

Explore queries,
page 773

Explore reports,
page 777

25 Explore an Access 2010 Database

In this chapter, you will learn how to

✔ Work in Access 2010.

✔ Understand database concepts.

✔ Explore tables.

✔ Explore forms.

✔ Explore queries.

✔ Explore reports.

✔ Preview and print Access objects.

Microsoft Access 2010 is part of Microsoft Office 2010, so the basic interface—such as the Quick Access Toolbar, the ribbon, the Backstage view, and dialog boxes—should be familiar if you have used other Office 2010 programs. However, Access has more dimensions than many of those programs, so it might seem more complex until you become familiar with it.

Tip If you are upgrading from an earlier version of Access, you should refer to the introduction in *Microsoft Access Step by Step*, by Joyce Cox and Joan Lambert (Microsoft Press, 2010), to learn about differences between earlier versions and Access 2010.

Throughout this book, you'll be working with databases that contain information about the employees, products, suppliers, and customers of a fictional company. As you complete the exercises in this book, you will develop an assortment of tables, forms, queries, and reports, which are called *database objects*. These objects can be used to enter, edit, and manipulate the information in a database in many ways.

In this chapter, you'll explore the Access program window and learn about the concepts and structure of data storage in Access, including types of databases, types of database objects, and relationships between objects. You'll look at objects in a working database, learning about interesting features of Access as well as functionality that you'll explore in more depth in later chapters.

> **Practice Files** Before you can complete the exercises in this chapter, you need to copy the book's practice files to your computer. The practice file you'll use to complete the exercises in this chapter is in the Chapter25 practice file folder. A complete list of practice files is provided in "Using the Practice Files" at the beginning of this book.

Working in Access 2010

As with all programs in Office 2010, the most common way to start Access is from the Start menu displayed when you click the Start button at the left end of the Windows Taskbar. When you start Access without opening a database, the program window opens in the Backstage view, with the New page active. In the Backstage view, commands related to managing Access and Access databases (rather than their objects) are organized as buttons and pages, which you display by clicking the page tabs in the left pane. You can display the Backstage view at any time by clicking the colored File tab in the upper-left corner of the program window.

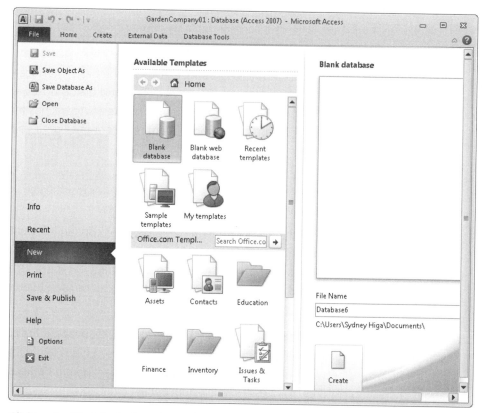

Clicking the File tab displays the Backstage view, where you can manage database files and customize the program.

From the New page of the Backstage view, you can create a blank database; or you can create a new database based on a template that comes with Access, on a template down-loaded from the Office.com Web site, or on a custom template saved on your computer or on your network. From the Backstage view, you can also open a database you worked in recently, or navigate to any database on your computer and open it.

When you create or open a database, it is displayed in the program window.

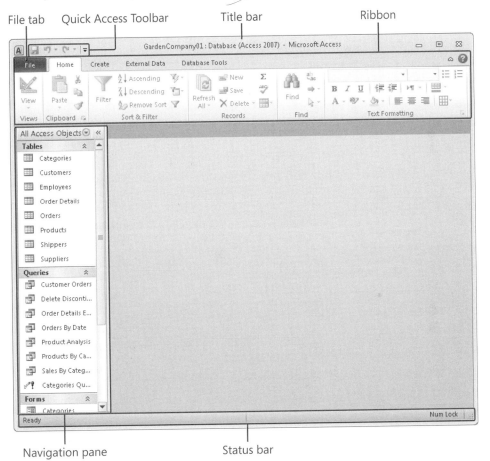

An Access database in the program window

Troubleshooting The appearance of buttons and groups on the ribbon changes depending on the width of the program window. For information about changing the appearance of the ribbon to match our screen images, see "Modifying the Display of the Ribbon" at the beginning of this book.

The database interface is designed to closely reflect the way people generally work with a database or database object. For those of you who are not familiar with this interface, which was first introduced with Microsoft Office Access 2007, here is a quick survey of the program window elements:

- The title bar displays the name of the active database. The designation *(Access 2007)* after the database name indicates that the database is in the .accdb format introduced with Access 2007. At the left end of the title bar is the Access icon, which you click to display commands to move, size, and close the program window. The Minimize, Restore Down/Maximize, and Close buttons at the right end of the title bar serve the same functions as in all Windows programs.

  See Also Windows 7 introduced many fun and efficient new window-management techniques. For information about ways to work with the Access program window on a Windows 7 computer, refer to *Windows 7 Step by Step,* by Joan Lambert Preppernau and Joyce Cox (Microsoft Press, 2009).

- By default, the Quick Access Toolbar appears to the right of the Access icon at the left end of the title bar, and displays the Save, Undo, and Redo buttons. You can change the location of the Quick Access Toolbar and customize it to include any command that you use frequently.

  Tip If you create and work with complicated databases, you might achieve greater efficiency if you add the commands you use frequently to the Quick Access Toolbar and display it below the ribbon, directly above the workspace. For information about Access 2010 features not covered in this book, refer to *Microsoft Access 2010 Step by Step* by Joyce Cox and Joan Lambert (Microsoft Press 2010).

- Below the title bar is the ribbon. All the commands for working with your Access database content are available from this central location so that you can work efficiently with the program.

- Across the top of the ribbon is a set of tabs. Clicking the File tab displays the Backstage view. Clicking any other tab displays a set of related commands represented by buttons and lists. The Home tab is active by default.

  Tip Don't be alarmed if your ribbon has tabs not shown in our screens. You might have installed programs that add their own tabs to the Access ribbon.

- On each tab, commands are organized into named groups. Depending on your screen resolution and the size of the program window, the commands in a group might be displayed as labeled buttons, as unlabeled icons, or as one or more large buttons that you click to display the commands within the group.

- If a button label isn't visible, you can display the command name and its keyboard shortcut (if it has one) in a ScreenTip by pointing to the button.

  Tip To control the display of ScreenTips, display the Backstage view, click Options to open the Access Options dialog box, and change settings in the User Interface Options area of the General page. You can also change the language of ScreenTip content on the Language page.

- Some buttons include an integrated or separate arrow. If a button and its arrow are integrated, clicking the button will display options for refining the action of the button. If the button and its arrow are separate, clicking the button will carry out the default action indicated by the button's current icon. You can change the default action by clicking the arrow and then clicking the action you want.

- Related but less common commands are not represented as buttons in a group. Instead they are available in a dialog box or task pane, which you display by clicking the dialog box launcher located in the lower-right corner of the group.

- To the right of the ribbon tab names, below the Minimize/Maximize/Close buttons, is the Minimize The Ribbon button. Clicking this button hides the commands but leaves the tab names visible. You can then click any tab name to temporarily display its commands. Clicking anywhere other than the ribbon hides the commands again. When the full ribbon is temporarily visible, you can click the button at its right end, shaped like a pushpin, to make the display permanent. When the full ribbon is hidden, you can click the Expand The Ribbon button to permanently redisplay it.

  Keyboard Shortcut Press Ctrl+F1 to minimize or expand the ribbon.

- Clicking the Access Help button at the right end of the ribbon displays the Access Help window, in which you can use standard techniques to find information.

  Keyboard Shortcut Press F1 to display the Access Help window.

  See Also For information about the Help system, see "Getting Help" at the beginning of this book.

- On the left side of the program window, the Navigation pane displays lists of database objects. By default, it displays all the objects in the database by type of object, but you can filter the list by clicking the pane's title bar and then clicking the category or group of objects you want to display. You can collapse and expand the groups in the list by clicking the chevrons in the section bars. If the Navigation pane is in your way, you can click the Shutter Bar Open/Close button in its upper-right corner to minimize it. To redisplay the Navigation pane, click the Shutter Bar Open/Close button again. You can drag the right border of the pane to the left or right to make it wider or narrower.

Keyboard Shortcut Press F11 to display or hide the Navigation pane.

● Across the bottom of the program window, the status bar displays information about the current database and provides access to certain program functions. You can control the contents of the status bar by right-clicking it to display the Customize Status Bar menu, on which you can click any item to display or hide it.

● At the right end of the status bar, the View Shortcuts toolbar provides buttons for quickly switching the view of the active database object.

The goal of all these interface features is to make working with a database as intuitive as possible. Commands for tasks you perform often are readily available, and even those you might use infrequently are easy to find.

In this exercise, you'll take a tour of the command structure in the Access 2010 program window.

 SET UP You need the GardenCompany01_start database located in your Chapter25 practice file folder to complete this exercise, but don't open it yet. Just follow the steps.

1. On the **Start** menu, click **All Programs**, click **Microsoft Office**, and then click **Microsoft Access 2010**.

   Access starts and displays the program window in the Backstage view. From this view, you manage your Access database files, but you don't work with the content of databases. For example, you can create a database, but not a database object. We'll talk about the tasks you can perform in the Backstage view in other chapters of this book.

2. In the left pane of the Backstage view, click **Open**. Then in the **Open** dialog box, navigate to your **Chapter25** practice file folder, and double-click the **GardenCompany01_start** database.

   The database opens in the program window. A security warning appears below the ribbon.

3. In the security warning bar, click **Enable Content**.

    Important Be sure to read the sidebar "Enabling Macros and Other Database Content" later in this chapter to learn about Access security options.

    Let's save the database so that you can explore it without fear of overwriting the original practice file.

4. Click the **File** tab to display the Backstage view, click **Save Database As**, and then in the **Save As** dialog box, save the database in your **Chapter25** practice file folder with the name **GardenCompany01**.

    Tip In this book, we assume you will save files in your practice file folders, but you can save them wherever you want. When we refer to your practice file folders in the instructions, simply substitute the save location you chose.

    In the program window, the title bar tells you that you can work with this database in Access 2007 as well as Access 2010. On the left, the Navigation pane displays a list of all the objects in this database. Spanning the top of the window, the ribbon includes five tabs: File, Home, Create, External Data, and Database Tools. The Home tab is active by default. Because no database object is currently open, none of the buttons on the Home tab are available.

    Tip Databases created with Access 2010 use the file storage format introduced with Access 2007, and their files have the .accdb extension. You can open database files created in earlier versions of Access (which have an .mdb extension) in Access 2010. You can then either work with and save them in the old format or work with and save them in the new format. If you convert them, you can no longer open them in versions prior to Access 2007. For more information about the ACCDB format, search for accdb in Access Help.

5. In the **Navigation** pane title bar, click **All Access Objects**, and then under **Filter By Group** in the menu, click **Tables**.

    The Navigation pane now lists only the tables in the database.

6. In the **Navigation** pane, under **Tables**, double-click **Categories**.

    The Categories table opens on a tabbed page. Because a table is displayed, two Table Tools contextual tabs (Fields and Table) appear on the ribbon. These contextual tabs are displayed only when you are working with a table.

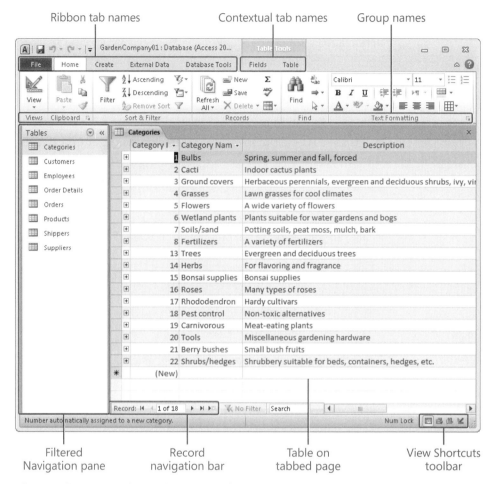

Ribbon tab names   Contextual tab names   Group names

Filtered Navigation pane   Record navigation bar   Table on tabbed page   View Shortcuts toolbar

The record navigation bar at the bottom of the table page tells you how many records the table contains and which one is active, and enables you to move among records.

Buttons representing commands related to working with database content are organized on the Home tab in six groups: Views, Clipboard, Sort & Filter, Records, Find, and Text Formatting. Only the buttons for commands that can be performed on the currently selected database object—in this case, a table—are active.

7. On the **Home** tab, click the **Text Formatting** dialog box launcher.

   The Datasheet Formatting dialog box opens.

   From this dialog box, you can access settings not available as buttons in the Text Formatting group, such as Gridline Color and Border And Line Styles.

8. In the **Datasheet Formatting** dialog box, click **Cancel**.

9. Click the **Create** tab.

   Buttons representing commands related to creating database objects are organized on this tab in six groups: Templates, Tables, Queries, Forms, Reports, and Macros & Code.

   The Create tab.

10. Double-click the **Create** tab.

Double-clicking the active tab hides the ribbon and provides more space for the current database object.

The ribbon is hidden.

11. Click the **External Data** tab.

The ribbon temporarily drops down, with the External Data tab active. Buttons representing commands related to moving information between a database and other sources are organized on this tab in four groups: Import & Link, Export, Collect Data, and Web Linked Lists.

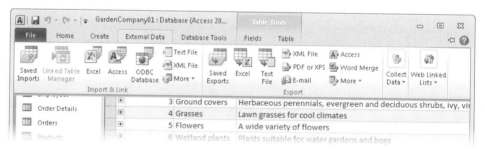

Clicking any tab—in this case, the External Data tab—displays the ribbon temporarily.

Tip To make the graphics in this book readable, we are working in a program window that is smaller than full-screen. As a result, the Collect Data and Web Linked Lists groups are represented in this graphic as buttons. For more information, see "Modifying the Display of the Ribbon" at the beginning of this book.

12. Click anywhere in the open table.

The ribbon disappears again.

13. Double-click the **Database Tools** tab.

Double-clicking a tab permanently displays the ribbon and activates that tab. Buttons representing commands related to managing, analyzing, and ensuring data reliability are organized on the Database Tools tab in six groups: Tools, Macro, Relationships, Analyze, Move Data, and Add-Ins.

The Database Tools tab.

14. To the right of the **Categories** table page tab, click the **Close** button to close the table without closing the database.

Clicking this button closes the active object.

15. Click the **File** tab to display the Backstage view, and then click **Close Database**.

When you close a database without exiting Access, the New page of the Backstage view is displayed so that you can open another database or create a new one.

Note that if you don't close the active database before opening another one, Access prompts you to save your changes and closes the active database for you. You cannot have two databases open simultaneously in a single instance of Access. If you want to have two databases open at the same time, you must start a new instance of Access.

Tip You can close Access entirely by clicking the Close button in the upper-right corner of the program window, or by clicking Exit in the Backstage view.

CLEAN UP Retain the GardenCompany01 database for use in later exercises.

Enabling Macros and Other Database Content

Some databases contain Microsoft Visual Basic for Applications (VBA) macros that can run code on your computer. In most cases, the code is there to perform a database-related task, but hackers can also use macros to spread a virus to your computer.

When you open a database that is not stored in a trusted location or signed by a trusted publisher, Access displays a security warning below the ribbon.

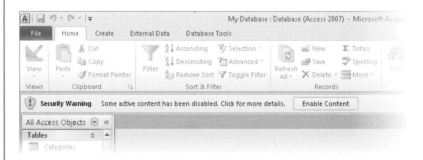

The security warning.

While the security warning is displayed, the macros in the database are disabled. You can enable macros in three ways:

- By enabling the macros in the database for use in the current database session.

- By adding the database publisher to the list of trusted publishers. This option is available only if the publisher's digital signature is attached to the database. Access will then automatically enable macro content in any database that is also signed by that publisher.

- By placing the database in a trusted location. Access automatically enables macro content in any database saved in that location. The trusted locations you specify within Access are not also trusted by other Office programs.

To enable macros for the current database session only:

- In the Security Warning area, click Enable Content.

To add the publisher of a digitally signed database to the trusted publishers list:

1. In the Security Warning area, click Some Active Content Has Been Disabled. Click For More Details.

2. On the Information About *<Database Name>* page, click the Enable Content button, and then click Advanced Options.

3. In the Microsoft Office Security Options dialog box, click Trust All From Publisher, and then click OK.

   Note that the Trust All From Publisher option is available only if the database is digitally signed.

To add the location of a database to the trusted locations list:

1. Display the Backstage view, and then click Options.

2. In the left pane of the Access Options dialog box, click Trust Center, and then click Trust Center Settings.

3. In the left pane of the Trust Center, click Trusted Locations.

4. On the Trusted Locations page, click Add New Location.

5. In the Microsoft Office Trusted Location dialog box, click Browse.

6. In the Browse dialog box, browse to the folder containing the current database, and then click OK.

7. In the Microsoft Office Trusted Location dialog box, select the Subfolders Of This Location Are Also Trusted check box if you want to do so, and then click OK in each of the open dialog boxes.

If you prefer, you can change the way Access handles macros in all databases:

1. Display the Trust Center, and then in the left pane, click Macro Settings.

2. Select the option for the way you want Access to handle macros:

   ○ **Disable All Macros Without Notification** If a database contains macros, Access disables them and doesn't display the security warning to give you the option of enabling them.

   ○ **Disable All Macros With Notification** Access disables all macros and displays the security warning.

   ○ **Disable All Macros Except Digitally Signed Macros** Access automatically enables digitally signed macros.

   ○ **Enable All Macros** Access enables all macros (not recommended).

3. Click OK to close the Trust Center, and then click OK to close the Access Options dialog box.

Understanding Database Concepts

Simple database programs, such as the Database component of Microsoft Works, can store information in only one table. These simple databases are often called *flat file databases*, or just *flat databases*. More complex database programs, such as Access, can store information in multiple related tables, thereby creating what are referred to as *relational databases*. If the information in a relational database is organized correctly, you can treat these multiple tables as a single storage area and pull information electronically from different tables in whatever order meets your needs.

A table is just one of the object types you work with in Access. Other object types include forms, queries, reports, macros, and modules.

Of all these object types, only one—the table—is used to store information. The rest are used to enter, manage, manipulate, analyze, retrieve, or display the information stored in a table—in other words, to make the information as accessible and therefore as useful as possible.

Over the years, Microsoft has put a lot of effort into making Access not only one of the most powerful consumer database programs available, but also one of the easiest to learn and use. Because Access is part of Office 2010, you can use many of the same techniques you use with Microsoft Word and Microsoft Excel. For example, you can use familiar commands, buttons, and keyboard shortcuts to open and edit the information in Access tables. And you can easily share information between Access and Word, Excel, or other Office programs.

In its most basic form, a database is the electronic equivalent of an organized list of information. Typically, this information has a common subject or purpose, such as the list of employees shown in the following table.

ID	Last name	First name	Title	Hire date
1	Anderson	Nancy	Sales Rep	May 1, 2003
2	Carpenter	Chase	Sales Manager	Aug 14, 2001
3	Emanuel	Michael	Sales Rep	Apr 1, 1999
4	Furse	Karen	Buyer	May 3, 2004

This list is arranged in a table of columns and rows. Each column represents a field—a specific type of information about an employee: last name, first name, hire date, and so on. Each row represents a record—all the information about a specific employee.

If a database did nothing more than store information in a table, it would be no more useful than a paper list. But because the database stores information in an electronic format, you can manipulate the information in powerful ways to extend its utility.

For example, suppose you want to find the phone number of a person who lives in your city. You can look up this information in the telephone book, because its information is organized for this purpose. If you want to find the phone number of someone who lives further away, you can go to the public library, which probably has a telephone book for each major city in the country. However, if you want to find the phone numbers of all the people in the country with your last name, or if you want to find the phone number of your grandmother's neighbor, these printed phone books won't do you much good, because they aren't organized in a way that makes that information easy to find.

When the information published in a phone book is stored in a database, it takes up far less space, it costs less to reproduce and distribute, and, if the database is designed correctly, the information can be retrieved in many ways. The real power of a database isn't in its ability to store information; it is in your ability to quickly retrieve exactly the information you want from the database.

Exploring Tables

Tables are the core database objects. Their purpose is to store information. The purpose of every other database object is to interact in some manner with one or more tables. An Access database can contain thousands of tables, and the number of records each table can contain is limited more by the space available on your hard disk than by anything else.

Tip For detailed information about Access specifications, such as the maximum size of a database or the maximum number of records in a table, search for *"Access 2010 specifications"* (including the quotation marks) in Access help.

Every Access object has two or more views. For tables, the two most common views are Datasheet view, in which you can see and modify the table's data, and Design view, in which you can see and modify the table's structure. To open a table in Datasheet view, either double-click its name in the Navigation pane, or right-click its name and then click Open. To open a table in Design view, right-click its name and then click Design View. When a table is open in Datasheet view, clicking the View button in the Views group on the Home tab switches to Design view; when it is open in Design view, clicking the button switches to Datasheet view. To switch to either of the two remaining table views (PivotTable view or PivotChart view), you click the View arrow and then click the view you want in the list. You can also switch the view by clicking one of the buttons on the View Shortcuts toolbar in the lower-right corner of the program window.

When you view a table in Datasheet view, you see the table's data in columns (fields) and rows (records). The first row contains column headings (field names). In this format, the table is often simply referred to as a *datasheet*.

Field names

Categories			×
Category ID ▾	Category Name ▾	Description	
1	Bulbs	Spring, summer and fall, forced	
2	Cacti	Indoor cactus plants	
3	Ground covers	Herbaceous perennials, evergreen and deciduous shrubs	
4	Grasses	Lawn grasses for cool climates	
5	Flowers	A wide variety of flowers	
6	Wetland plants	Plants suitable for water gardens and bogs	
7	Soils/sand	Potting soils, peat moss, mulch, bark	
8	Fertilizers	A variety of fertilizers	
13	Trees	Evergreen and deciduous trees	
14	Herbs	For flavoring and fragrance	
15	Bonsai supplies	Bonsai supplies	
16	Roses	Many types of roses	
17	Rhododendron	Hardy cultivars	
18	Pest control	Non-toxic alternatives	
19	Carnivorous	Meat-eating plants	
20	Tools	Miscellaneous gardening hardware	
21	Berry bushes	Small bush fruits	

Record: ◀ ◀ 1 of 18 ▶ ▶ ▶▦ ⚑ No Filter Search ◀ ⦙⦙⦙ ▶

Field   Record

Field names, fields, and records in a table.

If two tables have one or more field names in common, you can embed the datasheet from one table in another. By using an embedded datasheet, called a *subdatasheet*, you can see the information in more than one table at the same time. For example, you might want to embed an Orders datasheet in a Customers table so that you can see the orders each customer has placed.

In this exercise, you'll open existing database tables and explore the table structure in different views.

→ **SET UP** You need the GardenCompany01 database you worked with in the preceding exercise to complete this exercise. Open the GardenCompany01 database, ensure that tables are listed in the Navigation pane, and then follow the steps.

1. In the **Navigation** pane, double-click **Products**. Then at the right end of the **Navigation** pane title bar, click the **Shutter Bar Close** button so that you can see more of the table's fields.

The Products table is displayed in Datasheet view.

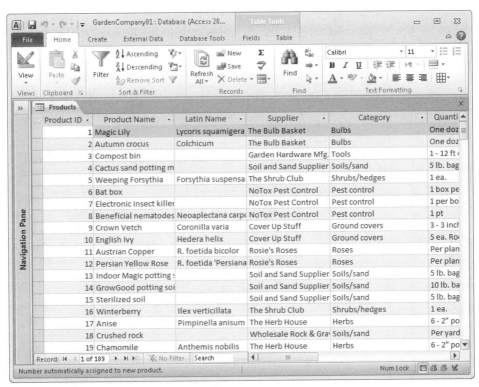

Each row in this table contains information about a product and each column contains one field from each record.

2. In the row of field names at the top of the table, point to the right border of the **Product Name** field name, and when the pointer changes to a double-headed arrow, double-click the border.

   Access adjusts the width of the field to accommodate its longest entry. Notice that Product 1, Magic Lily, and Product 2, Autumn crocus, are assigned to the Bulbs category.

3. Double-click the right border of the **Category** field name to adjust that field's width.

   Tip You can also resize a table column by pointing to the border and dragging it to the left or right.

4. In the **Navigation** pane, click the **Shutter Bar Open** button, and then double-click **Categories**.

   Tip From now on, open the Navigation pane whenever you need to work with a different object, but feel free to close it if you want to see more of the data.

The Categories table opens on a new tabbed page in Datasheet view. The Categories page is active, but the Products page is still open and available if you need it.

5. At the left end of the record for the **Bulbs** category, click the **Expand** button.

The Bulbs category expands to reveal a subdatasheet containing all the records from the Products table that are assigned to the Bulbs category. This is possible because a relationship has been established between the two tables.

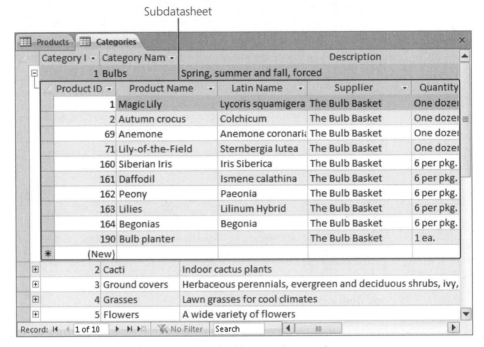

You can display records from two related tables simultaneously.

See Also For information about relationships, see "Creating Relationships Between Tables" in Chapter 26, "Create Databases and Simple Tables."

6. To the left of the record for the **Bulbs** category, click the **Collapse** button to hide the subdatasheet.

7. Click the **Close** button at the right end of the tab bar (not the Close button in the upper-right corner of the program window) to close the **Categories** table.

8. Close the **Products** table, and when Access asks whether you want to save your changes to this table, click **Yes**.

In steps 2 and 3, you changed the look of the table by changing the widths of columns. If you want those changes to be in effect the next time you open the table, you must save them.

9. In the **Navigation** pane, double-click the **Orders** table.

This table contains order-fulfillment information.

	OrderID ▾	CustomerID ▾	AccountRep ▾	OrderDate ▾	ShippedDate ▾	ShippedBy ▾
⊞	11079	LANER	Carpenter	1/5/2010	1/7/2010	Big Things Frei
⊞	11080	ACKPI	Carpenter	1/5/2010	1/6/2010	EZ Does It
⊞	11081	BROKE	Anderson	1/6/2010	1/7/2010	EZ Does It
⊞	11082	KHAKA	Anderson	1/6/2010	1/8/2010	Triple P Delive
⊞	11083	KOCRE	Carpenter	1/8/2010	1/9/2010	Triple P Delive
⊞	11084	COXBR	Anderson	1/12/2010	1/14/2010	Triple P Delive
⊞	11085	RAMLU	Emanuel	1/12/2010	1/13/2010	EZ Does It
⊞	11086	OVESC	DeGrasse	1/12/2010	1/13/2010	Triple P Delive
⊞	11087	THIRA	Carpenter	1/12/2010	1/13/2010	Big Things Frei
⊞	11088	MILFR	Emanuel	1/13/2010	1/14/2010	Triple P Delive
⊞	11089	ESTMO	Anderson	1/14/2010	1/16/2010	EZ Does It
⊞	11090	HOFRO	Emanuel	1/14/2010	1/16/2010	Big Things Frei
⊞	11091	HOLMI	Carpenter	1/15/2010	1/19/2010	EZ Does It
⊞	11092	ASHCH	Emanuel	1/16/2010	1/19/2010	Triple P Delive
⊞	11093	BENPA	Anderson	1/19/2010	1/21/2010	Big Things Frei
⊞	11094	BANMA	Carpenter	1/22/2010	1/23/2010	Fast Freddie's
⊞	11095	GANJO	Emanuel	1/22/2010	1/24/2010	Big Things Frei

Record: I◄ ◄ 1 of 87 ► ►I ►❋ 🏷 No Filter Search

The record navigation bar at the bottom of the window indicates that this table contains 87 records, and that the active record is number 1 of 87.

10. On the record navigation bar, click the **Next Record** button several times.

The selection moves down the OrderID field, because that field is active.

Keyboard Shortcuts Press the Up Arrow or Down Arrow key to move the selection one record at a time. Press the Page Up or Page Down key to move one screen at a time. Press Ctrl+Home or Ctrl+End move the selection to the first or last field in the table.

11. Click the record navigation bar, select the current record number, type **40**, and then press the Enter key.

The selection moves directly to record 40.

12. On the **View Shortcuts** toolbar, click the **Design View** button.

The Orders table structure is displayed in Design view, and the Table Tools Design contextual tab appears on the ribbon.

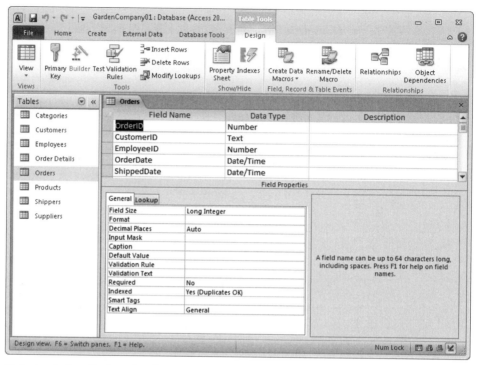

Datasheet view displays the data stored in the table, whereas Design view displays the underlying table structure.

See Also For information about table structure, see "Refining Table Structure" in Chapter 26, "Create Databases and Simple Tables."

 CLEAN UP Close the Orders table. Retain the GardenCompany01 database for use in later exercises.

Tabbed Pages vs. Overlapping Windows

By default, Access 2010 displays database objects on tabbed pages in the program window. If you prefer to display each object in a separate window rather than on a separate page, you can do so.

To switch to overlapping windows:

1. Click the File tab to display the Backstage view, and then click Options.

   The Access Options dialog box opens.

2. Display the Current Database page, and then in the Application Options area, under Document Window Options, click Overlapping Windows.

3. Click OK.

A message tells you that you must close and reopen the current database to put this change into effect.

4. Click OK. Then close and reopen the database.

When database objects are displayed on tabbed pages, a Close button appears at the right end of the tab bar. When objects are displayed in overlapping windows, the window of each object has its own set of Minimize, Restore Down/Maximize, and Close buttons at the right end of its title bar.

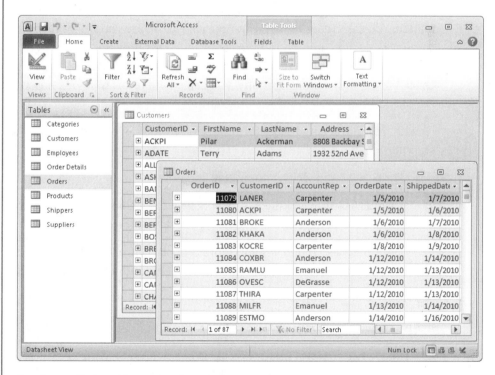

Two forms displayed in overlapping windows.

You can move object windows by dragging their title bars, and you can size them by dragging their frames. You can also arrange windows by using the options available when you click the Switch Windows button in the Window group. (This group is added to the Home tab when you select Overlapping Windows in the Access Options dialog box.)

Exploring Forms

Access tables are dense lists of raw information. Working directly with tables in a database you create for your own use might be quite simple for you, but it might be overwhelming for people who don't know much about databases. To make it easier to enter, display, and print information, you can design forms.

A form acts as a friendly interface for a table. Through a form, you can display and edit the records of the underlying table, or create new records. Most forms provide an interface to only one table, but if you want to use one form to interact with multiple tables that are related through one or more common fields, you can embed subforms within a main form.

Forms are essentially collections of controls that either accept information or display information. You can create forms by using a wizard, or you can create them from scratch by manually selecting and placing the controls. Access provides the types of controls that are standard in Windows dialog boxes, such as labels, text boxes, option buttons, and check boxes. With a little ingenuity, you can create forms that look and work much like the dialog boxes in all Windows programs.

As with tables, you can display forms in several views. The following are the three most common views:

- **Form** A view in which you display and enter data.

- **Layout** A view in which you can work with the elements of the form to refine the way it looks and behaves while also being able to see the data from the underlying table.

- **Design** A view that gives you more precise control over the look, placement, and behavior of elements of the form but that hides the underlying data.

See Also For more information about forms, see Chapter 27, "Create Simple Forms."

In this exercise, you'll explore forms, subforms, and the available form controls.

 SET UP You need the GardenCompany01 database you worked with in the preceding exercise to complete this exercise. Open the GardenCompany01 database, and then follow the steps.

1. In the **Navigation** pane, click the title bar to display the category list, and then under **Filter By Group**, click **Forms**.

   This group includes all the forms that have been saved as part of this database.

2. In the **Navigation** pane, double-click **Products**.

The Products form opens on a tabbed page.

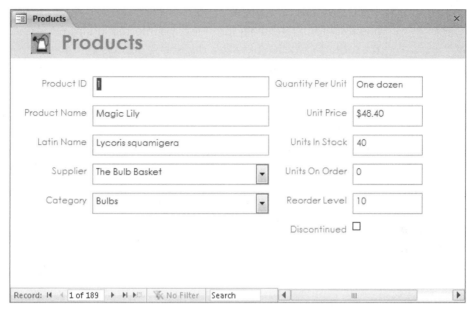

This form is the interface for the Products table.

3. Click the arrow adjacent to the **Supplier** box.

Access displays a list of all the company's suppliers.

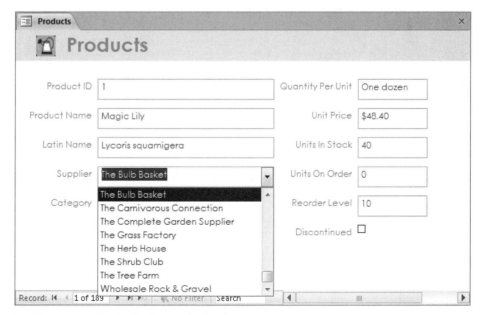

This is an example of a list box control.

4. In the **Navigation** pane, double-click **Categories**.

   The Categories form opens on its own tabbed page. This form includes a main form and a subform. The main form displays information from the Categories table, and the subform, which looks like a datasheet, displays information for the current record from the Products table.

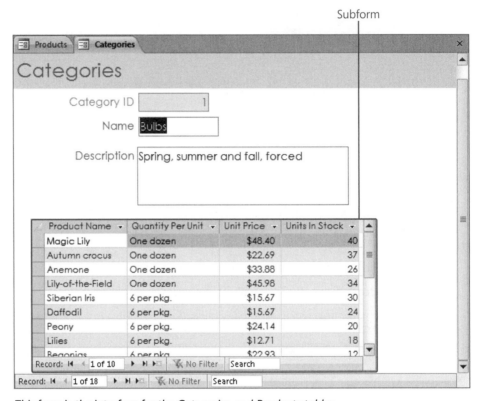

This form is the interface for the Categories and Products tables.

5. On the record navigation bar, click the **Next Record** button a few times to display the next few records.

   Notice that the subform changes with each click to display the products in each category.

6. In the **Navigation** pane, double-click **Customers**.

   The Customers form opens in Form view.

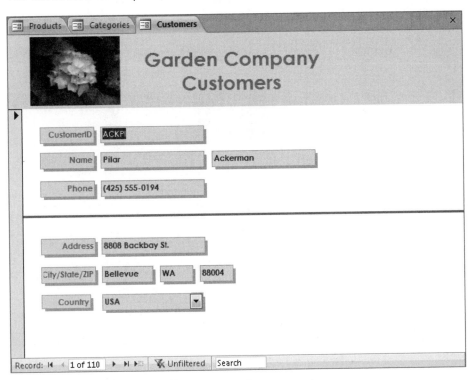

The purpose of this form is to edit or create customer records.

7. On the **Home** tab, in the **Views** group, click the **View** button.

   For forms, clicking the View button switches between Form view and Layout view.

8. In the **Views** group, click the **View** arrow, and then click **Design View**.

   Access displays the Customers form in Design view, and adds three Form Design Tools contextual tabs (Design, Arrange, and Format) to the ribbon. The contextual tabs are available only when you are working on the design of the form in either Layout view or Design view.

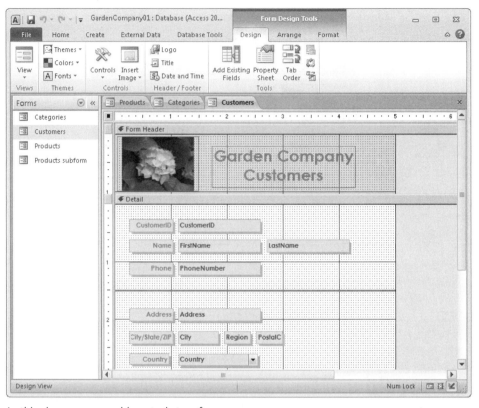

In this view, you can add controls to a form.

9. Switch between Form view, Layout view, and Design view, noticing the differences in the program window.

10. On the **Design** contextual tab, in the **Controls** group, display the **Controls** gallery.

Depending on the size of your program window, you might have to click the Controls button or the More button to display this gallery.

You can use these controls to assemble custom forms for your database.

11. Click away from the gallery to close it.

12. Right-click the tab of the **Customers** form, and then click **Close All**.

    All the open database objects close.

 CLEAN UP Retain the GardenCompany01 database for use in later exercises.

Exploring Queries

You can locate specific information stored in a table, or in multiple tables, by creating a query that specifies the criteria you want to match. Queries can be quite simple. For example, you might want a list of all products in a specific category that cost less than $10. Queries can also be quite complex. For example, you might want to locate all out-of-state customers who have purchased gloves within the last three months. For the first example, you might be able to sort and filter the data in the Products table fairly quickly to come up with a list. For the second example, sorting and filtering would be very tedious. It would be far simpler to create a query that extracts all records in the Customers table with billing addresses that are not in your state and whose customer IDs map to records that appear in the Orders table within the last three months and that include item IDs mapping to records classified as gloves in the Products table.

You can create queries by using a Query wizard, and you can also create them from scratch. The most common type is the select query, which extracts matching records from one or more tables. Less common are queries that perform specific types of actions.

Processing a query, commonly referred to as *running a query* or *querying the database*, displays a datasheet containing the records that match your search criteria. You can use the query results as the basis for further analysis, create other Access objects (such as reports) from the results, or export the results in another format, such as an Excel spreadsheet.

If you create a query that you are likely to want to run more than once, you can save it. It then becomes part of the database and appears in the list when you display the Queries group in the Navigation pane. To run the query at any time, you simply double-click it in the Navigation pane. Each time you run the query, Access evaluates the records in the specified table or tables and displays the current subset of records that match the criteria defined in the query.

Don't worry if this all sounds a bit complicated at the moment. When you approach queries logically, they soon begin to make perfect sense.

In this exercise, you'll explore two existing queries.

SET UP You need the GardenCompany01 database you worked with in the preceding exercise to complete this exercise. Open the GardenCompany01 database, and then follow the steps.

1. In the **Navigation** pane, display the **Queries** group.

   The group includes all the queries that have been saved as part of this database.

2. In the **Navigation** pane, right-click the **Delete Discontinued Products** query, and then click **Object Properties**.

   Access displays the properties of the query, including a description of its purpose.

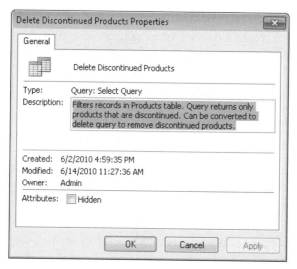

The icon at the top of the General tab indicates that this is a select query.

3. In the **Delete Discontinued Products Properties** dialog box, click **Cancel**.

4. Right-click the **Products By Category** query, and then click **Open**.

   Access runs the query.

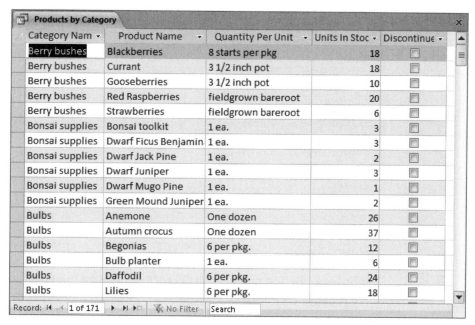

This datasheet displays the results of running the Products By Category query.

The record navigation bar indicates that 171 records are displayed; the Products table actually contains 189 records. To find out why 18 of the records are missing, you need to look at this query in Design view.

5. On the **View Shortcuts** toolbar, click the **Design View** button.

   Access displays the query in the Query Designer, and the Query Tools Design contextual tab appears on the ribbon.

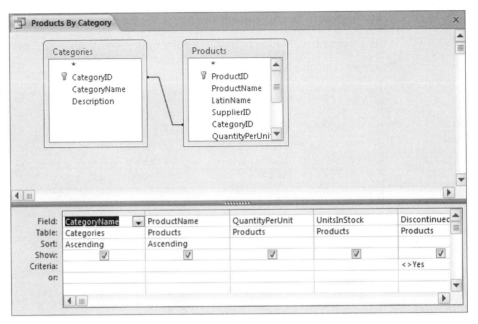

The Query Designer.

Two boxes in the top pane of the Query Designer list the fields in the tables this query is designed to work with. The line between the boxes indicates that before the query was created, a relationship was established between the two tables based on the fact that the CategoryID field is present in both of them. The relationship enables this query to draw information from both tables.

See Also For more information about relationships, see "Creating Relationships Between Tables" in Chapter 26, "Create Databases and Simple Tables."

The query is defined in the design grid in the bottom pane of the Query Designer. Each column of the grid refers to one field from one of the tables above. Notice that <> Yes (not equal to Yes) is entered in the Criteria row for the Discontinued field. This query finds all the records that don't have a value of Yes in that field (in other words, all the records that have not been discontinued).

6. As an experiment, in the **Criteria** row of the **Discontinued** field, replace **<>** with **=**. Then on the **Design** contextual tab, in the **Results** group, click the **Run** button.

Tip You can also run a query by switching to Datasheet view.

This time, the query finds all the records that have been discontinued. The 18 discontinued products account for the difference between the number of records in the Products table and the number of records displayed by the original query.

Run

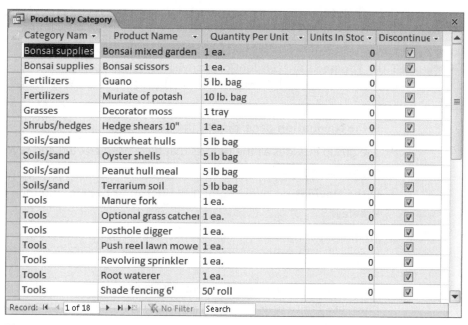

The new query results.

7. Close the **Products By Category** query. When a message asks whether you want to save your changes to the query, click **No**.

✖ **CLEAN UP** Retain the GardenCompany01 database for use in later exercises.

Exploring Reports

You can display the information recorded in your tables in nicely formatted, easily accessible reports, either on your computer screen or on paper. A report can include items of information selected from multiple tables and queries, values calculated from information in the database, and formatting elements such as headers, footers, titles, and headings.

You can look at reports in four views:

● **Report view** In this view, you can scroll through the information in the report without being distracted by the page breaks that will be inserted when it is printed.

● **Print Preview** In this view, you see your report exactly as it will look when printed.

● **Layout view** This view displays the data in the report (similar to Print Preview) but enables you to edit the layout.

● **Design view** In this view, you can manipulate the design of a report in the same way that you manipulate a form.

In this exercise, you'll preview a report as it will appear when printed. You'll also examine another report in Design view.

 SET UP You need the GardenCompany01 database you worked with in the preceding exercise to complete this exercise. Open the GardenCompany01 database, and then follow the steps.

1. In the **Navigation** pane, display the **Reports** group.

   The group includes all the reports that have been created and saved as part of this database.

2. In the **Navigation** pane, right-click **Customer Labels**, and then click **Print Preview**.

   Troubleshooting If a message tells you that some data may not be displayed because of column widths and spacing, for the purposes of this exercise, simply press OK to continue.

   The Customer Labels report opens, displaying a full page of labels in a view that is much like Print Preview in other Office programs. The ribbon now displays only the Print Preview tab.

   Tip Access provides a wizard that can help you create a mailing label report. You can also create labels like these by using the Customers table as a data source for the Word 2010 mail merge tool.

3. Move the pointer over the report, where it changes to a magnifying glass. Then with the pointer over the middle label at the top of the report, click the mouse button.

   The zoom percentage changes to 100%, as indicated on the Zoom Level button in the lower-right corner of the window. You can click this button to switch back and forth between the current and previous zoom levels.

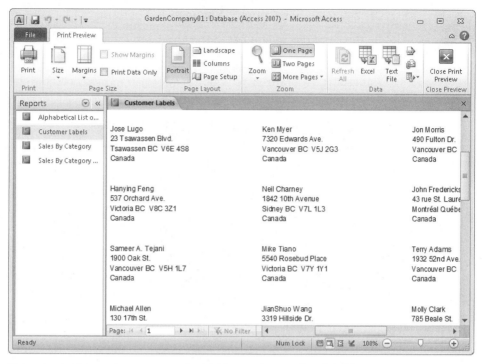

This report prints customer names and addresses in a mailing label format.

If the report is too small to read in Print Preview, you can adjust the zoom percentage by clicking the Zoom In button (the plus sign) at the right end of the Zoom slider in the lower-right corner of the window, or by dragging the Zoom slider. You can also click the Zoom arrow in the Zoom group on the Print Preview tab and then click a specific percentage.

4. In the **Navigation** pane, right-click the **Sales By Category** report, and then click **Print Preview**.

5. Use any method to zoom the page to 100 percent.

6. On the page navigation bar in the lower-left corner of the page, click the **Last Page** button.

This report generates nine pages of information by combining data from the Categories table and the Products table.

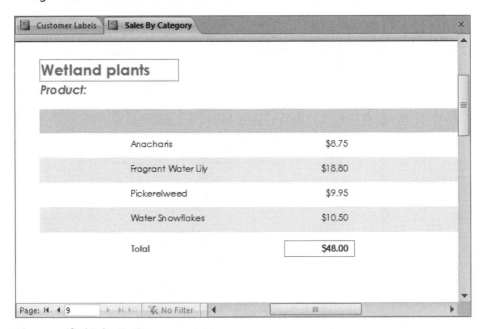

The magnified Sales By Category report.

7. Click the **Previous Page** button a few times to view a few more pages of the report.

8. On the **View Shortcuts** toolbar, click the **Design View** button.

Access switches to Design view and displays four Report Design Tools contextual tabs (Design, Arrange, Format, and Page Setup) on the ribbon. In this view, the report looks similar to a form.

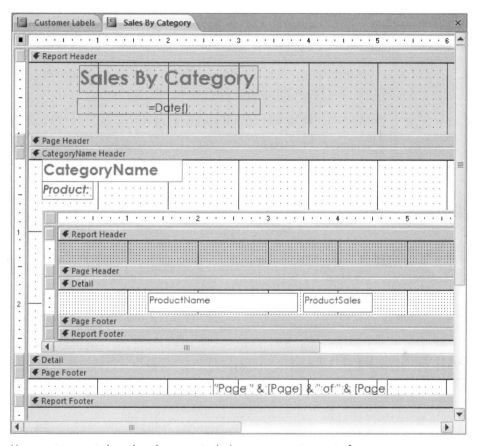

You create reports by using the same techniques you use to create forms.

 CLEAN UP Close the open reports. Retain the GardenCompany01 database for use in the last exercise.

Previewing and Printing Access Objects

Because Access is a Windows application, it interacts with your printer through standard Windows dialog boxes and drivers. This means that any printer that you can use from other programs can be used from Access, and any special features of that printer, such as color printing or duplex printing, are available in Access.

The commands for printing database objects are available from the Print page of the Backstage view. From this page, you can do the following:

- Print the active object with the default settings.
- Display the Print dialog box, where you can select the printer you want to use, as well as adjust various other settings appropriate to the active object and the current view.
- Display the active object in Print Preview.

In this exercise, you'll explore the printing options for a table and a form.

 SET UP You need the GardenCompany01 database you worked with in the preceding exercise to complete this exercise. Open the GardenCompany01 database, and then follow the steps.

1. In the **Navigation** pane, display the **All Access Objects** category.
2. In the **Tables** group, double-click the **Employees** table to open it in Datasheet view.

   This table contains information about nine employees. Some of the columns are too narrow to display all their data, and even with the program window maximized, depending on your screen resolution, some of the fields might not fit on the screen.
3. Adjust the widths of all the columns so that all the values in the fields are visible.

   Access will not print data that is not visible.
4. Click the File tab to display the Backstage view.

5. In the left pane, click **Print**.

The Print page displays the available print options.

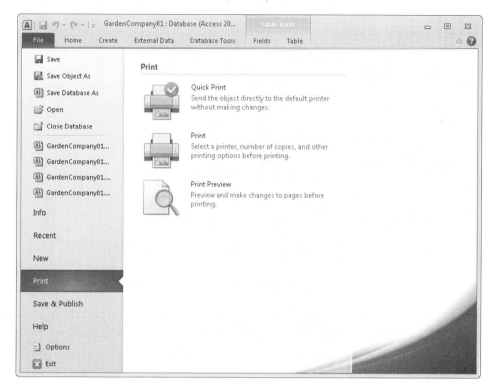

The Print page of the Backstage view.

6. In the right pane, click **Print Preview**.

The first page of the Employees table is displayed in Print Preview.

Tip This is the only way to preview a table, a query results datasheet, or a form. There is no Print Preview command available when you right-click one of these objects, and there is no Print Preview button on the View Shortcuts toolbar or in the View button list, as there is for reports.

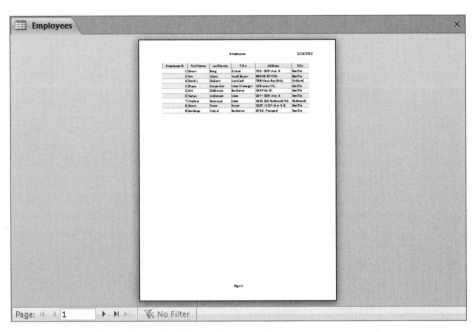

The Employees table in the default Portrait orientation.

7. On the navigation bar at the bottom of the window, click the **Next Page** button. Then click the **First Page** button to move back to page 1.

   If you print this datasheet with the current settings, it will print as two short, vertically oriented pages.

8. On the **Print Preview** tab, in the **Page Layout** group, click the **Landscape** button. Then click the **Next Page** button.

   In Landscape orientation, the datasheet still fits on two pages, with only one field on the second page.

9. In the **Page Size** group, click the **Margins** button, and then click **Narrow**.

   On the page navigation bar, the buttons are now gray, indicating that the Employee list fits on one page.

   Tip You can set custom margins by clicking the Page Setup button in the Page Layout group and then adjusting the Top, Bottom, Left, and Right settings on the Print Options page of the Page Setup dialog box.

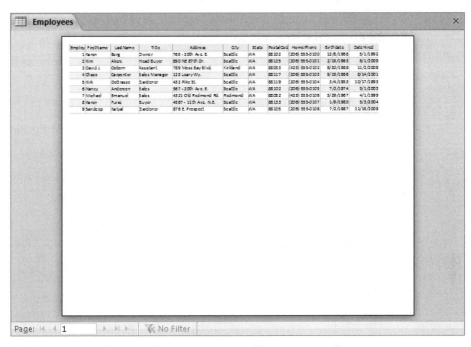

The Employees table in Landscape orientation with narrow margins.

10. In the **Print** group, click the **Print** button.

The Print dialog box opens.

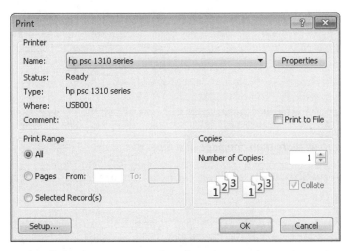

In this dialog box, you can select the printer and set print options such as the pages or records to print, and the number of copies.

11. Click **Cancel** to close the **Print** dialog box, and then in the **Close Preview** group, click the **Close Print Preview** button.

12. In the **Navigation** pane, under **Reports**, double-click **Alphabetical List of Products**.

The report opens in Report view.

13. Display the Backstage view, click **Print**, and then click **Print Preview**.

Access displays a preview of the information that will be printed.

 14. On the **Print Preview** tab, in the **Zoom** group, click the **Two Pages** button.

Access displays the first two pages in the report side by side.

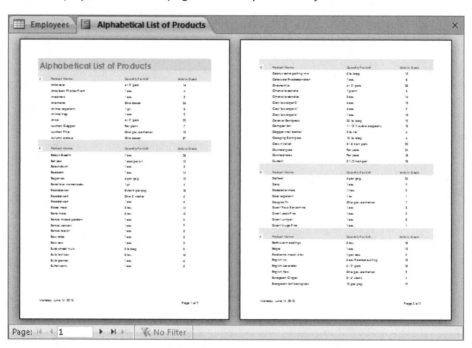

You can preview more than one page at a time.

 15. On the **View Shortcuts** toolbar, click the **Report View** button to return to that view.

CLEAN UP Save your changes to the Employees table, and close both the table and the report. Then close the GardenCompany01 database.

Key Points

- The basic Access interface objects work much the same as in other Office or Windows programs.

- A database is the computer equivalent of an organized list of information.

- Tables are the core database objects. Access data is organized in tables made up of columns and rows, called *fields* and *records*.

- In a relational database, tables can be related based on common fields, enabling the retrieval of information from more than one table at the same time.

- The purpose of the other database objects—forms, reports, queries, macros, and modules—is to interact with one or more tables.

- Every Access object has two or more views. For example, you view data in a table in Datasheet view and define how the data is structured in Design view.

- If you want to print a database object, be sure the information you need is visible on the screen before you print.

Chapter at a Glance

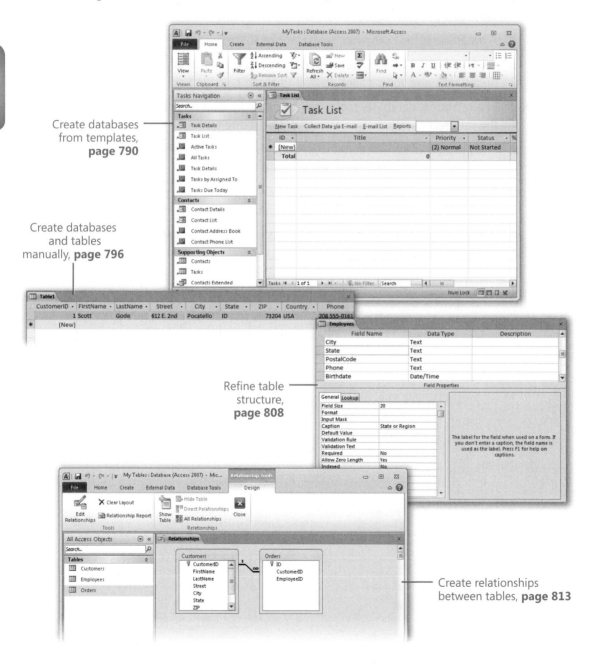

Create databases from templates, **page 790**

Create databases and tables manually, **page 796**

Refine table structure, **page 808**

Create relationships between tables, **page 813**

26 Create Databases and Simple Tables

In this chapter, you will learn how to

✔ Create databases from templates.

✔ Create databases and tables manually.

✔ Manipulate table columns and rows.

✔ Refine table structure.

✔ Create relationships between tables.

Creating the container for a database is easy. But an empty database is no more useful than an empty document or worksheet. It is only when you fill a database with data in tables (known as populating a database) that it starts to serve a purpose. As you add forms, queries, and reports, it becomes a useful tool. If you customize it by adding a startup page and organizing the various objects into categories and groups, it moves into the realm of being a database application.

Not every database has to be refined to the point that it can be classified as an application. Databases that only you or a few experienced database users will work with can remain fairly simple. But if you expect someone without database knowledge to enter data or generate their own reports, spending a little extra time in the beginning to create a solid foundation will save a lot of work later. Otherwise, you'll find yourself continually repairing damaged files or walking people through seemingly easy tasks.

Microsoft Access 2010 takes a lot of the difficult and mundane work out of creating and customizing a database by providing database applications in the form of templates that you modify and populate with your own information. Access 2010 also provides templates for common elements that you might want to plug into a database. These application parts consist of sets of objects—a table and related forms, queries, or reports—that together provide a complete, functioning part of a database. All you have to do is fill in your data. If none of the templates meet your needs, you can create tables manually.

In this chapter, you'll create a database from a template and create a table manually. Then you'll adjust the display of a data table to fit your needs. By the end of this chapter, you'll have a database containing a few tables and you'll understand a bit about how the tables in the databases you will use for the exercises in the remaining chapters of the book were created.

> **Practice Files** You don't need any practice files to complete the exercises in this chapter. For more information about practice file requirements, see "Using the Practice Files" at the beginning of this book.

Creating Databases from Templates

A few years ago (the distant past, in computer time), creating a database structure involved first analyzing your needs and then laying out the database design on paper. You would decide what information you needed to track and how to store it in the database. Creating the database structure could be a lot of work, and after you created it and entered data, making changes could be difficult. Templates have changed this process, and committing yourself to a particular database structure is no longer the big decision it once was.

A template is a pattern that you use to create a specific type of database. Access 2010 comes with templates for several databases typically used in business and education, and when you are connected to the Internet, many more are available from the Microsoft Office Online Web site at office.microsoft.com. By using pre-packaged templates, you can create a database application in far less time than it used to take to sketch the design on paper, because someone has already done the design work for you.

Using an Access template might not produce exactly the database application you want, but it can quickly create something that you can customize to fit your needs. However, you can customize a database only if you know how to manipulate its basic building blocks: tables, forms, queries, and reports. Due to the complexity of these templates, you probably shouldn't try to modify them until you're comfortable working with database objects in Design view and Layout view. By the time you finish this book, you will know enough to be able to confidently work with the sophisticated pre-packaged application templates that come with Access.

In this exercise, you'll create a database application based on the Tasks template. This template is typical of those provided with Microsoft Access 2010, in that it looks nice and demonstrates a lot of the neat things you can do in a database.

SET UP You don't need any practice files to complete this exercise. Close any open databases, and then with the New page of the Backstage view displayed, follow the steps.

1. In the **Available Templates** area, click **Sample Templates**.

   Access displays a list of the templates that shipped with the program and are installed on your computer.

2. Click the **Tasks** template icon.

   In the right pane, you can assign a name to the database and browse to the location where you want to store the database.

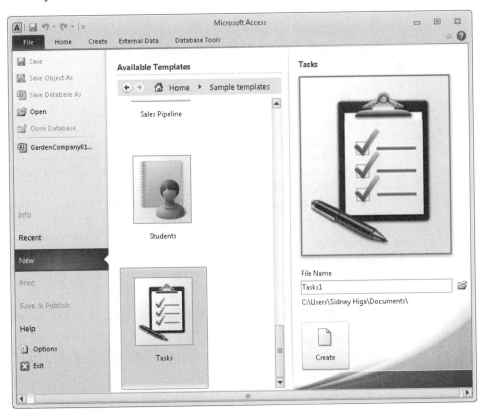

The Tasks template is supplied with Access.

3. In the **File Name** box, type **MyTasks**.

   Tip Naming conventions for Access database files follow those for Windows files. File names cannot contain the following characters: \ / : * ? " < > |. By default, file name extensions are hidden, and you shouldn't type the extension in the File Name box. (The extension for an Access 2010 database file is .accdb. For information about this file format, which was introduced with Access 2007, search for *accdb* in Access Help.)

4. Click the adjacent **Browse** button, and then in the **File New Database** dialog box, navigate to your **Chapter26** practice file folder.

    You use the same navigational techniques in this dialog box that you would use in any Open or Save dialog box.

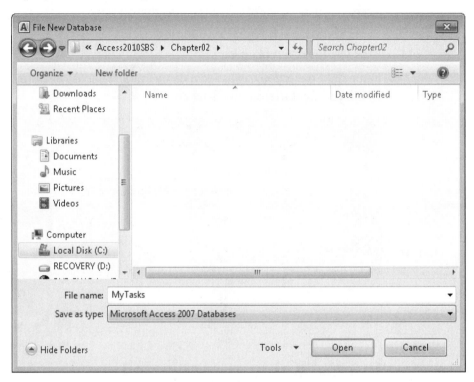

The File New Database dialog box.

5. With **Microsoft Access 2007 Databases** selected in the **Save as type** box, click **OK**.

    The path to the specified folder is displayed below the File Name box.

    Tip By default, Access creates new databases in your Documents folder. You can change the location when you create each database, as you did here, or you can change the default save folder. To specify a different default folder, click the File tab to display the Backstage view, click Options, and then on the General page of the Access Options dialog box, under Creating Databases, click the Browse button to the right of Default Database Folder. In the Default Database Path dialog box, browse to the folder you want to be the default, and then click OK in each of the open dialog boxes.

6. Click the **Create** button.

Access briefly displays a progress bar, and then the new database opens, with the Task List form displayed in Layout view.

Tip Below the form name is a toolbar with commands created by embedded macros. These commands are an example of what makes this a database application rather than a simple database. The topic of macros is beyond the scope of this book. For information, search for *macros* in Access Help.

7. If the **Navigation** pane is closed, click the **Shutter Bar Open** button at the right end of its title bar to open it. Then if any of the groups are collapsed, click their chevrons to open them.

The Navigation pane displays a custom Tasks Navigation category.

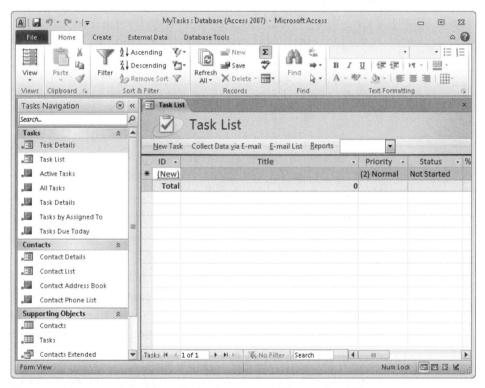

The custom category has custom Tasks, Contacts, and Supporting Objects groups.

Troubleshooting The appearance of buttons and groups on the ribbon changes depending on the width of the program window. For information about changing the appearance of the ribbon to match our screen images, see "Modifying the Display of the Ribbon" at the beginning of this book.

8. In the **Navigation** pane, click the **Tasks Navigation** title bar, and then in the category and group list, click **Object Type** to list all the objects in this database.

9. In the **Tables** group, double-click **Contacts**.

The empty Contacts table is displayed. You could now start entering data in this table.

10. Right-click the **Contacts** tab, and click **Close All**.

11. On the **Create** tab of the ribbon, in the **Templates** group, click the **Application Parts** button.

The Application Parts gallery appears.

The Application Parts gallery.

You can add various types of forms and several sets of related tables and other database objects to this or any other database. These ready-made objects give you a jump start on creating a fully functional database application.

12. Click away from the gallery to close it.

13. Continue exploring the objects that are part of the **MyTasks** database on your own.

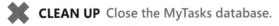 **CLEAN UP** Close the MyTasks database.

Web Databases

Several of the templates in the Sample Templates gallery and many of the templates available from the Microsoft Office Online Web site are designated as Web databases. A Web database is one that is compatible with the new Web publishing capabilities of Access 2010.

If Access Services are installed on your organization's Microsoft SharePoint server, you can now publish a database to Access Services. Publishing converts tables to SharePoint lists stored on the server and makes it possible to work with the database either in Access or in a Web browser.

You can create a Web database based on a Web template or build a new one from scratch by choosing Blank Web Database on the New page of the Backstage view. You can also publish a regular database as a Web database, although the tables in the database must conform to Web database requirements for publication to be successful. Because of these requirements, if you work for an organization where future deployment of Access Services is a possibility, you might want to consider creating a Web database to ensure that your database can be published to Access Services in the future.

In a Web database, you can create two kinds of objects:

- **Web objects** These can be created and viewed in either a Web browser or Access.
- **Non-Web objects** These can be created and viewed only in Access.

When you are working with a Web database from a browser, you are working with the database on the server. When you are working with it from Access, you are working with a local copy of the database that is synchronized with the database on the server. For both types of objects, you can make design changes only in Access and only when connected to the server.

These days, more and more companies have employees and clients in different geographic locations, and more and more people are working away from company offices. Web databases make it possible for people to access company databases from wherever they are and from any computer, whether or not it has Access installed.

Creating Databases and Tables Manually

Suppose you need to store different types of information for different types of people. For example, you might want to maintain information about employees, customers, and suppliers. In addition to the standard information—such as names, addresses, and phone numbers—you might want to track these other kinds of information:

● Employee identification numbers, hire dates, marital status, deductions, and pay rates

● Customer orders and account status

● Supplier contacts, current order status, and discounts

You could start with a template, add fields for all the different items of information to a single Contacts table, and then fill in only the relevant fields for each type of contact. However, cramming all this information into one table would soon get pretty messy. It's better to create a new database based on the Blank Database template and then manually create separate tables for each type of contact: employee, customer, and supplier.

When you create a new blank database or insert a new table into an existing database, the table is displayed on a tabbed page in Datasheet view with one empty row that is ready to receive data. Because the active object is a table, Access adds the Table Tools contextual tabs to the ribbon so that you can work with the table.

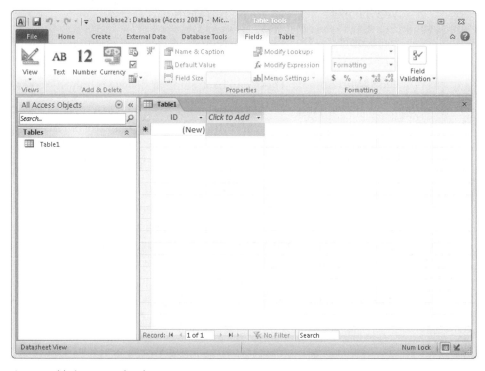

A new table in a new database.

If you close the table at this point, it will disappear, because it contains no data and it has no structure. The simplest way to make the table part of the database is to create at least one record by entering data, which simultaneously defines the table's structure.

Tip You can also define the structure of the table without entering data. For information about table structure, see "Refining Table Structure" later in this chapter. For information about Access 2010 features not covered in this book, refer to *Microsoft Access 2010 Step by Step* by Joyce Cox and Joan Lambert (Microsoft Press, 2010).

Obviously, to create a record, you need to know how to enter information in Datasheet view.

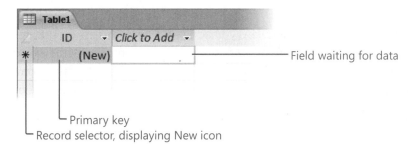

Field waiting for data

Primary key
Record selector, displaying New icon

The first record in a new table, before data is entered.

Every table has an empty row that is ready to receive a new record, as indicated by the New icon (the asterisk) in the record selector at the left end of the row. By default, the first field in each new table is an ID field designed to contain an entry that will uniquely identify the record. Also by default, this field is designated as the table's *primary key*. No two records in this table can have the same value in this primary key field. Behind the scenes, the data type of this field is set to AutoNumber, so Access will enter a sequential number in this field for you.

Tip As you'll see in a later exercise, the primary key field does not have to be the default AutoNumber type. If you need to you create your own primary key field, then anything meaningful and unique will work.

See Also For information about data types, see "Refining Table Structure" later in this chapter.

The first field you need to be concerned about is the active field labeled *Click To Add*. You enter the first item of information for the new record in the first cell in this field, and then press the Tab or Enter key to move to the first cell in the field to the right. Access then assigns the value 1 to the ID field, assigns the name Field1 to the second field, and moves the Click To Add label to the third field. The icon in the record selector at the left end of the record changes to two dots and a pencil to indicate that this record has not yet been saved, and the New icon moves to the record selector of the next row.

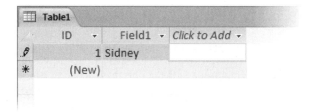

The first record in a new table, after data has been entered in the first field.

When creating a new table in Datasheet view, you need to save the first record after entering the first item of data. If you don't, Access increments the ID value for each field you add to that record. For example, if you add seven fields, Access assigns the value 7 to the ID field of the first record. To avoid this problem, you simply click the icon in the record selector after you enter your first value in the first record. This saves the record with the value 1 assigned to the ID field, and subsequent records will be numbered sequentially.

Having entered the first item of data and saved the record, you continue entering items of information in consecutive cells and pressing Tab or Enter. When you finish entering the last item for the first record, you click anywhere in the row below to tell Access that the record is complete.

After you complete the first record of a new table, you will probably want to change the default field names to something more meaningful. To rename a field, you simply double-click its field name and then type the name you want.

At any time while you are entering data in a new table, you can save the table by clicking the Save button on the Quick Access Toolbar and naming the table. If you try to close the table without explicitly saving it, Access prompts you to save the table. If you click No, Access discards the table and any data you have entered.

After you have saved the table for the first time, Access automatically saves each record when you move away from it. You don't have to worry about losing your changes, but you do have to remember that most data entries can be undone only by editing the record.

Databases almost always contain more than one table. You can create additional empty tables by clicking the Table button in the Tables group on the Create tab of the ribbon. If you need to create a table that is similar in structure to an existing one, you can copy and paste the existing table to create a new one. When you paste the table, Access gives you the option of naming the table and of specifying whether you want the new table to have the existing table's structure or both its structure and its data.

For some kinds of tables, Access provides Quick Start fields that you can use to add common sets of fields or kinds of fields to a table. The Quick Start options take the work out of defining these fields and can be very useful when you know exactly what type of field you need.

In this exercise, you'll create a blank database, enter information into the first record of its default table, assign field names, add another record, and save and close the table. Then you'll copy that table to create a second one. Finally, you'll create a new table and experiment with Quick Start fields.

 SET UP You don't need any practice files to complete this exercise. Close any open databases, and then with the New page of the Backstage view displayed, follow the steps.

1. In the center pane of the **New** page, in the **Available Templates** area, click **Blank Database**.

2. In the right pane, click the **File Name** box, and type **MyTables**. Then click the **Browse**
 button, navigate to your **Chapter26** practice file folder, and click **OK**.

   Tip You can't create a blank database without saving it. If you don't provide a file name and location, Access saves the file with the name *Database* followed by a sequential number in the default location (your Documents folder, unless you have changed it).

3. In the right pane, click the **Create** button.

   Access creates the blank database in the specified location, opens the database, and displays a new blank table named *Table1*.

4. With the empty field below **Click to Add** selected, type **Scott**, and then press Tab to move to the next field.

   The icon in the record selector changes to indicate that this record has not yet been saved. The value 1 appears in the ID field, the name of the second column changes to Field1, and the Click To Add label moves to the third column.

5. Click the icon in the record selector to save the record before you move on.

   Tip Clicking the record selector is necessary only after you enter the first value in a new table. This action sets the ID field value to 1.

6. Click the cell under **Click to Add**, and type the following information into the next seven cells, pressing Tab after each entry:

> **Gode**
>
> **612 E. 2nd**
>
> **Pocatello**
>
> **ID**
>
> **73204**
>
> **USA**
>
> **208 555-0161**

As the cursor moves to the next cell, the name of the field in which you just entered data changes to *Field* followed by a sequential number.

The first complete record.

Tip Don't be concerned if your screen does not look exactly like ours. In this graphic, we've scrolled the page and adjusted the widths of the columns so that you can see all the fields. For information about adjusting columns, see "Manipulating Table Columns and Rows" later in this chapter.

7. Double-click the **ID** field name (not the ID value in Field5), and then type **CustomerID** to rename it.

Tip Field names can include spaces, but the spaces can affect how queries have to be constructed, so it is best not to include them. For readability, capitalize each word and then remove the spaces, or use underscores instead of spaces.

8. Repeat step 7 for the other fields, changing the field names to the following:

Field1	FirstName	**Field4**	City	**Field7**	Country
Field2	LastName	**Field5**	State	**Field8**	Phone
Field3	Street	**Field6**	ZIP		

The table now has intuitive field names.

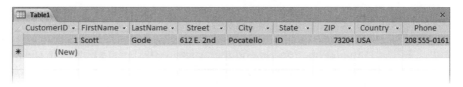

The renamed fields.

Tip Again, don't worry if your screen doesn't look exactly like this graphic, because we've made adjustments so that you can see all the fields.

9. Add another record containing the following field values to the table, pressing Tab to move from field to field:

FirstName	John	**City**	Montreal	**Country**	Canada
LastName	Frederickson	**State**	Quebec	**Phone**	514 555-0167
Street	43 rue St. Laurent	**ZIP**	(press Tab to skip this field)		

10. At the right end of the tab bar, click the **Close** button.

11. When Access asks whether you want to save the design of the table, click **Yes**.

    Important Clicking No will delete the new table and its data from the database.

    Access displays the Save As dialog box.

You must save the table before closing it.

12. In the **Table Name** box, type **Customers**, and then click **OK**.

    Access closes the table, which is now listed in the Tables group on the Navigation bar.

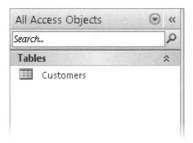

The database now contains one table.

Tip You can rename a table by right-clicking it in the Navigation pane and then clicking Rename. You can delete a table by right-clicking it, clicking Delete, and then confirming the deletion in the message box that appears. (You can also delete a table by selecting it in the Navigation bar and then clicking the Delete button in the Records group on the Home tab or pressing the Delete key.)

13. In the **Navigation** pane, click the **Customers** table to select it.

14. On the **Home** tab, in the **Clipboard** group, click the **Copy** button. Then click the **Paste** button.

Keyboard Shortcuts Press Ctrl+C to copy data. Press Ctrl+V to paste data.

The Paste Table As dialog box opens.

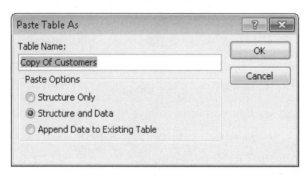

If you need to create a table that is similar to an existing table, it is sometimes easier to customize a copy than to create it from scratch.

15. In the **Table Name** box, type **Employees**. In the **Paste Options** area, click **Structure Only** to capture the fields from the **Customers** table but none of the customer information. Then click **OK**.

The new Employees table appears in the Navigation pane.

Tip You can also use the Copy and Paste commands to append the information in the selected table to another existing table. In that case, in the Paste Table As dialog box, type the name of the destination table in the Table Name box, click Append Data To Existing Table, and then click OK.

16. Double-click **Employees** to open it in Datasheet view so that you can view its fields. Then close the table again.

17. On the **Create** tab, in the **Tables** group, click the **Table** button.

Access creates a new table containing an ID field and a Click To Add field placeholder.

18. With the **Click to Add** field active, on the **Fields** contextual tab, in the **Add & Delete** group, click the **More Fields** button.

The More Fields gallery appears.

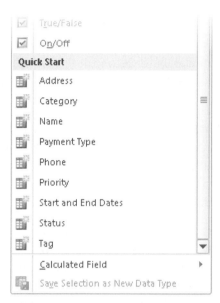

The Quick Start fields are at the bottom of the More Fields gallery.

19. If necessary scroll to the bottom of the gallery, and then under **Quick Start**, click **Name**.

Access inserts ready-made LastName and FirstName fields.

20. Repeat steps 18 and 19 to add the **Address** fields from the **Quick Start** list.

Access inserts ready-made Address, City, State Province, ZIP Postal, and Country Region fields.

21. Close the table, saving it with the name **Shippers** when prompted.

✖ CLEAN UP Retain the MyTables database for use in later exercises.

Database Design

In a well-designed database, each item of data is stored only once. If you're capturing the same information in multiple places, that is a sure sign that you need to analyze the data and figure out a way to put the duplicated information in a separate table.

For example, an Orders table should not include information about the customer placing each order, for two significant reasons. First, if the same customer orders more than once, all his or her information has to be repeated for each order, which inflates the size of the table and the database. Second, if the customer moves, his or her address will need to be updated in the record for every order placed.

The way to avoid this type of problem is to put customer information in a Customers table and assign each customer a unique identifier, such as a sequential number or unique string of letters, in the primary key field. Then in the Orders table, you can identify the customer by the unique ID. If you need to know the name and address of the customer who placed a particular order, you can have Access use the unique ID to look up that information in the Customers table.

The process of ensuring that a set of information is stored in only one place is called *normalization*. This process tests a database for compliance with a set of normalization rules that ask questions such as "If I know the information in the primary key field of a record, can I retrieve information from one and only one record?" For example, knowing that a customer's ID is 1002 means you can pull the customer's name and address from the Customers table, whereas knowing that a customer's last name is Jones does not mean that you can pull the customer's name and address from the table, because more than one customer might have the last name Jones.

The topic of normalization is beyond the scope of this book. If you need to design a database that will contain several tables, you should search for *Database design basics* in Access Help to learn more about the normalization process.

Manipulating Table Columns and Rows

In Chapter 25, "Explore an Access 2010 Database," we showed you how to quickly adjust the width of table columns to efficiently display their data. In addition to adjusting column width, sometimes you might want to rearrange a table's fields to get a better view of the data. For example, if you want to look up a phone number but the names and phone numbers are several fields apart, you will have to scroll the page to get the information you need. You might want to rearrange or hide a few fields to be able to simultaneously see the ones you are interested in.

You can manipulate the columns and rows of an Access table without affecting the underlying data in any way. You can size rows and size, hide, move, and freeze columns. You can save your table formatting so that the table will look the same the next time you open it, or you can discard your changes without saving them.

In this exercise, you'll open a table and manipulate its columns and rows.

 SET UP You need the MyTables database you worked with in the preceding exercise to complete this exercise. Open the MyTables database, and then follow the steps.

1. In the **Navigation** pane, double-click the **Customers** table to open it in Datasheet view.

2. In the field name row, point to the right border of the **Street** field name, and when the pointer changes to a double-headed arrow, drag to the right until you can see all of the street addresses.

3. Double-click the right border of any column that seems too wide or too narrow to adjust the column to fit its contents.

   This technique is particularly useful in a large table where you can't easily determine the length of a field's longest entry.

4. Point to the border between any two record selectors, and drag downward.

   When you release the mouse button, Access increases the height of all rows in the table.

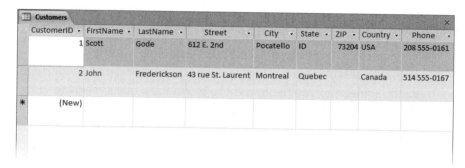

You cannot adjust the height of a single row.

5. On the **Home** tab, in the **Records** group, click the **More** button, and then click **Row Height**.

The Row Height dialog box opens.

You can set the rows to the precise height you want.

6. In the **Row Height** dialog box, select the **Standard Height** check box, and then click **OK**.

Access resets the height of the rows to the default setting.

7. Click anywhere in the **FirstName** field. Then in the **Records** group, click the **More** button, and click **Hide Fields**.

The FirstName field disappears, and the fields to its right shift to the left.

Tip If you select several fields before clicking Hide Fields, they all disappear. You can select adjacent fields by clicking the field name of the first one, holding down the Shift key, and then clicking the field name of the last one. The two fields and any fields in between are selected.

8. To restore the hidden field, in the **Records** group, click the **More** button, and then click **Unhide Fields**.

The Unhide Columns dialog box opens.

You can select and clear check boxes to control which fields are visible.

Tip If you want to hide several columns that are not adjacent, you can display the Unhide Columns dialog box and clear their checkboxes.

9. In the **Unhide Columns** dialog box, select the **FirstName** check box, and then click **Close**.

   Access redisplays the FirstName field.

10. If you can see all of the fields in the table, for the purposes of this exercise, adjust the size of the program window until some of the fields are no longer visible.

11. Point to the **CustomerID** field name, hold down the mouse button, and drag through the **FirstName** and **LastName** field names. With the three columns selected, click the **More** button in the **Records** group, and then click **Freeze Fields**.

12. Scroll the page to the right until the **Phone** field is adjacent to the **LastName** field.

    The first three columns remain in view as you scroll.

13. In the **Records** group, click **More,** and then click **Unfreeze All Fields** to restore the fields to their normal condition.

    Tip The commands to hide, unhide, freeze, and unfreeze columns are also available from the shortcut menu that appears when you right-click a field name.

14. Click the **Phone** field name to select that field. Then drag the field to the left, releasing the mouse button when the thick black line appears to the right of the **LastName** field.

15. Close the **Customers** table, clicking **Yes** to save the changes you have made to the column widths and order. If you see a warning that this action will clear the Clipboard, click **Yes**.

✖ **CLEAN UP** Retain the MyTables database for use in later exercises.

Refining Table Structure

Although you can create the structure of a database in Datasheet view, some structural refinements can be carried out only in Design view. When you are familiar with tables, you might even want to create your tables from scratch in Design view, where you have more control over the fields. You can open a new table in Design view by clicking the Table Design button in the Tables group on the Create tab.

When you open an existing table in Design view, the tabbed page shows the underlying structure of the table.

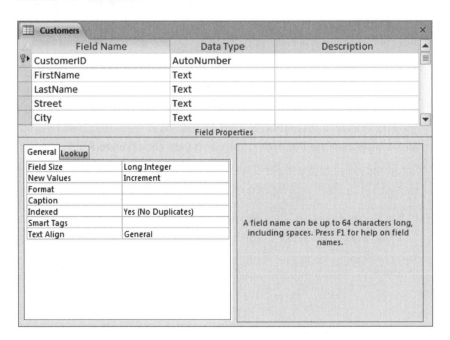

The table design page.

- **Selector** You can click the shaded box at the left end of a row to select the entire field. You can then insert a row above the selected one, delete the row (thereby deleting the field), or drag the row up or down to reposition its field in the table.

  The selector also identifies the primary key field of the table by displaying the Primary Key icon (a key with a right-pointing arrow).

  Tip If you don't want a table to have a primary key (for example, if none of the fields will contain a unique value for every record), select the field designated as the primary key, and on the Design contextual tab, in the Tools group, click the Primary Key button to toggle it off. If you want to designate a different field as the primary key, select the new field, and click the Primary Key button to toggle it on. (You don't have to remove the primary key from the current field first; it will happen automatically.)

- **Field Name column** This column contains the names you specified when you created the table. You can edit the names by using regular text-editing techniques. You can add a new field by typing its name in the first empty cell in this column.

- **Data Type column** This column specifies the type of data that the field can contain. By default, the ID field in a new table is assigned the AutoNumber data type, and all other fields are assigned the Text data type. With the exception of fields with the OLE Object and Attachment data types, you can change the type of any field by clicking its Data Type entry, clicking the arrow that appears, and clicking a new data type in the list.

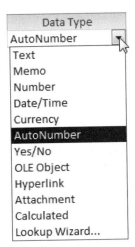

The list of data types.

- **Description column** This column contains an optional description of the field.

The Field Properties area at the bottom of the design page displays the properties of the field selected in the top part. Different properties are associated with different data types. They can determine such things as the number of characters allowed in a field, the value inserted if the user doesn't type an entry, and whether an entry is required. Properties can also assess whether an entry is valid and can force the user to select from a list of values rather than typing them (with the risk of errors).

All fields, no matter what their data type, can be assigned a Caption property that will appear in the place of the field name in tables or in other database objects. For example, you might want to use captions to display the names of fields with spaces, such as First Name for the FirstName field.

See Also For a comprehensive list of data types and properties, search on *data types* in Access Help.

In this exercise, you'll open a table in Design view, add and delete fields, change a data type, set field sizes, and add a caption.

SET UP You need the MyTables database you worked with in the preceding exercise to complete this exercise. Open the MyTables database, and then follow the steps.

1. In the **Navigation** pane, right-click the **Employees** table, and then click **Design View**.

   Access opens the table with its structure displayed. Because you created this table by copying the Customers table, you need to make some structural changes.

2. With **CustomerID** highlighted in the **Field Name** column, type **EmployeeID**, and then press the Tab key twice.

3. In the **Description** column, type **Unique identifying number**.

4. Click the **Country** field's selector, and then on the **Design** contextual tab, in the **Tools** group, click the **Delete Rows** button.

5. In the empty row below the **Phone** field, click the **Field Name** cell, and type **Birthdate**. Then click the **Data Type** cell.

   Access assigns the default Text data type to the new field.

6. Click the arrow at the right end of the **Data Type** cell, and in the list, click **Date/Time**.

7. Repeat steps 5 and 6 to add another **Date/Time** field named **DateHired**.

8. Select the **ZIP** field name, change it to **PostalCode**, and then change its data type to **Text**.

Tip If you use only five-digit ZIP codes, the Number data type is fine. But setting it to Text allows you to enter ZIP+4 codes or the letter-number postal codes used in Canada and other countries.

The properties in the Field Properties area at the bottom of the design page change to those that are appropriate for this type of field.

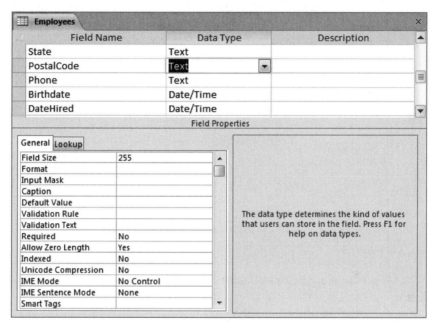

The properties for the Text data type.

9. In the box to the right of **Field Size**, double-click **255**, and type **10**.

You are specifying that this field can contain no more than 10 characters.

10. Change the **Field Size** property of the following fields as shown:

FirstName	50	**City**	50	**Phone**	30
LastName	50	**State**	20		

Tip Sometimes changing the field properties of a table that already contains data can produce unanticipated results. If you make a change to a field property that might cause data to be lost (for example, if you make the Field Size property smaller than one of the field's existing values), Access warns you of this problem when you attempt to save the table.

11. Click the **State** field. Then in the **Field Properties** area, click the **Caption** box, and type **State or Region**.

The Field Name remains State, but in Datasheet view, the column heading will be *State or Region*.

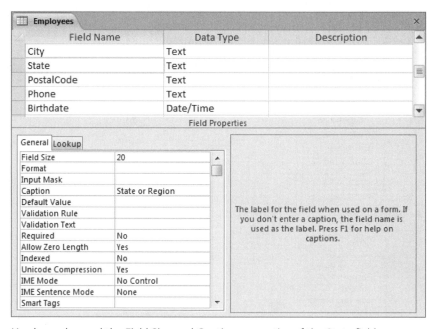

You have changed the Field Size and Caption properties of the State field.

12. On the **Design** tab, in the **Views** group, click the **View** button to switch to Datasheet view.

Access tells you that you must save the table before leaving Design view.

13. In the message box, click **Yes** to save the table.

Access saves the table and displays it in Datasheet view.

14. With the table displayed in Datasheet view, click the **LastName** field name. Then on the **Fields** contextual tab, in the **Add & Delete** group, click the **Text** button.

A new field called *Field1* that has the Text data type is inserted to the right of the LastName field.

Tip You can also create a new field with a specific data type by clicking the Click To Add label to the right of the last field in the field name row. Then in the list that appears, you can click the data type you want.

15. With **Field1** selected, type **Title**, and press Enter.

16. Click the **Title** field name. Then in the **Properties** group, in the **Field Size** box, click **255** to select it, type **50**, and press Enter.

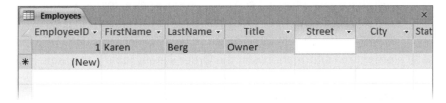

17. Type the following information in the first record:

FirstName	Karen
LastName	Berg
Title	Owner

    The Employees table is now ready for you to start entering data.

The first record of the Employees table.

✖ CLEAN UP Close the Employees table. Retain the MyTables database for use in the last exercise.

Creating Relationships Between Tables

In Access, a relationship is an association between common fields in two tables. You can use this association to link the primary key field in one table to a field that contains the same information in another table. The field in the other table is called the *foreign key*. For example, if customer accounts are assigned to specific sales employees, you can establish a relationship by linking the primary key EmployeeID field in the Employees table with the foreign key EmployeeID field in the Customers table. Each customer account is assigned to only one employee, but each employee can manage many customer accounts, so this type of relationship—the most common—is known as a *one-to-many relationship*.

Similarly, if every order is associated with a customer, you can establish a relationship by linking the primary key CustomerID field in the Customers table and foreign key CustomerID field in the Orders table. Each order is placed by only one customer, but each customer can place many orders. So again, this is a one-to-many relationship.

Less common relationships include:

- **One-to-one** In this type of relationship, each record in one table can have one and only one related record in the other table. This type of relationship isn't commonly used because it is easier to put all the fields in one table. However, you might use two related tables instead of one to break up a table with many fields, or to track information that applies to only some of the records in the first table.

- **Many-to-many** This type of relationship is really two one-to-many relationships tied together through a third table. You might see this relationship in a database that contains Products, Orders, and Order Details tables. The Products table has one record for each product, and each product has a unique ProductID. The Orders table has one record for each order placed, and each record in it has a unique OrderID. However, the Orders table doesn't specify which products were included in each order; that information is in the Order Details table—the table in the middle that ties the other two tables together. Products and Orders each have a one-to-many relationship with Order Details. Products and Orders therefore have a many-to-many relationship with each other. In plain language, this means that every product can appear in many orders, and every order can include many products.

The most common way of creating a relationship between two tables is to add the tables to the Relationships page displayed when you click the Relationships button in the Relationships group on the Database Tools tab. You then drag a field in one table to the common field in the other table and complete the relationship definition in the Edit Relationships dialog box. In this dialog box, you are given the opportunity to impose a restriction called *referential integrity* on the data, which means that an entry will not be allowed in one table unless it already exists in the other table.

After you have created a relationship, you can delete it by deleting the line connecting the tables on the Relationships page. You can clear all the boxes from the page by clicking the Clear Layout button in the Tools group on the Relationship Tools Design contextual tab.

Tip The coverage of relationships in this topic is deliberately simple. However, relationships are what make relational databases tick, and Access provides a number of fairly complex mechanisms to ensure the integrity of the data on either end of the relationship. For a good overview, search for *Guide to table relationships* in Access Help.

In this exercise, you'll create relationships between one table and two other tables. Then you'll test the referential integrity of one of the relationships.

SET UP You need the MyTables database you worked with in the preceding exercise to complete this exercise. Open the MyTables database, and then follow the steps.

Table

1. On the **Create** tab, in the **Tables** group, click the **Table** button to create a new table.

   Before we add fields to this table, let's save it.

2. On the Quick Access Toolbar, click the **Save** button, name the table **Orders**, and click **OK**.

3. To the right of **Click to Add**, click the arrow, and in the data type list, click **Number**. Repeat this step to create a second field with the **Number** data type.

4. Double-click **Field1**, and type **CustomerID**. Then double-click **Field2**, and type **EmployeeID**.

   Each order in the Orders table will be placed by one customer and will be handled by one employee. Let's create relationships between the Orders table and the Customers and Employees tables so that we don't create records for orders from customers who don't exist or that seem to have been handled by employees who don't exist.

5. Close the **Orders** table.

   Tip You cannot create a relationship for an open table.

Relationships

6. On the **Database Tools** tab, in the **Relationships** group, click the **Relationships** button.

   The Show Table dialog box opens so that you can indicate the tables for which you want to create a relationship.

The Tables page of the Show Table dialog box.

Troubleshooting If the dialog box doesn't open automatically, click the Show Table button in the Relationships group on the Design contextual tab.

7. With **Customers** selected on the **Tables** page, click **Add**. Then double-click **Orders**, and click **Close**.

Access displays the Relationships page and adds a Relationship Tools contextual tab to the ribbon.

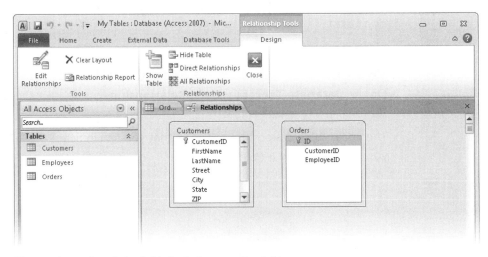

The two boxes list all the fields in their respective tables.

8. In the **Customers** field list, click **CustomerID**, and drag it down and over **CustomerID** in the **Orders** field list, releasing the mouse button when two little boxes, one containing a plus sign, appear below the pointer.

The Edit Relationships dialog box opens.

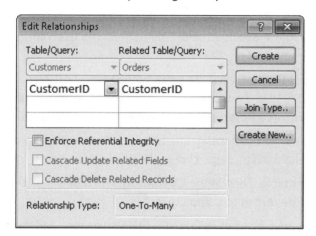

At the bottom of the dialog box, Access indicates that this will be a one-to-many relationship.

9. Select the **Enforce Referential Integrity** check box, and then click **Create**.

Access creates the link between the primary key in the Customers table and the foreign key in the Orders table, and a line now connects the two field lists on the Relationships page.

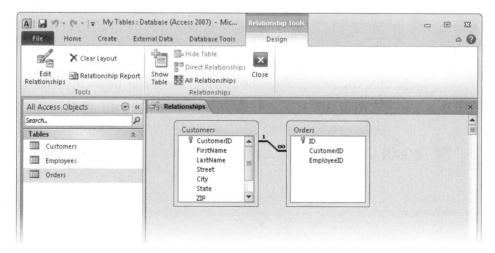

The symbols at each end of the line indicate that each Customer ID value appears only once in the Customers table but can appear many times in the Orders table.

Show Table

10. On the **Design** contextual tab, in the **Relationships** group, click the **Show Table** button. Then in the **Show Table** dialog box, double-click the **Employees** table, and click **Close**.

    Access adds a box listing all the fields in the Employees table to the Relationships page.

11. On the page, drag the title bars of the three field lists to arrange them so that they are side by side and equidistant.

12. In the **Employees** field list, click the **EmployeeID** field, and drag it down and over the **EmployeeID** field in the **Orders** field list. Then in the **Edit Relationships** dialog box, select the **Enforce Referential Integrity** check box, and click **Create**.

13. After Access draws the relationship line between the primary key and the foreign key, close the Relationships page, clicking **Yes** to save its layout.

14. Open the **Orders** table. Then in the **CustomerID** field of the first record, type **11**, and click below the record to complete it.

    Access displays a message box telling you that you cannot add the new record to the table.

The value in the CustomerID field in the Orders table must match a value in the primary key CustomerID field in the Customer table.

15. Click **OK**. Then change the value to **1**, and click below the record to complete it.

    This time, Access accepts the value because there is a record with the value 1 in the primary key CustomerID field of the Customers table.

 CLEAN UP Close the Orders table, and then close the My Tables database.

Key Points

- Access 2010 includes templates to help you create databases and application parts to help you add related tables and other database objects.

- Rather than storing all information in one table, you can create different tables for each type of information, such as customers, orders, and suppliers.

- You can create a simple table structure by entering data and naming fields in Datasheet view. You can also set the data type and certain properties.

- You can manipulate or hide columns and rows without affecting the data.

- In Design view, you can modify any table, whether you created it manually or as part of a template.

- Data types and properties determine what data can be entered in a field, and how the data will look on the screen. Caution: changing some properties might affect the data.

- You can create a relationship between the primary key field of one table and the foreign key field of another so that you can combine information from both tables.

Chapter at a Glance

Create forms by using the
Form tool, **page 822**

Change the look of
forms, **page 829**

Change the
arrangement
of forms, **page 837**

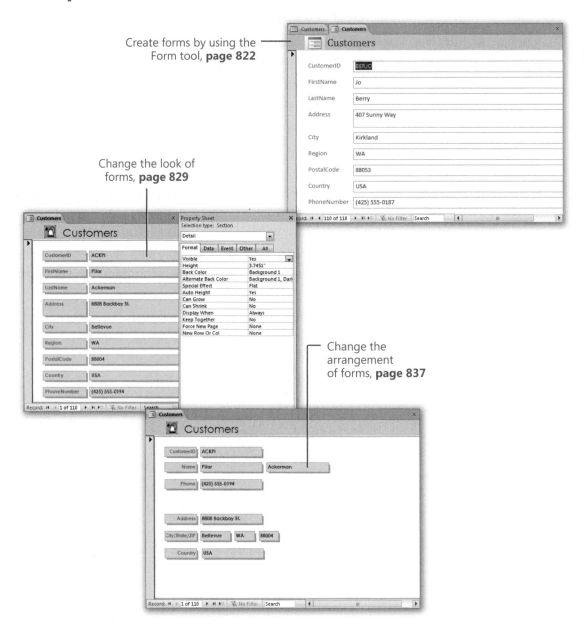

27 Create Simple Forms

A database that contains the day-to-day records of an active company is useful only if it is kept current and if the information stored in it can be found quickly. Although Microsoft Access 2010 is fairly easy to use, entering, editing, and retrieving information in Datasheet view is not a task you would want to assign to someone who's not familiar with Access. Not only would these tasks be tedious and inefficient, but working in Datasheet view leaves far too much room for error, especially if details of complex transactions have to be entered into several related tables. The solution to this problem is to create and use forms.

A form is an organized and formatted view of some or all of the fields from one or more tables. Forms work interactively with the tables in a database. You use controls in the form to enter new information, to edit or remove existing information, or to locate information. The controls you will use most frequently in an Access form are:

● **Text box controls** You can view or enter information in these controls. Think of a text box control as a little window through which you can insert data into the corresponding field of the related table or view information that is already in that field.

● **Label controls** These tell you the type of information you are looking at in the corresponding text box control, or what you are expected to enter in the text box control.

Tip An Access form can also include a variety of other controls, such as list boxes, that transform the form into something very much like a Windows dialog box or wizard page. For information about Access 2010 features not covered in this book, refer to *Microsoft Access 2010 Step by Step* by Joyce Cox and Joan Lambert (Microsoft Press, 2010).

In this chapter, you'll discover how easy it is to create forms to view and enter information. You'll also modify forms to suit your needs by changing their appearance and the arrangement of their controls.

> **Practice Files** Before you can complete the exercises in this chapter, you need to copy the book's practice files to your computer. The practice files you'll use to complete the exercises in this chapter are in the Chapter27 practice file folder. A complete list of practice files is provided in "Using the Practice Files" at the beginning of this book.

Creating Forms by Using the Form Tool

Before you begin creating a form, you need to know the following:

- Which table the form should be based on
- How the form will be used

After making these decisions, you can create a form in the following ways:

- By clicking the table you want in the Navigation bar, and then clicking the Form button in the Forms group on the Create tab. This method creates a simple form that uses all the fields in the table.

- By using a wizard. This method enables you to choose which of the table's fields you want to use in the form.

- Manually in Layout view where you can see the underlying data or Design view where you have more control over form elements.

    See Also For information about manipulating forms in Layout view, see the other two topics in this chapter.

    Tip When creating forms for a Web database, you must use Layout view. You can use Layout view or Design view for non-Web databases.

You will usually want to start the process of creating forms that are based on tables by using the Form tool or a wizard—not because the manual process is especially difficult, but because it is simply more efficient to have the tool or a wizard create the basic form for you and then refine that form manually.

In this exercise, you'll use the Form tool to create a form based on a table. You will then enter a couple of records by using the new form and refresh the table to reflect the new entries.

SET UP You need the GardenCompany03_start database located in your Chapter27 practice file folder to complete this exercise. Open the GardenCompany03_start database, and save it as *GardenCompany03*. Then follow the steps.

Important The practice file for this exercise contains tables that look similar to those in the practice file for Chapter 25. However, to simplify the steps, we have removed the relationships between the tables. Be sure to use the practice database for each chapter rather than continuing on with the database from an earlier chapter.

1. In the **Navigation** pane, display **All Access Objects**, and then in the **Tables** group, double-click **Customers**.

    The Customers table opens in Datasheet view.

CustomerID	FirstName	LastName	Address	City	Region	P
ACKPI	Pilar	Ackerman	8808 Backbay S	Bellevue	WA	88
ADATE	Terry	Adams	1932 52nd Ave.	Vancouver	BC	V4
ALLMI	Michael	Allen	130 17th St.	Vancouver	BC	V4
BANMA	Martin	Bankov	78 Riverside Dr	Woodinville	WA	88
BENPA	Paula	Bento	6778 Cypress P	Oak Harbor	WA	88
BERKA	Karen	Berg	PO Box 69	Yakima	WA	88
BOSRA	Randall	Boseman	55 Grizzly Peak	Butte	MT	49
BRETE	Ted	Bremer	311 87th Pl.	Beaverton	OR	87
BROKE	Kevin F.	Browne	666 Fords Land	Seattle	WA	88
CAMDA	David	Campbell	22 Market St.	San Francisco	CA	84
CANCH	Chris	Cannon	89 W. Hilltop D	Palo Alto	CA	84
CHANE	Neil	Charney	1842 10th Aven	Sidney	BC	V1
CLAMO	Molly	Clark	785 Beale St.	Sidney	BC	V1
COLPA	Pat	Coleman	876 Western A	Seattle	WA	88
CORCE	Cecilia	Cornejo	778 Ancient Rd	Bellevue	WA	88
COXBR	Brian	Cox	14 S. Elm Dr.	Moscow	ID	73
CULSC	Scott	Culp	14 E. University	Seattle	WA	88

Record: 1 of 108   No Filter   Search

The record navigation bar shows that there are 108 records in this table.

Notice the CustomerID field, which contains a unique identifier for each customer and is the primary key field. In this case, the unique identifier is not an auto-generated number, but the first three letters of the customer's last name combined with the first two letters of his or her first name.

2. On the **Create** tab, in the **Forms** group, click the **Form** button.

Access creates a simple form based on the active table and displays the form in Layout view. In this view, you can make adjustments to the layout and content of the form by clicking the buttons on three Form Layout Tools contextual tabs.

Tip You don't have to open a table to create a form based on it. You can simply click the table in the Navigation pane to select it and then click the Form button in the Forms group on the Create tab. But it is sometimes useful to have the table open behind the form so that you can verify the form contents against the table contents.

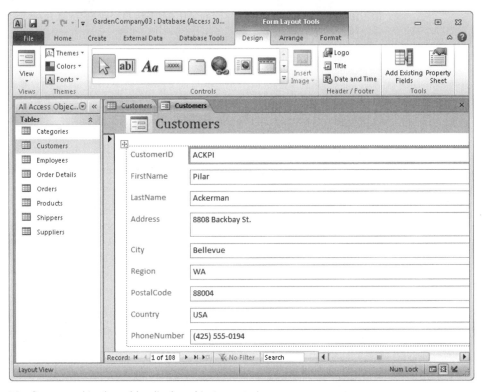

The first record in the table, displayed in Layout view.

Troubleshooting The appearance of buttons and groups on the ribbon changes depending on the width of the program window. For information about changing the appearance of the ribbon to match our screen images, see "Modifying the Display of the Ribbon" at the beginning of this book.

The Form tool has configured all the field names in the table as labels and all the fields as text boxes. In the header at the top of the form, the name of the table appears as a title, and the form icon appears as a placeholder for a logo.

3. Move the mouse pointer over the form, and click any label or text box control.

In Layout view, you can adjust the controls on the form, so any control you click becomes selected, ready for manipulation.

4. On the **View Shortcuts** toolbar, click the **Form View** button. Then move the mouse pointer over the form, and click the **City** label.

In Form view, the Form Layout Tools contextual tabs are no longer displayed. Clicking a label doesn't select the label for manipulation; instead it selects the entry in the adjacent text box, ready for editing.

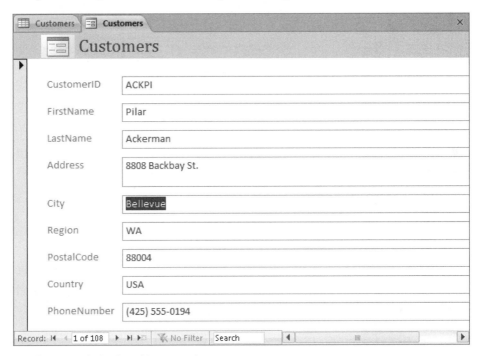

The first record, displayed in Form view.

5. In the record navigation bar at the bottom of the form, click the **Next Record** button.

Access displays the second record in the table.

6. Use the record navigation bar to display a few more records.

Tip You can easily compare the information shown in the form to that in the table by alternately clicking the Customers table tab and the Customers form tab to switch back and forth between their pages.

7. At the right end of the record navigation bar, click the **New (Blank) Record** button.

Access displays a blank Customers form, ready for you to enter information for a new customer.

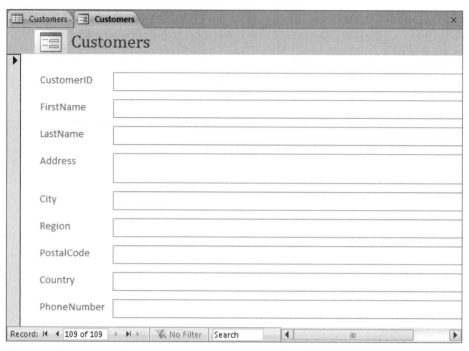

The record navigation bar shows that this will be record number 109.

8. Click the **CustomerID** label.

   The text box to the right now contains the cursor.

9. Type **ASHCH**, and press Tab.

   When you start typing, the icon that indicates a record is receiving data (two dots and a pencil) appears in the bar to the left. When you press Tab or Enter, the cursor moves to the next text box.

10. Type the following information, pressing the Tab key to move to the next text box.

FirstName	Chris
LastName	Ashton
Address	89 Cedar Way
City	Redmond
Region	WA
PostalCode	88052
Country	USA
PhoneNumber	(425) 555-0191

11. When you finish entering the phone number, press Enter.

Because you just typed the last field value in the record, Access displays another blank record. The record navigation bar now shows that this will be the 110th record in the table.

12. Type the following information, pressing the Tab key to move from text box to text box.

CustomerID	**BERJO**
FirstName	**Jo**
LastName	**Berry**
Address	**407 Sunny Way**
City	**Kirkland**
Region	**WA**
PostalCode	**88053**
Country	**USA**
PhoneNumber	**(425) 555-0187**

13. When you finish entering the phone number, press Enter. Then in the record navigation bar, click the **Previous Record** button.

Access cancels the new record and displays the record you just created.

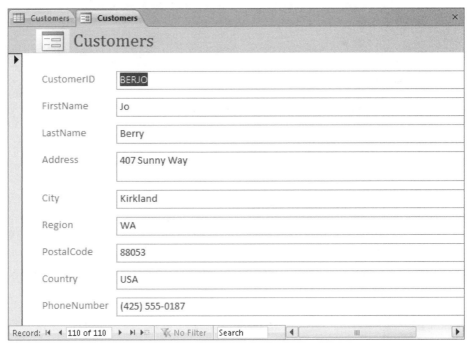

The information you entered for record number 110.

14. Click the **Customers** table tab, and on the record navigation bar, click the **Last Record** button.

The two records you entered in the form do not appear at the bottom of the table, and the record navigator bar indicates that there are only 108 records in the table.

15. On the **Home** tab, in the **Records** group, click the **Refresh All** button.

Access synchronizes the form data input with the table, updates the record navigator bar to show 110 records, and displays the top of the table.

CustomerID	FirstName	LastName	Address	City	Region	P
ACKPI	Pilar	Ackerman	8808 Backbay S	Bellevue	WA	88
ADATE	Terry	Adams	1932 52nd Ave.	Vancouver	BC	V4
ALLMI	Michael	Allen	130 17th St.	Vancouver	BC	V4
ASHCH	Chris	Ashton	89 Cedar Way	Redmond	WA	88
BANMA	Martin	Bankov	78 Riverside Dr	Woodinville	WA	88
BENPA	Paula	Bento	6778 Cypress P	Oak Harbor	WA	88
BERJO	Jo	Berry	407 Sunny Way	Kirkland	WA	88
BERKA	Karen	Berg	PO Box 69	Yakima	WA	88
BOSRA	Randall	Boseman	55 Grizzly Peak	Butte	MT	49
BRETE	Ted	Bremer	311 87th Pl.	Beaverton	OR	87
BROKE	Kevin F.	Browne	666 Fords Land	Seattle	WA	88
CAMDA	David	Campbell	22 Market St.	San Francisco	CA	84
CANCH	Chris	Cannon	89 W. Hilltop D	Palo Alto	CA	84
CHANE	Neil	Charney	1842 10th Aven	Sidney	BC	V'
CLAMO	Molly	Clark	785 Beale St.	Sidney	BC	V'
COLPA	Pat	Coleman	876 Western A'	Seattle	WA	88
CORCE	Cecilia	Cornejo	778 Ancient Rd	Bellevue	WA	88
COXBR	Brian	Cox	14 S. Elm Dr.	Moscow	ID	73
CULSC	Scott	Culp	14 E. University	Seattle	WA	88

Record: ⬅ ◀ 1 of 110 ▶ ▶⬛ ▶⬛ No Filter Search

The two new records now appear in alphabetical order based on their CustomerID field values.

16. Close the **Customers** table.

17. On the Quick Access Toolbar, click the **Save** button. Then in the **Save As** dialog box, click **OK** to accept *Customers* as the form name.

Access saves the form. The Forms group appears on the Navigation bar, listing Customers as the only form in the database.

CLEAN UP Close the form. Retain the GardenCompany03 database for use in later exercises.

Changing the Look of Forms

When you create a form by using the Form tool, as you did in the previous exercise, the form includes every field in the table on which it is based. Each field is represented on the form by a text box control and its associated label control. The form is linked, or *bound*, to the table, and each text box is bound to its corresponding field. The table is called the *record source*, and the field is called the *control source*.

Forms and their controls have properties that determine how they behave and look. A form inherits some of its properties from the table on which it is based. For example, each text box name on the form reflects the corresponding field name in the source table. The text box label also reflects the field name, unless the field has been assigned a Caption property, in which case it reflects the caption. The width of each text box is determined by the Field Size property in the table.

Even though a form is bound to its table, the properties of the form are not bound to the table's properties. After you have created the form, you can change the properties of the form's fields independently of those in the table. You might want to change these properties to improve the form's appearance—for example, you can change the font, font size, alignment, fill color, and border.

One of the quickest ways to change the look of a form is to change the theme applied to the database. A theme is a combination of colors and fonts that controls the look of certain objects. In the case of a form, it controls the color and text of the header at the top of the form and the text of the labels and text boxes. By default, the Office theme is applied to all databases based on the Blank Database template and their objects, but you can easily change the theme by clicking the Themes button in the Themes group on the Design contextual tab, and then making a selection from the Themes gallery. While the gallery is displayed, you can point to a theme to display a live preview of how the active database object will look with that theme's colors and fonts applied.

If you like the colors of one theme and the fonts of another, you can mix and match theme elements. First apply the theme that most closely resembles the look you want, and then in the Themes group, change the colors by clicking the Colors button or the fonts by clicking the Fonts button.

Tip If you create a combination of colors and fonts that you would like to be able to use with other databases, you can save the combination as a new theme by clicking Save Current Theme at the bottom of the Themes gallery.

If you like most of the formatting of a theme but you want to fine-tune some elements, you can do so in Layout view. In this view, you can see the records from the table to which the form is bound, so when you make adjustments, you can see the impact on the data. (Changes to the data can be made only in Form view.) You might also want to add your organization's logo or a small graphic that represents the form's contents.

In this exercise, you'll change the form properties that control its colors and text attributes. You'll also add a logo to the form.

SET UP You need the GardenCompany03 database you worked with in the preceding exercise and the Logo graphic located in your Chapter27 practice file folder to complete this exercise. Open the GardenCompany03 database, and then follow the steps.

1. In the **Navigation** pane, under **Forms**, right-click **Customers**, and then click **Layout View**.

   The Customers form opens in Layout view.

2. On the **Design** contextual tab, in the **Themes** group, click the **Themes** button.

   The Themes gallery appears.

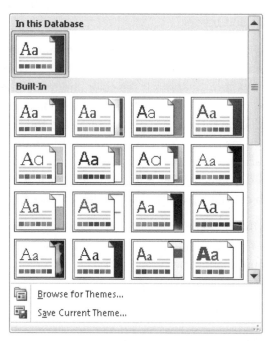

Each thumbnail represents a theme. By default, the Office theme is applied to this database.

3. Point to each thumbnail in turn, pausing to see its name in the ScreenTip that appears and the live preview of the form header and text.

4. Click the **Austin** thumbnail to apply that theme.

5. On the **Design** tab, in the **Header/Footer** group, click the **Logo** button.

6. With the contents of your **Chapter27** practice file folder displayed in the **Insert Picture** dialog box, double-click the **Logo** picture.

The logo replaces the form icon to the left of the title in the form header.

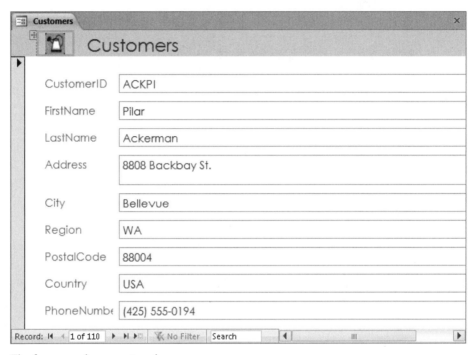

The form now has a custom logo.

Now let's experiment with individual properties.

7. On the **Customers** form, click the **CustomerID** label (not its text box).

The label is surrounded by a thick orange border.

8. On the **Format** contextual tab, in the **Font** group, click the **Font Size** arrow, and then in the list, click **8**.

The label text is now significantly smaller.

9. Click the **CustomerID** text box (not its label), and then on the **Design** contextual tab, in the **Tools** group, click the **Property Sheet** button.

Keyboard Shortcut Press Alt+Enter to display the Property Sheet.

The Property Sheet for this form opens and displays the properties for the object whose name appears in the text box at the top of the pane. Above the box, the type of object is identified. The properties are organized below the box on four pages: Format, Data, Event, and Other. You can display all the properties on one page by clicking the All tab.

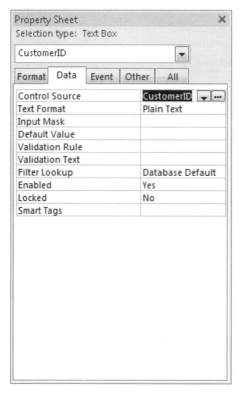

The Data properties of the CustomerID text box control.

> **Tip** Don't change the properties on the Data page until you know more about controls and their sources.

10. In the **Property Sheet**, click the **Format** tab.

All the commands available in the Font group on the Format tab of the ribbon (plus a few more) are available on this page of the Property Sheet.

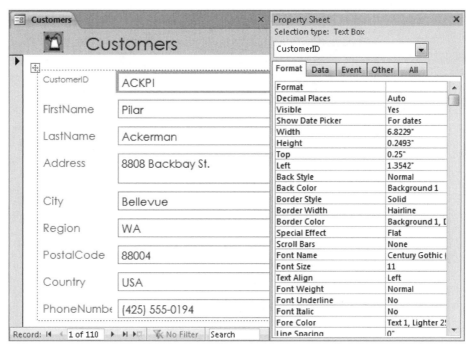

The Format properties for the CustomerID text box control.

11. On the **Format** page, click **Font Size**, click the arrow to the right of the adjacent property, and in the list, click **8**.

12. Set the **Font Weight** property to **Bold**.

On the form, the entry in the CustomerID text box reflects your changes.

> **Tip** Sometimes the Property Sheet might obscure your view of the controls on the form. You can change the width of the Property Sheet or of any task pane by dragging its left border to the left or right. You can undock the Property Sheet from the edge of the window and move it elsewhere by dragging its title bar. Double-click the title bar to dock it again.

13. At the right end of the box at the top of the **Property Sheet**, click the arrow, and then in the object list, click **Label3**.

The FirstName label is now selected. You can display the properties of any object on the form, including the form itself, by clicking the object you want in the object list.

14. Repeat step 11 to change the font size of the **FirstName** label to **8** points.

    You have now made changes to three controls on this form.

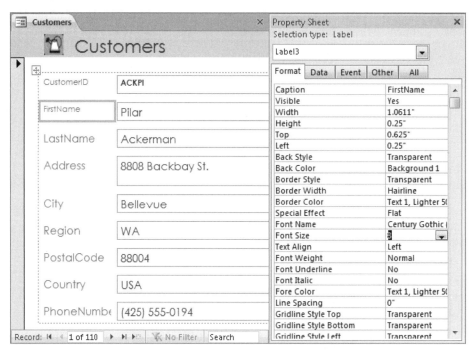

You have applied character formatting to the CustomerID label and text box control, and to the FirstName label.

These different ways of selecting a control and changing its properties provide some flexibility and convenience, but it would be a tedious way to make changes to several controls in a form. The next two steps provide a faster method.

15. In the upper-left corner of the dotted frame surrounding all the controls on the form, click the **Select All** button.

    All the controls within the dotted frame are now surrounded by thick orange borders to indicate that they are selected. In the Property Sheet, the selection type is *Multiple selection*, and the box below is blank. Only the Format settings that are the same for all the selected controls are displayed. Because the changes you made in the previous steps are not shared by all the selected controls, the Font Size and Font Weight settings are now blank.

16. Repeat steps 11 and 12 to set the **Font Size** and **Font Weight** properties of the selected controls to **8** and **Bold**.

17. With the controls still selected, set the **Back Style** property to **Normal**.

    Although you can't see any change, the background of the labels is no longer transparent.

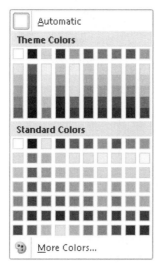

18. Click the **Back Color** property, and then click the **Ellipsis** button at the right end of the property.

    This Ellipsis button has different names and serves different purposes for different properties. In this case, clicking the Ellipsis button displays a color palette.

The colors in this palette reflect the color scheme that is part of the Austin theme.

19. Under **Theme Colors** in the palette, click the third box (**Light Green, Background 2**).

    The background of all the controls changes to light green.

    Tip If the Back Color palette doesn't include a color you want to use, click More Colors at the bottom of the gallery, select a color on the Standard or Custom page of the Colors dialog box, and then click OK to set the color and add it to the list of recent colors at the bottom of the gallery.

20. Set the **Special Effect** property to **Shadowed**, and the **Border Color** property to the fifth box under **Theme Colors** in the color palette (**Green, Accent 1**).

21. In the form, click away from the selected controls to release the selection.

You can now see the results.

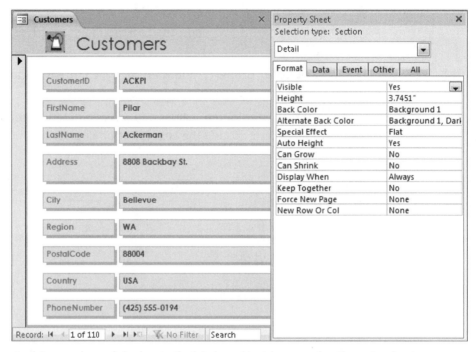

Applying a color and shadow to the labels and text boxes makes them stand out.

22. In the form, click the **FirstName** label. Then in the **Property Sheet**, click the **Caption** property, change **FirstName**: to **First Name**, and press Enter.

23. Repeat step 22 to change **LastName** to **Last Name** and **PhoneNumber** to **Phone**.

> **Tip** Changing the Caption property of the form does not affect the Caption property of the table.

 24. On the Quick Access Toolbar, click the **Save** button to save the design of the **Customers** form, and then close it.

The Property Sheet attached to the form also closes.

 CLEAN UP Retain the GardenCompany03 database for use in the last exercise.

Changing the Arrangement of Forms

Forms generated with the Form tool are functional, not fancy. By default, they are arranged in the Stacked layout, which arranges all the label controls in a single column on the left and all their corresponding text box controls in a single column to their right. All the boxes of each type are the same size, and in the boxes, the text is left-aligned.

If it suits the needs of your data better to display records in a tabular layout much like that of a table in Datasheet view, you can click Tabular in the Table group on the Arrange contextual tab.

If the default layout doesn't suit your needs or preferences, you can customize it. Most of the rearranging you are likely to want to do can be accomplished in Layout view, where you can see the impact on the underlying data. If you want to make more extensive changes to the layout of a non-Web database, you can switch to Design view.

In Layout view, you can do the following to improve the form's layout and make it attractive and easy to use:

- Add and delete a variety of controls
- Change the size, color, and effects of controls
- Move controls
- Change text alignment
- Change control margins

Tip The order in which you make changes can have an impact on the results. If you don't see the expected results, click the Undo button on the Quick Access Toolbar to reverse your previous action, or click the Undo arrow, and click an action in the list to reverse more than one action.

In this exercise, you'll size, align, and rearrange the label and text box controls in a form.

SET UP You need the GardenCompany03 database you worked with in the preceding exercise to complete this exercise. Open the GardenCompany03 database, and then follow the steps.

1. In the **Navigation** pane, under **Forms**, right-click **Customers**, and click **Layout View**.

   Because the Property Sheet was open when you last closed the form, it opens with the form.

2. Click the **CustomerID** label (not its text box), and on the **Arrange** contextual tab, in the **Rows & Columns** group, click the **Select Column** button.

   Tip You can also point above the selected control, and when the pointer changes to a single downward-pointing arrow, click to select the column of controls.

3. With all the labels selected, on the **Format** page of the **Property Sheet**, set the **Text Align** property to **Right**.

   All the labels are right-aligned in their boxes. The Property Sheet indicates that by default, the Width property of the labels is 1.0611".

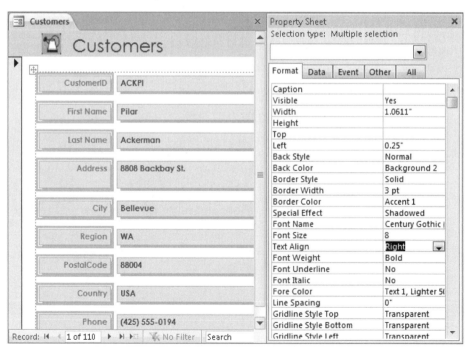

You can efficiently adjust the alignment of multiple controls by changing the Text Align property in the Property Sheet.

4. Point to the right border of the **CustomerID** label, and when the pointer changes to a two-headed horizontal arrow, drag to the left until **CustomerID** just fits in its box.

5. In the **Property Sheet**, adjust the **Width** property to **0.8"**, and press Enter.

   Tip It is often easier to adjust the size of controls visually and then fine-tune them in the Property Sheet than it is to guess what property settings might work.

6. Select the **CustomerID** text box (not its label), and change its **Width** property to **1.5"**.

   Tip Throughout this book, we refer to measurements in inches. If your computer is set to display measurements in centimeters, substitute the equivalent metric measurement. As long as you are entering the default units, you don't have to specify the unit type.

   The width of all the text box controls is adjusted, not just that of the CustomerID text box.

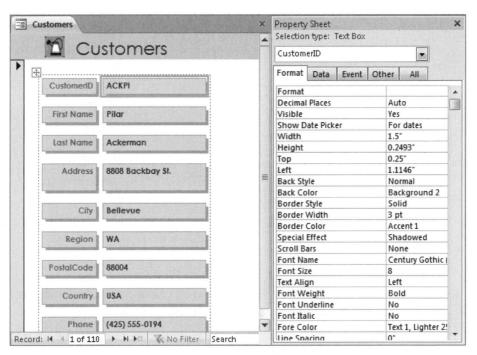

In a Stacked layout, all the controls in each column are the same width.

Notice that the controls are different heights. We'll fix that next.

7. Above the upper-left corner of the dotted border that surrounds all the controls, click the **Select All** button to select all the controls within the border. Then in the **Property Sheet**, set the **Height** property to **0.25"**.

8. On the **Arrange** contextual tab, in the **Position** group, click the **Control Margins** button, and then click **Narrow**.

Now all the controls are the same height and width and have the same interior margins.

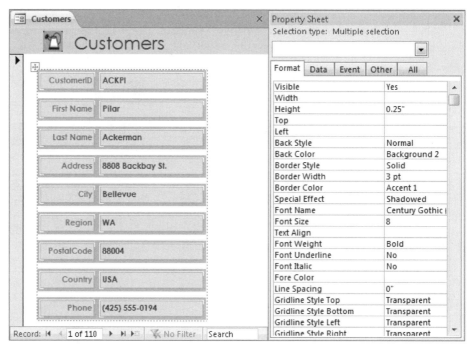

You can control not only the size of the controls but also the distance from the control's border to its text.

9. Click the **Phone** label (not its text box), and on the **Arrange** contextual tab, in the **Rows & Columns** group, click the **Select Row** button.

Tip You can also point to the left of the selected control, and when the pointer changes to a single right-pointing arrow, click to select the row of controls.

10. Point anywhere in the selection, and drag upward, releasing the mouse button when the insertion line sits below the **Last Name** label or text box.

    The Phone label and text box move to their new location. As you can see, it is easy to move controls within the structure of the Stacked layout. But suppose you want to rearrange the form so that some controls are side by side instead of stacked.

11. Point to the selected label and text box, and try to drag it to the right of the **Last Name** controls above.

    The controls will not move out of their columns. They are confined by the Stacked layout applied to the form. To make more extensive layout adjustments, you need to remove the layout from the form.

12. Above the upper-left corner of the dotted border, click the **Select All** button. Then right-click the selection, click **Layout**, and click **Remove Layout**.

    The dotted border disappears, and the form is no longer constrained by the Stacked layout.

13. Click the **Last Name** label, and then press the Delete key.

14. Click the **LastName** text box, point to the **A** in *Ackerman*, and when the pointer is shaped like a four-headed arrow, drag up and to the right until the pointer sits slightly to the right of the **FirstName** text box.

    When you release the mouse button, the control snaps to an invisible grid that helps maintain consistent spacing on the form.

15. In the **Property Sheet**, adjust the **Left** property to **2.7"**.

16. Hold down the Shift key, and click the two adjacent controls to add them to the selection. Then top-align the controls by setting the **Top** property to **0.6"**.

17. Click the **First Name** label, and change the label's **Caption** property to **Name**.

18. Rearrange the remaining controls in logical groupings on the form, and then close the **Property Sheet**.

    We adjusted the position of the phone controls and then grouped and sized the address controls.

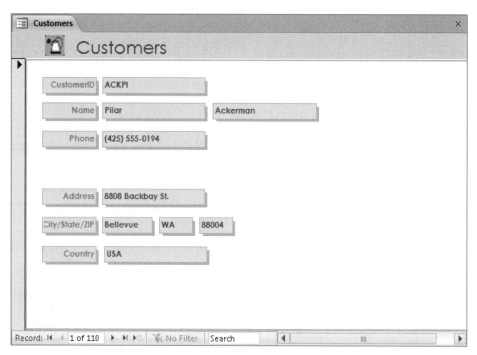

In Layout view, this kind of arrangement can be achieved only if you remove the default layout, which constrains the controls in columns.

Tip If you rearrange controls or add new controls to a form and then find that pressing Tab jumps around erratically instead of sequentially from one control to the next, you can change the tab order. When working in Layout view, you click the Other tab in the Property Sheet and set the Tab Index property for each control in the tab order you want. When working in Design view, you click the Tab Order button in the Tools group on the Design tab to display the Tab Order dialog box, where you can drag fields into the correct order.

19. Close the **Customers** form, clicking **Yes** when prompted to save its layout.

 **CLEAN UP** Close the GardenCompany03 database.

Key Points

- The quickest way to create a form that includes all the fields from one table is by using the Form tool. You can then use the form to view and enter records.

- A form that is based on a table is bound to that form. The table is called the *record source.*

- By default, the form displays one text box control and its associated label control for each field in the table.

- Each text box control is bound to its field, which is called the *control source.*

- Each control has several properties that you can change in Layout view or Design view to improve the look and layout of the form.

Chapter at a Glance

Sort information in tables, **page 846**

Filter information in tables, **page 851**

Filter information by using forms, **page 855**

Locate information that matches multiple criteria, **page 859**

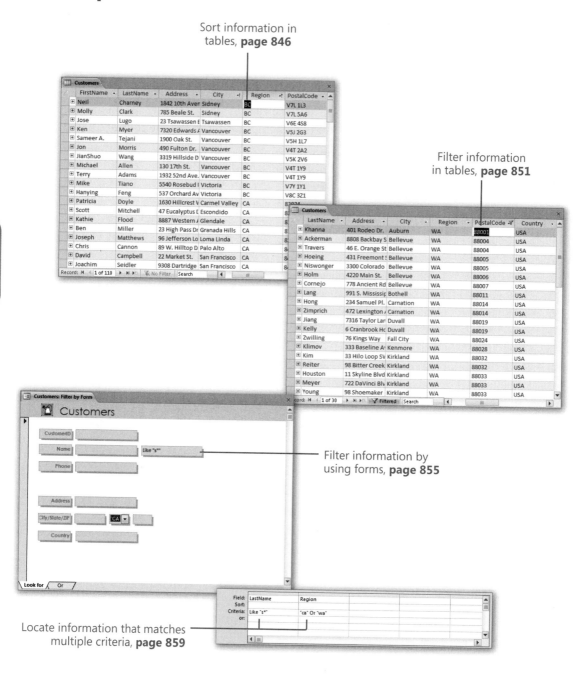

28 Display Data

In this chapter, you will learn how to

✔ Sort information in tables.

✔ Filter information in tables.

✔ Filter information by using forms.

✔ Locate information that matches multiple criteria.

A database is a repository for information. It might contain only a few records or thousands of records, stored in one table or multiple tables. No matter how much information a database contains, it is useful only if you can locate the information you need when you need it. In a small database, you can find information simply by scrolling through a table until you find what you are looking for. But as a database grows in size and complexity, locating and analyzing information becomes more difficult.

Microsoft Access 2010 provides a variety of tools you can use to organize the display of information stored in a database. For example, you can organize all the records in a table by quickly sorting it based on any field or combination of fields. You can also filter the table so that information containing a combination of characters is displayed or excluded from the display.

In this chapter, you'll first sort information in a table based on one and two columns. Then you'll explore three ways to filter tables and forms to display only the records that meet specific criteria.

> **Practice Files** Before you can complete the exercises in this chapter, you need to copy the book's practice files to your computer. The practice file you'll use to complete the exercises in this chapter is in the Chapter28 practice file folder. A complete list of practice files is provided in "Using the Practice Files" at the beginning of this book.

Sorting Information in Tables

You can sort the information stored in a table based on the values in one or more fields, in either ascending or descending order. For example, you could sort customer information alphabetically by last name and then by first name. This would result in the order found in telephone books.

Last Name	First Name
Smith	Brian
Smith	Denise
Smith	Jeff
Taylor	Daniel
Taylor	Maurice

Sorting a table groups all entries of one type together, which can be useful. For example, to qualify for a discount on postage, you might want to group customer records by postal code before printing mailing labels.

Access can sort by more than one field, but it always sorts sequentially from left to right. You can sort by the first field, and if the second field you want to sort by is to the right of the first, you can then add the next field to the sort. If you want to sort by more than one field in one operation, the fields must be adjacent, and they must be arranged in the order in which you want to sort them.

See Also For information about moving fields, see "Manipulating Table Columns and Rows" in Chapter 26, "Create Databases and Simple Tables."

Tip You can sort records while viewing them in a form. Click the field on which you want to base the sort, and then click the Sort command you want. You can't sort by multiple fields at the same time in Form view, but you can sort by one field and then the next to achieve the same results.

In this exercise, you'll sort records first by one field, and then by multiple fields.

SET UP You need the GardenCompany04_start database located in your Chapter28 practice file folder to complete this exercise. Open the GardenCompany04_start database, and save it as *GardenCompany04*. Then follow the steps.

1. With **All Access Objects** displayed in the **Navigation** pane, under **Tables**, double-click **Customers**.

    The Customers table opens in Datasheet view.

2. Click the arrow to the right of the **Region** field name.

    A list of sorting and filtering options appears.

The list at the bottom includes check boxes for every unique value in the field.

3. Click **Sort A to Z**.

Access rearranges the records in alphabetical order by region.

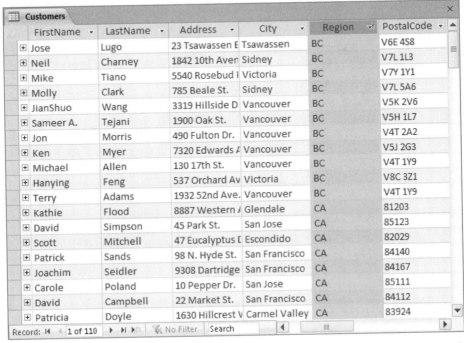

The upward-pointing arrow at the right end of the Region field name indicates that the table is sorted in ascending order on this field.

4. To reverse the sort order by using a different method, on the **Home** tab, in the **Sort & Filter** group, click the **Descending** button.

   The sort order reverses. The records for customers living in Washington (WA) are now at the top of the list, and the arrow at the right end of the field name is pointing downward.

   In both sorts, the region was sorted alphabetically, but the City field was left in a seemingly random order. Suppose you want to see the records arranged by city within each region. You can do this by sorting the City field and then sorting the Region field.

5. Click the arrow to the right of the **City** field name, and then click **Sort A to Z**.

   Access sorts the records alphabetically by city.

6. To finish the process, right-click anywhere in the **Region** column, and then click **Sort A to Z**.

   The two fields are now sorted so that the cities are listed in ascending order within each region.

Both the City and Region field names have upward-pointing arrows.

7. On the **Home** tab, in the **Sort & Filter** group, click the **Remove Sort** button to clear the sort from both fields.

The table reverts to the previously saved sort order. Now let's sort both columns at the same time.

8. Click the **City** field name, hold down the Shift key, and click the **Region** field name. Then in the **Sort & Filter** group, click the **Ascending** button.

Because the City field is to the left of the Region field, Access cannot achieve the result you want.

The City sort is overriding the Region sort.

9. Clear the sort, and then click away from the **City** and **Region** fields to clear the selection.

10. Click the **Region** field name, and drag the field name to the left of the **City** field name, releasing the mouse button when a heavy black line appears between the **Address** and **City** field names.

11. With the **Region** field selected, hold down the Shift key, and click the **City** field name to include that field in the selection.

12. In the **Sort & Filter** group, click the **Ascending** button.

Access arranges the records with the regions in ascending order and the cities in ascending order within each region.

13. Experiment with various ways of sorting the records to display different results. Then close the **Customers** table, clicking **No** when prompted to save the table layout.

 CLEAN UP Retain the GardenCompany04 database for use in later exercises.

How Access Sorts

The concept of sorting seems quite intuitive, but sometimes the way Access sorts numbers might seem puzzling. In Access, numbers can be treated as either text or numerals. Because of the spaces, hyphens, and punctuation typically used in street addresses, postal codes, and telephone numbers, the data type of these fields is usually Text, and the numbers are sorted the same way as all other text. In contrast, numbers in a field assigned the Number or Currency data type are sorted as numerals.

When Access sorts text, it sorts first on the first character in the selected field in every record, then on the next character, then on the next, and so on—until it runs out of characters. When Access sorts numbers, it treats the contents of each field as a single value, and sorts the records based on that value. This tactic can result in seemingly strange sort orders. For example, sorting the list in the first column of the following table as text produces the list in the second column. Sorting the same list as numerals produces the list in the third column.

Original	Sort as text	Sort as numerals
1	1	1
1234	11	3
23	12	4
3	1234	11
11	22	12
22	23	22
12	3	23
4	4	1234

If a field with the Text data type contains numbers, you can sort the field numerically by padding the numbers with leading zeros so that all entries are the same length. For example, 001, 011, and 101 are sorted correctly even if the numbers are defined as text.

Filtering Information in Tables

Sorting the information in a table organizes it in a logical manner, but you still have the entire table to deal with. For locating only the records containing (or not containing) specific information, filtering is more effective than sorting. For example, you could quickly create a filter to locate only customers who live in Seattle, only items that were purchased on January 13, or only orders that were not shipped by standard mail. When you filter a table, Access doesn't remove the records that don't match the filter; it simply hides them.

The Filter commands are available in the Sort & Filter group on the Home tab, on the menu displayed when you click the arrow at the right end of a field name, and on the shortcut menu displayed when you right-click anywhere in a field's column. However, not all Filter commands are available in all of these places.

To filter information by multiple criteria, you can apply additional filters to the results of the first one.

Tip You can filter records while displaying them in a form by using the same commands as you do to filter records in a table.

In this exercise, you'll filter records by using a single criterion and then by using multiple criteria.

 SET UP You need the GardenCompany04 database you worked with in the preceding exercise to complete this exercise. Open the GardenCompany04 database, and then follow the steps.

1. In the **Navigation** pane, under **Tables**, double-click **Customers** to open the **Customers** table in Datasheet view.

2. In the **City** field, click any instance of **Vancouver**.

 3. On the **Home** tab, in the **Sort & Filter** group, click the **Selection** button, and then in the list, click **Equals "Vancouver"**.

Access displays a small filter icon shaped like a funnel at the right end of the City field name to indicate that the table is filtered by that field. The status bar at the bottom of the table has changed from *1 of 110* to *1 of 6* because only six records have the value Vancouver in the City field. Also on the status bar, the Filter status has changed to Filtered.

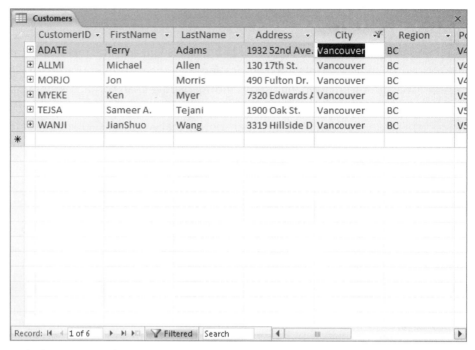

Only the six records for customers who live in Vancouver are displayed in the table.

Tip In the list displayed when you click the arrow to the right of a field name (or the Filter button in the Sort & Filter group) are check boxes for all the unique entries in the active field. Clearing the Select All check box clears all the boxes, and you can then select the check boxes of any values you want to be displayed in the filtered table.

In the Sort & Filter group on the Home tab, the Toggle Filter button is now active. You can use this button to quickly turn the applied filter on and off.

4. In the **Sort & Filter** group, click the **Toggle Filter** button.

   Access displays all the records. If you click the Toggle Filter button again, the filter will be reapplied.

   Now let's display a list of all customers with postal codes starting with 880.

5. Click the arrow to the right of the **PostalCode** field name, and point to **Text Filters** in the list.

A list of criteria appears.

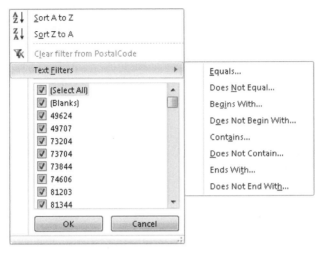

You can specify criteria for the text you want to find.

Tip The sort and filter options displayed when you click the arrow to the right of a field name (or when you click the Filter button in the Sort & Filter group) are determined by the data type of the field. The PostalCode field is a Text field to allow for ZIP+4 codes. If you display the sort and filter list for a field that is assigned the Number data type, the sort and filter list includes Number Filters instead of Text Filters, and different options are available.

6. In the list, click **Begins With**.

The Custom Filter dialog box opens.

The name of the text box is customized with the field name and the filer you chose.

7. In the **PostalCode begins with** box, type **880**. Then click **OK**.

Access filters the table and displays only the records that match your criteria.

Only the 30 records for customers who live in postal codes starting with 880 are displayed in the table.

8. In the **Sort & Filter** group, click the **Toggle Filter** button to remove the filter and display all the records.

   Now let's display only the records of the customers who live outside of the United States.

9. In the **Country** field, right-click any instance of **USA**, and then click **Does Not Equal "USA"**.

   Tip In this case, it is easy to right-click the text you want to base this filter on. If the text is buried in a large table, you can quickly locate it by clicking the Find button in the Find group on the Home tab, entering the term you want in the Find What box in the Find And Replace dialog box, and then clicking Find Next.

   Access displays the records of all the customers from countries other than the United States (in this case, only Canada).

10. Remove the filter, and close the **Customers** table, clicking **No** when prompted to save your changes.

11. Open the **Orders** table in Datasheet view.

12. In the **EmployeeID** field, right-click **7**, and then click **Equals 7**.

    Twenty records are displayed in the filtered table.

13. In the **OrderDate** field, right-click **2/1/2010**, and then click **On or After 2/1/2010**.

    Tip To see a list of the available options for date filters, right-click any cell in the OrderDate field, and then point to Date Filters.

    You now have a list of the orders customers placed with the selected employee on or after the specified date. You could continue to refine the list by filtering on another field, or you could sort the results by a field.

14. Close the **Orders** table, clicking **No** when prompted to save the table layout.

 CLEAN UP Retain the GardenCompany04 database for use in later exercises.

Filtering Information by Using Forms

When you want to filter a table based on the information in several fields, the quickest method is to use the Filter By Form command, which is available from the Advanced Filter Options list in the Sort & Filter group on the Home tab. When you choose this command with a table displayed, Access displays a filtering form that resembles a datasheet. Each of the cells in the form has an associated list of all the unique values in that field in the underlying table.

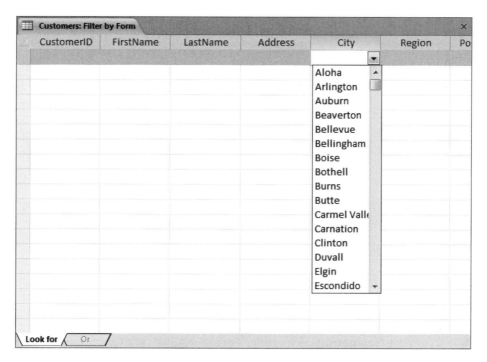

Using the Filter By Form command with a table.

For each field, you can select a value from the list or type a value. When you have finished defining the values you want to see, you click the Toggle Filter button to display only the records that match your selected criteria.

Using Filter By Form on a table that has only a few fields, such as the one shown above, is easy. But using it on a table that has a few dozen fields can be cumbersome, and it is often simpler to find information in the form version of the table. When you choose the Filter By Form command with a form displayed, Access filters the form the same way it filters a table.

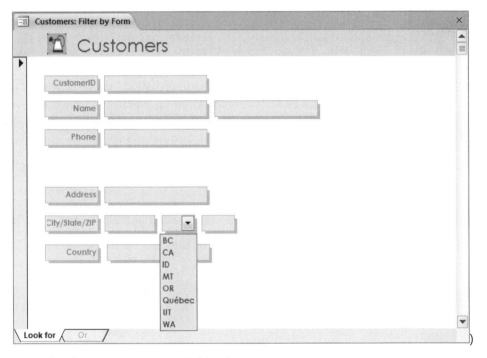

Using the Filter By Form command with a form.

After you have applied the filter, you move between the matched records by clicking the buttons on the record navigation bar at the bottom of the form page.

In this exercise, you'll filter a form by using the Filter By Form command.

SET UP You need the GardenCompany04 database you worked with in the preceding exercise to complete this exercise. Open the GardenCompany04 database, and then follow the steps.

1. In the **Navigation** pane, under **Forms**, double-click **Customers**.

   The Customers form opens in Form view.

2. On the **Home** tab, in the **Sort & Filter** group, click the **Advanced Filter Options** button, and then in the list, click **Filter By Form**.

   The Customers form is replaced by its Filter By Form version, which has two pages: Look For and Or. Instead of displaying the information for one record from the table, the form now has a blank box for each field.

3. Click the second text box to the right of the **Name** label (the box that normally displays the customer's last name), type **s***, and then press Enter.

   The asterisk is a wildcard that stands for any character or string of characters. Access converts your entry to *Like "s*"*, which is the proper format, called the *syntax*, for this type of criterion.

   See Also For information about wildcards, see the sidebar "Wildcards" following this topic.

4. In the **Sort & Filter** group, click the **Toggle Filter** button.

   Access displays the first record that has a LastName value starting with *S*.

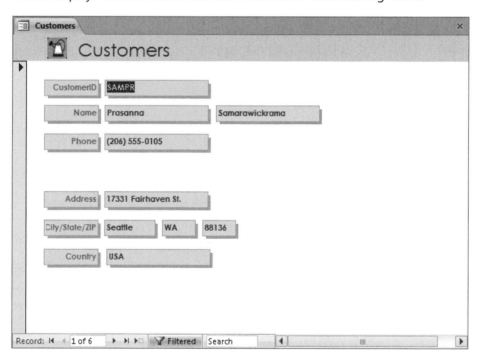

The record navigation bar shows that six records match the filter criterion.

5. Click the **Advanced Filter Options** button and then click **Filter By Form** to redisplay the filter form.

   Your filter criterion is still displayed in the form.

Tip No matter what method you use to enter filter criteria, the criteria are saved as a form property and are available until they are replaced by other criteria.

6. Click the second box to the right of the **City/State/ZIP** label (the box that normally displays the state or region), click the arrow that appears, and then in the list, click **CA**.

You are instructing Access to find and display records that have both a Region value of CA *and* LastName values starting with *S*.

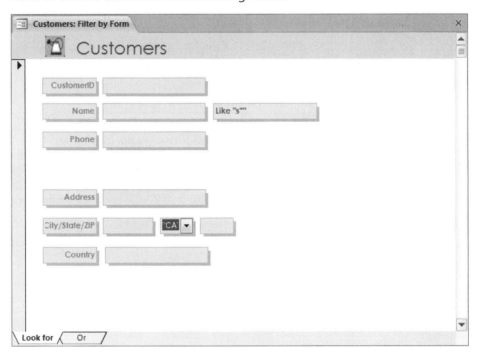

Only records matching both of the criteria will be displayed.

7. Click the **Toggle Filter** button.

Access displays the first of three records that meet the filtering criteria.

8. Switch back to the filter form, and at the bottom of the form page, click the **Or** tab.

The criteria you entered on the Look For page are still there, but on this page, all the fields are blank so that you can enter alternatives for the same fields.

Tip When you display the Or page, a second Or tab appears so that you can include a third criterion for the same field if you want.

9. Type **s*** in the second **Name** box, and click **WA** in the list for the second **City/State/ZIP** box.

You are instructing Access to find and display records that have either a Region value of CA *and* LastName values starting with *S*, *or* a Region value of WA *and* LastName values starting with *S*.

10. Click the **Toggle Filter** button.

11. Use the record navigation bar to view the six records in the filtered **Customers** form.

12. Click the **Toggle Filter** button to remove the filter. Then close the form.

 CLEAN UP Retain the GardenCompany04 database for use in the last exercise.

Wildcards

If you want to filter a table to display records containing certain information but you aren't sure of all the characters, or if you want your filter to match variations of a base set of characters, you can include wildcard characters in your filter criteria. The most common wildcards are:

- ***** The asterisk represents any number of characters. For example, filtering the LastName field on *Co** returns records containing *Colman* and *Conroy*.

- **?** The question mark represents any single alphabetic character. For example, filtering the FirstName field on *er??* returns records containing *Eric* and *Erma*.

- **#** The number sign represents any single numeric character. For example, filtering the ID field on *1##* returns any ID from *100* through *199*.

Tip Access supports several other wildcards. For more information, search for *wildcards* in Access Help.

When searching for information in a Text field, you can also use the Contains text filter to locate records containing words or character strings.

Locating Information That Matches Multiple Criteria

As long as your filter criteria are fairly simple, filtering is a quick and easy way to narrow down the amount of information displayed in a table or to locate information that matches what you are looking for. But suppose you need to locate something more complex, such as all the orders shipped to Midwestern states between specific dates by either of two shippers. When you need to search a single table for records that meet multiple criteria, or when the criteria involve complex expressions, you can use the Advanced Filter/Sort command, available from the Advanced Filter Options list.

Choosing the Advanced Filter/Sort command displays a design grid where you enter filtering criteria. As you'll see, filters with multiple criteria are actually simple queries.

See Also For information about Access 2010 features not covered in this book, refer to *Microsoft Access 2010 Step by Step* by Joyce Cox and Joan Lambert (Microsoft Press, 2010).

In this exercise, you'll filter a table to display the data for customers located in two states. Then you'll experiment with the design grid to better understand its filtering capabilities.

SET UP You need the GardenCompany04 database you worked with in the preceding exercise to complete this exercise. Open the GardenCompany04 database, and then follow the steps.

1. In the **Navigation** pane, under **Tables**, double-click **Customers** to open the **Customers** table in Datasheet view.

2. On the **Home** tab, in the **Sort & Filter** group, click the **Advanced Filter Options** button, and then in the list, click **Advanced Filter/Sort**.

   The CustomersFilter1 page opens, displaying the Query Designer with the Customers field list in the top pane and the design grid in the bottom pane.

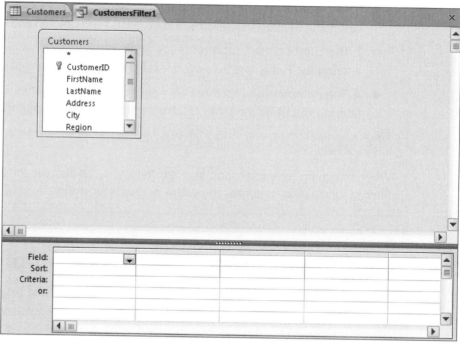

Clicking the Advanced Filter/Sort button displays the Query Designer.

3. In the **Customers** field list, double-click **LastName** to copy it to the **Field** row of the first column of the grid.

4. In the **Criteria** row of the **LastName** field, type s*, and then press Enter.

   Because you have used the * wildcard, Access changes the criterion to *Like "s*"*.

5. In the **Customers** field list, double-click **Region** to copy it to the **Field** row of the next available column of the grid.

6. In the **Criteria** row of the **Region** field, type **ca or wa**, and then press Enter.

> **Tip** If you want to find the records for customers who live in California or Oregon, you cannot type *ca or or*, because Access treats *or* as a reserved word. You must type *ca or "or"* in the Criteria row. Anytime you want to enter a criterion that will be interpreted as an instruction rather than a string of characters, enclose the characters in quotation marks to achieve the desired results.

Your entry changes to *"ca" Or "wa"*. The query will now filter the table to display the records for only those customers with last names beginning with the letter *S* who live in California or Washington.

The grid with two criteria.

7. In the **Sort & Filter** group, click the **Toggle Filter** button to display only records that match the criteria.

Access switches to the Customers table page and displays the filter results.

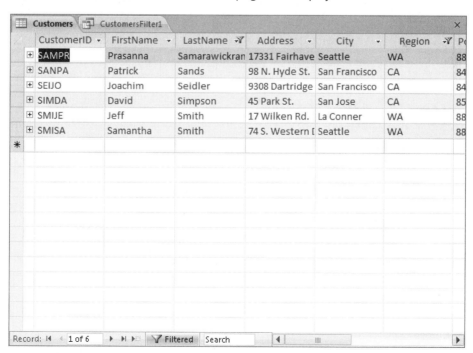

Six customers with last names beginning with S live in either California or Washington.

8. Click the **CustomersFilter1** tab to switch to the filter page.

9. In the **or** row of the **LastName** field, type **b***, and then press Enter.

   We want to filter the table to display only the records for customers with last names beginning with the letter *S* or *B* who live in California or Washington.

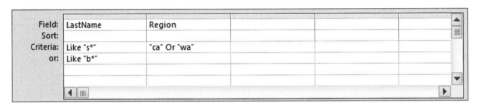

Field:	LastName	Region				
Sort:						
Criteria:	Like "s*"	"ca" Or "wa"				
or:	Like "b*"					

The design grid with three criteria.

10. In the **Sort & Filter** group, click the **Toggle Filter** button to apply the filter.

    On the Customers table page, the result includes records for all customers with last names that begin with *S* or *B*, but some of the *B* names live in Montana and Oregon.

11. Click the **CustomersFilter1** tab to switch to the filter page, and look carefully at the design grid.

    The filter first works with the two criteria in the Criteria row and searches for customers with names beginning with *S* who live in California or Washington. Then it works with the criteria in the Or row and searches for customers with names beginning with *B*, regardless of where they live. To get the results we want, we need to repeat the criterion from the Region field in the Or row.

12. In the **or** row of the **Region** field, type **ca or wa**, and then press Enter.

13. Apply the filter.

    Access switches to the Customers table page and displays only the records for customers with last names beginning with S or B who are located in California or Washington.

14. Close the **Customers** table, clicking **Yes** when prompted to save changes to the design of the table.

 CLEAN UP Close the GardenCompany04 database.

Tip If you are likely to want to use a filter again, you can save it as a query. On the Home tab, in the Sort & Filter group, click the Advanced Filter Options button, click Save As Query, assign the query an appropriate name, and click OK. Then you can run the query to display the filtered results at any time.

Generating Reports

You generate and work with reports in ways that are similar to forms. However, unlike forms, which are used to enter, view, and edit information, reports are used only to extract information. And unlike filters and queries, whose results you usually view only on the screen, reports are often intended to be printed.

Just as you can create a form that includes all the fields in a table by using the Form tool, you can create a report that includes all the fields by using the Report tool, which is located in the Reports group on the Create tab. But such a report is merely a prettier version of the table, and it does not summarize the data in any meaningful way. You are more likely to want to create a report based on only some of the fields, and that is a job for the Report wizard.

The Report wizard leads you through a series of questions, including how you want to group and sort the data. For example, in a report based on a Products table, you might want to group products by category and then sort the products in each category alphabetically. After you finish specifying the report, the wizard creates the report layout, adding a text box control and its associated label for each field you specified.

You can use the Report wizard to get a quick start on a report, but you will frequently want to modify the report to get the result you need. As with forms, the report consists of text box controls that are bound to the corresponding fields in the underlying table and their associated labels. You can adjust the layout and content of reports in either Layout view or Design view. For simple adjustments, it is easier to work in Layout view, where you can see the layout with live data, making the process more intuitive. You can add labels, text boxes, images, and other controls, and you can format them, either by using commands on the ribbon or by setting their properties in the report's Property Sheet.

See Also For information about using Property Sheets, see "Changing the Look of Forms" in Chapter 27, "Create Simple Forms." For information about more advanced report modification techniques, refer to *Microsoft Access 2010 Step by Step* by Joyce Cox and Joan Lambert (Microsoft Press, 2010).

Before printing a report, you will want to preview it, paying particular attention to how the pages break. In a grouped report, you can control whether group headings are allowed to appear at the bottom of a page with no data and whether groups are allowed to break across pages. You can make changes to the margins and orientation of your report pages from the Page Setup contextual tab in Layout view or from the tab displayed when you switch to Print Preview. You can also click the Page Setup button to display the Page Setup dialog box, where you can change all these settings in one place, as well as make additional refinements.

Key Points

- You can sort a table in either ascending or descending order, based on the values in any field (or combination of fields).

- You can filter a table so that information containing a combination of characters is displayed (or excluded from the display).

- You can apply another filter to the results of the previous one to further refine your search.

- The Filter By Form command filters a table or form based on the information in several fields.

- You can use the Advanced Filter/Sort command to search a single table for records that meet multiple criteria.

Part 8

Microsoft
Publisher 2010

Chapter at a Glance

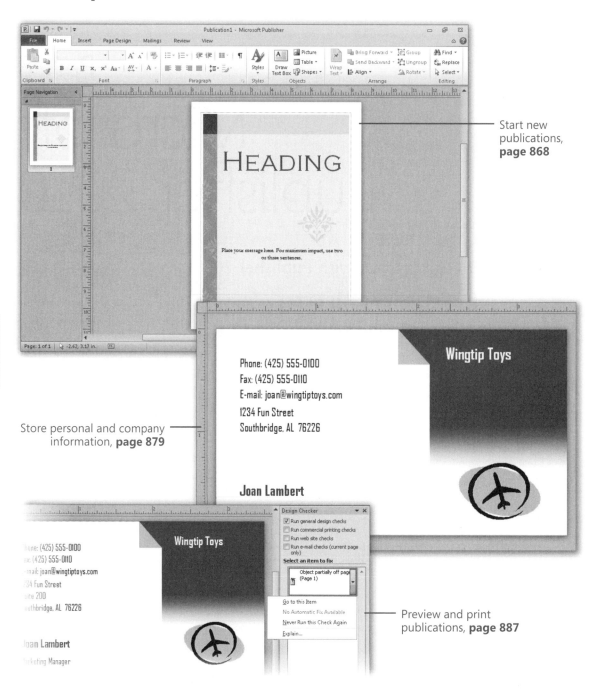

Start new publications, **page 868**

Store personal and company information, **page 879**

Preview and print publications, **page 887**

29 Get Started with Publisher 2010

In this chapter, you will learn how to

✔ Start new publications.

✔ Store personal and company information.

✔ Preview and print publications.

When you use a computer or typewriter to create text documents, you are *word processing*. When you use a specialized computer program to create professional-quality documents that combine text and other visual elements in non-linear arrangements, you are *desktop publishing*. Microsoft Publisher 2010 is designed specifically to handle the various desktop publishing needs of individuals and small organizations. Publisher makes it easy to efficiently create a wide range of publications, from simple flyers to complex brochures. Even novice users will be able to work productively in Publisher after only a brief introduction.

In this chapter, you'll first learn various ways to create blank publications and publications based on existing content. You'll then store standard contact information in Publisher for later use. Finally, you'll preview and print a publication.

> **Practice Files** Before you can complete the exercises in this chapter, you need to copy the book's practice files to your computer. The practice files you'll use to complete the exercises in this chapter are in the Chapter29 practice file folder. A complete list of practice files is provided in "Using the Practice Files" at the beginning of this book.

Starting New Publications

When you start Publisher without opening a publication, the New page of the Backstage view is displayed. From this page, you can start a new publication either from scratch or based on one of the many publication templates that are available.

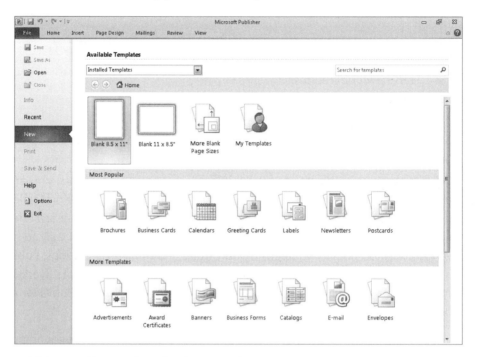

Publisher provides templates for almost anything you might want to create.

The New page of the Backstage view provides several options for starting a new publication, including the following:

● If you need help designing the publication layout, you can base the publication on one of the design templates that comes with Publisher. If none of these templates meets your needs, you can download a sample publication from Microsoft Office Online and then customize it. You can also base publications on your own custom templates.

See Also For information about creating your own templates, see the sidebar "Custom Templates," later in this chapter.

Tip New publications are continually being added to Office Online, so visit the site occasionally to see what's new.

- If you have an existing publication that is close enough in content and design to be a good starting point, you can save a copy of that publication as the starting point for the new one.

- If your content is in a Microsoft Word document, you can import the document into Publisher and then lay out the text as you want it.

- If you want to manually design the publication, you can create a blank publication and specify the page size you want.

See Also For information about creating a blank publication, see "Working with Text Boxes" in Chapter 30, "Create Visual Interest."

Using Templates

Creating a publication from a blank page is time-consuming and requires quite a bit of design skill and knowledge about Publisher. Even people with intermediate and advanced Publisher skills can save time by capitalizing on the work someone else has already done. On the New page of the Backstage view, you can choose a publication type, preview thumbnails of the available designs of that type, and experiment with different color schemes and font schemes.

Tip The templates that come with Publisher, as well as those that are available from Office Online, have associated keywords. You can type a keyword in the Search For Templates box at the top of the Getting Started window and then click the Search button (the green arrow to the right of the search location list) to display thumbnails of templates to which that keyword has been assigned.

When you create a publication based on a template, you are not opening the actual template file; instead, you are creating a new file that includes all the placeholders, graphic elements, and formatting of the template. You customize the publication with your own information, typing text and placing graphics and other elements in the placeholders provided. The new file is temporary until you save it.

Custom Templates

Throughout Part 8 of this book, you'll learn techniques for personalizing the content and layout of publications. If you create a special publication that you might want to use as the basis for future publications, you can save the publication as a custom template and then use it just as you would an installed or online template.

To save a publication as a template:

1. In the left pane of the Backstage view, click Save & Send.

2. In the File Types section of the Save & Send page, click Change File Type.

3. In the Publisher File Types section of the Save Publication list, click Template (*.pub).

4. At the bottom of the Save Publication list, click the Save As button.

   The Save As Template dialog box opens, displaying the contents of your default Templates folder.

   Important You can change the location in which you save your template, but if you do so, it will not appear in the My Templates category of the New page in the Backstage view. If you store a template in a different folder, you can create a publication based on the template by browsing to that folder in Windows Explorer and double-clicking the template file.

5. In the File Name box, type a generic name for the publication template.

6. If you want to assign the template to a specific template category, click the Change button. In the Template Category dialog box that opens, select the category from the list. Then click OK.

   Tip On the My Templates page, you can change the category of a template by right-clicking the template and then clicking Edit Category.

7. In the Save As Template dialog box, click Save.

To create a new publication based on the custom template:

1. On the New page of the Backstage view, click My Templates.

   The My Templates page displays templates stored in the default Templates folder, organized by category.

2. In the center pane, click the template you want, and then click Create.

   Publisher opens a new publication based on your custom template.

The simplest way to change a custom template after you save it is to create a publication based on the template, make the changes, and then save the revised publication as a template with the original template name, overwriting the old one.

Importing Word Documents

To import the text of a Word document into a publication, you click Import Word Documents in the More Templates section of the New page and then choose a document design, page size, and column layout. (If you prefer, you can forego the design and choose only a generic page size or a paper format such as those available from Avery.) Publisher converts the document and inserts it into a new publication, adding as many pages as necessary to hold the complete document. You can then add a title and replace any other placeholders that are part of the design, or you can add new elements to suit the purpose of the publication.

Tip You can create a simple publication directly from a Word document. In the Backstage view, click the Open button. Then with All Publisher Files selected as the file type in the Open Publication dialog box, locate and double-click the Word document you want to use. The new publication contains the document text but doesn't have a template applied.

In this exercise, you'll create a publication based on a ready-made template that comes with Publisher. You'll also import a Word document.

SET UP You need the Importing document located in your Chapter29 practice file folder to complete this exercise.

1. Click the **Start** button, click **All Programs**, click **Microsoft Office**, and then click **Microsoft Publisher 2010**.

   Publisher starts and displays the New page of the Backstage view.

   Tip If you are already working on a publication, you can display the New page by clicking the File tab to display the Backstage view, and then clicking New in the left pane.

   The page is divided into sections displaying blank publication templates, "most popular" publication template categories, and other available template categories.

2. At the top of the **New** page, in the template location list under the **Available Templates** heading, click **Installed Templates**.

   Publisher displays only those templates that were installed on your computer when you installed Publisher or the Microsoft Office Professional 2010 software suite.

3. In the **More Templates** section of the **New** page, click **Quick Publications**.

The New page displays the publication templates in the Quick Publications category. The category is shown on the gray bar near the top of the page.

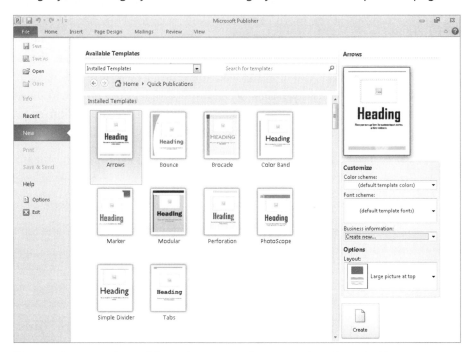

You can choose a color and font scheme, as well as a template, from the New page.

The left pane of the New page displays thumbnails of the publication templates in the Quick Publications category. The selected publication is indicated by an orange frame. The right pane displays a larger thumbnail of the selected template, and any available customization options.

4. In the left pane, click the **Brocade** thumbnail.

   The right pane displays a larger thumbnail of the Brocade publication template and the customization options that you can set before you create the publication.

   See Also   For information about creating information sets, see "Storing Personal and Company Information" later in this chapter.

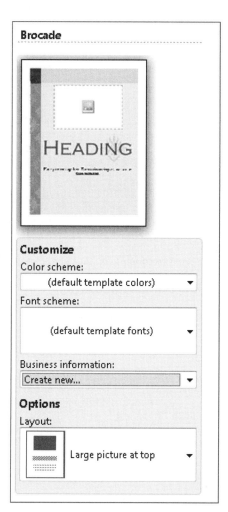

From the Business Information list, you can select an information set to prepopulate the publication with names, addresses, telephone numbers, and a logo.

5. In the right pane, under **Options**, click the **Layout** arrow (to the right of the **Large picture at top** setting).

The Layout list displays available layout options for this template.

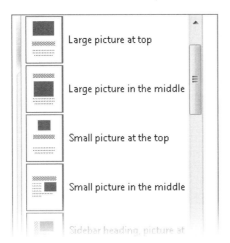

When choosing a layout, consider the types of content you intend to include in the publication.

6. In the **Layout** list, click **Large picture in the middle**.

   All the thumbnails change to show this layout option.

7. At the bottom of the right pane, click **Create**.

   A one-page publication based on the selected template opens in the Publisher program window. The picture placeholder shown in the template thumbnail is not visible on the page.

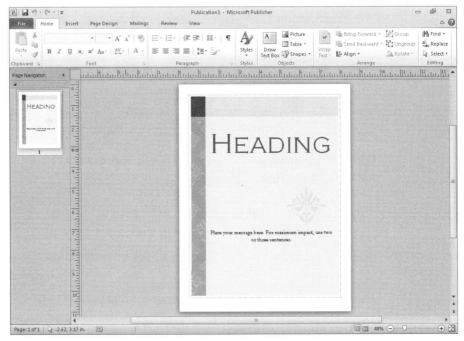

Until you save a new publication, Publisher assigns it a generic name such as Publication1.

Troubleshooting The appearance of buttons and groups on the ribbon changes depending on the width of the program window. For information about changing the appearance of the ribbon to match our screen images, see "Modifying the Display of the Ribbon" at the beginning of this book.

8. Point to the center of the page, below the heading, where the picture placeholder was shown in the template thumbnail.

   A picture placeholder appears on the page.

You can insert a graphic by clicking the picture placeholder.

9. On the **Page Design** tab, in the **Template** group, click **Change Template**.

   From the Change Template window that opens, you can apply a different Quick Publication template to the open publication, or you can switch to an entirely different type of publication.

10. In the **More Installed Templates** section of the left pane, click **Layers**. Then in the lower-right corner of the **Change Template** window, click **OK**.

    The Change Template window closes.

Troubleshooting In some instances, the Change Template dialog box opens. From this dialog box, you can apply the selected template to the current publication or create a new publication based on the selected template.

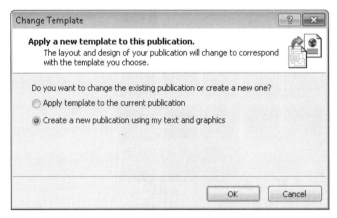

If the Change Template dialog box opens, click Apply Template To The Current Publication, and then click OK.

The fonts, colors, and arrangement of the existing content change to reflect the new template.

11. Display the Backstage view and then, in the left pane, click **New**.

12. In the **More Templates** section of the **New** page, click **Import Word Documents**.

The left pane of the New page displays thumbnails of document templates. The right pane displays a larger thumbnail of the selected template, and the available customization options.

13. In the **Installed Templates** list, click **Crossed Lines**.

14. Scroll down the right pane if necessary. In the **Options** section, click the **Columns** arrow (to the right of the **1** option) and then, in the **Columns** list, click **2**.

All the thumbnails change to show a two-column layout.

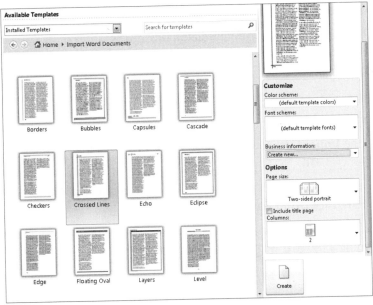

When importing a document, the right pane displays options for text-intensive layouts.

15. In the **Options** section of the right pane, select the **Include title page** check box.

    The Import Word Documents gallery changes to display the title page templates associated with each template.

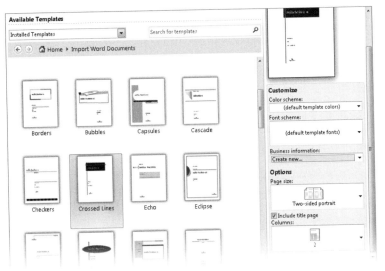

You can choose a title page template other than the selected publication template.

16. At the bottom of the right pane, click **Create**.

    The Import Word Document dialog box opens.

17. In the **Import Word Document** dialog box, navigate to your **Chapter29** practice file folder.

    Because Publisher is searching for a Word document, the publications saved in this folder are hidden.

18. In the **Import Word Document** dialog box, click the **Importing** document, and then click **OK**.

19. For the purposes of this exercise, in the **Microsoft Publisher** dialog box that opens, click **Don't Save**.

    Publisher creates a new publication, based on the Crossed Lines template, that contains the text of the Importing document.

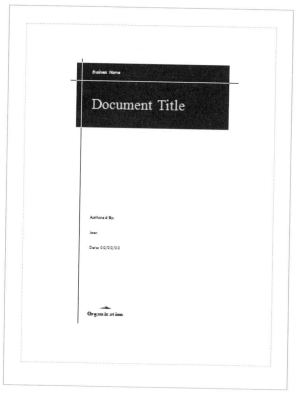

The first page of the publication is a title page.

20. In the **Page Navigation** pane, click the **Page 2** thumbnail.

Publisher has inserted the contents of the imported Word document in two columns on the second page.

Publisher flows the content to fit in each column, which doesn't always create the most appealing column breaks.

 CLEAN UP Close the publication without saving your changes.

Storing Personal and Company Information

Many of the publications you create by using Publisher will include the same personal or company contact information, such as a name, a mailing address, a telephone number, and an e-mail address. Instead of entering this information for each new publication, you can save it as an information set. Then whenever a new publication includes an item from the information set, Publisher automatically pulls it from the stored record and inserts it in the publication. Similarly, to update personal or company information throughout the publication, you need only update it once, in the information set.

In this exercise, you'll create two information sets and apply them to a publication.

 SET UP You need the Logo image located in your Chapter29 practice file folder to complete this exercise. Display the New page of the Backstage view, and filter the page to display only installed templates. Then follow the steps.

1. On the **New** page, in the **Most Popular** section, click **Business Cards**.

   Publisher displays the available business card templates.

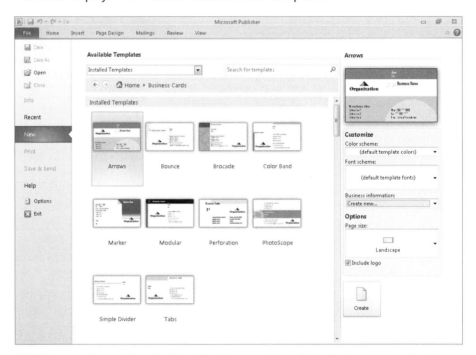

Publisher provides a wide selection of business card templates that you can customize.

2. In the **Installed Templates** section, double-click **Marker**.

   Publisher creates a business card containing placeholders for standard information. The user name you provided when first configuring Office or an Office program might already be shown on the card.

Information icon   Stored Office user information

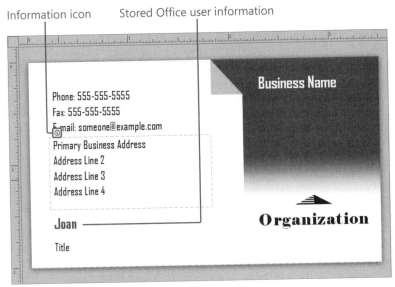

Pointing to a text box displays an Information icon if that information is pulled from an information set.

3. Point to the text box containing the phone number, and click the information icon that appears.

   A list of information set options appears.

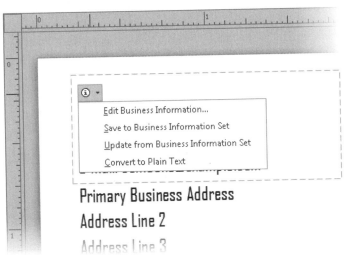

Options for working with the information set.

4. In the list, click **Edit Business Information**.

The Create New Business Information Set dialog box opens.

This dialog box contains any information already available to Publisher, and placeholders for other standard information.

Troubleshooting The Create New Business Information Set dialog box appears only if you have not previously created an information set. If you already have an existing information set, the Business Information dialog box appears. You can click New in the Business Information dialog box to display the Create New Business Information Set dialog box.

5. Fill in the information in all the boxes other than the **Logo** and **Business Information set name** boxes. Delete the placeholder for any information that does not apply.

For example, if you are filling in personal information, delete the entries in the Job Position Or Title and Organization Name boxes and remove the logo.

6. Below the **Logo** box, click **Change**.

The Insert Picture dialog box opens. You navigate in this dialog box the same way you do in the Save As or Open dialog box.

7. Navigate to your **Chapter29** practice file folder, and then double-click the **Logo** file.

The selected logo appears in the Logo preview pane.

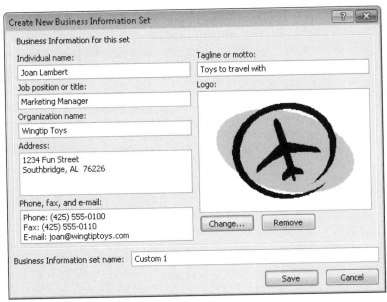

By including a logo in your business information set, it will automatically be added to new publications.

8. In the **Business Information set name** box, replace **Custom 1** with a name that represents the information you just entered. (For example, you might enter *Company* or *Personal.*) Then click **Save**.

The Business Information dialog box opens.

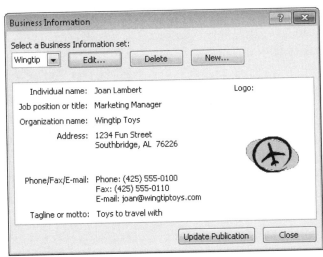

If you have multiple information sets, you can display a specific information set by clicking its name in the Select A Business Information Set list.

9. In the **Business Information** dialog box, review the information you just entered, and then click **Update Publication**.

The business card now appears with your information in place.

Phone: (425) 555-0100
Fax: (425) 555-0110
E-mail: joan@wingtiptoys.com
1234 Fun Street
Southbridge, AL 76226

Wingtip Toys

Joan Lambert

Marketing Manager

You can update the information set at any time.

10. Click the address block to activate it, and make a change to the address. (For example, you could add a suite or apartment number.)

11. Click the information icon and then, in the list, click **Save to Business Information Set**.

The business card doesn't change.

Tip After you insert an item into a publication from the information set, you can add to it or delete parts of it without affecting the way it is stored in the information set. Similarly, if an item such as a tagline or motto is not included in the information set, you can replace the corresponding placeholder in a publication with text without affecting the saved information set. Unless you click the Save To Business Information Set command, the changes exist only in the specific publication and are not part of the information set.

12. Click the information icon and then, in the list, click **Edit Business Information**.

The Business Information dialog box opens. The information you changed directly on the card is shown in the dialog box and is now part of the saved information set.

Tip From the Business Information dialog box, you can create, edit, or delete information sets.

13. In the **Business Information** dialog box, click **New**.

    The Create New Business Information Set dialog box opens. The dialog box contains the information you supplied earlier in this exercise. *Custom 1* appears in the Business Information Set Name box.

14. In the **Create New Business Information Set** dialog box, enter a different set of information, again deleting any elements that are not relevant.

    For example, if you previously entered your company information, you might want to enter personal information this time.

15. In the **Business Information set name** box, type an appropriate name, and then click **Save**.

    The Business Information dialog box reflects your changes.

16. In the upper-left corner of the dialog box, click the **Select a Business Information set** arrow.

    The two information sets you've created are available in the list.

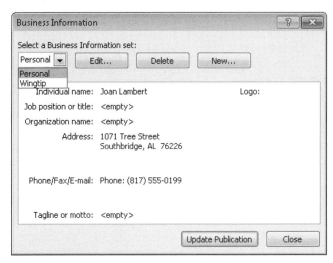

You can display any saved information set by selecting it in the list.

17. In the **Business Information** dialog box, click **Close**.

    The information shown on the business card remains unchanged.

18. On the **Insert** tab, in the **Text** group, click the **Business Information** button.

   The Business Information pane expands, displaying the information saved in the current information set.

19. In the **Business Information** gallery, point to your name.

   The selected information field is highlighted.

You can insert an individual piece of information from an information set into a publication by clicking it in the Business Information gallery.

20. At the bottom of the **Business Information** gallery, click **Edit Business Information**.

The Business Information dialog box opens.

Tip You can also edit the current information set from the Info page of the Backstage view.

21. In the **Business Information** dialog box, in the **Select a Business Information set** list, click the name of the second information set you created. Then click **Update Publication**.

Publisher updates the business card publication to reflect the new information set.

You can easily update a publication by editing the associated information set.

CLEAN UP If you want to, save the publication with the name *BusinessCard* in your Chapter29 practice file folder for later reference. Then close the publication without exiting Publisher.

Previewing and Printing Publications

When you are ready to print a publication, you can print to your computer's default printer with the default settings by clicking the Print button on the Print page of the Backstage view. From the same page, you can choose a different printer or change the print settings.

See Also For information about print settings in Office 2010 programs, see Chapter 7, "Preview, Print, and Distribute Documents."

Checking Publications

In the right pane of the Print page of the Backstage view, Publisher displays a preview of how your publication will look on paper when printed with the current print settings. You can page through multipage publications by clicking the Next Sheet and Previous Sheet buttons at the bottom of the preview pane.

In addition to visually checking your publication in the preview pane, you can locate possible problems by using the Design Checker, which is available from the Info page of the Backstage view.

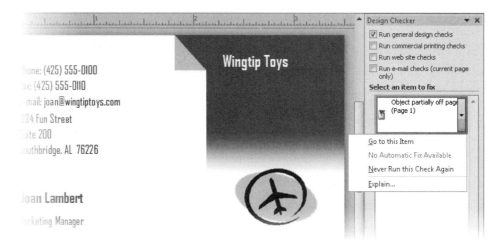

The Design Checker identifies issues with the placement and integrity of publication elements.

Working with Advanced Printer Settings

Usually the simple settings in the left pane of the Print page will meet your needs. When you want to print only a few copies of a publication, using your own printer is quick and easy. If you need many copies, you will often save time and money by going to a copy shop or professional printer. If you're preparing a publication for a professional printer, you can access advanced settings by clicking Commercial Print Settings on the Info page of the Backstage view.

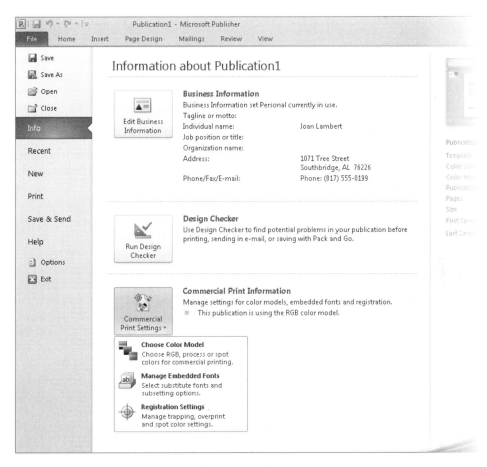

Check with your commercial printer for their specific requirements.

From the Commercial Print Settings menu you can choose any of the following commands:

- **Choose Color Model** In the Color Model dialog box, you can define the colors in your publication as RGB colors, single color, spot colors, CMYK process colors, or a combination of spot and process colors.

- **Manage Embedded Fonts** From the Fonts dialog box, you can embed fonts into the publication so that the text of your publication will display the same on all computers.

- **Registration Settings** From the Publication Registration Settings dialog box, you can add registration settings (marks that define the area to be printed and provide other necessary information to commercial printers) to your publication.

In this exercise, you'll run the Design Checker, preview a publication, and then print the publication.

 SET UP You need the Printing_start publication located in your Chapter29 practice file folder to complete this exercise. Ensure that your computer is connected to a printer. Open the Printing_start publication, and save it as *Printing*. Display the Backstage view, and then follow the steps.

1. On the **Info** page of the Backstage view, click the **Run Design Checker** button.

   The Design Checker task pane opens. Publisher checks the publication for possible issues and displays two in the Select An Item To Fix list.

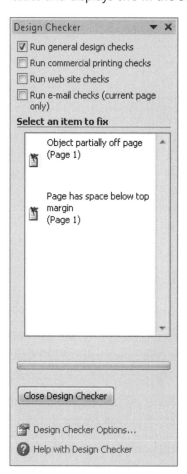

By default, the Design Checker examines the publication only for general types of errors. You can expand the search for errors specific to commercial printing, Web display, and e-mail display.

2. In the **Select an item to fix** list, point to **Object partially off page (Page 1)**, click the button that appears, and then click **Go to this Item**.

In the lower-right corner of the first page of the publication, Publisher selects the OTSI company logo.

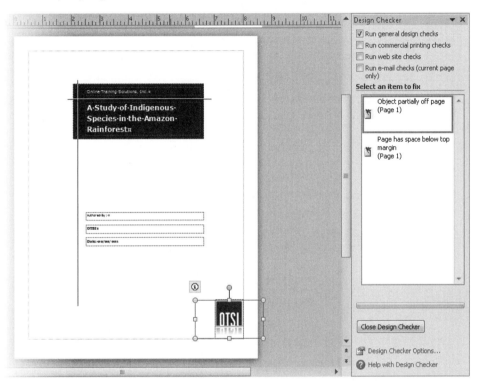

The inserted image depicting the logo has white space on both sides that runs off the side of the page.

3. In the **Select an item to fix** list, point to **Page has space below top margin (Page 1)**, click the button that appears, and then click **Go to this Item**.

Publisher selects all the objects on the page so that if you wanted to, you could move them upward to decrease the white space at the top of the page.

4. In the **Design Checker** task pane, select the **Run web site checks** check box.

Additional errors appear in the Select An Item To Fix list.

5. Scroll down the **Select an item to fix** list, point to **Picture does not have alternative text (Page 5)**, and then click the button that appears.

The menu of options includes a suggested fix for the problem.

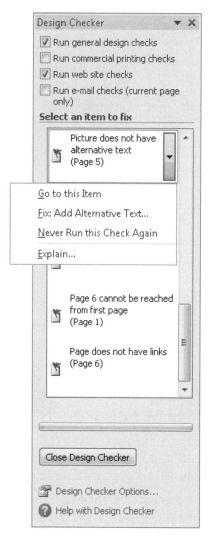

If Publisher can't fix a problem for you, No Automatic Fix Available appears on the menu in place of a suggestion.

6. On the menu, click **Go to this Item**.

   Publisher selects the graphic on page 5 of the publication.

7. In the **Select an item to fix** list, point to **Picture does not have alternative text (Page 5)**, click the button that appears, and then click **Fix: Add Alternative Text**.

   The Format Picture dialog box opens, displaying the Web page.

8. In the **Alternative text** box, enter Image depicting a variety of Microsoft Office documents and features.

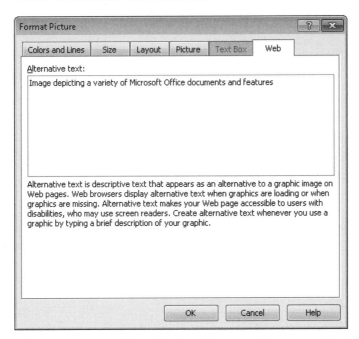

When you create a Web publication, it's a good idea to provide alternative text for images; this alternative text appears in place of the image if the viewer's computer doesn't support the display of the image.

9. In the **Format Picture** dialog box, click **OK**.

   The selected error disappears from the Select An Item To Fix list.

10. Close the **Design Checker** task pane.

11. In the left pane of the Backstage view, click **Print**.

    The Print page of the Backstage view displays information about the current publication and printer.

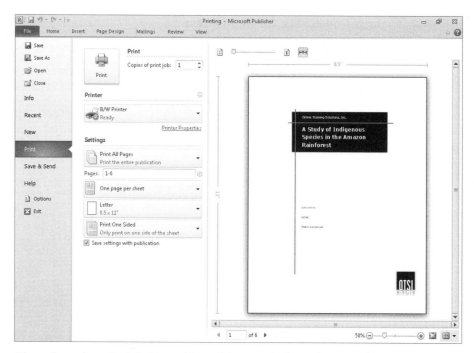

Dimensions along the left side and top of the page indicate the page size.

12. In the lower-right corner of the **Print** page, click the **View Multiple Sheets** button. In the **Multiple Sheets** gallery that appears, point to the sheet icon at the intersection of the second row and third column.

    The Multiple Sheets gallery heading changes to *2 x 3* to reflect the selected page view.

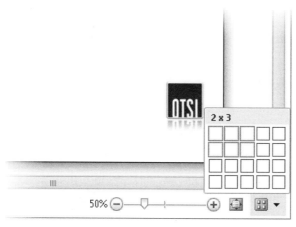

You can display up to 25 pages in the Print Preview window.

13. In the **Multiple Sheets** gallery, click the selected sheet icon.

The preview pane changes to display the six pages of the publication in the selected layout. The page dimensions are indicated to the left and above the currently active publication page.

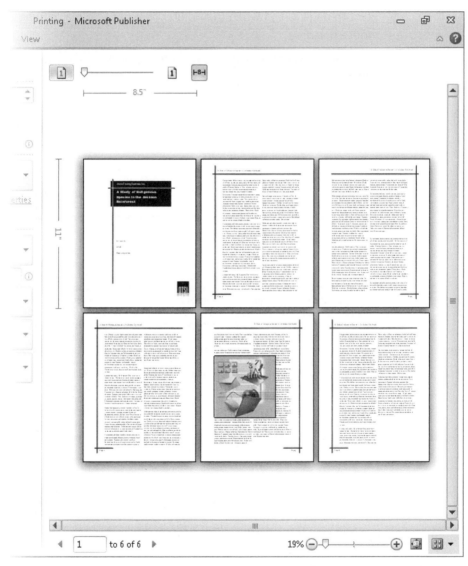

In the preview pane, pages are not specifically displayed in spreads as they are in the Page Navigation pane.

Tip You can turn off the display of the dimensions by clicking the Ruler button located at the top of the preview pane.

14. At the top of the preview pane, to the right of the slider, click the **Show Page Numbers** button.

    In the preview pane, a page number appears on each sheet of the publication.

    Tip You can darken or lighten the page numbers by moving the slider.

15. Point to page **3**, and when the pointer changes to a magnifying glass, click the mouse button.

    Publisher displays the part of page 3 that you clicked at a magnification level of 100 percent.

When showing page numbers, the page number appears in the center of the magnified page, but will not be printed.

16. Click the magnified page **3** to return to the previous view.

17. In the lower-right corner of the **Print** page, click the **Fit to Sheet** button.

    The preview pane displays only page 1, which is currently active in Publisher.

18. In the **Settings** section of the left pane of the **Print** page, click **Print All Pages** and then, in the list, click **Print Custom Range**.

    The page range 1-6 appears in the Pages box.

19. In the **Pages** box, replace **1-6** with **2**, and then press Tab or Enter.

    Page 2 appears in the preview pane.

    Important Because publications are usually carefully laid out before they are printed, it is unlikely that you will want to change settings such as the paper size and orientation from the Print page of the Backstage view. Instead you should change them from the Page Design tab of the ribbon so that you can see the effects on your publication before you print it.

20. If you have more than one printer available and you want to switch printers, click the **Printer** arrow and then, in the list, click the printer you want to use.

21. In the **Copies of print job** box, change the setting to **2**. Then click the **Print** button.

    Publisher prints two copies of the second page of the publication on the designated printer.

    Tip When you print multiple copies of the entire publication, you can choose to have Publisher collate the copies (print one entire set of pages before printing the next) or print the publication on both sides of the paper.

 CLEAN UP Close the Printing document without saving your changes.

Key Points

- From the Backstage view, you can create a publication based on one of the many purpose-specific templates that come with Publisher. You can specify fonts, colors, and layout options before creating the publication.

- Publisher doesn't have multiple views, but because publications often consist of many different elements, it is important to know how to zoom in and out to check details or to get an overview of the entire publication.

- You can store sets of personal and company information for Publisher to automatically enter in all the appropriate places in your publications.

- You can check the placement of elements within your publication before printing the publication.

Chapter at a Glance

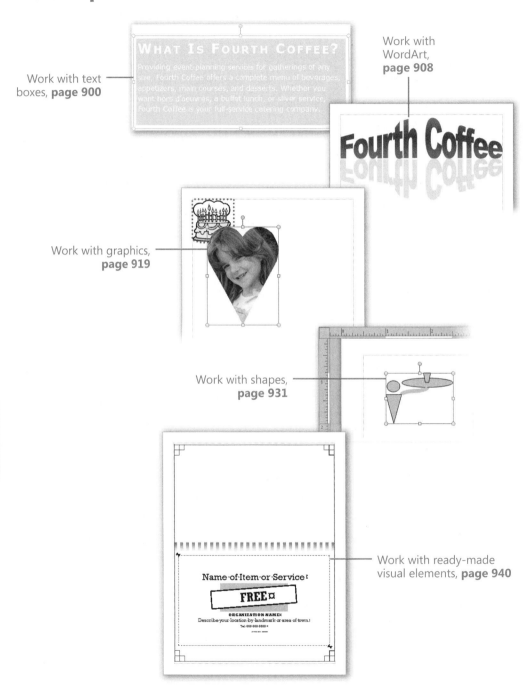

Work with text boxes, **page 900**

Work with WordArt, **page 908**

Work with graphics, **page 919**

Work with shapes, **page 931**

Work with ready-made visual elements, **page 940**

30 Create Visual Interest

In this chapter, you will learn how to
- ✔ Work with text boxes.
- ✔ Work with WordArt.
- ✔ Work with graphics.
- ✔ Work with shapes.
- ✔ Work with ready-made visual elements.

Microsoft Publisher 2010 is specifically designed to make it easy to create publications that contain a mixture of text and visual elements arranged on the page. Knowing basic techniques for inserting and manipulating visual elements such as photographs, illustrations, and decorative images is key to quickly assembling impressive publications.

Publications are most effective when you achieve a balance of text and graphics that is appropriate for your purpose. Some publications convey information through text and include visual elements only to catch the reader's eye or to reinforce or illustrate a point. At the other end of the scale, some publications include almost no text and instead rely on visual elements to carry the message.

In this chapter, you'll first create a text object and see how to enhance the text with color and formatting. Then you'll use WordArt to create fancy, stylized text for those occasions when regular formatting doesn't quite meet your needs. Next, you'll insert clip art graphics and pictures, add borders, and change the size, color, and position of the images. You'll draw, connect, and group shapes. Finally, you'll insert ready-made design elements from the Building Block Library.

Practice Files Before you can complete the exercises in this chapter, you need to copy the book's practice files to your computer. The practice files you'll use to complete the exercises in this chapter are in the Chapter30 practice file folder. A complete list of practice files is provided in "Using the Practice Files" at the beginning of this book.

Working with Text Boxes

When you create a document by using a word processing program such as Microsoft Word, you enter text on the page in the area defined by the margins. When you create a publication by using Publisher, however, you place a text box on the page and enter text into the text box. The text box is an object that can be sized to fit the text it contains, and can be moved with its contents intact. You can create text boxes or manipulate the text boxes that are part of a Publisher template. You can type text directly into the text box, paste text from another file, or insert the entire contents of another file.

Tip In Publisher, the text in a text box is called a story. A story is any discrete block of text that occupies a single text box or a set of linked text boxes. It can be a single paragraph or multiple paragraphs.

Manipulating Text Boxes

After you create a text box, or when you click a text box to make it active, you can move it by dragging its frame.

Keyboard Shortcut To create a copy of a text box and its contents, hold down the Ctrl key while you drag the text box to the location where you want the copy.

You can drag the handles of the frame to change the size or shape of the box. If you want a specific size or shape, you can change the settings on the Drawing Tools Format contextual tab or the Text Box Tools Format contextual tab. On these tabs, you can also specify:

● The background color of the text box, whether it has a border, and the color of the border.

● Whether the text box has a shadow or three-dimensional effects.

● The position of the text box on the page, and how text in adjacent frames flows around this text box.

● The vertical text alignment, the margins, and whether Publisher can automatically adjust the size of the text box to fit the amount of text you insert in it.

When a text box is active, a green rotating handle is attached to its upper-middle handle. You can drag this handle to change the angle of the text box and the text within it.

Tip You can rotate a text box and its contents by clicking the Rotate button in the Arrange group on the Drawing Tools Format contextual tab and then clicking the rotation option you want. You can change the direction of only the text within the text box from horizontal to vertical by clicking the Text Direction button in the Text group on the Text Box Tools Format contextual tab.

Formatting Text for Visual Impact

Brief segments of text, such as those on a postcard or flyer, need to have more visual impact than longer blocks of text, such as those in a newsletter. You can vary the look of text by changing the character formatting. Here are some things about character formatting to be aware of:

- All text is displayed in a particular font consisting of alphabetic characters, numbers, and symbols that share a common design.

- Almost every font comes in a range of font sizes, which are measured in points from the top of letters that have parts that stick up (ascenders), such as h, to the bottom of letters that have parts that drop down (descenders), such as p. A point is approximately 1/72 of an inch.

- Almost every font comes in a range of font styles. The most common are regular (or plain), italic, bold, and bold italic.

- Fonts can be enhanced by applying font effects, such as underlining, small capital letters (small caps), or shadows.

- You can choose from a palette of harmonious font colors, and you can also specify custom colors.

- You can alter the character spacing by pushing characters apart or squeezing them together.

Tip The instructions in the exercises assume that you're working in a blank publication so that you can focus on the techniques you're learning. However, you can easily adapt the instructions to any type of publication.

In this exercise, you'll create a blank publication, add a text box, and then insert the contents of an existing Word document. You'll then format the text box by filling it with color and format the text by changing its character formatting.

 SET UP You need the Text document located in your Chapter30 practice file folder to complete this exercise. Display the New page of the Backstage view, and then follow the steps.

1. In the **Home** section of the **New** page, click **More Blank Page Sizes**.

2. On the **More Blank Page Sizes** page, under **Standard**, click the **Letter (Portrait)** thumbnail. Then, in the right pane, click the **Create** button.

   Publisher creates a blank publication of the selected size. Blue margin guides designate the margins of the publication.

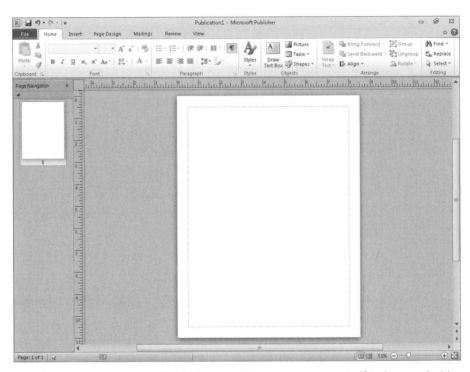

By default, the page margins for the letter publication are set to a half inch on each side.

Troubleshooting The appearance of buttons and groups on the ribbon changes depending on the width of the program window. For information about changing the appearance of the ribbon to match our screen images, see "Modifying the Display of the Ribbon" at the beginning of this book.

Tip Throughout this chapter, we work with letter-size publications, but you can choose any size you want. You might want to try a different size for each exercise to see some of the available options.

3. Save the publication as **TextBox** in your **Chapter30** practice file folder.

4. On the **Home** tab, in the **Objects** group, click the **Draw Text Box** button.

Tip The Draw Text Box button is also available from the Text group on the Insert tab.

5. Move the cross-hair pointer over the blank page, and when the pointer is slightly to the right of the left margin guide and slightly below the top margin guide, hold down the mouse button, and drag to the right and down, without releasing the mouse button.

Don't release the mouse button yet.

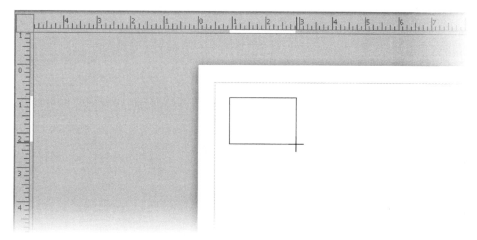

The white areas of the rulers indicate the height and width of the area you've defined.

As you drag, Publisher displays the exact coordinates of the upper-left corner (the anchor point) of the text box and its exact dimensions at the left end of the status bar.

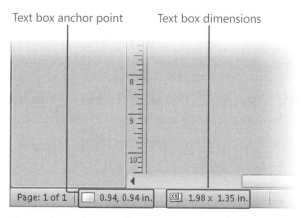

The anchor point coordinates are expressed in relation to the upper-left corner of the page.

6. Release the mouse button when the text box dimensions are **5.00 x 2.00 in**.

The Drawing Tools Format contextual tab and the Text Box Tools Format contextual tab appear on the ribbon.

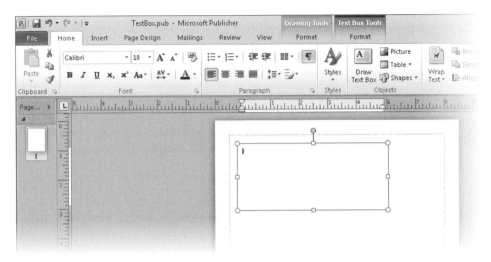

A blinking cursor in the text box shows where any text you type will appear.

Tip We've minimized the Page Navigation pane so it's less distracting.

7. Without clicking anything else, on the **Insert** tab, in the **Text** group, click the **Insert File** button.

The Insert Text dialog box opens, displaying the contents of your Documents library.

8. If necessary, navigate to your **Chapter30** practice file folder. Then double-click the **Text** document.

Publisher inserts the contents of the document into the text box.

9. On the **View** tab, in the **Zoom** group, click the **100%** button.

The inserted text is now a legible size.

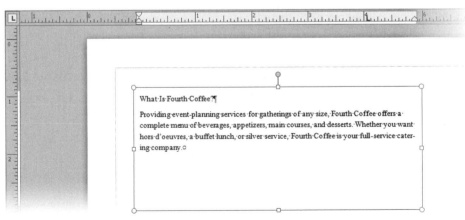

The default alignment for text you insert in a text box is Top Left.

10. Point to the frame around the text box, and when the pointer changes to a four-headed arrow, drag the frame down and to the right, releasing the mouse button when the text box coordinates shown on the status bar are **2.00, 2.00 in.**

   Tip Publisher can display measurements in inches, centimeters, picas, points, or pixels. You can change the unit of measure in the Display section of the Advanced page of the Publisher Options dialog box.

11. With the text box still selected, on the **Drawing Tools Format** tab, in the **Shape Styles** group, click the **Shape Fill** arrow. Then in the **Standard Colors** palette, click the **Orange** square.

   See Also For information about applying a different color scheme and using custom colors, see "Creating Folded Cards" in Chapter 31, "Create Colorful Cards and Calendars."

12. Click anywhere within the text in the text box. On the **Home** tab, in the **Editing** group, click the **Select** button and then, in the **Select** list, click **Select All Text in Text Box**.

   Keyboard Shortcut Press Ctrl+A to select all the text in the active text box.

13. On the **Home** tab, in the **Font** group, click the **Font** arrow. Then scroll down the **Font** list and click **Verdana**.

   Keyboard Shortcut After expanding the Font list you can press the V key to scroll the list to the fonts that begin with the letter V.

14. In the **Font** group, click the **Increase Font Size** button twice, to increase the font size to **12** points.

   Keyboard Shortcut Press Ctrl+> to increase the font size of the selected text.

   Tip If the font is too big, you can click the Decrease Font Size button or press Ctrl+<. You can select a specific point size by clicking the Font Size arrow and clicking the size in the list, or by selecting the number in the Font Size box and then entering the font size you want.

15. In the **Font** group, click the **Font Color** arrow, and in the **Scheme Colors** palette, click the white square (**Accent 5**). Then click anywhere in the text box to release the selection.

   Tip To apply the color currently shown on the Font Color button, simply click the button (not its arrow).

16. Drag the bottom handle (the square box in the center of the bottom frame) of the text box frame upward, releasing the mouse button when the text box dimensions shown on the status bar are **5.00 x 1.50 in**.

   The Fit Text button appears on the right side of the text box and the text box handles turn red to indicate that it is too small to fit its contents. We'll leave that for now.

Troubleshooting If the dimensions don't change but the coordinates do, you missed the handle and moved the text box by dragging its frame instead of the handle. (When dragging the handle, the cursor shape changes to a two-headed arrow. When dragging the frame, the cursor shape changes to a four-headed arrow.) Click the Undo button on the Quick Access Toolbar, and then try dragging the handle again.

17. Select the heading **What Is Fourth Coffee?** by dragging across or triple-clicking it.

18. In the **Font** group, click the **Increase Font Size** button five times to increase the font size to **22** points. Then click the **Bold** button.

19. With the heading still selected, click the **Font** dialog box launcher.

The Font dialog box opens.

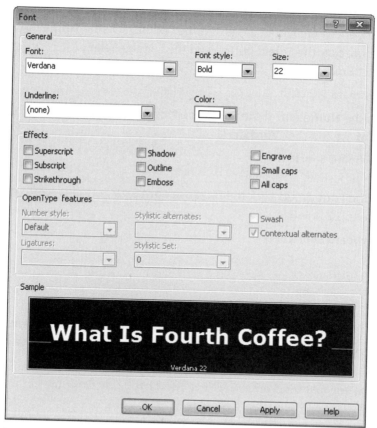

The Font dialog box includes font formatting options that are not available from the Font group on the Home tab.

The Sample pane shows the formatting applied to the selection. As you make changes to settings in the dialog box, the sample changes to show how the selection will look if you click Apply or OK. (Clicking Apply implements the current settings without closing the dialog box; clicking OK implements the changes and closes the dialog box.)

20. In the **Effects** section, select the **Small caps** check box. Then click **OK**.

   Tip You can use the commands in the Format group on the Home tab to change the font style of text, but to apply font effects, you have to use the commands in the Font dialog box. If you want to apply several attributes to the same text, it is often quicker to open the dialog box and apply them all from there.

21. In the **Font** group, click the **Character Spacing** button and then, in the **Character Spacing** list, click **Very Loose**.

   Tip To copy the formatting of one word or phrase to another, select the text whose formatting you want to copy, click the Format Painter button on the Standard toolbar, and then select the text onto which you want to "paint" the formatting.

22. Click outside the text box.

   The text box handles disappear.

The text doesn't currently fit within the text box.

23. Click anywhere in the text box to select it.

24. On the **Text Box Tools** tab, in the **Text** group, click the **Text Fit** button and then, in the **Text Fit** list, click **Grow Text Box to Fit**.

The text box expands vertically to fit its contents.

To expand a text box horizontally, you need to drag the side handles.

 CLEAN UP Save the TextBox publication, and then close it without exiting Publisher.

Working with WordArt

If you want to add a fancy title to a publication, and you can't achieve the effect you want with regular text formatting, you can use WordArt. With WordArt, you can visually enhance text in ways that go far beyond changing a font or font effect, simply by choosing a style from a set of thumbnail images arranged in a gallery.

Tip For the best results, use WordArt to emphasize short phrases, such as *Customer Service*, or a single word, such as *Welcome*. Overusing WordArt can clutter your publication and draw attention away from your message.

You add stylized text to a publication by clicking the WordArt button in the Text group on the Insert tab. You then select a style from the WordArt gallery, enter your text, and apply any additional formatting. Publisher inserts the text in your publication as a WordArt object that you can size and move like any other object. You can also change the shape of the object to stretch and form the letters of the text in various ways.

In this exercise, you'll add a WordArt object to a publication and then modify the appearance of the WordArt text.

SET UP You need the Blank_start publication located in your Chapter30 practice file folder to complete this exercise. Open the Blank_start publication, and save it as *WordArt*. Then follow the steps.

1. On the **Insert** tab, in the **Text** group, click the **WordArt** button.

    The WordArt gallery opens, displaying the available styles.

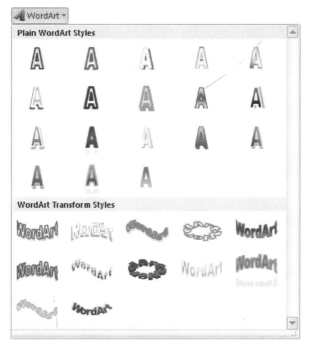

The WordArt gallery includes plain styles that format only letters and transform styles that control the shape of text phrases.

2. In the **WordArt Transform Styles** section of the **WordArt** gallery, click the **Gradient Fill – Red, Curved** icon (the second icon in the third row).

    The Edit WordArt Text dialog box opens. The dialog box contains sample text for you to replace with the text you want to format.

You can't format existing text in a text box as WordArt; WordArt objects are separate from other objects, such as text boxes and images.

3. With the placeholder text selected, type **Fourth Coffee**, and then click **OK**.

The formatted text appears as an object in the center of the page.

The WordArt Tools Format contextual tab appears on the ribbon.

4. Point to the word **Fourth**. When the pointer changes to a four-headed arrow, drag the WordArt object up toward the top of the page until the top margin changes from a light blue and white dotted line to a light blue and dark blue dotted line that spans the entire page.

   This indicates that the top of the WordArt object is aligned with the top margin of the page.

Until you release the mouse button, the WordArt object stays in its original location and a shaded version represents the object in its new location.

5. Release the mouse button to move the object to the top of the page.

6. Point to the lower-left sizing handle of the WordArt object. When the pointer changes to a diagonal double-headed arrow, drag the sizing handle to the left, until the dotted line representing the left edge of the object is aligned with the left page margin.

   Tip The pointer position is always shown on the horizontal and vertical rulers. When dragging an object's sizing handle, you can use the pointer position to align the sizing handle with the ruler units.

7. Drag the lower-right sizing handle down and to the right, until the WordArt object spans the full width of the page and is about two inches high.

   It's not necessary to set the height exactly; we'll use another method to do so.

   Tip To create a WordArt object consisting of existing text, select the text, click the WordArt style you want, and then click OK in the Edit WordArt Text dialog box. Publisher then creates a WordArt object separate from the original text.

The location and dimensions of the selected WordArt object are indicated on the status bar and in the Size group on the WordArt Tools Format tab.

8. On the **WordArt Tools Format** tab, click the **Size** dialog box launcher.

The Format WordArt dialog box opens, displaying the Size page.

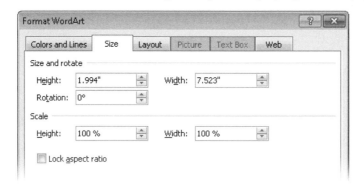

You can precisely specify the size and location of a WordArt object in the Format WordArt dialog box.

9. In the **Size and rotate** section of the **Size** page, replace the measurement in the **Height** box with **2**, and replace the measurement in the **Width** box with **7.5**. Then click the **Layout** tab.

The Layout page of the Format WordArt dialog box displays settings that control the position of the WordArt object on the page in relation to other page elements.

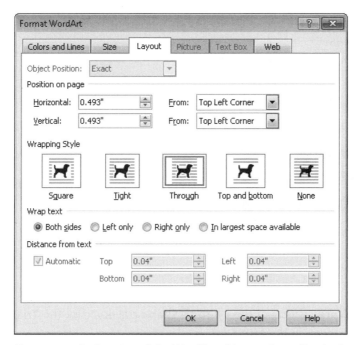

You can set the location of the WordArt object and specify whether text near the object wraps around the object or runs through it.

10. In the **Position on page** section of the **Layout** page, replace the measurements in the **Horizontal** and **Vertical** boxes with **0.5**. Then click **OK**.

    Your changes are reflected in the Size group on the WordArt Tools Format tab.

    The position that you specify on the Layout page of the Format WordArt dialog box is the position of the upper-left corner of the WordArt object frame. Notice that because of the curve of the letters, the left and right edges of the words *Fourth Coffee* currently extend beyond the left and right page margins.

11. On the **WordArt Tools Format** tab, in the **WordArt Styles** group, click the **Change Shape** button.

    The Change Shape gallery displays a variety of shapes. The current shape, Arch Down (Curve) is selected.

You can form a WordArt object into any shape shown in the Change Shape gallery.

12. In the **Warp** section of the **Change Shape** gallery, click the **Triangle Up** icon (the third icon in the fifth row).

The shape of the WordArt object changes.

The WordArt object now fits within the page margins.

Troubleshooting If you click outside the WordArt object, it is no longer active, and the WordArt toolbar disappears. Click the WordArt object once to reactivate it and display the toolbar.

13. On the **WordArt Tools Format** tab, in the **WordArt Styles** group, click the **Shape Fill** button.

The Shape Fill gallery opens.

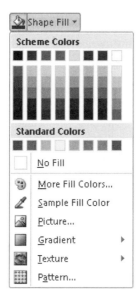

You can fill a WordArt object with a solid color, a picture, a gradient, a texture, or a pattern.

14. At the bottom of the **Shape Fill** gallery, click **Gradient**.

The Gradient gallery displays options for working with gradient fill colors. The gallery currently displays one-color gradient options, with a single color (blue) fading to white or black.

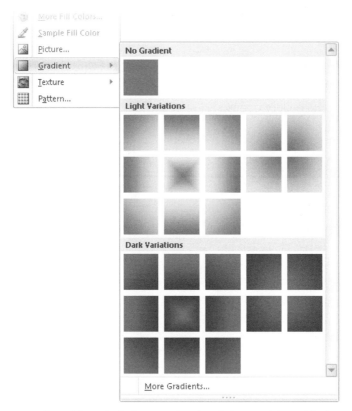

A gradient fill can include one color that fades to white or black, or two colors that fade into each other.

15. At the bottom of the **Gradient** gallery, click **More Gradients**.

The Fill Effects dialog box opens, displaying the Gradient page. The page displays gradient settings based on the existing color of the selected WordArt object.

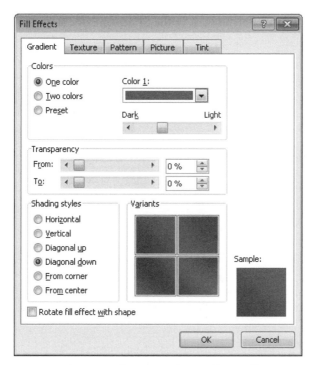

You can select a gradient from the Gradient gallery or precisely specify gradient attributes from the Fill Effects dialog box.

16. In the **Colors** section, click **Two colors**.

    A Color 2 list appears below the Color 1 list.

17. Click the **Color 1** arrow and then, in the top row of the **Scheme Colors** palette, click the medium-blue **Accent 3** icon (the fourth icon). Click the **Color 2** arrow and then, in the top row of the **Scheme Colors** palette, click the violet **Followed Hyperlink** icon (the seventh icon).

    As you select colors, the previews in the Variants pane update to display the effects of your selections.

18. In the **Shading styles** area, click **Horizontal**. In the **Variants** box, click the lower-left thumbnail. Then click **OK**.

    The WordArt object reflects your changes.

19. On the **WordArt Tools Format** tab, in the **Shadow Effects** group, click the **Shadow Effects** button.

    The Shadow Effects gallery displays options for applying standard shadows to the letters of the WordArt object.

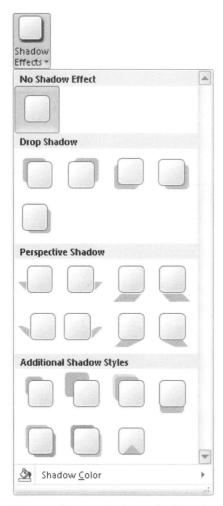

You can choose a shadow color from the list at the bottom of the gallery.

20. In the **Additional Shadow Styles** section of the **Shadow Effects** gallery, click the **Shadow Style 17** icon (the fourth icon in the first row). Then click away from the WordArt object to display the full effect.

    The shadow appears below the WordArt object.

When selecting a shadow effect, ensure that it fits within the page margins.

 CLEAN UP Save the WordArt publication, and then close it without exiting Publisher.

Working with Graphics

Publisher 2010 provides access to hundreds of professionally designed pieces of clip art—license-free graphics that often take the form of cartoons, sketches, or symbolic images, but can also include photographs, audio and video clips, and more sophisticated artwork. In a publication, you can use clip art to illustrate a point you are making or as eye-pleasing accompaniments to text. For example, you might insert an icon of an envelope to draw attention to an e-mail address, or a picture of mountains to set a "back to nature" tone.

To search for a clip art image, you display the Clip Art task pane and enter a keyword. You can search a specific clip art collection in the Microsoft Clip Organizer; search for specific media types, such as photographs; and search for images on the Microsoft Office Online Web site.

Tip To open the Microsoft Clip Organizer, click Start, All Programs, Microsoft Office, Microsoft Office 2010 Tools, and then Microsoft Clip Organizer; or enter clip in the Start menu Search box and then, in the results list, click Microsoft Clip Organizer.

You can add illustrations created and saved in other programs or scanned photographs and illustrations to your publications. Images such as these, saved as graphic files, are referred to as pictures. Like clip art, pictures can be used to make your publications more attractive and visually interesting. However, pictures can also convey information in a way that words cannot. For example, you might display photographs of your company's products in a catalog or brochure.

After you insert a graphic into a publication, you can move and size it just as you can any other object. When a graphic object is selected, Publisher displays the Picture Tools Format contextual tab on the ribbon. You can use the commands on this tab to modify the appearance of the selected graphic in various ways, including the following:

- Rotate the graphic to any angle.

- Crop away the parts of the graphic that you don't want to show in the publication, or crop the graphic into a shape. (The graphic itself is not altered—parts of it are simply not shown.)

- Compress the image to minimize the file size.

- Adjust the brightness, contrast, and color of the image, and apply color variations such as grayscale (shades of gray), sepia (to give the image an old-fashioned look), and washout (muted shades of the original colors).

- Add a border, shadow, or preformatted frame effect.

- Make parts of the graphic transparent.

And if you decide you don't like the changes you have made to a graphic, you can restore the original image by clicking the Reset Picture button.

In this exercise, you'll insert and modify a clip art image, and then insert and crop a picture. Then you'll decrease the file sizes of the two graphics by compressing them.

 SET UP You need the Blank_start publication and BirthdayGirl image located in your Chapter30 practice file folder, and an Internet connection, to complete this exercise. Open the Blank_start publication, and save it as *Graphics*. Then follow the steps.

1. On the **Insert** tab, in the **Illustrations** group, click the **Clip Art** button.

   Tip If you are designing the layout of a publication and know you will want to insert some sort of graphic later, you can click Picture Placeholder to insert a graphic placeholder.

   The Clip Art task pane opens.

2. In the **Search for** box at the top of the **Clip Art** task pane, type **birthday**. Then define the scope of your search, as follows:

   ○ If **All media file types** doesn't already appear in the **Results should be** box, click the **Results should be** arrow and then, in the list, select the **All media types** check box.

   ○ If the **Include Office.com content** check box isn't already selected, select it.

3. In the **Clip Art** task pane, click **Go**.

Thumbnails of clip art, photographs, movies, and sounds with the keyword *birthday* appear in the task pane.

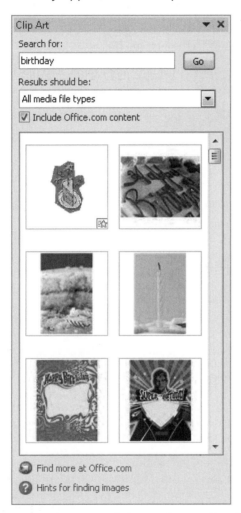

You can locate specific images by searching for associated keywords.

Troubleshooting If you do not select the Include Office.com Content check box or do not have an active Internet connection, your search might return zero results.

Icons indicate special properties of the images. For example, a yellow star icon in the lower-right corner of a thumbnail indicates an animated image, and a globe icon in the lower-left corner of a thumbnail indicates an image that is available from the Microsoft Office Online Web site rather than from the clip art collection stored locally on your computer.

4. In the **Clip Art** task pane, point to the first image.

A vertical button appears on the right side of the image, and a ScreenTip displays information about the image.

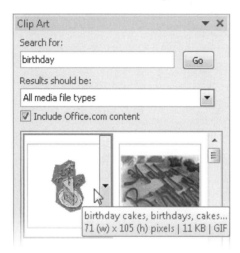

Pointing to an image displays the beginning of the list of keywords associated with the image, its dimensions and file size, and its format.

Tip The file size of a publication that contains graphics can become quite large. You can shrink the size of a graphic file (without affecting the displayed graphic) by using the Compress Pictures feature. Depending on the resolution setting, you might lose some visual quality when you compress a picture. You choose the resolution you want for the pictures based on where or how the presentation will be viewed—for example, on the Web or printed. You can also set other options, such as deleting cropped areas of a picture, to achieve the best balance between quality and file size. This is especially important when you intend to distribute a publication electronically, because the file size affects how long it takes to transmit or download.

5. Click the button that appears on the right side of the active image.

A menu of actions you can take with the image appears.

Copying an image to a clip art collection stores a copy of the image on your computer.

6. On the menu, click **Edit Keywords**.

The Keywords dialog box opens. From this dialog box, you can display the keywords for all the clip art images currently returned by your search. The number of images is shown above the Preview box.

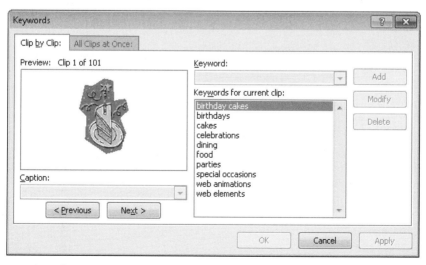

Searching for any of the words in the Keywords For Current Clip list will locate this image.

7. Below the **Preview** box, click the **Next** button several times to display other images and their keywords. Then click **Cancel**.

    Troubleshooting The Add, Modify, and Delete buttons are active only when viewing the keywords for an image that is stored in your collection.

8. In the **Clip Art** task pane, enter **birthday cake** in the **Search for** box. Click the **Results should be** arrow, clear the **All media types** check box, and select the **Illustrations** check box. Then click **Go**.

    The clip art shown in the task pane changes to display only drawings.

9. Scroll down the list, locate an image of a birthday cake that you like, and click the image.

    The image appears on the page, and the Picture Tools Format tab appears on the ribbon.

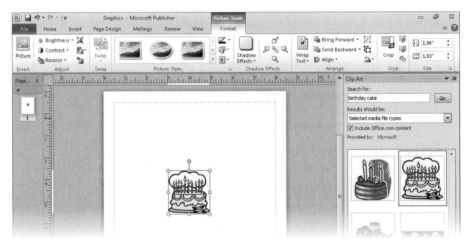

You can edit image aspects, such as the style and shadow effects, from this tab.

10. On the **Picture Tools Format** tab, in the lower-right corner of the **Picture Styles** gallery, click the **More** button.

    The Picture Styles gallery expands to display all the style options.

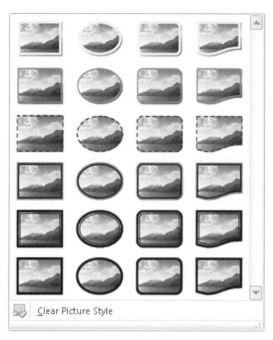

After applying a picture style, you can modify it.

11. Point to each of the thumbnails in the **Picture Styles** gallery to preview the effect of applying that style to the clip art image.

    Tip If necessary, move the image down on the page so you can see the effect when previewing the styles.

12. In the **Picture Styles** gallery, click **Picture Style 24** (the last style in the gallery).

    A shaped, thick black frame appears around the image. Areas of the image that don't fit within the frame are not visible.

 13. In the **Picture Styles** group, click the **Picture Border** arrow (not the button) and then, on the menu below the color galleries, click **Sample Line Color**.

    The cursor changes from an arrow to an eyedropper.

14. With the eyedropper, click a color in the birthday cake clip art image you chose.

    The color of the shaped frame changes to the color you clicked, and the cursor shape changes back to an arrow.

15. On the **Picture Border** menu, click **Dashes**, and then on the **Dashes** submenu, click **Round Dot** (the first dotted option).

The shaped frame changes to a dotted frame.

16. In the **Arrange** group, click the **Align** button.

Because no other objects are selected, only one alignment option is available.

17. In the **Align** list, click **Relative to Margin Guides**. Then click the **Align** button again.

All the alignment options are now available.

18. In the **Align** list, click **Align Top**. Then in the **Align** list, click **Align Left**. Then click a blank part of the page to release the selection.

The modified clip art graphic is now located in the upper-left corner of the printable area of the page.

You can modify many aspects of a basic clip art image.

19. Experiment with other settings on the **Picture Tools Format** tab, and then close the **Clip Art** task pane.

20. On the **Insert** tab, in the **Illustrations** group, click the **Picture** button.

The Insert Picture dialog box opens, displaying the contents of your Pictures library.

Troubleshooting If you don't release the selection before clicking the Picture button, the picture will replace the clip art image.

21. Navigate to your **Chapter30** practice file folder, and double-click the **BirthdayGirl** photo.

The photo is inserted on the page, and the Picture Tools Format tab appears on the ribbon. The photo occupies nearly the entire page.

22. On the **Picture Tools Format** tab, click the **Size** dialog box launcher.

The Format Picture dialog box opens, displaying the Size page.

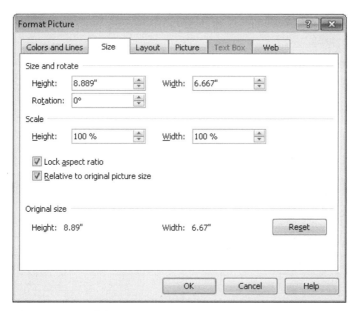

The Size page of the Format Picture dialog box displays the current size and scale of the selected object.

23. In the **Scale** section of the **Size** page, ensure that the **Lock aspect ratio** check box is selected. Then change the **Height** to **50**, and press Tab.

    Because the aspect ratio is locked, the Width setting also changes to 50%.

24. In the **Format Picture** dialog box, click **OK**.

    The photograph is resized to half its original height and width.

The position of the upper-left corner of the photo remains constant when you rescale it.

25. In the **Arrange** group, click the **Align** button, and then click **Distribute Horizontally**.

    The photo moves to the horizontal center of the page.

26. In the **Picture Styles** group, click the **Picture Shape** button.

    The Picture Shapes gallery expands.

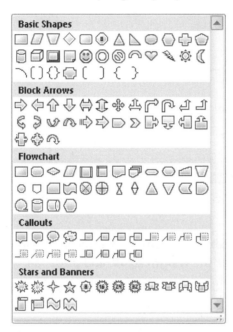

You can form a photo or other image into any shape in the gallery.

27. In the **Basic Shapes** section of the **Picture Shapes** gallery, click **Heart** (the fourth icon from the right end of the second row).

    The photo is shaded, and crop handles appear on its sides and corners. A clear area in the center of the photo indicates the area that will be visible when you apply the shape.

While the crop handles are visible, you can move the photo within the shape or change the dimensions of the shape.

28. Click a blank area of the page, and then point to the photo.

The photo appears to be cropped in the shape of a heart. Pointing to the cropped photo displays the outline of the original photo.

29. Drag the heart-shaped photo to overlap the birthday cake.

Although the original photo still exists, the parts that have been cropped away are not at all visible, and do not impede your view of the clip art image.

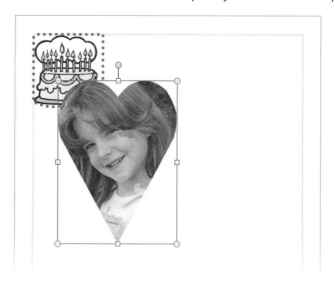

When the sizing handles are visible, you can resize the image but not change the relationship of the picture to the crop frame.

30. With the photo still selected, click the **Compress Pictures** button in the **Adjust** group on the **Picture Tools Format** tab.

The Compress Pictures dialog box opens.

You can compress a single image or all images in the publication.

Notice the current size of the image files and the estimated size after compression using the default settings.

Important Unless you select the Apply To Selected Pictures Only check box, Publisher will compress all the pictures in the publication, not only the selected picture.

31. In the **Target Output** section of the dialog box, click **Web**.

The estimated size after compression changes to a much smaller size. The resolution necessary for displaying graphics on the Web is much lower than the resolution for printing.

32. In the **Compress Pictures** dialog box, click **Compress**. Then in the **Microsoft Publisher** dialog box that opens, click **Yes** to apply picture optimization.

Publisher compresses the images and deletes the cropped parts of the photo. If you were to save the file now, the compressed pictures would result in a smaller file size.

 CLEAN UP Save and close the Graphics publication without exiting Publisher.

Working with Shapes

Publisher provides tools for creating several types of shapes, including lines, arrows, ovals, rectangles, stars, banners, and many more. With a little imagination, you will discover countless ways to create drawings by combining shapes.

When you create a shape in Publisher, you drag the pointer across the page to define the size of the shape. After you draw the shape, it is surrounded by a set of handles, indicating that it is selected. (You can select a shape at any time by simply clicking it.) When a shape is selected, the Drawing Tools Format contextual tab appears on the ribbon. Using the commands on this tab, you can change an existing shape, add text to the shape, apply a preformatted visual style, fill the shape with color, give the shape a three-dimensional appearance, and apply other formatting options.

You can easily insert text within a shape. Simply select the shape by clicking it, and then start typing. Publisher treats the text area of the shape as a text box. (A separate text box is not created.) You can then format the text by selecting it and using the commands in the Font group of the Text Box Tools Format contextual tab that appears.

Manipulating Shapes

You move and copy shapes just as you do other page elements. To move a shape from one location to another on the same page, you simply point to the shape, and when the pointer becomes a four-headed arrow, drag the shape to its new location, using the coordinates shown on the status bar to position it precisely. (You can create a copy of a selected shape by dragging it while holding down the Ctrl key.) You can also reposition a shape by changing settings on the Layout page of the Format AutoShape dialog box.

Keyboard Shortcut Hold down the Shift key while moving a shape to restrict the position change to a horizontal or vertical movement.

The handles around a selected shape serve the same sizing and rotating purposes as those around any other object. You can use the dimensions shown on the status bar to adjust the size precisely, or you can set the size of the shape in the Size group on the Drawing Tools Format tab or on the Size page of the Format AutoShape dialog box. You can rotate it by using the Rotate Or Flip command on the Arrange menu.

After drawing a shape, you can fill it with color, change the color and width of the border, or apply a Shape Style by using the commands in the Shape Styles group on the Drawing Tools Format tab.

Tip Having made changes to one shape, you can easily apply the same attributes to another shape by clicking the shape that has the desired attributes, clicking the Format Painter button in the Clipboard group on the Home tab, and then clicking the shape to which you want to copy the attributes. If you want to automatically apply the attributes of a shape to all future shapes in the same publication, right-click the shape, click Format AutoShape, and on the Colors And Lines page of the Format AutoShape dialog box, select the Apply Settings To New AutoShapes check box.

Connecting and Grouping Shapes

To show a relationship between two shapes, you can connect them with a line by joining special handles called *connection points*. Moving a connected shape also moves the line, maintaining the relationship between the connected shapes.

When you create a drawing composed of multiple shapes, you can group them so that you can edit, copy, and move them as a unit. While shapes are grouped, you can still change some of the attributes of an individual shape within the group by selecting only that shape. You can ungroup the grouped shapes at any time and regroup them after making changes.

In this exercise, you'll draw several shapes of the same color. Then you'll connect two shapes and format the connection line. Finally, you'll group the shapes.

SET UP You need the Blank_start publication located in your Chapter30 practice file folder to complete this exercise. Open the Blank_start publication, and save it as *Shapes*. Then follow the steps.

1. On the **Insert** tab, in the **Illustrations** group, click the **Shapes** button.

   The Shapes gallery expands.

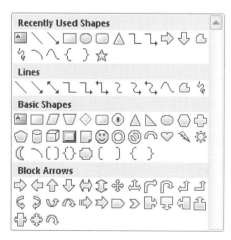

You can insert any shape from the gallery into your publication and modify it by applying styles and inserting text.

Keyboard Shortcut To draw a circle or square, click the Oval or Rectangle shape, and hold down the Shift key while you drag.

2. In the **Basic Shapes** section of the **Shapes** gallery, click **Isosceles Triangle** (the eighth shape in the first row).

3. Move the pointer over the page, and starting about 1 inch below the top margin guide, drag to draw a triangle about 1 inch tall and 0.5 inch wide.

   Tip Use the rulers to determine the location of the pointer and size of the shape.

4. On the **Drawing Tools Format** contextual menu that appears, in the **Arrange** group, click the **Rotate** button and then, on the menu that appears, click **Flip Vertical**.

   The triangle is now upside down.

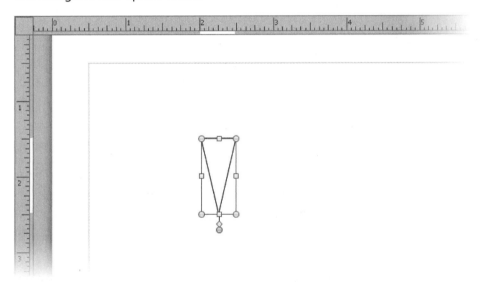

You can resize the shape by dragging the light-blue shape handles, rotate it by dragging the green rotation handle, or change its angle by dragging the yellow angle handle.

5. Click the **Shape Styles** dialog box launcher.

   The Format AutoShape dialog box opens, displaying the Colors And Lines page.

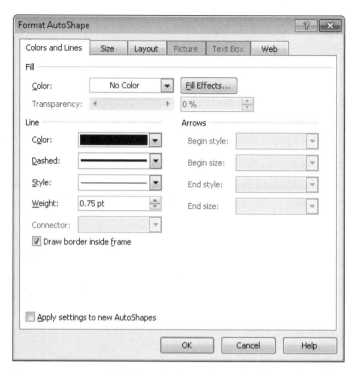

You can more precisely format a shape from the Format AutoShape dialog box.

6. In the **Fill** section of the **Colors and Lines** page, click the **Color** arrow and then, in the **Standard Colors** palette, click the **Orange** square.

7. At the bottom of the **Colors and Lines** page, select the **Apply settings to new AutoShapes** check box. Then click **OK**.

8. On the **Drawing Tools Format** tab, in the **Insert Shapes** gallery, click the **Oval** icon. Then hold down the Shift key, and drag to draw a circle above the triangle with a diameter slightly smaller than the triangle's side.

   When you release the mouse button, Publisher fills the circle with the orange color you specified for all shapes in this publication.

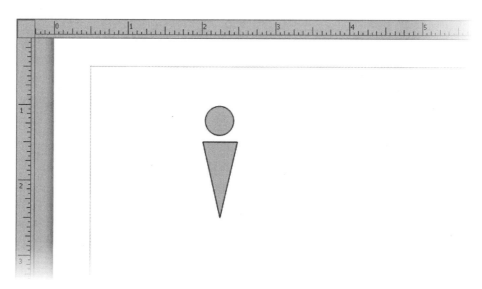

All shapes you draw in this publication will have the same fill color.

Tip If you click a shape icon in the Insert Shapes gallery and then change your mind, you can release the shape by pressing the Esc key.

9. In the **Insert Shapes** gallery, click the **Oval** icon. Then drag to draw an oval about 1.5 inches wide to the right of the circle.

10. In the lower-right corner of the **Insert Shapes** gallery, click the **More** button.

    The full Insert Shapes gallery expands.

11. In the **Lines** section, click **Curved Connector** (the seventh shape in the row).

12. Point to the triangle.

    Because you have selected a connector, blue dots appear at the ends and midpoints of each line of the triangle.

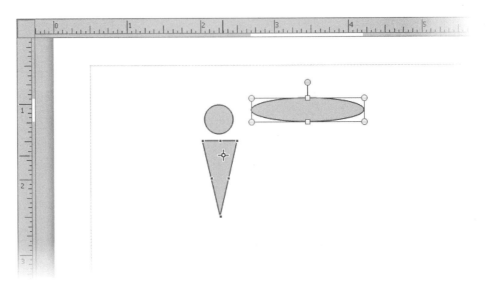

When drawing a connection, the pointer shape changes from an arrow to a crosshair.

13. Drag to draw a line from the connection point at the upper-right corner of the triangle to the connection point at the bottom of the oval.

    Publisher joins the two shapes with a curved connecting line. Red handles appear at each end of the line, indicating that the shapes are connected.

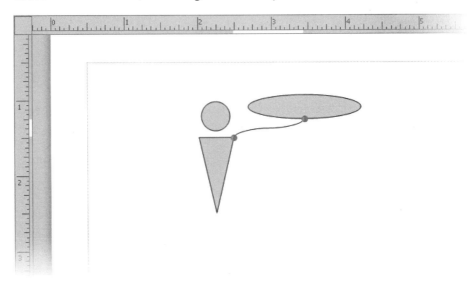

When a curved line is long enough to support it, a yellow diamond-shaped handle in the center of the line provides a means to adjust its curve.

14. With the line selected, click the **Shape Outline** arrow (not the button) in the **Shape Styles** group on the **Drawing Tools Format** tab.

15. On the **Shape Outline** menu, click **Weight**.

    The Weight submenu displays examples of various line weights, or thicknesses.

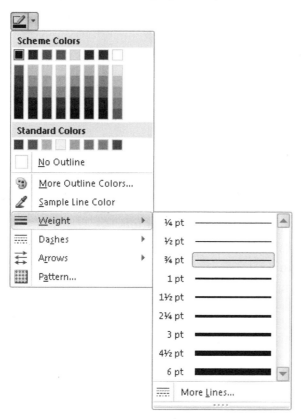

The Shape Outline menu and line weight options.

16. On the **Weight** submenu, click **6 pt**. Then on the **Shape Outline** menu, in the **Standard Colors** palette, click the **Orange** square.

    The color and weight of the curved connector changes.

17. Drag the oval shape to the left, close to the circle.

    Publisher adjusts the length and curve of the connecting line.

18. Select the four shapes by holding down the Shift key as you click each one in turn.

    Notice that each shape has its own set of handles.

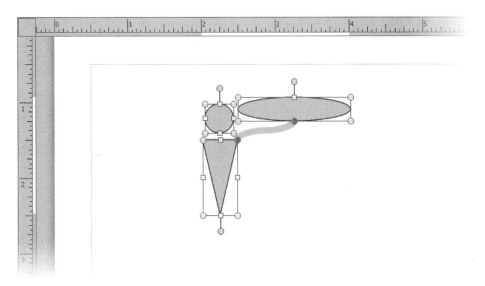

Select the individual shapes you want to group.

19. In the **Arrange** group, click the **Group** button.

    Publisher groups the shapes together with only one set of handles around the edge of the entire group.

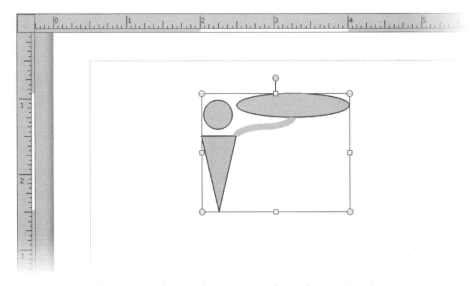

When grouped objects are selected, the Ungroup Objects button is active.

20. Point to any shape in the group, and when the pointer changes to a four-headed arrow, drag the grouped object to the upper-left corner of the page until the **Object Position** on the status bar is **1.00, 1.00 in**.

> **Tip** If you have difficulty positioning the shape by dragging, you can set the position on the Layout tab of the Format AutoShape dialog box.

The entire group moves.

21. Drag the lower-right handle of the group up and to the left until the **Object Size** shown on the toolbar is **1.50 x 1.00 in**.

> **Tip** If you have difficulty resizing the shape by dragging, you can set the position on the Size tab of the Format AutoShape dialog box or in the Size group on the Drawing Tools Format tab.

22. Click a blank area of the page to see the results.

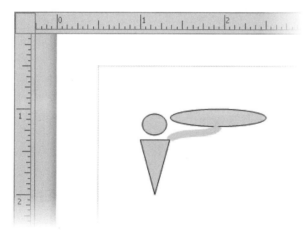

By combining shapes, you've created a cartoon waiter.

23. On the **Insert** tab, in the **Basic Shapes** section of the **Shapes** gallery, click **Trapezoid** (the fourth shape in the first row).

24. Draw a small "cup" on top of the oval "tray." Then hold down the Shift key, click any of the other shapes, and click the **Group** button in the **Arrange** group.

Publisher adds the cup shape to the group.

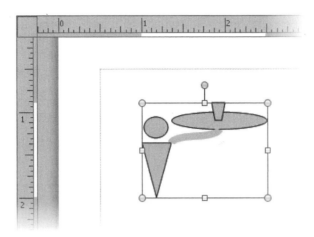

To remove an individual shape from a group, click the Ungroup button, select all the shapes other than the one you want to remove, and then click the Group button.

 CLEAN UP Save and close the Shapes publication without exiting Publisher.

Working with Ready-Made Visual Elements

Publisher excels at helping you create visually exciting publications. One of the ways it provides assistance is by offering hundreds of ready-made visual elements, called *building blocks*, that you can insert in a publication with a couple of clicks.

To simplify the use of these visual elements, Publisher 2010 organizes them in categories in the Building Block Library. Many of the elements have a common design and color scheme to give your publications a consistent look. When you are more familiar with color schemes and themes, you will be able to customize the colors of these elements, but for now, we will show you how to use the default building blocks to add professional touches to your publications.

See Also For information about applying a different color scheme and using custom colors, see "Creating Folded Cards" in Chapter 31, "Create Colorful Cards and Calendars."

You cannot add a customized element to the Building Block Library, even if you originally inserted it in your publication from that gallery. If you want to reuse a customized building block, or any other object, you can copy and paste it between publications.

In this exercise, you'll insert ready-made elements from three categories of the Building Block Library into a publication.

 SET UP You need the Blank_start publication located in your Chapter30 practice file folder to complete this exercise. Open the Blank_start publication, and save it as *Design*. Then follow the steps.

1. On the **Insert** tab, in the **Building Blocks** group, click the **Borders & Accents** button.

   The Borders & Accents gallery expands, displaying some of the available preformatted border options.

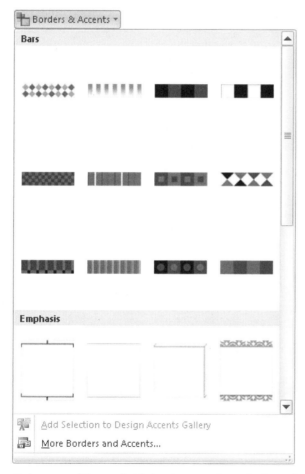

   Only some of the available borders are shown in the gallery.

2. Below the **Borders & Accents** gallery, click **More Borders and Accents**.

The Building Block Library dialog box opens, displaying the Borders & Accents page.

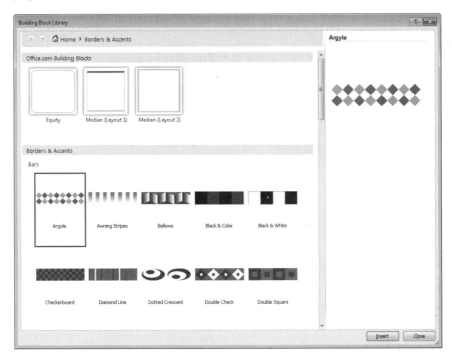

The border and accent options are divided into groups: Bars, Boxes, Emphasis, Frames, Lines, and Patterns. Options that are available from the Microsoft Office Online site are shown at the top of the page.

Tip The available borders and accents all depict a red, white, blue, and black color scheme, but you can change the colors after you insert the object.

3. Scroll down the **Borders & Accents** page. In the **Frames** section, click the **Stacked Corners** thumbnail. Then in the **Building Block Library** dialog box, click **Insert**.

The Building Block Library dialog box closes and Publisher inserts an asymmetrical border around the perimeter of the page.

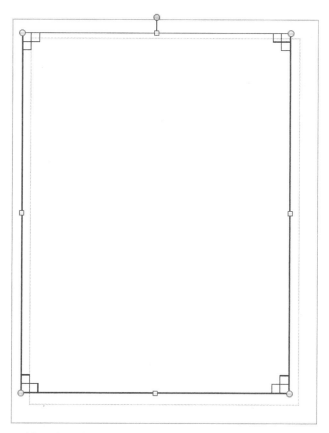

Unlike other objects you insert, the border was not inserted in the center of the page.

4. With the border selected, press the Right Arrow and Down Arrow keys repeatedly until the border is approximately centered within the blue margin guides.

   The border consists of sets of overlapping rectangles. You can move the entire border because all of its components are grouped to form one object that can be treated as a single unit.

   See Also For information about grouping objects, see "Connecting and Grouping Shapes," earlier in this chapter.

5. Repeat steps 1 and 2 to redisplay the **Borders & Accents** page of the **Building Block Library** dialog box. In the **Bars** section, double-click **Awning Stripes**.

   Publisher inserts the bar in the center of the page. The Awning Stripes bar consists of a series of blue and white rectangles.

6. With the bar selected, drag one of its left corner handles to the left until a pink line indicates that the left edge of the bar is at the left page margin. Then repeat this step to extend the right edge of the bar to the right page margin.

   The number of rectangles in the bar increases to fill the designated space.

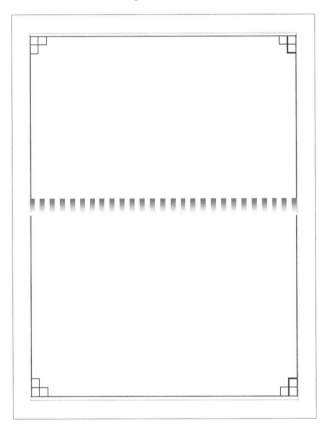

The bar graphic overlaps the border graphic, hiding the border.

7. Select the bar graphic. On the **Drawing Tools Format** tab, in the **Arrange** group, click the **Send Backward** button (not its arrow).

   Tip You can send an object backward one layer at a time, or send it directly to the back of the stack by clicking the Send Backward arrow and then clicking Send To Back.

   The bar graphic moves behind the border graphic, so the entire border is visible.

8. On the **Insert** tab, in the **Building Blocks** group, click the **Advertisements** button.

   The Advertisements gallery expands, displaying some of the available black-and-white advertisement elements.

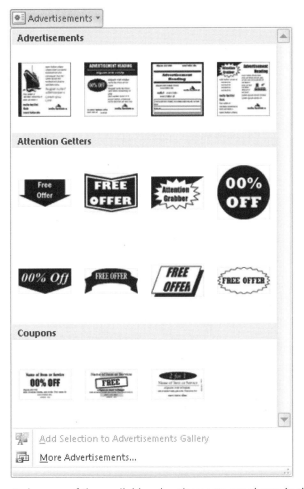

Only some of the available advertisements are shown in the gallery.

9. Below the **Advertisements** gallery, click **More Advertisements**.

The Building Block Library dialog box opens, displaying the Advertisements page.

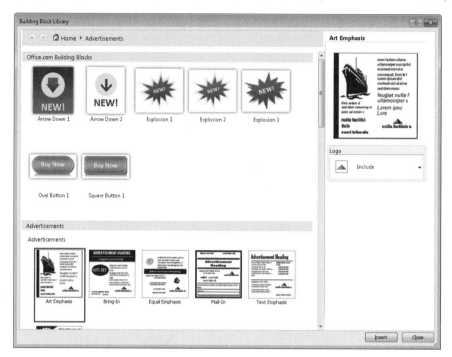

The advertisement options are divided into groups: Advertisements, Attention Getters, and Coupons. Options that are available from the Microsoft Office Online site are shown at the top of the page.

Tip You can switch between pages of the Building Block Library dialog box by clicking Home at the top of the dialog box and then clicking the category of building blocks you want to display: Advertisements, Borders & Accents, Business Information, Calendars, Page Parts, or More Categories.

10. Scroll down the **Advertisements** page. In the **Coupon** section, click the **Tilted Box** thumbnail.

The right pane displays a preview of the selected coupon and additional options.

11. In the **Border** list, click **Cutout dots**. Then click **Insert**.

The Building Block Library dialog box closes and Publisher inserts the coupon in the center of the page.

12. Drag the coupon to the area below the border row you inserted earlier. Then drag the corner handles to enlarge the coupon until it fills the available space.

By inserting the three ready-made objects from the Building Block Library, you have created a basic flyer.

Name·of·Item·or·Service

You can customize the color and appearance of the placeholder text and graphic elements as you want.

✖ CLEAN UP Save and close the Design publication.

Key Points

- Creating and manipulating visual elements is a basic Publisher skill that you will use when working in most publications.
- You can reposition most elements by dragging them, and you can resize elements by dragging their sizing handles.
- You can group elements together to manipulate them as a single unit.
- Before you spend time creating graphics, check for publicly available clip art and ready-made Building Block Library elements.

Chapter at a Glance

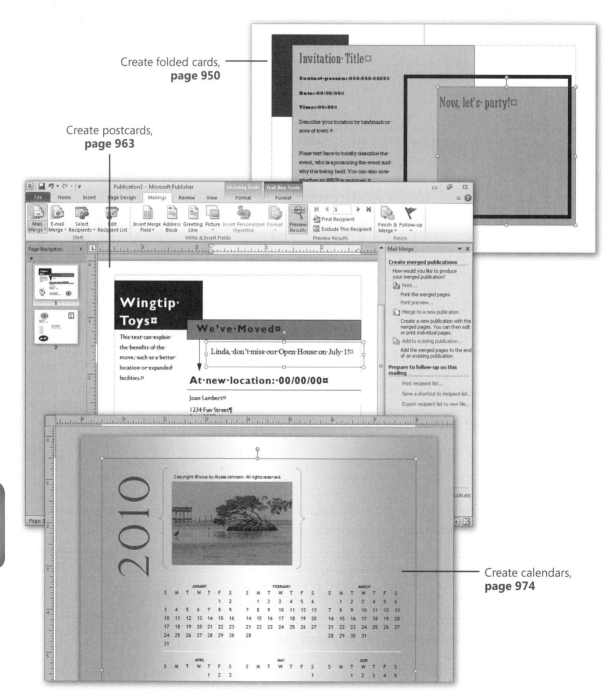

31 Create Colorful Cards and Calendars

In this chapter, you will learn how to

- ✔ Create folded cards.
- ✔ Create postcards.
- ✔ Create calendars.

Cards and calendars can be among the easiest publications to produce. Microsoft Publisher 2010 provides dozens of attractive templates from which you can create and personalize these items, perhaps to send to friends or clients. However, if you intend to distribute a lot of them, you might need to do some advance planning. Several of the decisions you need to make before creating cards and calendars for large-scale distribution revolve around the cost, in time and money, of printing the final product.

In this chapter, we discuss issues such as layout, color, paper, printing, and mailing, while showing you how to produce a folded card, a postcard, and three types of calendars. You also learn how to save time when creating a multipage publication by applying formatting to the underlying master page.

> **Practice Files** Before you can complete the exercises in this chapter, you need to copy the book's practice files to your computer. The practice files you'll use to complete the exercises in this chapter are in the Chapter31 practice file folder. A complete list of practice files is provided in "Using the Practice Files" at the beginning of this book.

Creating Folded Cards

The cards that you buy in a store are usually folded publications with text and graphic elements on all sides. You can print cards that you create in Publisher on both sides of the paper, or you can simulate this effect by printing the content on one side of the paper and then folding it in four. Publisher 2010 comes with many templates for two types of folded cards: Greeting Cards and Invitation Cards. In addition, five tent-fold templates are available in the Postcards category (along with dozens of flat card templates).

Tip Publisher 2010 includes templates that are specifically designed for pre-cut folded card stock from paper manufacturers such as Avery. You can purchase card stock and then, from the bottom of the Greeting Card, Invitation Card, or Postcard page of the Available Templates window, select the card stock by its model number.

Choosing a Design or Layout

After you choose a publication type on the New page of the Backstage view, thumbnails for two kinds of templates appear in the center pane:

- **Design templates** Templates such as the Thank You type of greeting card or the Party type of invitation card are based on classic Publisher designs, such as Accent Box, Capsules, or Quadrant. When you click one of these templates, the Page Size and Layout settings under Options in the right pane are unavailable, so you cannot change the design.

- **Layout templates** Templates such as the Birth Announcement type of greeting card or the Birthday Party type of invitation card are based on a layout, such as Frames, Portal, or Radius. When you click one of these templates, the Page Size and Layout settings under Options in the right pane are available, so you can change them.

The Page Size option determines whether your publication will occupy a quarter page or a half page, with the fold on the top or on the side. The Layout option determines which page layout will be applied to the card. You can change the page size and customize the layout after you create the card, but with so many options to choose from, you can save time by choosing the template that is closest to the effect you want.

If you click a layout template and then change the Page Size option, most of the layout thumbnails in the center pane change to reflect the size you selected. If you change the Layout option, most of the thumbnails change to reflect the layout you selected. In this way, you can get a good idea of the range of possibilities. (A few layout templates are fixed and don't change when you select a different option.)

Tip Each time you choose a template category from the New page of the Backstage view, it displays the template thumbnails with the default settings. You can experiment with changes to the color scheme, font scheme, page size, and layout until you find the combination you want.

Every publication, even a blank one, has a color scheme, a font scheme, and a set of information associated with it. You can change these options after you create a publication, but you can save time by specifying all three at the time of creation.

Changing the Color Scheme

A color scheme consists of eight complementary colors designed to be used for the following elements of a publication:

- The Main color is for the text.
- The Accent 1 through Accent 5 colors are for objects other than text.
- The Hyperlink color is for indicating hyperlinks that have not been clicked.
- The Followed Hyperlink color is for indicating visited hyperlinks.

Understanding color schemes can help you create professional-looking publications that use an appropriate balance of color. You are not limited to using the colors in a publication's color scheme, nor are you limited to using the color schemes that come with Publisher, but because they have been selected by professional designers based on good design principles, using them ensures that your publications will be pleasing to the eye.

The Color Scheme list in the Customize pane that appears when you select a publication type displays four of the eight colors in each scheme—Accent 1 through Accent 4—to give you an idea of the feeling evoked by that combination of colors. (By default, the Main text color is always black.) When you select a color scheme in the Customize pane, all the thumbnails in the center pane change to reflect that color scheme.

After you create a publication, you can switch to a different color scheme by clicking a color scheme in the Schemes gallery on the Page Design tab.

Tip If the default color schemes don't meet your needs, you can create your own by selecting a starting color scheme (preferably one that is close to what you want), clicking Create New Color Scheme at the bottom of the Schemes gallery, and then choosing colors in the Create New Color Scheme dialog box. After you save the scheme with a name of your choosing, it appears in the Schemes gallery, and you can apply it to any publication in the usual way.

Using Non–Color-Scheme Colors

Although working with the eight colors of a harmonious color scheme simplifies the process of designing a publication, you might want to use a larger palette of colors. You can add colors that are not part of the color scheme by selecting the element whose color you want to change and then choosing from the almost infinite spectrum of colors available from the Colors dialog box.

After you use a non–color-scheme color in a publication, it becomes available on all the palettes that appear when you click buttons that apply color—for example, the Font Color button. The color remains on the palettes associated with the publication—even if you stop using the color or change the color scheme applied to the publication.

Choosing Text

Most publications that you create based on Publisher templates include placeholders for text. The placeholder text might be suggested wording or simply indicate the type of information to insert in that text box. When you create an invitation, Publisher suggests text that is appropriate to the invitation template you choose. You can change the text to your own words, or choose from suggested verses (divided into categories, including business, personal, and holiday occasions) designed to adorn the cover and interior of a folded card.

In this exercise, you'll create a folded card based on a layout template. You'll change the color scheme before and after you create the publication, change the verse, apply different colors, and change the stacking order of elements on the page.

 SET UP You don't need any practice files to complete this exercise. Display the New page of the Backstage view, and select Installed Templates in the Available Templates list. Then follow the steps.

1. In the **More Templates** section of the **Available Templates** page, click **Invitation Cards**. Then scroll the center pane to see the range of invitation card templates that are available.

2. In the **Party** category of the **Invitation Cards** page, click (don't double-click) the **All Party** folder.

   Publisher displays the 72 invitation card templates that are installed with the program. The templates are divided into five categories: Party, Theme Party, Holiday Party, Birthday Party, and Housewarming.

3. In the **Party** category, click the **Blends** thumbnail.

In the Customize pane, the Page Size and Layout options are unavailable (dimmed), indicating that this is a design template rather than a layout template.

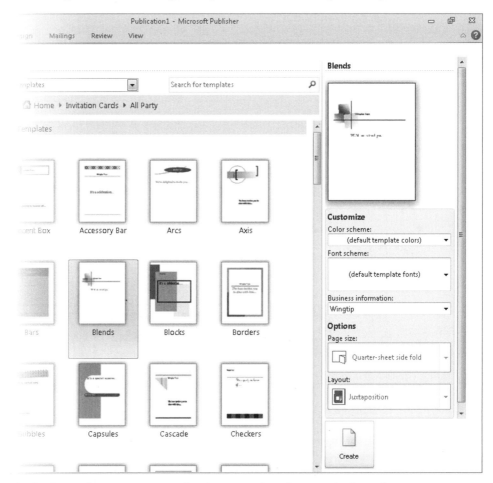

In the Customize pane, you can also choose a color scheme and a font scheme.

4. Scroll down the **Invitation Cards** page. In the **Theme Party** category, click the **Dinner Party 2** thumbnail.

   In the Customize pane, the Page Size and Layout options become available, indicating that this is a layout template rather than a design template.

5. In the **Options** section of the **Customize** pane, click the **Page size** arrow and then, in the **Page size** list, click **Quarter-sheet top fold**. Then click the **Layout** arrow, scroll to the top of the **Layout** list, and click **Juxtaposition**.

   The preview thumbnail at the top of the Customize pane and the Theme Party category thumbnails change as you select each option.

6. Scroll up and down the **Invitation Cards** page.

   Publisher has applied your choices to the thumbnails of all templates that do not have a fixed layout.

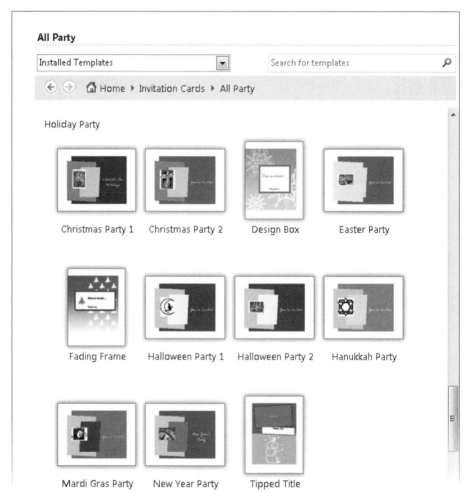

Horizontally oriented thumbnails represent layout templates that do not have a fixed layout.

7. In the **Customize** pane, click the **Color scheme** arrow, and then scroll down the **Color scheme** list, noting all the different options.

8. In the **Color scheme** list, click **Oriel**, and then scroll up and down the **Invitation Cards** page.

   Publisher has applied the Oriel color scheme to all the templates.

9. In the **Party** category, double-click the **Blocks** thumbnail.

Publisher creates an invitation card divided into four pages (the front of the card, the inside spread, and the back of the card). The publication reflects the Oriel color scheme you selected, but because Blocks is a design template, the publication is a half-sheet side-fold card instead of the quarter-sheet top-fold orientation that you selected in step 5.

Tip Although you cannot change the orientation and size of this design template from the Customize pane of the New page, you can change them after you create the card by setting the Orientation and Size from the Page Setup group on the Page Design tab. Be aware however, that the layout of this design is tailored specifically to a vertical half-page card. If you change the orientation or size, you will need to manually adjust the layout to fit your selection.

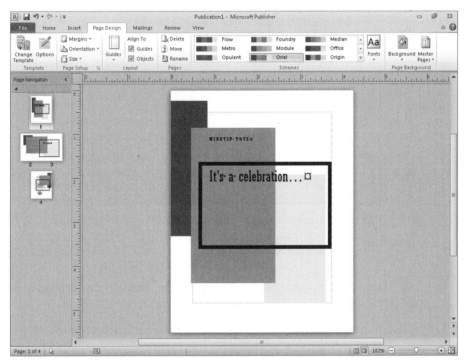

If you have already saved text in an information set as we did in Chapter 29, "Get Started with Publisher 2010," your organization name appears on page 1 above the invitation text, and on page 4.

Troubleshooting The appearance of buttons and groups on the ribbon changes depending on the width of the program window. For information about changing the appearance of the ribbon to match our screen images, see "Modifying the Display of the Ribbon" at the beginning of this book.

Troubleshooting The information set does not automatically replace the placeholder text in templates that you download from Microsoft Office Online. To replace or update a placeholder with text or a logo saved in an information set, point to the placeholder, click the action button that appears, and then click Update From Business Information Set.

See Also For information about information sets, see "Storing Personal and Company Information" in Chapter 29, "Get Started with Publisher 2010."

10. In the **Page Navigation** pane, click the **Page 2 and Page 3** thumbnail to display the interior spread.

11. On the **Page Design** tab, in the **Template** group, click the **Options** button.

    The Suggested Verse dialog box opens.

Publisher includes suggested greeting card verses in 23 categories.

12. Click the **Category** arrow, and scroll up and down the **Category** list to see the available categories of greeting card text categories. Click any category to see the messages associated with that category. Then, in the **Category** list, click **General Party**.

13. In the **Available messages** list, click **We've worked hard.**

    Publisher displays the message text that will appear on the front page of the card in the First Message Part pane, and the text that will appear inside the card in the Second Message Part pane.

14. In the **Suggested Verse** dialog box, click **OK**.

    The text on pages 1 and 3 change to reflect your choice.

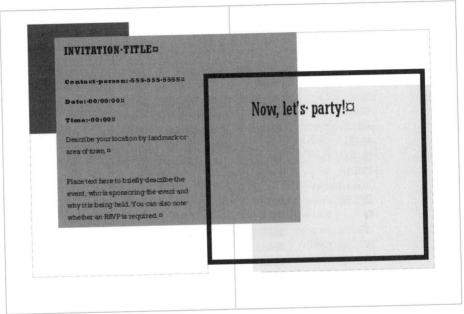

You can customize the messages and the other text on the card to suit your needs.

15. In the **Page Navigation** pane, click the **Page 4** thumbnail.

    If you completed the exercise at the end of "Storing Personal and Company Information" in Chapter 29, "Get Started with Publisher 2010," the information you stored in your information set is displayed on this page, which is the back for the card.

16. On the **Page Design** tab, in the **Schemes** gallery, click various color schemes and observe their effect on the card.

    Notice that the first color in each scheme (Accent 1) is always assigned to the vertical block at the right edge of the card, the second color (Accent 2) is assigned to the middle block, and the fourth color (Accent 4) is assigned to the left block.

17. In the **Schemes** group, click the **More** button in the lower-right corner of the **Schemes** gallery.

    The Schemes gallery expands to display all the available color schemes. The Built-In section includes 21 color schemes, and the Built-In (Classic) section includes an additional 71 color schemes.

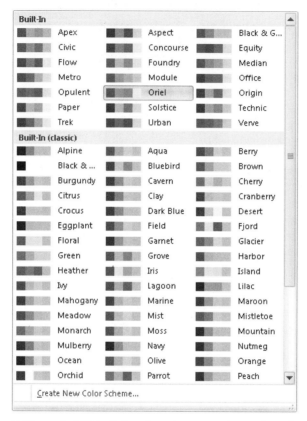

With nearly 100 built-in color schemes to choose from, it's likely that one will fit your needs.

18. In the **Built-In (classic)** section of the **Schemes** gallery, click **Desert**.

    Publisher applies the selected color scheme to the publication.

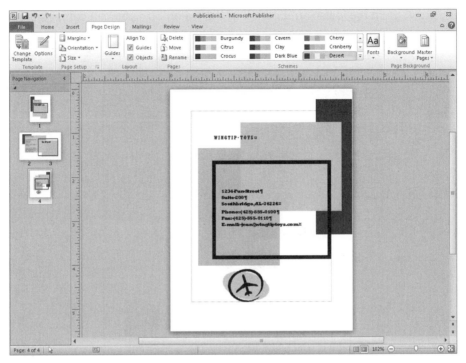

The color scheme coordinates with the company logo that is saved as part of the information set.

19. Display the inside page spread. In the black rectangle, click **Now, let's party!** Then, if necessary, press Ctrl+A to select the entire sentence.

    The Drawing Tools Format contextual tab and the Text Box Tools Format contextual tab appear on the ribbon.

20. On the **Text Box Tools Format** tab, in the **Font** group, click the **Font Color** arrow and then, on the **Font Color** menu, click **More Colors**.

    The Colors dialog box opens, displaying the Standard page.

21. In the **Colors** spectrum, click the brown hexagon that is one to the right of the lower-left corner of the spectrum.

In the lower-right corner of the dialog box, you can compare your selection to the current font color.

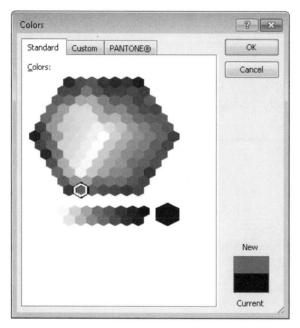

With color ranges grouped together, it's easy to choose one shade lighter or darker in the same color family.

22. In the **Colors** dialog box, click **OK**.

    The color of the selected text changes.

23. With the text still selected, on the **Home** tab, in the **Clipboard** group, click the **Format Painter** button once.

    Tip Format Painter is a nifty tool that you can use to copy multiple formatting characteristics from one element to another. To copy formatting to only one element, click the Format Painter button once. To copy formatting to multiple elements, double-click the Format Painter button. The feature will then remain active until you either press the Esc key or click the Format Painter button again.

24. In the yellow rectangle, click anywhere in the phrase **INVITATION TITLE**.

    The text changes to the same font, color, and size as the text in the right square.

25. In the **Font** group, click the **Decrease Font Size** button three times, and then click a blank area of the publication to see the results.

26. In the center of the page spread, click the left edge of the yellow rectangle that contains the invitation details.

    Publisher selects the grouped objects on the page spread.

27. Click the left edge of the yellow rectangle a second time.

    Publisher selects only the large square, as indicated by the gray handles.

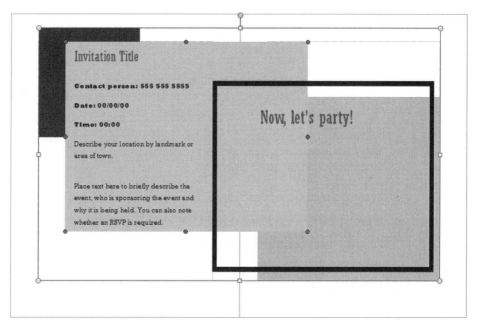

You can now make changes to the Invitation Title box.

> **See Also** For information about grouped objects, see "Working with Shapes" in Chapter 30, "Create Visual Interest."

28. On the **Drawing Tools Format** tab, in the **Shape Styles** group, click the **Shape Outline** arrow.

    The brown color you applied in step 22 from the Colors dialog box appears in the Recent Colors section of the Shape Outline menu.

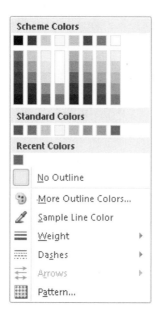

*The selected non–color-scheme color is available
for use with all color formatting tools.*

29. In the **Recent Colors** section of the **Shape Outline** menu, click the brown square.

    A brown outline appears around the yellow rectangle.

30. On page 3, click an area of the gray square that is outside of the black square to select the gray square.

31. In the **Shape Styles** group, click the **Shape Fill** arrow and then, in the **Scheme Colors** gallery on the **Shape Fill** menu, click the **Accent 3, Darker 25%** square (the second square from the bottom of the fourth column).

    Tip Pointing to a color displays the purpose and the name or value of the color in a ScreenTip.

    The gray square changes to a light green square.

32. On the **Drawing Tools Format** tab, in the **Arrange** group, click the **Ungroup** button.

    The grouped objects on the page ungroup and become individually selected.

33. Click a blank area of the page to clear the selections, and then click an area of the green square that is outside of the black square to select it.

34. In the **Arrange** group, click the **Bring Forward** button.

    The green square overlaps the yellow rectangle.

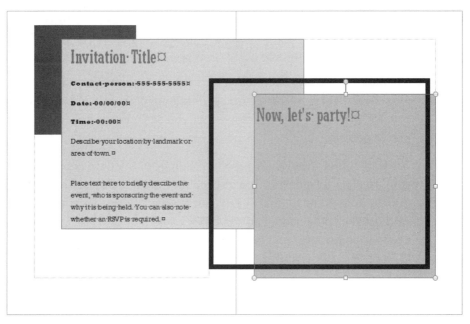

The text is now easier to read because it all appears on one background.

35. Use what you have learned about color to enhance the card in various ways. You might also want to use the skills you learned in Chapter 30, "Create Visual Interest," to create eye appeal by adding graphic elements.

✖ CLEAN UP Save the publication in your Chapter31 practice file folder as *Invitation*, and then close it without exiting Publisher.

Creating Postcards

Postcards provide a simple format to send information to customers, club members, family, or friends. Publisher comes with many templates for two-sided postcards. Most are designed to occupy a quarter page, but a few have quarter-page or half-page options. All have a primary side named Side 1 and a secondary side named Side 2. Most of the layout options for Side 2 include space for an address and postage.

Using Mail Merge

If you communicate with customers or members of an organization by means of post-cards and other marketing pieces that are sent to everyone on a mailing list, you might want to use a process called *mail merge*. This process combines the static information you enter in a publication with the variable information in a data source (a mailing list or any other type of database) to create one copy of the merged publication for every record in the data source.

The data source is a structured document, such as a Microsoft Word table, a Microsoft Excel worksheet, a Microsoft Access database table, or a Microsoft Outlook contact list. You can use an existing data source, or you can create a new one as part of the mail merge process.

To tell Publisher what information to pull from the data source and where to put it, you insert data fields into the publication. These fields correspond to the field names (usually column headings) in the data source. For example, the address area of a postcard usually contains an address block consisting of fields for the name and address of each recipient. After you enter the data fields in the publication, each field is enclosed in chevrons—for example, «FirstName».

After you specify the data source you want to use and insert the appropriate data fields into the publication, you can either send the merged publications directly to the printer or you can merge them one after the other into a new publication, as separate pages. If you merge to a new publication, you have another chance to review and, if necessary, edit the merged copies before sending them to the printer.

This might sound like a complicated process, but Publisher makes it simple with the Mail Merge Wizard, a three-step wizard that leads you through the mail merge process from start to finish.

Using Catalog Merge

Publisher offers several booklet-style catalog templates into which you can insert product information. If this information is stored in an Excel workbook or an Access database, you can use catalog merge to merge the product information into the catalog publication at printing time.

Catalog merge works pretty much the same way as mail merge. You can link to an existing data source or create a new one. When using an existing data source, you can filter the information or exclude specific records. This means you can tailor each printing of the catalog—for example, for a particular occasion or season.

If you frequently use catalogs as a marketing tool, it is worth taking the time to set up your product or service information in a workbook or database so that you can maintain it in one location and avoid having to retype it every time you need it. You might even consider storing information such as team or membership lists this way so that you can use Publisher and catalog merge to produce professional-looking rosters.

In this exercise, you'll create a postcard, insert data fields based on an existing data source, and then perform a mail merge operation to create copies with preprinted names and addresses, ready for mailing.

SET UP You need the DataSource workbook located in your Chapter31 practice file folder to complete this exercise. Display the New page of the Backstage view, and then follow the steps.

1. In the **Most Popular** section of the **Available Templates** page, click the **Postcards** thumbnail and then, in the **Marketing** section of the **Postcards** page, click the **All Marketing** folder.

2. Scroll down the **All Marketing** page to see the available templates.

   Tip The templates display the color scheme you applied most recently. If you completed the previous exercise, the templates display the Oriel color scheme.

   The postcard templates are divided into 13 categories: Informational, Special Offer, Sale, Event, Invitation, Holiday Party Invitation, Holiday Greeting, Holiday Thank You, Thank You, We've Moved, Announcement, Reminder, and Tent Fold.

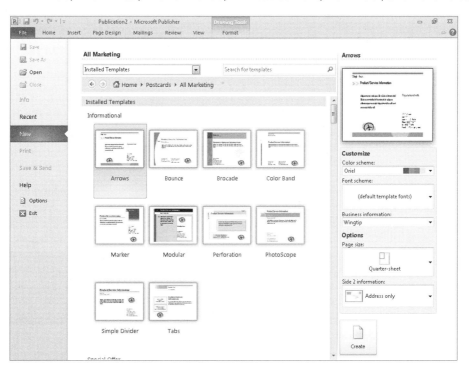

Publisher installs nearly 150 postcard templates.

3. In the **We've Moved** category, click the **Compass Point** thumbnail.

A preview of and options for the selected postcard appear in the Customize pane.

4. In the **Color scheme** list, click **Sapphire**, and in the **Side 2 information** list, click **Promotional text**. Then, at the bottom of the **Customize** pane, click **Create**.

Publisher creates the postcard with the specified settings.

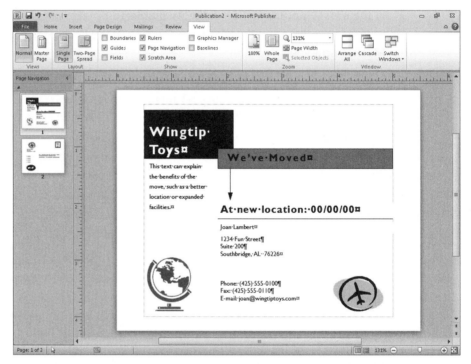

If you have already created an information set, the saved information appears on both sides of the postcard.

See Also For information about creating information sets, see "Storing Personal and Company Information" in Chapter 29, "Get Started with Publisher 2010."

5. In the **Page Navigation** pane, click the **Page 2** thumbnail.

6. Click the **Mailings** tab.

The Mail Merge button is active (yellow) because this publication contains mail merge fields.

Mail
Merge ▾

7. On the **Mailings** tab, in the **Start** group, click the **Mail Merge** arrow and then, in the **Mail Merge** list, click **Step by Step Mail Merge Wizard**.

   The Mail Merge task pane opens, displaying step 1 of the Mail Merge Wizard.

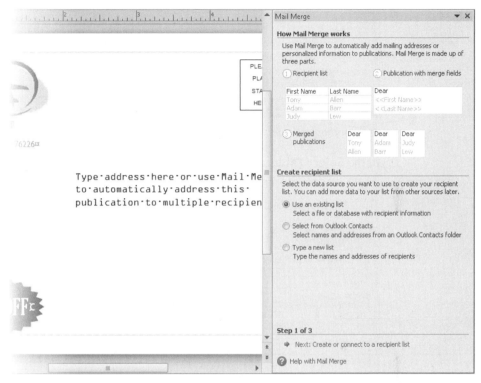

Step 1 requires that you create or connect to a recipient list.

8. With the **Use an existing list** option selected under **Create recipient list**, click **Next: Create or connect to a recipient list** at the bottom of the task pane.

   The Select Data Source dialog box opens, displaying the contents of a folder, named QUERIES, that was created when you installed Microsoft Office 2010 Professional.

9. In the **Select Data Source** dialog box, navigate to your **Chapter31** practice file folder and double-click the **DataSource** workbook.

   The Select Table dialog box opens.

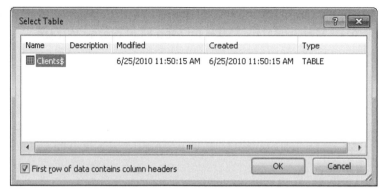

The workbook contains only one data table.

10. In the **Select Table** dialog box, with the **Clients$** sheet and the **First row of data contains column headers** check box selected, click **OK**.

The Mail Merge Recipients dialog box opens.

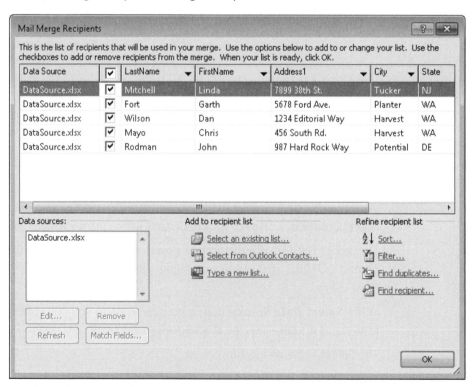

The data table contains five records.

If you use mail merge often, you will want to explore this dialog box to see how you can refine the mail merge process. For the purposes of this exercise, we will use the default settings.

11. In the **Mail Merge Recipients** dialog box, click **OK**.

The Mail Merge task pane displays step 2 of the Mail Merge Wizard.

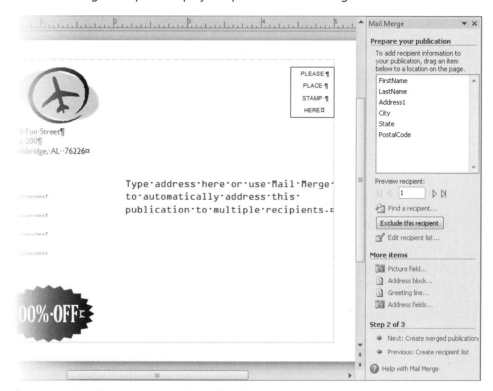

Step 2 requires that you prepare the publication.

12. On page 2 of the postcard, click the sentence that begins **Type address here**.

Publisher selects all the text in the address area.

13. Press the Delete key.

The address area of the postcard is now empty other than the end-of-line marker (the placeholder character within a text frame or table cell, which is visible only when hidden characters are displayed).

14. In the **Mail Merge** task pane, under **More items**, click **Address block**.

   Tip You can also insert an address block by clicking the Address Block button in the Write & Insert Fields group on the Mailings tab.

   The Insert Address Block dialog box opens. From this dialog box, you can refine the format of the fields that constitute the name and address.

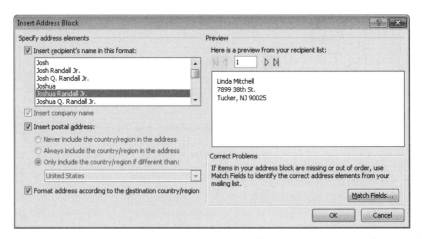

The text in the Preview pane indicates that the fields in your recipient list match those required for the address block.

15. In the **Insert Address Block** dialog box, above the **Preview** pane, click the **Next** button.

   The Preview pane displays information for the second recipient defined in the recipient list you selected in step 1 of the wizard.

16. Notice the name and address options you can set. Then click the **Previous** button to redisplay the first recipient, and in the **Insert Address Block** dialog box, click **OK**.

A field code that represents the address block appears in the address area of the postcard.

Field codes that will be replaced in the merged publication by recipient information are indicated by double chevrons.

17. Display page 1 of the postcard, and insert a text box below the **We've Moved** box and to the right of the downward-pointing arrow.

    See Also For information about inserting text boxes, see "Working with Text Boxes" in Chapter 30, "Create Visual Interest."

18. With the insertion point in the new text box, on the **Mailings** tab, in the **Write & Insert Fields** group, click the **Greeting Line** button.

The Insert Greeting Line dialog box opens.

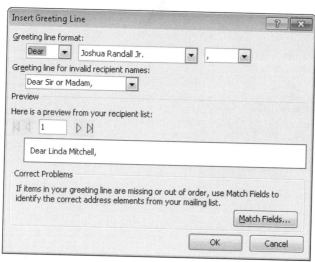

The text in the Preview pane indicates that the fields in your recipient list match those required for the greeting line.

19. Under **Greeting line format**, click the arrow to the right of the first box, and click **(none)**. Then click the arrow to the right of the second box, scroll down the list, and click **Joshua**.

20. In the **Greeting line for invalid recipient names** list, click **(none)**. Then in the **Insert Greeting Line** dialog box, click **OK**.

    A field code that represents the greeting line appears in the text box.

21. On the **Mailings** tab, in the **Preview Results** group, click the **Preview Results** button.

    Publisher displays the greeting for the first recipient in the selected recipient list.

22. Click after the comma, press the Spacebar, and type **don't miss our Open House on July 1!** Then click away from the text box.

    The postcard is now ready for merging.

23. At the bottom of the **Mail Merge** task pane, click **Next: Create merged publication**.

Step 3 of the Mail Merge Wizard appears in the Mail Merge task pane.

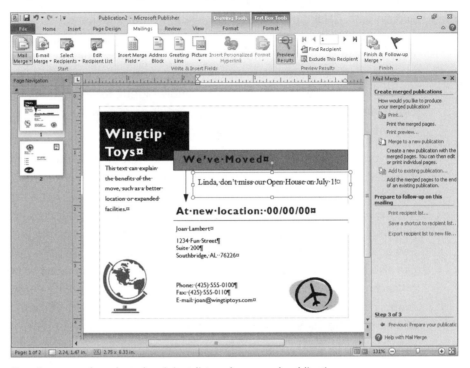

Step 3 merges the selected recipient list and prepared publication.

24. In the task pane, click **Merge to a new publication**.

Publisher creates a new publication that includes two pages for each of the five records in the selected recipients list.

25. Scroll through the publication pages to see the personalized postcards.

You can edit each copy as necessary in this publication before printing it. You can also save the publication for future use.

❌ **CLEAN UP** Close the merged publication without saving your changes. Then save your postcard as *Postcard*, and close it without exiting Publisher.

Creating Calendars

Although various technologies are now available to track appointments and schedules electronically, many people still prefer to use printed calendars to keep them organized and on time. Calendars can be an excellent promotional item because they keep your information in front of the recipient for the entire calendar period. You can include information about promotions and events, or if you create a calendar for friends and family members, you can include information about personal events such as birthdays. You can use Publisher to create a calendar for a single month, for a range of months, or for an entire year. Various designs are available in full-page or wallet sizes, or you can build a custom-sized calendar from a blank publication.

After you choose a calendar template from the New page of the Backstage view, you can specify whether each calendar page displays a month or a year, and which months or years the calendar includes. (If you don't select a year, Publisher creates a calendar for the current year.) Publisher creates a calendar consisting of one page specific to each month or year in the selected range. For example, setting a starting month of January and an ending month of June of the same year produces a six-page publication. You can also add a Schedule Of Events section, which is a text box next to the calendar grid on each page in which you can insert information, by selecting the Include Schedule Of Events check box at the bottom of the Customize pane before you create the calendar. You can change the Schedule Of Events text box header to represent information other than events.

Tip You can insert a one-month calendar object from the Building Blocks Library into any type of publication. For information, see "Working with Ready-Made Visual Elements" in Chapter 30, "Create Visual Interest."

Adding Captions, Credits, and Copyrights

Some calendar templates include placeholders for photographs or other artwork. If you are creating a calendar for distribution to other people and you select one of these templates, think carefully about the ownership of the artwork you plan on using. If you insert your own photographs, do you want to indicate ownership in some way? If you plan to use artwork created by other people, do you have the right to distribute those materials without infringing on the owner's rights?

Many people assume that if a graphic is available on the Web, it is part of the public domain. However, it is wise to err on the side of caution whenever you use artwork in your publications, unless you know it is not protected by a copyright. For example, the clip art that comes with Publisher and that is available from Microsoft Office Online is not copyrighted and can be used by anyone for any purpose. Materials that are copyrighted are usually accompanied by a variation of the following statement:

Copyright © 2010 by Online Training Solutions, Inc. All rights reserved.

If you want to use artwork that you have been given by someone else, it is wise to acknowledge the source. Otherwise, hard feelings can result if it appears to the owner that you are trying to claim credit for his or her work. You can add captions, credits, and copyrights to your publications in unobtrusive text boxes, so don't be tempted to omit them only because you think they might detract from your design.

Changing Page Backgrounds

In Publisher, you can customize the background of any page by adding a solid color, a color gradient, a texture, or even a picture. This type of formatting is particularly effective in full-page publications such as calendars, because the background holds the objects on the page together with a cohesive design element.

A color gradient is a visual effect in which a solid color gradually changes from light to dark or dark to light. Publisher offers several gradient patterns, each with several variations. You can also choose a preset arrangement of colors from professionally designed backgrounds in which different colors gradually merge.

Tip Be cautious when using preset color arrangements with calendars. It is important that the background be subtle and that it not compete with the other objects for attention or make them difficult to read.

If you want something fancier than a gradient, you can give the background a texture, or you can even use a picture. Publisher comes with several textures that you can easily apply to the background of your pages.

Working with Master Pages

When you create a publication, the pages take on the characteristics of the template on which it is based. You can then make changes to individual pages. In a multipage publication, making the same change to the design of every page can be tedious. For efficiency and precision, you can make the change to the publication's master page instead.

The design of the master page controls the look of all the pages in the publication. Anything that appears on the master page appears on every page. (For example, you might want to add your company logo or a watermark to every page.) Most master page elements can be changed only on the master page. (An exception is the background; you can override a master page background on an individual publication page.) For this reason, most publications created with Publisher templates have a blank master page—the design elements are individually inserted on each page so that you can easily change them.

To make changes to a publication's master page, you click the Master Page button in the Views group on the View tab to display the master page and the Master Page tab.

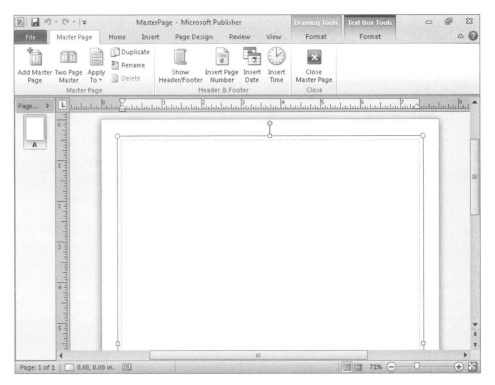

While the master page is displayed, you can choose commands from menus and click buttons on the Home, Insert, Page Design, Review, and View tabs to insert and format the elements you want to appear on every page of the publication.

By clicking buttons on the Master Page tab, you can do the following:

● Create additional one-page or two-page master pages.

● Change a one-page master page to a two-page master page (a spread) or vice versa.

● Apply a master page to one page, all pages, or a range of pages in the current publication.

● Duplicate or rename the active master page, or delete it if there is more than one.

● Display and add content to the header and footer areas of the master page.

Clicking the Close Master Page button on the Master Page tab, or the Normal button in the Views group on the View tab returns you to the publication so you can check the effects of changes you make to the master page.

In this exercise, you'll first create a full-page calendar for the entire year, with a custom photograph and copyright statement. You'll then change the background on the master page, and change the background of the calendar object.

 SET UP You need the Peaceful picture located in your Chapter31 practice file folder to complete this exercise. Display the New page of the Backstage view, display only the installed templates, and then follow the steps.

1. On the **Available Templates** page, in the **Most Popular** section, click **Calendars**, and then scroll the **Calendars** page to see the broad range of available design templates.

   The templates are divided into two categories: Full Page and Wallet Size.

   Tip The templates display the color scheme you applied most recently. If you completed the previous exercise, the templates display the Sapphire color scheme.

2. In the **Full Page** category, click **Photo Album**.

   Publisher displays a preview of the Photo Album calendar, with the default settings, in the Customize pane.

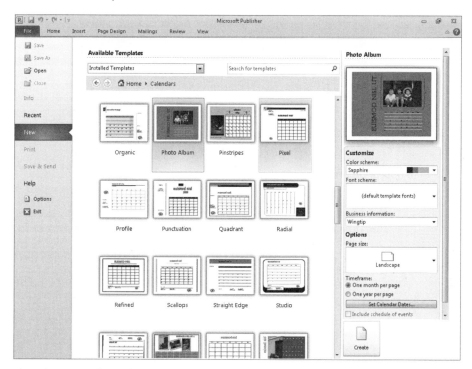

If you have saved an information set, it is available in the Business Information list.

3. In the **Customize** pane, set the **Color scheme** to **Aqua**. Under **Options**, change the **Page size** to **Portrait** and the **Timeframe** to **One year per page**. Then click **Create**.

   Publisher creates a full-page, vertical, 12-month calendar based on the selected design template.

You can change the space occupied by the picture on the page by selecting the picture and then dragging its resize handles or using the commands on the Picture Tools Format tab.

4. Save the publication as **Calendar** in your **Chapter31** practice file folder.

5. On the **View** tab, in the **Zoom** group, click the **100%** button. Then scroll to the top of the page.

6. Right-click the existing picture, click **Change Picture**, and then click **Change Picture**.

   The Insert Picture dialog box opens, displaying the contents of your Pictures library.

7. In the **Insert Picture** dialog box, navigate to your **Chapter31** practice file folder, and double-click the **Peaceful** picture.

   The selected picture replaces the original picture, and the Picture Tools Format contextual tab appears on the ribbon.

   See Also For information about inserting and manipulating pictures, see "Working with Graphics" in Chapter 30, "Create Visual Interest."

8. On the **Picture Tools Format** tab, in the **Picture Styles** group, click the **Caption** button.

   The Caption gallery expands, displaying many options for caption positions.

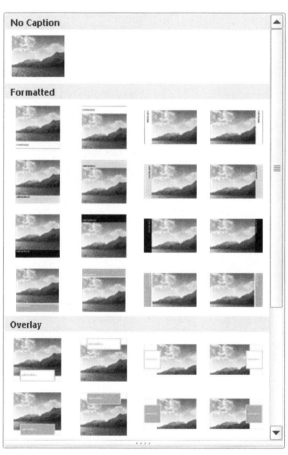

From the Caption gallery, you can attach a caption or copyright notice to a picture that is inserted in a publication.

9. Scroll down the **Caption** gallery to see the available options. Point to captions to display a preview of their effects on the selected photo. Then, in the **Simple** category, click the **Simple – Layout 2** thumbnail (the second thumbnail from the left).

Publisher inserts a generic caption in the selected location.

10. Click **Picture caption** to select the entire caption. Then type **Copyright (c) 2010 by Alyssa Johnson. All rights reserved.**

Tip When you press the Spacebar after typing *(c)*, Publisher substitutes the copyright symbol, because the Replace Text As You Type check box is selected in the AutoCorrect dialog box. For information about AutoCorrect, see "Correcting Spelling and Grammatical Errors" in Chapter 3, "Edit and Proofread Text."

The caption runs over onto a second line.

The caption is an integral part of the photo.

11. Press Ctrl+A to select the entire caption. On the **Home** tab, in the **Font** group, click the **Decrease Font Size** button twice. Then click an empty area of the page to see the results.

    The caption now fits on one line.

12. On the **View** tab, in the **Views** group, click the **Master Page** button.

    The master page is currently blank.

13. On the **Page Design** tab, in the **Page Background** group, click the **Background** button.

    The Background gallery expands.

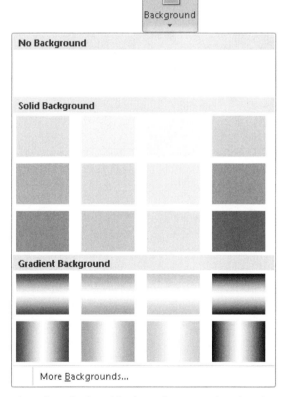

The colors displayed in the gallery are related to the colors in the current page layout template.

14. In the **Gradient Background** section of the **Background** gallery, click the **Accent 2 Vertical Gradient** thumbnail (the second thumbnail in the second row).

    The master page background changes.

15. On the **Master Page** tab, in the **Master Page** group, click the **Apply To** button and then, in the **Apply To** list, click **Apply to Current Page**.

16. In the **Close** group, click the **Close Master Page button**.

    The selected gradient has been applied to the page background, but not to the calendar object in the center of the page.

The edges of the calendar object are visible against the gradient background.

17. Click a blank area of the calendar. On the **Drawing Tools Format** tab, in the **Shape Styles** group, click the **Shape Fill** arrow, click **Gradient**, and then click **More Gradients**.

    The Fill Effects dialog box opens, displaying the Gradient page.

18. In the **Shading styles** section, click **Vertical**.

    In the Colors section, One Color is selected and the base color specified by the color scheme appears in the Color 1 box.

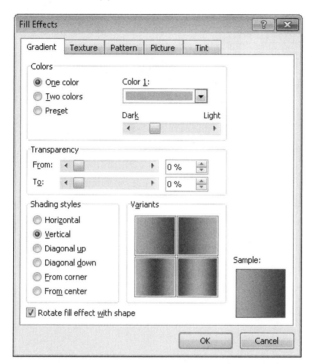

The default one-color gradient is from the base color to black.

19. In the **Colors** area, move the slider all the way to the right (toward **Light**).

    The thumbnails in the Variants area change to display gradients from aqua to white.

20. In the **Variants** area, click the lower-left thumbnail. Then click **OK**.

    The calendar object background changes to match the page background.

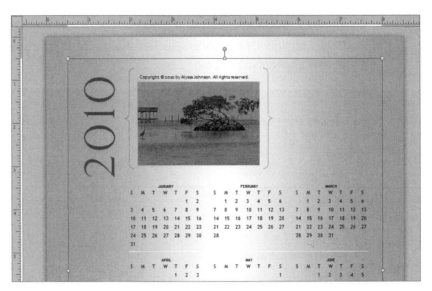

Choosing colors that blend with objects you insert, such as this photo, creates a cohesive appearance.

 **CLEAN UP** Save and close the Calendar publication.

Key Points

- With so many templates to choose from, you can save time by selecting the one that is closest in size and layout to the publication you want.

- Although all the templates come with a default color scheme, you can switch to a different scheme at any time. And you can expand the scheme by adding custom colors.

- Printing is a big consideration whenever you need more than just a few copies of a publication. Design with the printing method—and your budget—in mind.

- If you need to send a publication to a large group of people, save time by merging their contact information directly into the publication.

- Subtle backgrounds can unify a publication. In a multipage publication, the background belongs on the master page.

Index

Symbols & Numbers

A

E

M

Q

R

About the Authors

Joyce Cox

Joyce has 30 years' experience in the development of training materials about technical subjects for non-technical audiences, and is the author of dozens of books about Office and Windows technologies. She is the Vice President of Online Training Solutions, Inc. (OTSI).

As President of and principal author for Online Press, she developed the *Quick Course* series of computer training books for beginning and intermediate adult learners. She was also the first managing editor of Microsoft Press, an editor for Sybex, and an editor for the University of California.

Joan Lambert

Joan has worked in the training and certification industry for more than a decade. As President of OTSI, Joan is responsible for guiding the translation of technical information and requirements into useful, relevant, and measurable training and certification tools.

Joan is a Microsoft Office Master (MOM), a Microsoft Certified Application Specialist (MCAS), a Microsoft Certified Technology Specialist (MCTS), a Microsoft Certified Trainer (MCT), and the author of more than two dozen books about Windows and Office (for Windows and Mac).

Curtis Frye

Curtis Frye is a writer, speaker, and performer living in Portland, Oregon. He is the sole or lead author of more than 20 books, including *Microsoft Excel 2010 Plain & Simple*, *Microsoft Access 2010 Plain & Simple*, and *Excel 2007 Pocket Guide*. In addition to his writing, Curt presents keynote addresses on Excel and motivational topics.

The Team

This book would not exist without the support of these hard-working members of the OTSI publishing team:

- Kathleen Atkins
- Jan Bednarczuk
- Jenny Moss Benson
- Rob Carr
- Susie Carr
- Jeanne Craver
- Patty Gardner
- Elizabeth Hansford
- Kathy Krause
- Marlene Lambert
- Patty Masserman
- Brianna Morgan
- Jaime Odell
- Jean Trenary
- Liv Trenary
- Elisabeth Van Every

We are especially thankful to the support staff at home who make it possible for our team members to devote their time and attention to these projects.

Devon Musgrave and Joel Panchot provided invaluable support on behalf of Microsoft Learning.

Online Training Solutions, Inc. (OTSI)

OTSI specializes in the design, creation, and production of Office and Windows training products for information workers and home computer users. For more information about OTSI, visit:

www.otsi.com

What do you think of this book?

We want to hear from you!

To participate in a brief online survey, please visit:

microsoft.com/learning/booksurvey

Tell us how well this book meets your needs—what works effectively, and what we can do better. Your feedback will help us continually improve our books and learning resources for you.

Thank you in advance for your input!

Stay in touch!